JEWS AND JEWISH IDENTITIES IN LATIN AMERICA

Historical, Cultural, and Literary Perspectives

Jewish Latin American Studies

Series Editor: Darrell B. Lockhart (University of Nevada, Reno)

ACADEMIC
STUDIES
PRESS

JEWS AND JEWISH IDENTITIES IN LATIN AMERICA

Historical, Cultural, and Literary Perspectives

EDITED BY Margalit Bejarano, Yaron Harel,
Marta F. Topel, Margalit Yosifon

Coordinator
Ora Kobelkowsky (Dahan Center, Bar Ilan University)

Boston
2017

Library of Congress Cataloging-in-Publication Data

Names: Bejarano, Margalit, editor. | Merkaz le-tarbut, òhevrah òve-òhinukh be-moreshet Yahadut Sefarad a. sh. Aharon òve-Raòhel Dahan

Title: Jews and Jewish identities in Latin America : historical, cultural, and literary perspectives / edited by Margalit Bejarano, Yaron Harel, Marta F. Topel, Margalit Yosifon; coordinator (Dahan Center, Bar Ilan University), Mrs. Ora Kobelkowsky.

Description: Boston: Academic Studies Press, [2017]

Series: Jewish latin american studies | Includes bibliographical references and index.

Identifiers: LCCN 2017034062 (print) | LCCN 2017034354 (ebook) | ISBN 9781618116499 (e-book) | ISBN 9781618116482 (hardback: alk. paper)

Subjects: LCSH: Jews—Latin America—History—20th century—Congresses. | Jews—Latin America—History—21st century—Congresses. | Jews—Latin America—Identity—Congresses. | Latin America—Ethnic relations—Congresses.

Classification: LCC F1419.J4 (ebook) | LCC F1419.J4 J515 2017 (print) | DDC 980/.004924—dc23

LC record available at https://lccn.loc.gov/2017034062

© Academic Studies Press, 2017
ISBN 978-1-61811-648-2 (hardcover)
ISBN 978-1-61811-649-9 (electronic)

Book design by Kryon Publishing Services (P) Ltd.
www.kryonpublishing.com

On the cover: "Homenaje a la migración sefaradí en México," by Arnold Belkin. 1979. Mural decorating the building of Sociedad de Beneficencia Alianza Monte Sinai in México City.

Published by Academic Studies Press in 2017
28 Montfern Avenue
Brighton, MA 02135, USA
P: (617)782-6290
F: (857)241-3149
press@academicstudiespress.com
www.academicstudiespress.com

Table of Contents

Introduction

THE JEWISH COMMUNITIES OF LATIN AMERICA

The history of the Jews in Latin America is marked by contradictions. During the colonial era, the Spanish and Portuguese monarchies prohibited any Jewish presence, but the Jews were able to create modern Jewish communities in the Dutch and British Caribbean. The Inquisition persecuted crypto-Jews, and their descendants were assimilated into the Catholic societies. In recent years, however, we have witnessed the proliferation of groups that consider themselves *Bnei anusim* (descendants of *marranos*), around Recife—which was part of the Dutch colony in Brazil, as well as in Peru, Mexico and Colombia.

The first Jewish immigrants to reach the Latin American republics after independence settled in the Caribbean port cities of Venezuela, Colombia, and Panama. They prospered economically, but tended to intermarry and assimilate. Their traces, however, did not disappear, and, in some cases, they laid the foundations for the future organization of their respective communities.

The forerunners of the Sephardic communities in Brazil were Moroccan Jews from Tétouan and Tangier, who immigrated during the nineteenth century, and penetrated into the Amazon region as a result of the rubber boom. The decline of the rubber industry brought many of them to Rio de Janeiro and São Paulo. In recent years, groups of Amazonians of Moroccan descent have reclaimed their Jewish identity.

During the period of mass migration, the countries of the Southern Cone—Argentina, Brazil, Uruguay, and Chile—tried to attract European immigrants, especially agricultural workers. Argentina thus became the focus of an organized attempt to solve the problem of Russian Jewry through a massive agricultural project sponsored by Baron Maurice Hirsch. The agricultural colonies became a hotbed nurturing the leadership of Jewish Argentina, and provided the narrative of the local roots of the "Jewish Gauchos," but, from a practical point of view, Jewish agriculture disappeared within two generations.

Nevertheless, the Jewish agricultural settlements, which today house a very small number of Jews, did not escape from a new form of contemporary Jewish identity. Thus, in recent decades, the colonies created by Baron Hirsch have been transformed into memory landmarks of the Argentine Jewish community. We may claim, then, that they operate as the foundational myth of the Argentine Jewish community, competing with other myths of origin and "mother lands," such as *Eretz Israel* or the communities in Europe and the Middle East, from which the first immigrants to Argentina arrived. Jewish schools organize visits to these colonies and small villages, and there are organized tours for members of the Jewish communities and the general Argentine public. These demonstrate the ability of the largest Jewish community of Latin America to recreate its Judaism, incorporating its Jewish past into the history of Argentina as well as to its Jewish present through creative strategies.

With the decline of the Ottoman Empire, Sephardic Jews began to immigrate to Latin America in large numbers. Jews from Syria, Turkey, and the Balkan countries dispersed throughout the continent since the beginning of the twentieth century, establishing communal infrastructures based on sub-ethnic affiliation.

During the 1920s, large numbers of Jews from Poland and other East European countries immigrated to Latin America. From a historical perspective, the United States quota acts led to Latin America becoming a destination for Jewish mass migration. The closing of the gates of America resulted in the growth of the Jewish communities in the Southern Cone, as well as in Mexico and Cuba. During the Holocaust, the countries of Latin America became potential havens for Jewish refugees from countries under Nazi rule, creating a contradiction between law and practice: while all the countries implemented a restrictive legislation that legally closed their gates, they did not necessarily deny unofficial procedures for rescue. In fact, there is no correlation between the capacity for absorption and the number of refugees who entered each country.[1]

Jewish institutional life was established on a voluntary basis, and was influenced by the model of the communities of origin as well as by the different circumstances in the new countries. Larger communities were able to create more elaborate infrastructures, but the patterns of organization were similar. The Ashkenazi Jews created religious institutions, even though most of them

---

1 Haim Avni, "The Spanish Speaking World and the Jews, the Last Half Century," in *Terms of Survival: The Jewish World since 1945*, ed. Robert S. Wistrich (Abingdon, UK: Routledge, 1995), 358–82; "Latin America and the Jewish Refugees: Two Encounters, 1945 and 1938," in *The Jewish Presence in Latin America*, ed. Judith Laikin Elkin and Gilbert W. Merkx (Boston: Allen and Unwin, 1987), 58–68.

were secular. They developed educational networks, as well as social and cultural institutions that reflected the political conflicts between Zionists, Bundists, and Communists. The *Landsmanschaftn* (institutions for persons coming from the same town) characterized the first generation, and were substituted gradually by a general Ashkenazi identity, unlike the Sephardic Jews, who tended to preserve sub-ethnic divisions. The Sephardic institutions are based on centralized communities that maintain divisions between Ladino speakers, Aleppans (*Halebis*), Damascenes (*Shamis*), and Moroccans.

The Judaism of the immigrants, which differed significantly from the Judaism recreated by the first and second generations born in Latin America, reveals rich and complex phenomena in the social, political, religious, and cultural development of the Jewish communities from different countries. Social, cultural, and political transitions challenged the institutional infrastructures created by the immigrant generation. Processes of integration and assimilation were influenced by the ethnic composition and attitudes toward religious diversity and multiculturalism that require specific analysis for each individual country. Intergenerational conflicts, mixed marriages, and the growing identification with the non-Jewish environment alienated large segments of the Jewish population from the organized communities, especially in countries with large European populations and with an ideological openness toward pluralism—Brazil being a paradigmatic case. In countries with large indigenous populations, such as Mexico and Peru, where immigrants and their descendants were small minorities, the Jews tended to be auto-segregated in their own communities, and, to this day, are more involved in communal life.

For many years, the Jews of Latin America—particularly the Ashkenazi Jews—tended to be secular. From the 1940s on, Jewish identity was constructed around two axes: Zionism and the Holocaust. In the words of historian Judith Laikin Elkin, the Jews of Latin America were "a secular minority attached to Zionism as a substitute for its ancestral religion."[2] This situation has changed totally in the last fifty years. The Conservative movement became a focus of religious attraction that spread from Argentina throughout the continent, converting the *Seminario Rabínico de Buenos Aires* into an exporter of rabbis to all the Spanish-speaking communities, including those in the United States, as well as to Brazil. More recently, global ultra-Orthodox movements are gaining strength among the Jewish communities, under the impact of *shlichim*

2 Judith Laikin Elkin, *The Jews of the Latin America 3rd Edition* (Boulder, CO: Lynne Rienner Publishers, 2014), 293.

of Chabad Lubavitch or Latin American graduates of *yeshivot* in Israel and the United States. While large segments of the Jewish population are totally integrated into the Latin American environment, with a high percentage of intermarriage, the presence of ultra-Orthodox Jews, Ashkenazi and Sephardic, has been very visible in the public sphere from the 1980s on.

The growing role of religion in Jewish life has diminished the importance of Zionism as a manifestation of Jewish life—a phenomenon known as de-Zionization. Following its establishment, the State of Israel contributed to legitimizing local identities, and provided a respected *madre patria* for the rootless Jews. Gradually, however, Israel was transformed from a source of self-confidence to a source of danger, as manifested in the 1990s' bombings of the Israeli Embassy and the AMIA (Asociación Mutual Israelita Argentina—the Ashkenazi Jewish Community) in Buenos Aires, or in the anti-Semitic treatment of the Jewish community by the Chávez administration in Venezuela.

Political and economic crises in Latin American countries motivated waves of emigration that resulted in the emergence of transnational Jewish Latin American communities in Israel, the United States, and Europe. New problems now confronted the descendants of the immigrants who had found a haven from persecutions and poverty in Latin America. During the period of the military dictatorships, a relatively large number of Jews, particularly in Argentina, but also in Brazil, Chile, and Uruguay, were involved in underground activities. While many became *Desaparecidos*, others were able to escape to exile. At the same time that the countries of the Southern Cone experienced a return to democracy, other countries—such as Colombia, Peru, and Venezuela—faced political violence that threatened personal security, which became a major cause for emigration. In addition, the impoverishment of the middle classes under neo-liberal governments shattered the economic situation of the Jewish communities, leading to the departure of many Latin American Jews from Latin America.

***

Many of the early studies on Latin American Jewry were monographs prepared by local researchers, some academic, but many conducted by community activists, who wrote testimonies, memoirs, and histories of their own immigration and regions—works that came to light through books, magazines, and the community presses, and, in many cases, which were characterized by their apologetic tone.

One of the early initiatives to professionalize Jewish studies was the creation of the Program for Jewish Studies at the University of São Paulo in the late 1960s.

During the same period, the Institute of Contemporary Jewry of the Hebrew University of Jerusalem introduced the study of Latin American Jewry with the pioneering studies of Haim Avni. The starting point for Avni's approach was the need to understand the current existential problems of the Jews in Latin America through a combined analysis of the economic, social, and political reality in their respective countries, and the Jewish context at both the local and global levels.

Avni's students were among the founders of *Agudat Mitmachei Iahadut Latinoamerica* (AMILAT), an Israeli association of researchers of Latin American Jewry that organizes the Latin American section in the World Congresses of Jewish Studies, which take place every four years in Jerusalem. It also publishes the volumes of *Judaica Latinoamericana*, thus contributing to the inclusion of Latin America in the framework of Jewish studies.

While many of the early studies focused on one country, particularly Argentina, Judith Laikin Elkin was the first to present Latin American Jewry as a complex, pointing out the comparative perspective. Her book, *The Jews in the Latin American Republics* (1980), became the basic textbook for the study of Latin American Jewry in the United States. In 1980, she founded LAJSA— the Latin American Jewish Studies Association, which became an international forum for scholars interested in the field, with biannual conferences.

Latin American Jewish studies expanded gradually, with a growing crop of research, not only in history but also in literature, political science, sociology, anthropology, and art. Many of the researchers, particularly those based in the United States, became interested in the Jewish case from the perspective of general Latin American studies. A revisionist approach emerged, criticizing the "Zionist approach" of Haim Avni and his disciples. Its main representatives are Raanan Rein and Jeffrey Lesser, who argue that most of the old studies focus on the organized communities and ignore the nonaffiliated. They emphasize the local identity, using the term "Argentine Jews" instead of Jewish Argentineans, and stress the similarities between Jews and other minorities.[3]

This revisionist approach was challenged in Avni, Bokser Liwerant, DellaPergola, Bejarano and Senkman, *Pertenencia y alteridad. Judíos en/de América Latina: Cuarenta años de cambios* (*Belonging and Otherness: Jews in/ from Latin America: Forty Years of Change*) (2010), which makes a comparative

---

3 Jeffrey Lesser and Raanan Rein, eds., *Rethinking Jewish-Latin Americans* (Albuquerque: University of New Mexico Press, 2008); Ranaan Rein, *Argentine Jews or Jewish Argentines* (Leiden: Brill, 2010).

analysis of both the history and the historiography of Latin American Jews between 1967 and 2008.

✳ ✳ ✳

The collection of articles in this volume is based on an international conference that took place in São Paulo in September 2012. The conference was organized in Israel by the Dahan Center of the Bar-Ilan University and the Academic College in Ashkelon, and, in Brazil, by The Program for Hebrew Language, Jewish Literature, and Culture, and the Center for Jewish Studies of the University of São Paulo. Half of the articles in the volume deal with Brazil, reflecting the growing importance of studies on Brazil in Latin American Jewish studies, thus contributing to a more proportionate balance between studies on Argentina, as the largest Jewish community, and Brazil, as the second.

In this collection, the reader will find a wide range of subjects reflecting all the historiographical approaches mentioned above, as well as various scholarly perspectives, such as social history, anthropology, sociology, and literary criticism. There are studies using comparison versus monographs; studies based on the inside perspective of the individual communities versus analyses of the Jewish case in the general context; papers focused on the Jewish communities versus those focused on the relationship between these groups—or the diasporas—and the State of Israel. The common denominator of all the works included in the present volume is the aim to understand the singularity of contemporary Judaism and Jewishness in Latin America.

Some of the articles reflect the way in which scholars of Jewish studies in Israel are exposed to subjects such as the emergence of the new orthodoxy, Jewish education in the Diaspora, *aliyah*, and kibbutzim, or to Latin American literature from an Israeli point of view. Indeed, both lay Israelis and the Israeli academic community continue to regard Latin America as an "exotic" and distant space studied almost exclusively by researchers from various academic institutes dedicated to Latin American studies or to Latin American Jewish studies. In their efforts to overcome this tendency, the contribution of Israeli authors to this volume is an important step in demystifying stereotypes that were consolidated in Israeli society over several decades. At the same time, they raise awareness of the importance of Latin America in the global context, and the relevance of the different Jewish communities and their special relations to the State of Israel.

We would like to extend our thanks and appreciation to Dr. Shimon Ohayon of the Dahan Center, for his support and encouragement over the years. Our thanks also go to Dr. Gabriel Steinberg, head of the Center for Jewish Studies of the University of São Paulo, for giving us the backing needed for the successful accomplishment of the conference; to our students, Amilkar Henrique Gonçalves de Moura and André Galvão Soares, who worked with enthusiasm and efficiency on the last-minute details; and, finally, to Robert Bánvölgyi, who did the simultaneous translation of conferences presented in Hebrew into Portuguese. Above all, we would like to thank Mrs. Ora Kobelkowsky, who, on an almost daily basis over more than three years, ably and painstakingly oversaw the editing of the articles. She was the connecting link between the contributors to this volume and us, and did it so graciously.

We hope that the contents of this volume will be of interest to both scholars and laypersons who care about Jewish life in Latin America.

Margalit Bejarano, Israel
Yaron Harel, Israel
Marta F. Topel, São Paulo

Part One

Globalization, Transnationalism, and Latin American Judaism and Jewishness

CHAPTER 1

Expansion and Interconnectedness of Jewish Life in Times (and Spaces) of Transnationalism: New Realities, New Analytical Perspectives

JUDIT BOKSER LIWERANT

Latin American Jews live, move, build, and interact in a global world. Resulting from increasing interconnectedness and sustained migration flows, new processes of redefinition and reshaping of Latin American Jewish experiences and identities are taking place in both the known and the new geographical and social territories. Organizational and ideational patterns develop through a process of reaffirmation, transferral, or re-transferral between home and new settings. Thus, novel realities emerge that require a broad analytical scope that relates to and differentiates between Diaspora and transnationalism both as social processes and conceptual tools.

Singular to Jewish life has been the worldwide dynamics of interaction and closeness. The diasporized patterning across time and space has encompassed dense institutional networks situated within localities, across them, and as part of a Jewish world system. Through a historic process of being attached to different shifting and overlapping external centers–homelands, real and concrete, imaginary and symbolic, Latin American Jews have experienced crossing borders. A path simultaneously evincing strong connections of transnational solidarity, as well as a dependent or peripheral character of communities in the process of becoming an ethno-national Diaspora, affected these relationships. Political concepts, values, aspirations, and organizational entities brought from diverse parts of the world played fundamental roles in the process of cultural and institutional formation of Jewish communities in Latin America.

Latin American Jewish realities point to convergences and divergences between identities within a singular common trait: a close interaction between ethno-cultural identity and the national dimension in the mold of diasporic Jewish nationalism under progressive Zionist hegemony. The permanent struggle between world visions, convictions, strategies, and instrumental needs fostered the Zionist idea and the need for the State of Israel to become a central axis around which identity was built and communal life structured and developed. Thus, the State of Israel and the Jewish/Zionist ethos have played a unique role as hegemony builders and catalysts.

However, today's processes of globalization, the growing scope and intensity of worldwide interaction, and the emigration waves from the continent point to new models of transnational ties, and the emergence of transnational social fields and spaces. We suggest that Diaspora and Transnationalism may be seen as key concepts for approaching the Latin American Jewish contemporary condition. The borders of Latin American and Jewish life have expanded beyond the region, and acquired great significance as factors of social transformation. Processes of migration and relocation to new geographical and social territories reshape experiences and identities (see Figure 1.1).

Transnationalism becomes a stable condition that goes beyond the subjects that move and create expanded social spaces and realities. It therefore challenges the "methodological nationalism" of prevailing social theories that equate society

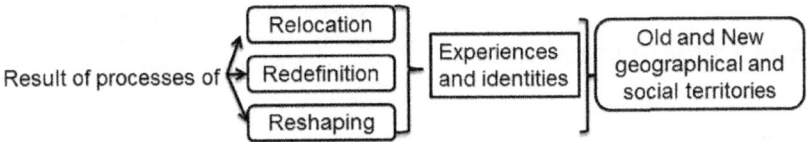

Changes (migration, relocation, return, dual residency, dispersal, renewal)⟶impact domains of community and public life:

- Inclusion and exclusion within broader communal and societal contexts

- Shifting ideological commitments

- Construction, resilience, transformation, contesting and reconstitution of individual and collective Jewish life

- Building, imagining, reformulating and adjusting-redefining individual and collective identities

Figure 1.1 Latin American Jewish Trends.

with the boundaries of a particular nation-state. Social processes, cultural inter-actions, and identity building operate across borders.[1] From this perspective, we observe traits and trends of the Latin American Jewish ethno-national Diaspora becoming an ethno-transnational one, in which bordered and bounded social and communal units are transnationally constituted spaces interacting with one another while creating new extended spaces (see Figure 1.2).[2]

While singular in certain respects, the Jewish case exhibits traits that may help us to redefine the character and significance of transnational ethnicities in a broader sense. It enables us to grapple with issues that have developed in scholarly discourse and to fill in some gaps. Comparatively, Jews are understudied in contemporary Diaspora research, where they seem to have lost their historical resonance.[3] This article affords an opportunity to redress that imbalance. Similarly, there is a relative dearth of discourse about communal institutional underpinnings in the available literature on transnational social relations.

---

1 Cf. Ulrich Beck, "La condition cosmopolite et le piège du nationalisme méthodologique," in *Les Sciences Sociales en Mutation,* ed. Michel Wieviorka (Auxerre, FR: Cedex, 2007); Nina Glick Schiller et al., "From Immigrant to Transmigrant: Theorizing Transnational Migration," *Anthropological Quarterly* 68, no. 1 (1995).

2 Judit Bokser Liwerant, "Latin American Jews. A Transnational Diaspora" in *Transnationalism,* ed. Eliezer Ben-Rafael et al. (Leiden: Brill, 2009).

3 Roger Brubaker, "The 'Diaspora' Diaspora," *Ethnic and Racial Studies* 28, no. 1 (2005).

Multidimensional nature

Jewish identities in a context of identity revival, transformation, negotiation, or even fading away and loss

Dialectic of de-territorialization and re-territorialization
Historical and current *moments* of a transnational world can be located among Latin American Jews and their communities

- In Latin America- Abroad

- Implications for social morphology as expressed in the changing character of social/communal formations

- Past- present

- Historical development of Latin America Jewish and changing conditions

Key concept to approach historical development of ethno-national Jewish Diasporas in LA + present condition
Bordered and bounded social and communal units as transnationally constituted spaces interacting with one another

Figure 1.2 Conceptual Renewal of Territory and Community (Material + Symbolic): Transnationalism.

TRANSNATIONALISM AND GLOBAL DIASPORAS: THE CONCEPTUAL AXES

Both concepts refer to similar processes and actors, and sometimes are used interchangeably, reflecting different intellectual genealogies; that is, different ways in which theoretical traditions deal with the place of structures and agency in a world on the move: population movements, migratory processes, and classical or historical dispersions, as well as a new Diaspora.

The changing contours of diasporas and their profusion have led to new formulations that recover and redefine classical dimensions. Indeed, while older notions of Diaspora mainly concern enforced dispersal, today this concept covers diverse groups like migrants, expatriates, refugees and displaced peoples, temporary migrant workers, groups of exiles, or ethnic communities, thus leading to extreme responses such as the questioning of its heuristic value.[4]

---

4 Rainer Bauböck and Thomas Faist, eds., *Diaspora and Transnationalism: Concepts, Theories and Methods* (Amsterdam: Amsterdam University Press—IMISCOE Research, 2010);

The research on Diaspora, despite the potentially indiscriminate use of the term, has highlighted three essential components: a) dispersion of its members, b) orientation toward an ethno-national center, real or imaginary, that is considered to be a homeland, and c) host country maintenance of the group's ethno-cultural borders.[5] It has gradually pointed to the dynamics both of boundary maintenance and boundary erosion, of continuity and change, and widened the concept of return to include old–new dynamics of interaction and interconnectedness. Moreover, in its wide parameters, the national and transnational dimensions interact, shift, and overlap.

Transnationalism, for its part, has focused mainly on more recent migration movements. While it has emphasized hybridity over distinctiveness and border maintenance as its characteristic, it complements and apprehends the current transformation of diasporas, allowing new readings of the past trajectory of the Jewish dispersion. The coexistence of an original home—mythic, symbolic, real—with interconnections between communities of dispersion, plus the fact that migration is no longer a unilateral movement that proceeds from the homeland to a land of destination, exhibits, rather, greater recurrence and circularity in its destinations—and points toward a novel convergence of processes, such as the diasporization of communities of migrants, or the de-diasporization, re-diasporization, and also the conversion of ethno-national diasporas into transnational ones. Multiple spatial, labor, social, and cultural displacements imply a change in analytical approaches, thus providing new perspectives.

Indeed, the potentiality of these conceptual axes points to common grounds and specificities of the Jewish case as well as to other equally relevant processes of today's Jewish life, concerning complex patterns of continuity and change in communal/national/transnational spaces. Basic conceptual and methodological dilemmas stand before us. In Diaspora studies, the Jewish case has been attenuated and has lost centrality,[6] whereas transnational studies tend to lose sight of boundary maintenance and the diasporic density present in

Douglas Nonini, "Diasporas and Globalization," in *Encyclopedia of Diasporas*, ed. Melvin Ember et al. (Boston: Springer Verlag, 2005); Brubaker, "The 'Diaspora' Diaspora."

5   Erik H. Cohen, *Youth Tourism to Israel: Educational Experiences of the Diaspora* (Clevedon, UK: Channel View Publications, 2008); Daniel Peter O'Haire, *Diaspora* (Charleston, SC: Booksurge Publishing, 2008); Frederic Brenner, *Diaspora: Homelands in Exile* (Abingdon, UK: Routledge, 2008); Milton J. Esman, *Diasporas in the Contemporary World* (London: Polity Press, 2009).

6   Robin Cohen, *Global Diasporas: An Introduction* (Seattle: University of Washington Press, 1997); Brubaker, "The 'Diaspora' Diaspora."

contemporary migratory movements. On the contrary, the latter is subsumed under the critique of the "ethnic lens."[7] Transnational studies have typically focused on individuals, their links and networks of social relations being the principal units of analysis.[8]

The Jewish case, however, is grounded necessarily in the collective dimension, in the institutional underpinnings of globality and its structural effects. The individual and communal levels interact through dense and stable Jewish associational and institutional channels that enhance informal ethnic threads (and also family links and networks). At the collective level, however, associative resources re-elaborate and reorient organized Jewish life.[9] The degree of formalization or institutionalization is characterized as well by a strong collective historical experience that brings together time dimensions as expressed by *longue durée* trends.

On the other hand, significant work in social sciences research of contemporary Jewry tends to leave out the global dimension of Jewish life, focusing on national cases and thus underscoring exceptionalism.[10] Therefore, while the historical Jewish experience does not equate social processes with national or state frontiers, it has contributed to overcoming the limitations of methodological individualism that focuses on the migrants and their networks as the exclusive unit of analysis.[11]

The concepts of Diaspora and transnationalism can now be reexamined, revealing the remarkable partnership of the "awkward partners," as

---

7 Glick Schiller et al., "From Immigrant to Transmigrant"; Peggy Levitt and Mary Waters, eds., *The Changing Face of Home: The Transnational Lives of the Second Generation* (New York: Russell Sage Foundation, 2002).

8 Luis Eduardo Guarnizo and Michel Peter Smith, "The Location of Transnationalism," in *Transnationalism from Below*, ed. Michel Peter Smith and Luis Eduardo Guarnizo (New Brunswick, NJ: Transaction Publishers, 1998); Alejandro Portes et al., "The Study of Transnationalism: Pitfalls and Promise of an Emergent Research Field," *Ethnic and Racial Studies* 22, no. 2 (1999); Ludger Pries, "Transnational Societal Spaces: Which Units of Analysis, Reference and Measurement," in *Rethinking Transnationalism: The Meso-link of Organization*, ed. Ludger Pries (Abingdon, UK: Routledge, 2008).

9 Pierre Bourdieu, "The Forms of Capital," in *Handbook of Theory and Research for the Sociology of Education*, ed. John G. Richardson (New York: Greenwood Press, 1986); James S. Coleman, "Social Capital in the Creation of Human Capital," *American Journal of Sociology* 94 (1988).

10 Judit Bokser Liwerant, "Jewish Diaspora and Transnationalism: Awkward (Dance) Partners," in *Reconsidering Israel-Diaspora Relations*, ed. Eliezer Ben Rafael et al. (Leiden: Brill, 2014).

11 Portes et al., "The Study of Transnationalism."

Bauböck and Faist defined them.[12] In particular, the dialectics of boundary maintenance/boundary erosion complements the analysis of practices of émigré ethnic communities centered only in processes of cultural hybridization, fluidity, and Creolization, as well as religious syncretism. Rogers Brubaker warns about such ambivalence found in the literature on transnationalism, for which the predominant orientation toward hybridism resists diasporic practices that have highlighted the principle of boundary maintenance. It is worthwhile underlining the fact that a major theorist of Diaspora and immigrant assimilation is aware of the need to maintain the perspective of boundary maintenance as a resource that explains interaction with society as a whole:

> Boundaries can be maintained by deliberate resistance to assimilation through self-enforced endogamy or other forms of self-segregation... [Boundary-maintenance] that enables one to speak of a diaspora as a singular "community," held together by a distinctive, active solidarity, as well as by relatively dense social relationships, that cut across state boundaries and link members of the diaspora in different states into a single "transnational community."[13]

Valuable achievements can be found in current sociological work aiming to develop and benefit from the transnational analytical paradigm.[14] As part of the conceptual shift suggested, an important line of inquiry relates to the interaction between integration, innovation, and continuity.

While deterritorialization and porous borders geographically detach communities and social sectors, transnational networks, spaces and social

---

12   Bauböck and Faist, *Diaspora and Transnationalism*;   Thomas Faist, *The Volume and Dynamics of International Migration* (New York: Oxford University Press, 2000); Thomas Faist, "Transnationalization and Development," in *Migration, Development and Transnationalization: A Critical Stance*, ed. Nina Glick Schiller and Thomas Faist (New York: Berghahn Books, 2010); Peggy Levitt and Nina Glick Schiller, "Conceptualizing Simultaneity: A Transnational Social Perspective on Society," *International Migration Review* 38, no. 145 (2004).

13   Brubaker, "The 'Diaspora' Diaspora," 6.

14   Eliezer Ben Rafael and Yitzhak Sternberg, eds., *Transnationalism: Diasporas and the Advent of a New (Dis)order* (Leiden: Brill, 2009); Shmuel Noah Eisenstadt, "The New Religious Constellation in the Framework of Contemporary Globalization and Civilizational Transformation," in *World Religions and Multiculturalism*, ed. Eliazar Ben Rafael and Yitzhak Sternberg (Leiden: Brill, 2010).

circles are created and bolstered.[15] In this sense, diasporas and transnational social formations are both cause and effect of global and multicultural macro social contexts. Current experiences imply the revision of the classic assimilation process, including segmented assimilation that often involved a gradual relaxing or reshaping of the social and cultural boundaries of migrants vis-à-vis the absorbing society. It is precisely this trend that acquires a new dynamic in light of boundary reinforcement and even boundary creation vis-à-vis the country of origin and original identities; it necessarily refers to the interplay of multiple identities (Jewish, national/country of origin, new/country/city of relocation/transnational).

The Latin American Jewish case is an apt choice in that regard if we look at Latin American Jewish immigrants in the United States who have invested strongly in establishing the institutional underpinnings for a collective identity. Individuals interact at the communal level in dense and stable associational venues. These resources elaborate and reorient organized Jewish life. Moreover, a relatively high degree of formalization and institutionalization is supra local; that is, this group's organizations and institutions embrace far more than local communal needs and attachments. The patterns observed among the migrants to the United States and elsewhere echo practices in the home communities in Latin America, where strong collective historical bonds that transcend national borders and find expression in transnational practices have characterized Jewish communal life.

BEING GLOBAL–GOING GLOBAL:
THE REGION AND THE JEWISH WORLD

Latin America may be seen from a historical global perspective; that is, it is transiting from a past global condition to a new insertion into globalization. Latin America's trajectory represents a pathway to globality as a result of the world's expansion and the extension of Europe. The conquest, colonization, and the European encounters with native peoples and civilizations produced societies that differed from the "original model," thus marking the complex and heterogeneous character of a global world in the making. Historically, the region has been constituted and incorporated into the world configuration by the export and extension of the modern European

---

15 Sanjeev Khagram and Peggy Levitt, eds., *The Transnational Studies Reader* (Abingdon, UK: Routledge, 2008); Steven Vertovec, "Conceiving and Researching Transnationalism," *Ethnic and Racial Studies* 22, no. 2 (2009).

experience to the Americas. However, following S.N. Eisenstadt's analysis, the Americas became not just "fragments of Europe" (Heartz), nor replicas of one another. They were civilizations and societies in their own right, and thus the first case of multiple modernities.[16] Through a peripheral connection of Latin American's countries to external centers—rightly conceptualized as a "global immersion"[17]—a sustained global dynamic developed. Their being part of the West but differing from it led Latin American cultures to global awareness and reflexivity. Territorial, national, cultural, socioeconomic, and political diversity certainly underline the region's internal variation.

In the final decades of the last century, however, a new phase claims globalization in unprecedented ways. Trends are closely related and underscore aspects of the same phenomenon. Time and space cease to have the same influence on the way in which social relationships and institutions are structured, and economic, social, and political arrangements do not depend on distance or on borders, nor do they have the same impact on the final shaping of institutions and social relations.

The presence and strength of transnational, supranational, or global actors and institutions radically transform the known organizational frameworks. A reconsideration of their links with communities and identities goes beyond national borders, and reconnects the links between the local, the national, and the global. States face new forms of civil society regrouping, of political participation—individual and collective—and of building and rebuilding citizenship. As shown in Figure 1.3, these processes cannot be seen exclusively in terms of continuity and evolution, but must be approached also in terms of discontinuity and breakdown. Profound tensions, contradictions, and paradoxes arising from the emergence of globally interconnected realities have characterized Latin America and affected the dynamics of inclusion and exclusion of collective identities and the constitution of the public sphere.[18] Today's extensive presence and encounters with new milieus widens the challenges derived from building collective identities.

---

16 Shmuel Noah Eisenstadt, "Multiple Modernities," in *Daedalus Journal of the American Academy of Arts and Sciences* 129, no. 1 (2000); Judit Bokser Liwerant, "Thinking Multiple Modernities from Latin America's Perspective: Complexity, Periphery and Diversity," in *Varieties of Multiple Modernities: New Design of the Research*, ed. Gerhard Preyer and Michael Sussman (Boston, MA, and Leiden: Brill, 2016), 177–205.

17 Luis Roniger, "Global Immersion: Latin America and Its Multiple Modernities," in *Globality and Multiple Modernities: Comparative North American and Latin American Perspectives*, ed. Luis Roniger and Carlos Waisman (Brighton, UK: Sussex Academic Press, 2002).

18 These two analytical axes were central to Eisenstadt's theoretical formulations.

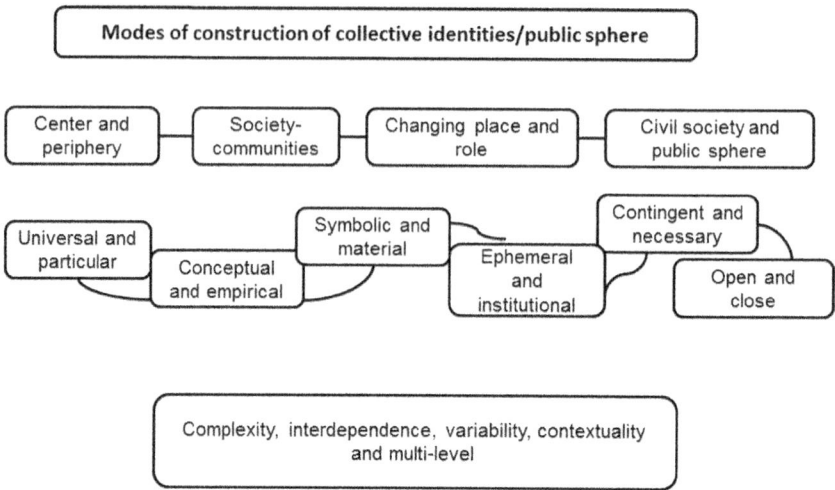

Figure 1.3 Discontinuity, Breakdowns and Tensions.

Economic and political changes, as well as social instability, have led to inner changes and substantive reconfigurations, as well as to emigration. The increasing migratory trends reflect not only regional trends but also ongoing global undercurrents and longer-term historical constraints and opportunities. It is our contention that migration today must be seen as a sustained social process and a source of social change.

Latin America, which constituted a hub of immigration, has become an exit region for broad social sectors. In parallel to processes of growing pluralism—political, institutional and cultural—and the ensuing affirmation of civic commonalities, recurrent economic crises, political instability, high levels of public violence, and lack of security have acted as main processes that lead to exit. Simultaneously, a global and interconnected world opens up opportunities to move and benefit from professional opportunities and entrepreneurial expansion in increasingly interconnected markets.

Over the past forty years, between 150,000 and 250,000 Jews from Latin American countries undertook cross-border migrations, both inside the region and outside of it. The majority moved to the United States and Israel, and, to a lesser extent, to Canada or countries in western Europe, such as Spain.[19] This

---

19 Sergio DellaPergola, "International Migration of Jews," in *Transnationalism: Diasporas and the Advent of a New (Dis)order*, ed. Eliazar Ben-Rafael et al. (Leiden: Brill, 2009); and Sergio

has led to a significant drop in the number of Jews living in Latin America, from 514,000 in 1970 to 390,000 in 2010.[20]

Estimates updated to 2011–12 indicate that Jews currently residing either in Latin America or in an array of new destination countries total about 617,000 (defining "Jewish" by a core definition of birth and current identification), or 841,000 (an enlarged population, based on currently Jewish as well as currently non-Jewish members of Jewish households). Given these global figures, it appears that close to 36–37 percent, respectively, now live outside the region.[21]

The size, timing, and social profile of migrant communities might be analyzed in terms of "waves" of migration, which in turn may be grouped under the heading of the Latin American region's "migration crises." This refers to emigration, dispersal, and regrouping of migrant communities shaped worldwide by macro-level forces, both political and economic.[22] Successive migration crises affecting Latin Americans took place during the second half of the twentieth century. The first phase began with the Cuban revolution in 1959 and continued intermittently, chiefly during the 1970s in Chile under Allende's socialist government, and later under the authoritarian regime of Pinochet (1973–90). Emigration also ensued during the era of military dictatorships in Brazil (1964–85), Argentina (1976–83), and Uruguay (1973–85). The later phases of the "migration crisis" (mid-1980s and the 1990s) were provoked by the combined effects of neo-liberal economic policies and globalization that twice affected Argentina, as well as Uruguay. Colombian Jews emigrated during that period due to a general atmosphere of domestic violence. More recently (mainly since 2000), Jews of Venezuela have emigrated under the impact of the populist regime initiated by Hugo Chávez, and continued under Nicolás Maduro. Emigration from Mexico was quite stable during these decades (see Figure 1.4).

DellaPergola, *Jewish Population Policies: Demographic Trends and Options in Israel and in the Diaspora* (Jerusalem: The Jewish People Policy Institute, 2011).

20 Estimates vary between 227,500 based on the core population definition, and 303,000 considering the enlarged population definition.

21 DellaPergola, *Jewish Population Policies*; and Sergio DellaPergola, "¿Cuántos somos hoy? Investigación y narrativa sobre población judía en América Latina," in *Pertenencia y Alteridad. Judíos en/de América Latina: Cuarenta Años de Cambio*, ed. Haim Avni et al. (Madrid: Veruvert-Iberoamericana, 2012), 305–40.

22 Nicholas Van Hear, *New Diasporas: The Mass Exodus, Dispersal and Regrouping of Migrant Communities* (Seattle: University of Washington Press, 1998).

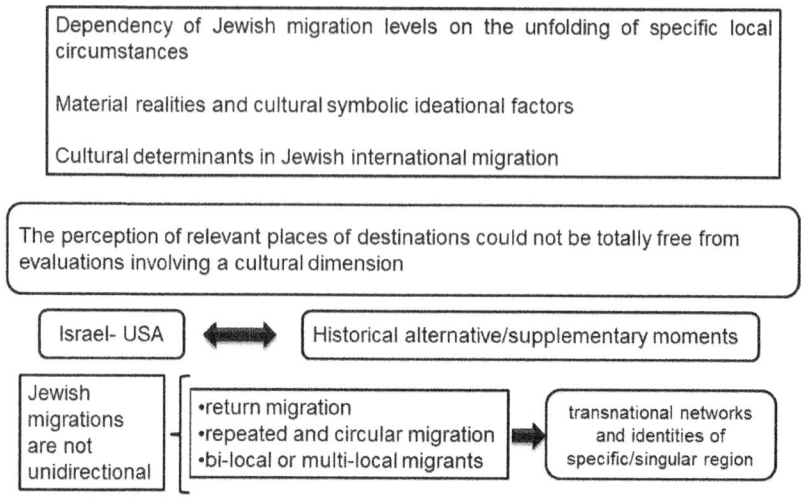

Figure 1.4 Migration Crisis and Jewish Migration.

As a result, over the course of two generations, Latin American Jews have gone from being primarily communities of immigrants to being communities of locally born citizens and, simultaneously, of expatriates and emigrants.

According to the US Census Bureau, nearly forty million US residents were foreign-born in 2010.[23] Those born in Latin America and the Caribbean, who totaled 21,224,087, represented just over half of that migratory mosaic.[24] Newcomers from the region joined veteran immigrants as well as their offspring, including second and third generations. Between 1990 and 2007, the number of emigrants from Latin American countries increased by 257 percent (from 1.9 to 4.9 million). Out of the 4.9 million, 4.2 million, or 84.3 percent of the total migrants from the region, migrated to the United States.[25] Because of both its

---

23 According to the Pew Forum (2010), there are 42.8 million migrants, including unauthorized immigrants and people born in US territories. While the United States has taken in more immigrants than any other country, the proportion of the US population that is foreign-born (13 percent) is about average for Western industrial democracies. See Pew Research Center's Forum on Religion and Public Life, "Where International Migrants Have Gone: Migrants' Destinations by Region," in *Global Religion and Migration Database 2010*, http://features.pewforum.org/religious-migration/world-maps/weighted-gone.php.

24 This figure contrasts with smaller migrant populations: 11,283,574 from Asia, 4,817,437 from Europe, and 1,606,914 from Africa. See *American Community Survey and State and County QuickFacts*, US Census Bureau, 2010, http://quickfacts.census.gov.

25 Latin America and the Caribbean showed the highest levels of relative growth of qualified migrants to OECD countries, while the latter's qualified migrant population increased by

proximity to Latin America and the opportunities it offers, the United States attracts a significant number of professionally qualified migrants. At the beginning of the twenty-first century, there were 494,000 scientists of Latin American descent working in the United States; this number represents 15 percent of all foreigners incorporated into science and technology fields in the United States.[26]

Although we have no precise figures for the number of Latin American Jews in the United States, estimates range between 100,000/133,000 (core and enlarged definitions)[27] and 156,000.[28] Considering the gamut of experiences of Latin American Jews in North American society in terms of their integration and mobility in their new milieus, and in terms of their sociocultural distinctiveness— with respect both to their culture of origin and their Jewishness—different scenarios regarding patterns of relocation and identity building can be found.

Jews migrating across and out of Latin America are in the process of becoming dispersed and regrouped simultaneously—with both the pluralization of migrant populations and the recovery of a historic trajectory of ethnic and ethno-national migration patterns. This conjunction between two interrelated factors implies an enhancement of Jewish globalization and, at the same time, the reinforcement of particular, local aspects of the Jewish experience. This, therefore, requires a dual terminology: Diaspora and transnationalism are related concepts that are applicable to the contemporary itinerary of Jewish dispersion in the "new global ethnic landscape," as Appadurai calls it.

Mobility and relocation set the stage for the potential reconstitution of an enlarged, redefined ethno-religious and national/transnational Diaspora.

---

111 percent, from 12.3 to 25.9 million. Fernando Lozano Ascencio and Luciana Gandini, "Skilled-Worker Mobility and Development in Latin America and the Caribbean: Between Brain Drain and Brain Waste," *The Journal of Latino-Latin American Studies* 4, no. 1 (2012): 7–26.

26 In 2007, 229 Mexicans, 180 Brazilians, 141 Argentines, and 121 Colombians obtained their PhDs in the United States. In 2003, naturalized individuals or nonresidents constituted 19 percent of those who graduated with a PhD or engineers employed in the United States. UNESCO-International Social Science Council, *World Social Science Report. Knowledge Divides* (Paris: UNESCO, 2010).

27 DellaPergola, *Jewish Population Policies.*

28 For an extended analysis of the relocation and transnational dynamics of Latin American Jews in the United States, see Bokser Liwerant, "Latin American Jews in the United States: Community and Belonging in Times of Transnationalism," and "Transnational Expansions of Latin American Jewish Life in Times of Migration: A Mosaic of Experiences in the United States," in *Research in Jewish Demography and Identity*, ed. Eli Lederhendler and Uzi Rebhun (Brighton, MA: Academic Studies Press, 2015); Ira M. Sheskin and Arnold Dashefsky, *Jewish Population in the United States, 2011*, Current Jewish Population Reports, North American Jewish Data Bank, 2011, accessed May 23, 2017, http://www.bjpa.org/Publications/details.cfm?PublicationID=13458.

Latin Americans Jews do not simply replicate social relationships transferred from country of origin to destination society.[29] Rather, their subjective and socially expressed experiences are quite diverse. Boundary maintenance between origin groups may be complicated (undercut, refracted, blurred) by interaction and by the plausibility of multiple identities: a sense of being Latin American may thus coexist simultaneously with a sense of being Jewish, Colombian, Mexican, or Venezuelan, Latino/Hispanic, or perhaps a more general awareness of "being immigrant Jews on the way to becoming Americans."[30]

Current literature on transnationalism questions whether the newer transnational diasporas will have a multigenerational effect. Therefore, the case of Latin American Jews in their new emigrant Diaspora provides new insights related to the hypothesis of *longue durée*. Ongoing research reveals various permutations, including reaffirmation, intermingling and disentanglement, as variegated subgroups deploy in and around concurrent ethno-cultural-national (country of origin) boundaries in common spaces, intergenerationally and communally.

Incorporation into a new society entails mutual "objective" and "subjective" ways of being similar/being different that relate to the particular place and the relative weight of changing national, sub-ethnic, and social collective belongings. The criteria by which migrant groups are classified, and the underlying assumption of Jewish communal life—either as a mosaic of experiences or as a homogeneous and uniform collective entity—are then at stake. One may thus ask how a thick package of old-country cultural norms and intense/enduring links across national borders influences social spatialities in specific ways, such that both integration and reshaping of communal, educational, and religious models take place? To what extent does the singular trajectory of being Latin American and Jewish point to new convergences and divergences between the instrumental and ideational connectedness with home(s)—including countries and communities—and their way of building their national/Jewish identity(ies) in the new settings?

---

29 Peggy Levitt, *The Transnational Villagers* (Berkeley, CA: University of California Press, 2001); Douglas Nonini, "Introduction: Transnational Migrants, Globalization Processes and Regimes of Power and Knowledge," *Critical Asian Studies* 34, no. 1 (2002): 3–17.

30 Interviews with Paul Harriton, October 2011, Miami; and Fanny Herman, April 2012, Chicago.

SPACES, PATTERNS, AND INTERACTIONS

Different identification/cultural/geographical moments of the transnational world can be distinguished among Latin American Jews and their communities. Transnational trends have a relevant influence on restructuring life in the region and in the new satellite centers that have grown out of it.

Narratives and parameters of Jewish identities may take place in a context of identity revival, transformation, negotiation, or even fading away and loss. This dialectic may entail "the loss of the natural relation of culture to geographical and social territories and, at the same time, a certain relative, partial territorial relocation of old and new symbolic productions."[31] We certainly face the diversification of Jewish life in Latin American settings and abroad. A new dialectic between homogeneity and diversity is taking place inside the Jewish world, as reflected in communal spaces and identity-building processes.

Latin American Jews in the United States live in a variety of different environments, and their experiences vary accordingly. Miami–Dade County in southern Florida and San Diego in southern California may serve as foci for analyzing the collective profile of this resettlement that contrast with settings such as the Northeast and the Midwest, with a greater transitional individualized profile. They typically live in "stacked social spaces" characterized by high proportions of foreign-born population. In Miami–Dade, 51.1 percent of the population was born outside the United States. Smaller but nonetheless significant percentages of the foreign-born characterize Los Angeles (39.6 percent), New York City (36.8 percent), Broward County, Florida (30.9 percent), Boston (27.2 percent), and San Diego (23.1 percent).[32] These metropolitan locales, which share certain socio-demographic and ethnic–racial contexts, constitute a figurative set of separate spaces; that is, they are situated and grouped in certain, noncontiguous parts of the United States, which lends significance to locality and concentration—as opposed to models that exemplify a symbolically unitary "conjunction of the social and the spatial."[33]

---

31 Néstor García Canclini, *Consumidores y ciudadanos. Conflictos multiculturales de la globalización* (Barcelona: Grijalbo, 1995).

32 In percentage terms, San Diego (32 percent) has a larger Hispanic/Latino population than Broward, Chicago (28.9 percent), and New York City (28.6 percent), while this population is far larger in Los Angeles (48.5 percent).

33 Pries, "Transnational Societal Spaces," 5.

Convergent settlement patterns shape encounters between Latino and North American Jews. Indeed, great numbers of Latin American Jews have relocated to areas with significant Jewish populations, such as the Northeast, the Midwest, southern California, and southern Florida. The Hispanic/Latino population of Broward County, FL is smaller, for example, than in Miami–Dade (25.1 percent), but the Jewish population of Broward is larger, thus reflecting the movement by Latin American Jews northward to Broward County and Palm Beach, outside the borders of Dade County.[34] In addition to the socioeconomic stratification that influences the urban section of metropolitan areas vis-à-vis suburban patterns of residence, relative size plays a role in determining the visibility of the new immigrants' communities, and shapes the nature of the encounters between their members and veteran American Jews in their environment. Thus, one might expect a lower visibility in a place like New York, where the number of Jewish residents is almost 1.5 million.

Moreover, the migrants themselves are apt to perceive distinctions among various locations and communities. There are cities in the United States where the size of the Jewish population may closely approximate the scale that new immigrants experienced in their countries of origin. The Jewish communities in Washington, DC, Boston, and Chicago (200–300,000), for example, loosely resemble the approximate size of Argentine Jewry (182,300 in 2011),[35] 85 percent of whom live in Buenos Aires. San Diego's Jewish population of 89,000 is larger than Mexico's Jewish community (estimated at 40,000), but here again the perceived similarity of scale may be an important factor in community life.

Encounters between Latin American Jews and other Jewish migrant groups exemplify a Jewish world on the move.[36] When evaluating mobile populations,

---

34 Margalit Bejarano, "From Havana to Miami, the Cuban Jewish Community," in *Judaica Latinoamericana. Estudios Histórico-Sociales*, vol. 3 (Jerusalem: AMILAT, 1997).

35 DellaPergola, *Jewish Population Policies*.

36 In Miami, it is estimated that 30.8 percent of adults in Jewish households are foreign-born. In addition to the 7.3 percent who were born in South America, 4.6 percent were born in Central America (generally including Mexico, other countries of Central America, and the Caribbean), 4.5 percent in the Middle East, and 4.5 percent in eastern Europe (excluding the Former Soviet Union [FSU]). A similar percentage (4.3 percent) was born in the FSU while 3 percent are of western European origin. Another 2.6 percent were born in other foreign countries. See Ira M. Sheskin, *Population Study of the Greater Miami Jewish Community* (Miami, FL: Greater Miami Jewish Federation, 2004). The majority of Hispanic Jews born in South American countries, including Colombia, Venezuela, and Argentina live in North Dade (10 percent), in contrast to Hispanic Jews born in Cuba, who are more concentrated in the Beaches (7.1 percent compared to 3.9 percent in South Dade and 1.5 percent in North Dade). In North Dade, other countries of origin include: Poland, Germany, Romania, Canada, Israel, and Russia.

we need to consider temporary residents. Mexican Jews living in San Diego travel regularly to Tijuana/Mexico City. Venezuelans and Mexicans travel from Miami to Caracas and Mexico City. The well-established business connections of Venezuelan and Mexican Jews living in Florida highlight the way that current economic conditions afford opportunities for transitory migration. In Miami, 7 percent of Jewish households live in the area for 3–7 months of the year (considered to be part-year households); 2 percent, for 8–9 months; 4 percent, for 10–11 months of the year; and 87 percent, for 12 months (year-round households).[37]

San Diego has become an important destination and second home abroad for Mexican Jews. Some 600–700 Mexican Jewish immigrant families, or 2,400 individuals, are currently living in San Diego (private estimates).[38] It is a border city and, partially as a consequence, overlapping migratory and social networks (family, ethnic, and increasingly professional, business, and generationally younger) have developed. The total San Diego population born in Mexico stands at over 40 percent. In turn, San Diego is part of a larger American reality in which Mexico stands out as having exceptionally high migration fluxes: close to thirty million Hispanics are of Mexican origin.[39]

In times of transnationalism, encounters between communities enable cultural circulation, interaction, and mutual influence. An examination of American Jewry and Latin American Jewish communities reveals contrasting models of Jewish collective life inside a different–similar dynamic.

The Jewish congregational model developed in the United States on the basis of denominational pluralism, and as part of a society in which religion was constitutionally separated from the state. Jewish organizational life outside the synagogue is based largely on local, regional, and national membership associations and social–welfare federations, interwoven with the Jews' other associational habits and social connections in a pluralistic and individualized manner.[40] Until fairly recently, religion was assumed to be the primary axis of

---

37 Sheskin, *Population Study of the Greater Miami Jewish Community*.
38 According to data provided by the Pew Hispanic Center, 48,348,000 Hispanics live in the United States. Of this total, 31,674,000 are Mexican (based on self-described family ancestry or place of birth). From the approximately 11.5 million undocumented migrants in the United States, 6.5 million are Mexican, representing 57 percent of the total; see B. Lindsay Lowell et al., "La demografía de la migración México a Estados Unidos," in *Mexico-US Migration Management: A Binational Approach*, ed. Agustín Escobar Latapí and Susan F. Martin (Lanham, MD: Lexington, 2008).
39 Glick Schiller et al., "From Immigrant to Transmigrant."
40 Bruce Phillips, "American Judaism in the Twenty-First Century," in *American Judaism*, ed. Dana Evan Kaplan (Cambridge: Cambridge University Press, 2005), 397–416; Chaim Waxman, *American Jews in Transition* (Philadelphia, PA: Temple University Press, 1983).

distinction among Americans, yet the unique dynamics between religion and ethnicity frequently led to the acceptance of the former as a way of expressing the latter. Individualized Jewish religiosity developed around the synagogue–congregation, and was gradually embedded in a public Jewish "civil religion," understood either as a set of civic tenets or as a Jewish ethno-national solidarity that, in the view of some observers, attained quasi-sacralized status.[41]

For their part, and in contrast to the American Jewish pattern, Latin American Jews have often sought to recreate an all-embracing *kehillah* structure, born in pre-migration Jewish social centers in the Old World, transplanted to the Latin American environment, and recovered with changing sociological meanings in the new countries of their Diaspora. Suggestive of a corporate experience, the trend in Latin American Jewish life led to an ethno–religious–national, secularized, institutionalized, and cohesive Jewish community.

In view of these background characteristics, it is important to note several indicators that point to differences as well as commonalities that shaped the migrants' individual, family, and group paths of incorporation into American Jewish communities. Overall, the rates of Jewish affiliation with ethno–communal institutions in Latin America are higher than in the United States. While the gap between Mexico City and San Diego is striking (85 percent and 30 percent, respectively), Jews in cities in Brazil and Argentina typically have far lower affiliation rates (45–50 percent), closer to the US national Jewish average for synagogue affiliations. Intermarriage rates rose among American Jews during the second half of the twentieth century, eventually reaching about 50 percent.[42] Whereas this rate (strikingly higher in the western states) contrasts with much lower rates in Mexico and Venezuela (less than or just above 10 percent), it is similar to those prevailing in Argentina and Brazil (surpassing 45 percent).

Both North and Latin American Jewish communities have been transformed by general social patterns, with distinct implications for continued collective communal life. These include: transitions from individualization to collective affirmation, and their subsequent reversal; from congregational

---

41 Shlomo Fischer and Suzanne Last Stone, *Jewish Identity and Identification: New Patterns, Meanings and Networks* (Jerusalem: Jewish People Policy Institute, 2012); Jonathan S. Woocher, "Sacred Survival Revisited: American Jewish Civil Religion in the New Millennium," in *American Judaism*, ed. Dana Evan Kaplan (Cambridge: Cambridge University Press, 2005), 283–97.

42 DellaPergola, *Jewish Population Policies*; Steven T. Katz, *Why Is America Different? American Jewry on Its 350th Anniversary* (Lanham, MD: University Press of America, 2010).

Past	Present
• Ethno-national Diaspora • Communal endeavors • Sub-ethnicity as identity and organizational axes • Secularization and politicization: plural transnational cultural baggage • Zionist idea and the State of Israel as central axes • Educational networks developed as a replica of the different ideological and political currents that were created overseas • Religious institution not brought over from Europe but 'imported' from the United States	• De-secularization and religious growing and diversified profile • Orthodox groups and new religious congregations • Educational system: dramatically change expressing religious and cultural developments • An increase in religiosity and observance constitute part of the meaningful current changes in Latin American Jewish life

Figure 1.5 Latin American Jewish Life: Old and New Patterns.

to communal models, albeit simultaneously witnessing a growing role for synagogues; from secularization to rising expressions of some forms of religiosity, even as secularism continues to gain ground; from privatization to communal revival. These trends are not linear but rather reflect changing moments, fluctuations, and interacting paths. These changes are both cause and effect of a transnational overall interconnection (see Figure 1.5).

Resulting from the interaction between the organized American Jewish communal spaces, migrants' associational initiatives within their quotidian life spheres, as well as prevailing patterns of ongoing home–abroad attachments, the social capital of American/Latin American Jewry is being restructured in a context that displays aspects of both mobility and permanence.

Latin American Jewish societies and communities have experienced radical changes in the region in their social, political, and cultural lives in terms of local and global dynamics. National culture has stopped referring to symbolic processes that set the boundaries and hierarchies between the "inside" and the "outside," and has transformed into a wide horizon/market of shared cultural goods. Inside this horizon, the transnational nature of Jewish life has gained legitimacy. The multifaceted interplay between globalization and multiculturalism allows the public manifestation of particularism and, simultaneously, widens the exposure to new forms of identification that seriously compete with the Jewish national identity referent. The pluralizing of referents does not operate in a linear or substitutive form; it rather presents an intricate pattern that points to new conceptions and practices. Indeed, we may affirm that the region is confronting a singular convergence of transitions to democracy and transnationalism that confer legitimacy to the links with external centers, be it the State of Israel or other centers, such as North American Jewry. The latter has gained relevance among the Jewish communities, extending its political concern to the region as well as its economic and philanthropic help. Paralleling political efforts, North American support has been channeled to communities in distress through a variety of institutions that have taken on an increased role, where historically the Jewish Agency for Israel was almost the exclusive actor.

INTEGRATION, DISTINCTIVENESS, AND CONTINUITY

Expressions of both continuity and adaptability characterize the display of being Latin American through one's Jewishness and one's Jewishness via Latin American–style communal patterns. Among other fields, education and communal life exemplify the range of experiences reported by Latin American Jews in the United States.[43]

Education played a central role in shaping Latin American Jewish life. Although it initially reflected the gamut of secularized political and ideological currents that shaped the Latin American Jewish communities in the early to mid-twentieth century, in more recent decades, following global Jewish trends, religious traditionalism has become more influential. The highest growth rates have been observed for religious and ultra-Orthodox (*haredi*) schools.[44]

---

43 See n. 27.

44 The *haredi* schools in Mexico, serving 26 percent of the student population, show the highest population growth—55 percent in the last eight years. The Ashkenazi schools show the greatest decrease (28 percent) and the Maguen David schools (Aleppo community schools) the highest growth rate, with 46 percent of the total student population. Of this group, 40 percent attend *haredi* schools. In Argentina, too, the highest population growth is registered among the religious schools. See Sergio DellaPergola, Judit Bokser Liwerant, Leonardo Senkman, and Yossi Goldstein, *The Transnational Jewish Educator (TNJE). Second Year Final Research Report* (Jerusalem: The Hebrew University of Jerusalem, 2014). In São Paulo, five religious schools were founded in the last decade, while there is a growing incorporation of Orthodox teachers into secular schools. See Marta F. Topel, *Jerusalém and São Paulo: A nova ortodoxia Judaica em cena* (Rio de Janeiro: Topbooks Editora, 2005), and AMIA and Vaad Hajinuj, *Profile of Jewish Education in Argentina* (working document, AMIA, Buenos Aires, 2013).

In the United States, until recent decades, education in private communal institutions was the exception rather than the rule, as most Jewish families sent their children to public schools. Today, the somewhat heightened levels of Jewish education have to be understood in light of changing trends in the Jewish world, including the demographic growth of the Orthodox sector, which tends to favor comprehensive private day school education. Less than 15 percent of the schools are non-Orthodox, 20 percent are modern Orthodox, and 60 percent are *haredi*.[45]

The relative density of Latin American Jewish populations, socioeconomic stratification, and the general availability of high-quality public education are among the factors that influence enrollment. Both in Miami and San Diego, a growing number of Latin American Jews of non-Orthodox background have been admitted into Orthodox schools (such as Hillel, Soille San Diego Jewish Day School, Chabad) through strategies of adopting selective religious practices. Cohesive social environments attract Latin American Jewish parents to schools espousing greater levels of religiosity than those they attended in their home countries, though there too the levels of religiosity have been raised. In the US, Jewish day schools, integration and mutual influence are related to the ratio of immigrants in the framework of changing trends.[46]

Social boundaries are maintained, though bifurcation and overlapping occurs—as expressed through distinctive and active solidarity, as well as by relatively dense social relationships. Being Jewish in a school or extracurricular

---

45 It is estimated that there were 60,000 students in Jewish day schools in 1962, while by 1982–83 the student population increased to 104,000 (10 percent of the Jewish school-age population). In 2000, it reached approximately 200,000; that is, nearly one-quarter of all Jewish school-age children attended day school. Recent studies show that today's total enrollment nationwide is 242,000. In 1998, the numbers were 20 percent non-Orthodox, 26 percent modern Orthodox, and 47 percent *haredi*. The growth in ultra-Orthodox or *haredi* school enrollment, including both Hasidic and non-Hasidic schools, reflects high birthrates and contrasts with modern Orthodox schools, which are essentially holding their own. At the same time, there has been a severe drop (35 percent) in Solomon Schechter (Conservative movement) school enrollment. In 1998, the first year AVI CHAI foundation examined student enrollments, the Schechter attendance totaled 17,563 students in 63 schools nationwide. This year, their school enrollment is just 11,338 students in 43 schools. See AVI CHAI, *Report on Education* (New York: The AVI CHAI Foundation, 2012).

46 At both Hillel and Sinai schools in Miami, a relatively high proportion of students are of Latin American origin. In the first case, according to one interviewee, the increase of Latin Americans in the student body has led to the relaxing of the school's religious environment. In the second case, Spanish was incorporated into the curriculum. In San Diego, a bilingual setting characterizes the Jewish Academy, where more than a third of the population is Mexican.

program in the new environment may promote a revised articulation of social and cultural markers, as in the case of family unity, ideational connectedness with the State of Israel, and memorialization of the Holocaust—referents that are so central to Latin American Jewry. However, these values—once perceived as flowing from the Latin American Jewish experience—may now come to be regarded as more universally Jewish. Transnationalism means integration via American Jewish schools even as cross-border connections are maintained.[47] At the same time, incorporation into specifically Jewish spaces allows for the maintenance of a generalized Latin American or a particularized Mexican (or Colombian/Venezuelan/Cuban) communal tie, legitimizing multiple identities.

Particular interactions sometimes occur that involve new relations in educational and communal spaces. The case of charter schools in New York and Miami illustrates the split from the mainstream Jewish education system by a small number of families for socioeconomic (middle-class Jews looking for more affordable options) and cultural reasons (a secular–cultural Jewish/Israeli environment).[48] In some instances, they become spaces for Israeli influence, illustrated by the teaching of Hebrew and Israel's culture, a trend that influences the redefinition of a one-center model vis-à-vis a radial configuration of the current Jewish Diaspora.

As for community groups, both associational and organized communal settings constitute porous containers of primordial and elective belonging. Such bordered spaces provide alternative/complementary routes into maintaining distinctiveness. The *ken* (i.e., "nest" in Hebrew, as the name of the local branch of Jewish/Zionist youth movements) in San Diego and the Hebraica/Jewish Community Center (JCC) in Miami may be conceived as ethno-national/transnational autonomous magnets. They provide contexts where immigrants can reproduce Latin American Jewish social practices—language, food, and Zionist attachments.

---

47 This may be exemplified by the Montessori school in San Diego, founded and headed by a Mexican-born educator in the 1980s. Intersections between being American and being Latin American occur in the immediate, quotidian sphere of social interaction.

48 Charter schools have become particularly attractive to Israelis and Argentines in Miami, who regard them as an "alternative" model to the synagogue-congregational one, as they are secular and cost-free institutions that are "non-elitist" and "open." Ben Gamla's Hollywood school, which opened in 2007, was the first Hebrew-English language charter school in the United States. More recently, schools with a "bilingual, bi-literate and bi-cultural curriculum" have opened in Plantation, Boynton Beach, and Kendall. A fifth school was scheduled to open in St. Petersburg, FL, in August 2012. These public schools are state-funded but privately operated. See http://www.begamla-charter.com.

Diaspora, transnationalism, and multiculturalism have shaped the lives of the newcomers and the receiving communities in complex ways. Israel has a peculiar salience as a target of economic support and political advocacy. Further study is needed in order to determine the significance of social practices such as donations to Israel. In Miami and San Diego old (pre-migration) and new patterns coexist. Direct individual–family donations and financial support are channeled through American Jewish organizations with a strong pro-Israel agenda (e.g., the Jewish National Fund, Friends of Israel Defense Forces, the United Jewish Federation, NACPAC –Pro Israel National Action Committee, and SunPac– Florida Hispanic Outreach). However, migrants also sustain regular links with their original communities, partly through the maintenance of affiliation to Jewish institutions (mainly among Mexican and Venezuelan families); therefore, resources intended for Israel-related and other overseas assistance continue to be transferred through Latin American institutional channels.

To some degree, Latin American Jewish migration to the United States implies an altered posture vis-à-vis the connection to Israel. A geographically diverse transnationalism replaces older binary connections between Latin American Jews and Israel. This does not necessarily imply the weakening of attachments but rather their re-signification.

MULTILEVEL TRANSNATIONALISM AND DIASPORA CONFIGURATIONS

Amidst new transnational trends, religion is one of the main actors in the unbinding of culture from its traditional referents and boundaries and its reattachment in new space-time configurations. It plays a major part in the revitalization of tradition, and, along with ethnicity (and nationalism), it plays a central role in the maintenance of the inter-subjective worlds where meaning, identity, a sense of place, and belongingness emerge.

Thus, one may see the widening of transnational spheres in the cultural exchange fostered under the aegis of the Conservative Jewish synagogue movement in both North and South America, in a feedback loop that ends up in the north. In the 1960s, the Conservative movement spread from North to South America, providing the first congregational model that was imported from the United States (instead of Europe), thereby establishing what may be considered a new phase of "old Transnationalism." In a regional context of scarce religious functionaries, the Seminario Rabínico Latinoamericano in Argentina assumed a pivotal role in the Conservative religious leadership.

The Conservative movement adapted to local conditions (communal over congregational model) that dated back to the earliest days when a low synagogue profile prevailed in mainly secular communities. This movement brought the synagogue to the forefront of communal and societal life in Latin American Jewry by mobilizing thousands of otherwise nonaffiliated Jews.[49]

In Argentina, the movement trained the rabbinical personnel that presently serve throughout Latin America and the United States. In the United States, nearly two dozen rabbis arrived due to the new possibilities associated with regional migration.[50] Conservative rabbis trained in Latin America currently serve in various locations, such as New York (including Forest Hills and Jamaica Estates, apart from the Manhattan congregation mentioned); Hartford, Connecticut; River Forest and Deerfield, Illinois; Vineland, New Jersey; La Jolla and San Diego, California; Boca Raton, North Miami Beach, and Plantation, Florida; Pittsburgh and Narberth, Pennsylvania; Omaha, Nebraska; Fort Worth, Texas; Atlanta, Georgia; and Roanoke, Virginia.

Latin American rabbis and their participation in new settings in the United States enhance the community model over the congregational one and, simultaneously, maintain transnational practices by traveling back and forth to their communities of origin to lead services. As mobile agents of change across national borders, they recreate a congregational–communitarian matrix. In both Miami and San Diego, Latin American Orthodox, Conservative, and Reform rabbis do not necessarily address Latin American audiences: many of them are not "Latin rabbis" but "rabbis of the community."[51] Latin American and North American rabbis collaborate in religious settings, thus symbolizing the bringing together of Latin and English-speaking American Jewish publics.

---

49 Daniel J. Elazar, *People and Polity: The Organizational Dynamics of World Jewry* (Detroit, MI: Wayne State University Press, 1989).

50 An exemplary case of the presence and wide influence of the Argentine model that integrates Conservative Judaism and social issues–human rights is Temple B'nai-Jeshurun in Manhattan, which became a vibrant religious and social space for nearly 2,000 households under the leadership of Rabbi Marshall Meyer. In 2001, Rabbi Felicia Sol (first woman rabbi) joined the congregation. See http://www.seminariorabinico.org.ar/nuevoSite/website/contenido.asp?sys=1&id=50.

51 Such rabbis include Conservative rabbis Mario Rojzman (Beth Torah), Marcelo Bater (Temple Beth Israel) and Hector Epelbaum (Beth David); Orthodox rabbis Shea Rubinstein (The Shul at Barl Harbour Chabad), Shloime Halsband (California Club Chabad), Yossi Srugo (Aventura Chabad); Reform rabbi Arturo Kalfus (Beth Am). Sources: Interview with Juan Dierce, October 2011, Miami, FL; and "Find a Rabbi," Greater Miami Jewish Federation, http://jewishmiami.org/resources/find_rabbi/.

Orthodox groups have gained fresh impetus in founding new religious congregations and supplying communities with rabbinical leadership. The spread of Chabad and the establishment of their centers in large and small cities in the United States is striking, as is the fact that thousands of Chabad representatives (known as *shluchim*) are currently working around the world. Close to eighty Chabad centers have developed in Latin America alone.[52] The increased presence and influence of transnational Chabad is evident in both California and Florida, where it reaches members by creating educational networks, social welfare services, intricate religious campaigns, legal assistance, and support for finding jobs.[53]

Although extreme religious and self-segregation strategies are still marginal to Jewish life in Latin America, their growing presence corresponds to ongoing world Jewish patterns. In fact, there has been a redefinition of identification components such as place of origin, the dilution of political ideologies—formerly the source of "hard-core" values—and the consequent emergence of spiritual calls. In recent years, both in the United States and in Latin America, new forms of religious sociability, less institutional and more individualized, have emerged. In certain ways, Buenos Aires, São Paulo, and Miami display similarities along the transnationally constituted religious sphere.

Throughout the twentieth century, Latin America has been able to contribute one of the most powerful models of Jewish corporate experience—the ethno-cultural, secularized, cohesive Jewish *kehillah*: clarity in the definition of boundaries, richness of institutions, unmistaken Jewish content—even through a significant acceptance of the social norms of the surrounding society and its priorities. These were common patterns within the internal distinction between more and less integrated societies concerning the general role of ethnicity and social stratification among the majority.

---

52 While the presence of Chabad in Mexico is marginal at best, there are more than fifty synagogues, study houses, *kollelim* and *yeshivot*, more than thirty of which were established in the last twenty-five years. Fourteen of the twenty-four existing *kollelim* belong to the Syrian *halabi* community. In Brazil—where liberal Judaism, secularity, and the syncretism of the society had a strong influence—fifteen Orthodox synagogues, three *yeshivot*, two *kollelim*, and five religious schools were established in the last fifteen years (Topel, *Jerusalém and São Paulo*).

53 In the case of Israelis, joining Chabad in Miami, New York, and Los Angeles may be a way of belonging to a more familiar home setting, in part because Conservative or Reform Judaism are still small movements in Israel (Steven J. Gold and Bruce A. Phillips, "Israelis in the United States," in *American Jewish Yearbook* (New York: The American Jewish Committee, 1996). In Miami, Chabad also has a Venezuelan "nucleus" (Topel, *Jerusalém and São Paulo*).

We observe a newly expanding claim of religious experience, but an experience that is connected in relevant and practical ways with and within the known universe of Jewish community institutions and patterns transnationally connected.

The emerging pattern could be described as a disappointment and diffidence facing the secular and political alternatives within the Jewish realm, but it is also a questioning of the basic paradigm of peaceful integration into the local national–civic mainstream, of being equal while at the same time preserving a significant amount of Jewish community autonomy.

Are we facing the growing role and visibility of the Jewish religion as a manifestation of despair or as a creative experience? Is such a revival of religion directed from the local community, or is it better characterized as joining the local community with a transnational community of believers under one superior authority, usually located in the United States or in Israel?

Changes have a determinant impact on the centrality of Israel. They can be reformulated both in terms of the changing meanings of its centrality as well as an expression of decentralization and the pluralizing of centers. Certainly, Israel's actual place is not necessarily mediated by the classical Zionist paradigm(s) while, it must be stressed, there is a search for new types of interaction that have totally overcame the mediation that organized Zionism used to offer through institutions and individual leaders.

For Latin American Jews, besides its condition of national sovereignty and a creative cultural center, Israel has historically been a vital space for those who are in need. Necessity and ideology interacted in particularly interesting ways, as expressed through waves of migration and selected places of destination. Regional and national trends point to dependency of *aliyah* (and Jewish migration in general) on the unfolding of specific local circumstances, varying recurring economic crises, political unrests, and returns to normalcy; in some cases, these factors tend to form repeated cycles.[54] There also emerge some sub-regional similarities. The situation in the country of origin was by far the most powerful determinant of *aliyah*, although one cannot neglect the intervention of successful absorption in the country of destination as a further explanatory factor. The fact that Israel is ranked significantly above every Latin American society, according to the Human Development Index, is certainly compatible with making that

---

54 Sergio DellaPergola, "International Migration of Jews," in *Transnationalism: Diasporas and the Advent of a New (Dis)order*, ed. Eliazar Ben-Rafael and Yitzhak Sternberg, with Yosef Gorni and Judit Bokser Liwerant (Leiden: Brill, 2009), 213–36.

choice consonant with the routine preference of most international migrants to move from poorer to better environments. More than 100,000 Jews have made *aliyah*, and the different moments and profiles point to the weight of their ideational motive.

Israel has been a focal point. However, when asked today about their country of preference in case of emigration, other destinations appear. We may look further into this variation through the angle of educational trips to Israel, an indicator that reveals the unique convergence of modern nationalism and postmodern transnationalism in the Jewish world and the region or, in other words, the changing role of the national homeland to guarantee the continuity of the Diaspora. Seen from the perspectives of interaction and circulation, trips oscillate between links and bonds to the nation-state and Diaspora-building.[55] However, the latter must be seen from a regional lens that focuses on the process of becoming an ethno-transnational Diaspora. Ethnic diasporas—the "exemplary communities of the transnational moment"—are today engaged in a renewed geography of dispersion.[56] These trips and their function—based on a complex logic of interdependence, disjuncture, and convergences between Israel and Diaspora —are closely related to the institutional density, the social capital, and the communal legacy of the diverse communities. Accordingly, Israel plays a varied central role.

Redefining and reconnecting their attachments, Latin American Jews are involved in processes of Diaspora making and Diaspora unmaking. Diverse scenarios are available to them as they experience de-socialization from their country and community of origin, and re-socialization in the country and community of destination, a dialectic of Diaspora making and Diaspora unmaking.[57]

Greater Miami mirrors the cycles of migration crises in the region; it became a host location to the first Jewish Cuban collective migratory/exiled wave. Successive migration crises in the region led to the thinning-out of an ethno-national Diaspora under stress (e.g., Venezuela) and the expansion of a transnational community in new frontier areas such as Caribbean Florida or the American Southwest. Multiple ways of retaining connections with communities and countries of origin have developed, and trans-local entrepreneurs from Colombia, Venezuela, and Mexico exemplify these ties. We observe complex

55 Shaul Kelner, *Tours That Bind: Diaspora, Pilgrimage, and Israeli Birthright Tourism* (New York: New York University Press, 2010).

56 Kaching Tölölyan, "Rethinking Diaspora(s): Stateless Power in the Transnational Moment," *Diaspora* 5, no. 1 (1996).

57 Van Hear, *New Diasporas*.

dynamics grounded in patterns that are particular to each national group but are generalized also within a large population.

In San Diego, an ethno-national enclave with a transnational character took shape among Mexican Jews, leading to what may be termed a secondary Diaspora. In contrast, the Latin American Jewish community of Miami has a multinational composition.[58] In this case, a shared sense of living in a community with other Latin Americans, the existence of communal organized spaces that represent group continuity, and the presence of a critical mass enhance new social regrouping by allowing migrants to establish and bolster formal and informal networks based on their common origins.

From a comparative perspective, the migrant experience in the Northeast–Midwest triangle and its counterpart in Texas are of particular interest as they represent individual–professional (e.g., medical students, interns, and doctors) cases, rather than collective migration patterns. Age, gender, and household composition—selectively younger and nuclear—provide interesting doors of entry and mapping routes into associational connections. We may thus question further and analyze a scenario of de-diasporization that could lead to either individual integration or new prevailing criteria and axes of regrouping.

Migration movements and diasporas and their transnational links involve maintaining communities, having collective homes away from home, and building new ones. Diasporas may be conceived simultaneously in terms of "mobility and fixity, closeness and distance"; they connect the Jewish world and exist "only through circulation."[59] Thus, building Jewish life consists not only of rootedness but also of exchanges of dynamic cultural practices.

There is certainly a diversity that results from our focus on particular units of analysis (e.g., families, ethnicities and sub-ethnicities, social classes, values, institutions and organizations, identities), units of reference (e.g., nation-states, regions, world Jewish system), and units of measurement (e.g., norms, rituals, flows and circulation of information, households), thus calling our attention to the need for a

---

58 Of the Jewish adults who consider themselves to be Hispanic, the majority (29 percent) come from Cuba; 18 percent, from Argentina; 16 percent, from Colombia; and 15 percent, from Venezuela. Other countries from Latin America and the Caribbean with smaller percentages include Mexico (4 percent), Uruguay (2.2 percent), Peru (1.4 percent), Brazil (1.3 percent), Dominican Republic (0.7 percent), Guatemala (0.7 percent), Chile (0.5 percent), Ecuador (0.3 percent), Jamaica (0.3 percent), Nicaragua (0.3 percent), Panama (0.3 percent) and Bolivia (0.2 percent). See Sheskin, *Population Study of the Greater Miami Jewish Community.*

59 James Clifford, "Diasporas," *Cultural Anthropology* 9, no. 3 (1994): 388.

new theoretical and methodological framework that combines a cross-national, world Jewish system and transnational studies.[60]

Jewish collective life is built in multiple institutional arenas—territorial, communal, religious, national, cultural—and political–ecological settings— local, regional, national—within a global world in which identities intersect and overlap, and their components become re-linked.[61]

Therefore, our subject calls for conceptual lenses of multiple identities, meaning the need to understand the continuous process of construction, fragmentation, and diversification of identities that lead to new dimensions that do not necessarily imply erosion and decline. Following this line of thought, not only continuity but also diversity and pluralism become cultural and normative requirements to define Jewish collective identity today. Amidst an inner differentiated culture, we may need to make parallel approaches to multicultural environments and develop neighborly relations on the basis of what Margaret Levi calls "contingent consent, that is, a consent less situational than that implied when actors are treated as economist rational maximizers pursuing instrumental self-interests but less uniform, fixed and definite than when actors belong to single cultures characterized by unselfish shared norms."

Through migration waves and beyond, by crossing material and symbolic borders, Latin American Jewish life transcends the region's frames of reference, encounters the culture(s) of the United States and, through diversified interactions and exchanges, widens the experience of being Jewish in the twenty-first century. The prevalence of manifold scenarios and their differential impact explain the increasing complexity of experiences, but they also point to broadly shared trends that bring together different worlds.

Looking at Latin American societies, globalization, and transnationalism, as well as local factors such as democratic pluralism and identity, politics have enhanced the apparent contradictory processes of assimilation and ethnicitization of diasporas.[62] The region has witnessed the development and legitimate expression of a new transnational consciousness—somewhat

---

60   Pries, "Transnational Societal Spaces"; Judit Bokser Liwerant, Sergio DellaPergola, and Leonardo Senkman, *Latin American Jews in a Transnational World: Redefining Experiences and Identities in Four Continents* (Jerusalem: The Hebrew University of Jerusalem, 2010).

61   Shmuel Noah Eisenstadt, "The Constitution of Collective Identity. Some Comparative and Analytical Indications," in *A Research Programme; Preliminary Draft* (Jerusalem: The Hebrew University of Jerusalem, 1995).

62   Arjun Appadurai, "Disjuncture and Difference in the Global Cultural Economy," in *Theory, Culture and Society*, vol. 7 (London: Sage, 1990).

recovering an earlier stage of "diaspora consciousness" among descendants of earlier migrants—marked by multiple identifications as well as an awareness of decentralized and multiple attachments. Thus, amidst a general diasporization, the Jewish one—home and abroad—has gained visibility and legitimacy. Indeed, there is an unprecedented respectability granted to diasporas in the public spheres of modern Latin American nation-states, basically due to migration movements and the role of civil society in countries that have successfully transitioned from dictatorships to democratic coexistence. Whereas in regimes with strong states that are stable and democratic, the conception of civil societies led to a redefinition of the role of the state and favored a new political–institutional equilibrium, new democratized scenarios of civil society aim to legitimize diasporic formations seen as emerging social movements that contribute to cultural pluralism and diversity.[63] However, societies that have not yet consolidated democratic transitions channel the lion's share of their efforts into implementing and strengthening their traditional republican institutions, as well as streamlining their political efficiency for improved governability and reform of the state. Indeed, external transnational processes in Latin America have validated diasporic formations far more than the political horizon of liberal democracy and civil coexistence, or new civic conceptions. In other words, the legacy of the national constitutional order, reestablished within the republican democratic tradition, lukewarmly legitimized traditional diasporas; and if these were actually revitalized, it was because of processes exterior to the local political system, such as the impact of globalization processes and the expansion of transnational networks.

Drawing comparative insights into encounters in different times and spaces certainly leads to diversified scenarios. Transnationalism may extend its conceptual utility to historical changes. A full circle may be drawn when applying the concept of Transnationalism to the analysis of the Latin American Jewish experience. Its capacity differentially to encompass past and present trends in changing and supplementary spaces widens its explanatory potential. While new types have emerged, diverse models of interaction have redefined and reshaped the original attachment of Jewish life in the region to external centers.

---

63 Judit Bokser Liwerant and Leonardo Senkman, "Diasporas and Transnationalism: New Inquiries Regarding Latin American Jews Today," in *Judaica Latinoamericana*, vol. 7 (Jerusalem: Magnes Press, 2013).

REFERENCES

American Community Survey and State and County QuickFacts, US Census Bureau, 2010, http://quickfacts.census.gov/.

AMIA, and Vaad Hajinuj. *Profile of Jewish Education in Argentina*. Working document, AMIA, Buenos Aires, 2013.

Appadurai, Arjun. "Disjuncture and Difference in the Global Cultural Economy." In *Theory, Culture and Society*, 295–310. Vol. 7. London: Sage, 1990.

AVI CHAI, *Report on Education* (New York: The AVI CHAI Foundation, 2012).

Bauböck, Rainer, and Thomas Faist, eds. *Diaspora and Transnationalism. Concepts, Theories and Methods*. Amsterdam: Amsterdam University Press–IMISCOE Research, 2010.

Beck, Ulrich. "La condition cosmopolite et le piège du nationalisme méthodologique." In *Les Sciences Sociales en Mutation*, edited by Michel Wieviorka, 223–26. Auxerre, FR: Cedex, 2007.

Bejarano, Margalit. "From Havana to Miami, The Cuban Jewish Community." In *Judaica Latinoamericana. Estudios Histórico-Sociales*, 113–30. Vol 3. Jerusalem: AMILAT, 1997.

Ben Rafael, Eliezer, and Yitzhak Sternberg, eds. *Transnationalism: Diasporas and the Advent of a New (Dis)order*. Leiden: Brill, 2009.

Bokser Liwerant, Judit. "Thinking Multiples Modernities from Latin America's Perspective: Complexity, Periphery and Diversity," in *Varieties of Multiple Modernities: New Design of the Research*, ed. Gerhard Preyer and Michael Sussman, 177–205. Boston, MA, and Leiden: Brill, 2016.

———. "Jewish Diaspora and Transnationalism: Awkward (Dance) Partners." In *Reconsidering Israel-Diaspora Relations*, ed. Eliezer Ben Rafael, Judit Bokser Liwerant, and Yosi Gorny, 369–404. Leiden: Brill, 2014.

———. "Latin American Jews in the United States: Community and Belonging in Times of Transnationalism." *Contemporary Jewry* 33 (2013): 121–43.

———. "Latin American Jews. A Transnational Diaspora." In *Transnationalism*, ed. Eliezer Ben-Rafael, Yitzhak Sternberg, Judit Bokser Liwerant, and Yossi Gorny, 81–105. Leiden: Brill, 2009.

———. "Transnational Expansions of Latin American Jewish Life in Times of Migration: A Mosaic of Experiences in the United States." In *Research in Jewish Demography and Identity*, ed. Eli Lederhendler and Uzi Rebhun, 198–240. Brighton, MA: Academic Studies Press, 2015.

Bokser Liwerant, Judit, and Leonardo Senkman. "Diasporas and Transnationalism: New Inquiries Regarding Latin American Jews Today." In *Judaica Latinoamericana*. Vol. 7 (Jerusalem: Magnes Press, 2013).

Bokser Liwerant, Judit, Sergio DellaPergola, and Leonardo Senkman. *Latin American Jews in a Transnational World: Redefining Experiences and Identities in Four Continents*. Jerusalem: The Hebrew University of Jerusalem, 2010.

Bourdieu, Pierre. "The Forms of Capital." In *Handbook of Theory and Research for the Sociology of Education*, ed. John G. Richardson, 241–58. New York: Greenwood Press, 1986.

Brenner, Frederic. *Diaspora: Homelands in Exile*. Abingdon, UK: Routledge, 2008.

Brubaker, Roger. "The 'Diaspora' Diaspora." *Ethnic and Racial Studies* 28, no. 1 (2005): 1–19.

Clifford, James. "Diasporas." *Cultural Anthropology* 9, no. 3 (1994): 302–38.

Cohen, Erik H. *Youth Tourism to Israel: Educational Experiences of the Diaspora.* Clevedon, UK: Channel View Publications, 2008.

Cohen, Robin. *Global Diasporas: An Introduction.* Seattle: University of Washington Press, 1997.

Coleman, James S. "Social Capital in the Creation of Human Capital." *American Journal of Sociology* 94 (1988): 95–120.

DellaPergola, Sergio. "¿Cuántos somos hoy? Investigación y narrativa sobre población judía en América Latina." In *Pertenencia y Alteridad. Judíos en/de América Latina: Cuarenta Años de Cambio,* ed. Haim Avni, Judit Bokser-Liwerant, Sergio DellaPergola, Martalit Bejarano, and Leonardo Senkman, 305–40. Madrid: Veruvert-Iberoamericana, 2012.

DellaPergola, Sergio. *Jewish Population Policies: Demographic Trends and Options in Israel and in the Diaspora.* Jerusalem: The Jewish People Policy Institute, 2011.

——. "International Migration of Jews." In *Transnationalism: Diasporas and the Advent of a New (Dis)order,* ed. Eliazar Ben-Rafael and Yitzhak Sternberg, with Yosef Gorni and Judit Bokser Liwerant, 213–36. Leiden: Brill, 2009.

DellaPergola, Sergio, Judit Bokser Liwerant, Leonardo Senkman, and Yossi Goldstein. *The Transnational Jewish Educator (TNJE). Second Year Final Research Report.* Jerusalem: The Hebrew University of Jerusalem, 2014.

Eisenstadt, Shmuel Noah. "The New Religious Constellation in the Framework of Contemporary Globalization and Civilizational Transformation." In *World Religions and Multiculturalism,* ed. Eliazar Ben Rafael and Yitzhak Sternberg, 21–40. Leiden: Brill, 2010.

——. "Multiple Modernities." *Daedalus. Journal of the American Academy of Arts and Sciences* 129, no. 1 (2000): 1–30.

——. "The Constitution of Collective Identity. Some Comparative and Analytical Indications." In *A Research Programme; Preliminary Draft.* Jerusalem: The Hebrew University of Jerusalem, 1995.

Elazar, Daniel J. *People and Polity: The Organizational Dynamics of World Jewry.* Detroit, MI: Wayne State University Press, 1989.

Esman, Milton J. *Diasporas in the Contemporary World.* London: Polity Press, 2009.

Faist, Thomas. *The Volume and Dynamics of International Migration.* Oxford: Oxford University Press, 2000.

——. "Transnationalization and Development." In *Migration, Development and Transnationalization. A Critical Stance,* ed. Nina Glick Schiller and Thomas Faist, 63–99. New York: Berghahn Books, 2010.

Fischer, Shlomo, and Suzanne Last Stone. *Jewish Identity and Identification: New Patterns, Meanings and Networks.* Jerusalem: Jewish People Policy Institute, 2012.

García Canclini, Néstor. *Consumidores y ciudadanos. Conflictos multiculturales de la globalización.* Barcelona: Grijalbo, 1995.

Glick Schiller, Nina, Linda Basch, and Christina Blanc-Szanton. "From Immigrant to Transmigrant: Theorizing Transnational Migration." *Anthropological Quarterly* 68, no. 1 (1995): 43–68.

Glick Schiller, Nina, and Ayse Çaglar. *Locating Migration: Rescaling Cities and Migrants*. Ithaca, NY: Cornell University Press, 2011.

Gold, Steven J., and Bruce A. Phillips. "Israelis in the United States." In *American Jewish Yearbook*, 51–101. New York: The American Jewish Committee, 1996.

Guarnizo, Luis Eduardo, and Michel Peter Smith. "The Location of Transnationalism." In *Transnationalism from Below*, ed. Michel Peter Smith and Luis Eduardo Guarnizo, 3–34. New Brunswick, NJ: Transaction Publishers, 1998.

Katz, Steven T. *Why Is America Different? American Jewry on Its 350th Anniversary*. Lanham, MD: University Press of America, 2010.

Kearny, Michael. "The Local and the Global: The Anthropology of Globalization and Transnationalism." *Annual Review of Anthropology* 24 (1995): 547–65.

Kelner, Shaul. *Tours That Bind: Diaspora, Pilgrimage, and Israeli Birthright Tourism*. New York: New York University Press, 2010.

Khagram, Sanjeev, and Peggy Levitt, eds. *The Transnational Studies Reader*. Abingdon, UK: Routledge, 2008.

Levitt, Peggy, and Nina Glick Schiller. "Conceptualizing Simultaneity: A Transnational Social Perspective on Society." *International Migration Review* 38, no. 145 (2004): 595–629.

Levitt, Peggy, and Mary Waters, eds. *The Changing Face of Home: The Transnational Lives of the Second Generation*. New York: Russell Sage Foundation, 2002.

Levitt, Peggy. *The Transnational Villagers*. Berkeley, CA: University of California Press, 2001.

Lowell, B. Lindsay, Carla Perdezini, and Jefrey S. Passel. "La demografía de la migración México a Estados Unidos." In *Mexico-US Migration Management: A Binational Approach*, ed. Agustín Escobar Latapí and Susan F. Martin. Lanham, MD: Lexington, 2008.

Lozano Ascencio, Fernando, and Luciana Gandini. "Skilled-Worker Mobility and Development in Latin America and the Caribbean: Between Brain Drain and Brain Waste." *The Journal of Latino-Latin American Studies* 4, no. 1 (2012): 7–26.

Pew Research Center's Forum on Religion and Public Life. "Where International Migrants Have Gone: Migrants Destinations by Region." In *Global Religion and Migration Database 2010*. http://features.pewforum.org/religious-migration/world-maps/weighted-gone.php.

Phillips, Bruce. "American Judaism in the Twenty-First Century." In *American Judaism*, ed. Dana Evan Kaplan, 397–416. Cambridge: Cambridge University Press, 2005.

Pries, Ludger. "Transnational Societal Spaces. Which Units of Analysis, Reference and Measurement." In *Rethinking Transnationalism. The Meso-link of Organization*, ed. Ludger Pries, 1–20. Abingdon, UK: Routledge, 2008.

Nonini, Douglas. "Diasporas and Globalization." In *Encyclopedia of Diasporas*, ed. Melvin Ember, Carol Ember, and Ian Skoggard, 559–70. Boston: Springer Verlag, 2005.

———. "Introduction: Transnational Migrants, Globalization Processes and Regimes of Power and Knowledge." *Critical Asian Studies* 34, no. 1 (2002): 3–17.

O'Haire, Daniel Peter. *Diaspora*. Charleston, SC: Booksurge Publishing, 2008.

Portes, Alejandro, Luis Guarnizo, and Patricia Landolt. "The Study of Transnationalism: Pitfalls and Promise of an Emergent Research Field." *Ethnic and Racial Studies* 22, no. 2 (1999): 217–37.

Pries, Ludger. "Transnational Societal Spaces. Which Units of Analysis, Reference and Measurement." In *Rethinking Transnationalism. The Meso-link of Organization,* ed. Ludger Pries, 9–67. Abingdon, UK: Routledge, 2008.

Robertson, Roland. *Globalization: Social Theory and Global Culture.* London: Sage Publications, 1992.

Roniger, Luis. "Global Immersion: Latin America and Its Multiple Modernities." In *Globality and Multiple Modernities: Comparative North American and Latin American Perspectives,* ed. Luis Roniger and Carlos Waisman, 79–105. Brighton, UK: Sussex Academic Press, 2002.

Scholte, Jan Aart. "The Globalization of World Politics." In *The Globalization of World Politics: An Introduction to International Relations,* ed. John Baylis and Steve Smith, 13–30. Oxford: Oxford University Press, 1997.

Sheskin, Ira, and Arnold Dashefsky. *Jewish Population in the United States, 2011.* Current Jewish Population Reports, North American Jewish Data Bank, 2011. Accessed May 23, 2017. http://www.bjpa.org/Publications/details.cfm?PublicationID=13458.

Sheskin, Ira M. *Population Study of the Greater Miami Jewish Community.* Miami, FL: Greater Miami Jewish Federation, 2004.

Tölölyan, Kaching. "Rethinking Diaspora(s): Stateless Power in the Transnational Moment." *Diaspora* 5, no. 1 (1996): 3–36.

Topel, Marta F. *Jerusalém and São Paulo: A nova ortodoxia Judaica em cena.* Rio de Janeiro: Topbooks Editora, 2005.

UNESCO–International Social Science Council. *World Social Science Report. Knowledge Divides.* Paris: UNESCO, 2010.

Van Hear, Nicholas. *New Diasporas: The Mass Exodus, Dispersal and Regrouping of Migrant Communities,* Global Diaspora Series. Seattle: University of Washington Press, 1998.

Vertovec, Steven. "Conceiving and Researching Transnationalism." *Ethnic and Racial Studies* 22, no. 2 (2009): 447–62.

Waters, Malcolm. *Globalization.* Abingdon, UK: Routledge, 1995.

Waxman, Chaim. *American Jews in Transition.* Philadelphia, PA: Temple University Press, 1983.

Woocher, Jonathan S. *Sacred Survival: The Civil Religion of American Jews.* Bloomington, IN: Indiana University Press, 1986.

———. "Sacred Survival Revisited: American Jewish Civil Religion in the New Millennium." In *American Judaism,* ed. Dana Evan Kaplan, 283–97. Cambridge: Cambridge University Press, 2005.

CHAPTER 2

Changing Identities in a Transnational Diaspora: Latin American Jews in Miami[1]

MARGALIT BEJARANO

D ade Country—the metropolitan area of Miami—is a kaleidoscope of ethnic groups in constant movement. Under the impact of continuous waves of migration, particularly from Latin America, the city has been undergoing processes of Latinization that are transforming its social and cultural texture. A similar phenomenon is occurring among the Jews of Miami, who were dominated until recently by English-speaking Ashkenazim. Their demographic decline was accompanied by the arrival of new waves of immigrants from the former Soviet Union (FSU), the Middle East, and particularly from Latin America, which changed the profile of Miami Jewry. The Latin Americans are the largest group among the Jews born outside the United States to reside in Miami–Dade. Their history is related closely to that of the non-Jewish Cubans and Latinos who have transformed Miami over the past fifty years.

The turning point in the history of Miami was the arrival of the massive Cuban exodus following the Castro revolution of 1959. The United States opened its doors to the Cuban immigrants, recognizing them as refugees from a Communist regime. The Cubans participated in the development of Dade County—the metropolitan area of Miami—achieving a remarkable economic

---

1 This paper is part of the research project of the Liwerant Center for the Study of Latin America, Spain, Portugal and their Jewish Communities at the Hebrew University on transnationalism of Latin American Jews in four continents.

success as well as gaining political power. Miami offered the Cuban exiles an economic, social, political, and cultural substitute for their homeland, and they became a paradigm of a successful insertion of Hispanics into the American host society.[2]

The Cubans were the pioneers in the development of Latin American transnational diasporas in Miami. Under the impact of processes of globalization that affected the Latin American countries, Miami became a lodestone, not only for low income Hispanics trying to improve their economic situation but also for middle and upper class immigrants from Central and South America seeking permanent or transitory stability in periods of crises, as well as new business opportunities, tropical tourism, and an American lifestyle in a Spanish-speaking environment. The largest groups of unskilled economic migrants came to Miami from Puerto Rico and Nicaragua, while immigrants from Colombia and Venezuela included also members of the white elite, escaping political violence.[3]

The migratory flows into and out of Miami in different periods can be viewed as indicators of political transitions, economic movements, and waves of violence in the different homelands.[4] In the case of the Cubans, the migration was unidirectional and irreversible; despite their auto-definition as exiles (*el exilio*), they created a permanent transnational Diaspora of Cuban-Americans.[5] Other migrations from Latin America were bi- or multidirectional, causing the phenomenon of "blurred borders."[6] Latin American Jews followed the footsteps of their conationals in creating transnational diasporas in Miami.

---

2 The use of the term "insertion" instead of "integration" is based on Eliezer ben Rafael, "Collective Identities and Transnationalism," in *Transnationalism: Diasporas and the Advent of a New (Dis)order*, ed. Eliezer Ben-Rafael, Yitzhak Sternberg, Judit Bokser Liwerant, and Yosef Gorny (Leiden: Brill, 2009), 124–25; see also Alex Stepick, Guillermo Grenier, Max Castro, and Marvin Dunn, *This Land Is Our Land: Immigrants and Power in Miami* (Berkeley, CA: University of California Press, 2002), 8–10, 21–22, 34–39.

3 "Latinos Become Largest Racial Group in Miami–Fort Lauderdale–Palm Beach Metro Area," *The Higley 1000*, February 15, 2010, accessed December 16, 2013, http://higley1000.com/archives/241.

4 Stepick, Grenier, Castro, and Dann, *This Land Is Our Land*, 20.

5 David Rieff, *Exile: Cuba in the Heart of Miami* (New York: Simon and Schuster, 1996), 26–30.

6 Jorge Duany, *Blurred Borders: Transnational Migration between the Hispanic Caribbean and the United States* (Chapel Hill, NC: University of North Carolina Press, 2011); Judit Bokser Liwerant and Leonardo Senkman, "Diásporas y transnacionalismo, nuevas indagaciones sobre los judíos latinoamericanos hoy," in *Judaica Latinoamericana: Estudios históricos, sociales y literarios*, vol. 7 (Jerusalem: Magnes Press, 2013), 36.

In their case, they had to redefine the borders of their ethnic and religious identity vis-à-vis their English-speaking coreligionists, whom they considered as part of the white Anglo mainstream. Most of Miami's Jews, however, were recent immigrants from other parts of the United States or foreign-born Jews, mainly from Europe.[7]

From the 1980s, the demographic profile of Jewish Miami became more diversified with the arrival of immigrants from the FSU, from Israel, and from North Africa (many of them via France or Canada).[8] The largest group of foreign born, as mentioned above, came from Latin America, constituting 12 percent of the total Jewish population.

In the eyes of others, the Latin American Jews may seem to be a homogenized group. In reality, however, they are divided into different communities, with different relations with their homelands, with their conationals in Miami, and with their Jewish communities of origin. They bring to the United States their former historical experiences, social patterns, and ideologies, in most cases with a deep commitment to Israel. Their insertion into the Jewish life of Miami is marked by tensions between trends of continuity and adaptation with far-reaching consequences for the Anglo-Jewish host society.

This article focuses on four groups: Cubans, Colombians, Argentineans, and Venezuelans. Its objectives are: 1) to analyze the interaction of Spanish- and English-speaking Jews, and its influence on the formation of a Jewish-Latino transnational Diaspora in Miami; 2) to compare the Jewish-Cuban experience with more recent migrations; 3) to examine the patterns of identity of the Latino Jews in Miami with their countries of origin, with their former communities, with the United States, and with Israel.

THE ETHNIC TRANSFORMATION OF MIAMI

During the second half of the twentieth century, Miami developed from a tourist resort town into a bustling metropolis, a crossroad of international trade and finance, a vibrant center of leisure and entertainment, and a shelter for political refugees. The large waves of immigration converted Miami into a

---

7 In 1984, 4 percent of the Jewish adults were born in Dade County, 73 percent were born in the United States, and 80 percent of the foreign born came from eastern and central Europe; Ira M. Sheskin, *A Demographic Study of the Great Miami Jewish Community, Summary Report* (Miami, FL: Greater Miami Jewish Federation, 1984), 7.

8 Ira M. Sheskin, *The 2004 Greater Miami Jewish Community Study* (Miami: Greater Miami Jewish Federation, 2005), 4–12.

mosaic of ethnic communities and a frontier city between the United States and Latin America.

Over the past fifty years, the demographic profile of Miami has changed dramatically. The rate of white English-speaking Americans has decreased from 80 percent to 15 percent; the population of the African Americans has increased slightly, from 15 to 19 percent; and the Hispanic population has increased from 5 to 65 percent. More than two-thirds of the Hispanics are Cubans, and the rest are divided into small groups of less than 4 percent each, coming mainly from Colombia, Nicaragua, Puerto Rico, Dominican Republic, Honduras, Mexico, Venezuela, and Argentina.[9]

Miami–Dade attracted Jewish tourists and investors from New York, Chicago, and other parts of the United States, many of whom lived there only during the winter season. It also became home to many Holocaust survivors and their children.[10] When the Cuban immigration began, half of the Jewish population lived in Miami Beach, which attracted elderly Jews from the North who preferred to retire in a tropical climate. Miami Beach at that time was 80 percent Jewish, and was divided geographically according to social classes: the wealthy Jews resided in fancy condominiums in North Beach, while the poor lived south of Lincoln Road.[11] Gradually, however, poor Hispanics took the place of the poor Jews in South Beach. The Jewish population started to move northward, creating two major centers, in Broward County and Palm Beach, outside the borders of Dade County.[12]

The arrival of the Jews from Cuba coincided with the peak of the Jewish presence in Miami Beach. While most of the non-Jewish Cubans created their center near downtown Miami, in the area known as *Calle Ocho* or Little Havana, the Cuban Jews settled in the Jewish neighborhood of Miami Beach, moving gradually from South Beach to North Beach.[13]

---

9 Alejandro Portes and Alex Stepick, *City on the Edge: The Transformation of Miami* (Berkeley, CA: University of California Press, 1993), 211; figures for 2007 are taken from: *Miami Dade County Quick Facts from the US Census Bureau*, US Census Bureau, accessed September 5, 2012, *quickfacts.census.gov/qfd/states/12/12086.html*.

10 Andrea Greenbaum, *Jews of South Florida* (Waltham, MA: Brandeis University Press, 2005), xiii.

11 Deborah Dash Moore, *To the Golden Cities: Pursuing the American Jewish Dream in Miami and L.A.* (New York: The Free Press, 1994), 54.

12 Ira Sheskin, "Ten Percent of American Jews," in *Jews of South Florida*, ed. Andrea Greenbaum (Waltham, MA: Brandeis University Press, 2005), 5–6; Henry A. Green, *Gesher Vakesher: Bridges and Bonds: The Life of Leon Kronish* (Atlanta, GA: Scholars Press, 1995), 122–23.

13 Green, *Gesher Vakesher*, 131–32.

A FIRST ANGLO-HISPANIC JEWISH ENCOUNTER:
THE CUBAN EXODUS

The immigration of Cuban Jews was part of the larger exodus of the Cuban bourgeoisie that followed the Castro revolution. It was motivated by the nationalization of businesses, the loss of personal security, and political threat.[14] Approximately 80 percent of the Jews living in Cuba migrated during the first three years of the revolution. In January 1963, it was estimated that only 2,500 remained on the island.[15]

The Cuban exiles tended to concentrate in south Miami, but the Jews remained in the margins of their social and political frameworks, and created their own enclave in Miami Beach. For the Cuban Jews, the encounter with their English-speaking coreligionists was disappointing. The Anglo Jews ignored their plight—an insult that was never forgotten. Synagogues and Jewish schools demanded full membership and tuition, looking down on the Spanish-speaking Jews and taking no account of their difficult situation as newly arrived refugees. The only exception was Rabbi Meir Abramowitz of Temple Menorah, who offered free services and sympathy to the Cubans—a favor that proved rewarding to his congregation in the long run.[16]

Feeling rejected by the local Jewish institutions, the Cuban Jews formed separate organizations, with the objective of continuing their former Jewish life. Unable to recreate the rich institutional network that had existed in Jewish Havana, they adapted the religiously centered American model, founding the Ashkenazi Cuban Hebrew Congregation and the Sephardic Congregation of Florida. Their Zionist activities took place in the framework of the Latin Division created by the Jewish Federation of Greater Miami for Spanish-speaking Jews.[17]

---

14 For personal testimonies of emigrants, see Margalit Bejarano, *The Jewish Community of Cuba: Memory and History* (Jerusalem: Magnes Press, 2014).

15 Dover to Malat, 14 January 1963, Israel State Archive, hz3440/28. For personal testimonies of emigrants, see Bejarano, *The Jewish Community of Cuba*, 309–11.

16 Caroline Bettinger-Lopez, *Cuban Jewish Journeys: Searching for Identity, Home and History in Miami* (Knoxville, TN: University of Tennessee Press, 2000), 3–31; Margalit Bejarano, "From Havana to Miami: The Cuban Jewish Community," in *Judaica Latinnoamericana*, vol. 3 (Jerusalem: Magnes Press, 1997), 125–27.

17 Bettinger-Lopez, *Cuban Jewish Journeys*, 36–60; Interviews with Rafael and Rebeca Kravec, Israel Bichachi, Oscar Boruchin, Juan and Rebeca Matalon (Miami, 1991), and Alberto Behar (Miami, 1993). All the interviews are deposited in the Archive of the Oral History Division, A. Harman Institute of Contemporary Jewry, Hebrew University of Jerusalem.

The Cuban Jews in Miami tended to socialize within their own group, and their families remained knit together even in the second generation. They redefined their identity as "Jewbans," marking the boundaries that separated them both from the Anglo Jews and from the Gentile Cubans.[18] As a new transnational Diaspora, they cultivated relations with other Diaspora communities of Cuban Jews, but they disconnected themselves from the Jews remaining in Cuba. Being exposed to the local Spanish media, which was strongly anti-Castro, the Jews tended to adopt the official policy of the anti-Communist Cuban exile.[19]

The Cuban immigrants of the early 1960s enjoyed remarkable economic success, some becoming owners and managers of large business firms, as well as senior bank executives. The prosperity in tourism and housing was influenced by the growth of the Cuban population, and by the visits of Latin Americans who made Miami their second home. Knowledge of Spanish became an important asset for business success, and was not necessarily an indicator of ethnic identity.

The Cuban Jewish community, after being uprooted from its homeland, had transplanted to Miami together with its leadership. Cuban Jews who relocated to other parts of the United States or migrated to a third country, like Puerto Rico or Venezuela, gradually made their way to Miami, which became the largest concentration of Cuban Jews. Emigration from Cuba was a one-way journey, burning the bridges with the former homeland, while creating a strong collective identity in the new Diaspora.

THE LATINO JEWS: A NEW TRANSNATIONAL DIASPORA

The case of the Cuban Jews who arrived in the United States as refugees from a Communist regime was different from that of other Jews from Latin America, who arrived individually or in small groups. The migration of the Latin American Jews was voluntary, often without viewing Miami as the final destination. Arriving in the 1970s and 1980s, many of them from affluent backgrounds, the new immigrants were able to purchase fancy apartments in Northern Miami Beach or in Aventura, as a second home or as an insurance policy for future crises.[20]

---

18 Cuban Hebrew Congregation of Miami, *El Nuevo Jew-Ban* (*JEW-ish-cuBAN*), *Anuario 1970* (Miami: Magnes Press, 1970); Hannah Schiller Wartenberg, "Cuban Jewish Women in Miami: A Triple Identity," in *Ethnic Women: A Multiple Status*, ed. Vasilieki Demos and Marcia Texler Segal (Dix Hills, NY: General Hall, 1994), 186–99.

19 Abraham D. Lavender, "Sephardic Political Identity: Jewish and Cuban Interaction in Miami Beach," *Contemporary Jewry* 14 (1993): 116–32.

20 Margalit Bejarano, "Report on Spanish-Speaking Jews in Miami and Their Special

Taking the Colombians as an example of the Latino-Jewish transnational Diaspora, we see that their migration was motivated primarily by personal insecurity. The Jews in Colombia belonged to the upper middle class, and were exposed to the violence of the guerrilla movements, particularly during the drug wars. Many Jews were victims of assaults and kidnappings for ransom that induced them to move to Miami.[21] Some started by sending their wives and children, and remained behind to look after their businesses, before deciding to settle in Miami permanently.

Interviews show that the identification of the Colombian Jews with their homeland is quite weak. In Miami, they have no contacts with their conationals, who mostly belong to the lower classes. They tend to socialize with other Spanish-speaking Jews, regardless of their country of origin, and they see themselves as Jews and Latinos, not necessarily as Colombians.[22]

A different experience is that of Argentinean Jews, who feel more attached to their fellow countrymen than to their coreligionists: "The heritage that one brings from the country one comes from is very powerful, it is beyond religion. We have many Argentinean friends who are not Jewish, and we feel very close to them, maybe more so than to a Jew from Colombia."[23]

Argentinean Jews who were active in clandestine movements did not seek a haven in Miami during the "Dirty War" of the military dictatorship that ruled the country between 1976 and 1983. This may have been due to the difficulty in obtaining an American visa by individuals identified with the political left, as well as to the image of the United States as an imperialist and capitalistic country that collaborated with the junta. Several Argentinean Jews moved to Miami in the late 1970s, at the height of the military dictatorship, but they were motivated by personal rather than political reasons. Some of these immigrants returned to Argentina, and those who remained have a similar socioeconomic profile to that of other Latino Jews.[24]

Educational and Cultural Necessities, June 1984" (manuscript in Hebrew, prepared for the Department of Education in the Diaspora, World Zionist Organization, in hands of author).

21 Yehudit Ben Guigui, *Yahadut Colombia: Mikehila mesagseget lekehila bemashber* (*Colombian Jewry: From a Successful Community to a Community in Crisis*) (MA diss., Hebrew University of Jerusalem, 2013).

22 Interviews with Broncha Kleinbaum, Alex Halberstein (Miami, 2010), Rachel Lapidot, and Clarita Kassin (Miami, 2011); Survey 2012.

23 Interview with Edgar Halac (Miami, 2011).

24 Interviews with Sarah Elnecave (Miami, 2010), Adriana and Edgar Halac (Miami, 2011); Survey 2012.

A large and different wave of migration from Argentina arrived in the early 2000s, following the economic crisis that hit the middle classes and led to their pauperization. Admitted as tourists, the new immigrants were not allowed to work unless they found an American employer ready to hire them legally. In order to assist the new arrivals, the Jewish Federation of Greater Miami created Latin American Migration Program (LAMP) that saw the legalization of the immigrants' status as its first priority.[25] In some cases, women were the first to obtain a green card, due to their qualifications as teachers in Jewish schools.[26] According to an official report, LAMP assisted more than 2,500 immigrants, 80 percent of whom came from Argentina. Through LAMP, Jewish day schools granted the needy Latino parents a special reduction on tuition.[27]

Not all the Argentineans of the early 2000s were able to find legal employment, and, with the economic improvement in their homeland and the real estate crisis in the United States, many decided to return.[28] Oral histories show that Argentinean Jews have a very strong identity with their homeland and prefer to socialize with their conationals—Jews and non-Jews: "An Argentinean, no matter how many years he is in the United States, remains an Argentinean."[29]

The Argentinean migration was followed by that of the Venezuelans, who became the largest group among the Latino Jews in Miami. Their migration in small numbers began several years before Chávez came to power, but has reached significant proportions in recent years. Like the Cuban exiles, the Venezuelans tend to idealize their life prior to the "Bolivarian revolution," pointing out the internal unity and the protective framework of the communal Jewish enclave. Most of them had little interest in Venezuelan politics, but they could not remain indifferent to the present regime. Under Chávez, political violence, assassinations, and kidnappings reached unprecedented proportions, and personal security

---

25   Bruce J. Yudewitz, "Coming to Miami: The Domestic Impact of the Crisis in Argentina," *Journal of Jewish Communal Service* 79, no. 2–3 (Winter-Spring 2002–2003), accessed January 23, 2014, accessed May 23, 2017, http://www.bjpa.org/Publications/details.cfm?-PublicationID=1222; Interview with Juan Dircie (Miami, 2010).

26   Interview with Juan Dircie (Miami, 2010), Adriana Halac (Miami, 2011), ICJ.

27   Larry Luxner, "Miami is a Gateway to Latin Jews," *Jewish Telegraphic Agency*, July 17, 2003, accessed January 23, 2014, http://www.jta.org/2003/07/17/life-religion/features/miami-is-gateway-for-latin-jews.

28   Interviews with Juan Dircie, Rabbi Yosef Galimidi (Miami, 2010).

29   Interview with Rabbi Yosi Smierk (Miami, 2010). See also interview with Adriana and Edgar Halac.

became the main trigger for the emigration of the Venezuelan bourgeoisie.[30] The Jews, however, were threatened also by the anti-Semitic and anti-Zionist policies of the government, and their solidarity with Israel undermines their legitimacy as loyal Venezuelans. It is still too early to assess if the death of Chávez will change the situation, but there are signs that the situation of the Jewish community has not improved, and that immigration figures keep growing.[31]

The migration of Venezuelan Jews was a gradual process: tourists who bought a second home in Miami went through a transitory period of living in two homes, moving frequently between the business in Caracas and the family in Aventura. Though life in Miami is more costly, the Venezuelans had enough economic resources to open their own businesses and thus to resolve their legal status. In view of the insecure future under Chávez — and now under Maduro — Miami is becoming the first home of many Venezuelan Jews, whose second home is still in Caracas. Like the Latino Jews who preceded them, they are looking for ways to insert themselves into the local Jewish community.

PATTERNS OF IDENTITY AND COMMUNAL ORGANIZATION

Miami was transformed into the "Capital of Latin America" by the Cuban immigrants of the early 1960s, who opened it up for Spanish-speaking tourists, immigrants, and businessmen. Like their conationals, the Jews of Latin America took advantage of the opportunities offered by Miami, but they did not consider the Cuban Jews as mediators in the process of their insertion into the American Jewish way of life. When seeking religious services, the Jewish immigrants from Latin America refrained from joining the Cuban Ashkenazi congregation, located in South Beach, where none of them resided. In the early 1980s, this congregation was struggling against the decline in its membership. In an attempt to attract young members, the congregation hired an American rabbi and joined the Conservative movement.[32] The self-imposed assimilation into the English-speaking environment was uncomfortable for the immigrants of the older generation, and at the same time failed to attract the second generation, which

---

30 Interviews with Alberto Gross, Annabel Blum, Dora Amram, and Anita Lepco (Miami, 2010).

31 Editorial, "Precedent Chavez: What the Future Looks Like for the Jews of Venezuela," *The Commentator*, March 24, 2013, accessed January 23, 2014, http://www.thecommentator.com/article/3025/precedent_chavez_what_the_future_looks_like_for_the_jews_of_venezuela.

32 Interview with Oscar Boruchin (Miami, 1991).

preferred the "real" Conservative synagogues, such as Temple Menorah, to its Cuban imitation.

The case of the Sephardic Cubans was somewhat different. Due to the lack of Sephardic synagogues in Miami, the Cuban congregation, Temple Moses (now Torat Moshe) was the best option for the Sephardim from Latin America.[33] Better situated than its Ashkenazi counterpart, it also maintained Spanish as its official language. The special place of the Sephardic Cuban community in Miami in around 1980 found expression in the words of its president: "Latin America and its Sephardic congregations are looking toward us. We give them security in the face of possible political uncertainties, and we urge them not to lose contact with us, and to tighten our fraternal ties."[34]

The growth of the Sephardic population, and the opening of new synagogues in North Miami Beach and Aventura that offered diverse sub-ethnic traditions with different degrees of religious observance, led to the decline of the Cuban Sephardic congregation as a Latino center.[35]

The tendency of the Jews from Latin America not to intermingle with the Cubans resulted in the creation of two separate transnational diasporas— Jewbans and Latino Jews. While the Cubans tried to perpetuate their separate communal organization, founding their own religious congregations, the Latino Jews were ready to join the Anglo religious infrastructure, but they continued to cultivate their distinct patterns of identity.

The analysis of the patterns of identity of Latino Jews in Miami is based on 30 interviews and 200 responses to a questionnaire (cited in the footnotes as Survey 2012). Though it is not a statistical sample, the division between countries of origin of the respondents roughly corresponds to the demographic study conducted by Ira Sheskin in 2004 for Greater Miami Jewish Federation (GMJF). The main differences between the two sources reflect the changes between 2004 and 2012—the considerable increase in the number of Venezuelan Jews and the relocation of immigrants from Argentina and Colombia.

Most of the respondents to the questionnaire work in business or the liberal professions. A large proportion (83 percent) holds academic degrees.[36]

---

33 Interviews with Sara Elnecavé (2010), Clarita Kassin (Miami, 2011).

34 Israel Bichachi, "De la presidencia," *Boletín Informativo* 2 (September 1980), Cuban Sephardic Hebrew Congregation.

35 For a list of the Sephardic congregations and their location see Green, "Transnational Identity and Miami Sephardim," in *Contemporary Sephardic Identity in the Americas*, eds. Margalit Bejarano and Edna Aizenberg (Syracuse, NY: Syracuse University Press), 139.

36 A total of 24 percent obtained a degree in their specialization; 42 percent a university degree (*licenciatura*); 29 percent MA, and 12 percent PhD.

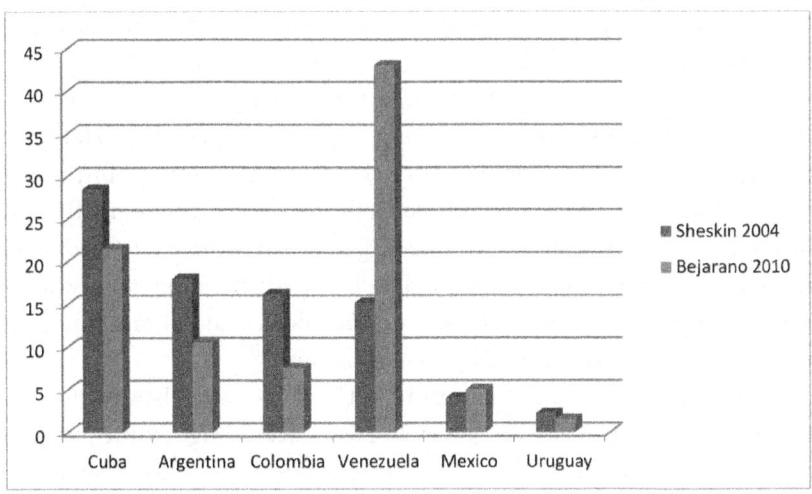

Figure 2.1 Selected Countries of Origin in Latin America (percent).
Ira M. Sheskin, *2004 Population Study of the Greater Miami Jewish Community*, released by Greater Miami Jewish Federation, sample of 338 cases, accessed May 23, 2017, http://www.jewishdatabank.org/study.asp?sid=18420&tp=2. Bejarano 2012, Questionnaire, answered randomly. 200 cases.

In addition to their high educational profile, Cuban and Latino Jews arrived in Miami with a strong Jewish background, acquired in day schools or in Zionist youth movements. In their country of origin, 89 percent of the respondents were affiliated to a Jewish organization and most were married to a Jewish spouse.[37]

Those who came from Cuba, Venezuela, Mexico, Colombia, or Peru grew up in a Jewish enclave, with little contact with the Gentile environment. Others, like the Argentineans, Chilean, Uruguayans, and Brazilians, were integrated to a much greater degree into their homeland. Regardless of the country of origin, oral histories reflect strong Jewish identity and a liberal attitude toward religion.[38] Of the respondents to the survey, 69 percent stated that their Jewish identity did not change with immigration, 29 percent that it was reinforced, and only 2 percent felt that their Jewish identity weakened in Miami.

---

37 Of those who married in their homeland, 82 percent had a Jewish spouse, 7 percent married a non-Jew who converted, and only 3 percent were married to a non-Jew. Most of the "others" stated that they married a Jewish spouse after immigration or that they did not marry.

38 Interviews with Nelson Menda, Beatriz Eisenstadt, Anita Lepco (Miami, 2011).

The experience of Latino Jews, especially in the last twenty years, has been totally different from that of the Cubans who arrived in the 1960s. With the "white flight" from Miami–Dade to other parts of South Florida, Jewish congregations that were losing their Anglo members started to cater to a Spanish-speaking audience, employing Latino rabbis, mostly from Argentina.[39] The Conservative Beth Torah is a paradigmatic case: two rabbis—one American and one Argentinean—share the leadership, assisted by a cantor from Uruguay. The Latin American members have a growing impact on the services and on the social and cultural functions, creating a common space for Anglos and Latinos.[40]

Immigration forced the Latino Jews to adapt themselves to the local institutions, and to redefine their Judaism according to the religious movements of American Jewry. Congregations were selected for their geographic vicinity, the quality of their schools, the presence of other Latino Jews, or the similarity to their former religious tradition. Interviewees conclude that it is much easier to live a full Jewish life in Miami than it was in their homeland.[41] Of the respondents to the survey, 32 percent became more religious, while only 9 percent became less religious.

Table 2.1 shows a pattern of continuity in the religious tendencies of the Latino Jews. Interviewees referred to the search for synagogues that were similar to those of their communities of origin. At the same time, they observed that while, in Latin America, most of the Jews were affiliated with synagogues to which they did not necessarily go, in Miami many of those who are not affiliated participate in services on High Holidays.

The Venezuelans, who are now the largest Spanish-speaking group, belonged to Orthodox congregations, and many of them joined Chabad in Miami. This may be part of a global process of growing orthodoxy, in which Chabad-Lubavitch and the Aleppan congregations are playing a central role.[42] The Safra synagogue in Aventura, like Chabad, offers a supportive and friendly

---

39 Alexandra Alter, "Outreach in Spanish Grows Temple Ranks: As South Florida's Jewish Population Ages, Temples Expand their Congregations by Offering Services in Spanish," *The Miami Herald*, October 3, 2005, interview with Dror and Sigal Gershoni (Miami, 2011).
40 Interview with Rabbi Mario Rojzman, Rabbi of Beth Torah (Miami, 2010), Marcos Kerbel (Miami, 2011); interviews with Juan Dircie, Adriana and Edgar Halac.
41 Interviews with Simon Chocron (Miami, 2010) and Alberto Franco (Miami, 2011).
42 On the impact of global orthodoxy on Mexico, see Liz Hamui Halabe, *Transformaciones en la religiosidad de los judíos en México* (Mexico: Noriega, 2005); on São Paulo see Marta F. Topel, *Jerusalem and São Paulo: The New Jewish Orthodoxy in Focus* (Lanham, MD: University Press of America, 2008).

Table 2.1 Changes in religious trends (percent)*.

	In country of origin	In Miami
Orthodox Ashkenazi	36	34
Orthodox Sephardic	16	11
Conservative	36	28
Other synagogues	6	11**
Reform	–	3
Not affiliated	13	23

*Some respondents were/are affiliated with more than one synagogue and therefore
the total is more than 100 percent.
**More than half of the "other" belongs to Chabad.

space to the newly arrived immigrants, in their own language and mentality, and subsequently strengthens their religiosity.[43] It is evident that the passage from Latin America to the United States reinforces the religious dimension in Jewish identity.

INTERRELATIONS BETWEEN SPANISH AND ENGLISH SPEAKERS

In the early 1980s, a group of Latino Jews in Miami tried to found Hebraica, a social club modeled after similar organizations in Latin America that unite the local Jews around activities of sport, recreation, and culture. The attempt to import a social model from Latin America and recreate it in Miami was short-lived.[44] The failure of Hebraica as an independent Latin American organization was due to financial problems, but also to other reasons, such as the constant mobility of the Latino Jewish population, the large attraction of Jewish and non-Jewish recreational organizations, and the desire of the younger generation to integrate into the English-speaking host society.[45]

Hebraica was reorganized as a section of the Michael Ann Russell Jewish Community Center in North Miami Beach. The integration between the declining center of Anglos, whose members were mostly pensioners, and the young families from Latin America looking for a local version of their previous Jewish clubs,

---

43 Interview with Rabbis Yosef Smierk and Yosef Galimidi.
44 Bejarano, "Report on Spanish-Speaking Jews."
45 Patricia Duarte, "Hispanic Jews: One Faith, Many Accents," *The Miami Herald*, November 28, 1985; Interviews with Clarita Kassin, Marcos and Linda Ackerman (Miami, 2011), Rafael Kravec (Miami, 1991).

became a success story. The Hebraica section of the JCC was converted into the focus of Latino Jewish social life in Miami with around 2,000 members, mostly families with children. In addition to sport and recreation, they have a Maccabi youth movement, and conduct cultural activities with Zionist content, organized by a special *shaliach* from Israel.[46]

The most important annual events are the *Maccabiada* games, in which teams play under the flags of their homelands—Argentina, Brazil, Venezuela, etc., but also the United States and Israel. The activities, which until recently took place in Spanish, are now in English, and also attract Anglo and Israeli children. Through their contributions, the Latinos are able to influence the policy of the JCC. Ariel Bentata, the first Latino president of the organization, stated that the social involvement of the Latinos serves as a model for the American Jews.[47]

On a political level, the major arena of contact between the Anglo and Latino Jews is the Jewish Federation of Greater Miami—the umbrella organization for fundraising and for allocation of funds to Israel and local institutions. The federation did very little to help the Cuban Jewish refugees on their arrival, but, since they were used to working on behalf of Israel, it created for them the Latin Division as a framework for their Zionist activities. The first director of the Latin Division was Sender Kaplan, a prominent Zionist leader from Cuba, and activities were held in Spanish with little contact with the Anglos.

The growing economic power of the Cubans and the arrival of the Latino Jews prompted the federation to attract them to its activities. They appointed as director of the Latin Division the Israeli Dr. Rachel Lapidot, who worked very successfully in this capacity for fifteen years. In her interview, she criticized the Anglo leadership of the federation for their arrogance, lack of sensitivity, and discriminatory attitude toward the Spanish-speaking Jews. The latter were able to buy their respect only through generous donations: money was the key of entry into the Jewish host society.

The decline of the Anglo-Jewish population increased the dependence of JFGM on its Cuban and Latino donors. Isaac Zelcer, a Cuban Jew, was elected as president of the federation in 1996. Nevertheless, the JFGM is still dominated by English speakers, although a number of Cuban and Latino Jews figure among the members of the board of directors.

---

46 Interviews with Dror and Sigal Gershoni, Juan Dircie, Clarita Kassin; "About Hebraica," accessed February 4, 2014, http://www.hebraicamiami.org/modules.php?op=modload&name=info&file=index&info_id=aboutus.

47 Interview with Ariel Bentata (Miami, 2011).

The Cuban and Latino Jews who are active in the federation have been living in Miami for a long time. From the respondents to the 2012 survey, only 31 percent are affiliated to the federation. According to George Feldenkreis, a Cuban board member of JFGM, there is a small number of Latino activists who are generous donors to the federation, but many of the Latino Jews do not contribute according to their economic capacity.[48] The insertion into the local Jewish mainstream by way of the federation is a gradual process.

CONFRONTING MULTIPLE IDENTITIES

The Cuban and Latino Jews have very strong ties with Israel, some of them referring to it as a homeland. Interviews show that formal and informal Jewish education in Latin America shaped their Zionist outlook. Although only a few consider actually moving to Israel, they follow the news, are exposed to Israel's culture, and contribute to Israeli causes. According to Sheskin's data, 70 percent of the Hispanic households are "extremely/very attached" to Israel, compared to 61 percent of the non-Hispanic households.[49]

The attachment to Israel finds expression in donations to Israeli causes, and a constant exposure to the news. Of the respondents, 25 percent have lived in Israel for some time, and 66 percent have visited. According to Rabbi Rojzman, the ties of Latino Jews to Israel are deeply rooted, and are strengthened by the frequent visits of Israeli politicians and artists to Aventura.

Voting patterns in the United States are often influenced by the candidate's policy toward Israel. However, only 27 percent of the respondents to the 2012 survey were involved in political activities on behalf of Israel in American frameworks. The involvement of Latino Jews in local politics is a relatively new phenomenon. Latino leaders, such as Juan Dircie of the American Jewish Committee, are working to defend Israel in the Spanish media and create links of collaboration with Hispanic politicians, whose importance is growing constantly.[50]

Most of the respondents to the survey defined their identity prior to immigration as Jews with a hyphen of their homeland. Grading their different identities, it is evident that their Jewish identity is the most important.

---

48 Interview with George Feldenkreis (Miami, 2011).
49 The non-Hispanics include Israelis, 91 percent of whom are strongly attached to Israel; Sheskin, *Miami Jewish Community Demographic Study*, p. 1010.
50 Interviews with Juan Dircie, George Feldenkreis, Marcos Ackerman, Paul Kruss (Miami, 2011).

Table 2.2 Grading Identities.

	Very important	Important	Not so important	Unimportant
Jewish	118	20	2	3
Homeland	45	43	20	22
United States	33	42	26	16
Latin	29	39	22	23
Hispanic	23	26	28	25

Cubans, more than any other group, have adopted the American identity, but it is a hybrid identity of an uprooted group. In 1991, an ex-president of the Cuban Hebrew Congregation described the situation of the Cuban-born generation: "We forgot to speak Spanish, but we didn't learn to speak English."[51] The generation of his children became bilingual, but he expected the third generation to be totally Americanized.

The Hispanization of Miami, however, influenced the process of Americanization—which does not exclude the maintenance of Latino culture. When asked about the future of their children, 69 percent of the respondents to the survey stated that they would preserve their Jewish and Latino identities, or that they would maintain their Jewish and Latino identities but would also consider themselves as Americans.

CONCLUSION

The study shows that, over the past fifty years, the relations between the Anglos and the Latinos have undergone many changes. The English speakers received the Jewban transnational Diaspora that emerged in Miami with indifference, ignorance, and even hostility, and were prepared to recognize their common ethnicity with "Hispanics" only if the latter were ready to assimilate.

The demographic transformation of Miami, and the decline of the Anglo-Jewish population, changed the relations between Anglos and Latinos. The former became dependent on the latter for their institutional survival, and are now prepared to negotiate the adoption of Jewish-Latino social patterns. As in the case of the general Miami population, the hegemony is still in the hands

---

51 Interview with Oscar Boruchin.

of the English speakers, but the Spanish speakers are gradually taking a growing share of the leadership.

The Cuban Jews paved the way for their coreligionists from Latin America, but the two Cuban congregations failed in their efforts to attract Latino members. Geographical distances, social and cultural differences, as well as prejudices, left the Jewbans as a separate transnational Diaspora. Comparison between Cubans and more recent immigrants shows that the former differed from other Latino groups, being a transplanted community that had burnt the bridges with its homeland. While many Gentile Cubans have been traveling to their homeland, and reestablishing contacts with their families, several Jewbans still hold a non-compromising attitude toward the Jews living on the island. Their Cuban identity is still nurtured by memories of pre-revolutionary Cuba, whose influence is gradually declining.

The Jewbans, however, are a paradigmatic case in presenting the inevitable process of integration into the host society, even though this society is in a constant state of transformation. Like the Cuban Gentiles, the Cuban-born Jews speak Spanglish, and their cultural and social patterns have been Americanized, creating a new combination. Their children and grandchildren often study in universities in other parts of the United States, and are gradually losing their Cuban identity.

For Jewbans and Latino Jews alike, it is evident that their Jewish identity is much more profound than their other identities, and that their national identity, as Cubans, Colombians, Argentineans, and Venezuelans, is deeply connected with their hyphenated identity as Jews in their homeland. With respect to Israel, there is a consensus on its centrality among all the Spanish-speaking groups. Both Cuban and Latino Jews are united by a deep commitment to Israel. While this commitment is translated infrequently into political activism, the Jewbans and Latinos play a central role in building a bridge between Jews and Hispanics in the United States.

CHAPTER 3

Globalization, Education, and Jewish Community Life: Latin American Transnational Jewish Educators—Toward a New Paradigm?

YOSSI J. GOLDSTEIN

This paper aims to investigate the extent and ways in which a transnational educational approach could contribute to an increase in the intellectual and social capital of the Jewish communities in Latin America in order to meet the challenges of the twenty-first century. Its theoretical–conceptual framework arises from the central research project of the Liwerant Center for the Study of Latin America, Spain, Portugal, and its Jewish communities, at the Hebrew University of Jerusalem, entitled: "Latin American Jews in a Transnational World: Redefining Experiences and Identities in Four Continents." The starting point for this approach is the change of paradigms reflected in research work published during the last decade, in times of globalization and transnationalism.[1,2]

Our interest lies in a broad and holistic concept of the Jewish educator who received training in one of the Latin American countries—especially in

---

1 Judit Bokser Liwerant, Sergio DellaPergola, Haim Avni, Margalit Bejarano, and Leonardo Senkman, "Cuarenta Años de Cambios: Transiciones y Paradigmas," in *Pertenencia y Alteridad—Judíos en/de América Latina: cuarenta años de cambios*, ed. H. Avni, J. Bokser Liwerant, S. DellaPergola, M. Bejarano, and L. Senkman (Madrid: Iberoamericana Vervuert—Bonilla Artiga Editores, 2011), 13–83.
2 Ibid., 59–64.

Argentina—and migrated to other countries of the world, based on a prospect of circulation of knowledge and people in a globalized world.[3]

The study of Jewish community life in Latin America has evolved as a function of various epistemological and conceptual paradigms. To understand this evolution, it seems necessary first to define the concept of paradigm, and then to compare between two very different paradigms. The first paradigm was forged in the early years of the existence of the State of Israel in the context of the "Cold War," and the second was created in the era of globalization since the 1990s, a phenomenon that we define as the transnational paradigm.

DEFINITION OF THE CONCEPT OF "PARADIGM"

The term paradigm means "example" or "model." In the scientific, religious, or other epistemological context, paradigm may indicate the concept of a formal organizational scheme, and be used as a synonym for a theoretical framework or set of theories.

The philosopher and scientist Thomas Kuhn gave this term its contemporary significance when he adopted it to refer to the set of practices that define a scientific discipline during a specific period. Kuhn defines the scientific paradigm as "a complete constellation of beliefs, values, and techniques, etc., shared by the members of a given community." Kuhn adds the following assertion:[4] "I consider the paradigms as universally recognized scientific achievements that, for a certain period of time, provide models of problems and solutions to a scientific community."[5] The paradigm is a model, or example, that a scientific community chooses to follow, from the problems that need to be solved all to way to how solutions are offered.

The paradigm shift is not a mere revision or transformation of an isolated theory, but a change in the way in which we define terminology, the manner in which scientists address their object of study, and, perhaps more importantly, the type of questions considered valid, as well as the rules used to determine

---

3 Lucas Luchilo, ed., *Más allá de la fuga de cerebros: Movilidad, migración y diásporas de argentinos calificados* (Buenos Aires: Universidad de Buenos Aires, 2011); J-B Meyer and J. Charum, "¿Se agotó el *Brain Drain*? Paradigma perdido y nuevas perspectivas," *Inmigración, Ciencia y Tecnología* 1 (1994): 47–54.

4 Thomas S. Kuhn, *The Structure of Scientific Revolutions* (Chicago: University of Chicago Press, 1962), vii–xiv; Thomas S. Kuhn, *The Structure of Scientific Revolutions*, 2nd ed. (Chicago, University of Chicago Press, 1970), viii.

5 Kuhn 1962, x; Kuhn 1970, 175.

the truth of a particular theory. Kuhn emphasized the fact that paradigms play a central role in scientific research, providing models for the solution of problems accepted by a scientific community.

When applying Kuhn's definition to a social sciences context, we should discuss the issue of whether you can talk about paradigms, scientific revolutions, or paradigm shifts in the sociological field. Kuhn argued that this is impossible, and that this concept emphasizes the enormous difference between natural and social sciences.

Our hypothesis is that this implementation is feasible and necessary, taking into account the fact that the transnational perspective has been transformed into a field with clear signs of paradigm shift around key conceptual axes, such as Nation–State, People–Diaspora, Citizenship–Nationality, primary identity–multiple identities in permanent construction.

M. L. Handa raised the concept of "social paradigm" in the 1980s, in order to analyze the change of paradigms in the social sciences. It is clear that social transformations change the perspective according to which societies and individuals face reality and the interpretation of its meanings. It was not merely a subjective perception, however, or a personal worldview, but mainly its impact on research and scientists who analyze these new realities. The central question that emerges from this new analytical perspective is the following: What determines the acceptance of a "dominant paradigm" within a scientific community? Obviously, the main factor is the historical and cultural context of a given society. Yet, in our times, scientific communities are not restricted to a particular country. By their nature, these transnational bodies cross borders and attract scientists with shared interests and viewpoints. Scientific communities certainly fostered ties beyond political boundaries following the European scientific revolution of the seventeenth century. However, we believe that the information and technological revolution in the era of globalization from the 1990s on has qualitatively affected the development of scientific communities, virtual and real. This development can be seen both in cyberspace and through scientific congresses and classroom visits facilitated by the development of means of transport, the support of universities and academic funds, and the publication of numerous scientific journals, many of them in the virtual space.[6]

---

6 M. L. Handa, "Peace Paradigm: Transcending Liberal and Marxian Paradigms," paper presented at The International Symposium on Science, Technology and Development, New Delhi, India, March 20–25, 1987, mimeographed at O.I.S.E., University of Toronto, Canada.

In 2005, Alain Touraine, a prominent French sociologist and a critic of modernity, published a book entitled *A New Paradigm for Understanding the World of Today*.[7] Touraine noted the evolution of paradigms to interpret and understand social reality in the modern era. He argued that we have evolved from a political paradigm to an economic and social one, and are witnessing the development of a new "cultural paradigm," characteristic of an individualistic era and marked by the information revolution, in which the main struggle is the claim of cultural rights.[8]

The works of Eliezer Ben-Rafael and, in particular, of Judit Bokser Liwerant in recent years—following steps established by the theoretical sociologist S. N. Eisenstadt—have contributed greatly to the understanding of Jewish identities in an era of "multiple modernities." Their point of departure is the wide spectrum and cultural diversity, which are never "organic" but which generate various options to build collective identities, leaving the image of total homogeneity. These identities are not uniform but dynamic, and represent a plurality of parameters with changing trends within a "broad space of identity," flowing into different streams and taking shape according to dynamic structures.[9] At the same time, the socio-demographic perspective developed by Sergio DellaPergola, departing from a vision of contemporary Jewry that faces all the components of Jewish life, includes various forms of Jewish identity and socioeconomic aspects as migratory processes, from a global comparative perspective.[10]

There are conflicting paradigms around new approaches to Latin American research of Jews and Judaism. We may assume that we are facing a confrontation of theoretical models that offer different answers to the problems and challenges when we try to analyze Jewish life in Latin America and study Latin American Jews scattered throughout the world.[11]

---

7 A. Touraine, *Un Nouveau Paradigme* (Paris: Librairie Arteme Fayard, 2005); A. Touraine, New *Paradigm for Understanding Today's World* (Cambridge: Polity, 2007).

8 See its introduction, ibid., 1–6.

9 Shmuel N. Eisenstadt, "New Transnational Communities and Networks: Globalization Changes in Civilizational Frameworks," in *Transnationalism: Diasporas and the Advent of a New (Dis)Order*, ed. E. Ben-Rafael, Y. Sternberg, J. Bokser Liwerant, and Y. Gorny (Leiden: Brill, 2009), 29–46; J. Bokser Liwerant, "Latin American Jewish Identities: Past and Present Challenges: The Mexican Case in a Comparative Perspective," in *Identities in an Era of Globalization and Multiculturalism. Latin America in the Jewish World*, ed. J. Bokser Liwerant, E. Ben-Rafael, Y. Gorny, and R. Rein (Leiden: Brill, 2008), 81–105; Bokser Liwerant and DellaPergola, et al., "Cuarenta Años de Cambios," Introduction, 59–64.

10 Ibid., 73–100.

11 Bokser Liwerant and Senkman, "Diásporas y transnacionalismo," 11–71; Sergio DellaPergola, "National Uniqueness and Transnational Parallelism: Reflections on the

The wide range of research and approaches is reflected clearly in publications that specialize in the study of Latin American Jews, such as *Judaica Latinoamericana* (JL)—an initiative of the Israeli Association of Latin American Researchers of Latin American Jews (AMILAT). Prior to 2013, AMILAT published seven volumes of articles based on papers presented at the International Congress of Jewish Sciences, held at the Hebrew University of Jerusalem every four years. JL highlights the fruits of researchers addressing Jewish life from various disciplinary perspectives, from the national level to a comparative level. The seventh volume, published in the year 2013, by way of example, accentuates the new trends in research and the need to review concepts such as "Diasporas," or "National Uniqueness," from a view that incorporates regional and transnational studies. We can find various articles on migration studies, Jewish colonization, the impact of the Holocaust, the interaction with the environment in national contexts, the impact of international contexts, and studies on literature and identity in this volume.[12]

A new generation of researchers has also emerged in Latin America, for instance, the nucleus of Jewish studies of IDES—Institute of Economic and Social Development of Buenos Aires—which has successfully promoted the academic studies on the Argentine Jewish collective in various disciplines, with emphasis on social history and sociology.[13] The diversity of approaches is also reflected in other publications and essays, such as those compiled under the title "Thinking about Jewish Questions in Argentina of the Twenty-First Century."[14]

The research of Jewish life in Latin America has faced great challenges in the last few years, raised by researchers who cast doubts on old conceptions. These include questioning the concept of Jewish community,[15] or the

---

Comparative Study of Jewish Communities in Latin America," in *Judaica Latinoamericana*, vol. 7 (Jerusalem: Magnes Press, 2013), 73–100.

12 AMILAT, *Judaica Latinoamericana—Estudios Históricos, Sociales y Literarios*, vol. 7 (Jerusalem: Magnes, 2013).

13 E. Kahan, L. Schenquer, D. Setton, and A. Dujovne, eds., *Marginados y consagrados—Nuevos Estudios Sobre la Vida Judía en la Argentina* (Buenos Aires: Lumiere, 2011), 21–26.

14 A. Dujovne, D. Goldman, and D. Sztajnszrajber, eds., *Pensar lo judío en la Argentina del Siglo XXI* (Buenos Aires: Capital Intelectual, 2011).

15 For example, see my work on the concept of Jewish community in the Latin American context: Yossi J. Goldstein, "De Kehilá a Comunidad: Enfoques acerca de la vida comunitaria judía en la Argentina y el Brasil hacia fines del Siglo XX," in *Judaica Latinoamericana*, vol. 5 (Jerusalem: Magnes, 2005), 27–47; "Jewish Communal Life in Argentina and Brazil at the End of the 20th century and the Beginning of the 21st: A Sociological Perspective," in *Identities in an Era of Globalization and Multiculturalism: Latin America in the Jewish*

paradigm focused on institutionalized life, as well as Zionism and the links with Israel, instead of searching for the enormous mass of Jews marginalized from any community institution, or slightly identified with organized frameworks. Raanan Rein and Jeffrey Lesser lead this critical line, departing from the view of the multicultural ethnicity, accentuating the profound processes of integration of Latin American Jews, and seeking different voices of individual Jews or Jewish groups that mark innovative tendencies.[16] Rein has clamored for the "normalization of the historiography of Latin American Jews," emphasizing that there are "gaps" in investigation.[17] We believe, on the contrary, that a balanced overview will show that there is already a "pluralization" and a "kaleidoscopic diversity" in these studies.[18]

Perhaps there is no question of a confrontation of paradigms in the strict sense of Kuhn's concept, but surely we are facing a diversification of academic approaches addressed in an interdisciplinary way, which is based on various assumptions, either on a national level as international or in individual versus community and ethnic dimensions. If we adopt the concept of a paradigm as "a model or example to be followed by a scientific community," a "revision of terminology," a change in "the type of questions considered valid," and "how we will offer solutions to diverse challenges," as defined by Kuhn—then there is no doubt of the validity of application of such a concept in the field of social sciences and education.

This confrontation of theoretical models or analytical paradigms has given great impetus to recent research on Latin American Jewry. The approach we have adopted in this work is based on the transnational paradigm, assuming the importance of analyzing processes of de- and rediasporization as a product of the migratory patterns of Latin American Jews in recent decades.[19] Quoting the Argentinean sociologist Elisabeth Jelin, we may speculate that "the inquiry of the

World, ed. J. Bokser Liwerant, E. Ben-Rafael, Y. Gorny, and R. Rein (Leiden: Brill, 2008), 185–202.

16 Raanan Rein, "Waning Essentialism: Latin American Jewish Studies in Israel," in *Identities in an Era of Globalization and Multiculturalism*, ed. J. Bokser Liwerant, Y. Gorny, and R. Rein (Leiden: Brill, 2008), 109–24; J. Lesser and R. Rein, eds., *Rethinking Jewish-Latin Americans* (Albuquerque, NM: University of New Mexico Press, 2008), ch. 1, Introduction, 1–22, and ch. 2, "New Approaches to Ethnicity and Diaspora," 23–35; R. Rein, *Argentine Jews or Jewish Argentines? Essays on Ethnicity, Identity, and Diaspora* (Leiden: Brill, 2010).

17 R. Rein, "Historiografía judeo-latinoamericana: desafíos y propuestas," in Kahan et al., *Marginados y consagrados*, 27–44.

18 Concepts of Edna Aizenberg, cited by R. Rein, "Historiografía judeo-latinoamericana," 26.

19 Liwerant and Senkman, "Diásporas y transnacionalismo," 15.

Jew has necessarily to pass permanently, round-trip, on a bridge that links the community with various societies where the Jews lived in their multiple levels, from a small local community until the global society, and all the intermediate levels."[20]

PARADIGMS IN EDUCATION AND IN JEWISH EDUCATION (JE)

T. Husén (1988) developed the idea of applying the concept of paradigm for research in the field of education, alluding to the development of a "post-Kuhn era" in the philosophy of science.[21] A field of research in education developed in the 1990s based on the model of educational paradigms, the most prominent of which is perhaps Thomas C. Reeves (1996),[22] who differentiated between four paradigms for research in the field of education, namely:

1) *Empiric–Positivist–Quantitative Paradigm:* this paradigm leads in the field of research in education and social sciences.

2) *Constructivist–Hermeneutic Paradigm,* Interpretative–Qualitative: this paradigm, developed in the 1990s, emphasizes the need to put any analysis in a specific context, presenting interpretations of various groups and individuals interested in the results of any educational process.

3) *Praxis Paradigm* of critical theory, neo-Marxist–Postmodern: focuses on issues of power, control, and epistemology as a construction total that benefits a minority. It arises from the educational theories of Paulo Freire and Ivan Illich in the 1970s.

4) *Eclectic–Pragmatic Paradigm:* preferred by Reeves, because it uses elements of the other paradigms to solve problems. This paradigm seeks the complexity of educational processes, and is based on the recognition of the need to implement multiple disciplines in any analysis, choosing the most appropriate analytical tool for each studied phenomenon.[23]

---

20 E. Jelin, "Prólogo—La cuestión judía como paradoja de la inclusión y la diferencia," in Kahan et al., *Marginados y consagrados,* p. 16.

21 Torsten Husén, "Research Paradigms in Education," *Interchange* 19, no. 1 (Spring 1988): 2–13.

22 Tom Reeves, "Educational Paradigms" (1996). On the following link, retrieved on May 4 2017. http://wikieducator.org/images/f/f3/Educational_paradigms.pdf. See also T. C. Reeves, "Established and Emerging Evaluation Paradigms for Instructional Design," in C.R. Dills and A. Romiszowski, eds., *Instructional Development Paradigms* (Englewood Cliffs, NJ: Educational Technology Publications, 1997), 163–78.

23 See also J. F. Soltis, "Inquiry Paradigms," in *Encyclopedia of Educational Research,* ed. M. C. Alkin (New York: Macmillan, 1992), 620–22. See a much more sophisticated analysis, applied

According to research in the sciences of education, the need to change the paradigm of education was made even more prominent in the twenty-first century by two researchers in the world of education, Marc Prensky[24] and Ken Robinson. The starting points for these thinkers are digital education, the implementation of interactive games for education, creativity, and imagination as a target for educational processes, and the search for relevance in education geared toward the learner. According to Robinson, we should abandon the educational paradigm of the era of Enlightenment and industrialization, oriented toward the teacher, individual study, and focused on physical spaces such as the school (associated with a factory). We should instead adopt a paradigm in keeping with the twenty-first century, based on collaboration, group study, the use of technology in learning processes, flexible and informal study spaces, and the centrality of the student.[25]

The reconsideration of JE in a context of globalization has been manifested clearly in the last decade.[26] This in turn is reflected in the *International Handbook of Jewish Education* (Springer 2011), two volumes containing about 1,300 pages with interdisciplinary studies that cover a wide range of thematic importance such as: philosophy of JE; curriculum development; links with the Jewish community and with national environments; education toward multiple identities; pluralism in JE; visions of JE; teaching of different subjects and content such as Bible, Talmud, the Hebrew language, studies of Israel, or the Holocaust; the impact of environmental studies in JE; gender and JE; trips to Israel; the impact of technology and the digital revolution in JE; between day schools and congregational schools; non-formal JE; training and professional development of teachers for JE; Orthodox-*Haredi* Education, etc.

In the first volume of this monumental work, we find a pioneering study of Jonathan Woocher of Jewish Educational Services of North

to the South American context: Lidia Sandman, *Paradigmas en Ciencias de la Educación* (Montevideo, UY: Edición de la autora, 2002), 22–34.

24 Marc Prensky, *Digital Game-Based Learning* (New York: McGraw-Hill, 2001); and "Changing Paradigms: From Being 'Taught' to Learning on Your Own with Guidance," in *Educational Technology* (July–August 2007), accessed May 23, 2017, http://www.marc-prensky.com/writing/Prensky-ChangingParadigms-01-EdTech.pdf

25 Sir Ken Robinson, *Changing Education Paradigms*: TED Talks (December 2010), accessed May 23, 2017, http://www.ted.com/talks/ken_robinson_changing_education_para-digms.html; Ken Robinson, *The Element: How Finding Your Passion Changes Everything* (New York: Viking Books, 2009).

26 A. Pomson and H. Dietcher, eds., *Jewish Day Schools, Jewish Communities: A Reconsideration* (Oxford: The Littman Library for Jewish Civilization, 2009), introduction, 1–28.

America (JESNA) on the need to develop a new practice in planning for the twenty-first century. Woocher calls for a systematic search for a "Planning Paradigm," addressing JE as a "complex adaptive system," and focusing on changes in educational practice: Practice Planning and Action Research. Woocher defines Michael Fullan as "the leading academic figure in the world of educational reform," who based his revolutionary theory on the model of "complexity theory," i.e., the presumption that "rapid change is endemic and inevitable in postmodern society." This contrasts with the perception of conventional rational planning.[27] In terms of T. Reeves, we found in this analysis a convergence of the Praxis and the Eclectic–Pragmatic Paradigm in education.

The plurality of approaches and paradigms in education had its impact on Jewish education, and emerged from a theoretical debate carried out in the United States in the framework of the prestigious *Journal of Jewish Education*. In 2012, this journal of the Network for Research in Jewish Education launched as its main focus of debate the search for a new paradigm in JE, based on a challenging article written by Jonathan Woocher, the main theme of which is the need to "reinvent the Jewish education for the twenty-first century."[28] Woocher clamored for a paradigm shift, based on the following elements: education focused on the learner and his family, encouragement of interactive relationships, and relevance of JE to real life. Without referring to Prensky or Robinson, Woocher adopts the same conclusions that these authors offered previously, emphasizing the importance of taking a holistic approach to education in general and Jewish education in particular. Woocher demands not only a change in teaching practice but also a reorganization of the entire Jewish community education system. Also, in this case, priority is given to the innovation and application of new technologies in addition to systematically incorporating the use of the internet as an educational tool. That article generated intense debate among researchers, thinkers, and scholars of Jewish education, as reflected in the next volume of the *Journal of Jewish Education*.[29] The associate editor, Joseph Reimer, summed up the questions and criticisms of various

---

27 J.S. Woocher, "Planning for Jewish Education in the Twenty-First Century: Toward a New Praxis," in *International Handbook of Jewish Education*, ed. H. Miller, L. D. Grant, and A. Pomson (Dordrecht, NL: Springer, 2011), part one, 247–65. Fullan's quotation on p. 256 was taken from M. Fullan, *Change Forces: The Sequel* (Philadelphia, PA: The Falmer Press, 1999), 3.

28 J. Woocher, "Reinventing Jewish Education for the 21st Century," *Journal of Jewish Education* 78, no. 3 (2012): 182–226.

29 For example, see the editor's note to J. Reimer. "Is a New Paradigm the Need of the Hour," *Journal of Jewish Education* 78, no. 4 (Fall 2012): 291–93.

specialists in Jewish education in the United States, the first and most important of which is the following question: Is it logical and appropriate to create a new uniform and unified paradigm for the whole Jewish community school system? The conclusion, based on the general debate, is that we need different paradigms according to the ideology and idiosyncrasies of each stream and each place, based on a pluralistic view of education. In the context of the sciences of education, we may conclude that the concept of "paradigm" is used as a framework or model, oriented to interpret the changing reality and offer solutions to new challenges.

THE CLASSIC PARADIGM AND ITS PROJECTIONS IN JEWISH EDUCATION

Jewish education (JE) in Latin America has faced new challenges and transformations in the past two decades.[30] Its historical foundations emanate from the impact of the ideological currents developed in Europe, and the community structure adjusted to the new social and cultural contexts, and crystallized after the period of the Holocaust and the creation of the State of Israel.

The classic paradigm of Jewish education is manifested in the public discourse of the leadership and in the main publications of the native community. We can sum it up via the following components:[31]

1) Nation–state Zionism, with emphasis on central and organized community; the centrality of Israel as a Jewish state, and the predominance of Zionist parties in Jewish life; Jewish education in formal frameworks—school, youth movements (*tnuot noar*),

---

30 Yossi J. Goldstein assisted by Drori Ganiel, "Jewish Education in Latin America: Challenges, Trends and Processes," in *International Handbook of Jewish Education*, ed. H. Miller, L. Grant, and A. Pomson (Dordrecht: Springer, 2011), part two, 1253–70; Yossi J. Goldstein, "Jewish Education in Latin America: A Socio-Historical Comparative Perspective," in *Paths in Pluralistic Jewish Education*, ed. N. Chamo and Y. Dror, in honor of Naama Sabar Ben Yehoshua (Tel Aviv: Tel Aviv University, 2012), 23–42.

31 Based on my following articles: Yossi J. Goldstein, "La Educación Judía en Argentina y Brasil: Balance histórico y abordaje sociológico," in *Pertenencia y Alteridad—Judíos en/de América Latina: cuarenta años de cambios*, ed. H. Avni, J. Bokser Liwerant, S. DellaPergola, M. Bejarano, and L. Senkman (Madrid: Iberoamericana Vervuert— Bonilla Artiga Editores, 2011), 503–27; "El Judaísmo argentino de fin de siglo XX: del olvido a la recuperación de la memoria colectiva," in *Memoria y Representación: Configuraciones culturales y literarias en el imaginario judío latinoamericano*, ed. Ariana Huberman and Alejandro Meter (Rosario, AR: Editorial Beatriz Viterbo, 2006), 41–63; "Israel in Jewish Communal Life—South America," in *Contemporary Jewries: Convergence and Divergence*, ed. E. Ben-Rafael, Y. Gorny, and Y. Ro'i (Leiden: Brill, 2003), 291–305.

or Jewish social and sports clubs —with gaps or almost chasms between each sector.

2) Center–periphery relations with Israel as the nation state of the Jewish people; a cultural and policy-making center for the entire Jewish people—with attempts to impose Hebrew-language education and Jewish life as a function of the political hegemony of Zionist parties; the predominance of comprehensive day schools with teachers (*morim*) trained locally or regionally, and with educational emissaries (*shlichim*) from Israel or *morim* trained in Israel—particularly in the Greenberg Institute of Jerusalem and at the Midrasha or Mijlelet Shazar of Buenos Aires.

3) *Aliyah* (immigration to Israel) as a main objective, or at least as a long-term aspiration; support to new immigrants to Israel (*olim hadashim*); and identification with the decision to immigrate to Israel, taken in general as a rational and ideological act, beyond a recognition that Jews with economic difficulties can seek practical solutions in the Jewish State.

4) Zionist Jewish communities in the political sense of unwavering support to Israel. Centrality of the alleged threat of anti-Semitism—at least in the collective memory, with the association to the Holocaust (*Shoah*) and its commemoration based on the Zionist model of *Shoah* and resurrection or *Shoah* and heroism, understood as armed struggle or rebellion against Nazism.

Was this paradigm real or an imaginary reflection of the community leadership? First, the paradigm is more Argentine that Latin American, although it was shared by lay community leadership from several countries, such as Mexico and Uruguay. However, it was not adopted systematically in Brazil, for example, where the anti-Semitic factor was less significant, and the orientation toward progress, the future and a multiracial and multiethnic system has dominated in modern times. Brazil is a country where the attempt to impose Hebrew and Zionist Jewish education and a system of Israeli *shlichim* (emissaries) failed.[32]

---

32 Yossi J. Goldstein, "El Estado de Israel, el Movimiento Sionista y la educación judía en Brasil, 1948–1955," *Kivunim-Revista de Sionismo y Judaísmo* 3 (May 2000): 173–200.

יוסף ח. גולדשטיין, " התנועה הציונית והחינוך היהודי בברזיל: 1955–1948," בתוך יהדות זמננו-שנתון לעיון ולמחקר, המכון ליהדות זמננו, כרך 8 (תשנ"ג): 39–66.

The gaps between the school and the Jewish pioneering Zionist movements were abysmal, and prevented an influx of young people and content to both sectors. The young Jewish student was socialized according to the objective of preserving Jewish continuity and affiliation to central Jewish institutions. The Zionist youth movements viewed education toward *aliyah* to Israel as a central premise, in particular *aliyah* to kibbutz as a space for innovation and pioneering, implementing idealistic values. They defined this goal as the "only truth," and defied the Zionist community leadership by considering it to be declarative, without consistency, at the level of realization of the Zionist ideal—*hagshama.*

In this context, the journey of local educators to Israel was regarded as an important stage in their vocational training, and, if it resulted in *aliyah,* as the realization of the Zionist ideal; it was legitimized by the community public discourse. In this sense, the model of "brain drain" does not apply to the Jewish community context. The primacy of the Jewish national identity was clear, considering those who fell outside this paradigm as "assimilated" Jews.

In the Orthodox sector, this paradigm was expressed in complex forms, thus perpetuating the classic confrontation between the Zionist parties— including the Zionist Orthodox stream of Hamizrachi and the Mafdal (the National Religious party of Israel)—and the ultra-Orthodox and anti-Zionist party "Agudat Israel." The weight of orthodoxy in Argentine Jewry was very low before the 1990s, when some movements began to grow steadily—like Chabad-Lubavitch—with great impact on JE.

THE NEW TRANSNATIONAL PARADIGM

From the 1990s, and in particular during the last decade, a new paradigm linked to the transformations of the globalized world was developed; the opening of borders and mass migrations; the rise of the importance of skilled labor; the circulation of highly skilled professionals throughout the world; the information revolution, and the development of new technologies in information and communications. Saskia Sassen contributed enormously to understanding this new world stage by coining the concept of "Global Cities," organized on the basis of transnational networks and urban systems, which she defined as a new theoretical model for understanding the processes of globalization. On the other hand, Michel Laguerre raised another concept essential to an analysis of the new transnational paradigm, defining the Jewish people as a "Transglobal

Network Nation."[33] Laguerre called for a review of the relationships model between a national homeland and a Diaspora, i.e., between a "homeland" and a "Hostland."[34] Michelle Laguerre applied this model to Jewish neighborhoods in Paris, London, and Berlin, believing that they have emerged as "global social formations," interconnected with other Jewish diasporas and with Israel, forming a kind of "Transglobal Urbanism" and "Diasporic Global Cities."[35]

Transnationalism—understood as shared spaces and interactions that are sustained across community and national borders—is a key condition to approaching Jewish life in Latin America in the twenty-first century. Transnational entities can be effective agents for micro and macro changes both in the countries of origin and in the new countries of migration.[36]

One of the axes of community studies that can best contribute to understanding the new patterns of Jewish life in the region is Jewish education, as a mechanism of socialization and facing Jewish identity from the perspective of collective identities in interaction between social units that cross national borders.

Our analytical model is based on the transnational paradigm, applied to the field of Jewish education in terms of the four "Commonplaces" of the educational practice and curriculum theory developed by Joseph J. Schwab.[37] These commonplaces refer to the following dimensions:

1) The Educator

The educator in the era of globalization is no longer a "Jewish schoolteacher" without academic training but a person with a great dedication and vocation. Today, there is a great demand for a highly trained professional. Training was

---

33   S. Sassen, *The Global City: New York, London, Tokyo*, 2nd ed. (Princeton, NJ: Princeton University Press, 2001,), xix; *A Sociology of Globalization* (New York: Norton2007).

34   M. S. Laguerre, "The Transglobal Network Nation: Diaspora, Homeland and Hostland," in E. Ben-Rafael and Yitzhak Sternberg (2009), op. cit., 195–210.

35   M. S. Laguerre, *Global Neighborhoods: Jewish Quarters in Paris, London and Berlin* (Albany, NY: State University of New York Press, 2008), xii and 2.

36   Bokser Liwerant, DellaPergola, and Senkman (2011), op. cit., 61f.

37   Joseph J. Schwab. "The Practical 4: Something for Curriculum Professors to Do," *Curriculum Inquiry* 13, no. 3 (1983): 239–65; Joseph J. Schwab and Thomas W. Roby, "The Practicals 5 and 6: Finding and Using Commonplaces in Literature and Psychology," archived at the Museum of Education, University of South Carolina, 1986. On J. Schwab see: http://education.stateuniversity.com/pages/2401/Schwab-Joseph-1909-1988.html

questioned or reduced following the closure of the Greenberg Institute or the Gold Institute in Jerusalem, and Teacher Training Institutes for Jewish schools in the Diaspora, especially for small Jewish communities in Latin America and Europe, due to the decline of the Jewish Agency, the decreased or canceled subsidies, and the decline of the centrality or image of Israel because of the Second Intifada, the Second Lebanon War, and the wars or military operations in the Gaza Strip. On the one hand, this new era raises the demand for certification and systematic training, but, on the other, this is not reflected in any increase in salary or improvement of the social status of the Jewish educator, which largely depends on the status of teachers in general and of national wage policies.

The crisis in the Jewish Agency had an impact on the continuing decline in the number of *morim–shlichim*, emissaries of Israel with clear educational tasks within the school environment, and cultural integration in the countries where they were born. The clear consequence was the slow decline of Hebrew-language teaching in Jewish schools, especially in Argentina—one of the factors that contributed to the closure of the Greenberg Institute, without forgetting the economic factor, of course. The new teacher training frameworks for Jewish schools include matching education schemes with Israeli universities (e.g., The Melton Center with the Institute Melamed of Buenos Aires, or Melton with Hebraica University of Mexico, or The Lookstein Center of Bar-Ilan University with various schools in South America), agreements with local universities, and a constant search to match the teaching certificate or degree in Jewish studies with the teachers of other areas or general education.

2) The Learner

The learner or young students in the new era are no longer passive receivers of information but "digital natives" and technophiles, critical of hierarchies and pedagogic authority—including the paternal authority—covered by parents and society's demand to adapt the curriculum to the demands of the professional market and higher education. In fact, they have become an important factor in the educational processes of the twenty-first century, and it was not to no avail that one of the axes of the new paradigm suggested by thinkers such as Ken Robinson or J. Woocher places the learner in the center, and focuses on the pursuit of relevance from the students' perspective.

3) The Content and Didactic Materials

The educator of our times cannot be satisfied with school textbooks; he must go into the world of the information superhighway with searches in Google, YouTube, and Wikipedia, etc. We noticed a constant change and adaptation to the exposure of knowledge and information, marked by the problem of validating data authenticity and sources. The teaching materials used in Jewish education do not have a single source, Israel in particular, but are produced in various countries, and are used as a function of their potential as teaching methods, and can be applied in various languages. The perspective of these materials is multi- and interdisciplinary, with special emphasis on the visual impact. This is a challenge for both the educator and the learner.

4) The Social Environment and Its Impact on the Educational Frameworks

It is impossible to understand today the processes of socialization and education without further analysis of the TICs (technology, information, and communications tools), and their impact in the era of globalization.[38] Social networks constitute an axis of grouping and reference, although they are not always translated into knowledge networks or virtual communities in the full sense of the word. In recent years, we have noticed an increase in the legitimacy and validity of non-formal education in parallel with a rise in the sense of crisis and decline in the school (Jewish and non-Jewish).

These four commonplaces interact on a permanent basis; all educational processes should consider them and, as part of a new paradigm for Jewish education, should provide a model of deliberative dialogue and interaction, providing solutions to the major challenges faced by communities or ethnic diasporas in an era of globalization.

LATIN AMERICAN JEWISH EDUCATORS IN AN ERA OF GLOBALIZATION AND TRANSNATIONALISM

Migratory processes characteristic of the era of globalization also affect community life and Jewish identities. Well-trained Jewish educators with community experience are seeking new horizons with a view to ensuring a

---

38 Manuel Castells, *The Information Age: Economy, Society and Culture*, 2nd ed., vol. 2 of *The Power of Identity* (Hoboken, NJ: Wiley–Blackwell, 2010), see especially xxix–xxxii; Sassen, *A Sociology of Globalization*, chs. 6 and 7.

respectable career in countries that can provide employment opportunities. A look from the perspective of the modern era will prove that this is a "brain drain," i.e. community professionals in Jewish education who found the possibility of upward social mobility in countries that not only provide better wages but also a possibility of community building. This paradigm was forged in the 1960s, and was characterized by the migrations of scientists and qualified professionals from developing countries to the more developed states; it was considered a transfer of national investment in human capital. Yet, from the perspective of the new paradigm in education, we wonder if this is a brain drain, or a flow of knowledge and professional experiences?[39] The new paradigm no longer focuses on the idea of a "brain drain," but a "brain gain," based on a perspective of open borders and transnational relations, which can also benefit the country of origin of these professionals, generating a diaspora of knowledge.[40]

The impact of these technologies can be different according to the sectors that make up the Jewish collective in each country. However, we note that Orthodox sectors, like Chabad-Lubavitch, have taken the information revolution in a systematic manner and applied it as tool to disseminate their ideological and theological vision, and attract new adherents. Rabbi Zvi Grunblatt of Buenos Aires, in a personal interview given at the Ohalei Jinuj Jewish School of Buenos Aires in March 2012,[41] expressed this perspective. Rabbi Grublatt stressed the fact that "the matter of transnationalism has always been a foundation of our education."

Transnationalism is understood by the rabbi in charge of the Chabad movement in Argentina as a commitment to travel the world as part of a training mission in the Jewish and educational community—by emissaries "Shlujim," as well as the use of online networks and communication technologies in the service of the "mission of the Rebbe."

A similar process occurred in the Conservative-Masorti movement since Rabbi Marshall Meyer's arrival in Argentina in 1959, and his huge contributions to the development of Conservative communities and rabbinical training in the framework of the Latin-American Rabbinical Seminar (SRL). Rabbi Abraham Skorka, dean of the SRL, in an interview conducted

---

39 Luchilo, *Más allá de la fuga de cerebros*, introducción, 9–17.
40 Jean Baptiste Meyer, "La sociología de las diásporas del conocimiento," in Luchilo, ibid., 91–114. This perspective of analysis will be expanded and analyzed in my article, to be published in the forthcoming volume of *Judaica Latinoamericana* (Magnes, Hebrew University of Jerusalem).
41 Interview conducted in Hebrew with Batia Nemirovsky, on March 23, 2012.

in Buenos Aires in March 2012,[42] emphasized that the circulation of rabbis and educators is in the DNA of the Conservative movement. Beyond the migration of rabbis in the Jewish world, the movement has failed to develop networks of work and study, except for the Latin American Rabbinical Assembly, which addresses another role and is not intended to further the development of study networks. However, the executive director of the Federation of Conservative-Masorti Communities in Latin America, Ariel Blufstein, emphasized the efforts being made to develop a network of conservative communities throughout Latin America, including social and virtual networks. According to him, the goal is to digitize all the contacts and exchanges, and develop distance education as well as teaching materials for those communities and congregations belonging to the Masorti movement in Latin America.[43]

A pilot research project was carried out in 2011 in the framework of the Liwerant Center at the Hebrew University of Jerusalem. It focused on the study of Argentinean and Uruguayan educators—without disregarding those of other Latin American origins—who received training in their country of origin and migrated to other countries, where they continued to exercise their educational mission, developing a career with professional development. The research[44] was intended to analyze and understand the impact of globalization in this professional field, based on the concept of the "transnational Jewish educator." That is to say, educators connected with their country of origin and with professional peers in the world, who have incorporated elements of culture and identity of the new countries in which they live, enabling them to reside in another country, or to return to their country of origin. The Jewish educator in the framework of this research is defined in a holistic way, including the formal and the non-formal, as well as community work in the educational framework of congregations and synagogues.

To illustrate this point, let us look at Brazil, and in particular the large cities such as San Paulo, Rio de Janeiro, and Porto Alegre. These cities became poles of attraction for professionals of other South American countries, especially

---

42 Interview conducted in AMIA, with Anita Weinstein, on March 22, 2012.
43 Interview with Ariel Blufstein in Buenos Aires, March 21, 2012.
44 From the beginning of 2012, this research was reshaped and expanded and has become a project led by the Liwerant Center of the Hebrew University of Jerusalem in cooperation with the Vaad Hajinuj (Educational Committee), the Universidad Hebraica of Mexico, and the AMIA–Jewish community in Argentina, with the support of the Pincus Fund for Jewish Education in the Diaspora.

Argentina and Uruguay, who had played central roles in their original Jewish communities, whether in synagogues or religious congregations, Jewish schools, and social–sports clubs. This phenomenon is reflected, for example, in the concentration of non-Brazilian Jewish educators in the metropolis of San Pablo, regarded as one of the forty global cities of the world, being a financial center, telecommunications node, and site for transnational networks between South America, United States, Europe, and Japan.[45]

The concept of "transnational Jewish educator" is novel, and we believe that it is part of the paradigm shift in Jewish education in general, and in Latin America in particular. Judging from the cases studied in the pilot research, this educator is characterized by the following (not necessarily present in all cases):[46]

1) Professional mobility: the educators do not wish to return to their countries of origin; they are mostly willing to migrate to another destination, to advance their professional career.

2) Imprint of trips to Israel and a positive relationship with the Jewish state on the part of the Jewish educator. Most do not intend to immigrate (*aliyah*) to Israel, or to settle in another country after having lived and studied in Israel. In any case, they are committed to community- building and continuity in the Jewish world or in their countries of origin.

3) Israel is viewed as a spiritual component vital and necessary in the Jewish identity, and an important stage of professional development.

4) Ability to grow professionally, and adjustment to changes or new conditions of life. We found a consciousness of the importance of innovation and professional renewal, with projections toward the community dynamics.

5) Positive attitude toward knowledge networks, without being involved systematically in networks of Jewish learning.

The impact of processes of globalization and transnationalism in Jewish education is reflected more clearly and systematically in the Hebrew University

---

45 S. Sassen, ed., *Global Networks—Linked Cities*, 3rd ed. (Abingdon, UK: Routledge, 2006), see "Introduction: Locating Cities on Global Circuits," 1–36; Sueli Ramos Schiffer, "São Paulo: Articulating a Cross-border Region," in Sassen, ibid., 209–36.

46 The pilot research included 120 Latin American educators and rabbis outside their country of origin and training; it was not published due to its incorporation into the larger project of the Liwerant Center at the Hebrew University of Jerusalem from March 2012.

Liwerant Center's research, carried out from 2012–14, based on a questionnaire sent to electronic databases of educators from Mexico, Argentina, and other Latin American educators circulating in the Jewish world, including Israel. This research enjoyed the leadership of Sergio DellaPergola (Hebrew University of Jerusalem) and Judit Bokser Liwerant (UNAM, Mexico).

This study of Latin American Jewish educators comprised 1,379 respondents, mostly reached through an Internet survey. This is the largest in-depth study ever attempted of the personnel undertaking the daily mission of socializing the new generation of Jews rooted in Latin America either because they live in the continent, or because—after moving to other countries—their peculiar blend of culture and identity remained with them. The study covered 606 educators in Argentina (out of 1,497 identified there, at a response rate of 40.5 percent), and 636 educators in Mexico (out of 1,074, at a response rate of 59.2 percent). Another 137 respondents with Latin American origins were interviewed in other countries, 70 in Israel (at a response rate of 33.3 percent), and 67 elsewhere in Latin America, North America, and Europe (at a response rate of 27.2 percent). Close to 88 percent of the respondents in Mexico answered the entire questionnaire (around 140 questions). This percentage was also high for respondents in Israel and other countries (between 71 and 73 percent). The number of completed questionnaires was lower in Argentina (55 percent). While the sample in Mexico, and to some extent in Argentina, responds to acceptable statistical criteria (within the limits of self-selection and non-response), the sub-samples in Israel and elsewhere are only indicative.[47]

There were two important findings of the general research related to the transnational dimension, as follows:

1) Regarding changes in educational practices, about one-third of respondents said that the internet had totally changed their habits, although only for one-tenth of the respondents did this happen through professional networks of educators. The respective values for *haredi* educators are 13 percent and 5.5 percent.

2) Faced with the possibility of participating in programs of e-learning and teaching from a distance, about 70–75 percent of the respondents were in favor on both accounts. In this matter, differences across

---

47   The following findings and conclusions are based on the final report presented to community partners and to the Pincus Foundation in September 2014.

countries, across orientations, and across types of activity fulfilled within the educational system were minor.

3) There is a shared trend toward a growing *haredi* world. The extreme difference between Jewish educators in Mexico and in the other countries concerning the presence of a *haredi* orientation—with a much higher share in Mexico—reflects a particularly strong effort undertaken to cover those institutions that initially were not enthusiastic about participating in the study. Also worth mentioning are the fundamental differences in the representation of the *haredi* and the Orthodox sector among educators; in all countries, the traditionalist orientation appears to be most widespread.

The final results of the research were published toward the end of 2015.[48]

CONCLUSIONS

By way of general conclusion, we may establish that the impact of globalization and the development of networks of communication and interaction are reflected in transnational processes of training and professional development, changes in identity, and in the definition of the professional role of the Latin American Jewish educators. In this context, it seems to us that the process of transformation of the classic paradigm in Jewish education is deep, though still not noted in a practical and systematic manner, with clear impacts on the design of new educational policies at the level of Jewish community lay leadership. Nevertheless, we did not investigate this level of lay leadership, a vital and key dimension for future policy planning.

It seems to us that a change in paradigm regarding the level of Latin American Jewish educators is already in sight, reflected in the following manifestations: diminishing Israeli influence and a decline of the model of center–periphery is one of the main findings in this research, but without a break with the State of Israel. Professional formative processes are based and focused on the local reality, so we may assume the gradual influence of global transformations at the level of professional attitudes of educators who are involved in educational projects or community teaching in Jewish community

---

48 Judit Bokser Liwerant, Sergio DellaPergola, Leonardo Senkman and Yossi Goldstein, *El Educador Judío Latinoamericano en un Mundo Transnacional – Informe de Investigación*, (Mexico City: 2015).

frameworks. One of the main challenges lies in the design of educational policies based on the professionalization of the Jewish educator, the promotion of knowledge networks with transnational linkages and teacher training programs, as well as professional development of the Jewish educator through education at a distance.

Ultimately, we may not explore the process of transformation of the paradigm of Jewish education in Latin America without the design of new educational policies and the mobilization of financial resources from the voluntary and professional leadership. This is both at the level of specific institutions or communities understood as autonomous entities, whether school, religious congregations, sports and social Jewish clubs, community centers, etc., or at the macro level, starting from the design of consensual policies by roof organizations. This transformation must take into account the four components of all educational processes and curricula: the educator, the learner, the learning materials, and the social environment.

In conclusion, we believe that no serious transformation will be possible without involving Jewish educators in a serious and systematic way, including Jewish educators who have migrated to other countries. We should recognize them as a key agent in the new dynamics of change, taking into consideration the development of a new educational paradigm that reflects patterns and dynamic processes of the twenty-first century.

CHAPTER 4

Informal Jewish Education: Argentina's Hebraica Society

SILVIA SCHENKOLEWSKI-KROLL

"The Ideological Transnationalism of Zionism: Theoretical Aspects and Their Implementation in Informal Jewish Education in Latin America as of 1968" is a research project, the subject of which is informal education in the Jewish community centers of Argentina, Uruguay, Brazil, and Chile. It takes as its starting point the events, guidelines, and changes that have taken place in the past forty or so years, as much in communitarian spaces as in the World Zionist Organization, and the interconnection between each sector—especially as they relate to the ideological transnationalism that links them.[1]

Before embarking on the subject at hand, I would like to propose a theoretical framework to define ideological transnationalism and its place in the historiography of the Jewish people; "the history of the present," and the type of required documentation, given that we are studying recent decades; and, lastly, the place of community centers within informal education.

"Ideological transnationalism may be defined as the transmission of ideas and their realization as actions within a certain ethnic group that is geographically dispersed, taking into account relations between periphery and center, center and periphery, and the peripheries among themselves."[2] This definition is based on Yosef Gorny's study, which asks if the transnational

---

1   This paper pertains to the main project of the Liwerant Center for the Study of Latin America, Spain, Portugal, and Their Jewish Communities at the Hebrew University of Jerusalem, the subject of which is "Latin American Jews in a Transnational World: Redefining Experiences and Identities on Four Continents."

2   Author's definition; see "Zionism's Ideological Transnationalism: Theoretical Aspects and Implementation in Informal Education in Latin America since 1968," Liwerant Center, http://www.liwerantcenter.huji.ac.il/research-projects.

Jewish Diaspora has retained its uniqueness—taking into account the fact that the past one hundred and fifty years have seen two conflicting movements, one divisive and the other unifying, the latter gaining strength mainly due to the solidarity felt by most Jewish ideologies following the establishment of the State of Israel. Gorny defines the establishment of the State of Israel as a "singular normalization," in the sense, unlike previous eras, that it has a hub of origin and reference that is materialized in a concrete national entity—much as it was in classic transnationalism.[3] Judit Liwerant makes use of sociological methodology in her investigation of transnationalism in Latin America's Jewish diasporas. Taking off from the premise that transnationalism is an inherent aspect of these diasporas, with European-born patterns brought to a new continent, it is evident that they are a part of the Jewish world both in terms of identity and organization. She concludes that the influence of the environment does not supersede Jewish transnationalism, which remains unchallenged.[4] This position corroborates the historiographic view of Simón Dubnow, who studied the question of "the relation between local dimensions and the universal dimensions in Jewish history."[5] Despite the difference

---

3 Among the divisive elements in the nineteenth century were assimilation, Reform Judaism, and the Bund, while those with a uniting effect were the development of Jewish solidarity expressed through the establishment of the Alliance Israelite Universelle, and especially the rise of Zionism, a movement that despite its diverse ideological and organizational components had a broad common denominator. In the twentieth century, the two trends continued. On the divisive side, at one extreme, was the establishment of the Agudat Yisrael movement, and, at the other, that of the anti-Zionist American Council for Judaism. However, during that century the trend toward solidarity continued: the participation of non-Zionists in the Jewish Agency and the acceptance by Reform groups of the idea of the establishment of a Jewish state are two examples. Yosef Gorny, "Is the Jewish Transnational Diaspora Still Unique?" in *Transnationalism: Diasporas and the Advent of a New (Dis)order*, ed. Eliezer Ben-Rafael and Yitzhak Sternberg, with Judit Bokser Liwerant and Yosef Gorny (Boston, 2009), 237–50. In the introduction to this work, the editors define a transnational entity: "They may include linguistic groups, religious communities, regional populations or nomadic people. Some stem from relations of migrations and migrants' retention of relations with homelands—real or virtual; others may be the outcome of changes in inter-state borders that divide a culturally homogeneous population," Introduction: Debating Transnationalism, ibid., 2; Silvia Schenkolewski-Kroll, "Changes in the Transnational Relationship of the World Zionist Organization and Latin American Jewry: Informal Education, 1968–2006," in *Judaica Latinoamericana*, vol. 7, ed. Margalit Bejarano, Florinda Goldberg, and Efraim Zadoff (Jerusalem: Magness Press, 2013), 465–85 (hereafter: Schenkolewski, "Changes in the Transnational Relationship").
4 Judith Bokser Liwerant, Latin American Jews: A Transnational Diaspora (Leiden: Brill, 2009), 351–74; Schenkolewski-Kroll, "Changes in the Transnational Relationship."
5 David Engel, "Dubnow on the Particular and Universal Elements in Jewish History" [Heb], *Zion* 77, no. 3 (2012): 307–15.

between the concept of the universal and that of the transnational, and with their content as an investigative tool, the distinction between the two today seems more semantic than substantial. In the past, the term "universal" was used to discuss phenomena such as the Jewish people's diasporas and immigration that in our day are considered transnational.[6] Dubnow saw first the spiritual unification of the Jewish people in its common past, to which he added the shared and parallel organizational dimensions that characterized Jewish organizations of the Diaspora. Despite local particularities, this organization created linked, autonomous centers.[7] Without explicitly mentioning transnationalism, Shulamit Volkov analyzes historiographic studies that view Jewish history as part of the history of each country, and those that view Jewish history as a national narrative of the entire People of Israel. Volkov also looks at the tension, in Dubnow, between local "tendencies" and that of *klal Israel*. She concludes that the national narrative, in the cultural, ethnic sense, prevails in Dubnow.[8]

Another facet to be taken into account is that this paper is part of what is defined as a "history of the present," meaning a history that is part of the past and the memories of people who are alive today. The historian and archivist Anne Perrotin Dumon uses this methodology to research Latin American military regimes that caused trauma and left scars among individuals and in society.[9] The epistemology and methodology of this historical genre is sufficiently elastic that it can serve to analyze contemporary socio-historic phenomena of the lived past and present, including such that do not result in trauma or, to the contrary, even such phenomena that in their intention and consequences are positive phenomena,

---

6　For example, Patrick Manning, *Migration in World History* (Abingdon, UK: Routledge, 2013); Robin Cohen, *Global Diasporas: An Introduction* (Abingdon, UK: Routledge, 2008); C. Leggewie, "Transnational Citizenship: Cultural Concerns," in *International Encyclopedia of the Social and Behavioral Sciences*, vol. 23, ed. Neil J. Smelser and Paul B. Baltes (Amsterdam: Elsevier, 2001), 15857–62; D. F. Eckelman, "Transnational Religious Identities (Islam, Catholicism, and Judaism): Cultural Concerns," in ibid., 15862–66.

7　Ibid., note 5.

8　Shulamit Volkov, "Jews among the Nations: A Unique National Narrative or a Chapter in National Historiographies," *Zion* 61, no. 1 (1996): 91–111. *Klal Israel* means considering the Jewish people as a whole.

9　Anne Perotin Dumon, "El pasado vivo de Chile en el año del Informe sobre la Tortura," *Nuevo Mundo, Nuevos Mundos*, May 23, 2005, http://nuevomundo.revues.org/954. The "history of the present" makes extensive use of oral histories, classified documents, and all elements that provide testimony of the present and recent past.

as in the case of community centers.[10] Therefore, from the methodological point of view, we may define these as "history of the present."

Within the informal education of children and youth, Kahane defines community centers as organisms with a high degree of control on the part of the adults who act as agents for pause mechanisms (recreation), consumption, or immediate gratification. To this definition, we must add elements that Kahane defines as characteristics of youth movements, such as, given the role of *madrichim* in community centers, "the creation of creative roles."[11]

What could serve as a model for all of the above? In the ethnic-cultural sense, community centers in the various diasporas form part of the local Jewish institutional complex. Among other things, the ideological transnational network of Zionism in its current iteration, the Joint Distribution Committee, which is parallel but associated through various projects with Zionism, which generates connections and disseminates ideological and organizational content that creates a common denominator between community centers in a specific geographical area, adapting them to local conditions?[12]

The available sources for this paper are the historical archive of World Maccabi, which keeps documents belonging to the organizations affiliated with the Maccabi World Union, especially prior to the 1990s, including these organizations' publications.[13] More recently, the dearth of information is due to the lack of preservation of documents. As a result, oral history interviews with persons involved with the *Sociedad Hebraica Argentina* (SHA) in the past and present, conducted both in Israel and in Argentina, are of major importance.[14] Similarly, the importance of published information made accessible directly by the SHA cannot be overstated. This material is complemented by internet sites and digital publications about or by the organization.[15] This situation differs from

---

10 See below.

11 Reuven Kahane, *Youth and the Code of Informality* [Heb], ed. Mosad Bialik (Jerusalem, 2007), 24–27.

12 See Schenkolewski, "Changes in the Transnational Relationship," n. 3; for example, see Anita Weiner, *Renewal. Reconnecting Soviet Jewry to the Jewish People (AJJC). Activities in the Former Soviet Union, 1988-1998* (Lanham, MD: University Press of America, 2003); Abby Pitkowsky, "Just Like Henry" (electronic resource): The Power of Jewish Caring across Borders" (New York: American Jewish Joint Distribution Committee, 2006).

13 *Joseph Yekutieli Maccabi Sports Archive.*

14 Interviewees: David Fleischer, president of SHA during the Argentine military dictatorship (1976–83); Beto Kaplan Krep, head of the Department of Physical Education; Jessica Rozenblum, head of the Department of Youth; Alberto Senderey, Director General (1976–87).

15 www.hebraica.org.ar; Iton Gadol, www.itongadol.com.ar.

classical historical research based on the analysis of conventional documents, and focuses its analysis and interpretation on material that was accessible to the public from the moment of its publication, on interviews in which there is interaction between the interviewee, the object of the study, and the researcher. As stated, this is "history of the present."

The *Sociedad Hebraica Argentina*, founded in 1926 as an association whose aim was to nourish Jewish culture and encourage the relationship between the Jewish public and Argentine culture, is the oldest communal center in Argentina. Over several decades, the SHA attained its objective through courses, conferences, publications, theater, and a significant library. At the same time, it developed sports activities for children and youth that we may define as informal education.[16]

To understand the context in which Hebraica was established as a specific institution, we need to take into account Argentina's socio-political situation, to undertake an adequate analysis of the abovementioned transnationalism of the Zionist movement and of the Joint, and to reach an understanding of Hebraica's place within the world of Argentina's community centers.

Argentina has passed through various periods during Hebraica's eighty-seven-year life span, starting with the "radical democracy" of its inception, through the so-called Infamous Decade of the 1930s and the first Perón government, to the vicissitudes of democracy and the military regimes that followed it.[17] In terms of the SHA, Argentina's goal of nurturing the relationship between Jewish and Argentine cultures, a specific study could determine the influences on changes in SHA policies, activities, and structures of the Argentine environment during determined periods.

---

16 *Hebraica. Crónica de una creación permanente, 1926–2001* (Buenos Aires, 2001); *Sociedad Hebraica Argentina, 85 años, 1926–2011, Crece junto a vos, Memoria y Balance 2010–2011* (Buenos Aires, 2011); *Entrevistas*, see note 14.

17 Leonardo Senkman and Mario Sznajder, eds., *El legado del autoritarismo* (Jerusalem: The Hebrew University of Jerusalem, 1995); Bernardo Kliksberg, "Una comunidad judía en peligro. Los inquietantes interrogantes del judaísmo argentino y latinoamericano," *Policy Forum* 23 (2002): 22–31; Andrés Bisso, *El Antifascismo Argentino* (Buenos Aires: CeDInCI Editores/Buenos Libros, 2007), 14–97; David Rock, *Argentina, 1516–1987: From Spanish Colonization to Alfonsin* (Berkeley, CA: University of California Press, 1987), 199–376; Ricardo Falcón, *Nueva Historia Argentina: democracia, conflicto social y renovación de ideas (1916–1930)* (Buenos Aires: Penguin Random House Grupo Editorial Argentina, 2000); Alejandro Cattaruzza, *Nueva Historia Argentina: crisis económica, avance del estado e incertitubre política (1930–1943)* (Buenos Aires: Editorial Sudamericana, 2002); Daniel James, *Nueva Historia Argentina: violencia, proscripción y autoritarismo (1955–1976)* (Buenos Aires: Editorial Sudamericana, 2001); Juan Suriano, *Nueva Historia Argentina: dictadura y democracia (1976–2001)* (Buenos Aires: Penguin Random House Grupo Editorial Argentina, 2005).

The SHA always maintained a democratic attitude, while constantly safeguarding the neutrality required by the circumstances.[18] As we know from previous eras, some branches of Hebraica were partially responsible for the security of the Jewish community at certain critical times. During the time of the military regime (1976–82), its building was a place of refuge for those in danger, a repository for "prohibited books," and a witness to the burning of compromising documents.[19]

Another aspect of the context is the Zionist movement, considered by its nature and the way it is transmitted to be an example of ideological transnationalism. Like other Jewish ideologies, the Zionist idea arrived in Latin America together with immigration; one of its characteristics in the New World is that it developed alongside communal organization from its earliest stages. In Argentina, as regards Hebraica, it can be said that the Zionist movement, its political parties, and institutions conquered the communal establishment at the time of the establishment of the State of Israel.[20] Today, there is no overt anti-Zionism among Argentine Jews. Nevertheless, in certain circles, to synthesize the identity of the Argentine Jew, Zionism as such remains unmentioned and is referred to only as a part of a wider system of Judaism. This state of affairs accords with the development of the history of ideas within Zionism starting with the Second Program of Jerusalem in 1968. Being a Zionist does not imply *aliyah*. This definition contradicts that of David Ben-Gurion in the First Program of Jerusalem of 1951, which defined as a Zionist only the individual who actually made *aliyah*. Therefore, today, a Jew can be a Zionist identified with Israel as the state of the Jewish people while continuing to reside in his or her original place of residence. "To be a Zionist in the Diaspora" is a current example of Zionism's transnational ideology.[21]

---

18 I will mention only of the period in question, starting in 1968.

19 *Hebraica. Crónica de una creación permanente*, 53–54. Electronic interview with Alberto Senderey, July 3, 2012.

20 Silvia Schenkolewski-Kroll, "Cambios en la relación de la Organización Sionista Mundial hacia la comunidad judía y el movimiento sionista en Argentina, hasta 1948," *Judaica Latinoamericana* (Jerusalem, 1988), 14–66; Silvia Schenkolewski-Kroll, *The Zionist Movements and the Zionist Parties in Argentina, 1935–1948* [Heb] (Jerusalem: Magnes Press, 1996), 115–17; Schenkolewski, "La conquista de las comunidades: el movimiento sionista y la Comunidad Ashkenazí de Buenos Aires [1935–1949]," in *Judaica Latinoamericana*, vol. 2 (Jerusalem: Magnes Press, 1993), 191–201; *idem*, "Zionism's Ideological Transnationalism: Theoretical Aspects and Implementation in Informal Education in Latin America since 1968," Liwerant Center, http://www.liwerantcenter.huji.ac.il/research-projects.

21 *Idem*, "Tradición y cambio: la relación de las Organización Sionista Mundial con la comunidades de América Latina," in *Pertinencia y alteridad: los judíos en América Latina*, ed. Haim Avni et al. (Madrid: Iberoamericana Vervuert, 2011), 457–75; ibid., note 3.

Based on this concept of Zionism in the Diaspora, one can analyze the connection to the Diaspora itself, the development of ideas, and the changes that took place in the SHA— especially in the past forty or so years. This prism is especially useful to understand ideological transnationalism, its influence in the configuration of Hebraica's framework, and its expression in the institution's activities.

Together with Hacoaj and Macabi, the SHA is one of three principal Jewish communal centers in Buenos Aires. The three have already celebrated several jubilees and are approaching a centenary. Each was founded in specific circumstances and for different reasons. Macabi (established in 1930) was the transitional movement of an old-world sports-oriented organization to a new continent. Hacoaj (established in 1935) was created as a consequence of the rejection Jews faced in their general environment. Hebraica, as stated above, was founded in order to establish cultural ties between the Jews and the Argentines. All three eventually promoted informal education, initially via sport and later transmitting content with Jewish identity, each in its own rhythm at a specific time, and according to its circumstances.[22]

Among the prominent factors defining this informal education when compared with the traditional youth movements, is the initiation of activities at a very early age, and the ongoing nature of engagement and its continuation beyond the years of childhood (i.e., even for young people older than twenty). The crucial difference is that, unlike the case of the youth movements, at no time did any of these three organizations stipulate *aliyah* as an aim.[23] Without embarking on an exhaustive comparison, the common denominator unifying the SHA, Macabi, and Hacoaj is in their response to the need for some sort of Jewish identity in various strata of the Jewish community in Buenos Aires and its surroundings. To complete the picture, from the point of view of the

---

22 See note 16; *Club Naútico Hacoaj, 70 Aniversario. Un sueño, una pasión, una realidad* (Buenos Aires, 2005); Archive of World Maccabi, f-4-7-20, *40 Años de Macabi* (Buenos Aires, 1970).

23 A youth movement emerged in Macabi that justified its own chapter. The same could be said about a comparison between the three community centers mentioned here; Silvia Schenkolewski-Kroll, "Los movimientos juveniles: una faceta carente en la historiografía sionista de la Argentina," in *Judaica Latinoamericana*, ed. Florinda Goldberg, Yossi Goldstein, and Efraim Zadoff, vol. 5 (Jerusalem: Magnes Press, 2005), 209–19; Shlomo Bar Gil, *At First Was the Dream: Graduates of Pioneering Youth Movements in Latin America in the Kibbutz Movement, 1946–1967* [Heb] (Sde Boqer, 2005); idem, *Juventud, visión y realidad: movimientos jalutzianos en Argentina, de Dror y Gordonia a Ijud Habonim, 1934–1973* (Buenos Aires: Milá, 2008).

financial resources of its members and its effect on each organization, Hacoaj is on the highest economic level, followed by Hebraica and Macabi.[24]

The SHA is the result of the fusion of two organizations that preceded it: the Association of Israelite Youth and the Hebraica Association. These were established by the first generation of young people born in Argentina and by those who arrived in the country in their infancy. These young people formed an intellectual elite whose aspiration was to achieve a cultural synthesis between Judaism and Argentineness. The spirit they hoped to inculcate in the institution was already detectable a year earlier (1925), in the invitation to visit Argentina extended by the Hebraica Association to Albert Einstein. In its first decades, the SHA hosted preeminent writers, artists, and foreign and Argentine intellectuals, both Jewish and non-Jewish. For example, a figure no less famous than Arthur Rubinstein debuted at the Colón Theater, followed by a recital at the SHA. These activities can be defined as transnational culture.[25]

Due to the economic boom that Argentina experienced during World War II, The Israelite Mutual Association of Argentina (AMIA)[26] constructed and inaugurated its building on Pasteur Street during the same years of the Holocaust that the SHA erected its building on Sarmiento Street. With the passage of time, the SHA increased the scope of its activities, including a theater and a cinematheque. It published the literary journal *Davar* over a fifty-year period (1945–95). Each journal was on a high intellectual and professional level not only in reference to Judaism, but also in Argentine and universal terms. The SHA became a top-tier component of Argentine culture. Given the place it came to occupy in the general world of Argentina's intellectual life, it is possible to describe the SHA as a pioneer of the pluralism that began with the democratization of the 1980s.[27]

---

24 This assessment is the result of interviews and visits conducted by the author to the three institutions. See J. C.–R, "Tres grandes organizaciones juveniles: Hebraica, Macabi y Hacoaj," in *Anales de la Comunidad Israelita de Buenos Aires, 1963–1968* [Yiddish], ed. Isaac Janasovich (Buenos Aires: Asociacion Mutual Israelita Argentina, 1969), 353–66.

25 *Hebraica, Crónica de una creación permanente* (Buenos Aires: Sociedad Hebraica Argentina), 12–15; Haim Avni, *Judaísmo de Argentina. Posición social y configuración institucional* [Heb] (Jerusalem: The Hebrew University of Jerusalem, 1972), 82–83.

26 Ashkenazi community of Buenos Aires. See, for example, Silvia Schenkolewski-Kroll, "La conquista de las comunidades: el movimiento sionista y la comunidad ashkenazi de Buenos Aires (1935–1949)," in *Judaica Latinoamericana*, vol. 2, ed. Silvia Schenkolewski-Kroll and Leonardo Senkman (Jerusalem: Magnes Press, 1993), 191–201.

27 This contention deserves its own study. *Hebraica. Crónica de una creación permanente*, 19–20, 31–38; ibid., note 25.

With respect to Zionism, despite the activity of prominent members of the SHA in the Committee for a Hebrew Palestine, it maintained a reserved and neutral disposition, far from any defined political position, until the establishment of the State of Israel. In a plenary session at the time of the proclamation of the Jewish National Fund and the creation of the State of Israel, the SHA resolved to abstain from donations to the JNF and to refrain from asking its members to participate in any way. In response to this resolution, a group within the SHA initiated an electoral campaign that won the 1949 vote, and changed the organization's policies regarding Israel and the aid it should be granted.[28] In his doctorate, Yossi Goldstein addresses the SHA's position vis-à-vis Israel and Zionism during the first ten years of the state's existence. For the SHA's intellectual members, Israel represented reparation for generations of Jewish suffering that simultaneously created a new image of the Jew and shone its light on the Diaspora as a whole. On the other hand, the SHA's elite members could be counted among those Jews who continued to live in their countries of origin, and for whom Israel was the sun that radiated the spirituality that kept them close to Jewish tradition.[29] Despite the fact that, for practical purposes, identification with Israel and support for it existed over the course of the years, it was only in 1986 that a statute reformed the institution's basic aim to "strengthen cultural and spiritual ties with Israel."[30] In the SHA's case, we are discussing a spiritual Zionism in the manner of Ahad Ha'am and American Zionism, without any evidence of direct influence from the United States—rather, circumstances that engendered similar ideologies.[31] Although we have no in-depth study, it appears that despite changes and differing circumstances with the passage of time, these basic assumptions remain relevant today.

---

28 Ibid., 18–24, note 25.

29 Yossi Goldstein, "The Influence of the State of Israel and the Jewish Agency on Jewish Life in Argentina and Uruguay, 1948–1958" [Heb] (PhD dissertation, The Hebrew University of Jerusalem, 1993), 70, 77, 79, 82.

30 *Hebraica, Crónica de una creación permanente*, 12, note 25 above. In the same document, the SHA declared itself a community center. See "Afiliación a la Organización Sionista. Hebraica adhiere e informa a sus asociados," *Semana a semana* (April 1987): 3–12.

31 Gideon Shimoni, *The Zionist Ideology* (Hanover, NH: Brandeis University Press, 1995), 104–12, 270–78; Alon Gal, "Envisioning Israel—The American Jewish Tradition," in *Envisioning Israel: The Changing Ideals and Images of North American Jews*, ed. Alon Gal (Jerusalem: Magnes Press, 1996), 13–37; Jonathan D. Sarna, A Projection of America as it Ought to Be: Zion in the Minds of American Jews (Detroit, MI: Wayne State University Press, 1996), 41–59.

In addition to Zionism, the other transnational factor that influenced the SHA was the Joint. The Joint had a history of ties with Argentina's communitarian establishment, a subject that has been partially studied up to 1948, especially as a result of the ideological distancing of local Zionist elements, reinforced by anti-American sentiment directed at the Joint.[32] Alfredo Berlflein, an Argentine Jew who had studied in the United States and worked there for the JDC, was director of the Argentine office of the Joint in the early 1970s. In view of the poor financial state of the local Jewish institutions, and what the Joint officials considered necessary to assist Argentine Jewry during Berlflein's administration, he worked together with the Jewish Agency to support the socio-athletic associations. This involvement influenced the founding of the Argentine Federation of Maccabean Community Centers (FACCMA), inculcating the Joint's ideology of maintaining communities as a priority above the realization of Zionism. This in no way conflicted with accepted diasporic Zionism after 1968; it was this fact that legitimated cooperation with the Jewish Agency.[33]

Athletic activity was part of the SHA from its inception. According to participants, the level of instruction never reached the levels or the influence that the cultural branch achieved in the Argentine ecosphere; above all, it was a place where young members could go for recreational activities. In the early 1960s, the SHA underwent a period of crisis, losing members, in part due to the lack of a country club property that would have enabled it to compete with Hacoaj and Macabi. In 1963, the SHA acquired a parcel of land in the Buenos Aires suburb of Pilar, which was inaugurated as a country club in 1968. This responded to the necessity of granting its members a campus for weekend

---

32 The ties between the Joint and the Jewish community of Argentina since 1948 have yet to be studied. See Schenkolewski-Kroll, *The Zionist Movement and the Zionist Parties in Argentina* (Jerusalem: Magnes Press, 1996), 250–78; Silvia Schenkolewski-Kroll, "Comunistas y no sionistas en la Argentina y la ayuda a las víctimas de la Segunda Guerra Mundial desde el prisma del Joint," in *Judaica Latinoamericana*, ed. Margalit Bejarano, Florinda Goldberg, and Yossi Goldstein, vol. 6 (Jerusalem: Magnes Press, 2009), 337–50; Ralph I. Goldman, "El rol del profesional en el desarrollo e implementación de políticas y estrategias en la comunidad judía," in *Cuadernos de Capacitación*, vol. 4, Joint executive for Latin America (Argentina, 1981). Notwithstanding its later publication date, this reflects the Joint's ideology. See also Alberto Senderey, "Informe: El Joint en América Latina desde la década del setenta," in *Pertinencia y Alteridad. Judíos en de América Latina: cuarenta años de cambios*, ed. Haim Avni, Judit Bokser Liwerant, Sergio DellaPergola, Margalit Bejarano, and Leonardo Senkman (Madrid: Iberoamericana Vervuert, 2011), 457–83 (see *Joint*, bibliography, note 12).
33 Schenkolewski, *Tradición y cambio*, 457–75, note 12. Interview with David Fleischer, former president of SHA, November 2, 2011; Alberto Senderey, former director general of SHA, July 3, 2012. Note 21.

leisure activities. In this way, the nucleus of a new community was established and new sports arenas were opened.[34] As regards the informal education of children and youth, the Department of Minors and Cadets operated its first summer camp in 1947. In 1962, the SHA founded a leadership school and, ten years later, included a School for Instructors and Institutional Professionals (EDITTI in its Spanish acronym), which was founded by the Argentine Maccabean Foundation (FAM) and was sponsored by the Jewish Agency. From the 1960s, graduates of the leadership school were sent to Jerusalem's *Machon L'Madrichei Chutz La'Aretz*. By the early 1970s, the SHA was host to a *shaliach*—an Israeli emissary.[35] All this is testimony to strong links with Israel.

The great change that caused tumult in the SHA's concept and structure took place in 1976, when, following the recommendation of Alfredo Berlflein, Alberto Senderey was named the SHA's executive director. Senderey himself was the product of 1960s-era SHA informal education; he was a graduate of its leadership school and, as a *madrich*, had already attempted to bring about changes in the activities of SHA youth. He was the youngest member ever to have served in the Executive Committee. From his new post, he became the SHA's delegate to the newly created Argentine Jewish Youth Council, of which he became the first secretary and subsequently the president. In 1971, he went on to study at the Hebrew University of Jerusalem, focusing on international relations. At the same time, the Jewish Agency's department of youth and pioneers hired him to direct the Winter Machon for Latin American youth that arrived for six weeks: two at a kibbutz, two at a seminary, and two traveling around Israel. He returned to Argentina in 1974 and was invited to become a member of the SHA's executive committee.[36] Using American and European Jewish community centers as a model, the SHA transformed itself into an institution whose primary aim was informal Jewish education via groups of all ages: athletic activities and cultural expressions of all sorts. Members went from a passive role to actively participating as Hebraica "citizens." The slogan used by Senderey was "be a key member, join the committees, voice your opinion, speak up, interact, propose themes you'd like to study and activities that you'd like to undertake." This is part of a wider citizenship in the community and in the country. Following this principle, the same individual can be considered to possess multiple citizenships.[37]

---

34 Interviews with D. Fleischer and A. Senderey, see note 32; *Hebraica. Crónica de una creación permanente*, 41–46.

35 D. Fleisher interview, see note 32.

36 Interviews with Alberto Senderey, July 3, 2012, July 10, 2012.

37 *Hebraica. Crónica de una creación permanente*, 50–55. Senderey employs the term "citizen-

A question to be asked is if the post Yom Kippur War crisis regarding Israel and the prevailing situation in Argentina also influenced the institutional changes? One response is that of David Fleischer, then SHA's president. According to him, no educational changes occurred after the Six-Day War. This follows on what has already been discussed in previous papers, and the World Zionist Organization's new youth programs that were hindered by Argentina's political climate of that time. Fleischer recalls that a portrait of Che Guevara was on the wall at a 1973 *kabalat shabbat* service for eight- to nine-year-olds, as it was for adolescents. To improve the atmosphere, he decided to dissolve the team and send a group of instructors to the camp held by the Coordinating Committee for Non-Partisan Entities sponsored by the Jewish Agency. The SHA was no different at that time from what was taking place in the other youth movements.[38]

According to Fleischer, the SHA always maintained a Zionist line and its informal education conformed to what he calls "the program is the reading of reality." It was following this reading of that reality that Alberto Senderey was appointed executive director. Senderey remained in the post from 1976 to 1987; he was, therefore, head of the SHA during all the years of the military regime. Some testimonies recall that participants in activities organized by the youth department related to these activities as an escape valve for everything that could not be expressed outside. It is significant that the focus on *rikudim* (Israeli folk dancing) began during this time and grew throughout the entire period. The SHA transformed itself into a refuge. But not just a refuge—it was also an example. Given the circumstances of the era, the SHA was forced to self-censor the content of its activities. According to Senderey, every possible limit was reached, and in this way, despite the difficult state of affairs, an example was provided to the youth. Another example occurred following two anti-Semitic attacks against the building on Sarmiento Street, when the SHA's leadership decided to continue all its activities undeterred, because it was impossible to educate a new generation of young Argentine Jews in an

---

ship" to signify its active use in different circles. The definition accords with the concept of identity; see 52.

38 This theme needs to be studied at greater depth. Interview with David Fleischer, November 2, 2011. See Ariel Noyjovich, "Alienated at Home: Zionist Youth Movements and State Terrorism in Argentina in the Seventies" [Heb] (MA thesis, Faculty of Humanities, University of Haifa, November 2010), 21–56, 99–103; Schenkolewski, "Changes in the Transnational Relationship."

atmosphere of fear.[39] I have seen no documents indicating any criticism or offering factual evidence to doubt these testimonies of the SHA's operations during the military dictatorship. From the institution's contextual prism, they appear to be true.

Senderey inherited a bankrupt SHA, with only 4,000 paying members and 10,000 non-paying life members. His reform enabled him to bring in 17,000 paying members, including the life members. One of his first decisions was to dismiss the *shaliach* and, since that time, there have been no *shlichim* at the SHA.[40] This act demonstrates a new conceptualization of what we may define as independence and self-sustainment in everything to do with informal education, including Jewish and Zionist content.

According to Senderey, the SHA went from being a socio-athletic club with a youth department that did no more than mimic the youth movements, with people coming to practice sports and older persons who attended lectures, to being an organic community center providing services for all ages from cradle to grave.[41] In this paper, I mention only children, adolescents, and youth. Senderey conceived of an integrated system of departments and put it into practice, one for children and another for adolescents, which included—in the same space—the educational content that belonged to the *madrichim*, dance classes, music, theater, and professionals from the athletic schools. In line with that programming, the head of each department was in charge of interdisciplinary teams specializing in specific age groups that received appropriate instruction. One example of the lasting changes brought about by Senderey had to do with Passover. The theme had been addressed in a conceptual way according to age groups and following the principles of evolutionary psychology. Regarding the Passover Seder, the reform was

---

39 See notes 36 and 37.

40 See note 36. Interview with Jessica Rozenbaum, SHA's youth director, November 1, 2011.

41 Among the many journals and publications that provide information about the SHA's activities for all ages, these are a few examples: Sociedad Hebraica Argentina, *100% Hebraica, Proyectos 2005; XVIII Aniversario del Country SHA, Jai-Vida,* Sociedad Hebraica Argentina, Centro Comunitario, November 1982; Sociedad Hebraica Argentina, *85 Años, 1926–2011, Memoria y Balance 2010–2011.* Despite the extraordinary character of Sociedad Hebraica Argentina, *100% Hebraica, 2005,* which was published following the failed union with the Club Náutico Hacoaj, and despite the fact that not all projects were realized, the text fleshes out the content and character of the SHA's activities. See the epilogue for information on the attempt to unify both community centers and, even more than the epilogue, a new preface, "La vida es el arte del encuentro." Regarding the amalgamation of Hebraica and Hacoaj, see *Hebraica, Crónica de una creación permanente* (Buenos Aires 2001), 117, 119.

institutional and involved the education of children and adolescents. Instead of a single, all-purpose Seder that the SHA traditionally organized, they set up thirty-two Sedarim, each planned for a specific age and activity group. Each Seder had a Hagaddah appropriate to its intended audience. As a result of this change, attendance at the Seder increased significantly, and was drawn from a much wider group.[42] The most completely realized change instituted by Senderey was evident between the years 1983 and 1986, when between 3,000 and 3,500 children were signed up for groups (*kvutzot*), served by a team of 200 *madrichim*. The reform was also felt in the SHA country club in the Pilar suburb. The construction of dorms and a youth hostel, and a change of regulations opening the use of the country club to those were not property owners, converted the Pilar campus into a second center of informal education benefiting from all the resources for group activities and sports practice.[43] The most significant support given to this project has been the school for *madrichim*, established in 1978 and in existence until the present, from which thirty-four classes of students have graduated after completing two years of studies. The graduates complete their education with a trip to Israel. During the course of Senderey's administration, until 1987, he himself traveled to Israel personally, to organize the study programs and tours that corresponded to the SHA's needs.[44]

There is no doubt that the years under Senderey's leadership established a road map for the institution. Some changes have taken place, but the basic plan endures. Hacoaj and Macabi took the system established in the SHA—and the experience that was acquired—as a role model.[45]

In the early years of the twenty-first century, even taking into account external factors that influenced the processes, the SHA's attitude can be analyzed through an ideological prism— educational, athletic, and social.

---

42 Interviews with Alberto Senderey, note 35; *Hebraica, Memorias 1983-1984 del centro comunitario más importante del país*, World Maccabi Historical Archive, 3C/11, 10–18, 27–33.

43 Ibid., note 35; Hugo Guinguis, "En el Country SHA el judaísmo es una forma de vida," in *XVIII Aniversario del Country SHA, Jai-Vida* (Buenos Aires: Sociedad Hebraica Argentina, Centro Comunitario, November 1982), 25–29; and Sergio Bergman, "Paso a la juventud," ibid., 38.

44 Ibid., note 35; Sociedad Hebraica Argentina, *Escuela de Madrijim, treinta años*, 2008; "Hebraica comenzó con el 35 ciclo de su escuela de Madrijim," *Iton Gadol*, accessed May 23, 2017, http://itongadol.com/noticias/val/70345/hebraica-comenzo-con-el-35°-ciclo-de-su-escuela-de-madrijim.html, April 15, 2013.

45 This estimation, transmitted by some interviewees, requires corroboration in a comparative study.

The transnational ideology that supports the SHA's informal education system is to develop a strong feeling of belonging with and close ties to Israel based on Zionist content, but not a realizable link, such as that determined by *aliyah*. The aim is to be active Diaspora Jews and to belong to Jewish organizations, working with them and for them.[46] Affiliated children and adolescents belong to Jewish families that generally are secular. The few Orthodox Jews who attend do so principally for athletic activities in a Jewish atmosphere. A minority belongs to the Conservative movement. In an indication of private home practices, some 20 to 30 percent responded positively when asked if they required kosher food in questionnaires for summer camp registration. On the other hand, as the SHA admits, exogamic couples also attend all types of activities. Another aspect that underscores pluralism—in this case of the economic variety—are the grants offered to children aged six to eleven and those proffered by the school for *madrichim*.[47] The majority of the SHA's child members attend a Jewish primary school, meaning that there is a mutual complement between their school and the SHA. Others acquire Jewish values only through the SHA. The SHA's place is all the more relevant in middle school, when the majority of adolescents attend non-Jewish schools. The above-mentioned trips of the students of the leadership school to Israel are a crucial factor in this process. During the 1990s, Tapuz Hadraja used programs combining elements of the Jewish Agency and the World Maccabi. For six years, Argentina's economic crisis and the intifada disrupted the graduates' trips to Israel. The program was renewed as of 2005.[48] Today, Bekeff Hadraja is in charge, and the "March of Life," a trip that includes visits both to Poland and to Israel, has been added.[49] Participation in the "March of Life" is contingent on a quiz on material learned by the *madrichim* and Holocaust education. It should be clear that the education of the *madrichim* also traverses continental transnationalism, with SHA *madrichim* attending continental seminars organized by JUMA, FACCMA, and Latin American Maccabi Confederation (CLAM). In November 2010, the fourth seminar was held in Argentina. Out of 140

---

46 See, for example, Sociedad Hebraica Argentina, *100% Hebraica, Proyectos* (2005); Sociedad Hebraica Argentina, *85 Años, 1926–2011, Memoria y Balance 2010–2011*, 9; *Hebraica. Crónica de una creación permanente*; an interview with Hebraica's former president, Jorge Breutman, 27–28; ibid., interview with Hebraica president José Scaliter, 114–15; ibid., interview with Alberto Senderey, 50–55.

47 Interview with Jessica Rozenbaum, SHA Youth Director, November 1, 2011; note 46; Interview with Hebraica president José Scaliter, 114–15.

48 Interview with Jessica Rozenbaum, SHA Youth Director, November 1, 2011.

49 From the 1990s until today, the SHA has organized the "March of Life" for Argentine adults and youth.

attendees, 52 were Argentines and 22 were SHA members.[50] Given that the event was held in-country, it is not surprising that local representatives were the majority. It is notable, however, that almost half belonged to the SHA. This is a demonstration of the institution's educational import.

Alongside the major Jewish consciousness-raising, a strong commitment to Argentine society exists and is nourished. This is perhaps not at the level of the large cultural awakening that always characterized the SHA, but rather by using *mitnadvim* (Hebrew: volunteers), the SHA identifies adolescents and youth who engage in community service in rural schools in many provinces, including Santa Fe, Corrientes, Cordoba, and Misiones. The symbiotic commitment to Argentine society and Jewish tradition was launched during Rosh Hashanah 2011 as a project entitled *Tikun Olam*. This involved bringing families together to participate in "A Roof for My Country" project, which assists in the construction of emergency residences for those in need. The call by youth *madrichim* to participating families includes young children.[51]

As part of informal education, sport is essentially formative and pedagogical. The competitive aspect is of minor importance. The goal is not to build champions—although they exist. The system is based on an athletic school in which children aged six to seven are rotated among the various sports, eventually choosing between them. Organization is an important factor in relations between the community centers, as it is in transnational relations within the continent sponsored by FACCMA and CLAM. The highpoint is the Maccabiah Games in Israel. In another point of contact with the Argentine ecosystem, the SHA belongs to national federations in fourteen athletic disciplines. According to participants, contact with the national athletic world is conducted with conventional mutual respect. In the case of certain specific sports clubs, though less so in the national federations, there have been documented cases of anti-Semitism.[52]

---

50 Ibid.; Sociedad Hebraica Argentina, *85 Años, 1926–2011, Memoria y Balance 2010–2011*, 10; EDMA Escuela de Madrijim, Sociedad Hebraica Argentina, *Iom Iom*, 425, September 30, 2011, 10; "Marcha por la Vida. Casi 400 argentinos vivenciaron Iom Hazicaron y Iom Haatzmaut en Israel," *Iton Gadol*, April 18, 2013, accessed May 23, 2017, http://www.iton-gadol.com.ar/noticias/val/70422/marcha-por-la-vida-casi-400-argentinos-vivenciaron-iom-hazicaron-y-iom-haatzmaut-en-israel.html.

51 *Mitnadev. A Volunteer Project* (document received during my visit to the SHA in November 2011); "El proyecto Mitnadev recibió un reconocimiento de DAIA," *Iom Iom* (September 2011), 8.

52 Interview with Beto Kaplan Krep, Director of the Department of Physical Education, November 14, 2011; Sociedad Hebraica Argentina, *100% Hebraica, Proyectos 2005*,

If we focus on the implementation of the Youth Department's programming for 2011, it is clear that the conceptual and concrete vision delineated by Alberto Senederey's road map remains in place. Among the values that guide these activities, critical thought, Jewish experiences, Jewish content (including knowledge of biblical sources), belonging to and identification with the institution, and the surrounding reality (a commitment to the national reality) stand out.[53] Though it is part of the program, a connection to Israel is not made explicit; it is tacitly included in Jewish experiences and content. Each of these values is adapted to the programming of the various age groups.

We are left with the question of what future lies ahead for the education received through the SHA. One approach arises from the testimony provided by thirty graduating classes of *madrichim*. Those who return from Israel work for almost four years as lay *madrichim*, a minority remains as professional staff, and the majority pursue the most common path, that of attending university. The former *madrichim* will forever continue to articulate what they have learned, and lean on experiences gained during their years at Hebraica, using these skills to cope with the many facets of life.[54] Despite the nostalgic quality of the abovementioned publication, it does appear to contain a basic truth, which is corroborated by other attestations. It is no small matter that the students of the school for *madrichim* (EDMA)'s motto is "forms you for life." In 2011, the school's central theme of self-identity was presented in a project entitled (in Hebrew— like the names of groups and projects) *Mi Ani?* (Who am I?). The many elements of identity are processed in the meetings, among them, roots, family, the past, relations, and identification with Judaism. The aim is for the future *madrich* to learn how to know himself or herself, and thus achieve the construction of an individual and a group identity.[55] There is no doubt as to the necessity of a sociological field study to investigate what former *madrichim* have done from the point of view of their Jewish

---

Educación física, 6–7, 19–20; Sociedad Hebraica Argentina, *85 Años, 1926–2011, Memoria y Balance 2010–2011*, 17–30; "Macabeada: Más de 9000 deportistas se reunirán en Jerusalem para participar en uno de los principales encuentros del mundo judío," *Iton Gadol*, March 6, 2013, www.itongadol.com.ar.

53 Interview with Jessica Rozenblum, November 1, 2011; Sociedad Hebraica Argentina, *85 Años, 1926–2011, Memoria y Balance 2010–2011*, 9–11.

54 Sociedad Hebraica Argentina, *Escuela de Madrijim, treinta años*, 2008; interview with Jessica Rozemblum, November 1, 2011; *Hebraica. Crónica de una creación permanente*, 103.

55 EDMA School of Madrichim, Sociedad Hebraica Argentina, *Iom Iom*, 425, September 30, 2011, 10.

identity, and its multiple ideological and social expressions. Such a work would investigate whether the ideal of the SHA's informal education, which posits a diasporic Judaism and a Zionism that does not abandon traditional values while nurturing a sense of Argentinism, passes the test of real life.

I have attempted to outline informal education as it exists in the most veteran of Argentine Jewish community centers. A clear line can be traced from Hebraica's genesis through the establishment of the State of Israel to our times, which is unified by the ideology that has characterized the organization since its foundation: the symbiosis of Judaism and Argentinism. To achieve this aim, the development of methods for the SHA's informal education have changed with the times. Although no fundamental changes took place following the Six-Day War, adjustments were undertaken as a result of the Argentine political climate in the 1970s. In addition, Hebraica underwent a major reform when it also became a community center. Each of these stages has a common denominator, which is the concept of Israel being seen as a historic–political–spiritual center shining its light toward the Diaspora, a pillar of Judaism alongside other traditions of the Jewish world that reinforce Jewish identity within a community rooted in and committed to its country of residence. In order to achieve this state of affairs, it also uses transnationalism—which, in the case of the SHA, has multiple facets that converge: diasporic Zionism, Israel, the Joint, and World Maccabi and its activities on the continental and global levels. Each of these elements forms a canvas for the transmission of informal education. In order to verify the common denominator of the many diasporas, as in Dubnow and Volkov, embodied in this case by community centers, a comparative study is necessary. Given the sourcing and the periods in question, this is an example of a "history of the present" lacking in trauma and misfortune.

Much remains to be analyzed by digging deeper into subjects addressed here and studying aspects yet to be tackled. Among others, this historic-ideological prism still requires a sociological study to complete and verify the results presented here.

CHAPTER 5

The Effect of the Global Economic Crisis on the Affordability of Jewish Lifestyle in Latin America

ELI GOLDSTEIN[*] AND OSNAT ISRAELI

This paper discusses the effect of the global economic crisis of recent years on the affordability of maintaining a Jewish lifestyle in general, and in Latin America in particular. The data show that in countries like Argentina, Uruguay, Venezuela, and others, tens of thousands of Jews are facing a decreasing disposable income, and have even slipped below the poverty line. The inability to afford a Jewish lifestyle ranges from being unable to pay school tuition and summer camp fees, to having problems with maintaining the affiliation with synagogues, paying Jewish Center memberships, purchasing kosher food, and observing other aspects of the traditional Jewish household.

This paper focuses on the effect of Jewish attendance at Jewish day schools, which is highly sensitive to the global and local economic crisis, and on Jewish lifestyle aspects, namely:

1) the percentage of intermarriage in the Jewish community;
2) the percentage of the Jewish population that has visited Israel; and
3) the percentage of Jewish immigrants to Israel.

The main conclusions are that attending Jewish day schools has a statistically significant negative effect on the first and third variables, and a positive, though weaker, influence on visits to Israel.

---

[*] Eli Goldstein acknowledges financial and research support received from the Ashkelon Academic College.

The aim of this work is to test empirically the relations that may exist between four main indicators, typical of a Jewish community, namely:

1) the percentage of Jewish children attending Jewish day schools in each country;
2) the percentage of intermarriage in the Jewish community;
3) the proportion of the Jewish population that has visited Israel; and
4) the percentage of Jewish immigrants (making *aliyah*) to Israel.

The paper is divided into three sections. The first section provides a survey of the relevant literature that deals with the correlations between the economic crisis and traditional Jewish lifestyle affordability, focusing on Latin America. The second section describes the econometric model constructed to deal with some of the questions introduced in the first section. It also discusses the data and the results. The last section summarizes the paper.

ECONOMIC CRISIS AND TRADITIONAL JEWISH LIFESTYLE AFFORDABILITY IN LATIN AMERICA[1]

Being a Jew affiliated with the Orthodox or traditional Jewish community means spending 25 to 35 percent of the individual's available income on Jewish traditional living, often at the expense of housing that is more adequate, a more comfortable lifestyle, or the accumulation of savings. Among other things, the costs involved include synagogue affiliation, intensive Jewish education, camps, federation and other Jewish charitable donations, and memberships in Jewish community centers and Jewish communal organizations.[2] The bulk of the literature on the cost

---

1 This paper is focused on the Jewish communities of Latin America and the Argentinean community in particular. For research on similar problems in other Jewish communities, focusing mainly on North America, see Ann G. Wolfe, *The Invisible Jewish Poor* (New York: American Jewish Committee, 1971), and Ellen G. Witman, "Economic Distress in the American Jewish Community," *Israel Horizons* (September–October 1984). Wolfe documented the extent to which a class of Jewish poor existed in North America. Witman wrote about the effect the harsh national economic conditions in North America in the 1970s and '80s had on the Jewish middle class, which resulted in many cases of disaffiliation from Jewish communities and Jewish life. She also documented how synagogues and Jewish schools felt the ramifications of the recession, and were unable to respond due to their own lack of resources. See also Jack Wertheimer, "Jewish Education in the United States: Recent Trends and Issues," in *American Jewish Year Book* (New York: American Jewish Committee, 1999).

2 See Aryeh Meir and Lisa Hostein, *The High Cost of Jewish Living* (New York: American Jewish Committee, 1992); and Jerry A. Winter and Lester I. Levin, *The Cost of Jewish*

of a Jewish traditional lifestyle has focused on Jewish day school education costs, which represent the major component in these expenses.

Toward the end of 2001, Argentina was sliding catastrophically downward, suffering from the worst social and economic crisis of its recent history.[3] Argentina is home to Latin America's largest Jewish community, whose history goes back to the era of the Spanish and Portuguese Inquisitions, when Jews fled to Argentina to escape persecution.[4] It also has the fifth largest Jewish population in the world.[5] From an economic perspective, the Latin American region as a whole proved not to be immune to the financial disaster stemming from the global financial and economic crisis of the first decade of the third millennium.[6]

The Jewish community in Argentina, like the rest of the Argentinean population, suffered from the effects of the economic crisis. More than a third of those previously considered to belong to Argentina's historical middle class were now considered to be among the so-called "new poor."[7] Moreover, the

---

Affiliation and Participation (New York: Council of Jewish Federations, 1985). For a case study dealing with the city of Philadelphia in the United States, see Rela Geffen Monson and Ruth Pinkenson Feldman, "The Cost of Living Jewishly in Philadelphia" (paper delivered at AJC Consultation on the High Cost of Living, 1991).

3 See, for example, Bernardo Kliksberg, *How to Cope with Poverty and Inequality? An International Perspective* (Buenos Aires: Ministry of Education of Argentine, UNESCO, 2013b), and idem, *Argentina: Facing the Crisis* (New York: American Jewish Joint Distribution Committee, September 2011). See also Barry Eichengreen, *Financial Crises and What to Do About Them* (Oxford: Oxford University Press, 2012). For previous economic crises in Latin America and their impact, see Karen L. Remmer, "The Political Impact of Economic Crisis in Latin America in the 1980s," *American Political Science Review* 85 (1991), and idem, "Democracy and Economic Crisis: The Latin American Experience," *World Politics* 42 (1990).

4 Cohen (J. X. Cohen, *Jewish Life in South America: A Survey Study for the American Jewish Congress* [New York: Bloch Publishing Company, 1941]) reports that Jews arrived in South America before Jewish life was established in North America, and the first Jewish community in New York was actually created by Jews fleeing from Brazil. See also Bernardo Kliksberg, *Social Justice: A Jewish Perspective* (Jerusalem: Gefen Publishing House, 2003).

5 For an extensive socio-demographic survey on the Jewish population in Argentina, and in Buenos Aires in particular, see Adrian Jmelnizky and Ezequiel Erdei, *The Jewish Population in Buenos Aires: Socio-demographic Survey* (Buenos Aires: AMIA [MEIDA: Research Center for the Latin American Jewish communities] and the Joint, 2005).

6 Eduardo Levy-Yeyati and Luciano Cohan, "Latin America Economic Perspectives: Innocent Bystanders in a Brave New World," *Latin America Initiative at Brookings* (Washington, DC: Brookings Institution, 2011).

7 Kliksberg, *Argentina: Facing the Crisis*, 8; Bernardo Kliksberg, *How to Cope with Poverty and Inequality? An International Perspective* (Buenos Aires: Ministry of Education of Argentine, UNESCO, 2013b); Bernardo Kliksberg, *Towards an Intelligent State* (Amsterdam: International Institute of Administrative Sciences, IOS Press, 2001), 105–96.

Jewish banks, which had served as the community's economic base and had heavily subsidized the Jewish educational system, had collapsed four years earlier, shocking Argentina's Jewish educational infrastructure.[8]

Although the situation in Argentina has improved since 2001, it has not fully recovered. Today, in Argentina, an estimated 65,000 people of a Jewish population of 290,000 are still living in poverty.[9] In this continuing fragile environment, Argentina's Jewish educational system remains critical. At its height, more than a decade ago, there were more than sixty Jewish day schools, featuring Jewish-Zionist education and the Hebrew language at the core of their curriculum, with an enrollment of 22,000 students—representing 65 percent of the total Jewish youth population. In 2003, however, there were only approximately 16,000 students in the day school system, representing a nearly 30 percent attrition rate over the previous decade. However, enrolment has begun to increase, as 18,000 students attended Jewish day schools in 2006.

At this time, the entire Jewish formal and informal educational system reaches only 40 percent of the young community, and only approximately 30 percent of the Jewish population is involved in Jewish communal life. Maintaining connections within Jewish educational frameworks is critical. They are often the only link that the young have with the Jewish community.

Although the economic crisis is subsiding, the situation for middle-aged men and women —those who head households, and upon whom the burden of supporting families rests—has not substantially improved. Many families are still struggling financially. In light of these financial difficulties, the tuition payments for a private Jewish day school or a supplementary educational program, fees for a youth movement camp, or the cost of a long-term Israeli study program, remain an unmanageable financial burden.

Yet, as Barack Fishman and Fisher claimed in their work,[10] the future and survival of the Jewish community in the Diaspora depends extensively

---

8 Yossi Goldstein, Drori Ganiel, and Kaeren Fish, "Latin America—Jewish Education in Latin America: Challenges, Trends and Processes," *International Handbook of Jewish Education* (New York: Springer, 2011).

9 Kliksberg, *Argentina: Facing the Crisis*.

10 Sylvia Barack Fishman and Shlomo Fischer, *Learning Jewishness, Jewish Education and Jewish Identity* (Jerusalem, Israel: The Jewish People Policy Institute, 2011). For another very interesting research on the ties between education and Jewish identity, see Shaul Kelner, "Who Is Being Taught? Early Childhood Education's Adult-Centered Approach," in *Family Matters: Jewish Education in an Age of Choice*, ed. Jack Wertheimer (Waltham, MA: Brandeis University Press, 2007), 59–79.

on education. They have demonstrated that a strong Jewish social network in the teen years is a predictor for the choice of Jewish marriage partners in adulthood. The greater the number of Jewish educational activities and experiences, such as a Jewish supplementary school combined with Jewish summer camps, the greater the impact each one of them has on the given child or teenager and on the Jewish family as a whole.[11]

Indeed, marrying out is a common phenomenon among most of the Jewish Diaspora communities. The out-marriage ratio is between 10 and 80 percent. In the largest Jewish community, that of the United States, this ratio stands at 54 percent. DellaPergola (2003) focuses on out-marriages in the Jewish communities of Mexico and Venezuela.[12] He reports that, as expected, the highest incidence of out-marriage appears among non-affiliated Jews, noting that out-marriages are more often associated with persons displaying a somewhat weaker Jewish identification, whether as a cause or a consequence of the out-marriage itself. Other studies high-lighted the impact of Jewish elementary school education on adult identity, identification, and behavior.[13]

The relationship between economic conditions and in-marriage or out-marriage, however, is not linear. At the most religious end of the Orthodox Jewish community, we can find a sector that lives in poverty but continues to hold true to its tradition and beliefs.

Another effect of the economic crisis over the Jewish lifestyle may derive from the fact that organized communal institutions, which rely on the members of that community for contributions, are often unable to muster the resources needed to bring a young *shaliach* from Israel, or to provide local teachers with the continued training necessary to keep their knowledge and proficiencies current with the latest educational methodologies.

---

11 For further discussion on this issue see Alice Goldstein and Sylvia Barack Fishman, "When They Are Grown They Will Not Depart: Jewish Education and the Jewish Behavior of American Adults," *Research Report* 8 (Waltman, MA: Brandeis University, Cohen Center for Modern Jewish Studies, 1993), and Harold Himmelfarb, "Agents of Religious Socialization," *Sociological Quarterly* 20 (1979).

12 Sergio DellaPergola, "Jewish Out-Marriage: Mexico and Venezuela" (paper presented at the International Roundtable on Intermarriage, Brandeis University, December 18, 2003). See also Sergio DellaPergola, "Jewish Out-marriage: A Global Perspective," International Roundtable on Intermarriage, Brandeis University, December 18, 2003.

13 See Geoffrey E. Bock, "Does Jewish Schooling Matter?" (New York: Jewish Education and Jewish Identity Colloquium Papers of the American Jewish Committee, 1976); and Steven M. Cohen, "The Impact of Varieties of Jewish Education upon Jewish Identity: An Inter-generational Perspective," *Contemporary Jewry* 16 (1995).

DATA AND RESULTS

In this section, we attempt to test empirically several assumptions about the effect of Jewish day school attendance on several characteristics of the Jewish lifestyle. The data used for the empirical analysis includes data on twelve countries. For each country, we checked several variables: the percentage of Jews who attend private Jewish day schools, the percentage of marriage to non-Jews, the percentage of Jews who have visited Israel at least once, and the percentage of Jews who immigrated to Israel in 2011. The data regarding those variables was collected from publications produced by the Jewish People Policy Institute.[14] A table presenting a summary of the statistics of these variables is given in Appendix 5.1. As mentioned before, we test the effect of Jewish day school attendance on several characteristics of the Jewish lifestyle. We assume that the economic situation affects enrollment to private schools, such as Jewish day schools, as the tuition cost entailed is high.[15] Attending a Jewish private school, in turn, affects the connection of the individual to the Jewish religion[16] as, we assume, would be expressed in fewer inter-religion marriages. It could also possibly affect the connection to Israel, as expressed in more visits to Israel. As for the relationship between attending Jewish schools and immigration to Israel, we believe that a better economic situation, which enables enrollment in Jewish private schools, means that the Jewish identity and tradition may be preserved in the current place of residence, and immigration to Israel (in order to achieve those objectives) is not required. Moreover, individuals emigrate, in most cases, for economic reasons, i.e., in order to improve their economic situation. This, too, is not necessary when the individual is well-off. Thus, we would expect to find a negative relationship between the economic situation and immigration to Israel. Following the above assumptions, we have performed some statistical tests intended to check the following connections: we investigated the effect of attending Jewish education on marrying non-Jews, on visits to Israel, and on immigration

---

14 *Annual Assessment 2011–2012* (Jerusalem: Jewish People Policy Institute, 2012); Sergio DellaPergola, *Jewish Demographic Policies: Population Trends and Options in Israel and the Diaspora* (Jerusalem: Jewish People Policy Institute, 2011).

15 See Jack Wertheimer, "The High Cost of Jewish Living," *Commentary Magazine* (2010); Rela Geffen Monson and Ruth Pinkenson Feldman, "The Cost of Living Jewishly in Philadelphia" (paper delivered at AJC Consultation on the High Cost of Living, March 1991); and Gary Schiff, "Funding by Federation and Non-Federation Sources for Jewish Education," *Journal of Jewish Education*, 54 (1986).

16 Sylvia Barack Fishman and Shlomo Fischer, *Learning Jewishness, Jewish Education and Jewish Identity* (Jerusalem: The Jewish People Policy Institute, 2011).

to Israel. We analyzed the connections between the different variables using two statistical tools, the Pearson correlation coefficient and regression analysis.

The Pearson correlation coefficient tests whether there is a linear relationship between two numeric variables, i.e., how well the data fit a straight line. The Pearson correlation coefficient lies between 1 and −1; when it is close to 1, it means that there is a positive correlation between the two variables. A value close to −1 implies a negative correlation. If the value is close to 0, we have no correlation. We also performed a hypothesis test, where the null hypothesis is that there is no correlation between the two variables. Two adjustments (Bonferroni and Sidak) are also performed to calculate significance levels. The results are presented in Table 5.1. We found a statistically significant negative correlation between attending Jewish schools and marrying non-Jews. This means that in a country where there are more Jews enrolling in Jewish schools, the percentage of marrying non-Jews is lower.

As for the connection between attending Jewish schools and visits to Israel, we found a positive correlation, as expected, but this correlation is not significant.

Another significant negative relationship is found, as we expected, between attending Jewish schools and immigration to Israel. Whether this is because there is no economic reason for emigration when the economic situation is good (as expressed, among other things, by a high attendance of private Jewish schools), or whether it is possible to preserve a Jewish identity when attending Jewish schools without the need to immigrate to Israel, it is clear that when the percentage of Jews at private schools rises, the percentage of Jews immigrating to Israel falls.

The other statistical analysis that we performed, a regression analysis, gives similar results, and we can see more accurately the effects of receiving a Jewish education on the different variables. In the first column in Table 2, we see that attending Jewish education significantly affects the marrying a non-Jew variable; a 1 percent increase in attendance decreases the marrying a non-Jew variable by 0.63 percent. The second column shows the results of a regression of Jewish education attendance on visits to Israel. The results imply that a 1 percent rise in attendance

Table 5.1 Pearson correlation coefficient.

	Pearson correlation coefficient
Marrying a non-Jew	−0.8880**
Visits to Israel	0.6267
Aliyah	−0.5836**

(**) indicates that the result is significant at a significance level of 95 percent.

Table 5.2 Regression results.

	Coefficient	Standard error	F-value of the Regression
Marrying a non-Jew	−.6315945**	.0907042	48.49**
Visits to Israel	.3726513*	.1638226	5.17*
Aliyah	−.0002051**	.0000903	5.17**

(*) indicates that the result is significant at a significance level of 90 percent.

(**) indicates that the result is significant at a significance level of 95 percent.

increases the percentage of Jews visiting Israel at least once by approximately a third of a percent. The effect of a Jewish education on the percentage of Jews making *aliyah* is also significant and, as before, negative, though very small.

CONCLUSION

The inability to afford a full, traditional Jewish lifestyle may force Jewish families to choose one of the two available alternatives:

1. To use most of their discretionary income to pay for a Jewish education, affiliation with synagogues and community centers, donations to Jewish charities, etc. These expenses, however, will eventually leave Jewish families with the effective income of a poor household, reducing their capability to obtain basic necessities. This could lead, however, to an increase in the aliyah to Israel variable, as we found a negative connection between this variable and attending Jewish schools.
2. Withdrawing altogether from a Jewish education and community affiliation would severely diminish the families' commitment to Judaism and to Israel, and weaken the bonds within the community itself. This distancing would increase the likelihood of intermarriage: as shown in the statistical data presented above, a 1 percent increase in Jewish school attendance decreases the marrying a non-Jew variable by 0.63 percent, and inversely when attendance decreases. We also found a statistically significant connection between Jewish school attendance and visits to Israel.

The Yiddish saying "Shver tzu zein a Yid" ("It's hard to be a Jew") historically referred to the misfortunes and prosecutions that befell Jews, such as racial discrimination, pogroms, prejudices, and other forms of anti-Semitism. Nowadays, however, this saying is as relevant as ever, referring to a new challenge—the financial burden. Due to deteriorating global macro-economic conditions, Jewish families are currently struggling in their attempt to remain affiliated and to continue maintaining an active community life. The question is—for how long can they do so?

APPENDIX 5.1

Summary statistics of the data

	Average	Standard deviation	Number of observations
Percentage attending Jewish day schools	37.375	26.73	12
Percentage marrying non-Jews	50.75	19.36	12
Percentage of Jews visiting Israel	60.5	13.89	8
Percentage of Jews making *aliyah*	0.0062	0.0094	12

REFERENCES

Argentina: Facing the Crisis. New York: American Jewish Joint Distribution Committee, September 2011.

Barack Fishman, Sylvia, and Shlomo Fischer. *Learning Jewishness, Jewish Education and Jewish Identity.* Jerusalem: Jewish People Policy Institute, 2011.

Bock, Geoffrey E. *Does Jewish Schooling Matter?* New York: Jewish Education and Jewish Identity Colloquium Papers of the American Jewish Committee, 1976.

Cohen, J. X. *Jewish Life in South America: A Survey Study for the American Jewish Congress.* New York: Bloch Publishing Company, 1941.

Cohen, Steven M. "The Impact of Varieties of Jewish Education upon Jewish Identity: An Intergenerational Perspective." *Contemporary Jewry* 16 (1995).

DellaPergola, Sergio. "Jewish Out-marriage: Mexico and Venezuela." Paper presented at the International Roundtable on Intermarriage—Brandeis University, December 18, 2003.

———. "Jewish Out-marriage: A Global Perspective." International Roundtable on Intermarriage, Brandeis University, December 18, 2003.

———. *Jewish Demographic Policies: Population Trends and Options in Israel and the Diaspora.* Jerusalem: Jewish People Policy Institute, 2011.

Eichengreen, Barry. *Financial Crises and What to Do about Them.* Oxford: Oxford University Press, 2012.

Goldstein, Alice, and Sylvia Barack Fishman. "When They Are Grown They Will Not Depart: Jewish Education and the Jewish Behavior of American Adults." In *Research Report 8.* Waltman, MA: Brandeis University, Cohen Center for Modern Jewish Studies, 1993.

Goldstein, Yossi, Drori Ganiel, and Kaeren Fish. "Latin America—Jewish Education in Latin America: Challenges, Trends and Processes." *International Handbook of Jewish Education* (2011): 1253–70.

Himmelfarb, Harold. "Agents of Religious Socialization." *Sociological Quarterly* 20 (1979).

Jewish People Policy Institute. "Annual Assessment 2011–2012." Jerusalem: Israel, 2012.

Jmelnizky, Adrian, and Ezequiel Erdei. *The Jewish Population in Buenos Aires: Socio-demographic Survey.* Buenos Aires: AMIA (MEIDA: Research Center for the Latin American Jewish Communities) and the Joint, 2005.

Kelner, Shaul. "Who Is Being Taught? Early Childhood Education's Adult-Centered Approach." In *Family Matters: Jewish Education in an Age of Choice*, edited by Jack Wertheimer. Waltham, MA: Brandeis University Press, 2007.

Kliksberg, Bernardo. *Towards an Intelligent State.* Amsterdam: International Institute of Administrative Sciences, IOS Press, 2001.

———. *Social Justice: A Jewish Perspective.* Jerusalem: Gefen Publishing House, 2003.

———. "Ethics for CEOs. Why Business and Countries Win with Corporate Social Responsibility." *Ethics and Economics Edition.* Buenos Aires: Temas (2013a).

———. *How to Cope with Poverty and Inequality? An International Perspective.* Buenos Aires: Ministry of Education of Argentine, UNESCO, 2013b.

Levy-Yeyati, Eduardo, and Luciano Cohan. "Latin America Economic Perspectives: Innocent Bystanders in a Brave New World." In *Latin America Initiative at Brookings* (Washington, DC: Brookings Institution, 2011).

Meir, Aryeh, and Lisa Hostein. *The High Cost of Jewish Living.* New York: American Jewish Committee, 1992.

Monson, Rela Geffen, and Ruth Pinkenson Feldman. "The Cost of Living Jewishly in Philadelphia." Paper delivered at AJC Consultation on the High Cost of Living, March 1991.

Remmer, Karen L. "Democracy and Economic Crisis: The Latin American Experience." *World Politics* 42 (1990).

———. "The Political Impact of Economic Crisis in Latin America in the 1980s." *American Political Science Review* 85 (1991).

Schiff, Gary. "Funding by Federation and Non-Federation Sources for Jewish Education," *Journal of Jewish Education* 54 (1986).

Wertheimer, Jack. "Jewish Education in the United States: Recent Trends and Issues." In *American Jewish Year Book.* New York: American Jewish Committee, 1999.

———. "The High Cost of Jewish Living." In *Commentary Magazine* (2010).

Winter, Jerry A., and Lester I. Levin. *The Cost of Jewish Affiliation and Participation.* New York: Council of Jewish Federations, 1985.

Witman, Ellen G. "Economic Distress in the American Jewish Community." In *Israel Horizons* (September–October 1984).

Wolfe, Ann G. *The Invisible Jewish Poor.* New York: American Jewish Committee, 1971.

Part Two

The Twentieth and Twenty-First Centuries: The Emergence of New Jewish Religious Identities, and the Creation of Singular Interactions Between Jews and Non-Jews

CHAPTER 6

Jerusalem, the Diaspora, and the Jewish Home: The Transfer of the *Axis Mundi* in Contemporary Judaism— The Case of São Paulo

MARTA F. TOPEL

THE SANCTIFICATION OF JEWISH SPACE:
ISRAEL, EXILE, AND DIASPORA

In the pages of his highly celebrated *The Sacred and the Profane*, Mircea Eliade analyzes the sacred space and the sanctification of the world. One of his conclusions—albeit with several reservations—assists us toward an understanding of the importance held by the sacred space for Judaism during various periods of history and in our own times. Thus:

> the religious man wished to live as close as possible to the Center of the World. He knew that his parents inhabited the center of the Earth; he also knew that his town constituted the navel of the Universe and, above all, that the Temple or Palace were the real Centers of the World; but he also wanted his own home to be located in the Center, and for it to be an "imago mundi."[1]

In Judaism, the center of the world, that very same navel of the world, was Jerusalem, not because Jerusalem was a holy city (a term that does not appear in the Jewish Bible), but rather because the Temple had been built in Jerusalem. The ark was kept in the Temple, and the ark contained the pact between God and the People of Israel: the Torah. The difference from other civilizations of antiquity, for which the sacred space was essentially sacred, is that for Judaism the sanctification of the space is a historical act—a historical sanctitude resulting from a biblical event.

Adopting a phenomenological approach, Gurevitch and Aran[2] state that, for Eliade, the sacred space is the opposite of chaos and the profane—this being the reason that the religious man aspires to live close to it. In the Jewish Bible, however, sacred space is not located in space, but beyond it, as God, the source, is the locus of the sacred and is not contained within the limits of the cosmos, being by definition outside space. In the Bible, the sacred is beyond space, as is the Voice,[3] which is the means by which the God of Israel created the universe and communicates with his people. Thus, although space is indispensable for the Jews and for Judaism, the real sacred center is the faith of the people to whom the book was given. This question is of fundamental significance, as the sanctification of Jerusalem

---

1 M. Eliade, *O sagrado e o profane: a essência das religiões* (São Paulo: Martins Fontes, 1999), 43.

2 Z. Gurevitch and G. Aran, "Never in Place: Eliade and Judaic Sacred Space," *Arch. de Sc. soc. des Rel.* 87 (1994): 137.

3 It is interesting to note that the Voice, the sound, manifests itself within time.

implies the sanctification of the Jewish people, which, after receiving the Torah, transformed itself into a people of priests: into the sacred people.[4] The People of Israel is, at the same time, the People of the Land and the People of the Book. For this reason, in Jewish tradition, the threefold People of Israel, Torah of Israel, and Land of Israel is indivisible. Students of the discipline state that the conception of Jerusalem as the *axis mundi* is an idea put forward by the Talmudic sages in the first centuries of the Common Era and, later, of the medieval legacy found in kabalistic texts and the *piyutim*.[5] In this new conception, the Temple already has the characteristics as analyzed by Eliade, and is described as being located exactly at the navel of the world. It is the first part of the world from which the universe was created, a perfect reflection of a celestial model,[6] the last defense against chaos that protects the cosmic order.[7] This new concept of Jerusalem allocated great importance to the destruction of the Temple, to the extent that it became less tangible. However, it should be emphasized that the two conceptions of Jerusalem, despite their incongruence, coexisted in Jewish thought and coexist today, even in the State of Israel.[8]

Approached from a different angle, it could be said that, throughout history, the Jewish people seem to have created a pattern in relation to the Promised Land (the Land of Israel, which is synonymous with Zion and with Jerusalem). This pattern is expressed in the arrival in the territory to sanctify it, its abandonment, usually caused by expulsion and the consequent painful exile, and the return, which brought with it the redemption of the Jewish people and of humanity. These three stages— the dismantling of the center of Jerusalem, that is, the move away from the religious–political center; the separation in distinct communities in the heart of alien societies; and the learning process of being a foreign people, are occurrences which the prophets present as being part of the divine plan. Thus, the conclusion that, as God does not actually destroy, a far greater plan of reconstruction must exist. The influence of exile on Israelite history

---

4 Gurevitch and Aran, ibid.; M. Orfali, "El significado de Jerusalon y Sion en la tradició judia medieval," *Anuario de Histoia de la Iglesia IV* (1995).

5 From the Hebrew: literary style developed by the Jews in the Middle Ages. Normally written in verse, the *piyutim* were included in the various books of Jewish liturgy.

6 In Jewish cosmology, there is a celestial Jerusalem (*Yerushalaim shel mala*) and a terrestrial Jerusalem (*Yerushalaim shel mata*).

7 L. Gliner, L. and Y. Shilhav, "Holy Land, Holy Language: A Study of an Ultraorthodox Jewish Ideology," *Language in Society* 20 (1991); Orfali 1995.

8 Gurevitch and Aran 1994.

is very strong, and the lessons it teaches are complex. Among these, the past exile of the Israelites has led to constant vigilance as to the future, inextricably linking the mythical past to the messianic future.[9]

The return, in the Jewish worldview, is a return to Jerusalem, to the *axis mundi*, to that fixed point where Jewish political and sociocultural life will blossom once again. The allusions to Jerusalem and to the destruction of the Temple appear here and there in the Jewish liturgy for ordinary days, such as in the *Amidah* prayer[10] and in the *Birkat Ha'Mazon*,[11] and in important celebrations in the Jewish calendar including the Jewish Passover and Day of Atonement, as well as in the marriage ceremony. In the Middle Ages, the catastrophe of the destruction of the Temple and the loss of Jerusalem is a constantly recurring theme in both the poetry and the prose, as, for example, Yehuda HaLevi's *Siónidas*.

In the nineteenth century, Zionism accepted the rabbinic view in relation to the pattern discussed above: arrival, expulsion, and return to the Promised Land—the return constituting the only possible solution that would allow Jews to live a fully Jewish existence, in both its private and public dimensions. The expression *shlilat ha'galut* ("denial of exile"), a fundamental element in all Zionist streams that wished to separate themselves from the Diaspora Jew by creating the *new Jew*, shows the importance of the Land of Israel to Zionism, albeit transformed into a secular and modern idiom.

However, although the "conquest–expulsion–return" pattern generally attempted to explain the characteristics of the Jews as a diasporic people throughout history, the reality is more complex. The Bible itself is a long tale of withdrawals, departures, and returns. Adam and Eve were expelled from paradise despite the existence of an interdict. Cain committed a notorious transgression, and was condemned to eternal exile. Abraham arrived in Canaan but abandoned it of his own accord and, centuries later, only a few of the Jews exiled in Babylon returned when Cyrus issued the edict permitting their return to the Land of Israel—the *axis mundi* of the Jewish people. It is true that the great majority of the Babylonian Jews did not wish to lose what they had achieved in the region—above all the freedom

---

9 Bernard Dov Hercenberg, *O exílio e o poder de Israel e do mundo* (São Paulo: Paz e Terra, 1996).

10 From the Hebrew: central prayer of the Jewish liturgy. *Amidah* means "to be standing," as the prayer is said standing up, facing in the direction of Jerusalem. It is also called *Shmone Esrei* ("eighteen," in Hebrew), as it initially contained eighteen prayers.

11 A prayer recited after meals.

of worship and the prospects for economic growth in an environment that was less turbulent than the Land of Israel in the sixth century BCE. They had established roots there and were to remain there until the mid-twentieth century.

In the Middle Ages, false messiahs appeared who tried to encourage Jewish communities to return to the Promised Land and, in modern times, despite the great and unquestionable achievement that the establishment of the State of Israel represents, the majority of Jews continue to live outside its borders. Furthermore, today's strategies to bring Jews to live in Israel face increasing difficulties and show little success. Thus, although Ben-Gurion pronounced the exile over with the foundation of the State, with only diasporas existing in its place, the reality is that for millions of Jews, including those who pray "next year in Jerusalem" three times a day, life in the Diaspora is preferable to life in Zion.

The tension generated by the space in Judaism has many facets, of which I have mentioned only a few. Others may be found, for example, in the fact that God created the Universe ex nihilo, although one of his names is *Ha'makom*.[12] Exile obliged the Jews to seek alternative sacred instances to replace the Temple.[13] Among these, the most significant are the sanctification of the body, as argued by Mary Douglas, or the affirmation that time and not space constitutes the quintessence of the sacred in Judaism. Heschel's famous phrase "the Shabbat is the cathedral of the Jewish people" is emblematic of this view. Nevertheless, the Temple was not eliminated from Jewish memory, and its reconstruction is considered by some religious groups to be the sine qua non condition for the process of redemption of the Jewish people.

But, if these constituted the guidelines that governed rabbinic thought, the assumptions on which the first nineteenth-century historiographic studies of the Jewish people (*Wissenschaft des Judentums*) were based, and the Zionist conception of the Jewish people and its territory—the reality and the worldview of the Jews themselves—were more complex, and the dichotomy between Jerusalem and exile was not always an irreconcilable confrontation between opposites. The very fact that the Jews were the

---

12 From the Hebrew: the "Place." Gurevitch and Aran, ibid.
13 Sidra DeKoven Ezrahi, *Booking Passage: Exile and Homecoming in the Modern Jewish Imagination* (Berkeley, CA: University of California Press, 2000).

People of the Book (of the portable book[14] and of the portable Temple[15]) resulted, as has been shown, in the sanctification of new entities. Regarding the sanctification of new spaces, we should not forget the transference of Jerusalem as the *axis mundi* to other places during exile. This was done by sanctifying the *tzadik*,[16] conceived of by various groups as a holy man and, consequently, as the center of the world.[17] In this conception, the town where the *tzadik* lived became a little Jerusalem. Examples of this strategy of sanctification of spaces in the Diaspora have been frequent among the Hasidim since the beginning of the movement in the eighteenth century up to the present day. Medziboz, Lublin, Bratislav, Kotkz, Umam, and Crown Heights were, and continue to be, places of pilgrimage, as Jerusalem was before the destruction of the Temple.[18] When I was conducting field research in São Paulo on the *teshuvah* movement,[19] I recall the wife of a *Binyan Olam* rabbi (a breakaway group from the *Aish Ha'Tora* Yeshiva in Jerusalem) being deeply moved by the success of the *teshuvah* movement in the city, and making the following prophecy: "Very soon we will have a little Jerusalem in São Paulo."

The "quasi-sacred space" definition used by Glinter and Shilhav[20] is useful for the analysis of the Judaization of public spaces and the creation of new Orthodox ghettos in São Paulo. Both strategies produce "quasi-sacred" spaces for observant Jews. According to the Jewish tradition, "Just as it is

---

14 Despite the synagogue being the place par excellence for the conducting of certain Jewish rites, a minimum quorum of ten adult males is required for them to take place, known as the *minyan*. No public Jewish ritual can be performed without a *minyan*.

15 I think it is relevant here to mention the research that affirms that the Talmud itself was transformed into a sacred space for the Jews in exile: "Text, then, becomes a space in which collective identity can be formed without territory, and consequently it can be a metaphor for exile and homelessness" in C. E. Fonrobert and V. Shemtov, "Introduction: Jewish Conceptions and Practices of Space," *Jewish Social Studies* 11, no. 3 (2005): 3.

16 From the Hebrew: the "just," used in this context as a reference to the Great Rabbis who, in addition to their erudition, were considered just men by their followers. With the emergence of Hasidism in Eastern Europe (a revivalist religious movement of the early eighteenth century), the leaders of the various Chasidic groups—charismatic by definition—were venerated by the community, who saw them as just (*tzadikim*).

17 Grinert and Shilhav 1991; H. Goldschmidt, "Crown Heights Is the Center of the World: Reterritorializing a Jewish Diaspora," *Diaspora* 9, no. 1 (2000).

18 Green 1977; Goldschmidt 2000.

19 M. Topel, *Jerusalem and São Paulo: The New Orthodoxy in Focus* (New York: UPA, 2008).

20 Glinter and Shilhav, 1991, 79.

a sin to leave the Holy Land for Babylonia, it is a sin to leave Babylonia to go to other places." The underlying idea here is also that in Babylonia, that is, in exile, the Jews created academies to make a systematic study of the Law. Metaphorically, therefore, Babylonia becomes any place where a Jewish community organized according to halakhic precepts exists, which brings us back once again to the principle that in Judaism the sanctitude of any given place is not inherent to that place; it is historically and culturally created by living in strict accordance with the precepts of Jewish law. According to Glinter and Shilhav,[21] this is the engine that drives the territorialization of Orthodox Judaism that oscillates between Jerusalem and the reality of exile. Writers point out that the eschatological element here is of varying relevance. The return to the Land of Israel is a utopia; before its realization at the end of days, all the Jews can do is await the Messiah and strictly observe Jewish law. More precisely: "Thus, *Haredim*[22] are instructed that a place and its environment must be assessed according to what they contain. The *Haredim* can fully express themselves only in a space that is defined as *Haredi* quasi-sacred territory."[23]

Another strategy for the sanctification of spaces in the Diaspora was the creation of *midrashim*[24] that detected signs of divine providence in places where the Jews settled in exile. In recent decades, another phenomenon has been observed: the sanctification of Jewish neighborhoods and the Jewish home in the Diaspora. I will return to this point shortly.

As regards the *midrashim* of names, newly documented sources and analysis of popular legends have revealed that Poland was conceived not only as a place for a new Jewish settlement, but also as a metaphysical location.[25] This phenomenon occurred with other places where the Jews

---

21 Ibid.

22 From the Hebrew: "fearing" God, referring to Orthodox and ultra-Orthodox Jews.

23 Glinter and Shilhav, 1991, 79.

24 From the Hebrew: term for the body of homiletic stories told by Jewish rabbinic sages to explain passages in the Hebrew Bible. *Midrash* is a method of interpreting biblical stories that goes beyond simple distillation of religious, legal, or moral teachings. It fills in gaps left in the biblical narrative regarding events and personalities that are only hinted at. The interpretation of contemporary events through the lens of the Jewish religious tradition is also a *midrash*.

25 H. Bar-Itzhak, "A Materialized Settlement and a Metaphysical Landscape in Legends of Origin of Polish Jews," in *Jewish Topographies, Visions of Space, Tradition of Space* (Farnham, UK: Ashgate, 2008), 165–66.

settled for long periods. These *midrashim* show how the Judaization of place names allowed the Jews, to a certain extent, to appropriate the places in which they settled, making them less foreign.[26] Two examples of *midrashim* follow, the intention of which was the symbolic appropriation of a foreign territory: one *midrash* interprets the name of the Polish town Ostróg as *Os Toire* (in Yiddish: "a mark of the Torah"), and another the name of Poland ("Polin" in Hebrew) as *Po-lin* (in Hebrew "here we should remain"). In the second case, an element of divine intervention is added, which explains why the Jews remained in Poland despite the ruthless persecution to which they were subjected. As Bar Itzhak states: "In other words, the geography of Poland became the geography of the Jewish imagination."[27]

In recent years, in the field of social sciences, a number of studies have aimed at a greater understanding of the Jewish Diaspora, or, to be more precise, the transformation of the Jewish diasporas and the way they are represented by social agents. Another much-discussed topic is the link that these diasporas have with Israel. Safran, the founder of the academic magazine *Diaspora*, in his article "The Jewish Diaspora in a Comparative and Theoretical Perspective," published in 2005, states that in a number of cases, such as that of the Jews, a relocation of the native land may occur, producing a certain degree of confusion and superposition. With this in mind, the author asks himself: For the North American Jews, is the native land Israel, Romania, Poland, or Russia? We may ask the same question in the Brazilian context. The answer, depends on the specific conditions that existed in each of these countries and the period of time spent there— which can result in the native land being the subject of nostalgia (which is very common) or of rejection (as occurred in the case of many Jews who were expelled from Arab countries in 1948, and of many others who survived the Holocaust).[28]

Of further interest to this topic is the reflection of DeKoven Ezrahi, who in his book *Booking Passage: Exile and Homecoming in the Modern Jewish Imagination*, states that the Holocaust probably transformed the European exile from a place in which the home (Israel) was imagined, into a real home that could only be evoked from another location, and reconstructed from the

---

26 Ibid.
27 Ibid.
28 William Safran, "The Jewish Diaspora in a Comparative and Theoretical Perspective," in *Israel Studies* 10, no. 1 (2005), 39.

fragments. In retrospect, paradoxically, in the case of the Jews of Europe, the destruction territorialized the exile as a lost home.[29]

Another singularity of the Jewish case pointed out by Safran (2005) is the survival of the diasporas alongside the creation and consolidation of the Center, a phenomenon that led to a change in the type of relationship between the diasporas and the Homeland (Israel).[30]

Cohen (2008), in turn, discerns three types of diaspora by focusing attention on the relationship that they maintain with the native land: the solid, the ductile, and the liquid. According to the author, the Jewish Diaspora in recent years has gone from being a solid Diaspora to a ductile one as a consequence of a process of de-Zionization, due, among other things, to the criticism from a number of Jewish groups of the policies of the State of Israel. Another important variable that would explain the difficulty of the State of Israel in bringing Jews back is that, despite incidences of anti-Semitism, the diasporas largely have become safe places for Jews at the present time.[31]

The connections between the homeland and the diasporas are contextual and episodic: different events may activate the strategies of the diasporas for greater approximation or otherwise. Regarding the São Paulo community, the empirical data points to a weakening of the State of Israel as the native land, the national home, as the Jewish space par excellence to which, at some point in time Jews will return, or wish to return. At the same time, various forms of Judaization of the public local space may be observed. It is my hypothesis that the increase in orthodoxy in São Paulo, its growing visibility, and the attracting of new members to the group, constitute some of the significant factors that explain these two phenomena.

---

29 DeKoven Ezrahi, 2000, 16.
30 Relations between Israel and the Diaspora are reciprocal. Here, the importance of the ethno-symbols of the Diaspora for Israel should be remembered, like the *mimuna* of North Africa. Regarding spaces, one could mention the construction of Kfar Chabad as a replica of the center of Chabad's operations in Brooklyn. The typical Jewish form of organization in the Diaspora, the *Landmannschaften*, was adopted by Israel in the past and is adopted today by the new Russian immigrants and some Anglo-Saxon groups that are recognized—and wish to be recognized—as originating from their respective countries.
31 R. Cohen, "Sólidas, dúcteis e líquidas: noções em mutação de "lar" e "terra natal" nos estudos da diaspora," *CADERNO CRH* 21, no. 54 (2008); B. Sorj, "Diáspora, judaísmo e teoria social," accessed on October 24, 2012, http://www.bernardosorj.com.br/pdf/diasporajudaismoeteoriasocial.pdf.

Orthodoxy and the Reevaluation of the Diaspora in the Twentieth and Twenty-First Centuries: The Case of São Paulo

Despite the existence of various Orthodox streams in São Paulo, Chabad constitutes the most important group, not only in the process of attracting lay and liberal Jews to Orthodox Judaism and in the number of synagogues, but also in what I term the Judaization of the city's public space. This phenomenon may be observed, for example, in two streets that were renamed Chabad and Lubavitch, and in the *chanukiyot*[32] that are placed in public thoroughfares, squares, and shopping malls during the Chanukah festival.

What is interesting about this new initiative of São Paulo Judaism is that, in addition to the placing of *chanukiyot* in public spaces, members of the Jewish community who are not associated with the Chabad movement are invited to light the candles. In addition, authorities from the municipal and state governments, such as city mayor Gilberto Kassab and state governor José Serra, were invited in December 2009 to light the third candle of the gigantic *chanukiyah* placed in the Avenida Paulista, one of the nerve centers of the city. At the event, Rabbi Yossi Alpern[33] thanked all the guests for their presence and expressed the desire that "the light of Chanukah bring peace to all peoples of whatever origin."[34] According to the Chabad website: "The event was given prominence on the evening news of TV Cultura and Globo, as well as in the newspapers that covered the event the following day: *O Estado de S. Paulo, A Folha de S. Paulo, O Jornal da Tarde,* and *São Paulo Agora.*"[35]

Placing *chanukiyot* in public spaces constitutes a strategy of Judaization of these spaces, and opens up vistas from which a series of questions arise. Why should a group that tries to isolate itself from society as much as possible by the creation of ethnic neighborhoods; the strict observance of endogamy; by the establishment, in recent years, of a vast network of schools (primary

---

32 From the Hebrew: candelabra with eight branches used during the celebration of Chanukah, the Feast of Lights.

33 One of the most important rabbis of the Chabad movement in Brazil—the first to establish a Chabad synagogue in São Paulo.

34 http://www.chabad.org.br/datas/chanuca, accessed April 24, 2017.

35 Ibid.

and secondary), as well as *yeshivot* and *kollelim*;[36] a group that recommends that the young should not study at the universities in order to avoid mixed marriages and the much feared assimilation be interested in the Judaization of a public space used as a thoroughfare by the non-Jewish citizens of São Paulo? And, lastly, what are the reasons that led it to adopt this new practice during recent decades?

The answer to the last question may be found in the approval and support, from the mid-1970s on, of the Lubavitcher Rebbe for the placing of monumental *chanukiyot* in public places.[37] In a gradual process, Chabad centers around the world followed the North American example. Large-scale *chanukiyot* were placed beside the Eiffel Tower, in the Kremlin, in Bangkok, in a football stadium in Buenos Aires, and in numerous other cities, signaling not only the miracle of Chanukah, but also the phenomenon of the globalization of the Chabad movement.[38] With regard to the placing of *chanukiyot* in public spaces, it may well be that the intention is to follow the *mitzvah Pirsum Ha'Nes* (from the Hebrew: "the commandment that requires the proclamation of the miracle"). An additional interpretation is related directly to the date of Chanukah, which often coincides with Christmas. Considering this last point, we could speculate that the Chabad rabbis want Jewish citizens, like their Christian counterparts, to have a series of festival days at this time of year, and for the *chanukiyah* to serve as a Jewish symbol, as the Christmas tree does for Christians.[39] Another possibility is that the joy implicit in the ritual awakens curiosity among secular Jews about Judaism.

Whatever the intentions of the Chabad rabbis, it is important to mention that not all Jews agree with the placing of *chanukiyot* in public spaces. Groups of secular and liberal Jews in the Unites States have led to court actions in the various cities in which this occurred, arguing that these occurrences infringe the first amendment of the United States Constitution, which stipulates the separation of church and state. Similar situations have

---

36 From the Hebrew, plural of *kollel*: academy of rabbinic studies for adult and married men.

37 M. Katz Balakirsky, "Trademarks of Faith: Chabad and Chanukah in America," in *Modern Judaism* (May 2009); S. Fishkoff, *The Rebbe's Army: Inside the World of Chabad-Lubavitch* (New York: Schocken Books, 2005).

38 Fishkoff 2005; D. Lehmann, "Religion and Globalization!" in *Religion in the Modern World: Traditions and Transformations*, ed. Linda Woodhead, Paul Fletcher, Hiroko Kawanami, and David Smith (Abingdon, UK: Routledge, 2009).

39 Fishkoff, 2003, 287.

occurred in Great Britain and Canada. In all these cases, however, appeals to a higher court gave Chabad the right to continue placing *chanukiyot* in public spaces.[40]

There were also halakhic[41] discussions as to the way in which the *mitzva Pirsum Ha'Nes* should be conducted. The main point of disagreement between the groups centered on the following question: Should the proclamation of the miracle of Chanukah occur in a private space, that is, in the Jewish home, lighting the candles beside a window, or in public spaces? A number of rabbis supported the first option, arguing that this had been the *minhag Israel*[42] throughout the centuries, the custom of the Jews of the Diaspora in the face of the persecution to which they were subjected. The Talmud explains that *chanukiyot* should not be lit in public spaces in times of danger. Regarding the question that concerns us here, the fact that Chabad ignored a centuries-old Jewish custom by placing *chanukiyot* in public spaces indicates a radical revision of its attitude toward the Diaspora; more precisely, the Diaspora is no longer a dangerous place and Jews can publicly pride themselves on their Judaism, just as their Israeli counterparts do. Fishkoff tells how an Orthodox Jew in North America, despite being against Chabad's innovation regarding the Chanukah festival, expressed his recognition of the merit of the Lubavitcher Rebbe for having eliminated the belief among the Jews of the United States that their religion should only be practiced in private.[43] Indeed, other North American Jewish tendencies have imitated Chabad's initiative, and today place *chanukiyot* in public spaces.

Balakirsky Katz (2009) also points to the fact that Chabad's *chanukiyot* have a specific design—in place of the traditional curved and rounded branches, they have upward-pointing diagonal ones—which permits the hypothesis of the "Chabadization" of North American Judaism, a hypothesis that, in my view, could be extended to the case of Brazil.

---

40 Fishkoff, 2003, 294–97; Balakirsky Katz, 2009, 8.
41 Halakhah: Jewish law. When different points of view arise in Judaism, it is common for rabbis to consult the halakhah to resolve them.
42 Literally: the custom of the People of Israel, referring to customs that go back centuries or millennia, which nevertheless function as religious precepts. A typical example of *minhag Israel* is the use of the skullcap by men.
43 Fishkoff, 2003, 298.

In São Paulo, although no differences of opinion have led to court action, it is interesting to learn what the two rabbis of the CIP[44] think about new custom. The criticisms involve two different dimensions of the religion: the political and the strictly religious. Rabbi Michel Schlessinger was against the placing of *chanukiyot* in public, i.e., non-Jewish spaces, arguing that the connections of the CIP with non-Jews are not restricted to a single week in the year. Rabbi Ruben Sternschein, referring to the *mitzvah* that requires the proclamation of the miracle, considers the environment of the home to be more appropriate, placing the *chanukiyah* beside the window, seeing no need to occupy the space of others.

The Judaization of public space in a number of cities in the Diaspora has acquired another facet in recent decades: the creation of *eruvin* in cities in the United States, Canada, Great Britain, South Africa, and Australia, among others. According to studies undertaken in recent years, there are currently over two hundred cities with *eruvin*.[45] The *eruv* is an imaginary line that surrounds a given space, with a few elements to signal its existence (such as small notices on power posts, stickers on trees, and/or posts placed there specifically for the purpose, natural settings such as rivers, lakes, and mountains). The idea of the *eruv* stems from the thirty-ninth interdiction related to the Shabbat, which forbids the transport from a private space to a public one and vice-versa of objects such as walking sticks, umbrellas, handbags, mobile phones, etc., as well as people, including children on laps or in pushchairs, and old people in wheelchairs, among others. The function of the *eruv* is to reclassify the public space as private space, allowing practicing Jews to escape confinement to their houses during the Shabbat and, obviously, to make the Shabbat easier to respect. This is the function of the *eruv* from the religious point of view. However, from the perspective of the construction, reformulation, and sanctification of space, we can also see it as a fence that ritually unifies the residents of the area, as if they lived in the

---

44 CIP—Congregação Israelita do Estado de São Paulo is the leading liberal synagogue in the city.

45 O. Valins, "Institutionalized Religion: Sacred Texts and Jewish Spatial Practice," *Geoforum* 31 (2000); "Stubborn Identities and the Construction of Socio-spatial Boundaries: Ultra-Orthodox Jews Living in Contemporary Britain," *Transnational Institute of British Geography* 28 (2003); C. E. Fonrobert, "The Political Symbolism of the *Eruv*," *Jewish Social Studies* 11, no. 3 (2005); A. Lang Susman, "Strings Attached: An Analysis of the *Eruv* under the Religion Clauses of the First Amendment and the Religious Land Use and Institutionalized Persons Act," *Race, Religion, Gender and Class* 9, no. 1 (2010).

same house.[46] For some secular Jews and for groups that oppose the *eruv* in the United States and in the United Kingdom, its institutionalization is reminiscent of the medieval ghetto. For these groups, the *eruv* is a spatial reconstitution that questions the universality of public space. This was the argument used by the groups that were against the establishment of the *eruv* in a number of cities in Great Britain and the United States. In some of these cases—as in the case of placing *chanukiyot* in a public space—the question was resolved by the courts. As Lang Susman makes a point of stating in relation to the controversies that arose with the establishment of *eruvin* in the United States:

> Both sides of the debate have labeled the other irrational and characterized the respective motivations of their opponents as nefarious. Interestingly enough, as the discourse of the debate becomes more contentious, both sides move away from their legal arguments and towards the language of difference, extremism, inclusion and exclusion, insiders and outsiders, and ultimately arrive at opposing visions of what it means to be "American." The eruv becomes a snowballing signifier for current debates on pluralism, multiculturalism and the place of religion in society.[47]

In the case of São Paulo, the initiative to create an *eruv* in the Jardins district[48] came from a few Orthodox rabbis at the request of practicing Jews who wanted the city to have an *eruv* similar to those existing in New York, London, and Antwerp. The initiative was reinforced when an important Israeli rabbi, a specialist in the halakhah of *eruvin*, visited São Paulo, and decided that — despite the city's size—it was legal to build an *eruv* there. The rabbis in charge negotiated the strategies that would be adopted for the construction of the first Brazilian *eruv* with the town council. The technical details, complex by definition, were also the subject of discussion and required the authorization of the local government. Thus, for example, in the case of São Paulo, power poles could not be used due to halakhic issues, requiring the installation of special ones. When I asked the rabbi who conceived the idea if he had no concerns due to the fact that the city is the constant victim of various types

---

46 Valins, 2000, 581.

47 A. Lang Susman, "Strings Attached: An Analysis of the Eruv under the Religion Clauses of the First Amendment and the Religious Land Use and Institutionalized Persons Act," *Race, Religion, Gender and Class* 9, no. 1 (2009): 192.

48 There are projects to create *eruvin* in Rio de Janeiro.

of vandalism, he replied in the affirmative way. Despite this, the *eruv* was constructed.[49] To a second question, he replied negatively: the FISESP[50] was not consulted about the creation of the *eruv* in São Paulo. He added ironically that perhaps it would have been a good idea.

It is a fair guess that the establishment of *eruvin* in the Jardins district and in Higienópolis has led to a significant increase in the value of property, as many Orthodox Jews probably prefer to live in neighborhoods where it is easier to respect the Shabbat. As a result, it is feasible to presume that the population of Orthodox Jews in the Jardins and Higienópolis districts will increase significantly.

I asked the same rabbi if there were not concerns that non-Jews would see the *eruv* as a means for the Jews to cut themselves off from the wider community. The answer was very clear: we are different and they know that we are different.

There are other points worthy of attention. On observing events in Avenida Paulista and in the *Pátio Higienópolis* shopping mall, it was clear that Chabad's agenda does not include explaining to Gentile passersby what the Jews are celebrating when they light the *chanukiyot*. More precisely, there are no posters to explain the Chanukah festival, and no explanatory leaflets are handed out. I asked several people if they understood the meaning of the *chanukiyah*, and they said that they did not have the slightest idea what the candelabra signified. Others, in Avenida Paulista, thought that the gigantic *chanukiyah* that stood at the entrance to the avenue was just another Christmas decoration.[51] In the *Pátio Higienópolis*, after talking with me, several people told me that they thought the gigantic golden candelabra surrounded by figurines[52] was a shopping mall decoration, while three others thought that it was an evangelical symbol.[53] Only the Jews who were

---

49 Currently (September 2013), there are two *eruvin* in São Paulo, one in the Jardins district and the other in the district of Higienópolis, both of which have large Jewish neighborhoods.

50 FISESP: Israelite Federation of the State of São Paulo, the umbrella institution for all the Jewish institutions in São Paulo, with the exception of those that are Orthodox or ultra-Orthodox.

51 At Christmas, the Avenida Paulista is completely decked out with Christmas decorations, attracting tourists from all over Brazil.

52 In addition to the *chanukiyah*, the Chanukah arrangement in the Pátio Higienópolis includes several figurines, representing the Maccabees.

53 It is important to note here that most of the Brazilian evangelical churches, above all the Neo-Pentecostal ones, use Jewish candelabra in their cults, in their publications, or as an ornament inside their churches.

walking around the mall and a few neighbors from Higienópolis identified the *chanukiyah* as a Jewish symbol.

Chabad began to put a further strategy of Judaization of public space into practice: on a number of days during the Jewish Festival of Lights, caravans of cars with a *chanukiyah* on the roof drove around the city neighborhoods with the highest Jewish populations. The caravan organized by Chabad to celebrate the Chanukah festival in 2013, although falling short of the organizers' expectations, left its imprint on the São Paulo cityscape for over an hour. A dozen or so cars left the Chabad synagogue in the Perdizes district in the direction of their synagogue in the Morumbi district. One of the cars transported a large *chanukiyah* on the roof; traditional songs of the Jewish Festival of Lights blared out from enormous loud speakers.

As was the case with the caravan organized for Chanukah by the Beit Yaacov synagogue in 2011, I noticed that the non-Jewish spectators had no idea what was going on, and paid no attention to the event. Considering the fact that São Paulo is a city with high levels of noise pollution and that the caravan was organized at a time close to Christmas (followed by New Year's Eve, followed by carnival), this is not surprising. In fact, some passersby and people watching from windows thought that it was a pre-carnival event organized by a local association. The blaring music, the lights, and what were seen through the lens of Brazilian culture as small carnival floats, left no doubt as to how the non-Jewish citizens of São Paulo interpreted the Chanukah caravan made up of cars belonging to the followers of the Lubavitcher Rebbe.

THE MANY JEWISH HOMES: SOME HYPOTHESES

It seems to me that the current situation contains an overlapping and an innovation regarding the spaces considered meaningful for the São Paulo Jewish community in addition to transforming the public space into a space in which it is important to make a mark. In this context, although the State of Israel continues to be a reference for the collective identity of the São Paulo Jews, the strategies of approximation to that country have been transformed over the last decades. Rather than *aliyah*[54] or trips to Israel lasting for long periods, the São Paulo Jews prefer short visits—which often include other Jewish spaces, such

---

54 From the Hebrew: literally "ascension," referring to immigration to the State of Israel.

as Poland, Toledo, and Prague—or to bring Israeli artists and writers to Brazil, among other options.[55]

As far as the Jewish neighborhoods are concerned, although we do not find the same degree of Judaization as that of Crown Heights, a reevaluation of the Diaspora nevertheless can be detected, as well as its "reterritorialization." This new conception of the Diaspora, according to Goldschmidt,[56] results in a very different Diaspora from that idealized by the Boyarin brothers (1993), conceived of as a collective awareness of sharing the diasporic space with other groups. Rather, the exclusive character of Chabad adepts in New York—similar to that observed in Orthodox groups in São Paulo—contradicts the ideal diaspora of postmodern theoreticians, who emphasize its hybrid, interstitial, polyphonic, and syncretistic traits.

To this, we should add the significance that the home itself has for some members of the community. The CIP rabbis and one of their wives indicated the home as being the most important Jewish space for them—in addition to the reemergence of their native homes in the consciousness of religious Jewish agents—such as the various towns and *shtetls*[57] of Central and eastern Europe, and certain towns in the Middle East.[58] The picture is extremely complex and reveals the existence of a hierarchy of Jewish spaces or sacred places rather than the classical dichotomy between *Eretz Israel* or the State of Israel versus exile or the Diaspora.

The Jewish home,[59] which is currently significant as an identity reference for a number of segments of the São Paulo Jewish community, is probably the outcome of a wider process known as the privatization of religion. The phenomenon can be observed among groups of moderates of various religions, whereas the fundamentalist groups try to dominate the scene and public scenario.

---

55 D. Douek, *Próximos e distantes: um estudo sobre as percepções e atitudes da comunidade judaica paulista em relação ao Estado de Israel (2006–2010)* (MA thesis at the Program of Jewish and Arab Studies, Departament of Oriental Literature, USP, 2012).

56 Goldschmidt 2000, 85–87.

57 From the Yiddish: Jewish village in Eastern Europe.

58 In recent years, groups of Jews have organized trips in search of their roots in central and eastern Europe, as well as in Rhodes, Turkey, and other countries where their parents and grandparents lived before settling in Brazil.

59 It should not be forgotten that the great majority of Jewish rituals are celebrated in the home (M.H. Danzger, *Returning to Tradition: The Contemporary Revival of Orthodox Judaism* [New Haven, CT: Yale University Press, 1989]).

In this context, it seems to me worthwhile—and ironical—to recall the famous words of A. D. Gordon to explain the faulty assimilation of the Jews in a nineteenth-century Europe that demanded of them: *"Heye adam betzeitkha viyehudi beohalekha"* ("Be Jewish at home and a man in the street"). Faced with this split in Jewish identity, the only solution for Zionists was the creation of a sovereign Jewish state in the Land of Israel. Today, however, the strategies for appropriation of public space in São Paulo and in other diasporas, like the return of the Orthodox ghetto, the placing of *chanukiyot* in streets, football stadiums, squares, and shopping malls during the festival of Chanukah, and the creation of *eruvin*, allow Jews to construct a public space in their own image and to develop a "complete Jewish identity"—the principle expressed in A. D. Gordon's words a century earlier. On many occasions, Orthodox Jews told me "just look at the amount of choice we have in Jewish education, recreation, and kosher food. Before it wasn't like that, before you only had this in Israel." Indeed, the kosher market has grown and diversified considerably in recent years, facilitating the life of São Paulo's Orthodox Jews.[60]

Furthermore, the Judaization of the public space may in some cases be interpreted as the *Israelization* of this space: a new strategy for being in Israel without having to travel there. Or, it could demonstrate the fact that in the Diaspora it is possible to be as good a Jew as in Israel.

This latter phenomenon is reflected in the existence of restaurants and bars with Hebrew names, such as *Pinati* (which sells traditional Israeli food) and *Matock* (a bakery and shop that sells Jewish and Israeli kosher food), and the large number of posters with Hebrew advertisements in the neighborhoods with the highest concentration of Jewish residents. It reveals the existence of a specific public whose Jewish identity is expressed via the Hebrew language, probably as a result of having lived in Israel or having spent long periods there.

The imagination and creativity that can be seen in these strategies, which, it should be pointed out, are the initiative of Orthodox Jewish congregations, are many. A novel example is the *Kupat Ha'ir*, the *Tzedakah* of the Teachers of Our Generation. This refers to establishing a *minyan* in Israel that meets at the Western Wall to pray, for a period of forty days, for all those Jews of the Diaspora

---

60 For further information on the exponential growth of the kosher market in São Paulo, see C. Gerlado, *Mercado Kasher em São Paulo* (MA thesis, the Post-Graduate Program in Hebrew Language, Literature and Jewish Culture, 2010).

prepared to pay for the service. Clearly, the idea is to "be" in one of the most sacred spaces of Judaism without actually being there. To delegate a religious ritual that, according to Jewish tradition, if carried out in Jerusalem and, even better at the Western Wall, will in all probability have a greater effect on those who seek "salvation" or "recovery," as the advertisements for the new strategy proclaim.[61]

If the place is the geography, and the space is the sociocultural construction, the examples analyzed show the construction of a new Jewish topography in the São Paulo community in which Israel and the Diaspora combine and intermingle. However, if it is possible to be as good a Jew in the Diaspora, as one would be in Israel, that is, in both the private and the public spheres, then, why organize *minyanim* in Jerusalem to pray for the Jews of the São Paulo community? The reply leaves no room for doubt: for observant Orthodox Jews—and for many others—Jerusalem continues to be the *axis mundi*, a sacred center, in which it is not necessary to live, and, in certain cases, not even to visit.[62] The social processes analyzed, to which must be added new concepts of distance resulting from new technologies, lead us to the conclusion that, unlike the "archaic" man analyzed by Eliade, the Jews of the Diaspora in the twenty-first century do not wish to build their homes as close as possible to the *axis mundi*.

In light of all this data, it is my hypothesis that, in the present historical context, the Jewish center par excellence, Jerusalem/Zion/Israel, has been shifted due to various types of saturation. This shift has resulted in a diversification of Jewish spaces and spaces sacred to Judaism. This phenomenon, perhaps, should not be surprising, given that studies of the space as a sociocultural configuration and construction reveal that the center does not always maintain the same configuration or affirm itself as exclusive; the configuration of a given center is the result of the specific characteristics of the society by which it is created.[63]

To sum up, I would like to draw attention to the dual approach taken by Orthodox Jews. On the one hand, they withdraw into ethnic neighborhoods and institutions that are increasingly exclusive, separating themselves from non-Orthodox Jews and the wider population, yet, on the other, they make considerable efforts to Judaize the public space, something never before considered by other segments of the São Paulo

---

61 *Nascente Magazine,* June 2013.
62 Here it is important to note that the seventh Lubavitcher Rebbe never visited Israel.
63 A. Teixeira Fernandes, "Espaço social e suas representações" (lecture presented at the VI Colóquio Ibérico de Geografia, Porto, September 1992).

Jewish community. These new phenomena still pose many questions, for example, what is the significance of the fact that an Orthodox stream invites leading members of the government to the lighting of the Chanukah candles when, in accordance with the halakhah, this *mitzvah* can only be performed by a Jew? How can this invitation of non-Jews be explained when it comes from a group that categorically denies the entry of non-Jews to their synagogues and *yeshivot*, even though these latter demonstrate interest in learning more and becoming acquainted with Judaism? And what happens to the non-Jewish residents of São Paulo who decode the symbol and the religious ritual from a Brazilian cultural viewpoint, identified to a high degree with evangelical movements that also use the *chanukiyah* in their cults? Moreover, what will be the reaction of secular Jews and non-Jews when they become aware of the existence of *eruvin* in the city? Lastly, how will the fact that the Jewish community, perceived as powerful but tightfisted, paid the municipal authorities just two *reais* for the São Paulo town council's permission to build the two *eruvin*, be manipulated by anti-Semitic elements in Brazilian society?

These questions are fundamental as they pose new conceptual challenges to social scientists, as well as producing new and different meanings for the diasporas themselves and for society in general. As Fonrobert and Shemtov affirm: "'space' has come to the foreground as a category of cultural analysis, at least as far as contemporary cultures are concerned. Accordingly, no political, social, or cultural space exists in isolation from others or can be considered in isolation from others."[64]

As regards the apparently contradictory findings of this study, it may be said that a tension exists between the centrifugal and centripetal forces of Orthodoxy represented by the Chabad movement. The centripetal force is seen at work in the creation of "pure" spaces, with the return of the Orthodox ghetto and the building of *eruvin*, in addition to the construction of innumerable institutions and the organization of activities specifically conceived for the Orthodox population (schools, *yeshivot*, *kollelim*, courses on the principles of the Jewish religion, exclusive trips for Orthodox Jews, etc.). The centrifugal movement is seen in the transnational network developed by Chabad, which allows us to conceive of Chabad not only as a transnational empire but also as a Diaspora without clear limits. Thus, Chabad is a Diaspora with hybrid characteristics, taking into consideration

---

64 Fonrobert and Shemtov, 2005, 2.

the fact that the *shluchim* (emissaries) of the Rebbe coexist alongside secular Jews and Gentiles in various regions of the world.

Lastly, despite the fact that so many questions exist, based on the data discussed it is possible to conclude that frontiers are essential for the definition of spaces, that spaces transform the locus of identity, and that identities in motion continually revise and reconfigure their concrete and conceptual frontiers. There can be no more pertinent reference than Van Gennep's famous *Rites of Passage*. He begins his analysis with the transfer from a territory that is known, or one's own, to one that is unknown, or that belongs to others, a process for which the prior demarcation of one's own territory is a sine qua non condition.

REFERENCES

Bar-Itzhak, H. "A Materialized Settlement and a Metaphysical Landscape in Legends of Origin of Polish Jews."In *Jewish Topographies, Visions of Space, Tradition of Space*.Farnham, UK: Ashgate, 2008.

Boyarin, D., and J. Boyarin, "Diaspora: Generation and the Ground of Jewish Identity." *Critical Inquiry* 19 (1993).

Cohen, R. "Sólidas, dúcteis e líquidas: noções em mutação de "lar" e "terra natal" nos estudos da diáspora." In *CADERNO CRH* 21, no. 54 (2008).

Danzger, M. H. *Returning to Tradition: The Contemporary Revival of Orthodox Judaism*. New Haven, CT: Yale University Press, 1989.

DeKoven Ezrahi, Sidra. *Booking Passage: Exile and Homecoming in the Modern Jewish Imagination*. Berkeley, CA: University of California Press, 2000.

Douek, D. *Próximos e distantes: um estudo sobre as percepções e atitudes da comunidade judaica paulista em relação ao Estado de Israel (2006–2010)*. MA thesis at the Program of Jewish and Arab Studies, Departament of Oriental Literature, USP, 2012.

Eliade, M. *O sagrado e o profane: a essência das religiões*. São Paulo: Martins Fontes, 1999.

Fishkoff, S. *The Rebbe's Army: Inside the World of Chabad-Lubavitch*. New York: Schocken Books, 2003.

Fonrobert, C. E. "The Political Symbolism of the *Eruv*." In *Jewish Social Studies* 11, no. 3 (2005).

Fonrobert, C. E., and V. Shemtov. "Introduction: Jewish Conceptions and Practices of Space,"*Jewish Social Studies* 11, no. 3 (2005).

Gerlado, C. *Mercado Kasher em São Paulo*. MA thesis at the Post Graduate Program in Hebrew Language, Literature and Jewish Culture, 2010.

Goldschmidt, H. "Crown Heights Is the Center of the World: Reterritorializing a Jewish Diaspora." *Diaspora* 9, no. 1 (2000).

Gurevitch, Z. , and G. Aran,. "Never in place: eliade and judaic sacred space," *Arch. de Sc. soc. des Rel.* 87 (1994).

Hercenberg, Bernard Dov.*O exílio e o poder de Israel e do mundo.* São Paulo: Paz e Terra, 1996.

Katz Balakirsky, M. "Trademarks of Faith: Chabad and Chanukah in America." *Modern Judaism* (May 2009).

Lang Susman, A. "Strings Attached: An Analysis of the *Eruv* under the Religion Clauses of the First Amendment and the Religious Land Use and Institutionalized Persons Act." *Race, Religion, Gender and Class* 9, no. 1 (2009).

Lehmann, D. "Religion and Globalization!" In *Religion in the Modern World: Traditions and Transformations,* ed. Linda Woodhead, Paul Fletcher, Hiroko Kawanami, and David Smith. London: Routledge, 2009.

Orfali, M. "El significado de Jerusalén y Sión en la tradición judía medieval,"*Anuario de Histoia de la Iglesia* IV (1995).

Rapoport, M. "Creating Place, Creating Community: The Intangible Boundaries of Jewish Eruv." *Environment and Planning D: Society and Space* 29 (2011).

Safran, William. "The Jewish Diaspora in a Comparative and Theoretical Perspective." *Israel Studies* 10, no. 1 (2005).

Shilhav, Y. "The Haredi Guetto: The Theology Behind the Geography." *Contemporary Jewry* 10, no. 20 (1989).

Shilhav, Y., and L. Gliner. "Holy Land, Holy Language: A Study of an Ultraorthodox Jewish Ideology," *Language in Society* 20 (1991).

Sorj, B. "Diáspora, judaísmo e teoria social." Accessed on October 24, 2012. http://www.bernardosorj.com.br/pdf/diasporajudaismoeteoriasocial.pdf.

Teixeira Fernandes, A. "Espaço social e suas representações." Lecture presented at the VI Colóquio Ibérico de Geografia, Porto, September 1992.

Topel, M. *Jerusalem and São Paulo: The New Orthodoxy in Focus.* New York: UPA, 2008.

Valins, O. "Institutionalized Religion: Sacred Texts and Jewish Spatial Practice." *Geoforum* 31 (2000).

————. "Stubborn Identities and the Construction of Socio-spatial Boundaries: Ultra-Orthodox Jews Living in Contemporary Britain." In *Transnational Institute of British Geography* 28 (2003).

Van Gennep, Arnold. *The Rites of Passage.* Chicago: University of Chicago Press, 1960.

CHAPTER 7

Blacks, Jews, and the Paradoxes of the Struggle against Racial Prejudice in Contemporary Brazil

MONICA GRIN

The commemoration of the International Day in Memory of Victims of the Holocaust, organized by the Israelite Confederation of Brazil and held in March 2012, in Salvador in the state of Bahia, brought a new atmosphere to one of the most symbolic events of the Jewish community both in Brazil and in the world as a whole. Salvador is the Brazilian city recognized as having the largest population of African descent. The black population in this city numbers around 745,000, while the population of Jews is no more than two thousand. The promoters of the event themselves were Jewish and included the Israelite Confederation of Brazil (CONIB) in conjunction with the Bahian state government, represented by Jacques Wagner, a man of Jewish descent. The organizers of this event in remembrance of the Holocaust, carried out in a city whose majority population consists of descendents of slaves, justified it with an argument that they considered unassailable: blacks and Jews alike were and are victims of racial prejudice. This event in Salvador sought to demonstrate to the city's population of African descent that, like the Jews, blacks were also victims of Nazism, according to the speech made by the history professor Luis Edmundo Moraes.[1]

The event in Salvador included a round table with the nation's president, Dilma Roussef, the governor of the state of Bahia, Jacques Wagner, representatives

---

1   On that occasion, historian Luis Edmundo Moraes presented a paper on the black victims of Nazi violence during the Third Reich, accessed May 23, 2017, http://www.conib.org.br/noticias/1217/homenagear-os-negros-d-ao-27-de-janeiro-um-carter-integrador-diz-professor-da-ufrrj.

Figure 7.1 The commemoration of the International Day in Memory of Victims of the Holocaust, Salvador, Bahia, 2012.

of CONIB, and the historian Luis Edmundo Moraes. Curiously, the opening round table of an event that explicitly sought to involve two historically victimized groups, Jews and blacks, under the theme of racial prejudice, included not a single participant of African descent.

Since the time of Fernando Henrique Cardoso's presidential administration (1994–2002), the narrative of victimization has become a particularly effective symbolic resource, which has been deployed to stir the government into action. The power of this victimization rhetoric is such that President Dilma Roussef, continuing a government tradition of expressing sensitivity to racial and ethnic causes, was present at the event commemorating Holocaust Remembrance Day, where she delivered a speech that emphasized racial victimization as a point of proximity between Brazil's black and Jewish people.[2]

---

2   The event appeared in several mainstream newspapers as well as in those published by the Jewish community. Curiously, the panel that celebrated the Holocaust Remembrance Day in the city of Salvador, where the black population is clearly a majority, had only white members. In her keynote speech, President Dilma Roussef stressed how significant the choice of Salvador was for this particular celebration, as it shelters the largest population of African descendants outside Africa, and for its role in historical struggles for the rights of minorities, as for instance the abolition of slavery. Dilma reaffirmed Brazil's commitment never

Historical victimhood has been the predominant argument in the black militant movement just as it has been among the leadership of various Jewish social movements, as in the case of CONIB (the Israelite Confederation of Brazil). Social movements have adjusted themselves to a new scenario, in which the notion that rights derived from "race" are valorized, recognized, and affirmed; in other words, these groups have made use of the principles of the multicultural paradigm, which has increasingly influenced the way in which ethnic or "racial" groups have represented themselves in Brazil.[3]

This article aims to reflect on a theme that is not often considered: the symbolic affinities and political interactions in the historical trajectory of blacks and Jews in Brazil in the larger context of post-abolition society. I would like to suggest that, in the present context of the promotion of the black "race," Jews have experienced a curious paradox. The more the Jews struggle for the consolidation of an ethnic society that is pluralist and tolerant—often founded on the collective memory of persecution and anti-Semitism—the more they can be identified by black Brazilians, in spite of the way they have chosen to represent themselves—as belonging to the white "race," and therefore, extending this logic, to the "white elite."

THE MULTICULTURAL CHALLENGE: THE CONSTRUCTION OF SIMILARITIES IN A NATION OF INEQUALITIES

The subject of Jewish ethnicity in the context of contemporary Brazil challenges observers, not because of the problems of survival and the preservation of identity, but rather because of the more recent challenges that the multicultural paradigm imposes on the ways in which ethnic identities are represented in Brazil.

In the wake of recent developments, such as the National Congress's approval of the Racial Equality Act (2010)[4] and the Supreme Federal Court's approval of racial quotas in public universities (2012), a clear shift in the identity paradigm has occurred in Brazil. Today, ethnic–racial representations are regulated normatively by the principles of multiculturalism, by the

---

to silence or fail to act to confront massacres such as the Holocaust. The president also reminded the public that Brazil has signed all international treaties to fight discrimination. See http://www.youtube.com/watch?v=NkZoOsqV0UY.

3 See Monica Grin, *Raça: Debate Público no Brasil* (Rio de Janeiro: Editora Mauad, 2010).

4 The Racial Equality Act is a set of judicial resolutions that aim to inhibit racial discrimination and to create policies to reduce social discrimination among the different racial groups. It became law in 2010 (Bill 12.288/10).

affirmation of differences and the recognition of "race" as the source of rights. Such a paradigm shift raises an interesting challenge, which is reflected in the way in which Jews have come to represent themselves as politically relevant actors involved in strategic alliances with other ethnic or racial actors.

At first glance, the multicultural paradigm seems quite tempting, especially for the Jewish leadership, because this paradigm suggests that the affirmation of difference and its political recognition by the state helps sustain and encourage the recognition of Jewish identity in the Diaspora, and makes viable a political scenario based on the belief that all are equal but different.

However, multiculturalism in a country like Brazil, which has experienced an extraordinary level of miscegenation, has brought about the introduction of a norm of racial differentiation that is not necessarily recognized by large segments of the Brazilian population. Under a multiculturalist paradigm, the "racial" division in Brazilian society between whites and nonwhites, or between persons of European descent and those of African descent, can take on an imperative for ethnic–racial representation, in spite of the presence of cultural and identity pluralism in Brazilian society, and especially within these groups.[5]

If this is the tendency, this situation in the Jewish case becomes especially interesting. In this new scenario of racial divisions, Jews, in theory, would become whites or persons of European descent, in distinction from the blacks, or persons of African descent.

In light of this polarizing, binary tendency to divide people between black and white, the leaders of the Brazilian Jewish community, by way of CONIB and the Israelite federations of individual states, have been adopting a strategy centered on the search for symbolic affinities with blacks, with the aim of transcending the limits imposed by multiculturalism because of the racial differentiation that it promotes. The alliance between these two groups has been constructed with an emphasis on their common struggle against racism and anti-Semitism, which has assigned Brazilian Jews a social status apart from whites in general: they are white yet still the victims of discrimination. Prejudice was thus transformed into a powerful common denominator that could unite blacks and Jews in a society that, according to the traditional logic of racial representation, has kept these groups socially separate. The proximity between blacks and Jews, however, is not a phenomenon that has existed historically, thinking back to the arrival of the Jews in Brazil in the early twentieth century.

---

5   Grin 2010.

The question arises, then: What is the history of the relationship between Jews and blacks in Brazil?

The interaction between blacks and Jews in Brazil following the arrival of waves of immigrants at the beginning of the twentieth century has failed to mobilize any major political or cultural dialogue—nor has it created any major crisis.[6] Historically, the circumstances that might have brought about political proximity between Jews and blacks have been rare. In a country marked by immense social inequalities, these two groups experienced quite different historical trajectories. While freed persons—many of whom remained in the vast rural areas and others who found themselves underemployed in cities[7]— found it difficult to integrate into the labor market, Jewish immigrants took up commercial occupations, mostly concentrating in urban areas and making use of an effective community network that helped ensure the survival of recently arrived Jewish immigrants in Brazil. These circumstances helped first-generation Brazilian Jews accumulate sufficient resources to permit them a measure of social mobility, above all by facilitating their search for an education for their children.

Despite restrictions on the entrance into Brazil of Jewish war refugees— particularly in the 1930s and '40s—this group generally experienced a certain social mobility. "Thus, despite occurring amid an anti-Semitic tide during the entire period of populist dictatorship in Brazil known as the Estado Novo (1937–45), the social status of the Jewish community did cause major modifications in the sociocultural standards in Brazilian social relations."[8] Under these circumstances, where anti-Semitism had such limited impact, the first generations of immigrant groups could benefit from the process of modernization that marked the emergence of a middle class in Brazil.[9]

From a symbolic point of view, the myth of racial democracy cultivated by the Brazilian government and intellectuals would facilitate Jewish integration

---

6 Jeffrey Lesser, *Welcoming the Undesirables* (Berkeley, CA: University of California Press, 1995).

7 Ana Lugão Rio and Hebe Mattos, *Memórias do Cativeiro* (Rio de Janeiro: Civilização Brasileira, 2005); Flavio Gomes and Petrônio Domingues (Eds.), *Políticas da Raça* (São Paulo: Selo Negro Edições, 2014).

8 Bernardo, Sorj. "Sociabilidade Brasileira e Identidade Judaica," in N. Bonder and B. Sorj, *Judaísmo para o Século XXI*, ed. Jorge Zahar (Rio de Janeiro: Centro Edelstein de Pesquisas Sociais, 2001), 159.

9 Roney Cytrynowicz, "Cotidiano, imigração e preconceito: a comunidade judaica nos anos 1930 e 1940," in *Os judeus no Brasil: inquisição, imigração e identidade*, ed. Keyla Grinberg (Rio de Janeiro: Civilização Brasileira, 2005).

into Brazilian society. Ethnicity, in theory, held little importance as a symbolically relevant category for the definition of national identity. In this case, the pedagogy of integration into Brazilianness, promoted by the national government under the presidential administration of Getúlio Vargas, was more threatening for an ethnic group that sought endogamy than was the possibility of that group's social exclusion. This country, since the 1950s but especially in the 1970s, showed a significant degree of economic growth and social mobility that produced enormous possibilities for the social ascent of many Jews who, in this process, did not have to confront displays of prejudice or explicitly racist sentiments.

At these moments, from a political perspective, the institutions that represent the Jewish community became involved in Brazilian society with at least two objectives in mind: 1) to combat any display of anti-Semitism; and 2) to defend the image of the State of Israel and Zionism. It is important to note here that these Jewish groups have adopted an ethnic survival strategy guided not by questions that are internal to Brazilian political dynamics but rather, and mainly, by the international context. This group's trajectory has been marked by the principle of minimal public visibility, although, within the community, they have taken up numerous initiatives and forms of sociability and ways of maintaining their group identity, such as through Jewish schools, synagogues, clubs, associations, and the encouragement of endogamous marriage.

The historical trajectory of blacks in Brazil has developed in a different way. During this same period, Brazil had only recently emerged from slavery and was marked by patriarchy and a politics that tended to neglect the country's growing social inequality. Particularly since the beginning of the twentieth century, any sort of social mobility became almost impossible for the poorest segments of the population, which included people of African descent, above all due to the absence of public policies aimed at poor populations and providing social safety nets in a brutally unequal society.[10] For these reasons, most people of color have enjoyed relatively low levels of social mobility, income, and education, and life expectancies, and have remained at the bottom of the Brazilian socioeconomic pyramid. From the social point of view, the chances that Jews and blacks would ever encounter each other in post-abolition Brazil—whether competing with each other in the job market or in spaces of sociability—have been minimal, given Brazil's profound social inequality. Moral indifference with respect to the fate of large, impoverished segments of the population would mark the social conscience of the Brazilian elite and middle classes, including, it is worth

---

10   Brodwyn Fischer, *A Poverty of Rights* (Stanford, CA: Stanford University Press, 2008).

noting, a large proportion of the Jews, who were already well positioned in the middle and upper segments of Brazil's socioeconomic structure.

In the case of black social movements and their representative institutions, one can observe a shift in the forms of political involvement and public visibility as a racial group. Until the 1970s, the black movement's political activists oriented themselves toward the open possibilities of integration into Brazilian society. The trajectory of the struggle for integration, generated in the wake of abolition in the late nineteenth century, was also a struggle for people of African descent to liberate themselves from the stigma of slavery. The poor population, and especially freed slaves, felt the challenges of citizenship in the new Brazilian republic most acutely. The persistence of the struggle for integration went through a visible transformation only in the 1970s, a period during which the influence of the Black Power movement would give this new group a more culturally aggressive discourse. Until then, the discourse of the black movement emphasized integration of blacks into Brazilian society mainly by way of their criticism of racial prejudice. The focus of the black movement in the 1980s, however, would come to shift its focus from the struggle against racial discrimination toward a struggle for reparation, for redistributive justice, for greater opportunities in the labor market and in education; in other words, for compensatory politics.[11]

In light of the brutal social inequality in Brazil, the black movement based its new emphasis on the demand for reparation on statistical data. In merging "brown-skinned people" ("*pardos*") and "blacks" ("*pretos*") in the national census into one single category—under the more generic term for persons of African descent, "*negro*"—a Brazil was revealed in which the most glaring social inequality was indeed racial. It thus became possible, statistically, that when seen through the country's social indices, Brazil should be understood by way of biracial categories. The movement adopted a version of Brazil's national statistics in which social inequality between blacks and whites was actually racial. Such a classificatory mechanism presupposes that blacks (*pretos*) and brown-skinned people (*pardos*) always lived under similar social conditions, which differentiated them from whites, and thus rendered them a single, cohesive group in opposition to whites. For the black movement, biracialism founded on statistics strengthened their struggle for justice and reparation for the centuries

---

11 Carlos Hasenbalg and Nelson do Vale Silva, *Relações Raciais no Brasil* (Rio de Janeiro: Rio Fundo Editora, 1992).

of enslavement and exclusion to which they had been subjected, and for having been deprived of opportunities for education and the possibility to compete in the labor market.[12]

The reframing of social inequality in Brazil as racial inequality clashes with the belief in the possibility of racial democracy, a cherished part of conventional Brazilian wisdom since the nineteenth century.[13] Equating social inequality with racial inequality also effectively calls into question the positive nature of the culture of "*mestiçagem*," or racial mixing, especially in intellectual and academic circles, as has been happening since the denunciations of racism initiated by the research on race in Brazil sponsored by UNESCO after World War II (Maio 1996). From the social and political perspective, therefore, nothing would suggest any kind of proximity between blacks and Jews in Brazilian society.

An Experiment in Solidarity between Blacks and Jews

The beginning of the 1990s, however, may be considered a turning point in the relations between Jews and blacks in Brazilian society. The context in which this proximity became visible would be marked by waves of explicit anti-Semitism and racism, whose impact was felt equally by blacks and Jews. This wave of racism was not rhetorical. Instigated by neo-Nazis, the so-called skinheads, this movement was characterized by forms of racial violence that are rare in Brazil. Demonstrations of anti-Semitism with the desecration of Jewish cemeteries, graffiti drawn on synagogues and schools, and revisionist readings of the history of the Holocaust are just some examples of the displays of prejudice carried out by this group. This racist militancy resonated in Brazil in the early 1990s, and sparked a public debate about ethnic groups and intolerance. Its principal targets included blacks, Jews, homosexuals, and people from the country's northeast,[14] some of whom were the targets of physical attack. Such events produced a never before seen anti-racist mobilization in civil society, and, for the first time, a political alliance between blacks and Jews was formed.

---

12 Ibid.

13 Joaquim Nabuco, *O Abolicionismo* (Rio de Janeiro: Editora Vozes, [1883] 1977).

14 *Nordestinos* is a general description for Brazilians who originate from Brazil's northeast region. Drought and chronic poverty in this region have triggered successive waves of migration from this area to the wealthier areas of the country, in particular the southeast, where the cities of Rio de Janeiro and São Paulo are located. *Nordestinos*, in general, take jobs as domestic help, in civil construction, or in retail. They may be white, *pardos*, or black. They often share a regional heritage, mostly connected to culture, folklore, music, or cuisine.

Such an alliance signaled a shift in the form of political action favored by the Jewish community in Brazil. The Jewish community's representative institutions together with black representatives demanded that the state take more vigorous action to prevent racist and anti-Semitic attacks. In civil society, the main effect of these events was the formation of the "Movement of Democratic Entities against the Resurgence of Nazism and All Forms of Discrimination" in São Paulo and the "Front Against Nazi-Fascist-Racism" in Rio de Janeiro. Local government responses to these racist events led to the creation of the Specialized Police Station for Racial Crimes in São Paulo in 1993 and the Nazareth Cerqueira Reference Center against Racism and Anti-Semitism (CERENA) in Rio de Janeiro in 2000, two characteristic examples demonstrating how such discussions can produce institutional antidotes to all forms of racism. One might say that the creation of this Specialized Police Station was unprecedented in the history of the struggle against racial discrimination in the country.

The novelty in this process of interethnic institution building resulted, in part, from the emergence of a political alliance between blacks and Jews, two ethnicities that until then had acted separately and came from worlds apart. Without a doubt, their collective effort eventually contributed to the debate around the challenge of constructing a democratic-pluralist regime and, at the same time giving due value, in the political realm, to Brazil's ethnic-cultural diversity. For the first time, Jews took public positions concerning national issues, allying themselves with other groups and proposing a more plural and tolerant society where all ethnic groups and minorities would be effectively respected. From a political perspective, the entities represented in the Jewish community transcended the world of silent discussions in boardrooms,[15] becoming visible in a democratic public space. The Jewish community, for the first time, believed itself to be living in a pluralist democracy. The most important thing that remained of this experience was that the political alliance between Jews and blacks highlighted what they had in common: a history of persecution and prejudice. Within the context of the struggle against racism, the social distance between these groups of different skin colors did not appear especially relevant. Yet, this episode of historical alliance against prejudice has been challenged by the growing seduction that multiculturalism[16] has been

---

15 Lesser, *Welcoming the Undesirables.*
16 For a forceful criticism of multiculturalism, see Pierre Bourdieu and Löic Wacquant, "On the Cunning of Imperialist Reason," *Theory, Culture and Society* 16, no. 1 (1999):41–58.

imposing on relevant segments of the black movement, meaningfully changing the way they perceive race relations in Brazil.

The Impact of the Durban Conference on the Alliance between Blacks and Jews

The third United Nations World Conference against Racism, Racial Discrimination, Xenophobia, and Related Intolerance took place in Durban, South Africa in 2001. It began a new chapter in the struggles of the black movement in Brazil. Now more organized, the black movement began to pressure the democratic government to assume clearer and more efficient positions with respect to demands for reparation, especially concerning the question of racial quotas in public universities and the labor market.

It may be said that this event marked the beginning of the common effort to combat racism that blacks and Jews mounted in the courts of the 1990s. The introduction in the Durban conference of the idea that Zionism is a form of racism led the leadership of the Brazilian Jewish community to regard the conference as a farce. A conference against racism that reinforced, from an international perspective, the demands of black movements in Brazil by incorporating the theme of Zionism, or anti-Zionism, disaffected an important ally of the Black cause: the Israelite Confederation of Brazil. According to their president at the time:

> History tells us that the Jew has always been the easiest target, the preferred victim of racial and religious hatred. To be anti-Zionist is a euphemism for declaring one's self anti-Semitic. Perhaps because it is not politically correct to say that one does not like Jews, or that Jews are to blame for this or that, to speak out against the State of Israel has become a poorly disguised way of revealing a certain anti-Semitic rancor. Brazilian Jews actively participated in the preparatory debates of the Brazilian delegation. In South Africa, Jews fought against the apartheid regime. South African Jews walked hand in hand with Nelson Mandela to break down the walls that separated Whites and Blacks. It was this fight for common goals that allowed us to realize, precisely in Durban, the scene of massacres of Black people, the conference against racism that now draws to a melancholy end.[17]

---

17 "O sionismo pode ser considerado uma forma de racismo? NÃO. A farsa de Durban, por Jack Terpins," accessed May 23, 2017, http://www1.folha.uol.com.br/fsp/opiniao/fz0809200109.htm.

Yet, in the estimation of some segments of the black movement, the Jews in Durban were insensitive to the struggles of black people. According to Samoury Mugabe of the Political Articulation of Black Youth:

> I get irritated seeing how those who suffered through the Holocaust have failed to understand the pain of the Black people. This became clear at this Conference. The youths who were protesting here in the name of the Jews broke the rules and were not even barred from the conference as a consequence, as we would certainly have been. I think that it is absurd to keep quiet while they accuse us of racism. Brazil should take a stronger position in this regard.[18]

Despite the distressing confrontation in Durban, Seppir—the government agency that supports policies to promote racial equality—invited the Brazilian Israelite Confederation, the national organization representing the Jewish community in Brazil, as well as many other institutions representing such minorities as Gypsies, indigenous peoples, Palestinians, and the like, to participate in the "Council" of the Secretariat of Policies to Promote Racial Equality. This was supposed to strengthen an agency that, with a consultative role within the government, represents Brazil's ethnic-racial diversity. Despite the participation of representatives of minorities, the promotion of the "black race" is clearly the main challenge of the Secretariat of Policies to Promote Racial Equality. The president of the Israelite Confederation at that time, Jack Terpins, the same person who had voiced his strong criticism during the Durban conference, enthusiastically defined the functions of the Council:

> A Ministry of Racial Integration was created in Brazil. Five ethnic groups are represented: Indians, Blacks, Gypsies, Jews, and Palestinians. As representative of the Jews, I maintain contact with the other communities. We cooperate with the Black delegates to reinforce the communal structures that they wish to develop. We envisage the possibility that scientists from this community will come from the Weizmann Scientific Institute to research illnesses that are particular to the Black race and for which there is still no cure. And I can also imagine the possibility that other professionals will come to know about the absorption of

---

18 Samoury Mugabe—Black Youth Political Articulation. See: https://avaliacaodurban2009. wordpress.com/tag/estatuto-da-igualdade-racial.

Ethiopian immigrants in Israel. We are planning a trip for twenty Black community leaders so that they can learn about the country.[19]

In these terms, the Israelite Confederation shows clearly their efforts to co-opt blacks in order to bring about a greater proximity of the position of these two groups around the question of Israel, affirming that this country is an important pole of cooperation for the interests of the black movement. The Jewish leadership is trying to engage the black movement in their efforts to reinforce the image of Israel and Zionism, as a counterpoint to the affinities that black militants have spontaneously developed for the Palestinian cause and Third-Worldism. In other words, the Israelite Confederation of Brazil, in participating in the council of that government secretariat, is recognizing the value of "race" as a subject of rights, in exchange for the acceptance of Israel and for the adoption of Zionism by the black militancy.

In summary, if, in the 1990s, the black movement had an interest in forming an alliance with the Jews to confront the racism of the skinheads, the Jews now need to gain the support of the blacks, in the realm of state politics, to shield Zionism and the State of Israel from its critics, especially those coming from the left.

REFERENCES

Bourdieu, Pierre, and Löic Wacquant. "On the Cunning of Imperialist Reason." *Theory, Culture and Society* 16, no. 1 (1999): 41–58.

Cardoso, Fernando H. "Construindo a Democracia Racial." Coleção Documentos da Presidência da República, *Presidência da República*, 1998.

Cytrynowicz, Roney. "Instituições de Assistência Social e Imigração Judaica." *História, Ciência, Saúde—Manguinhos* 12, no. 1 (January–April 2005): 169–84.

Grin, Monica. *Raça: Debate Público no Brasil*. Rio de Janeiro: Editora Mauad, 2010.

Grinberg, Keyla, ed. *Os judeus no Brasil: inquisição, imigração e identidade*. Rio de Janeiro: Civilização Brasileira, 2005.

Guimarães, Antonio S. *Racismo e anti-racismo no Brasil*. São Paulo: Editora 34, 1999.

Hasenbalg, Carlos. *Discriminação e Desigualdades Raciais no Brasil*. Rio de Janeiro: Graal, 1979.

Hasenbalg, Carlos, and Nelson do Vale Silva. *Relações Raciais no Brasil*. Rio de Janeiro: Rio Fundo Editora, 1992.

---

19 Jack Terpins, as published in *Boletim Edição* 14 (September 6, 2006), Confederação Israelita Brasileira.

Lesser, Jeffrey. *Welcoming the Undesirables: Brazil and the Jewish Question*. Berkeley, CA: University of California Press, 1995.

Maio, Marcos Chor. "Negros e Judeus no Rio de Janeiro: um ensaio de movimento pelos direitos civis." *Revista Estudos Afro Asiáticos* 25 (1993): 161–88.

Maio, Marcos Chor. "O Projeto Unesco e a agenda das ciências sociais no Brasil dos anos 40 e 50." *Revista Brasileira de Ciências Sociais* 14, no. 41 (October 1999).

Sorj, Bernardo. "Sociabilidade Brasileira e Identidade Judaica." In N. Bonder and B. Sorj, *Judaísmo para o Século XXI*. Edited by Jorge Zahar, 90–109. Rio de Janeiro: Centro Edelstein de Pesquisas Sociais, 2010.

———. "Diáspora, Judaísmo e Teoria Social." In *Experiência Cultural Judaica no Brasil: recepção, inclusão e ambivalência* ed. Edited by Monica Grin and Nelson Vieira. Rio de Janeiro: Topbooks, 2004.

CHAPTER 8

The Circulation of Jewish Agents and Jewish Symbolic Goods inside the Universal Church of the Kingdom of God

CARLOS ANDRADE RIVAS GUTIERREZ

An article in the British newspaper the *Guardian* highlighted the construction of a replica of Solomon's Temple by the Universal Church of the Kingdom of God, and affirmed that it "could cast a shadow over the statue of Christ the Redeemer" high above Rio de Janeiro and become the new symbol of Brazilian postcards.[1] The launching of the project, which is being built in São Paulo's Brás neighborhood, was reported by Brazil's largest newspapers, such as the *Folha de São Paulo* and *O Estado de São Paulo*, and even by international media like the *Guardian* and the *New York Times*.[2]

The project arose, according to church leaders, after a pilgrimage by Bishop Edir Macedo to Jerusalem,[3] who said at the time, "if I can't bring all the people here, then I can bring pieces of this land to them." While the bishop affirms that the project provides a way for the "people of the Universal Church to step on the Holy Ground," many representatives interviewed (bishops and pastors) maintained that it is not a "denominational" project but a way of

---

1 Tom Phillips, "Solomon's Temple in Brazil Would Put Christ the Redeemer in the Shade," *The Guardian*, July 21, 2010, accessed February 11, 2012, http://www.guardian.co.uk/world/2010/jul/21/solomon-temple-brazil-christ-redeemer.

2 Robert Mackey, "Rebuilding Solomon's Temp, in São Paulo," *The New York Times*, July 22, 2010, accessed February 9, 2012, http://thelede.blogs.nytimes.com/2010/07/22/rebuilding-solomons-temple-in-sao-paulo/

3 Since the 1980s, the IURD (*Igreja Universal do Reino de Deus*=The Universal Church of the Kingdom of God) has conducted what it calls caravans to Israel, as a regular practice of the institution.

promoting direct contact with God and presenting the Brazilian people with a "cultural landmark."

The construction will have a 650-square-meter memorial, which is is intended to be a cultural and "secular" space, according to the discourse of the Universal Church's bishops and pastors, which will be separate from the temple and will not be connected to it, since it will be underground.

> The Church's intention is to promote culture, the history of Israel, knowledge, for this reason, this is a secular space, it is cultural, it is not a religious issue, but one of history, of culture. There, one will be able to see what was inside the Old Temple in detail.... This idea for separation is in the design itself, so that it will also have a space presenting the history of Universal, the church's beginning, the arrest of the Bishop, everything that happened, but it is another itinerary for visits. Visitors have the option to see what they want. There is no requirement to enter the church space, or the temple. This space will be a show, with guides, lots of technology, interactivity, it will attract tourists from throughout the world. It will be as good as the Centro Cultural Jerusalém, in Rio de Janeiro. (Pastor João Lacerda).[4]

The space will also have a museum that will tell the history of the Universal Church of the Kingdom of God, beginning with its foundation, continuing through Edir Macedo's imprisonment, the construction of large cathedrals by the church, and other events considered influential, emphasizing the "circuit of conquest." According to Gomes,[5] this process involves distinct but intrinsically linked phases: persecution, revolt, sacrifice, and conquest. Thus, church leaders are also interested in creating a "memory" for the Universal Church, and, by so doing, appropriating the so-called "Israel myth" as its own history. According to various agents interviewed, from different positions, the "people of Universal" are seen as a continuation of the "Hebrew people/the Chosen People" of the biblical narrative. Since its foundation, the discourse of the religious agents of Universal have always made references to mythic Israel and Old Testament passages, so much so that many of the portions used in the services come from the Old Testament. This involves no rational calculation on the part of the leaders of the Universal Church of the Kingdom of God, or of its members, but a practical

---

4 To avoid any problems for those interviewed, the study will use pseudonyms for the bishops, pastors, "workers," and faithful who requested anonymity.

5 Edlaine Gomes, *A Era das Catedrais: a autenticidade em exibição* (Rio de Janeiro: Garamond, 2011).

understanding, incorporated by experience in a certain symbolic universe, conferring a *habitus* on the agents, "an infinite capacity to freely engender products, thoughts, perceptions, expressions and actions, which always have as limits the historically and socially situated conditions."[6]

The Universal Church has two large secular cultural centers (one in Rio de Janeiro and the other in São Paulo), which are physically and symbolically separated from the space considered religious–ritualistic, in a distancing promoted by the discourse of the agents interviewed. In 2008, the Universal Church inaugurated the 736-square-meter Centro Cultural Jerusalém (CCJ) (Jerusalem Cultural Center) in Rio de Janeiro, at the Catedral Mundial da Fé (World Cathedral of Faith), located in the Del Castilho neighborhood, which has an exhibition space and an auditorium. The CCJ is also rented out for various events: weddings, special services of other denominations, courses in theology, etc. "As a secular space there is no problem, they do not see (renters) as being part of the Universal Church. Moreover, we have to pay our bills without help from the Church, so we must rent. Now, if it is used for religious or cultural purposes that is not our problem" (Preacher Lucas Neves).

When asked about the bronze inscription "Igreja Universal do Reino de Deus" (Universal Church of the Kingdom of God) in the auditorium of the Cultural Center, the pastor was categorical: "Although it is a secular space, we must mark our presence as well, right? I do not think that this means it is not a secular space." The border between secular and religious is defined by agents who frequent and or operate in this space.

The Cultural Center also has a cybercafé and a souvenir store. At the latter, one can find a number of ostensibly Jewish symbolic goods for sale, like yarmulkes,[7] mezuzahs,[8] *tallitot*,[9] various oils from regions of Israel, waters from Israeli rivers, books in Hebrew and about Jewish culture, in addition to CDs with Israeli music, rings with Hebrew inscriptions, miniatures of Solomon's Temple, the Ark of the Covenant, and Torah scrolls, and various other items.[10]

---

6 Pierre Bourdieu, *Senso Prático* (Rio de Janeiro: Vozes, 2009), 91.

7 *Kipa* in Hebrew: a skull cap.

8 In Hebrew: a small case that is nailed to the right-hand post of a door, with a parchment inside that has biblical verses celebrating the oneness of God and his alliance with the Chosen People.

9 A religious accessory similar to a scarf, made of wool. In prayer, mainly in the *shacharit* (morning prayers), observant Jews cover themselves with this cloth. It is considered a means of isolation from the physical world. For this reason, it facilitates concentration during prayer.

10 Carlos Gutierrez, "Visita ao Centro Cultural Jerusalém," Review, *Ponto Urbe* 9 (2011), accessed May 23, 2017, https://pontourbe.revues.org/339

But more than symbolic Jewish goods can be found here. During field research, I accompanied a visit by the Israeli ambassador to Brazil, Rafael Eldad, to CCJ to attend his lecture about the media treatment of Israel and the importance of evangelicals in this process, entitled "An Outstretched Hand for Peace." The event attracted the presence of other figures considered important in Rio de Janeiro's Jewish community, for example, the vice president of the Israeli Federation of Rio de Janeiro (FIERJ), representatives of the Clube Israelita, and the "Pioneiras da Comunidade" (Community Pioneers) group, which brings Jewish women together.

The lecture was considered a success and was widely publicized by Universal, via the church's national television network, *Record*,[11] and its news portal, the R7. The center's institutional website also publicized the ambassador's visit and the presence of various agents related to Judaism, and even mentioned that the event was highlighted in the newspaper *Alef* and in the online journal of the magazine *Menorah*, both publications of the Brazilian Jewish community.

The promotion of events in its spaces said to be "secular-cultural" also attracts agents from other religious denominations. According to the pastor responsible for the CCJ, "many Evangelicals from other churches circulate through the space, participate in debates and even wind up going to the church at times." According to Presbyterians who attended the talk with the Israeli ambassador, the Universal Church has a very important role in the "positioning of Brazilian Evangelicals in relation to the State of Israel, and helps considerably to promote the culture of the Holy Land in Brazil." These Protestant agents see the place as "secular," but affirm that the participation of the members of the Jewish community in the spaces leads them to frequent the Universal Church during the "Holy Fire of Israel" faith campaigns, since they maintain that the presence of the Jews is an indicator that the names placed on the *tallitot* that are taken to Israel provide "a possibility that we do not have in our Church and the Holy Fire is something very strong, linked to the Holy Land, one can feel this," said Helena Alves, a Presbyterian and resident of the Zona Sul (southern zone) of Rio de Janeiro.

The members can take classes in the Brazilian language at the CCJ "in order to enhance their speech," as well as English, Hebrew, ethnology, multiculturalism, history, philosophy, political sciences, etc. "We are not stupid,

---

11 http://tv.r7.com/record-play/rio-de-janeiro/balanco-geral-rj/videos/embaixador-de-israel-no-brasil-se-encanta-com-maquete-gigante-de-jerusalem-no-rio-20102015.

we want to show that we know how to debate," says the director of the center. In the Solomon's Temple, in São Paulo, these kinds of courses will also be available for the members.

Thus, the central issues of this study include: the formulation of frontiers between "culture and religion"[12] in a constant re-elaboration through indirect interaction by specific agents, and the attempt by the Universal Church to present itself as a "culture" in the public space, producing a discursive arena to be studied. The debate about the concept of cultural heritage indirectly realized by the agents is essential in this process of movement from religion to culture. In 2005, then-senator Marcelo Crivella,[13] a bishop on leave from the Universal Church, presented a proposal in the Senate to alter Brazil's Rouanet law, which allows companies to make contributions to approved cultural entities in lieu of federal taxes. If this measure is approved, libraries, archives, and religious temples could also benefit from the Rouanet Law in addition to museums. The project has since been withdrawn from deliberation. Crivella defends the measure as follows:

> Nothing better expresses the formation of this culture than the melting pot of various religions, sects, cults and their syncretisms, which, for centuries, shaped the nation's civilizing process ... all of the beliefs, cults and religions, which, because they carry references to the identity, action and memory of Brazilian society, constitute an inseparable portion of the "Brazilian cultural heritage," and should thus be included in the larger objectives of the National Program for the Support to Culture.[14]

---

12 The project adopted the use of quotation marks when referring to culture and religion, because it involves an emic vision and not a cultural concept. Thus, it should be noted that it is necessary to separate the theoretical from the empiric plane, or to not substantialize statements proposed by the agents.

13 Crivella is currently minister of Fishing and Aquiculture, having given up his seat in the senate after being re-elected in 2010 for the period 2011–19.

14 Available at http://www.cultura.gov.br/o-dia-a-dia-da-cultura/-/asset_publisher/waaE236 Oves2/content/projeto-do-senador-crivella-inclui-igrejas-na-lei-rouanet-98474/10883? redirect=http%3A%2F%2Fwww.cultura.gov.br%2Fo-dia-a-dia-da-cultura%3Fp_ p_id%3D101_INSTANCE_waaE236Oves2%26p_p_lifecycle%3D0%26p_p_state% 3Dnormal%26p_p_mode%3Dview%26p_p_col_id%3Dcolumn-1%26p_p_col_count% 3D1%26_101_INSTANCE_waaE236Oves2_advancedSearch%3Dfalse%26_101_ INSTANCE_waaE236Oves2_keywords%3D%26_101_INSTANCE_waaE236Oves2_ delta%3D20%26p_r_p_564233524_resetCur%3Dfalse%26_101_INSTANCE_waa E236Oves2_cur%3D1185%26_101_INSTANCE_waaE236Oves2_andOpera- tor%3Dtrue. Accessed May 16, 2012.

According to Giumbelli, Crivella's argument raises the civilizing role of religion, relating the notion of heritage to culture. After a strong negative reaction from the artistic world, the senator restricted his formulation to temples denominated as "historic." In this way, only certain religious entities could receive the support. Giumbelli indicated that by restricting the benefit to historic monuments, Crivella accepted the subordination of the "religious" to the "cultural," thus indicating the existence of a form of presence of the "religious in the public space that involves culture and that can adapt itself to a generalist argument."[15]

We can problematize the construction of Solomon's Temple as a strategy by the institution to establish a cultural and "immaterial" heritage. According to Magnani, the sense of belonging, or the appropriation of the local as a point of reference by social actors, is the first step in the process of having a space recognized as a heritage: "The perception and later recognition as cultural heritage is due to the symbolic power of an episodic fact, which is highly dramatic, synthetic and easily remembered."[16]

In addition, the construction of spaces said to be cultural, which involve mythic Israel, can be understood as an attempt to construct an immaterial heritage by the Universal Church because it relates the group's past to the ancestry of the "Hebrew people," appropriating rituals and "traditions." Therefore, it becomes important to understand the construction of the cultural–religion dichotomy by sectors of the Universal Church and the effects of this indirect practice on the interaction of the Church with its various interlocutors.

The Universal Church of the Kingdom of God is Brazil's third largest evangelical institution in terms of numbers, with nearly two million members,[17] behind only the Congregação Cristã do Brasil (Christian Congregation of Brazil), and the Assembleia de Deus (Assembly of God). Its rapid growth in the late 1980s led to its involvement in many controversies and considerable media exposure, nearly always negative. The institution is classified as "neo-pentecostal," which means that it is different from historical pentecostal movements. These neo-pentecostal churches are well known in Brazil for their

---

15 Emerson Giumbelli, "A presença do religioso no espaço público: modalidades no Brasil," *Religião e Sociedade Rio de Janeiro* 28, no. 2 (*2008*): 80–101.

16 Jose Guilherme Cantor Magnani, *Cidade universitária: patrimônio e identidade* (São Paulo: EDUSP, Série Cadernos CPC, 2004).

17 Data from the Brazilian census: Censo 2000 (IBGE). The data for 2011 show a drop in this number, by nearly 400,000 faithful. Nevertheless, since the quantification was conducted by sampling, it is not possible to affirm this variation with certainty, because of the margin of error.

vision of postmillennialism: the kingdom of God is not in another world, nor will it take centuries to happen. It is "here and now." According to this belief, it is possible to "challenge" God, through your faith, in order to obtain material goods and financial prosperity. In fact, Universal is very much connected with this practice, and stands accused of misleading the poor people in Brazil and other countries. So, this theology is totally contrary to traditional ascetic Protestantism. The wordly pleasures are not rejected, but addressed as the main goals that people should seek and live in this life. This doctrine is called "prosperity theology," and is based on the belief that God's will is to increase material wealth and bless the financial life of his followers. According to this specific interpretation of the Bible,[18] there is a contract between God and men: if men have faith in God and donate money, they will be rewarded with prosperity. In this belief, it is necessary to make a sacrifice to God in order to obtain prosperity, and, nowadays, in their vision, money is the most important thing to be sacrificed. Actually, all these neo-pentecostal movements, including the Universal Church, are accused of misleading the poor, "brainwashing" and manipulating them, by promising them affluence and success. The Universal Church's new dialogue, presented in this paper, can be regarded as a strategy to improve its image in Brazilian society.

After establishing an extensive media apparatus (the TV Record network, the *Folha Universal* newspaper, Portal *R7*, and a network of radio stations, etc.), the Universal Church came to be perceived as one of the main religious institutions in the evangelical field. This was reflected in a large amount of academic literature in the 1990s. Authors like Freston[19] and Oro[20] highlight the use of the communication media and a supposedly "aggressive" approach, relating practices of the Universal Church to those of the "market." The core of the academic production focuses on the relationship between the "faithful" and the "sacred," as analogous to "clients–consumers" and "suppliers" (Prandi, Mariano, and Pierucci).[21] This paper will not attempt to fit the agents into pre-defined categories, nor will it address the practices by using pre-established categories based on the dichotomy between "demand and consumption."

---

18 Book of Malachi.
19 Paul Freston, "Breve história do pentecostalismo brasileiro," in A. Antoniazzi et al., *Nem Anjos Nem Demônios: Interpretações Sociológicas do Pentecostalismo* (Petrópolis: Vozes, 1996).
20 Ari Pedro Oro, *Avanço pentecostal e reação católica* (Petrópolis: Vozes, 1996).
21 F. Pierucci and R. Prandi, *A realidade social das religiões no Brasil* (São Paulo: Hucitec, 1996); R. Prandi, "Religião paga, conversão e serviço," in *Novos Estudos*, vol. 45 (São Paulo: Cebrap, June 1996); *Ricardo Mariano, Neopentecostais: Sociologia do novo pentecostalismo no Brasil* (São Paulo: Edições Loyola, 2005).

The intention of the study is to discuss a phenomenon that is new to anthropological literature: the presentation by agents of the Universal Church of the Kingdom of God of culture in the public sphere, and the establishment of frontiers between "religion" and "culture," according to the agents' discourses.

The use of these categories allows the formation of a distinct discursive space, in which the circulation and communicative exchange between various agents becomes possible. This group is highlighted by Jewish agents linked to institutions that support the State of Israel, which call themselves "promoters of Jewish culture."

The construction of these spaces, as well as that of Solomon's Temple, can be seen as an attempt to crystalize a memorial past through the establishment of a heritage. To do so, it is necessary to find resonance among the public. "By resonance, I refer to the power of an exposed object to reach a broader universe, beyond its formal frontiers, the power of evoking in the expectant the complex and dynamic cultural forces from which it emerged and for which, for the expectant, it is the representative."[22]

Considering that the classification of a certain cultural good as a heritage depends not only on an agency of the state, or exclusively on the socio-discursive explanation of the agent-groups, we can consider that the attempt at heritage declaration is an attempt to exercise a symbolic power, "the power to make see and make believe, to confirm or to transform the world view,"[23] in order to legitimate its discourse as "culture." In this way, in the view of the Universal Church leaders, the construction of the replica of Solomon's Temple and of the Universal Church Memorial is the promotion of a "cultural and secular" space for the population. In theory, this allows for the circulation of various agents and the production of discourses favorable to this initiative, as was the case of the president of the Juventude Judaica Organizada (Organized Jewish Youth), an institution that defines itself as secular and whose objectives are to fight anti-Semitism and defend the State of Israel. Persio Bider, in an interview with the "Blog do Bispo Macedo," said:

> Only by means of mutual knowledge can we eradicate any type of prejudice or discrimination on both parts, and thus, work together with what we have in common and respect the way we think and believe differently.

---

22 Stephen Greenblatt, "Resonance and Wonder," in *Exhibiting Cultures: The Poetics and Politics of Museum Display*, ed. Ivan Karp and Steven D. Lavine (Washington: Smithsonian Institution Press, 1991), 42–56.

23 Pierre Bourdieu, *O poder simbólico* (Rio de Janeiro: Bertrand Brasil, 2006), 14.

We have a lot in common and we need to join together so that it is possible to work actively in a more just, positive society that is focused on complete coexistence and inter-religiosity, the reason for which I believe that Bishop Macedo's initiative is very interesting. I understand he very much loves the land of Israel and the Jewish people.[24]

In fact, the Universal Church follows the dispensationalist doctrine that believes that God will reestablish his kingdom in Israel. In this view, Jesus Christ will rule the world from Israel. It is necessary, therefore, for the agents to support Israel politically, because Christ's return depends on the existence of the "Holy Land," i.e., the Israeli state. Indeed, Universal goes deeply inside dispensationalism and affirms that "Brazil must be a new Israel." In Rio de Janeiro, the main temple is called Templo da Glória do Novo Israel (Temple for the Glory of New Israel). They believe that it is important to promote the Israeli culture and to transform Brazil into a New Israel. According to Bishop Macedo, "it's very important to drive our thoughts to Israel." The mythical Israel is the basis for the creation of a real (in the Universal Church's perspective) secular state, without the "bad influence of the Catholic Church." Macedo gives an example of "Jesus' secular sense": when the Pharisees asked Jesus if it was right to pay tributes to Cesar, Jesus answered: "Then render to Caesar the things that are Caesar's; and to God the things that are God's" (Matthew 22:22). Therefore, Israel is more than a country for which everyone must fight, but it is a model for all the nations; furthermore, it is the Universal Church's most important symbolic mediator.

The promotion of Jewish agents' speeches is essential for the larger project, to establish the heritage and memory of the Universal Church. For this reason there is a concern for publicizing discourses like the one above and having certain agents circulate it in various media: institutional sites, blogs, the *Folha Universal* newspaper, the portal *R7* and the church's TV network *Rede Record*.

During my work on my master's thesis, I realized that many of the faithful of the neo-pentecostal churches and some pentecosts (Assembly of God and its various ministries and dissidences) put great value on objects linked to "the Holy Land," so much so that an unusual religious movement of neo-pentecostalism toward Judaism was found.[25] By establishing space said

---

24 Available at https://noticiasdauniversal.blogspot.fr/2010/07/projeto-do-templo-da-iurd. html Accessed on 12 November 2012.

25 Carlos Gutierrez, *Bnei anussim: uma experiência de judaísmo na periferia paulistana* (MA thesis, Anthropology Department, University of São Paulo, 2011), accessed May 23, 2017, http://www.teses.usp.br/teses/disponiveis/8/8134/tde-23052012-154251/pt-br.php.

to be secular and promoting the circulation of agents linked to Judaism, the Universal Church achieved considerable legitimacy in relation to the symbolic goods that it distributes or sells in its souvenir store, attracting faithful from other denominations to services and even pastors from other churches, who buy various objects in the CCJ.

It is interesting to emphasize that, at the same time as Universal creates spaces said to be secular, it denies itself as a religion. Churches come to be called cenacules[26] by both the religious media (television, social networks, radios, newspaper) and by its agents. In its blogs, institutional websites, and social networks, like Facebook, Universal denies the status of religion, defining this category as something negative, and relating to itself as a "way to make a covenant with God, a faith." In 2013, Universal changed its logo, excluding the words "Church" and "Kingdom of God"; the logo also underwent redesign. Many temples have started to make a similar change in the principal cities of Brazil and Latin America. The term "religion," according to the emic vision, is something that displeases many agents linked to Universal. "I hate religion; I'm fed up with religion. For me, religion is the most rotten thing on the face of the earth. The greatest enemy of God is religion. Religion is what separates people, makes people fight, struggle. The largest wars were fought because of religion" (Bishop Edir Macedo).[27]

The fact that the institution's main leaders deny that it is a religion is intimately linked to the use of symbolic goods that are ostensibly Jewish in the Universal Church services, based on the presumption of the Hebrew myth of the "direct pact with God."

Considering the size and visibility of the Universal Church in the public sphere, the problem to be analyzed is in consonance with the current debate promoted by sociology and anthropology of religion. The literature sees the presence of religion in the public sphere as being related to the notion of "market," in which the public sphere is a simple space for possible consumers. For these authors, religion has no place in the public sphere, and, for this reason, becomes "a commodity."[28] This concept is related to the Weberian concept of secularization.

In this sense, the debate is based on the implicit normative understanding that religion is out of place in the public sphere, and, for this reason, is becoming akin to merchandise. The theoretical problem of the relations between religions and the public sphere shifts to the normative domain, according to Montero,

---

26 Term used to refer to the location of Jesus's last supper with the apostles.

27 Available at http://www.youtube.com/watch?v=h0c3p1f03Vo; accessed May 23, 2017.

28 Paula Montero, "Secularização e espaço público: a reinvenção do pluralismo religioso no Brasil," *Etnográfica* 13, no. 1 (2009).

because the socio-anthropological field of religion is linked to the implicit ethical determinations in the Weberian paradigm of secularization, which has already been proved to be surpassed in various analyses (Casanova, Montero, and Habermas).[29] This study therefore focuses on the analysis of the relationship between religion and the public sphere, to contribute to the debate by analyzing statements made by the agents in their process of presenting the Universal Church as a culture, and how this process is constituted, beyond the establishment of frontiers between "culture" and religion, producing a new discursive arena and participating in a range of controversies, previously restricted to the Universal Church. The constitution of a space said to be "secular" establishes a different possibility for participation in controversies, given that the Universal Church, by means of these spaces, receives the option to participate as a "culture."

The Creation of Organizations and Participation in the Public Sphere

In 2012, the Universal Church of the Kingdom of God completed thirty-five years of existence. This occasion was the subject of a special TV *Record*'s report on "Domingo Espetacular." The show emphasized Universal's modest beginnings in a town bandstand, and its huge expansion all over the world. Nevertheless, the major point was its unique projects, unknown to the public, as, for example, Força Jovem (Teen Power), which develops cultural and sport activities among young people, the Raab group, which engages against domestic violence, etc. The theme of social assistance occupied most of the TV show, as well as Universal's cultural projects. What is viewed mainly as "religious," therefore, was diminished in the narrative constructed by television. The goal, therefore, was not the "religious rituals," but the varied forms of powerful technologies used to create docile followers (Foucault).[30] The formal education system set up by Universal, and its workshops for teenagers and adults, providing an adequate normative grammar to the public sphere, the way the public should have relationships, marry, and even have sexual relations is debated. The TV show "The Love School," owned by Universal, does not have a religious focus, but teaches men and women how to have a good marriage, "avoiding divorce and suffering." This allows the Universal Church agents to participate in many controversies, like the war against crack cocaine promoted by Força Jovem (Teen Power), the encouragement toward entrepreneurship, toward professional

---

29 J. Casanova, *Public Religion in the Modern World* (Chicago: University of Chicago Press, 1994); J. Habermas, *Entre Naturalismo e Religião* (Rio de Janeiro: Tempo Brasileiro, 2007); Montero, op. cit.

30 Michel Foucault, *Segurança, Território, População* (São Paulo: Martins Fontes, 2008).

requalification, with specific meetings on these themes. A good example is the "Ler e Escrever" (Read and Write) project, which teaches reading and writing, and provides preparatory workshops for the job market. Professor Isilda says that it is "about recovering the citizenship; these people learn more than reading and writing, they also learn how to be a citizen, to vote in a better way, they recover their dignity, and they have ethics in work and in their lives."

We may observe a complex engineering of power in service to governmentality. In Foucault's definition, this means the "government of people," exercised not in a territory, but a salvational power, used to care and protect, a "pastoral power," as defined by the author. This specific creation of bodies is publicized by such campaigns as "Eu sou a Universal" ("I am the Universal"), in which each member presents his or her trajectory, always emphasizing their academic standing and professional position, relating these to the fact of being a Universal member. This, in turn, makes access to the institution a potential for social and cultural improvement. To understand this complex involvement, composed of multiple elements, we need to digress. We have to present Universal as a producer of *habitus*, dispositions, and speeches, making a specific discursive arena possible, with its participation in a large number of public controversies,[31] as well as an attempt to occupy spaces that are understood as being unconnected with "religion."

The role of policy in the consolidation of Universal Church as a "culture" is fundamental to Universal, because this movement from "religion" to "culture" reflects the trend in the normative liberal state. The deputy George Hilton (pastor of Universal) has developed a legal project, PLC 160/09,[32] known as "Law of Religions," which defines religion as "part of Brazilian historical, artistic, and cultural patrimony, the material and immaterial patrimony of religious institutions is relevant to Brazilian cultural patrimony," as part of the process of Universal Church's patrimonialization and self-definition as a culture. Apart from these activities, there is also an important search for the mythic Hebrew world, in order to establish Universal as an immaterial patrimony. In São Paulo, the local deputy Gilmaci Santos (pastor of Universal) created a law, 225/2009, that establishes the festive week of Chanukah. This is another attempt on the part of the Universal Church to become part of national culture by using the Judaic tradition as its own.

31　The term "controversy" is used in this article to refer to disputes between social agents in the public sphere. Latour (2005) uses the term to explain conflicts that impose a final signification on a certain issue, and Habermas uses it to refer to themes that have become part of the juridical system, i.e., part of state policy.

32　Can be accessed at http://www.senado.gov.br/atividade/materia/detalhes.asp?p_cod_mate=92959; accessed May 23, 2017.

Therefore, the political ground is very important to Universal in its attempt to establish itself as a culture. These cultural courses and assistance projects are also fundamental to this attempt, because they produce organizations endowed with a specific framework, necessary to participate in the public sphere.

An interesting example may be found in the controversial project involving crack cocaine. In 2013, the governor of São Paulo state, Geraldo Alckmin, nominated Rogerio Haman of the Brazilian Republican Party (also known as Universal's party, because they represent a majority inside it) to the post of secretary of social development. Many members of Teen Power (Força Jovem) were present during the ceremony. This fact generated a considerable awareness among the media, because the group has a project called "Youth against Crack," through which they participate in this national controversy. The newspapers denounced this, and said that the government was adopting Universal's "crack policy." In fact, a pastor, who is also a politician, said that Universal would present their projects on the issue. Moreover, Universal is always promoting public demonstrations against crack, to prevent people from using it, "providing spiritual and material aid" to addicts, donating clothes and food, etc. This creation of organizations and the process of disciplinarization, creating a way of acting, ruling domestic life, and daily life, is responsible for providing agents with a normative grammar, adapted to the public sphere.

Talal Asad (2003) suggests that the anthropology of religion should not ask the meaning of belief, but rather how religions are created in the world through rhetoric. If we accept the idea that, in modern societies, rhetoric articulates places, people, things, and varied ideas, we can conclude that the historical conditions that created the concept of "belief" as a private conviction or something that a person or a group considers "truth" has changed considerably.

If we assume that Universal is concerned about ordering people's routine, it is necessary to emphasize the "government of people." This concept from Foucault decentralizes the analysis of control technologies and the power of specific institutions (hospitals, prisons, churches, etc.) to the procedures of classification, segregation, and alliances of these institutions. Foucault formulates the "pastoral power" model, introduced into Western society by the Catholic church, and defines it as the kind of power that is exercised not on a territory but over a multiplicity of people in flux.

This power is not related to policy, but to pedagogy and rhetoric; it seeks to control men's everyday lives. The controversies in which Universal is involved are linked to the government of people (the control of their bodies, time, relationships, and practices) and employ different techniques to obtain discipline, and create theological speeches and rules.

Universal has this capacity of producing and integrating itself into very different projects, even outside its own institution. According to Boltanski (2009), the "greatness" of an agent implies his capacity to connect to new projects. Therefore, adaptability is fundamental to network connections. Besides, how can we measure the value of a speech? Boltanski says that when something is publicized, and becomes public, it gains importance because it allows private causes, such as those of the Universal Church, to become public, and gain support from outside the institution. The capacity to act in the public sphere, therefore, is fundamental to participation in many social debates and to promoting a church, or a movement (in this case the use of Jewish symbolic items). These agents are connected to many others, thanks to their ability to interact with distinct points of a huge network, commonly seen as a "society," or "the social entity."

Solomon's Temple and the City

In a visit to the construction site, I was able to speak with workers (many of whom regard themselves as faithful to the Universal Church), who said that Bishop Macedo had asked them to "speed up" the pace of their work so that the temple would be ready before the 2014 World Cup. The religious leader believed that this event would be a unique opportunity to promote the location and its transformation into an international tourist attraction. "Truly, we also have this intention, because the Temple is a wonderful thing. So, it must be ready before the Cup so that the tourists can visit, and television and newspapers from abroad can show this to the world. I risk stating that Solomon's Temple will steal attention from the Itaquerão [stadium]!" (Pastor Marcelo).[33]

On Bishop Macedo's blog, there are posts[34] that affirm that the location would become a "cultural tourist attraction for people from around the world." According to Lehmann, neo-pentecostalism, as well as Islam and Judaism, "stand out as pillars of religious globalization because they break down political, linguistic and geographic frontiers, creating transnational communities."[35]

---

33 The stadium that will host the opening game of the 2014 World Cup, located in the Itaquera neighborhood of São Paulo.

34 Available at: http://www.bispomacedo.com.br/2010/07/15/projeto-do-templo-da-iurd.

35 David Lehmann, "Fundamentalism and Globalism," *Third World Quarterly* 19, no. 1 (1998): 13–14.

Thus, it is possible to expect the formation of a specific transnational evangelical circuit, or its penetration into already established circuits of religious tourism.

The temple project in São Paulo's Brás neighborhood will have a great impact on the region, so much so that the government has demanded various complementary projects. The Universal Church will have to widen the streets, alter the direction of traffic in some, and improve the traffic signs, affecting urban mobility. It is important to note that the temple is located in an area that already has a religious presence, including a large center of the Assembly of God and a Catholic church. The view from the front of the temple will be of these two institutions, separated only by Avenida Celso Garcia.

The model of the temple indicates there will be a large green space around the building, a food court, and a capacity of more than 10,000 people. In Rio de Janeiro, in addition to this same capacity, the Catedral Mundial da Fé has similar spaces for socializing, and walls covered with stones from Israel. The building in the city of Rio de Janeiro attracts many passersby, promoting different types of interaction: people who enter to touch the walls as they pray, or to place pieces of paper with requests in the cracks between the blocks; others use the local infrastructure for leisuretime activities and as a meeting place.

In a conversation with a technician at the worksite, I learned that the Universal Church has plans to build more parking spaces and even sidewalk malls around the temple. He said that the property had already been purchased, and the request to build the sidewalk mall had been sent to the municipal government. The international tourist potential is emphasized by Universal Church leaders, and research must be carried out to analyze how Solomon's Temple will be part of the local religious excursions, and the possibility of establishing a transnational itinerary.

CONCLUSION

It is important to note the argument made by the agents of the Universal Church in their attempt to present it as a "culture," and establish borders between "culture" and "religion." An analysis was conducted of the formation of the spaces said to be "secular–cultural," by agents linked to the Universal Church, and the implications of the uses of these categories. The circulation of ostensibly Jewish religious agents, who pass through these spaces, allows the legitimation of the production of ostensibly Jewish symbolic items, produced and distributed by the Church. This is an important factor in the appropriation of mythic Israel as the Universal Church's ancestral past for the crystallization of a "memory" of the Church.

The research identifies the formation of a "cultural heritage" by the Universal Church through its constructions and cultural centers, operationalized by agents of Universal in an attempt to impose a system of truths about the construction of an ancestral past and the meaning of its temples.

The existence of these spaces said to be secular, according to the discourse of the agents (the CCJ and also the future Memorial of Solomon's Temple), allow the Universal Church to present itself as a "culture" in the public sphere. For this reason, it is able to participate in controversies from a unique position, given that it is an entity with additional legal purposes, and thus legally separated from the Universal Church. Most of the controversies that involve the CCJ, for example, are related to the State of Israel, for which there is a plausible hypothesis: the attempt by the Universal Church of the Kingdom of God to take the lead among institutions that call themselves evangelical in issues related to the "Holy Land."

The translation of the religious arguments into nonreligious arguments is a way of adapting them for public argumentation, thus allowing the participation in debates in the public sphere.[36] For Habermas, the religious perspective needs to be translated into a publicly accessible language, and the participation of the Universal Church and its enunciations on the status of "culture" can logically permit a more expressive participation in public discussions.

The circulation of Jewish agents through Universal's "cultural" spaces, and its attempt to be recognized as an element of cultural heritage, indicates an extremely important process for the crystallization of the Universal Church as a culture, conferring memory and ancestry on the institution, in a process operationalized by the *habitus* of the agents related to it. In addition, the promotion of the circulation of these agents through environments linked to the Universal Church, as well as their discourses about Universal, are key elements in the church's efforts to cloak itself in a tradition, which is used to justify the fact that their practices are not religious.

REFERENCES

Almeida, R., and C. Mafra, eds. *Religiões e Cidades: Rio de Janeiro e São Paulo*. São Paulo: Terceiro Nome, 2009.

Almeida, R. "Religião na metrópole paulista." *Revista Brasileira de Ciências Sociais* 19, no. 56 (2004): 15–27.

---

36 Habermas 2007, 119.

Almeida, R. *A Igreja Universal e seus demônios: um estudo etnográfico*. São Paulo: Editora Terceiro Nome, 2009.

Almeida, Ronaldo, and Paula Montero. "Trânsito Religioso no Brasil." *São Paulo em Perspectiva* 15, no. 3 (2001; 2004).

Araújo, L. B. L. *Religião e modernidade em Habermas*. São Paulo: Loyola, 1996.

Asad, Talal. *Formations of the Secular: Christianity, Islam, Modernity*. Stanford, CA: Stanford University Press, 2003.

Asad, Talal. "Trying to Understand French Secularism." In *Political Theologies—Public Religions in a Post-secular World*, edited by H. de Vries and L. Sullivan. New York: Fordham University Press, 2006.

Boltanski, Luc. *L'Amour et la Justice comme compétences. Trois essais de sociologie de l'action*. Paris: Métailié, 1990.

Boltanski, Luc, and Ève Chiapello. *O novo espírito do capitalismo*. São Paulo: WMF Martins Fontes, 2009.

Bourdieu, Pierre. *Senso Prático*. Rio de Janeiro: Vozes, 2009.

———. *A Distinção*. São Paulo: Edusp, 2008.

———. *Razões práticas*. Campinas: Papirus, 1996.

———. *Coisas ditas*. São Paulo: Brasiliense, 2004.

———. *A economia das trocas simbólicas*. São Paulo: Perspectiva, 2005.

———. *O poder simbólico*. Rio de Janeiro: Bertrand Brasil, 2006.

Birman, Patrícia. "Imagens religiosas e projetos para o future." In *Religião e Espaço Público*, edited by P. Birman. São Paulo: Attar, 2003.

Casanova, J. *Public Religion in the Modern World*. Chicago: University of Chicago Press, 1994.

Casanova, J. "A Secular Age: Dawn or Twilight?" In Michael Warner, *Varieties of Secularism in a Secular Age*. Cambridge, MA: Harvard University Press, 2010.

———. "Public Religions Revisited." In *Religion: Beyond the Concept*, ed. Hent de Vries. New York: Fordham University Press, 2008, 101–19.

Dantas, Beatriz G. *Vovó nagô e papai branco: usos e abusos da África no Brasil*. Rio de Janeiro: Graal, 1988.

Durkheim, Émile. "As formas elementares da vida religiosa." In *Os pensadores*. São Paulo: Abril Cultural, 1978.

Freston, Paul. "Breve história do pentecostalismo brasileiro." In *Nem anjos nem demônios*, edited by Alberto Antoniazzi et al. Petrópolis: Vozes, 1996.

Foucault, Michel. *Segurança, Território, População*. São Paulo: Martins Fontes, 2008.

———. *Vigiar e punir: nascimento da prisão*. Translated by Raquel Ramalhete, 35th edn. Petrópolis: Vozes, 2008.

Giumbelli, Emerson. *O fim da religião*. CNPQ/PRONEX, 2002.

———. "A presença do religioso no espaço público: modalidades no Brasil." *Religião e Sociedade* 28, no. 2 (Rio de Janeiro, 2008): 80–101.

———. "Minorias religiosas." In *As religiões no Brasil—continuidades e rupturas*, edited by F. Teixeira and R. Menezes. Petrópolis: Vozes, 2006.

Gomes, Edlaine. *A Era das Catedrais: a autenticidade em exibição.* Rio de Janeiro: Garamond, 2011.

Gonçalves, José Reginaldo Santos. "Ressonância, materialidade e subjetividade: as culturas como patrimônios." *Horizontes Antropológicos* 2, no. 23 (Porto Alegre, January–June 2005): 15–36.

Gutierrez, Carlos. "*Bnei anussim: uma experiência de judaísmo na periferia paulistana.*" MA thesis, Anthropology Department, University of São Paulo, 2011.

————. "Visita ao Centro Cultural Jerusalém." *Revista Ponto Urbe* 9, no. 5 (2011).

Hall, Stuart. *Da diáspora: Identidades e mediações culturais.* Minas Gerais, BR: Editora UFMG, 2008

————. *A identidade cultural na pós-modernidade.* Rio de Janeiro: DP&A, 2006.

Habermas, J. *Entre Naturalismo e Religião.* Rio de Janeiro: Tempo Brasileiro, 2007.

————. *Era das transições.* Rio de Janeiro: Tempo Brasileiro, 2003.

————. *Direito e democracia: entre facticidade e validade* Vols. 1 and 2. Rio de Janeiro: Tempo Brasileiro, 1997.

————. *Consciência Moral e Agir Comunicativo.* Rio de Janeiro: Tempo Brasileiro, 1989.

————. *Teoría de la acción comunicativa I: racionalidad de la acción y racionalización social.* Madrid: Taurus, 1987.

Houtart, François. *Sociologia da religião.* São Paulo: Ática, 1994.

Latour, Bruno. *Jamais Fomos Modernos: Ensaio de Antropologia Simétrica.* Rio de Janeiro: Editora 34, 1994.

————. *Reassembling the Social.* Oxford: Oxford University Press, 2005.

Lavalle, Adrián Gurza. "Jurgën Habermas e a virtualização da publicidade." *Margem* 16 (December 2002): 65–82.

Lehmann, David. "Fundamentalism and Globalism." *Third World Quarterly* 19, no. 1 (1998).

Mariano, Ricardo. *Neopentecostais: sociologia do novo pentecostalismo no Brasil.* São Paulo: Edições Loyola, 2005.

Mauss, Marcel. *Sociologia e Antropologia.* São Paulo: Cosac Naify, 2005.

Montero, Paula. "Religião, pluralismo e esfera pública no Brasil." In *Revista Novos Estudos.* Vol. 74. São Paulo: Cebrap, 2006, 47–65.

————. "Jürgen Habermas: religião, diversidade cultural e publicidade." *Novos Estudos* 84 (2009).

————. "Secularização e espaço público: a reinvenção do pluralismo religioso no Brasil," *Etnográfica* 13, no. 1 (2009).

Negrão, Lísias. *Umbanda: entre a cruz e a encruzilhada.* São Paulo: Edusp, 1996.

Oro, Ari Pedro. *Religiões Pentecostais e Meios de Comunicação de Massa no Sul do Brasil.* Rio de Janeiro, Vozes, 1990. REB. v. 50, fasc. 198, 304–34.

————. *Avanço pentecostal e reação católica.* Petrópolis: Vozes, 1996.

Pierucci, Antônio Flávio. "Interesses religiosos dos sociólogos da religião." In *Globalização e religião,* ed. Ari Pedro Oro and Carlos Alberto Steil. Petrópolis/RJ: Vozes, 1997, 249-62.

————. "Reencantamento e dessecularização: A propósito do autoengano em sociologia da religião." In *Novos Estudos*. Vol. 49, 99–117. São Paulo: Cebrap, 1997.

————. "Representantes de Deus em Brasilia: A bancada evangelica na Constituinte." In *Ciências Sociais hoje*, ed. ANPOCS, 104–32. São Paulo, 1989.

Pierucci, F., and R. Prandi. *A realidade social das religiões no Brasil*. São Paulo: Hucitec, 1996.

Prandi, R. "Religião paga, conversão e service." In *Novos Estudos*. Vol. 45. São Paulo: Cebrap, June 1996.

Simmel, Georg. *Philosophie de la modernité*. Paris: Payot, 2004.

Topel, Marta. *Jerusalém and São Paulo. A nova ortodoxia judaica em cena*. Rio de Janeiro: Topbooks, 2005.

Tommaso, Venturini. "Building on Faults: How to Represent Controversies with Digital Methods." *Public Understanding of Science*. 2010.

————. "A inusitada incorporação do judaísmo em vertentes cristãs brasileiras: algumas reflex-ões. Revista Brasileira de História das Religiões." *ANPUH* 4, no. 10 (May 2011).

Velho, Otávio. "Comentários sobre um texto de Bruno Latour." *Mana* 11, no. 1 (2005).

Weber, Max. *Ensaios de sociologia*. 4th ed. Rio de Janeiro: Zahar, 1979.

————. *A ética protestante e o espírito do capitalismo*. São Paulo: Cia das Letras, 2004.

————. *Economia e Sociedade*. Vol. 2. São Paulo: Editora da Universidade de Brasília, 2004.

Wirth, Louis. "O urbanismo como modo de vida." In Otávio Guilherme Velho, *O fenômeno Urbano*. Rio de Janeiro: Guanabara, 1987.

CHAPTER 9

Identities, Migrations and Religious Practices: The Jews and Argentineans of Syrian and Moroccan Origin (from the Second Half of the Nineteenth Century to the Early Twenty-First century)

SUSANA BRAUNER

This article will analyze the flexible nature of the identities of the Jews and Argentineans of Arabic origin, especially those from Syria and Morocco, from the time of their arrival in Argentina in the second half of the nineteenth century to the early twenty-first century. Their beliefs and practices will be addressed comparatively, examining the similarities, diversities, and contrasts that originated as much on the national scene as in face of the twists and turns of the international scene. We will examine, therefore, the complexity of the processes that were undergone in the framework of the Argentine spectrum as a whole. In this context, we will focus on the nationalization processes, incorporating the experiences of those who stayed close to the central ethnic organizations and those who dissociated themselves from such organizations.[1] This way, despite the essentialized perspectives that prevail with regard to the identities of the Jews of Arabic origin, will highlight the wide range of practices—from traditionalism

---

1 According to one of the most recent investigations into this matter, roughly 61 percent of the Jewish population in Buenos Aires was dissociated from the community institutions (Ezequiel Erdei, and Adrián Jmelnitzki, *Población judía* [Buenos Aires: Amia-Joint, 2005]).

to secularization—that were adopted among both the ultra-Orthodox and the religious Orthodox. This framework will consider self-representations and representations that were constructed in different community and academic areas, and throughout intergenerational changes during this period of time.

The article forms part of the current discussions on the notions of ethnicity and diasporas. It is based on various sources, such as available internal records and files of the main community organizations, national and ethnic press, files and biographies of renowned leaders, and interviews carried out with the first-, second-, and third- generation protagonists themselves.

The Jews in Argentina are mostly of Ashkenazi origin, in other words, European Jews coming from the communities that developed in eastern Europe in particular. The Sephardic Jews (Sephardim), who include the descendants of those expelled from the Iberian Peninsula as well as those from the Middle East and the north of Africa, are a minority.[2]

Most Sephardic Jews from the Arab world speak Arabic, are of Syrian origin, and are from the cities of Damascus and Aleppo.[3] Those of Moroccan origin, mostly from Tetouan and Tangier, whose common language was *Haketia*[4] and/ or Spanish, make up the smallest group. Together they form the majority of Sephardic Jews, but at the same time they form minority groups within other minorities in Argentine society, on the one hand, within a Jewish community of multiregional origin, and, on the other, within the waves of immigrants of Arabic origin from different regions and faiths that settled in Argentina.

Although there are no official statistics to calculate the number of Jews from the Arab world who settled in Argentina, according to estimates by Israeli statistician Sergio DellaPergola in the mid-1980s, there were approximately 22,000 members, i.e., around 65 percent of the Sephardic Jews and more than 10 percent of the Jewish community in Argentina.[5]

---

2 The term *Sephardim* has led to different approaches. Which groups are included and which are excluded? For a discussion on the different perspectives that prevail on the subject and refer to Latin America, see M. Bejarano, "Sephardic Communities in Latin America—Past and Present," in *Judaica Latinoamericana* (Jerusalem: Magnes Press 2005), 9–26.

3 Some also came from Lebanon and Egypt.

4 *Haketia*: Judeo-Spanish-Arabic language, phonetically related to Andalusian and Spanish. During the years of the Spanish protectorate in Morocco (1913–56), modern Spanish was the language learned.

5 See M. Bejarano, "Los sefardíes en la Argentina: particularismo étnico frente a las tendencias de unificación," *Rumbos en el Judaísmo, Sionismo e Israel* 17–18 (1986): 145; M. Cohen, "Aspectos sociodemográficos de la comunidad sefardita de la Argentina," *Sefárdica* 2, no. 3 (August 1985): 57–78.

Research carried out into these groups and the Sephardic Jews on a global scale is limited. Both academic and community production and dissemination are narrow if compared to the vast literature on Judaism in Argentina, bearing in mind that most research into this field has been based on the study of the Ashkenazi Jews, and little or no attention has been paid to the Jews of Sephardic origin. So much so, that the image of the Jews in Argentina itself was built up based on identity characteristics attributed to Jews of European origin. In fact, they could be identified as "the other" in the "others."

Along these lines, from the 1960s until the early 1970s, under the influence of such concepts as the melting pot and secularization, the Jews from the Arab world were not a subject of particular interest. From the 1970s onward, and particularly in the 1980s, with the prevalence of more pluralist approaches and the recognition of cultural diversity, a small number of researchers began to study Jews from the Arab world as part of Sephardic subgroups settling in Argentina. These researchers placed emphasis on the strong religious identity of the Syrian Jews and the swift assimilation of the Moroccan Jews (Bejarano 1984; 1985; 1986; Mirelman 1988). The Center for Research and Dissemination of Sephardic Culture (CIDICSEF), which was founded in 1975, also began to show community and academic interest in studying the history of the Sephardic Jews in Argentina, including those hailing from the Arab world. Some case studies began to look into the Jews from Syria (Brauner 1999; 2000) and Morocco (Epstein 1993; 1995) from the 1940s onwards, while others looked into the Sephardic Jews more globally, and also included research on those coming from the Arab world (Ruben 1992). At the same time, the free-flowing links that developed among certain leaders of different faiths in the Syrian–Lebanese elite began to be addressed (Klich 1995), as did the similarity in models of immigration and economic integration of various groups (Klich and Lesser 1998). At the beginning of the twenty-first century, there was greater academic interest in this matter (Bejarano 2005; Epstein 2006; Brauner 2009; Rein 2011; Vagni 2012; Bejarano and Aizenberg 2012). However, the processes undergone by the Syrian and Moroccan Jews and their native descendants through the generational changes in Argentina have yet to be analyzed from a comparative perspective. This article, therefore, will provide a first approximation of the similarities and differences that characterize both groups. We will refer to the diverse migration flows reaching Argentina; the forms of socioeconomic integration; the indigenous identities and their consequences in the religious arena; and the relations with Arabs of other faiths and their ties with the State of Israel, Syria, and Morocco.

From Morocco and the Middle East to Argentina

Jews in the Muslim world belonged to those religious minorities that were tolerated and protected, and which—like other indigenous minorities— enjoyed a certain amount of autonomy, which was a distinct feature of the region. Their presence in the area dated back to ancient times, and was accepted as a natural situation by the Muslim majority. They became familiar with the cultural norms, the predominant languages, the food, the music, the clothing, the habits, the rules governing family relationships and gender, and the magic–religious beliefs and practices, such as that of the "evil eye" and the cult of sepulchres of venerated rabbis (Harel 2003; Stillman 1991; Laskier 1997; Simon et al. 2003; Castien Maestro 2004). Moreover, even though they practiced a different religion (which actually demanded a significant social distance from members of other faiths), like the rest of the population, they were very observant and fulfillment of religious precepts and traditions was not questioned. Indeed, religious beliefs and practices were part of the core values that governed the rules of everyday behavior of the population for both the Islamic majority and the minorities in the region (Brauner 2009). In other words, the Jews—not only from Morocco but also from the Middle East—may be considered a unique fragment of the local culture that included Muslims, Christians, and Jews alike.[6]

In this context, the Jewish immigrants from the Arab world arrived in Argentina from the latter half of the nineteenth century, and found a model of society that differed greatly from that prevailing in their regions of origin, in a country that, beyond the heterogeneity of prevailing conceptions, identified more with the prevailing values of the Western world. The cosmopolitan cities welcomed the constant flow of immigrants, especially from Europe and of the Christian faith, into a mainly Catholic society, where many considered very strict religious practices to be old-fashioned rituals that should be overturned on the path toward modernization (Brauner 2009).

Apart from their ethnic and regional characteristics and/or differences, the Jews from the Arab world, along with the other faiths that came from the

---

6 Juan I. Castien Maestro, "Las comunidades judías de Marruecos, entre la convivencia y la marginalidad," *Papeles ocasionales* 5 (2004), 7.

declining Ottoman Empire, such as the Christians, Druze, and Muslims, were perceived to be part of "exotic groups"[7] that did not fit into the preconceived ideas of identity expected by the Argentine elite. The Ashkenazi Jews saw them as bearers of identities that were rooted in "medieval" times. However, these images do not seem to have changed the Syrian and Moroccan perception of Argentina as a land of promise and a hospitable country, where they could build a better future and enjoy religious freedom.[8]

The first elements that gave rise to the migration from Morocco and the Middle East between the second half of the nineteenth century and the early twentieth century were economic concerns and the search for new horizons in the New World. In contrast, the causes behind the migration from the late 1940s until the early 1970s were more political, and were associated with the Arab-Israeli conflict together with the decolonization processes in the Levant and the north of Africa (Harel 2003; Zafrani 2005; Zenner 2000; Laskier 1990).

The Moroccans were the pioneers on their arrival in Argentina (Epstein 1995). The Spanish-Moroccan conflict between 1859 and 1860, along with political tensions and economic crises triggered the migration of Moroccans to various Latin American countries, including Argentina, Brazil, and Venezuela. In Argentina's case, this was the first group of Sephardic Jews to settle in Argentina as well as the smallest.[9] They came from Tetouan (the capital of the Spanish protectorate in Morocco between 1913 and 1956), Tangier, Ceuta, and Asilah, with a strong Spanish influence and in search of better prospects, just like the majority of immigrants who settled in Argentina in those days.

The progressive decline of the Ottoman Empire and its breakup after World War I, as well as the recurring economic crises that struck the region, produced relevant migration flows to the American continent. It was in this context that Jews from Damascus and Aleppo began to emigrate in search

---

7   "In the middle of the ghetto. . . . We saw a couple of thousand people flailing. . . . We saw dark faces, dull in color, deep-set eyes. . . . After a great effort to disperse the crowd, a few fanatics did not want to be separated from the coffin. . . . It was a strange sight indeed. . . . With crying and chanting: a multitude attended in cars and trucks. Curious scenes." This is how a newspaper article in the *Crítica* newspaper, of June 16, 1930, refers to the people who attended the funeral of Chief Rabbi Sitteon Dabbah.

8   N. Tawil, *La Nación*, October 6, 1928, 8.

9   According to the Argentine National Census of 1914, there were 802 Moroccans in total, of whom 92 percent were in urban areas and 8 percent were in rural areas. (D. Epstein, "Marroquíes de origen judío. Cohesión y dispersión comunitaria," in *Ponencia XII Jornadas Interescuelas* [Neuquén: Universidad del Comahue, 2009]).

of better economic opportunities, as did their compatriots of other faiths. So much so, that from the beginning of the twentieth century until the end of the 1920s, the Jewish-Syrian emigration became a significant demographic phenomenon, when the majority headed to the United States, Argentina, Mexico, Panama, Haiti, and Brazil. On the other hand, the fact that military conscription was imposed for men in 1909 also added to the factors that led to emigration. While they were Arabic speaking, some also spoke French and/or English due to their commercial activities in Europe, or their studies at the *Alliance Israélite Universelle* schools, or at Protestant schools that had settled in the region (Harel 2003; Brauner 2009).

From the 1930s onward, the immigration of Jews from the Arab world decreased.[10] Nevertheless, the increase of Arab nationalism, the creation of the State of Israel, and the independence of Syria, Lebanon, and Morocco in the mid-1940s and '50s, resulted in the arrival and settlement of Jewish immigrants from Morocco, Syria, and Lebanon in Argentina. These immigrants came from a different background to the first groups that settled in the country. In Syria under the French mandate, and in Morocco under growing European influence, these new waves of immigrants had come into greater contact with Western values and the most "refined" of European culture.[11] During this contact, the Jews had changed their way of dress, speech, work, and integration into the social environment to which they belonged.[12] In this context, the factors that motivated these migration flows were more of a political nature, and we may consider those involved a kind of "refugee," who had fled his country of origin out of a well-founded fear of being persecuted and having his civil and political rights threatened (Negrine 2013; Hillel Shulewitz 1999). However, it is important to highlight the contextual differences that led to the mass departure of Jews from both Morocco and Syria. While the Syrian Jews were subjected to strong harassment and government restrictions on emigrating, in Morocco they did not have to face such persecutions.

---

10 According to the Argentine National Census of 1960, the majority of Syrian Jews arrived in Argentina before 1929: 36 percent before 1919 and 47.5 percent between 1920 and 1929. According to Cohen, 11.5 percent arrived between 1930 and 1939, and 5 percent arrived between 1940 and 1960.

11 An interview conducted by the author S. Brauner and M. J. Cano with E. Benmaman, in November 2013.

12 A. Chouraqui, "Acerca de los judíos de África del Norte," in *En una Era de Transición* (Tel Aviv: Universidad Abierta, 1981), 36–37.

In any case, in Morocco too, at the time of the independence conflicts in North Africa, a strong anti-Western nationalism arose, which triggered uncertainty in the minorities and a fear of anti-Semitic attacks.[13] With this happening, mass emigration of the Jews as well as other European residents started. In short, beyond the coexistence that prevailed for long periods and the tolerant policies adopted by the royal dynasty, the Jews decided to migrate to different continents, leading to the disappearance of a once-thriving community with the greatest number of Jews in North Africa. So much so, that on the eve of independence it is estimated that around 255,000 Jews lived in Morocco, that is to say 2.5 percent of the local population.[14]

In short, the Jewish new immigrants who arrived in Argentina from the 1940s onward, whether from Morocco or Syria, were different from the pioneers. They belonged to higher socioeconomic levels, had received a better education, had undergone processes of secularization, and had become more open toward the values of Western Europe as well as the approaches toward the ideals of Zionism. Moreover, in Buenos Aires they found Jews of Syrian and Moroccan descent with their Argentinean descendants who had gone through a strong process of "Argentinization," as well as independently organized communities (the Moroccans, Aleppans, and the Damascenes). Under these circumstances, these waves of immigrants would give rise to new phenomena leading to the revitalization of beliefs and practices from their place of origin. So much so, that two religious leaders who came to Argentina from Morocco and Syria at the beginning of the 1950s, were appointed as chief rabbis. These two "recently arrived" leaders, with the support of certain sectors of the institutional elite, favored measures to strengthen their native traditions and higher levels of community cohesion.

Identities and Modes of Integration

The Moroccan Jews are identified as one of the Sephardic groups that integrated most quickly into Argentina, from the first native generations. According to Epstein, their command of Spanish, and, in some cases, the fact that they

---

13 An interview conducted by the author S. Brauner and M.J. Cano with J. Ovadia, in November 2013.

14 Chouraqui, "Acerca de los judíos de África del Norte," 28.

had surnames of Spanish origin, facilitated their integration and helped them not to be regarded as North Africans or Jews in Argentine society.[15] While the first generation stands out as being highly endogamic (Epstein 1995), there is supporting evidence to show that the younger generations distanced themselves from traditional norms and community centers.

On the other hand, the Syrian, Aleppan, and Damascene Jews preserved their traditions to a greater degree throughout their evolving generations. In fact, they became two independently organized groups in Buenos Aires. From their beginnings in Argentina to the present day, they are perceived as belonging to the most observant and traditional sectors, and as men of "strong faith" who recreated their identities preserving their religion and ethnic traditions as guiding principles of their lives (Brauner 2009). Nevertheless, even though they have so far maintained vigorous and highly organized communities, it is also worth noting that some sectors, which disagree with the religious norms established by the Orthodox and ultra-Orthodox leaders, have been dissociating themselves from these communities, and have joined other non-Orthodox Jewish groups, or have acculturated into Argentine society (Schammah and Brauner 2013).

The pioneers' strong identity resulted in these groups organizing themselves into three independent communities in the capital city: the Aleppans, the Damascenes, and the Moroccans. Their first objectives were to preserve the traditions of their homeland and to maintain community cohesion. In order to do so, they proposed providing religious and educational services, assistance for the needy, and a separate cemetery for each sector. Moreover, since they were so few in number, the small nuclei that had settled outside Buenos Aires or in other provinces began organizing themselves over time with Jews from other sectors. In other words, they were integrating themselves into entities that brought together Jews of different origins. In fact, the tendency to preserve one's ethnic origin appeared to be determined by the number and degree of population concentration registered in the different cities nationwide.

As regards employment, the first Moroccan Jews began their activities in the commercial sector, and some managed to achieve a strong economic status. Different paths were taken in order to achieve upward mobility in society, but in general, according to Epstein, they started out as street vendors, and later became small storekeepers or traders, financiers, or textile

---

15 Epstein, "Marroquíes de origen judío," 138.

businessmen. In other provinces of Argentina, they were employed by the public and private sectors to work on the construction of railways, drainage works, or in the forestry industry. They were also the first Sephardic Jews who became professionals, especially lawyers and accountants (Epstein 2009). In turn, the Syrian Jews also entered the labor market as street vendors, storekeepers, industrial workers, or importers of textile products using their transnational networks in Europe. Buenos Aires became the commercial and industrial center for Jews coming from Syria.[16] In this context, they tended to prefer commercial activities to education in order to advance their upward social mobility.

In other words, the Jews from the Arab world experienced modes of economic and social integration in Argentina similar to those undergone by the majority of immigrants from the Arab world of all faiths (Noufouri 2005). In this context, both the Moroccan and Syrian Jews, along with their descendants—who were connected mainly to the business and textile industries— were able to join the middle and upper-middle classes in society. However, their economic activities also diversified into the financial field, as well as into construction and real estate, among other industries. Furthermore, it should be noted that while the pioneers were associated with the banking institutions founded by Syrians of other faiths, the younger generations of Jews founded new credit institutions and cooperatives from the late 1950s. Such cooperatives were adopted as an instrument of mutual assistance, without any expressed political connotation, to secure the needs of their associates and to fulfill the functions of solidarity within the community, which later spread also to public institutions (Brauner 2004). In this process, some of the cooperatives of Syrian and Moroccan origin merged to form a cooperative bank, *Banco Mayo*, at the end of the 1970s. Until the late 1990s, this bank acted as one of the principal representatives for Sephardic Jews before the rest of the Jewish community, the Argentine society, and public authorities (Brauner 2009).

Nevertheless, it is important to highlight the fact that the Jews of Syrian and Moroccan descent, and/or their Argentine descendants, worked in other fields

---

16 This was the same for rest of the Jews in the country. According to the Argentine National Census of 1960, 84 percent of the Jews in Argentina lived in Buenos Aires and Greater Buenos Aires. The numerous community institutions founded by Jews of Syrian origin, which lasted for many years in comparison to those that were created or discontinued in other provinces, would also indicate the extremely high percentage of population concentration in this sector in Buenos Aires (Cohen 1985, 64).

too, not necessarily associated with commercial activities or classical liberal professions, for example, in the field of politics, arts, sports, and intellectual pursuits (Brauner 2009; 2012).

Religiousness and Rabbinical Leaderships: Between an Orthodoxy Close to Ultra-Orthodoxy[17] and an Orthodoxy Open to the Environment

In the mid-twentieth century, the Moroccan and Syrian Jews and their descendants experienced strong processes of "Argentinization," along with a distancing from the strict observance of biblical precepts and traditions. In this context, as mentioned earlier, it was decided to contact strong rabbinical personalities from Tetouan and Aleppo who had expert knowledge of their beliefs and regional practices. This developed in the context of the new situation of the Jews after World War II, the creation of the State of Israel, and the decolonization of Arab countries.

The Moroccans, who lacked rabbis to lead their temples,[18] took on Saadia Benzaquen. He was a young religious leader, born in Tetouan, who arrived in Argentina in 1951 from Morocco and remained as chief rabbi of the Moroccan community until his death in 1986 (Benmergui 2012). As for the Aleppans, the secular leadership designated the Orthodox rabbi Chehebar, a rabbinical leader who had escaped from Aleppo following the harsh persecutions of the Jews in the Middle East. He arrived in Buenos Aires in 1953, and remained as chief rabbi of the community until his death in 1990. Both rabbis, therefore, would remain in charge of the main community temples for many long years. Each sector was adamant that these periods were "flourishing" or "golden" (Rodgers 2005; Benmergui 2012).

---

17 The Orthodox and ultra-Orthodox movements, beyond their variants, promote the rigorous observance of the biblical precepts and religious traditions, while vindicating themselves as the only ones with the ability to ensure Jewish intergenerational continuity. Among others, see M. Friedman, *Society and Religion. The Non-Zionist Orthodox in Eretz Israel 1918–1936* [Heb] (Jerusalem: Ben Zvi Publications, 1988); T. Zohar, "Los Sabios de la Biblia y la Modernidad: la ortodoxia, los rabinos orientales y el movimiento Shas" [Heb], *Gilaion* (1996): 8–22; S. Brauner Rodgers, "Los judíos sirios en Buenos Aires: entre la revitalización de la religiosidad y la ultraortodoxia (1953–1990)" in *Anuario IHES* 17 (2002): 217–37.

18 Until Saadia Benzaquen's appointment, the Moroccans had not assigned rabbis to run their temples except for Shabetai Djaen. Although he only carried out rabbinical responsibilities for a short period, he was not in fact a proper rabbi or of Moroccan origin.

Saadia Benzaquen was an Orthodox rabbinical leader, but he maintained his position in a flexible manner and was open to surrounding values.[19] Even though he maintained his Orthodox religious orientation, he related to the more liberal sectors of Judaism and participated in inter-religious activities, radio and television shows (Benmergui 2012). He also offered his spiritual services to Jewish prisoners during the final military government (Brauner 2012).

As for Chehebar, he prompted a phenomenon that led to the revitalization of Orthodox religious norms and ethnic traditions, while reinforcing the rabbinical image. His influence over all religious and education matters was great. The functions conferred on him enabled him to prevent an act of matrimony that did not honor Orthodox norms, to examine the "legitimacy" of religious marriages of any community member "wherever they had been performed," to encourage traditional religious teaching, and to supervise and control everything related to *kashrut*.[20] Moreover, Chehebar was one of the leaders who would have to face Jewish religious groups that were more open to the modern world and Western values. Ultimately, Chehebar would have to set himself apart not only from the Orthodox rabbis like Saadia Benzaquen,[21] but also from ultra-Orthodoxy. However, the process that emanated from his religious leadership opened the doors to the ultra-Orthodox, and led also to the distancing of those who understood Judaism from a more liberal perspective.

After Chehebar's death in 1990, the Argentine descendants of the Jews from Aleppo and Damascus began to radicalize the process of becoming Orthodox and the re-signification of their ethnic traditions. On the other hand, after the death of Saadia Benzaquen, the Moroccan Jews continued with the modernization of their religious practices, vastly differentiating themselves in this respect from the Syrian Jews, who were connected to community organizations (Epstein 2009). Nonetheless, it is important to bear in mind that "the Orthodox revitalization of religiousness" that was being imposed on different sectors of the Jewish community in Buenos Aires also began to influence the Moroccan leadership, which, in recent times, after years of

---

19 Interviews conducted by the author S. Brauner and M. J. Cano with J. Ovadia, B. Benmergui, and E. Benmaman, in November 2013.

20 *Kashrut*: Jewish dietary laws referring to what may or may not be eaten. S. Rodgers, *Los judíos de Alepo en Argentina* (Buenos Aires: Nuevos Tiempos, 2005), 151–52.

21 While Saadia Benzaquen kept to the basic principles of Orthodoxy, unlike Chehebar he adopted less stringent measures in the face of conversions and intermarriage in the Moroccan community. See "Conversation with Rabbi Benzaquen" (interview published in 1971), Oral History Division, Hebrew University, Jerusalem.

inactivity, has been taking on rabbinical leaders linked to ultra-Orthodox sectors in their main temple. These rabbis favor the "rebirth" of religious beliefs and the respect and conservation of Moroccan traditions, as well as adopting the figure of Rabbi Saadia Benzaquen as one of the great religious leaders to have served the community.[22]

Beyond the orientations that prevailed in the central organizations, at the same time it is also worth pointing out the flexibility of the community frontiers. This flexibility was such that it gave rise to the dispersion and integration of the Argentineans of Moroccan origin into other Jewish and non-Jewish environments. Some were attracted to other groups: the ultra-Orthodox, such as Isaac Benchimol or Iosef Bitton (Benchimol 1999; Bitton n.d.); the more liberal Jewish groups, such as Mordejai Edery (Benmergui 2012); or the secular movements of the Jewish or national left wing.[23]

As for the Syrian Jews, while some of their more relevant rabbinical figures stood out and served in other Orthodox and ultra-Orthodox groups both nationally and internationally, we should also note the presence of other rabbis who joined religious variants that were more liberal, such as Rolando Matalon, Silvina Chemen, Ernesto Yattah, and José Faur. As with the Argentineans of Moroccan origin, a considerable number of youths were linked to the more modern religious groups, as well as the Jewish and non-Jewish left wing (Brauner 2012).

Relations with Arabs of Other Faiths and Alignments regarding the State of Israel, Syria, and Morocco

The relationships among Arabs of different faiths were more than cordial during the first half of the twentieth century. However, the new generations of Argentineans did not cultivate the same networks as their ancestors.[24] The intensification of the Arab–Israel conflict and the increasing persecutions experienced by the Jewish communities in the Arab world did not help the relationships constructed by the first immigrants in the institutional and economic environments,

---

22 See the magazine published by the Community, ACILBA (Latin Israelite Community Association of Buenos Aires): Argentine Judeo-Moroccan Community (Buenos Aires, 2014), 2–4.

23 In the 1960s and '70s, university students of Moroccan origin, like other Jews at that time, were linked to left-wing Zionist movements and to the national left wing, which was confronting the military government of the time. Some were forced to go into exile and others are still missing.

24 From the creation of the State of Israel, alignment with the Arab cause became a trend in the press of the time, Diario Sirio Libanés (the Syrian–Lebanese newspaper), October 20, 1947, 1.

and added to the mutual distrust of the younger generations. It was a time of "Argentinization" and "Zionization." In other words, even if the majority did not intend to emigrate, support for the nascent State of Israel was incorporated—but not in a uniform way. Although Damascus, Aleppo, Tetouan, and Tangier did not disappear from their collective memory, the Jewish state became another of their main overseas reference points. At that time, the younger generations undertook the defense of the Jews who were still residents in the Arab world as their own cause, particularly in Syria, where the country imposed serious constraints on Jewish emigration. Therefore, they organized themselves to put pressure on various entities and governments, such as the Jewish Agency, the Argentine Government, and the same Syrian authorities along with other international organizations dedicated to the defense of Jewish minorities in Arab countries. So much so, that they offered financial backing to facilitate the emigration of Jews to Argentina and supported activities led by DAIA[25] to that effect.

In fact, this cause managed to reunite the entire spectrum of entities representing Jews of Syrian origin in the country. This ranged from the most Orthodox sectors to the Zionist youths, who discredited the so-called "Syrian socialist regime" for acting as a dictatorship that was violating the human rights of the Jews who were still residing in Syria.[26] Syria continued to be one of their overseas reference points, and was a country that not so long ago had enjoyed freedom and tolerance: "We appeal to the Arab people once known for their noble virtues of generosity, hospitality and tolerance, inherited from our common father Abraham."[27]

While clandestine networks worked to help their emigration, the defense of the Jews still residing in Syria became a cause that had an impact on a global scale and was transnational, so much so that the Syrian Jews in Argentina intensified contacts with the rabbinical authorities in Lebanon, other Jewish diasporas in the Arab world,[28] and the main international organizations in the United States[29] that had assumed the defense of Jewish minorities residing in Arab countries.[30]

---

25 DAIA: *Delegación de Asociaciones Israelitas Argentinas* (Delegation of Argentine Israelite Associations)—the entity that represents Jews politically in Argentina, *Mundo Israelita*, September 8, 1972.
26 *Mundo Israelita*, November 13, 1971, 18.
27 Rabbi I. Chehebar, *Israel*, October 1968, 1.
28 Sephardic Congregation Act 932, *Memory*, July 7, 1971, 79–80.
29 The first organization established was the WOJAC (World Organization of Jews from Arab Countries). To analyze its role, see Shenhav (2002). Later, the JJAC (Justice for Jews from Arab Countries) was founded.
30 Y. Chehebar, *Rabbi Itzjak Chehebar: un visionario* (Buenos Aires: Congregación Sefardí, 1995), 227.

Today, of course, the main overseas points of reference of the Argentinean Jews of Syrian origin linked to major communities are in the State of Israel, and particularly in the rabbinical seminaries or sectors that represent the eastern Jews and the dispersed communities of Syrian Jews worldwide.

The positions of Moroccan Jews with respect to their homeland and the governing dynasty were and continue to be different. According to Vagni, as much in the Kingdom of Morocco as in the Diaspora, the Moroccan Jewish elite have preserved their feelings of patriotism toward Morocco and their loyalty to the Crown, which is considered a traditional protector of the community. In fact, the emphasis is on the "double loyalty" of the Jews: to the Moroccan culture and to the Jewish world in its entirety.[31] In accordance with this perspective, we should note, for example, the week of Moroccan culture that was organized in Buenos Aires in 2004, when the Moroccan ambassador described the Jews as an integral part of the social structure of Morocco.[32] What may also be taken into account is the participation of the community leaders and rabbis of the Moroccan community in the events organized by the Moroccan embassy for the traditional Throne Day, when the coronation of the King is commemorated.[33] Nevertheless, without detracting from the years of living together and politics of tolerance, there are other perspectives, that mention acts of open hostility against Jews carried out by Islamist groups as well as other sectors of the local population.[34]

FINAL CONSIDERATIONS

The purpose of this article has been briefly to shed light on the dynamics of the social processes of interaction in which Jews of Syrian and Moroccan origin have found themselves throughout their generations in Argentina. In order to understand the complexity of these processes, care has been taken to avoid relating the approaches that predominate in the subject matter, and that rebuild their ethnic attributes as monochromatic and almost frozen in

---

31 J. Vagni, "Los judeomarroquíes en Sudamérica: una migración africana bajo el signo de una identidad problemática," 2007, accessed May 23, 2017, http://www.redaepa.org.ar/jornadas/ixjornadas/resumenes/Se19.

32 J. Vagni, "La diplomacia cultural en la proyección exterior de Marruecos hacia Latinoamérica," *Mas allá del Medio Oriente. Las diasporas judía y árabe en América Latina*, ed. R. Rein, with M. J. Cano Pérez, and Rueda Molina (Granada, ES: University of Granada, 2012).

33 ACILBA, ibid., 24.

34 An interview conducted by S. Brauner and M. J. Cano with J. Ovadia, November 8, 2013.

time. In other words, we have avoided referring only to major community self-representations or academic representations. Instead, we also analyzed other simultaneous identifications that were constructed in the same community spaces by those people who distanced themselves from such spaces.

Therefore, in the case of the Moroccan Jews, it was important to present the overlooked and different processes of religious revitalization and community cohesion experienced in the times of Rabbi Saadia Benzaquen, as well as under the leadership of the ultra-Orthodox rabbis of the last few years.

As for the Aleppan Jews, beyond recognizing the processes that gave rise to the increase of their religious practices, what stood out, too, was the flexibility of community frontiers as well as the deinstitutionalization of those who opposed the norms that were being imposed in community spaces. Such deinstitutionalization meant the distancing of a considerable number of their members.

It is difficult to estimate the number of "deinstitutionalized" Jews from the Arab world. For reference purposes, according to the main records of the Jews from Aleppo, the average number of members who were heads of households would not be greater than 30 percent.[35] In this context, it could be pointed out that a significant number of the "deinstitutionalized" with Syrian roots not only integrated into different environments but also were conspicuous in different areas from the stereotypical "business" activities that are "attributed" to them. On the other hand, it should also be noted that some Moroccans and their descendants, at variance with the moderate religious criteria adopted in their community spaces, joined Orthodox and ultra-Orthodox groups (Benchimol 2009).

In short, the norms that prevailed then and now among Argentinean Jews of both origins have not been uniform. Nowadays, we can see a wide range of viewpoints that oscillate between ultra-Orthodoxy, Orthodoxy, traditionalism, secularization, and/or distancing from the community organizations.

Without wishing to exhaust the subject, the spectrum of beliefs and practices here presented provides merely a brief overview of the identities created and constructed in the framework of the pluralistic Argentine society amid the vicissitudes of the international scene. Ultimately, it shows the diversity of orientations and processes that question the aforementioned approaches, which dominate most of today's literature.

---

35 The membership varied according to which subjects were discussed. The average number of members who were heads of households between 1960 and 1998 was estimated to be around that percentage. AISA, *Asociación Israelita Sefaradí Argentina* (Argentine Sephardic Israelite Association), General Assembly Acts (1960–98).

REFERENCES

Bejarano, Margalit. "El Cementerio y la unidad comunitaria de los sefaradim de Buenos Aires." *Sefárdica* 3, no. 1 (1985): 13–20.

―――. "Los sefaradíes en la Argentina." *Sefárdica* 2 (1984): 37–43.

―――. "Los sefaradíes en la Argentina: particularismo étnico frente a las tendencias de unificación." *Rumbos en el Judaísmo, Sionismo e Israel* 17–18 (1986): 143–60.

―――. "Sephardic Communities in Latin America—Past and Present." In *Judaica Latinoamericana*, 9–26. Jerusalem: Magnes Press, 2005.

―――. "Un mosaico de identidades fragmentadas: los sefardíes en América Latina." In *Los Sefardíes una comunidad del exilio*. Buenos Aires: Simposio Internacional de Estudios Sefardíes, CIDICSEF, 2007.

Bejarano, Margalit, and Edna Aizenberg. *Contemporary Sephardic Identity in the Americas. An Interdisciplinary Approach*. Syracuse, NY: Syracuse University Press, 2012.

Benchimol, Isaac. *Contra viento y marea*. Buenos Aires: Benchimol, 1999.

Benmergui, Alicia Vischnivetzky. "Benzaquen Saadia," *Personalidades religiosas de la ciudad de Buenos Aires*. Gobierno de la Ciudad de Buenos Aires, 2012, 17–22.

―――. "Edery, Mordejai." *Personalidades religiosas de la ciudad de Buenos Aires*. Gobierno de la Ciudad de Buenos Aires, 2012, 83–88.

Bittón, Iosef. "Conversión al Judaísmo," Rabinato de la Comunidad Israelita del Uruguay, Uruguay, 1999.

Brauner Rodgers, Susana. "Los judíos sirios en Buenos Aires: entre la revitalización de la religiosidad y la ultraortodoxia (1953–1990)." *Anuario IHES* 17, Facultad de Ciencias Humanas–Universidad Nacional del Centro-Tandil-Argentina (2002): 217–37.

Brauner, Susana, Patricio Fraga, and Cristian Schuckman. "El cooperativismo de crédito en Buenos Aires: entre la neutralidad política y la religiosa, 1950–1966." *Grupo de Estudios Cooperativos Latinoamericanos*. Entre Ríos, UR: Instituto de Historia, Concepción del Uruguay, 2004.

Brauner, Susana, and Silvnia Schammah. "Más allá de las 'fronteras' comunitarias: los argentinos de origen sirio y judíos en tiempos de rebeldía y autoritarismo." In Las diásporas judías y árabes en las Américas, edited by R. Rein. Tel Aviv University–Universidad de Granada, Spain, 2012, 197–226.

Castien Maestro, Juan I. "Las comunidades judías de Marruecos, entre la convivencia y la marginalidad." *Papeles ocasionales* 5 (2004).

Chehebar, Yosef. *Rabbi Itzjak Chehebar: un visionario*. Buenos Aires: Congregación Sefardí, 1995.

Chouraqui, Andre. "Acerca de los judíos de África del Norte." In *En una Era de Transición*, vols. 10–11, 9–84. Tel Aviv: Universidad Abierta, 1981.

Cohen, Mario. "Aspectos sociodemográficos de la comunidad sefardita de la Argentina." *Sefárdica* 2, no. 3 (August 1985): 57–78.

Epstein, Diana. "Los judeo-marroquíes en Buenos Aires: pautas matrimoniales, 1875–1910." *EIAL* 6 (January–June 1995): 113–33.

————. "Aspectos generales de la inmigración judeo-marroquí a la Argentina, 1875–1930." *Temas de Asia y África* 2 (1993): 151–70.

————. "Judíos de Marruecos en Argentina. La inmigración política (1955–1970)." *EML* 59 (2006): 69–98.

————. "Marroquíes de origen judío. Cohesión y dispersión comunitaria." *Ponencia XII Jornadas Interescuelas*. Neuquén: Universidad del Comahue, 2009.

Erdei, Ezequiel, and Adrián Jmelnitzki. *Población judía*. Buenos Aires: Amia-Joint, 2005.

Erdei, Ezequiel. "La pertenencia: entre religión y cultura, afiliación o adhesión y endogamia y exogamia." In *Pensar en lo judío del Siglo XXI*, edited by Alejandro Dujovne et al, 41–51. Buenos Aires: Capital Intelectual, 2011.

Friedman, Menachem. *Society and Religion. The Non-Zionist Orthodox in Eretz Israel 1918–1936* [Heb]. Jerusalem: Ben Zvi Publications, 1988.

Hillel Shulewitz, Malka, ed. *The Forgotten Millions. The Modern Jewish Exodus from Arab Lands*. London: Cassell, 1999.

Klich, Ignacio. "Árabes, judíos y árabes judíos en la Argentina de la primera parte del novecientos." *EIAL* 6, no. 2 (Tel Aviv, July–December 1995): 109–43.

Klich, Ignacio, and Jeffrey Lesser, eds. *Arab and Jewish Immigrants in Latin America*. London: Frank Class, 1998.

Laskier, Michael M. *North African Jewry in the Twentieth Century: The Jews of Morocco, Tunisia, and Algeria*. New York: New York University Press, 1997.

Mirelman, Víctor. *En búsqueda de una identidad. Los inmigrantes judíos en Buenos Aires, 1890–1930*. Buenos Aires: Mila, 1988.

Negrine, Ralph. "Are Jews who Fled Arab Lands to Israel Refugees, Too?" *Media History* 19, no. 4 (2013): 450–63.

Noufouri, Hamurabi, ed. *Sirios, libaneses y argentinos: fragmentos de la diversidad cultural religiosa*. Buenos Aires: Cálamo-Fundación Los Cedros, 2005.

Rein, Raanan. "Judíos, árabes, sefardíes, sionistas y argentinos: el caso del periódico Israel." In *¿Judíos-argentinos o argentinos-judíos?Identidad, etnicidad y diáspora*, edited by R. Rein, 77–103. Buenos Aires: Lumiere, 2011.

Rodgers, Susana. *Los judíos de Alepo en Argentina*. Buenos Aires: Nuevos Tiempos, 2005.

Rubel, Yacov, ed. *Presencia sefaradi en Argentina*. Buenos Aires: Centro Educativo Sefaradí en Jerusalén y Centro de Estudios Históricos e Investigación Social de AMIA (CEHIS), 1992.

Schammah Silvina, and Susana Brauner. "Militancia y prácticas culturales contestatarias: las segundas generaciones de judíos procedentes del mundo árabe en la Argentina autoritaria." In *Archivo y memoria 1970-2010, Chasqui* 5, edited by Bonger Blanco and Gatzemeier De Toro, 45–61. Santiago: Grupo de Trabajo de Estudios de Memoria, Archivo y Cultura, 2013.

Shenhav, Yehouda. "Ethnicity and National Memory: The World Organization of Jews from Arab Countries (WOJAC) in the Context of the Palestinian National Struggle." *British Journal of Middle Eastern Studies* 29, no. 1 (2002): 27–56.

Simon, Reeva S., Michael M. Laskier, and Sara Reguer, eds. *The Jews of the Middle East and North Africa in Modern Times.* New York: Columbia University Press, 2003.

Stillman, Norman A. *The Jews of Arab Lands in Modern Times.* Philadelphia, pA: Jewish Publication Society, 1991.

Vagni, Juan J. "Los judeomarroquíes en Sudamérica: una migración africana bajo el signo de una identidad problemática," 2007. Accessed May 23, 2017. http://www.redaepa.org.ar/jorna-das/ixjornadas/resumenes/Se19.

———. "La diplomacia cultural en la proyección exterior de Marruecos hacia Latinoamérica." *Mas allá del Medio Oriente.* In *Las diasporas judía y árabe en América Latina,* edited by R. Rein, with M. J. Cano Pérez, and Rueda Molina, 282–315. Granada, ES: University of Granada, 2012.

Zafrani, Haim. *Two Thousand Years of Jewish Life in Morocco.* New York: Ktav, 2005.

Zenner, Walter P. *Global Community: The Jews from Aleppo, Syria.* Raphael Patai Series in Jewish Folklore and Anthropology. Detroit, MI: Wayne State University Press, 2000.

Zohar, Tzvi. "Los Sabios de la Biblia y la Modernidad: la ortodoxia, los rabinos orientales y el movimiento Shas" [Heb]. *Gilaion* (1996): 8–22.

NATIONAL AND ETHNIC PRESS

Crítica

Israel

La Nación

El Diario Sirio Libanés

El Mundo Israelita

CHAPTER 10

Brazilian Virtual Orthodox Jewish Education in the Twenty-First Century

DANIELA SUSANA SEGRE GUERTZENSTEIN

This article will present a discussion about modernity, the assimilation of values of the larger society, and how new technologies are being incorporated by members of the Brazilian city of São Paulo's Orthodox Jewish community, changing their behavior and identities in the early twenty-first century. For this purpose, the article will reveal educational models found in the Jewish doctrine and in the São Paulo Orthodox Jewish schools.

INTRODUCTION

To understand the social inclusion of the members of the Orthodox Jewish community in the larger society, it is important to reflect on their technological inclusion and access to different environments. One has to bear in mind the fact that the community in question is known to be closed to outsiders, and maintains very strict rules of interaction to ensure its privacy.

POSTMODERNISM AND ORTHODOX JEWISH IDENTITY

Postmodernism is characterized symbolically by a liquid modernity of fluid relationships as fast, momentary, and disposable situations among multiple choices (Bauman 1999; 2004; 2005) in a context where relationships are changed by fleeting specific interests. Self-identity in late modernity is determined by the transformation of intimacy, and social belonging as a result of personal choices, in a plurality of contexts of a cosmopolitan environment (Giddens 2002). Giddens argues that pure human relationships are developed through common interests above personal kinship qualities and commitments. Thus, the postmodern era is characterized by computerized databases that determine the possibilities of individuals in society (Postman 1994).

Rabbi Moses Schreiber, the Hatam Sofer (1762–1839), an important Orthodox rabbinical authority, banned the introduction of innovations into Jewish worship. The term "Orthodoxy" in Judaism defines the Jewish identity that imposes specific behaviors strictly in accordance with the standards of rabbinical exegetical and legal texts, in opposition to the Reform/Liberal Judaism that emerged in Germany and France under the cultural influence of Enlightenment inspirations.[1]

However, an Orthodox Jewish identity can be recognized by an Orthodox Jewish personal lifestyle, or by a specific consumer profile strictly in conformity with the laws dictated by the Orthodox religious authorities (see Figure 10.1).

The Orthodox Jewish identities reflect a modern behavior that originated with the Pharisees. The Parisees were the spiritual fathers of Judaism. The name "Pharisee," like other Hebrew names, reflects not merely the meaning assumed by its historical and linguistic context; the root of every Hebrew word has a meaning, for example, the Pharisees = *prushim* in Hebrew, which means "separated" in English.

Orthodox Judaism can be understood also as respect for a social behavior based on philosophical concepts written in the Jewish prayer books. For example:

1) The *Havdalah* (prayer that symbolizes the end of the Seventh Day / the Judaic Sabbath) contains this text to be read out loud: *lehavdil ben kodesh lechol, ben or lechoshech, ben Israel laamim, ben yom hashevii lesheshet yamei hamaase* = "differentiates between sacred and mundane, light and darkness, Israel from the people (i.e., Gentiles), the seventh day and working days";

2) Another Sabbath and Holy Days' prayer contains the text: *vekadshenu bemitsvotecha* = "separates us for a holy purpose (consecrates us) with its precepts (commandments)." The consecration through the Jewish commandments is interpreted by Orthodox Jews as being "enshrined in the practice of all the rabbinical laws and rites".

The different types of Jewish Orthodoxy are characterized by the ways in which the community members differentiate between themselves and others from outside their own specific Orthodox Jewish community. The level of Orthodoxy grows as avoidance of outsiders of their community strengthens,

---

1 Marta F. Topel, *A Nova Ortodoxia Judaica em Cena* (Rio de Janeiro: Topbooks Editora, 2005).

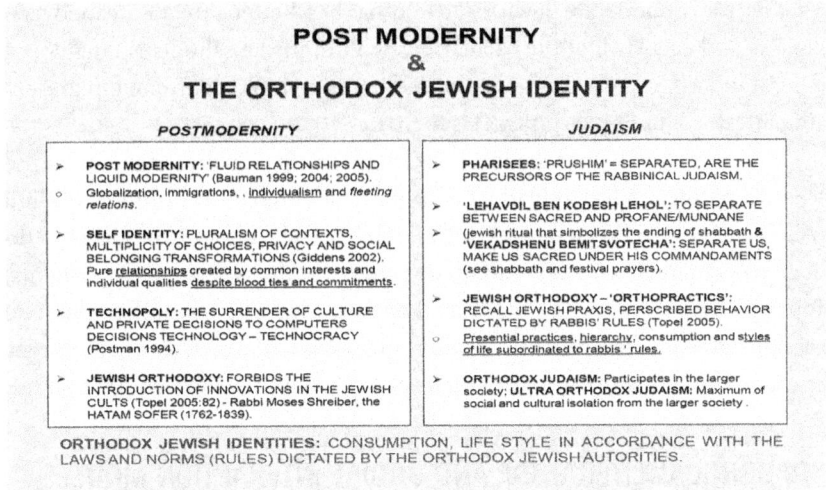

Figure 10.1 Postmodernism and Orthodox Jewish Identities.

and through the choice of being isolated and excluded from the larger society by the emphasis in some of their specific Orthodox Jewish tenets. The traditional hierarchy of the Orthodox rabbinical authorities dictates these practices and performances strictly in their communities. In such a narrow society with frozen interests, even connecting people with similar profiles around the world, it is not easy to be replaced.[2]

ORTHODOX JEWISH IDENTITIES

Orthodox Judaism can be divided into ultra-Orthodox Judaism, extreme-Orthodox Judaism (close to ultra-Orthodox Judaism), and moderate-Orthodox Judaism. The higher the standard of Jewish Orthodoxy in sociocultural isolation relates directly to the height of cultural provincialism (parochialism) in not sharing environments, and not getting involved with individuals outside their own community spaces.[3]

---

2 The levels of Jewish Orthodoxy, religious radicalism, and traditions in the communities themselves are not measured in a scale increasing from *left* to *right*, in order to avoid political associations, as written in M. Friedman, "The Market Model and Religious Radicalism", in *Jewish Fundamentalism in Comparative Perspective-Religion, Ideology and Crisis of Modernity*, ed. Laurence Silberstein (New York: New York University Press, 1993), 209.

3 The term "cultural provincialism" was chosen to avoid the word "parochial," as it is termed in Samuel Heilman and Steven M. Cohen, *Cosmopolitans and Parochial Modern Orthodox Jews in America* (Chicago: University of Chicago Press, 1989). "Parochial" is a Latin word commonly used in churches.

The more moderate Jewish Orthodoxy has better integration between religious and secular life; the secular curriculum in the schools is taught at a higher standard, and the cultural cosmopolitanism (interaction and integration with patterns of multiple cultures) is higher.

Therefore, the higher the level of Orthodoxy in Judaism, the lower is the access to public media; individual autonomy is diminished in order to fulfill the demands of the religious authorities. For example, ultra-Orthodox Jews do not attend cinemas, theaters, and do not enjoy products, share environments, adopt new behaviors that are proscribed by their own religious authorities. The decrease of the level of Jewish Orthodoxy increases social inclusion in the larger society, and assimilation into the larger society's contemporary cultural values.

RABBINICAL LITERATURE AND SOCIAL INTERACTION MODELS

The Jewish doctrine stands on the "Written Tradition" and the "Oral Tradition." In the fifth century BCE, Ezra the Scribe compiled, organized, and edited biblical manuscripts, scriptures, and copies of the Five Books of Moses, Judges, Prophets, and Scriptures that are known today as the Hebrew Bible. The biblical scriptures and manuscripts compiled by Ezra were consecrated and compiled, generation after generation, and are studied in the biblical Hebrew texts written in Assyrian script until today by the People of Israel, the Jews.

In the second century CE, the Prince of Judah (Rabbi Yehudah HaNassi) asked the generation of Jewish teachers known as *tannaim* to compile and edit the informal manuscripts of the Jewish oral tradition kept by the pharisaic leaders in order to prevent them from being forgotten. The oral tradition then began to be edited with the compilation of texts of the *Six Orders of the Mishnah* (composed in the Hebrew spoken in Judea at that time). The *Gemara*, composed in Aramaic by the Jewish teachers called *amoraim* and *savoraim*, was the continuation of the *Mishnah*. The *Gemara* is the Talmud. The Jerusalem Talmud preceded the Babylonian Talmud, but very little is known of the former, and it is considered less complete than the Babylonian Talmud. Rabbinical literature continues in Arabic and in a Hebrew heavily influenced by Arabic grammar in the era of the Jewish teachers known as *geonim* (the Sages), who flourished from the eighth century to the end of the first millennium CE.

The following centuries saw the first great rabbis, known as the *rishonim* ("the first"), including Maimonides, Nahmanides, and others, who literally illuminated the Jewish doctrine with extensive exegetic works during the dark European Middle Ages. In the following centuries, rabbinical literature continued through an extensive literary production of biblical and exegetic works of commentary, philosophical texts, and legal tractates. These works were written in medieval Hebrew, sometimes presenting a strong influence of a local language, or even written in Hebrew dialects by later rabbis around the world called *achronim* ("the later ones"). It is important to know that the Hebrew Bible does not shape Orthodox Jewish behavior, but, rather, the instructions and recommendations of the Orthodox Jewish leaders recognized as experts in rabbinical literature.

Models of cultural interaction, social integration, and professional Jewish schooling patterns are presented in the Babylonian Talmud. These models address human behavior conflicts in situations of multicultural contexts.[4]

1) *Torah Im Derech Eretz* / Torah with Secular Education

Torah Im Derech Eretz (or, *Torah U'Madda*) literally means religious insights into the ways of the world, religious insights, and secular knowledge. The Babylonian Talmud in Tractate Shabbat 33B states that:

> Rabbi Yehudah, Rabbi Shimon and Rabbi Yossi were together and Rabbi Yehudah praised the deeds of the people, the market, the bridges and the bathrooms. Rabbi Yossi forbore and Rashbi [Rabbi Shimon Bar Yochai] paused and replied that people did it for their own good: the markets for prostitution, the bathrooms to rejoice and the bridges to collect taxes.

Rabbi Yehudah represents the *Torah Im Derech Eretz* ("Judaism with the way of the land") model by integrating the benefits brought by the people into the Jewish doctrine.

Rabbi Samson Raphael Hirsch (1808–1888), explains *Torah Im Derech Eretz* as religion allied to progress. Following this idea as an educational model, secular studies improve the understanding of the Torah, even if the Torah is the driving force for Jewish knowledge as that which "teaches us how to see the world and how to listen to history."[5]

The *Torah Im Derech Eretz* educational model and *Torah U'Madda* (in English: Torah and Knowledge/Science) follows educational models for religious doctrine with the acquisition of secular knowledge. Moderate-Orthodox

---

4 Different levels and types of Jewish religious social patterns can be seen in the Torah and in the Jewish oral tradition (rabbinical literature).

5 Norman Lamm, *Torah U'Madda: The Encounter of Religious Learning and Worldly Knowledge in the Jewish Tradition* (Northvale, NJ: Jason Aronson Inc., 1990), 112–13.

Jews are closer to the secular world, and extreme-Orthodox Jews are closer to ultra-Orthodox Judaism.[6]

2) *Torah Veomanut* / Torah and a Job

The educational model *Torato Omanuto* is found in the Babylonian Talmud in Tractate Kiddushin 29, where it is stated that Rabbi Yehudah says: "He who does not teach his son a job is as if he taught to steal."

The educational model *Torah Im Derech Eretz* of the most extreme-Orthodox Jews may be equivalent to the ultra-Orthodox Jews' educational model, which requires a father to teach his son a professional skill, so that his son will be able to support himself following all patterns of Jewish doctrine.

3) *Torah Keneghed Kulam and Torato Omanuto* / Only Torah

In the Babylonian Talmud, Tractate Shabbat 33B, Rashbi (Rabbi Shimon Bar Yochai) emerged from the cave where he had been hiding from the Romans for twelve years, during which time he had studied Torah covered up to his neck by sand, wearing clothes only for the Sabbath and Festivals, and eating only locusts. Exiting the cave, his contempt for human undertakings was such that everywhere he looked he set ablaze. A heavenly voice then commanded him to return to the cave, where he stayed for over twelve months.

In the ultra-Orthodox Jewish educational model of *Talmud Torah KeNeghed Kulam* and *Torato Omanuto* ("Studying Torah as a Profession"), the disciplines studied are Jewish doctrinal topics only, with commentaries and teachings of their own rabbinical authorities in a context where secular subjects, abilities, and studies are minimized. The ultra-Orthodox Jews are characterized by their socio-cultural isolation, their voluntary exclusion of environments outside their communities, minimal or no secular curriculum in their schools, and by their local specific religious provincialism. However, any ultra-Orthodox Jewish community will reveal

---

6 The concept of Orthodox Judaism arose in Germany in the late eighteenth to the early nineteenth century to differentiate between Jews who strictly followed the path of the rabbinical literature, and not the social context of the Age of Enlightenment/Age of Reason that allowed for the Jewish Emancipation and the development of Reform and Liberal Judaism. Modern-Orthodox Judaism is a movement that synthesizes the observance of Jewish values with the secular/modern world. The term "Centrist-Orthodox Jew," which I used in my PhD thesis, is somewhere between ultra-Orthodox and moderate-Orthodox, perhaps extreme-Orthodox and just Orthodox are good equivalents. The concept "Centrist-Orthodox" is found in other authors as moderate-Orthodoxy, between non-Orthodoxy and ultra-Orthodoxy.

to outsiders that their educational curriculum educates their children toward God's fear, love, and sake; if needed, they must choose to live in a cave, covered by dust up to the neck, eating just locusts and they will be happy to study Torah all the time.

SÃO PAULO CITY JEWISH ORTHODOX SCHOOLS

There are an estimated 51,050[7] Jews in São Paulo, and about 3,000 more within 100 km of São Paulo, with three traditional Jewish schools:

1) Nova Escola Judaica Alef, which merged two earlier Jewish schools: Escola Renascença and Colégio Bialik;
2) Colégio I.L. Peretz, and;
3) Escola Beit Yaacov (founded and administrated by the Bank Safra group).

Figure 10.2 shows the chronological development of the Orthodox Jewish community and their schools in the city of São Paulo. Orthodox Jewish immigrants from Eastern Europe founded the first Orthodox Jewish schools after the Holocaust. Resulting from the renewed Islamic persecution against Israelis and Jews following the establishment of the State of Israel in 1948, new Jewish immigrants came to Brazil from Arab countries. These immigrants, with their Sephardic traditions, met European Jews with Ashkenazi traditions, - who discriminated against oriental practices. For this reason, and in order to preserve their own religious traditions, they began founding their own Orthodox Jewish schools.

São Paulo Jewish Orthodox schools:

1) Beth Chinuch - Iavne;
2) Yeshivá Or Torah and Mesivta;
3) Beth Jacob;
4) Talmud Torá Lubavitch and Gani;
5) Yeshivá Or Israel College;
6) Maguen Avraham and Beit Ester;
7) Yeshivá Tomchei Temimim - Lubavitch;
8) Benos Isroel;
9) Talmud Torá Hamaor;
10) Talmud Torá Or Menachem (Chabad Messianic School).

---

7 IBGE 2010: Brazilian Institute of Geography and Statistics.

EDUCATIONAL INSTITUITIONS OF THE SÃO PAULO ORTHODOX JEWISH COMMUNITY

20th CENTURY

1946: *Colégio Beth Chinuch – Iavne* male and female (from preschool till the end of the high school education). – *MODERATE ORTHODOX JEW ISH SCHOOL.*

1958: First *ieshiva* in São Paulo - *Yeshivá Or Torah* for males (from preschool till 18 years old - the age of ending the high school education). *** NO SECULAR CURRICULUM AFTER THE 4th GRADE – *ULTRA ORTHODOX JEWISH SCHOOL.*

1958: *Beth Jacob* fem. (from preschool till the end of the high school education). – *ULTRA ORTHODOX JEWISH SCHOOL WITH ALSO EXTREME ORTHODOX JEWS STUDYING THERE.*

1960: *Talmud Torá Lubavitch* male (from preschool till 5th grade – From 1995 from the 8th grade as *Yeshivá Tomchei Temimim* till the end of the high school education). – *ULTRA ORTHODOX JEWISH SCHOOL. WITH ALSO EXTREME ORTHODOX JEWS STUDYING THERE. SECULAR STUDIES TILL 6th GRADE,. *** OPTIONAL SECULAR STUDIES FROM THE 7th GRADE TILL THE END OF THE HIGH SCHOOL EDUCATION.*

1983: *Gani* fem. (from preschool till the end of the high school education). - *ULTRA ORTHODOX JEWISH SCHOOL WITH ALSO EXTREME ORTHODOX JEWS STUDYING THERE.*

1989: *Yeshiva Or Israel College* male. (from the 7th grade till the end of the high school education). – *MODERATE AND EXTREME ORTHODOX JEWS STUDYING THERE.*

1992: *Maguen Avraham* male; **1994:** *Maguen Avraham* female.(*Beit Esther*). (from preschool till th end odf the high school education). *ULTRA ORTHODOX JEWISH SCHOOL WITH ALSO EXTREME ORTHODOX STUDYING THERE.*

1995: *Yeshivá Tomchei Temimim – Lubavitch* male. (from the 7th grade till the end of the high school education – OPTIONAL SECULAR EDUCATION. *ULTRA-ORTHODOX JEWISH SCHOOL WITH SOME ORTHODOX JEWS STUDYING THERE.*

1995: *Benos Isroel* fem.. (from preschool till 7th grade) – *ULTRA ORTHODOX JEWISH SCHOOL.*

21st CENTURY

2002: *Yeshiva Gevohá Beer Avraham* male. (RABBINICAL HIGH EDUCATION).

2003: *Midrashet Orot* fem. (RABBINICAL HIGH EDUCATION). - *Shaarei Biná* in 2010.

2007: *Talmud Torá Hamaor* male. *ULTRA ORTHODOX JEWISH SCHOOL WITH EXTREME ORTHODOX JEWS STUDYING THERE*

2010: *Escola Or Menachem* male and female from kindergaten to high school (MESSIANIC CHABAD ULTRA-ORTHODOX HASSIDIC).

Figure 10.2 São Paulo Orthodox Jewish Schools and Learning Institutes.

The Orthodox Jewish community of São Paulo city kept growing with the immigration from Argentina, Israel, and other countries. It also increased through marriage, with a large number of Jews from secular families adopting an Orthodox Jewish lifestyle and, in addition, a considerable (and unrevealed) number of people from non-Jewish families who were converted in Israel or by ultra-Orthodox rabbis, and who adopted an ultra-Orthodox Jewish lifestyle and became part of their communities.

All official Orthodox Jewish schools in São Paulo city need to use Internet services in order to comply with local governmental obligations as registered institutions. To comply with these obligations, each Orthodox Jewish school has a financial office manager who is connected to the Internet by a private provider.

All Brazilian ultra-Orthodox, extreme-Orthodox, and moderate-Orthodox Jewish schools in the city of São Paulo introduced computers into the educational program, even if only used by teachers to type and print texts.

1) Beth Chinuch - Iavne

The Beth Chinuch - Iavne school was founded in 1946 in the Jardins neighborhood. This educational institution was the first Orthodox Jewish school in the city of São Paulo. This school was registered under the Jewish Religious Education Center, established by Mr. Benjamin Citron, an immigrant from eastern Europe.

The aim of this school has always been to accept children with traditional, religious, or Orthodox Jewish parents from any country. This school has classes for girls and boys from kindergarten to high school completion, and follows the moderate-Orthodox educational model of *Torah Im Derech Eretz* and *Torah U'Madda*.

The staff, teachers, and students have access to the Internet through Wi-Fi technology in a computer room monitored by the school's firewall. This school has a site on the Internet, and the students do some of their studies and homework relating to secular disciplines using Internet searches. The students learn about religion, but their abilities and knowledge in the Hebrew Bible, in rabbinical literature, and Jewish doctrinal practices are not high. However, this Orthodox Jewish school in the city of São Paulo is where the students can receive the best education, and be accepted into good universities in Brazil and abroad.

2) Yeshivá Or Torah and Mesivta

The Yeshivá Or Torah is a Hungarian ultra-Orthodox Hasidic Jewish school for boys with classes from kindergarten to 13-year-olds. Rabbi Elimelech Ashkenazi from Hungary founded the Yeshivá Or Torah in 1958. This institution started some years after the Mesivta educational program for boys aged thirteen to eighteen, under the leadership of Rabbi Avraham Meir Iliovits (Rabbi Ashkenazi's son-in-law). The Yeshivá Or Torah offers ultra-Orthodox Jewish studies from kindergarten to the end of the first half of the elementary school curriculum. The *Torah Im Derech Eretz* education of this institution is incomplete, and this educational complex therefore is managed under the ultra-Orthodox Hasidic Jewish educational model *Torah Keneghed Kulam* or *Torato Omanuto*. The predominant language spoken is Yiddish.

The students are strictly isolated from the outside world; in their religious community they speak Yiddish, and only with those whom their religious authorities allow them to talk. The students are not allowed to access the Internet. The parents believe that religious studies make their children so knowledgeable that they will be able to learn any profession at any time, should it become necessary.

3) Beth Jacob

In 1958, the ultra-Orthodox Hasidic Jewish school Beth Jacob was opened. Initially, this institution taught only Orthodox Jewish topics, and the secular education was conducted by the Beth Chinuch - Iavne school. Beth Jacob School was founded as an initiative of eastern Europe immigrants Jacks Moscovits and his wife. From 1969, Beth Jacob School began teaching a full-time educational program with Orthodox Jewish insights and secular studies. This school has a syllabus in accordance with the ultra-Orthodox Jewish *Torato Omanuto* educational model for girls, with classes from kindergarten to the end of high school and an optional year-program after high school, when most female students get engaged and married. Beth Jacob School teaches students to use Microsoft PC programs, but does not allow them to access the Internet. However, many of them access it elsewhere or at their homes.

4) Talmud Torá Lubavitch and Gani

Two brothers, born in Brazil but from an eastern European family, founded the Talmud Torá Lubavitch and Gani educational institution. The Begun brothers studied rabbinical doctrine in New York, and adopted Orthodox Jewish Chabad Hasidism. In 1960, they founded an educational institution in the city of São Paulo that, in 1983, became the first of the ultra-Orthodox Jewish Talmud Torah School: The Gani School with classes for girls from kindergarten to the end of high school and the Lubavitch School with classes for boys from kindergarten to the seventh grade (eighth year) of elementary education.

These two schools use the ultra-Orthodox *Torato Omanuto* Jewish school program, similar to the extreme-Orthodox Jewish educational model *Torah Im Derech Eretz*. For several years, the Talmud Torá Gani for girls had an optional half-year study course after completion of high school, until their students, if possible, were sent abroad to continue studying pedagogy, Orthodox Jewish laws, exegetical studies and traditions, or technical courses in the United States or Israeli ultra-Orthodox Jewish academic institutions.

Students from both schools are forbidden to access the Internet. The girls learn Microsoft PC programs at school. Many girls and boys, however, do access the Internet, and print homework for school with content from the Internet using their own computers and printers.

5) Yeshivá Or Israel College

The Yeshivá Or Israel College is a school for boys in a private campus with dorms founded in 1989 in the Cotia municipality, on the outskirts of São Paulo. From its foundation, Rabbi Raphael Shammah has been its principal. Jews from Aleppo (Syria) founded this school, but children from Arab and European Jewish families have been learning side by side from its beginning, despite a few conflicts during prayers and slightly different Jewish traditions.

The school program from the seventh grade (eight year) until the end of high school follows the extreme-Orthodox Jewish educational model *Torah Im Derech Eretz*, and has ultra-Orthodox, extreme-Orthodox, and moderate-Orthodox Jewish students who wish to learn Jewish Orthodox knowledge in order to continue rabbinical and secular studies and enable them to be accepted into Brazilian universities.

At school, the students are not allowed Internet access, but teachers encourage them to access the Internet for homework on free weekends. Students who live full-time in the school occasionally get permission to access the Internet at school, but only in the presence of a school supervisor.

6) Maguen Avraham and Beit Ester

In 1992, the Sephardic ultra-Orthodox Maguen Avraham school for boys of Jewish families from Arab countries was founded, and classes for girls were opened in 1994. This new division was renamed Beit Esther some years later. The educational model for these two schools is *Torato Omanuto*, under the coordination and leadership of Rabbi Isaac Dichi, the official rabbi of the Mekor Haim congregation. Maguen Avraham for boys and Beit Ester for girls have classes from kindergarten to the end of high school. The school for girls teaches Microsoft programs to the students. Both boys and girls use Microsoft programs to do homework. A small minority of the students in these schools plan to study in universities. Some of them plan to continue religious studies in Israel. Rabbi Dichi advises that students should get married before starting university studies.

The use of Internet by students of these two schools is prohibited, and its influence is regarded as an abomination, though most students have access to it outside school.

7) Yeshivá Tomchei Temimim - Lubavitch

The Yeshivá Tomchei Temimim - Lubavitch was founded in 1995, and its principal has always been Rabbi Shamai Ende, who is married to the daughter of Rabbi Henrique Begun (founder of the Talmud Torá Gani and Lubavitch school). The Yeshivá Tomchei Temimim - Lubavitch has classes for boys from the seventh grade (eight year) to the end of high school, and secular education is optional. Students are strictly prohibited from accessing the Internet and its supposed influence is regarded as an abomination, but most, nevertheless, have access to it.

The mission of the educational model is to fulfill the desires of those who wish to be experts on Hasidic Chabad texts and acquire knowledge in exegetical and rabbinical texts in order to be Orthodox Jewish leaders. This educational model may be classified as *Torato Omanuto*. However, this school does provide the option to learn secular studies. The quality of this option does not really enable this educational model to be understood as *Torah Im Derech Eretz*. Sometimes, it is a good idea to remember that learning some secular disciplines may help develop important abilities for someone who wishes to lead a religious community. This yeshiva has a "smicha program," which accepts students from all countries who wish to graduate as Lubavitcher rabbis.

8) Benos Isroel

The Benos Isroel girls' school was founded in 1995 by Mr. Benzion Feuerwerger for a number of ultra-Orthodox Hasidic Jewish families who speak mainly Yiddish, and who felt more ultra-Orthodox Hasidic Jewish than the ultra-Orthodox Jewish level of Beth Jacob School founded in 1959.

Today, this school has classes for girls from kindergarten to sixth grade (seventh year) of elementary school. This school can be classified as super-ultra-Orthodox Jewish, if such a term exists, as this is the religious concept embodied in the *Torato Omanuto* educational program with an incomplete educational environment of *Torah Im Derech Eretz*, instilled in its students and in their families. Internet use is prohibited, but these students and their families do not even know what Internet actually means, or what an Internet provider and services are. For example, some families use the VoIP (Voice Over Internet Protocol) phone service through a modem, a router and a telephone unit without connecting to a computer and/or other multimedia. The students do not have Internet access, and the parents of these students who have regular access to Internet are a minority.

9) Talmud Torá Hamaor

In 2007, the Ashkenazi Orthodox Jewish school Talmud Torah Hamaor was founded, under the leadership of Rabbi Shmuel Havlin, with classes for boys and girls from kindergarten through the first few years of elementary school. The educational model proposed is between the ultra- and extreme-Orthodox Jewish schooling model *Torah Im Derech Eretz*. There are ultra-Orthodox Jewish studies and secular disciplines, but the students are still young and the school is still too small. The children's parents claim to be ultra-Orthodox and extreme-Orthodox Jews who use the Internet, Microsoft programs, smartphones, Apple computers, and iPhones. Most of them say that they do not go to cinemas, but they do watch movies at home.

10) Talmud Torá Or Menachem (Chabad Messianic School)

Founded in March 2010, its educational program is as an ultra-Orthodox Messianic branch of the Chabad Lubavitch Hasidic Movement. Its members are taught to commit to the standards and ideals of their own ultra-Orthodox Chabad Hasidic Jewish authorities, with the goal of educating potential missionaries who will spread the belief that the Lubavitcher Rebbe is alive, who will know how to advise others to emancipate his revelations as the "Messiah Now."

The Internet is prohibited at school, but it is used to communicate with people of the same messianic group around the world, with family, or to practice their missionary objectives. Its educational model is *Torato Omanuto*, although they teach a few secular disciplines.

Figure 10.3 shows the virtual space of the Orthodox Jewish schools in the city of São Paulo.

THE VIRTUAL SPACE OF THE SÃO PAULO ORTHODOX JEWISH STUDENTS

The virtual interaction of the students under the actual names of the schools is not given in this article, in order to comply with the Brazilian law protecting the rights to privacy of minors.

Virtual Space and Orthodox Rabbis

There is no unanimous decision among the Orthodox rabbinical leadership regarding the use of digital equipment and the Internet. Digital devices with Internet-enabled access to newspapers, radios, events, activities, etc. also enable interaction with environments whose content has been prohibited by the rabbis. According to the Orthodox rabbis, the use of these new technologies changes the lifestyle of an Orthodox Jew, taking him away from his religious practices and changing his relationship (submission) via-à-vis the rabbinical authority.

The disagreements among the rabbis about the new technologies and the Internet occur because of the differences in their judgment regarding the importance of these tools in their relationship with the larger society, as a permitted aid to communication with members of their global religious community.

The followers of Rabbi Isaac Dichi (leader of the strictly religious Jewish Syrian–Lebanese Sephardic temple Mekor Haim and schools Maguen Avraham

THE VIRTUAL SPACE OF SÃO PAULO <u>ORTHODOX</u> <u>JEWISH SCHOOLS</u>
STUDENTS FROM THE 1st AND 2nd GRADE OF HIGH SCHOOL

EACH SCHOOL DETERMINES IT'S OWN RESTRICTIONS TOWARDS THE USE OF COMPUTERS AND INTERNET <u>IN AND OUTSIDE THE SCHOOL</u> BY IT'S STUDENTS

> THE ADMINISTRATIVE OFFICES OF THE SÃO PAULO ORTHODOX JEWISH SCHOOLS UTILIZE THE INTERNET, ALL OF THEM HAVE ROOMS WITH PCS FOR THEIR STUDENTS.

> <u>MODERATE ORTHODOX JEWS</u> – THE *COLÉGIO BETH CHINUCH - IAVNE* (MALE AND FEM) IS THE ONLY ORTHODOX JEWISH SCHOOL IN SÃO PAULO THAT HAS IT'S OWN INTERNET PROVIDER. IN THIS SCHOOL THE ACCESS TO THE INTERNET OCCURS THROUGH A FIREWALL PROGRAM. STUDENTS RECEIVE ORIENTATION ON HOW AND FOR WHAT PURPOSE TO USE THE PCs AND THE INTERNET IN GENERAL AND HOW TO PERFORM THEIR SCHOOL TASKS.

> <u>EXTREME ORTHODOX AND ULTRA ORTHODOX JEWS</u> – THE SCHOOLS *YESHIVÁ OR ISRAEL* COLLEGE (MALE), *GANI* (FEM), *MAGUEN AVRAHAM, BEIT ESTER* (FEM) AND THE *BETH JACOB* (FEM) IN ONE HAND THESE SCHOOLS REQUIRE TASKS AND HOME WORKS FOR THE SECULAR DISCIPLINES TO BE RESEARCH ON THE INTERNET – BUT – ON THE OTHER HAND THEY DO NOT PROVIDE THE ACCESS TO THE INTERNET AND VERY OFFEN EVEN FORMALLY FORBID THEIR STUDENTS TO ACCESS THE INTERNET... THE *YESHIVÁ TOMCHEI TEMIMIM* RABBINICAL LEADER FORBIDS THE JEWISH STUDENTS TO ACCESS THE INTERNET FOR ANY PURPOUSE.

· Controversial examples: 1) The Yeshivá Or Israel (MALE) is a dormitory school and some of it's students are permitted to access the Internet in the school office. 2) The Beth Jacob (FEM), the Maguen Avraham, Beit Ester (FEM) and Gani (FEM) the Internet is accessed by the students outside the school; always avoiding to mention the word 'Internet'. 3) The Yeshivá Tomchei Temimim (MALE) students accessed the Internet in the office without an official permission.

Figure 10.3 São Paulo Orthodox Jewish Schools' Virtual Space.

and Beit Ester) use telephone cards and forbid access to a multimedia Internet server. They pay for a local call and extra charges rather than take advantage of the cheap or even free VoIP service. The teachers at his schools remove references to the Internet from all printed lessons.

Rabbi Meir Iliovits (Satmer) and Rabbi David Horowitz use VoIP services without multimedia, and the term "Internet" must not even be mentioned. Rabbi Horowitz is completely sectary, against any new technologies, and has, he says, just a good cell phone (not a smartphone). Rabbi Iliovits has an Internet site (bka.com.br) about kosher food produced in factories under his supervision.

Other Orthodox rabbinical leaders of the Orthodox Jewish schools in São Paulo express themselves like Rabbi Yosef Shalom Eliashiv in Israel: they allow the use of technologies in a previously approved way. The use of cellular phones is permitted for a specific objective or a real need, but he restricts its use, for example, he does not allow his grandchildren to use smartphones: "Because the youth gets confused during the Torah studies."

VIRTUAL GHETTOS

It was found that 100 percent of students in ultra-Orthodox Jewish schools use personal computers at school and at home, even without access to the Internet.

These students informally adopt new habits like typing and printing texts, editing pictures and assimilated activities, such as playing digital games and watching movies, even if most of the films are ultra-Orthodox Jewish weddings and videos of their families' private parties.

Until 2008, some of the female ultra-Orthodox students were familiar with MSN (Windows Messenger) and Skype, according to them, in order to talk to their friends, members of their own community, and family, demonstrating that, at least sometimes, access to the Internet was possible. The habit of watching movies and the use of MSN demonstrate the formation of a "virtual ghetto." It can be understood that the cyberspace of the ultra-Orthodox Jewish students is constructed as a "virtual ghetto," a closed digital environment with no free or open access to outsiders.

Even though many ultra-Orthodox are opposed, rabbis advise the use of such communication programs as Skype, WhatsApp for smartphones and iPhones, the popularity of which is constantly growing.

CYBERSHTETLS

The extreme-Orthodox and moderate-Orthodox Jewish students frequently organize virtual communities in the social networking services. These virtual communities are like "virtual villages"; their users have public profiles and are not completely isolated from others, and their names and information are provided for public access. This "virtual village" is different from the "virtual ghetto," which is completely closed to outsiders.

In the first decade of the twenty-first century, students from Orthodox Jewish youth organizations created virtual communities for themselves known as "cybershtetels." These virtual communities used the Orkut virtual community in order to communicate with their friends from school and others who had moved to Israel or to other countries, and also to connect with people with similar Orthodox Jewish profiles around the world.

"Cybershtetl" is an allusion to the Jewish villages of eastern Europe prior to World War II, because reading the threads and seeing the houses and people in the streets of a "cybershtetl" was possible for outsiders. The term "virtual ghetto" was chosen because communication by messages is locked in a digital code, like a virtual space closed to outsiders.

The "Cybershtetl" is an allusion to virtual spaces like Facebook communities. The "Virtual Ghetto" is a method of private communications using chat services like the WhatsApp chat for cellphones.

CONCLUSIONS

Some of the students who are not permitted Internet access at school or in their homes learn unsanctioned and clandestine alternative methods of accessing the Internet. This unofficial access allows them to assimilate new information that may clash with their religious values. The personal virtual adventures of these students are an enigma, because they conceal themselves under fake profiles and shroud themselves in a veil of fear of rejection.

The use of new technologies increases every day in all the Orthodox Jewish organizations and among their members, even if just to communicate among themselves. Every individual who uses a computer or an iPod, even if only for private files, or a cellular phone to communicate with specific people, as advised by the ultra-Orthodox rabbis, needs to be aware of Internet program downloads that run automatically. These individuals also need to learn the universal digital technology language to know how to turn off the Wi-Fi or Bluetooth on their electronic devices. After all, if all download file upgrades are rejected, the device may stop working, and its services will be frozen.

The different types of Jewish religiousness and Jewish education presented in this article do not reflect personal levels of spirituality, faith, religiousness, or individual adherence to certain religious practices. Believers and followers who develop religious identities in their communities, and the rules on the social integration and interaction of their society's members maintain these practices.

The aim of this article is to open a discussion on Orthodox Jewish educational models (without the real need for terms created after the Jewish Enlightenment, like modern Orthodox), and to introduce the subject of the technological inclusion and development of transnational Jewish groups and their global communities, specifically the São Paulo Orthodox Jewish schools.

The importance of revealing the information gathered here represents a small part of the doctoral research written by the author of this article, which shows that the increase in technology has not yet made any significant difference to the professional conveyors of the ultra-Orthodox Jewish communities in São Paulo and their affiliations around the world.

It is important to take into consideration the fact that the author of this article is a community insider, and the main goal in revealing data was as a way to provide self- understanding for the members of this community. Educational, social, and new professional opportunities that can be adopted have been suggested in the doctoral thesis.

At some level, the citizens of Western countries may choose their own guides to follow a model of "selective technological inclusion" and "social self-exclusion," to shape their identities. It is relevant to mention that many Orthodox Jews justify their respect of the rabbis' guidance because they wish to preserve their symbolical religious identity like a ring attached to a very long Jewish chain and not because of religion or spiritual fear.

REFERENCES

Bauman, Zygmunt. *Amor Líquido*. Rio de Janeiro: Jorge Zahar, 2004.

————. *Globalização*. Rio de Janeiro: Jorge Zahar, 1999.

————. *Identidade*. Rio de Janeiro: Jorge Zahar, 2005.

Finkelman, Yoel. "Haredi Isolation in Changing Environments: A Case Study in Yeshiva Immigration." *Modern Judaism*, 22 (Oxford University Press, 2002): 61–81.

Friedman, M. "The Market Model and Religious Radicalism." In *Jewish Fundamentalism in Comparative Perspective Religion, Ideology, and Crisis of Modernity*, edited by Laurence Silberstein, 192-215. New York: New York University Press, 1993.

Giddens, Anthony. *Modernidade e Identidade*. Rio de Janeiro: Jorge Zahar, 2002.

Guertzenstein, Daniela S.S. *The Use of Computers and Internet by the São Paulo Orthodox Jewish Community*. PhD dissertation, University of São Paulo, 2008. Accessed May 23, 2017. http://www.teses.usp.br/teses/disponiveis/8/8152/tde-25092008-164332/en.php

Heilman, Samuel C., and Steven M. Cohen. *Cosmopolitans and Parochial Modern Orthodox Jews in America*. Chicago: University of Chicago Press, 1989.

Lamm, Norman. *Torah U'Madda: The Encounter of Religious Learning and Worldly Knowledge in the Jewish Tradition*. Northvale, NJ: Jason Aronson Inc., 1990.

Postman, Neil. *Tecnopólio: A Rendição da Cultura à Tecnologia*. São Paulo: Nobel, 1994.

Silberstein, Laurence J. "Religion, Ideology, Modernity: Theoretical Issues in the Study of Jewish Fundamentalism." In Laurence Silberstein, *Jewish Fundamentalism in Comparative Perspective: Religion, Ideology, and the Crisis of Modernity*, 3-26. New York: New York University Press, 1993.

Sokol, Moshe Z. *Rabbinic Authority and Personal Autonomy*. Jason Aronson, 1994.

Topel, Marta F. *A Nova Ortodoxia Judaica em Cena*. Rio de Janeiro: Topbooks Editora, 2005.

Talmud Bavli. The Schottenstein Edition Talmud Bavli. 1st ed. New York: Artscroll Mesorah Publications Ltd., November 2001.

Part Three

Zionism—Multiple Dimensions: History, Diplomacy, Politics, and Education

CHAPTER 11

The Beginnings of Brazilian Zionism: Historical Formation and Political Developments

MICHEL GHERMAN

INTRODUCTION

This article will present some of the formative elements of the Zionist movement in Brazil, specifically in the city of Rio de Janeiro. To do so, the analysis will focus on the processes through which Rio's Jewish-Zionist organizations became consolidated and institutionalized. Significantly, these processes were accompanied by the attempts of the first Jewish groups in Brazil, among which Zionists played an important role, to centralize and attain a position of political hegemony.

Fundamental to this examination will be the institutional configuration that arose in the Jewish community in the first three decades of the twentieth century. This article will take as its analytical point of departure the Jewish and Zionist educational structures that were founded in Rio at precisely this period. We will seek to understand some of the foundational and formative processes that marked these groups that defined themselves as Zionist in the city of Rio de Janeiro,[1] as well as the various stages through which they passed in the first decades of their activity.

This article also undertakes an analysis of the effective, possible, and potential connections and political relations that formed between the Jewish and Zionist institutions and groups in the city of Rio de Janeiro and the representative sites of the international Zionist movement. By way of the Zionist movement's representative on the global scene, the Zionist World Organization,[2] whose center of activities in the first decades of the twentieth century was concentrated on the European continent, in particular in central and eastern Europe, this relationship formed (or should have formed) a tendency that was to undergo a transformation in the following decades.

Finally, this article highlights the particularities demonstrated by Zionist groups in Rio de Janeiro between the 1910s and '20s. In addition to the activities organized by European immigrants who had already, back in their cities and countries of origin, begun to relate to Jewish nationalist perspectives, other initiatives also had a Zionist character. Here it is worth mentioning David Jose Peréz and Alvaro Castilho (the former a Moroccan Jew, whose family settled in northern Brazil, and the latter a non-Jewish Zionist sympathizer). By the second decade of the twentieth century, they had founded a newspaper that, despite being "strictly Zionist,"[3] was little known among the official structures of the Zionist movement.

ZIONISTS AND THEIR METHODS OF OPERATION IN RIO DE JANEIRO

With respect to the Jewish-Zionist organizations that arose in the early twentieth century in the city of Rio de Janeiro (and in Brazil as a whole), it is

---

1 Despite the specificities of various locations throughout Brazil, there are similarities and parallels between the different processes with Zionist organizations formed in Brazil as a whole. Some authors thus chose to emphasize Zionist "networks" and not to treat specific questions about the various Zionist organizations in different Brazilian cities. Thus, they discuss Zionist organizations in Rio and São Paulo as a formative part of Brazilian Zionism and of a Jewish "community" in formation. See Nachman Falbel, *Judeus no Brasil: Estudos e Notas* (São Pablo: Humanitas/EDUSP, 2008).

2 I refer here to the Zionist Organization, founded, as the result of Theodor Herzl's proposal, in the city of Basel in 1897. In 1960, the organization came to be called the World Zionist Organization, or WZO, and had as its initial goal the viability and guarantee of Jewish colonization in Palestine, and the creation of ties with Jewish life across the Diaspora. See Arthur Hertzberg, *The Zionist Idea* (Philadelphia: The Jewish Publication Society, 1997).

3 Jeffrey Lesser, *O Brasil e a Questão Judaica* (Rio de Janeiro: Imago, 1995), 81.

important to note that their activities represent a heterogeneous and pluralistic institutional reality. From their earliest years, there were two types of Jewish-Zionist groups, each one with its own distinctive nature, logic, and structure. Adherents of the first of these types defined themselves as "representatives of the national struggle for the Jewish people,"[4] making generalized claims about the group, functioning with the support of the Zionist Organization, being able to send delegates to this Organization's conventions, and having effective contacts with the international structure of the Zionist movement. One can perceive here the beginnings of the centralizing and hegemonic intentions of this group, which sought to determine the political direction and assume the leadership of future structures within the local community.[5]

Yet, since the earliest Zionist activities in the city (or at least since the appearance of an effective body of immigrant Jews in the 1910s to '20s),[6] there were also groups of a more ideological and militant nature. These organizations functioned in a more decentralized manner and had less general and more specific agendas.[7] This Zionist activism had a local nature, arising in cultural and political entities in the cities in which they operated. They established international connections by way of specific ideological perspectives—not just as the result of a general identification with the Zionist movement but rather by way of more singular and specific identities.

In this context, one can cite as examples socialist Zionism represented by the "Poalei Zion" party on the left, and "United Poalei Zion," revisionist Zionism, and

---

4 This concept, as used here, can be found in the newspaper *A Columna*, in issue No. 10, published on September 28, 1916, where there is a reference to "central, representative groups," which appear in contradiction to Zionist groups that have a profile of political action and militancy and a more specific and ideological agenda.

5 I refer here to Zionist organizations in Rio that attempted to maintain contact with the formal representation of international Zionism. In this phase, which Peter Demant calls the "pre-state period," the Zionist Organization presented itself as a "legitimate representative" of the Jewish nationalist, which would echo in the various Jewish communities around the world. In Rio, there were organizations that sought to have formal relations with the Zionist movement and presented themselves as general, centralized representatives of Zionism in their respective communities; Peter Demant, in *Israel-Palestina—A Construção da Paz vista de uma Perspectiva Global*, ed. Tullo Vigevani (São Paulo: UNESP, 2002), 201–62.

6 Lesser, *O Brasil e a Questão Judaica*, 22–60.

7 I refer here to the various ideological positions present in Zionism, which produced political and ideological militancy by way of a variety of political currents. Militant Zionists participated in the daily political life of political parties from an immense variety of political currents. See M. Howard Shachar, *A History of Israel: From the Rise of Zionism to Our Time* (New York: Alfred A. Knopf, 2010), 65–85.

the general Zionists, in addition to a wide range of ideological positions and parties that functioned within (and confronted) the Zionist Organization.

It is, thus, possible to affirm that beyond the central, homogenous structure, Brazilian Zionism became consolidated as a relevant political sector by way of contradictory and complex dynamics, disputes, and debates that show more variety than homogeneity and more conflict than consensus.

JEWISH IMMIGRANTS IN RIO DE JANEIRO: INTEGRATION AND IDENTITY

To understand the formation of the various groups that represented the "communal plurality" characterizing the institutional reality of the 1910s and '20s, it is necessary to understand the waves of immigration that gave rise to the diverse types of Jewish militancy, groups, bodies, and organizations in Brazil.

It will therefore be important here to analyze Jewish immigration since the first half of the twentieth century, especially after the beginning of World War I. This wave of immigration was largely made up of Jews of Ashkenazi origin, coming from eastern Europe, and generally arriving in Brazil with the "assistance"[8] of international Jewish institutions set up to aid immigration.

In the case of the processes through which Zionists groups in Brazil became institutionalized, one cannot ignore the immigrant stream made up of Jews of Sephardic origin, or "Oriental Jews"[9]—in other words Jews of non-European

---

8 As the Jewish community became larger in Brazil, the federal government imposed additional restrictions. During the presidential administration of Epitácio Pessoa, for example, the government insisted that, in order to immigrate to Brazil, candidates had to prove their ability to sustain themselves. Under these circumstances, it is important to understand the centrality of international organizations in assisting Jewish immigration to Brazil, and then creating communal structures in the country. As an example, one can cite the JCA (Jewish Colonization Association), an international aid agency that provided assistance for Jewish immigration and colonization that sent Rabbi Isaias Rafalovich as their representative to Brazil in the 1920s. Rafalovich was an important name in terms of political negotiation and international relocation, and had previously been responsible for a large relocation center in Liverpool. See Lesser, *O Brasil e a Questão Judaica*, 79.

9 The term used here to designate non-European Jews (not Ashkenazis) is insufficient, since the concept of Sephardic Jews is linked with Jews for whom Ladino was a lingua franca, which could include Dutch, Greek, or Turkish Jews. Despite the fact that there were Jews who emigrated from these places in the first waves of immigration to Brazil, in the case of the beginnings of the Zionist movement, we can observe the presence of precisely those non-Ashkenazi Jews who did not speak Ladino. These Jews originated in North Africa and the Middle East, and are called "Oriental Jews" or "Arabic Jews" in the new Israeli historiography. In Brazilian Jewish studies, such categories have not been incorporated, so I choose here to use both these terms—"Sephardic

origin, who arrived in Brazil from the end of the nineteenth century. This migratory group of Jews of Sephardic origin (from North Africa and the Middle East), which developed from the end of the nineteenth century and continued to grow until the beginning of World War I, was termed the "Old Immigration" by Falbel.[10]

The first Zionist groups arose in Brazil in the late nineteenth and early twentieth century precisely in these "older migratory waves," which also included isolated cases of Jews of Ashkenazi origin.[11] These immigrant waves are especially important because, alongside the first traditionalist, religious, and mutual aid organizations, Zionism stands out as one of the few modern Jewish currents to have some expression in northern Brazil.

If one might have expected the Zionist movement to draw Jews of Middle Eastern origin together politically in northern Brazil in view of the region's almost complete absence of Ashkenazi Jews, surprisingly, the Moroccan Jews were the first to correspond with the World Zionist Organization. These Moroccan Jews in northern Brazil were also the pioneers in the formation of Zionist groups, as in the case of Ohabei Sion, which even tried to organize the first financial campaigns for the international structures of Zionism from the city of Belém do Pará.

We may understand and analyze the history of the formation of those Jewish organizations in Brazil that later claimed their place at the helm of the "Jewish Brazilian groups" by examining their various references to belonging and the identities that each group assembled within itself. In fact, in a general sense, the Jewish Brazilian institutional design reproduced the dynamic of community formation that took place in other regions absorbing Jewish immigration, whether in Latin America, as in the cases of Uruguay and Argentina, or in North America, as in the case of the United States.

Jews" and "Oriental Jews"—to refer to Jewish groups of non-Ashkenazi origin. See Ella Sohat, *The Invention of the Mizrahim*, *Journal of Palestinian Studies* 29, no. 1 (Autumn 1999): 5–20.

10 Falbel points out those Jews who participated in communal life, including those who were part of the first directorship of the Colégio de Linha Sionista, or Hebreu Brasileiro. I consider these groups to be members of the old immigration that was connected to the Jews who arrived in Brazil before the end of World War I, or, effectively, before the 1920s. Generally classified by their place of origin, these immigrants were mostly Jews from North Africa (including many Moroccans who came to northern Brazil and then migrated to join communities in Rio de Janeiro and São Paulo), and Ashkenazi Jews from the borderland between France and Germany, in addition to Polish Jews. See Falbel, *Judeus no Brasil*, 343–44.

11 "We know that at the beginning of the twentieth century, in 1901 in Belém do Pará … Zionists were found who corresponded with groups in Europe [the Ohabei Sion group; founded in 1901 by Moroccan immigrants]"; see Falbel, *Judeus no Brasil*, 414–15.

It is important to note that the "Brazilian Jewish collectivity," like other communities in other places that were immigrant destinations, had ambivalent elements in their processes of formation and in their dynamics of communal aggregation, integration, and assimilation into Brazilian society.

Thus, the Brazilian Jewish community was made up of recent immigrants who integrated into the society that absorbed them, by way of gradual processes of assimilation and integration as one of their principal goals, as did numerous other immigrant communities recently arrived in Brazil.[12]

At the same time, the "Jewish-Brazilian community" of the first half of the twentieth century institutionally organized itself via an apparently contradictory dynamic that manifested just the opposite stance. On the one hand, these groups displayed a general dynamic of integration. Yet, on the other, there were very specific ties of ideology, identity, and community, which related back to the Jewish dynamics characteristic of processes of integration and modernization generally connected to Jewish realities of eastern Europe. Such ties proved fundamental to the political, cultural, and identity formation and integration.

Immigrants arriving in the New World brought with them not only hopes for a better future with improved living conditions for the generations to come but also ideas, aspirations, ideologies, and political ventures that included everything from debates about specific themes concerning the Jewish question to viewpoints indicating changes, ruptures, and broader social transformations. Each ideological trend and faction created by these immigrants regarded historical processes through their own perceptions, interpretations, ideological commitments, and intellectual ties. These, in turn, would determine how these groups would intervene in their community and their dynamics of political participation according to the variety of ideological positions that coexisted and competed with each other to gain favor among the Jewish immigrant communities in the city.

Thus, despite recent international historical developments (such as the Holocaust and the creation of the State of Israel), which strengthened the Zionist position among Rio's Jewish community, this should not be understood merely as the product of such developments. Furthermore, it is important to discuss here the configuration of the community and the conditions of Jewish immigration that had been underway since well before World War II, as well as the relations between different Jewish communities and the state, and with Brazilian society.

---

12 For examples of this migratory dynamic in Brazil, see Herbert S. Klein, *A Imigração Espanhola no Brasil* (São Paulo: Editora Sumaré/FAPESP, 1994).

Despite these momentous events, any consideration of the way Jewish organizations are structured—even the attempts to create a community dynamic between Jewish Brazilians in Rio de Janeiro—must include an analysis of the period before the Holocaust and the processes of Israel state formation became viable references, when Zionist forces and entities that identified with Jewish nationalism were already an important force in the Jewish collectivity, itself still in formation.

In this context, and despite contemporary debates that link any development in Jewish history with the perception of an "always present Holocaust,"[13] I propose that we disconnect ourselves from this "colonization of Jewish memory by this event"[14] and initiate a debate about the emergence of Zionism as a force in the Brazilian Jewish collectivity that was not conditioned by the Holocaust, or even by the creation of the State of Israel in the 1940s, but rather by the beginning of Jewish immigration in Brazil as early as the first decades of the twentieth century.

BRAZILIAN JEWS AND ZIONISM: POLITICAL ENTITIES AND MILITANCY

A dual dynamic marked the Zionist movement, established at the end of the nineteenth century. On the one hand, this dynamic included processes of institutionalization and international structuring from which deliberative forums and representative bodies of the Zionist movement arose.[15] On the other hand, the various Jewish communities in formation throughout the world went through phases of political expansion during this period. In this context, Zionism vied for space with other political concepts that became forms of ideological and community expression in the different regions of the world where Jewish immigrants came to settle.

Notably, Zionism was just one of the cultural, territorial, and social formulas adopted within the numerous historical and cultural strategies of the Jewish people. It was successful and managed to expand ideologically through various

---

13 Here I use the expression suggested by Avraham Burg. Despite having used this expression in an essay on the political usage of the Holocaust in Israeli society, it can also be useful in the context of Jewish studies in Brazil. See Avraham Burg, *The Holocaust Is Over: We Must Rise from Its Ashes* (New York: Palgrave MacMillan, 2008), 13–15.

14 Burg 2008.

15 For an analysis of the process of institutional construction of educational structures and international forums in the Zionist Organization at the end of the nineteenth and the beginning of the twentieth century, see Yoram Bar-Gal, *Propaganda and Zionist Education: The Jewish National Fund 1927–1947* (Rochester, NY: University of Rochester Press, 2003).

Jewish communities in the world, later bringing about Jewish colonization in Palestine and, finally, the formation of the Jewish state in this territory.[16]

Such success came about via complex processes of secularization of religious formulas, which were translated into political concepts that were intellectually and ideologically quite well defined. These processes led Jewish groups to adopt clear political agendas with national and political references, coming from a collective that until that time had defined itself by hegemonically religious and cultural references.[17]

Analysis of some of these groups, bodies, and institutions that, by the beginning of the twentieth century, were already active among Jewish immigrants who had settled in Brazil shows how Zionism became one of the unifying ideologies and a communal force at the start of the modern Jewish immigration to Brazil. It is important to note, however, that before Brazil became an important destination for the flow of immigrants, there were Jews who gathered around Zionist groups that presented themselves as available options in response to Jewish demands for modernization and integration.

This process occurred at the same time as the processes through which the Zionist movements themselves recruited adherents at the international level. At the very beginning of the international Zionist movement, groups identified with Zionism were already forming in places that were peripheral to the sites of Jewish immigration.[18] The establishment of these Zionist groups occurred in tandem with other community forces, with various political and ideological orientations. Among these, there were bodies whose perspectives were more traditional, as well as those that took more contemporary political positions and became adversaries of the groups that defended Jewish nationalism.

In this context, the study of Zionist groups and organizations is important for our understanding of the establishment of Jews within the Brazilian reality. As mentioned above, Brazil has many institutions that may be described as Zionist, or at least as Zionist militants, whose members have undertaken a considerable range of political activities since the beginning of the twentieth century.

---

16   See Pierre Birnbaum and Ira Katznelson, eds., *Paths of Emancipation: Jews, States, and Citizenship* (Princeton, NJ: Princeton University Press, 1995).

17   Yaakov Klatzkin, "La Diapora no es Perdorable," in *Fuentes Del Pensamiento Judio Contemporaneo* (Jerusalem: Organizacion Sionista Mundial, 1970), 72–73.

18   See Flavio Limoncic, "Imigração e Identidade Judaica o Brasil Contemporâneo," in *Os Judeus no Brasil*, ed. Keila Grinberg (Rio de Janeiro: Civilização Brasileira, 2005), 253–86.

With respect to the first Zionist organizations at the national level, the foundation of *Tiferet Israel* is especially noteworthy. The organization's early political activities at the outset of the Jewish communal organization in Brazil included the collection of funds under the ideological banner of the Zionist movement, to be sent to the Zionist World Organization[19] in Europe.

Founded in 1913, *Tiferet Israel's* directors, Jacob Schneider, Eduardo Horowitz, Júlio Stolzenberg, Marcos Kaufman, and Max Fineberg, all immigrants of Ashkenazi origin, were members of the "first waves of immigration to Brazil."[20] As an example of the activities connected to the collection of funds for the Zionist movement, one might cite the involvement of *Tiferet Israel* in the visiting representatives of the American Joint Committee[21] to Brazil.

When members of the American Joint came to Brazil in 1916, to undertake financial campaigns on behalf of Jews who had been displaced during World War I, *Tiferet Israel* applied various types of political pressure in order for the Zionist movement (i.e., the Zionist Organization) to receive some of the donations gathered in Brazil. The donations had been intended for the Jewish victims of World War I, and it would not have been possible to carry out two fundraising campaigns in such a small community. After multiple debates and exhaustive meetings, the non-Zionist Jews in Brazil lost the battle, and the Zionist Organization ended up receiving its share, an outcome that represented one of the Zionists' first political victories in the country.

It would be incorrect, however, to think of *Tiferet Israel* merely as a fundraiser for international Jewish nationalist concerns. Such an analysis does not take into account the organization's autonomy and its interest in transforming and controlling the Jewish community in Rio de Janeiro and Brazil. In addition to their fundraising efforts for the Zionist Organization, *Tiferet Israel* operated on numerous occasions in another area—one that

---

19 At this time, donations to the Zionist Organization were transferred by way of an intermediary in the National Fund for Israel (*Keren Hakayemet LeIsrael*—KKL). See Bar-Gal, *Propaganda and Zionist Education*, 16–17.

20 Falbel 2008.

21 I refer here to the Joint Distribution Committee of American Funds for the Relief of Jewish War Sufferers, founded in 1914 by members of the Jewish community of New York to help Jews who had been displaced during World War I. This organization competed for political space and donations with the Zionist movement, which had other interests and objectives; see www.jdc.org.

would have immense importance in the history of Jewish and Zionist bodies in the city, i.e., Jewish education.

In observing the Jewish educational development among other collectivities in Brazil, representatives of *Tiferet Zion* showed an interest in promoting the opening of Jewish schools with Zionist leanings from the earliest years of this institution's activity. Such an interest is demonstrated clearly in the excerpt below of a letter signed by Jaime Horowitz and Itshak Roitberg, respectively the president and the secretary of *Tiferet Zion*, in 1914:

> We report that in the Meeting on the 12th of Adar [March], we thought about founding a Hebrew school, and we considered taking advantage of the Purim holiday to create a fund for this school project … We also nominated as director of this fund for the Hebrew School Senhor Max (Sinai) Fineberg.[22]

Significantly, in the 1910s, Jewish educational initiatives in Brazil were restricted to two distinct tracks. On the one hand, there were school projects that catered to the sons of immigrant "colonists" in communities maintained by the Jewish Colonization Society (JCA),[23] in colonies that were found only in the southern state of Rio Grande do Sul; these schools were neither integrationist nor non-Zionist. In these schools, instruction was based on the Brazilian curriculum and taught in the Portuguese language; in addition, instruction was also given in the Yiddish language, Jewish culture, religion, and tradition.

---

22 From Horowitz and Roitberg to *Tiferet Zion*, 16 Adar 5674 (1914), Central Zionist Archives [CZA] Z3/85.

23 Baron Hirsch founded the Jewish Colonization Association in 1891, with the goal of assisting Jewish immigrants who had the foresight to emigrate from their countries of origin, in particular from Eastern Europe (where, generally, they had suffered oppression and persecution), and to move to countries offering better life opportunities. The JCA's goal was to direct immigrants to countries where there was a demand for them to establish agricultural colonies. The first destinations for immigrants aided by the JCA were Palestine and Argentina. The latter, where the scheme was well accepted by the local government, was part of the goal of Jews coming from a variety of countries.
The JCA also became active in Brazil, and was known as the ICA (around ten years later in Argentina), founding agricultural colonies in southern Brazil in the state of Rio Grande do Sul after 1904. The first colony, Philippson, absorbed some thirty-eight families from Bessarabia. With the apparent success of the first colony, the JCA acquired the Quatro Irmãos estate in 1909, located in the region of Passo Fundo. The first immigrants settled in this colony beginning in 1911 and came from Argentina and Bessarabia. The first years of Quatro Irmãos were promising and, on the eve of World War I, there were 350 families living on the estate. See http://www.ahjb.org.br/ahjb_pagina.php?ap=ica, accessed May 23, 2017.

On the other hand, some Jewish schools had a more traditional outlook. These schools were complementary and operated in cities like Rio de Janeiro, São Paulo, and Belo Horizonte. Such initiatives were similar to the European *chedarim* or the Middle Eastern complementary schools. Here, education focused around religious study, the main objective of which was to deepen the students' traditional learning and prepare children who did not study in Jewish schools for their *bar mitzvah*.

One must take into consideration here the definition of the Jewish school proposed by the documentation of the *Tiferet Israel* organization. It is important to note the importance held by the "school project," as an entity with clear political definitions, as in the case of the Zionist group in Rio de Janeiro. One must also bear in mind the fact that the text of this letter refers not only to the effort to open a general Jewish school. The *Tiferet Zion* activists, on the other hand, sought to establish a "Hebrew School" where the definition of identity was not simply linguistic or terminological, but also defined the broader education of the students, i.e., a Zionist school.

At a moment when both the Hebrew language and Zionist identity were far from hegemonic, in a community where most people spoke Yiddish and did not yet identify clearly with Zionism, this could have been a significant movement. One should remember that the attempt to open Jewish-Zionist schools was not a unique attribute of the Jewish community in Brazil. On the contrary, at around that time similar initiatives were implemented in other groups. One might even imagine that it was the position of the Argentine Zionists, who had the greatest contact with the World Zionist Organization, that gave rise to the first debates about Jewish education in Brazil.[24]

Another Zionist organization in Brazil in the early twentieth century was the previously cited newspaper, *A Columna* ("The Column—*Haamud*"). This periodical had some interesting characteristics that transformed it into a unique case among the first Zionist entities in the 1910s in Brazil. This periodical became a central point of reference for Brazil's Zionist community, while, at the same time, also becoming an important channel for dialogue with Brazilian society.

David Peréz and Alvaro Castilho founded the periodical in 1916, and served as co-editors. *Haamud* was established as the first Zionist entity in a large city, led by individuals who represented peripheral minorities in the Zionist

---

24 This information is based on the letters exchanged between Brazilian Zionists and Adolfo Crenovich, leader of the Argentine Zionist organization. These letters frequently expressed Crenovich's concern about the political and educational formation of Zionist Brazilians. See David José Peréz, *The Central Archives for the History of the Jewish People—Jerusalem. Carta de A. Crenovich* (15 February 1906) [document in Spanish].

movement. (There already were Zionist groups of Moroccan Jews in northern Brazil.) Peréz, who was from Morocco, and Castilho, a non-Jew, launched this Zionist publication, which aimed at being the first channel of communication between Brazilian Zionists and the wider society.

Everything seems to indicate that occupational mobility was the main factor that led David Peréz to move to the federal capital. Significantly, Peréz was not the only Moroccan Jew in northern Brazil to move to the large cities of the nation's southeast. In addition, many children of immigrants followed the same path after their parents' economical situation had improved, and went to study in cities like Rio de Janeiro and São Paulo.

Another unique facet of this newspaper, created in 1916, is that, in contrast with many Brazilian Jewish periodicals that emerged at that time, *A Columna* was written entirely in Portuguese, a fact that demonstrates Peréz's and Castilho's efforts to make the publication an important source of dialogue and information between the Jewish community and the Brazilian public. According to Jeffrey Lesser, the struggle for the "defense of the Jews in Brazil" was a fundamental one for the periodical, or, in his own words, "Peréz founded 'A Columna' with the intention of defending the interests of Jews in Brazil."[25]

The founding editorial of the newspaper confirms the above affirmation, in addition to demonstrating a deep concern over the lack of knowledge of Jews among Brazilians:

> It is not a fantasy to affirm that in our country, with the exception of the cultured classes, people do not have an exact idea of what a Jew is. It is truly haunting, fantastical, what we have been reading in our newspapers with respect to Judaism and its past. Even small historical facts are distorted and exaggerated. For this reason, the main purpose of this organization is to elucidate and explain these faults, to correct them, and to present the Jew such as he is in his religious, social, and political life. This is the first objective, but there is still another one that is, without a doubt, paramount: to establish an internal policy and to entrust in that the exhaustive task of separating the wheat from the chaff. Many people around here present themselves as Jews, but their bad behavior reflects on the whole community, which will never allow them into its bosom. [26]

---

25 Lesser, *O Brasil e a Questão Judaica*, 81.
26 *A Columna*, no. 1, January 14, 1916, 1.

The ideological tendencies in *A Columna* became clear from the very first edition, where the newspaper justified the Zionist identity while praising the leadership of Theodor Herzl, presented here in Portuguese, a rarity in the Jewish community at this time:

> Herzl: In the history of the Jewish people, this name represents the embodiment of the messianic ideal that has accompanied Israel for over twenty centuries. There is not a single Jew who knows the Zionist movement, and who does not have an extraordinary love and an almost mystical respect for Herzl. Even those who have disputed his sublime ideas recognize him as the most notable personality of the race. At the time when Herzl began his work, the Jews were divided into two large groups, well characterized: one where all of the factions could be found, from the reformists to the free thinkers. This large faction was called liberal. They did not want to know about the Past (even if they came from it), and many of their members avoided speaking of their origins. The other faction was more numerous and stronger, but for the most part was made up of elements that lived with a complete lack of culture and in a condition of almost miserable slavery. We can call this the conservative party: exacting in religious subjects, and waiting for someone miraculously to sound the savior *shofar*.

From this, one can infer that at that moment when someone wanted to speak of a nationalist movement, the person would find one that was disheartening and indifferent on the one hand, and ignorance and fanaticism on the other.

How then can we elevate the feeling among this people?

Herzl knew Jewish life well and diligently studied how to raise the spirits of his race, giving it a new, stronger soul.[27]

This excerpt shows the concern that the editors of *A Columna* had about what Lesser[28] calls the "public image of Zionism." The topic of "Jewish nationalism" should not be restricted to the Jewish community. With a certain frequency, the newspaper published explanatory texts, all in the Portuguese language, about the Zionist movement and the development of the international Zionist movement.

---

27 *A Columna*, op. cit., 5–6.
28 Op. cit.

It is clear, however, that at this period there was already an internal debate within the collectivity, where Zionism was just one of the forces that became central references in community activism. Here, the newspaper *A Columna* decided to establish relationships with other Zionist entities, maintaining contact with kindred organizations, as this excerpt of an article written for the newspaper by members of the Zionist group *Tiferet Zion* confirms:

> It is with the greatest pleasure that we publicize the terms of the congratulatory message and praise for this illustrious Jewish society, whose name serves as an epigraph for these lines. It is the first of its kind to express itself with respect to the value and the reasons behind the effort undertaken to create and firmly establish, in the most important social and intellectual center of Latin America, a specialized organization to defend the interests of the Jewish people in Brazil.... We are, as the children of the Maccabees, capable of fighting greater forces than our own; now the struggle is for the affirmation of our national pride, how powerful is the courage that we reveal, and the love for the past and dedication and faith in the truth. Our intention is to change the opinion held today about the Jew in Brazil.... I transmit these lines in the name of Tiferet Sion, in whose name I write. With greetings, from Zion—Max Fineberg, President.[29]

The above excerpt from the newspaper presents discursive references that are typical of the Jewish pioneering nationalism at the beginning of the twentieth century, in addition to exhibiting ideological similarities with the newspaper itself, which was always full of justifications and clarifications. One can thus recognize a clear institutional link between *Tiferet Israel* and the newspaper *A Columna*, which would be consolidated in the newspaper's next issues when its editor was elected honorary president of the Zionist organization. The results of the election in the Zionist Association *Tiferet Zion* were: Julio Stolzenberg and David Peréz were chosen as honorary presidents.[30]

Despite this link, one can recognize that the two entities, one made up of Ashkenazi immigrants and the other founded by a Moroccan Jew and other non-Jews who sympathized with Zionism, remained quite separate from one another. While *Tiferet Zion* maintained direct contact with Zionist leaders (whether from Argentina or from Europe), the directors of *A Columna* did not

---

29 *A Columna*, February 19, 1916, 24.
30 Ibid., May 5, 1916, 12.

have access to this channel of communication. On the contrary, the relationship between Peréz and Carilho was restricted to the local public, to Jews scattered throughout Brazil, as well as representatives of governments and a certain segment of the country's intellectual elite.[31]

Despite the "cultural differences" between the militant Ashkenazis of *Tiferet Zion* and the Sephardic Jews and the non-Jews and Brazilian Jews who were the leading lights of *A Columna*, both Brazilian Zionist entities formed a kind of Zionist unity. Two organizations with similar ideological perspectives and different community functions thus established an institutional front that would try to consolidate the collectivity into a unified whole.

The efforts to recognize the right of the Jewish people to a national homeland would justify both organizations' attempts to create a representative entity that was both Jewish and Zionist. This movement drew strength from the founding of the newspaper *A Columna* in 1916, and would remain after the newpaper discontinued its activities in 1917, when Castilho and Peréz entered more openly into the Zionist organization in Rio de Janeiro. This relationship appears to have remained in this form until the second half of the 1920s.

PERÉZ, *TIFERET ZION*, AND THE POLITICAL STRUGGLES OF ZIONISM

During the time when the newspaper *A Columna* existed, militant Zionism in Brazil was only peripheral, and held little relevance for the international scene. At this time, World War I had dried up the donations that Jewish communities could offer to the Zionist movement—which tried desperately to recuperate its lost territory and reestablish its prior dynamic of financial contributions. A poorly structured, small, and impoverished organization could not attain a position of importance. The movement's internal efforts, such as the establishment of a Zionist school, in the end were fruitless; the first of these Zionist schools would open only in 1922.[32]

This situation would only change substantially during the final phase of the conflict in Europe, at the end of 1917. This process was the result of efforts to gain British support for the creation of a Jewish state in Palestine. An important element in this part of the story was the relationship between Jews in Brazil, in particular

---

31 I refer here to contacts with Brazilian politicians and scientists, as in the case of Dr. Bulhões de Carvalho, who was responsible for the first national population census in the Brazilian Republic; see *A Columna*, February 24, 1916, 26–27.
32 Founded with the name Escola Maghen David in Rio de Janeiro in 1922, David Pérez was the school's first director; see Falbel, *Judeus no Brasil*, 332.

their Zionist movements like *Tiferet Zion*, and the efforts to gain international recognition for the right to a "Homeland for the Jewish people in Palestine," which came to be known as the "Balfour Declaration."

Of particular relevance here was the organization of the group that would come to serve as the official representative of the Zionist movement on the national level. This organization had its beginnings in an event organized on July 14, 1917, in Rio de Janeiro, where the fundamental mission of the "Jewish Congress" was supposed to be "to show national solidarity for the efforts to create a national Jewish state in Palestine,"[33] in addition to seeking to create a specifically Zionist organization in the Brazilian "Jewish community." These intentions were evident also in the final issues of the newspaper *A Columna*, where an article was published in August 1917 with the title, "The March," written by David Peréz, a Zionist activist and the editor of the newspaper:

> Various members of the Israelite colony have gathered in this city to try to summon a great display of national solidarity with their Jewish brothers, now agitating across the world for the definitive and firm reconstruction of their homeland in the territory of Palestine.[34]

This meeting was held in a room in the Sholem Aleichem[35] Library, and included some of the country's most important activists, such as Jacob Schneider, Julio Lerner, Max Finberg, and Sinai Finegold. It is important to note that the newspaper *A Columna* sent the non-Jewish journalist Alvaro de Castilho, the co-founder of the newspaper, as its representative.[36]

Despite the efforts to create a Zionist organization that was national in character by way of the "First Israelite Congress in Brazil," few representatives from other Brazilian states were there, and, effectively, no such institution was created in Brazil during this period. The relationship between the Zionist world movement and the Jewish community thus continued to be limited to a local institution, *Tiferet Zion*, which had only occasional contact with the Zionist leadership. In November 1917, it was *Tiferet Zion* that received a telegram with the famous text of the Balfour Declaration.

---

33 Falbel, ibid., 313.

34 *A Columna*, August 1917. In Falbel, ibid., 311.

35 It is important to note that this meeting occurred when the library had a great concentration of Zionist activists and progressives. A breach between these two organizations occurred in 1922.

36 Since the chief editor of the newspaper, David Pérez, was ill, Alvaro de Castilho represented him and came to express his Zionist positions. See ibid.

CONCLUSION

The 1910s marked the first efforts to structure a Zionist movement in Brazil. By way of a diverse and peripheral community that had few members, Brazilian Zionism ended up being marginalized among Brazilian Jewry. The Zionist leadership established in Brazil at this time was unable to meet the demands of the World Zionist Organization—principally, their request for more financing, which could not be met—ultimately affecting the image of Brazilian Zionism abroad.

Precisely because it was a weakened and peripheral group, Brazilian Zionism established an interesting and unique pattern in the first decades of the twentieth century. The more general and traditional organizations, similar to those that existed in other countries, were formed by European immigrants who arrived in Brazil already as "Zionists." Yet, beyond these more traditional organizations, local Zionism in Brazil would have as its central protagonist a figure who was doubly peripheral, David Peréz. Peréz was a Sephardic Jew, and came from the interior of the country. When he arrived in the nation's capital, however, he would found a periodical and create relationships with Brazilian society, in addition to making contact with Jews all over Brazil. Furthermore, Peréz and his faithful colleague, Castilho, would be pioneers in their thought about the future of the Jewish community, which was established outside the specific, determined sectors.

Peréz and Castilho thought not only about Ashkenazi Jews, Sephardim, Russian, Moroccan, or Polish Jews, nor did they distinguish between those who were religious and those who were secular; the two leaders envisioned a Jewish community that might establish itself beyond the members' individual national origin or religious practice. It was precisely Peréz and Castilho who, with their knowledge of the Portuguese language, would also display their leadership by establishing contacts between Zionist Jews and national leaders, in order to guarantee local support for the demands of a Zionist movement that was more optimistic after the war than at its beginning.

REFERENCES

Bar-Gal, Yoram. *Propaganda and Zionist Education: The Jewish National Fund 1927–1947.* Rochester, NY: University of Rochester Press, 2003.

Bartel, Carlos Eduardo. "Sionismo e Progressismo: Dois Projetos para o Judaísmo Brasileiro." *WebMosaica Revista do Instituto Cultural Judaico Marc Chagall* 2 (2010): 83–93.

Biale, David. *Power and Powerlessness in Jewish History.* New York: Schocken Books, 1986.

Birnbaum, Pierre, and Ira Katznelson, eds. *Paths of Emancipation: Jews, States, and Citizenship.* Princeton, NJ: Princeton University Press, 1955.

Burg, Avraham. *The Holocaust Is Over: We Must Rise from Its Ashes.* New York: Palgrave Macmillan, 2008.

Falbel, Nachman. *Judeus no Brasil: Estudos e Notas.* São Pablo: Humanitas/EDUSP, 2008.

Fridman, Fania. *Paisagem estrangeira. Memórias de um bairro judeu no Rio de Janeiro: Faperj.* Rio de Janeiro: Casa da Palavra, 2007.

Goldstein, Yossi. "Comunidad Voluntaria y Educacion Privada: Tendências en el Seno Del Judaísmo Argentino entre 1990 y 1995." In *Judaica Latino Americana,* vol. 4. Jerusalem: Editorial Universitária Magnes/Universidad Hebrea, 2001.

Lesser, Jeffrey. *O Brasil e a Questão Judaica.* Rio de Janeiro: Imago, 1995.

Sydenham, Lourenco N. "Imigrantes Judeus no Brasil: Marcos Políticos de Identidade." In *Lócus. Revista de História.* Juiz de Fora 14, no. 2 (2008): 223–37.

SOURCES

Archives

Arquivo da Federação Israelita do Estado do Rio de Janeiro

Arkhion Hatzioni Ha Merkazi

Arquivo Histórico Judaico Brasileiro

Periodicals

A Columna (1916–17)

Alef (1994–1998)

Aonde Vamos (1952–70)

Informe Fierj (1987–2000)

Nossa Voz (April 1947—May 1951)

Idishe Folkstsetung (popular Jewish newspaper) (1927–28)

Dos Idishe Vochemblat (1924)

Boletim Comemorativo da Escola Pertez de Santos

CHAPTER 12

The Creation of the Relations between Israel and Brazil from a Pioneering Perspective: Between Diplomacy and Kibbutz

MEIR CHAZAN

INTRODUCTION

In May 1953, the Israeli foreign minister, Moshe Sharett, visited Brazil. In his report to the government following his return from his South American tour, Sharett related that in his speech at the official, festive dinner held in his honor in Rio de Janeiro, he applauded several things that were being done in a similar manner in Brazil and in Israel. A settlement project was being carried out in Brazil, and in Israel: "There, they are pioneers, and so are we; they are a country surrounded by sister nations, but not of the same people, and we are, too." Brazil was a country that consisted of people who came from diverse cultures, and so was Israel. On the following day, the speech was praised in one of the Brazilian newspapers, although the writer noted that the comparison was original but questionable, since the foreign minister did not mention the difference between "us," the Brazilians, and them: "they," in Israel, "turn the desert into a blooming garden, while we turn a blooming garden into desert."[1]

---

1 Protocol of the Government of Israel, May 17, 1953, Israel State Archives, Jerusalem (hereafter ISA). Sharett spoke before representatives of the Brazilian Journalists Association in the presence of senior members of the Brazilian foreign ministry, including Osvaldo Aranha, the Brazilian ambassador to the United Nations who chaired the famous session of the United Nations General Assembly on November 29, 1947. For Sharett's speech and for the program of his visit to Brazil, see ISA, FO 6/236.

There is no need to adopt the teasing, disparaging analysis of the journalist or the unnecessary and stereotypical condescension that Sharett presented to his colleagues in the government of Israel disguised as a humorous anecdote. He added, on the same occasion, a few more disparaging words about "the well-known Brazilian laziness" in agricultural work,[2] in order to focus on what was perceived as one of the main issues on the Israeli agenda at that time — settlement in the frontier areas, and especially in the Negev region. This paper presents a bi-dimensional discussion, which will examine the development of Kibbutz Bror Hayil as a settlement in the northwestern Negev, in which immigrants of the pioneering Zionist youth movement Dror from Brazil concentrated in the 1950s, against the background of the early formation of Israel's diplomatic relations with Brazil. While the focus of the political aspect will be on the Israeli angle, the events concerning Bror Hayil will be anchored in two different points of view: that of the young pioneers, who were preparing for their *aliyah*, and that of the emissaries, who were facilitating the *aliyah* from Brazil on behalf of the *Ihud Hakvutzot Vehakibbutzim* kibbutz movement. The decision to focus the discussion on Bror Hayil stems from the fact that this kibbutz symbolized and expressed the continuous connection and attachment between Brazil and Israel, from both the Brazilian (Jewish and non-Jewish) and Israeli perspectives.[3]

The question presented for discussion here is what we can learn and conclude from observing Israel's national and Zionist experience in the early days of its independence by diverting the historical gaze from what happened in the new centers of the Israeli sovereign civil society and political power, to a combination of peripheral elements not dissociated from the mainstream but which conducted a dialogue with it, albeit from a secondary position. This combination of elements includes a youth movement—which was secondary on the Israeli scene; a kibbutz movement with little political importance; a distant land of emigration, lacking roots in Israel's reality; settlement in a region that was at the margins of Zionist consciousness; and establishing diplomatic relations with a country that was perceived as nonessential for securing the young State of Israel's existence. The implied assumption of this form of observation is that a discussion focusing on what was, admittedly, peripheral, may contribute to an understanding of various components in the general picture of Israel in its early days. Without dealing with these elements,

---

2 Protocol of the Government of Israel, May 17, 1953, ISA.

3 See Sigue Friesel, *Bror Chail: História do Movimento e do Kibutz Brasileiros* (Jerusalem: Organizacão Sionista Mundial, 1956); Avraham Milgram, ed., *Fragmentos de Memorias* (Rio de Janeiro: Imago, 2010).

we could miss important factors in understanding the nature and character of the process of structuring the new nation.

The issues we discuss constitute a layer in the historical writings about Israel–Brazil relations, and about the Jews who emigrated from Brazil to Israel in the second half of the twentieth century. The research of these subjects is in its initial stages. The topics discussed simultaneously touch on several spheres of research concerning the history of the Jewish minority as one of the minorities in the Latin American world, the manner in which Zionism and Israel were perceived in the Diaspora, the annals of the *aliyah* from South America and its absorption in Israel, and the history of the kibbutz.[4] In a key article written by Moshe Kitron in 1971, he noted that the immigrants from Latin America did not receive adequate preparation. This lack of preparation was apparent even in the areas of humor and sarcasm—which attested, in the Israeli immigration society experience, to a somewhat appropriate measure of attention to newcomers— except, maybe, for a pleasant smile on hearing their melodious accent. Kitron stressed this in light of the fact that, up to that time, about 37,000 Jews had come on *aliyah* from South America, compared to 25,000–30,000 Jews who had come from North America. According to his calculations, proportionate to the size of their respective Jewish populations, Latin America's contribution to *aliyah* was at least eleven times greater than that of North America. At a time when the hegemony of the labor movement was still at its peak, Kitron added that the South American *aliyah* contributed to increasing the population of the kibbutz settlement innumerably more than all the *aliyah* from the Western countries combined since the establishment of the state.[5] His words are still valid and appropriate today, and serve as a foundation for our discussion.

The time frame for the following discussion, from the late 1940s until the second half of the 1950s, is somewhat similar to that of the historian Nachman Falbel, who identified the years 1945–57 as one of the sub-periods in the history of Brazilian Jewry. The focus of Falbel's study, however, apart from the establishment of the State of Israel, was the immigration of Jews *to* Brazil (from

---

4 See, in the first three contexts, Donald L. Herman, *The Latin-American Community of Israel* (New York: Praeger, 1984); Raanan Rein, "Waning Essentialism: Latin American Jewish Studies in Israel," in *Identities in an Era of Globalization and Multiculturalism: Latin America in the Jewish World*, ed. Judit Bokser Liwerant, Eliezer Ben-Rafael, Yossi Gorny, and Raanan Rein (Leiden: Brill, 2008), 120–21; Misha Klein, *Kosher Feijoada and other Paradoxes of Jewish Life in São Paulo* (Gainesville: University Press of Florida, 2012).

5 Moshe Kitron, "Oley America Halatinit Beyisrael: Tahalichim, Shlabim Uve'ayot" ("The Immigrants from Latin America in Israel: Processes, Stages and Problems"), *Gesher* 69 (1971): 236–37.

Egypt and Hungary), rather than from Brazil to Israel, as in this study.[6] The historical writing about the Jews of Brazil in the twentieth century is constantly expanding, and it deals, simultaneously, with three kinds of Jews: those who were absorbed in Brazil, those who lived in Brazil, and those who emigrated from it to Israel. Jeffrey Lesser points to the immigration of Jews to Brazil and the complex diplomatic contacts that made this immigration possible in the period between the two world wars, as a basic means for understanding the duality that exists toward the Jewish community in contemporary Brazil. It includes latent and transient anti-Semitic elements, together with a warm, embracing attitude, stemming from the Brazilian mentality and cultural climate, as well as from an inherent interest in Brazilian politics to be portrayed in a positive light in the eyes of the world.[7] I intend partially to adopt the pattern of research discussion suggested by Lesser, albeit with a different objective, which is to examine the immigration from Brazil to Israel, and one of its factors, namely, the formation of diplomatic relations between the two countries. I will place the main emphasis regarding the topic of immigration on observing that part of it that originated in the youth movement and directed itself to the kibbutz.

A common tendency in the research of the history of the kibbutz during the period of statehood is marking the establishment of the State of Israel as a breaking point in the annals of, perhaps, the most original, revolutionary, and humane of the universal contributions of Zionism in the twentieth century. This quest generally prefers to focus on Degania and Ein Harod, on *Hashomer Hatzair* and *Hamahanot Haolim*, on *Hakibbutz Hemeuhad* and *Hakibbutz Haartzi*, on Tabenkin and Yaari. It is clearly reflected in the titles chosen by Henry Near, the most prominent historian of the kibbutz movement, for the chapters of his book, *Rak Shvil Kavshu Raglay: Toldot Hatnua Hakibbutzit (Just a Trail My Feet Cleared: History of the Kibbutz Movement)*. The book discusses the first decade after the establishment of the state: "The End of Pioneering" and "Politics and Crisis."[8] Indisputably, in terms of their status and influence, these were the dominant kibbutzim, personalities, and movements on the kibbutz scene.

---

6 Nachman Falbel, "A Propósito da Periodização da História dos Judeus no Brasil," in *Judeus no Brasil: Estudos e Notas* (São Paulo: Editora Humanitas, 2008), 27.

7 Jeffrey Lesser, *Brazil Vehashe'ela Hayehudit: Hagira, Diplomatia Vedeot Kdumot (Brazil and the Jewish Question: Immigration, Diplomacy and Prejudice)* (Tel Aviv: Loni Cohen, 1997). See also Keila Grinberg, ed., *Os Judeus no Brasil: Inquisição, Imigração e Identidade* (Rio de Janeiro: Civilização Brasileira, 2005).

8 Henry Near, *Rak Shvil Kavshu Raglay: Toldot Hatnua Hakibbutzit (Just a Trail My Feet Cleared: History of the Kibbutz Movement)* (Jerusalem: Bialik Institute, 2008), 422–68.

My claim, however, is that this perspective leads us to overlook a central dimension in the history of the kibbutz, without which a very important component in understanding the value and place of the kibbutz in the early days of the State of Israel, and its role as the bearer of the national message among the Jewish people, is missing. Although kibbutz life at that time was characterized by the tendency to improve the standard of living, preserving the movement framework of mutual guarantee, withdrawing inwardly, and shifting "the center of gravity of the kibbutz to its social destination as the nucleus of the future society,"[9] these represented the reality of only a part, however considerable, of the kibbutzim. The prominent sociologist of kibbutz research, Eliezer Ben-Rafael, pointed to the fact that a negative correlation developed in the 1950s between the processes of growth of the material wealth of the kibbutz and the gradual attrition of its social prestige and its national role as a revolutionary, pioneering avant-garde.[10] At the same time, however, we should note that in the young and gradually ripening periphery of kibbutz life, there were also kibbutzim that flourished, grew, and developed, in those very days, where the main emphasis was placed on pioneering, self-sacrifice, austerity, and adhering to the ideal spiritual life. This ideal lost its glamour, little by little, in the older and more established kibbutzim, and among a considerable part of the most prominent kibbutz activists and leaders. In absolute numbers, the kibbutz population grew during the first decade of the State of Israel from 49,140 persons to 78,634, a modest growth in proportion to the scope of the immigration in that period to Israel, which tripled its population, from 650,000 to 2,000,000. This was not the case, however, with regard to the number of kibbutzim. During this period, 106 new kibbutzim were established (more than half of them in the first year of the state), in addition to the 125 existing ones.[11] This new and young kibbutz periphery nourished and fertilized the kibbutz in a variety of ways, and served as a rousing and challenging element within it. While the pioneering flame faded in a substantial part of the older and relatively developed kibbutz settlements, it blazed anew in Mefalsim and

---

9 Anita Shapira, "Hakibbutz Vehamdina" ("The Kibbutz and the State"), *Iyunim Betkumat Israel*, 20 (2010): 195–99; Zeev Tzahor, *Itzuv Hayisraeliyut* (*The Formation of Israeliness*) (Am Oved, Tel Aviv, 2007), 107–12.

10 Eliezer Ben-Rafael, "The Kibbutz in the 1950s: A Transformation in Identity," in *Israel: The First Decade of Independence*, ed. S. Ilan Troen and Noah Lucas (Albany, NY: State University of New York Press, 1995), 269–72.

11 See Near, *Just a Trail*, 604–607; Henry Near, "The Crisis in the Kibbutz Movement, 1949–1961," in *Israel: The First Decade of Independence*, ed. Troen and Lucas, 245–51.

Gaash, in Kfar Szold and Kissufim, in Lehavot Haviva and Or Haner (and other kibbutzim—these are mentioned, among other reasons, because of their rousing names). In my opinion, the idealistic dreams of the members of the kibbutzim in this periphery, and their struggles to realize them, merit being part of the numerous factors to be considered in the description and analysis of the history of the kibbutz in the first decade of the State of Israel's existence. In order to identify and outline the potential of this way of looking at the history of the kibbutz in the period discussed here—which, of course, is worthy of being studied with a variety of emphases that exceed the bounds of the present discussion—we will examine below the creation of the close link between the Dror youth movement in Brazil and Kibbutz Bror Hayil.

BEGINNINGS

The Dror ("Freedom") youth movement was founded in Russia, in 1911. Its first branch in Brazil was established in the city of Porto Alegre on October 5, 1945. The Brazilian branch of *Dror* was created under the influence of the Argentinean one, led by Kitron; shortly thereafter, branches of the movement were opened in Rio de Janeiro and São Paulo. As was common among parties of the Israeli left, the youth movements associated with them also underwent numerous splits and unifications. Dror merged with the youth movement *Gordonia* in 1952, and was named *Ihud Hanoar Hahalutzi* ("The Union of Pioneering Youth"), and this movement merged with *Habonim* ("The Builders") in 1957, and created the *Ihud Habonim* movement. However, in the minds of its members in Brazil, the movement has always been, and remains to this day, identified by its first and original name—Dror,[12] and this is the name we will use below.

Carla Bassanezi Pinski described the process of the formation of the Dror movement in Brazil, focusing on the local social, ideological, and cultural factors, and relying on an extensive corpus of evidence.[13] Her work is compatible with

---

12 Vittorio Corinaldi, "Shishim Shana Dror, Gordonia, Habonim" ("Sixty Years *Dror, Gordonia, Habonim*"), in *Shishim Shana: Aliyah—Habonim Dror Brazil, Kibbutz Bror Hayil*, ed. Haim Zamir (Bror Hayil, 2008), 9; Haim Zamir, "Reshita shel Tnuat Dror Bibrazil" ("The Beginning of *Dror* Movement in Brazil"), ibid., 13–15; Friesel, *Bror Chail*, 19–20; Shlomo Bar-Gil, *Bereshit Haya Halom: Bogrey Tnuot Hanoar Hahalutziot Me'america Halatinit Batnua Hakibbutzit, 1946-1967* (*In the Beginning There Was a Dream: The Graduates of the Pioneering Youth Movements from Latin America in the Kibbutz Movement, 1946–1967*) (Kiryat Sde Boker: Ben-Gurion University Press, 2005), 28–29.

13 Carla Bassanezi Pinski, *Pássaros da Liberdade: Jovens, Judeus e Revolucionários no Brasil* (São Paulo: Contexto, 2000); hereafter: Pinski, *The Birds of Freedom*.

a common approach in the research of youth movements, as manifested in Shlomo Bar-Gil's book about the absorption of the graduates of the pioneering youth movements from Latin America in the kibbutz movements, and stressing the main elements that appear repeatedly, as a leitmotif, in their history. The first element was the optimistic view of reality that characterized these immigrants, who innocently believed that they were joining the realization of an ideological Zionist-socialist outlook, which was just and worthy from a humane point of view. Second, their unique interpretation of the term "pioneering" as an ideal and, at the same time, as an element that defined their individual and collective identity. Their pioneering was not manifested in innovativeness, nor was it perceived as clearing the path for others, but, rather, it was a strong expression of the extent of their commitment to the realization of the national goals of the Jewish society in Israel, which they valued over personal preferences and interests.[14] The actual embodiment of this kind of pioneering was reflected, in the early 1980s, in around 40 kibbutzim that contained groups of immigrants from South America, who were the core population in about ten of them.[15]

In December 1952, the first of eight *aliyah* groups of the graduates of the Dror youth movement in Brazil, which gave Bror Hayil its identity as "the Brazilian kibbutz," started its absorption there. Bror Hayil was founded on April 19, 1948, and it was the first kibbutz erected in the midst of the Israeli war of independence, and the last to be founded before the declaration of the establishment of the State of Israel on May 14.[16] The kibbutz is located about fifty kilometers north of Beer Sheva and fifteen kilometers east of Ashkelon. Its founders were immigrants from the Zionist movement in Egypt and numbered about 140. Due to economic difficulties, the end of the Zionist movement in Egypt—which had been intended to supply more human resources to the kibbutz—and the split within *Hakibbutz Hameuhad*, to which Bror Hayil belonged, the settlement experienced a severe crisis in 1951.[17] The kibbutz then joined the *Ihud Hakvutzot Vehakibbutzim*, which was created as a result of the split and was associated with Mapai, and was left with only fifty-six members and twenty-six candidates for membership, most from Egypt and the rest from Morocco. In a meeting held on November 26,

---

14 Bar-Gil, *In the Beginning There Was a Dream*, 2, 130, 138.
15 Roberto Soldinger, *The Absorption of Latin American Immigrants in Kibbutzim*, Research Report, June 1981, 3.
16 "A New Settlement in the Negev Controls, Since Yesterday, a Rioting Village which Disrupted Jewish Traffic," *Davar*, April 20, 1948; Near, *Just a Trail*, 380.
17 Dov Rosenhak, *Darki Bibror Hayil* (*My Way on Bror Hayil*) (Tel Aviv, 1988), 43–58.

1951, with the representatives of *Ihud Hakvutzot Vehakibbutzim,* the members of the executive of Bror Hayil (all from Egypt) said:

> Among the followers of *Mapam* who left last year there were many vet-
> eran, active members. Many of those who remained are irresponsible.
> In particular, many women don't want to work, and are here only because
> of their husbands—without whom the kibbutz cannot manage. The mem-
> bers don't want to accept responsibilities in this situation. The immigrants
> from Morocco should not be accepted. They come and leave, and turn the
> place into a transit camp. There is no hope for *aliyah* from Egypt in the near
> future, and so the conclusion is that it is necessary to bring to the kibbutz
> an organized group, preferably not from the Oriental countries, otherwise,
> they cannot survive in this place. They demand the Brazilian Group.[18]

If they refuse to come, they added, then they would be interested in getting other groups, but the members of Dror from Brazil were their first choice. In mid-1952, *Ihud Hakvutzot Vehakibbutzim* decided that the graduates of the youth movement Dror from Brazil would indeed serve as the alternative human reservoir that would enable Kibbutz Bror Hayil to survive and develop. They pre- viously had been intended to go to Kibbutz Mefalsim (near Gaza), and they even stayed there for some time. However, due to the tension that arose between them and the graduates of Dror from Argentina, who constituted most of the mem- bers of Mefalsim, most left, enlisted in the *Nahal,* and were sent for agricultural training, first on Kibbutz Kinneret, and, later on, Kibbutz Afikim. The choice of Afikim was not coincidental, but, rather, stemmed from its character as a large, nondoctrinaire kibbutz, with intellectual openness and economic diversity— elements that suited the mentality and frame of mind of the members of the Brazilian Dror movement, as well as their pioneering aspirations.[19] When *Ihud Hakvutzot Vehakibbutzim* confronted them with the dilemma of either estab- lishing a new kibbutz near Safed or returning to the Negev and joining an exist- ing kibbutz, the members of the Dror movement from Brazil chose the second option. Amir Plot, one of the Dror members waiting in Brazil for his or her turn to come on *aliyah,* relates in his memoirs that, deep in their heart, they hoped for two things: first, that the choice would be Bror Hayil, because of the attraction

---

18 Report of the visit of the Economic Committee of *Ihud Hakvutzot Vehakibbutzim* in Bror Hayil, September 11, 1951, Yad Tabenkin Archive (hereafter: YTA), 7/294/3; visit of the representa- tives of *Ihud Hakvutzot Vehakibbutzim* in Bror Hayil, November 26, 1951, ibid., 7/294/4.

19 Friesel, *Bror Chail,* 57–63; Rosenhak, *My Way,* 66–68; Corinaldi, "Dror," 11.

of realizing the vision of making the desert bloom, and secondly, that they would succeed in changing the name of the kibbutz, which was hard for them to pronounce, since the sound of the Hebrew letter *het* does not exist in Portuguese. In the tone characteristic of the dominant temperament among his associates in the movement, he summarized: "Well, you can't get anything in life... ."[20] But here we put the cart before the horse, and we should first turn to the Lapa Conference, in which the shape and uniqueness of the Dror movement in Brazil were formed.

THE CONFERENCE OF THE DROR MOVEMENT IN LAPA, SÃO PAULO

Numerically, at the beginning of their activity in the 1940s, the Zionist youth movements in Brazil consisted of a few hundred youths in their teens and early twenties. The formal Israeli body that maintained contact with the representatives of the youth movements in Brazil in the early 1950s was the JNF and its emissaries, who were constantly in touch with the Youth and Pioneer Department of the Zionist Organization. In the reports submitted to the Zionist institutions in Jerusalem, the activity of the pioneering youth movements, especially that of *Hashomer Hatzair* and Dror (which turned, in the meantime, into *Ihud Hanoar Hahalutzi*), was defined as "swimming against the current." According to the emissaries' estimates, the Jewish youth of the age addressed by the youth movements numbered about 13,000, and slightly more than 10 percent of them were active in those movements, i.e., 2,500 youngsters, about half of them members of *Hashomer Hatzair* and the other half members of Dror. Although their relative numbers were small, the youth movements were perceived as "the most dynamic factor in the Zionist life of Brazil, with all their weaknesses." The pioneering youth of the Dror Movement were proudly described by the senior activists of *Poalei Zion–Hitachdut* party (the world extension of Mapai) as "intending to accept the great heritage of the Zionist–socialist realization."[21]

---

20 Amir Plot, *Tamid Bitnua: Yoman Ishi Bamasa Hatzioni* (*Always in the Movement: A Personal Diary in the Zionist Journey*) (1998), 43.

21 See, for example, the letters of Yaakov Efrat to the Youth and Pioneer Department, January 3, 1950, February 19, 1950, Central Zionist Archives, Jerusalem (hereafter CZA), KKL5/17760 (the first quote is from here); letter of Itzhak Netter to the Chief Bureau of the JNF, January 20, 1951, ibid.; letter of Fishel Chernia, Y. Petter, and others to the Central Bureau of the JNF, November 13, 1953, ibid., KKL5/21074; K. Charmatz, "The First National Conference of *Poaley Zion—Hitachdut* Party in Brazil, *Davar*, March 5, 1950 (the second quote is from here).

At the beginning of 1949, funded by the Zionist Organization, three training farms were established in the state of São Paulo for the members of Dror, *Hashomer Hatzair*, and *Beitar*, in order to give them initial practical preparation for the collective and agricultural life that they were expected to lead in Israel. On the ideological level, the training farm was intended to reinforce the attachment of the members of the movement to the ideological framework to which they belonged, and to assist in consolidating their outlook on national phenomena and social problems in the Diaspora and in Palestine. It was also supposed to shape their personality, and sharpen their awareness of the link between rendering the Jewish economic life more productive and the patterns of the national Jewish existence. The Dror training farm, which was initially named Itufaba and later Ein Dorot, was located about fifteen kilometers from the town of Jundiai, and about seventy kilometers from São Paulo. Yaakov Efrat, the emissary of the Youth and Pioneer Department, reported to his superiors in Jerusalem about the training farms of *Hashomer Hatzair* and *Dror*:

> One can feel that there is a group of people here who have given up their studies in order to reach their destination. Life on both training farms is vigorous. Plans for the future are drafted, and agricultural programs are established, just like on a kibbutz in Israel.... Of course, both movements have many problems, and the main one is how to delay the process of assimilation, which is advancing fast among the Jewish youth. But the training farm is a ray of light in the Brazilian Jewish environment. Any investment is worthwhile in order to give these youth more possibilities to develop and to influence others.[22]

The establishment of the training farms did not come about without controversy. Due to the limited numbers of youth joining the pioneering movements in comparison to the numerical potential, Bernardo Cymeryng (later known as Dov Tsamir), one of the heads of Dror in São Paulo, maintained that *aliyah* should not be carried out prematurely, and that training farms should not be established at that time. Instead, the youth should stay longer in Brazil, and extensive ideological work should take place

22 Letter of Yaakov Efrat to the Youth and Pioneer Department, February 19, 1950, CZA, KKL5/17760. On the creation of the idea of the training farm, as a central tier in the life of a Zionist pioneering youth movement, see Israel Oppenheim, *Tnuat Hehalutz Bepolin, 1917-1929* (*Hehalutz Movement in Poland, 1917-1929*) (Jerusalem: Magnes Press, 1982), 239–305, 421–500.

among the Jewish youth during that time, in order to increase the number of members in the movement. *Aliyah* should start only after a few years of deepening the ideological education and expanding the circle of activists. The founders of the Dror Movement in Porto Alegre and Rio de Janeiro led the opposite trend. Prominent among them was Yosef Etrog, who claimed that if *aliyah* were postponed, it might never be carried out at all, and, moreover, since the members of the *Hashomer Hatzair* Movement in Brazil were getting organized for *aliyah*, in order to help the kibbutzim of their movement fighting in the war of independence, Dror should not lag behind. Cymeryng consulted on this matter with Yosef Almogi, a senior Mapai activist (and later, government minister and chairman of the Jewish Agency), who was visiting São Paulo. Almogi thought that *aliyah* should be carried out soon, but recommended that Cymeryng stay in Brazil and lead the movement for a little longer.[23] In the second national convention of the Dror Movement in Brazil, which was held in August 1948, the decision was made in favor of establishing the training farm, and the first group of members who were preparing for *aliyah* was formed. In retrospect, it seems that the training farm did not equip the graduates who were getting ready to leave for Israel with the professional and practical tools it had been meant to provide. However, from the individual point of view, staying there was valuable, since it detached the person from the psychological, emotional, and familial obstacles that, up to the last minute, hindered the realization of the crucial step of *aliyah*. For the Dror movement in general, the training farm expressed, symbolically and concretely, the movement's aspiration to create and develop one farming–agricultural settlement base associated with Israel.[24]

Nineteen members, who were part of the first pioneer group of the Dror movement, came on *aliyah* in January 1950. They were first accepted, as mentioned above, by Kibbutz Mefalsim, and in July they were followed by the rest of the first *aliyah* group, which altogether numbered forty-three members.[25] *Davar* newspaper reported that

> the departure of the pioneers of *Dror* turned into a national demonstration in honor of the State of Israel. Many came to the farewell party for

---

23 Dov Tsamir (Bernardo Cymeryng), "As Encruzilhadas no Caminho" (hereafter: Tsamir, "The Junctions on the Way to the Destination"), in Milgram, *Fragments of Memories*, 45–46.
24 Corinaldi, "Dror," 10.
25 Letter of Yaakov Efrat to the Youth and Pioneer Department, February 19, 1950, CZA, KKL5/17760; Friesel, *Bror Chail*, 28; Rosenhak, *My Way*, 72.

those who were leaving, and multitudes of Jews crowded the ports of Santos [the port town of São Paulo State] and Rio de Janeiro, and accompanied with applause the pioneering group of Jewish youth from Brazil, who were going for self-realization in the State of Israel.[26]

As mentioned above, this was the second group that departed, but it seems that an event that had taken place two months earlier was the main reason for the public attention it received.

The main challenge that the Dror movement faced, following the decision of the veteran and senior activists of the movement to immigrate to Israel, was the creation of an intergenerational system that would be self-nourishing and would repeatedly create a new, central team of activists, who would lead the movement until their turn for *aliyah* came, and so on. The actual dilemma was how to integrate the steps that had been agreed upon, of *aliyah* to Israel and joining the kibbutz, as an inherent part of the socialist Zionism in which they believed, within the greater whole of an ideological, mission-oriented, articulated, and binding system. The goal was for members of the movement of different age groups to see themselves within this framework, directly or indirectly, as part of a multifaceted fabric, which laid before them a continuous life course, in Brazil and in Israel alike.

On May 1, 1950, the central group of activists of the Dror movement, numbering about forty youngsters, assembled in order to discuss the question of where the movement was heading in light of the *aliyah* of its first graduates. Because of heavy rainfalls that day, the group could not meet in *São Bernardo* (a suburb of São Paulo), and the gathering was therefore moved to an unpopulated synagogue in Lapa, a São Paulo neighborhood. The guard on duty allowed the group to hold the meeting there, after its members explained to him that they came to protect him from injury by anti-Semitic bodies.[27] It was quite a strange meeting of interests between Judaism, nationalism, anti-Semitism, and socialism. The meeting lasted for three days, and focused on the dilemma presented by Cymeryng, who was later to serve as the internal secretary of *Ihud Hakvutzot Vehakibbutzim* in the second half of the 1960s. At that time, he was the secretary of the Dror movement in Brazil and its dominant personality. Should the central activists of the movement dedicate most of their time and energy to academic studies, and be involved with Zionism and movement education in their spare time, or should they rather devote

26 K. Charmatz, "Events of Brazilian Jewry," *Davar*, July 13, 1950.
27 Friesel, *Bror Chail*, 49–51.

themselves first and foremost to the activities of the movement? The second alternative required most of them to quit their academic studies, if they had already begun them, or to give up their intention of engaging in such studies for the next few years. The basic issue was whether the realization of Zionism meant, for them, *aliyah* and settlement in Israel, or whether it was a theoretical, abstract matter, which youngsters engaged in as part of their leisure culture. Personally, and on the family level, this burdensome dilemma compelled each one of them to decide whether the activity in Dror was, essentially, a pleasant but nonbinding ideological and philosophical discourse, or whether it meant a radical commitment to change their priorities and way of life. Cymeryng, who chaired the lengthy discussions, lost his voice at some point. He had to whisper, as if in a surrealist play, in the ear of David Perlov, his successor at Dror—who later became one of the pioneers of Israeli cinema—and the latter repeated, in his booming voice, the positions expressed by Cymeryng, who was tirelessly demanding that his comrades reach a clear-cut decision— "What do we do now?" Cymeryng's immediate objective was to urge a large group of graduates to undertake full-scale engagement in the activities of the movement, in order to spread its Zionist–socialist doctrine, and recruit new members, in their late teens, to its ranks. His main concern was that the more its members got used to seeing the existence of the State of Israel as a routine fact, the enthusiasm that characterized Dror's activity at that time would gradually wane. He feared that there would be a separation, in their life course between their ideological belief in Zionism and socialism, and the practice of academic studies, professionalization, starting a family, and getting settled in Brazil. On the spiritual level, he wanted to impress on them the idea that Zionism was at a revolutionary stage, which demanded personally from each one of the Dror members an immediate revolutionary decision regarding their future way of life.[28]

After a number of disagreements and crises, the resolution passed at the Lapa Conference was that the movement demanded of its members, excepting three, who were considered to be researchers with particularly promising potential, to dedicate themselves, for the time being, to the activities of the movement, and to relinquish their academic studies. The three exceptions were Vittorio Corinaldi (who was later the chief architect of the Planning Department of the United Kibbutz Movement), Jorja Sussman (later a professor of nuclear energy

---

28 Ibid., 44–54; Evyatar Friesel, *The Days and the Seasons* (Detroit: Wayne State University Press, 1996), 41–42; Pinski, *The Birds of Freedom*, 70–78; Tsamir, "The Junctions on the Way to the Destination," 46–47; Vitorio Corinaldi, "Há Caminhos que Levam de Roma a Jerusalém," in Milgram, *Fragments of Memories*, 128–30; "Testimony of Nuchem Fassa," interviewed by Markin Todder in Zamir, *60 Years*, 20.

at the Weizmann Institute of Science), and Yosef Kochinski (Katzir) (later the director of the premature babies' ward at Rambam Hospital in Haifa). In order to finance their activity, the members were required to undergo a process of "proletarization," as they called it, and find themselves a temporary livelihood, so they could allocate part of their income to a common fund that would help Dror operate. More than twenty members, headed by the leaders of the movement, immediately obeyed the Lapa Conference resolution. This decision aroused angry reactions from many of the activists' parents, who were upset that their children were giving up on the development of their personal careers for vague ideas. Nevertheless, within a short time, the Lapa Conference resolution turned Dror into a weightier factor than would have been warranted by its numerical size in the Jewish community of São Paulo. The movement was now perceived as a body with a clear and decisive worldview, with members who were determined to actually realize the values toward which they were educating the youth in the community, and whose time was fully dedicated to spreading their views, and to fostering everyday behavior that fit their values. It was a revolutionary move in their personal lives, and they felt entitled to be regarded as having actually joined the undercurrents of the Zionist revolution, while still in Brazil.[29] This was conspicuous in a fundamental article, expressing the movement temperament of Dror, which was published in the movement organ a few weeks after the Lapa Conference. The article, written by Nuchem (Nahum) Fassa, later the director general of *Kupat Holim Clalit* (general health services organization), clarified the meaning of the Lapa resolution for the members of Dror:

> We did what was right and what was needed. We and those who feel like us can certainly be satisfied, knowing that we follow the way of the youth who came on *aliyah* before us, who fight, and are still fighting fascism all over the world, the pioneering youth from the Warsaw ghetto, the pioneers of the Galilee, the Negev, and the Jerusalem hills ... and the youngsters who left the Hebrew University and joined the Haganah and Palmach.[30]

"The war on studies," according to Cymeryng, was indeed a difficult decision on both the personal and collective level, "but it purified the atmosphere of the movement, brought its activists closer together, and created uniform

---

29 See the sources in the previous note.
30 Nuchem H. Fassa, "O Unico Caminho," *Dror*, June 1950, in Milgram, *Fragments of Memories*, appendices (unnumbered).

psychological conditions in favor of pioneering." The concrete meaning of *aliyah* and agricultural settlement on kibbutz—following the path cleared by their predecessors, the settlers and fighters—placed this concept within the focus of the movement life of Dror. Although it stemmed from Dror's internal needs, it served as a lever for enhancing its presence in the Jewish community, and helped the movement establish itself in the Brazilian–Jewish landscape as a body aspiring to become "a mass movement," enlisting its activists to recruit more and more youngsters to their ranks, especially for the older age groups.[31]

THE MEETING BETWEEN PIONEERING ZIONISM AND CULTURAL DIPLOMACY

From the end of 1952, the members of the Brazilian Dror movement who immigrated to Israel began to be absorbed by Kibbutz Bror Hayil. A few months later, the members of the movement in Israel and its leadership in Brazil made a joint decision that the new immigrants would be directed only to Kibbutz Bror Hayil from then on. The Brazilian *Hashomer Hatzair* movement, on the other hand, preferred to distribute its graduates among a number of kibbutzim, hoping that it would facilitate their absorption and integration into the Israeli kibbutz reality. Several considerations guided Dror and Bror Hayil in their decision. First, they wanted to concentrate all the activists of the movement, tier upon tier according to their various age groups, in a kibbutz that identified with its method, and was committed to dedicating human and organizational resources to the realization of its outlook in everyday life. Second, they wished to preserve the practical and ideological cooperation between the members of the movement who were already in Israel and their comrades, who were engaged in educational activity in Brazil and in preparing the next groups for *aliyah*. Third, they sought to create a large kibbutz, with many members, which would promote a dynamic, continuous, and long-range process of building links between the motherland and a settlement with clear-cut Brazilian emphases, in terms of culture, mentality, language, and so on.[32]

The decision to anchor formally the link between the Brazilian Dror movement in its various forms and Bror Hayil was taken in mid-1953. At that time, there were indications of a certain wane in the initial enthusiasm that had followed

---

31 Dov Tsamir, "Kavim Ofyaniyim Behitpat'huta shel Hatnua Habrazilait" ("Characteristic Directions in the Development of the Brazilian Movement"), in *Kuntres* (periodical of *Ihud Hanoar Hahalutzi*) 28, July 14, 1956, YTA, 7/180/7 (hereafter: Tsamir, "Characteristic Directions").

32 Ibid.; Tzvi Chazan, *Netivim Vegaaguim* (*Paths and Longings*) (Tel Aviv, 2007), 106–7, 128–31.

the establishment of the State of Israel that was now replaced by the routine of ordinary days, which generated a crisis regarding the concrete meaning of Zionist awareness. As in other parts of the Diaspora, the circles of Zionist youth in Brazil were also burdened by a double dilemma: Did the establishment of the state mean that there was no more need for Zionism? And if, for various reasons, they could not implement their announced plan to immigrate to Israel, were they obligated to leave the ranks of the movement?[33] For Dror, which required its graduates to realize the obligation of *aliyah*, this situation necessitated a constant turnover of the central activists of the movement since the leaders immigrated to Israel with the groups. Numerically, this decision proved to have been justified, since the movement consistently succeeded in producing a new, worthy leadership out of its own ranks, and, at the same time, expanding its activity, as data from 1956 attest. In Argentina, with its 400,000 Jews, there were 23 branches of *Dror*, including 1,222 members, while in Brazil, which had a Jewish population of somewhat more than a quarter of that of Argentina, the Dror movement consisted of seven branches, with 1,020 members. From 1952–56, 378 graduates of Dror immigrated to Israel from Argentina (230 of them stayed on a training farm before their *aliyah*), and 234 came from Brazil (143 of them after staying on a training farm).[34]

The organizational–ideological approach was intended to ensure that a large group of Brazilians would live on one kibbutz, and that they would serve, for a long time, as a means of contact with the Jewish community in Brazil, and as the pioneering and dominant factor of Brazilian Jewry in Israel. This approach was supposed to feed the process of the gradual demographic development of Bror Hayil, and present to the members of Dror in Brazil a real and concrete pioneering ideal. This approach was not limited to the spheres of the kibbutz and the youth movement, however, but rather influenced the process of strengthening the relations of the Brazil's Jewish community with Israel, as well as the diplomatic relations between the two countries. A clear expression of this trend occurred in the areas of formal and informal cultural contact, in which the members of Dror and Bror Hayil played a somewhat passive role. From the perspective of the heads of the Jewish community of Brazil, the activity of the Zionist youth movements was one component in a wider array of Jewish community operations. In the Zionist context, these included the Jewish schools, in which part of the instruction was carried

---

33 K. Charmatz, "Hinuch Vetarbut Bibrazil" ("Education and Culture in Brazil"), *Davar*, February 16, 1953.

34 "Havrey Hatnua Behul" ("The Members of the Movement Abroad"), *Kuntres* 30, July 22, 1956, YTA, 7/180/7.

out in Hebrew, the educational activities initiated by the JNF emissaries, the fundraising campaign for Israel, the yearly Israel Independence Day ceremonies, and the Portuguese language monthly *Brazil–Israel*. This periodical, edited by Berta Kogan, was published in Rio de Janeiro in thousands of copies, and was likened in *Davar* newspaper to "the 'paper bridge' of Messianic times in Jewish legend," connecting "the faraway Brazilian Jewry and the State of Israel." As part of this aggregate, an institute for historical research of the Jewish settlement in Brazil, and another one for imparting Jewish culture, were founded in Rio de Janeiro, as well as the Union for Brazilian–Israeli Cultural Relations, which began operating in parallel to a similar body located in Tel Aviv.[35] Arie Aroch, a painter and diplomat, served as the director of the Section for Cultural Relations in the foreign ministry department of information (and was later Israel's third envoy to Brazil). He noted that the union founded in Rio de Janeiro, as well as its counterpart in Tel Aviv, undertook the role of distributing Brazilian culture in Israel, and not just the Israeli culture in Brazil— quite unlike similar bodies operating in other countries.[36] The sponsors of the rich activity of these unions were senior personalities in both countries. Thus, for example, the Brazilian foreign minister spoke at the opening ceremony of the institute in Rio de Janeiro, held in the auditorium of the Brazilian foreign ministry in the presence of senators and senior public figures. In Israel, the honorary president of the union was the minister of education, Ben-Zion Dinur. Its council included the painters Mordecai Ardon and Arie Aroch; the president of the Technion, Yaakov Dori; the brothers Aharon and Ephraim Katchalsky (Katzir), both professors at the Weizmann Institute of Science; Professor Gershom Scholem; the president of the Industrialists' Association, Arie Shenkar; Minister Yosef Burg; and Zalman Shazar. Binyamin Mazar, president and rector of the Hebrew University of Jerusalem, who headed the Union for Israeli–Brazilian Cultural Relations, reported that as part of the union's activities (which included exchanges of contacts and exhibitions in the areas of painting, architecture, photography, literature, and so on), its members

---

35 See, for example, Z. Ben-David, "Hayahadut Vehatzionut Bibrazil" ("Judaism and Zionism in Brazil," *Davar*, September 28, 1951; letter of the Latin American section in the foreign ministry to the Israeli legation in Rio de Janeiro, May 16, 1954, ISA, *Het Yzadi*-16/2390; Israel Amitai, "Mossad Tarbuti Brazil–Israel" ("A Brazilian-Israeli Cultural Institution"), *Davar*, June 20, 1954; letter of Aharon Faskin, director of the Institute for Hebrew Culture to the Head Bureau of the JNF, November 4, 1955, CZA, KKL5/22478.

36 Letter of Arie Aroch to the Israeli legation in Rio de Janeiro, April 2, 1954, ISA *Het Tzadi*-16/2390.

would visit "Bror Hayil, the kibbutz of immigrants from Brazil, in the northern Negev." Mazar updated the members of the union council:

> The members of this kibbutz, most of whom were born in Brazil and speak Portuguese as their mother tongue, have brought with them a little of the taste and culture of their country of origin, and our intention is to enable the members of the Union to breathe in some of this atmosphere.[37]

As part of the joint activities mentioned above, the well-known Brazilian writer and journalist José Lins do Rego visited Israel in August 1955, and consequently published a series of articles about Israel in the prominent Brazilian newspaper, O Globo (*The World*). His visit to Bror Hayil, which was guided by two Brazilian youths from São Paulo who had become members of the kibbutz, was, in his own enthusiastic words, one of the highlights of his stay in Israel—and not just because they talked to him about soccer, and "entertained him with the warm, human friendliness, typical of a Brazilian home." Through do Rego, millions of readers of the newspaper were exposed to the "kibbutz of the Brazilians," located in the Negev, which served as a model of a way of life in which "humanness, rather than brutality, is the essence, while giving each person responsibility, in a harmonious way." The writer, according to his own testimony, was deeply moved by what he saw on Bror Hayil—there, and not in any other place he visited throughout Israel, not even at the holy sites of his Christian religion in the West Bank. He sealed his ode with the statement that the social life created on the kibbutz was the closest and purest illustration he had ever seen of the Greek word "symphonia."[38]

From the Israeli public point of view, it seems that this cultural activity reached its peak in June 1956, with the exhibition opening of the works of the Brazilian painter Candido Portinari, considered the "Picasso of Brazil." The exhibition took place at the initiative of the two unions for cultural relations between Brazil and Israel, and enjoyed the patronage of the foreign minister, Moshe Sharett, one day before he left his office, on the eve of the Sinai campaign. About 160 of Portinari's oil paintings, drawings, reproductions, and photographs were exhibited for four months, successively, at the Bezalel Academy of Arts and Design in Jerusalem, the

---

37 Letter of B. Mazar and Y. Laron to the members of the council of the Union for Israeli–Brazilian Cultural Relations, April 19, 1955, ISA *Het Tzadi*-16/2390.

38 José Lins do Rego, *Roteiro de Israel* (*Centro Cultural Brasil – Israel*, Rio de Janeiro, 1955), 31–32. The efforts to bring do Rego to Israel lasted more than a year. See Amitai, "Mossad Tarbuti Brazil-Israel" ("A Brazil-Israel Cultural Institution"), *Davar*, June 20, 1954.

Tel Aviv Museum, the Museum of Contemporary Art in Haifa, and the Museum of Art, Ein Harod. In the catalog that accompanied the exhibition, the Brazilian envoy to Israel, Nelson Tabajara, noted that "Portinari is the faithful expression of Brazil." He commended the unions for the cultural relations between Brazil and Israel, which understood that "no other Brazilian artist can surpass him, both in terms of his level and in terms of his ability to be the faithful interpreter of all those things that make Brazil and its people so different from all the other nations of the American continent."[39] Portinari stayed in Israel for ten days on the occasion of the opening of his exhibition at Bezalel. He traveled to various places, and, on leaving, said that "on Kibbutz Bror Hayil, with its immigrants from Brazil, I felt at home" (he also gave the kibbutz one of his paintings as a gift), but added politely that "everywhere in Israel I felt at home." Following his visit, in December 1957, a book of paintings and drawings, based on his experience in Israel, was published, and it concluded with an impressive painting of kibbutz life.[40]

However, daily life on the dull frontier of the northern Negev lacked the luster of visiting dignitaries. Two days after Sharett reported to the government about his visit to Brazil, the executive of Bror Hayil asked the executive of *Ihud Hakvutzot Vehakibbutzim* for an urgent addition of buildings for the growing population of the immigrants of the Dror movement from Brazil. The request specified that the kibbutz had 118 members, who lived in 15 wooden shacks, comprising 38 housing units, and only 3 buildings, which included 12 housing units.[41] Throughout the 1950s, the prominent activists of Bror Hayil urged the bodies of the Jewish Agency that were in charge of new settlements, and the authorities of *Ihud Hakvutzot Vehakibbutzim*, to solve the burdensome housing problem, arguing that their kibbutz was "an absorbing, creative, and developing kibbutz, which serves as an educating model of *aliyah* from the South American countries." In a letter written in March 1956, Dov Tsamir, the kibbutz secretary

39 "Tzayar Brazilai Leyisrael" ("A Brazilian Painter to Israel"), *Davar*, April 19, 1956; "Taaruchat Portinari Nifteha Biyerushalayim" ("Portinari Exhibition Openedin Jerusalem"), ibid., June 17, 1956; "Nifteha Taaruchat Hatzayar Portinari" ("The Exhibition of the Painter Portinari Opened"), ibid., July 23, 1956; Nelson Tabajara, "Hakdama" ("Introduction"), in Portinari, *Tziurey Shemen Verishumim* [*Oil Paintings and Drawings*] *1940-1956* (Association of Museums in Israel, Israel, 1956). In May 1956, an exhibition with a similar format, of Brazilian architects, took place at the Bezalel Academy, sponsored by the unions for cultural relations between Brazil and Israel. On that occasion, a painting by Portinari was given to Bezalel as a gift. "Nifteha Taaruchat Architectim Brazilit" ("An Exhibition of Brazilian Architects Opened"), *Davar*, May 15, 1955.

40 "Hatzayar Portinari Azav et Haaretz" ("The Painter Portinari Left the Country"), *Davar*, June 26, 1956; Candido Portinari, *Israel* (New York, 1957), 141.

41 Letter of the Bror Hayil executive to the executive of *Ihud Hakvutzot Vehakibbutzim*, May 19, 1953, YTA, 7/294/4.

and its dominant personality, stated emphatically that Bror Hayil was "the first kibbutz of Brazilian Jewry, and, as of now, is the only address for this Jewish center, which enables us to attract a continuous stream of movement members, as well as relatives of our young members." In this spirit and "without excessive arrogance," he and his comrades demanded that the settling bodies examine their situation not according to the regular standards, but, rather, in light of the great opportunity presented by Bror Hayil serving as "a very serious center of attraction" for pioneering immigrants from Brazil, considering that "the people and the vision are there."[42] An indication of this was the swift increase in the population of Bror Hayil, despite the fact that the members of the Egyptian group were leaving one after the other. The kibbutz grew from 201 persons in 1955 to 471 in 1958, with an anticipated addition of 90 more in 1959. Its inhabitants nurtured the vision of developing a large-scale kibbutz in the Negev from the immigrants of the Brazilian Dror movement, like Afikim or Givat Brenner, with more than a thousand members. Tsamir and Nahum Fassa, the farm manager, utilized the leitmotif of "the Brazilian Kibbutz" to the utmost, as an argument for additional investments and grants being given to Bror Hayil. In a letter that they sent simultaneously to Levi Eshkol, the finance minister and head of the Department of Settlement of the Jewish Agency, and to Giora Yoseftal, the minister of labor, in June 1960, they wrote:

> Today we cannot accept applicants from Brazil or from Israel. This month, for example, we expect fifteen people from Brazil and four families from Israel who asked to join us, and many more will follow them. We do not know how to accommodate them. It is important to stress that it is not just that the kibbutz needs these people for its existence and development, but also, these people from Brazil, and others like them, can be absorbed now only on Bror Hayil, and about the importance of *aliyah* and absorption from South America there is, certainly, no need to elaborate.[43]

---

42 See, for example, letter of the executive of Bror Hayil to Raanan Weitz, director of the Department of Settlement of the Jewish Agency, January 16, 1956, YTA, 7/52/11; letter of Dov Tsamir, secretary of Kibbutz Bror Hayil, to Bassin, the Technical Department of the Jewish Agency, March 12, 1956, ibid.; Ephraim Bariah, the executive of Bror Hayil, to Raanan Weitz, September 29, 1956, ibid., 7/52/12; letter of Nahum Fassa, farm manager of Bror Hayil to Miriam Altmann, the Economic Committee of *Ihud Hakvutzot Vehakibbutzim*, April 21, 1960, ibid., 7/160/4.

43 Letters of Dov Tsamir and Nahum Fassa to Levi Eshkol and to Giora Yoseftal, June 9, 1960, YTA, 7/160/4; report of the Economic Committee of *Ihud Hakvutzot Vehakibbutzim* about its visit to Bror Hayil, July 16, 1957, ibid., 7/52/12. The local economic and social aspects

CONCLUSION

The tension between the sublime and romantic idealistic dream of creating a worthy and just lifestyle and life patterns, and the hard, meager rural reality, was an inseparable part of the process of the realization of Zionism, and was easily discernible by anyone who visited Bror Hayil in the 1950s. However, the Brazilian Dror movement members' personal and group ability to struggle with the challenges of the time and overcome the obstacles lurking on the sidelines was conditional on and reinforced by the cultural background and social temperament—the products of "the motherland"— which they had brought with them, and which united them in a single living environment on Bror Hayil. In the 1950s, about 470 members of Dror movement immigrated to Israel, and around 300 of them were absorbed in Bror Hayil. They constituted a considerable part of the Jewish immigration from Brazil to Israel during that period.[44]

In 1952, when the monthly *Brazil–Israel*, the prominent periodical of the Jewish community, marked two years of publication, several of the Israeli government ministers sent letters of congratulation. Yosef Burg, a member of *Hapoel Hamizrahi* party and the minister of health, who had visited Brazil in 1951, said in his greeting:

> Although Brazil has a great political tradition, nevertheless, its tasks in building its country have a distinctive "pioneering" character, meaning that only by devoting all the energy to the constructive projects of drying the swamps, eradicating illiteracy, and annihilating disease, especially tropical diseases, can settling the land be promoted. In this mission, which I called by its Hebrew name *halutziyut* ["pioneering"], there is something in common between the State of Brazil and the

---

of the reality on Bror Hayil go beyond the scope of our discussion in the present paper, and dealing with their actual context is basically trivial, since such problems were, naturally, common in any kibbutz settlement.

44 Ibid.; Pinski, *The Birds of Freedom*, 88. There is substantial disagreement between the data of different bodies concerning the extent of *aliyah* from Brazil during the period under discussion. While, according to Kitron, who relies on the data of the Jewish Agency, the *aliyah* from Brazil between May 1948 and December 1961 included about 1,600 persons, according to the Central Bureau of Statistics, only about 1,060 Jews came to Israel from Brazil between 1948 and 1960. See Kitron, "The Immigrants from Latin-America in Israel," 241; *The Central Bureau of Statistics*, vol. 57 (Jerusalem, 2006), 238–39.

State of Israel, and the Jews who live in the land of Brazil can play an important role in the contacts between the two countries, by exchanging information and experiences.[45]

Sharett (who also published a letter of congratulation in the same issue) probably took his comparison between Brazil and Israel, quoted in the beginning of this paper, from here. At around the same time, Sprinzak, the Speaker of the Knesset, wrote to Yosef Perlmutter, who was about to go to Argentina as an emissary. Perlmutter was a member of Kibbutz Mefalsim, which had absorbed immigrants from Argentina. Sprinzak wrote that "we need, once again, a new cycle of pioneering *aliyah*, a stream of daring young forces, who, together with our native Israelis, will attack all the difficulties of the historic mission [the establishment of the State of Israel], and invigorate all the active forces in Israel and among the Jewish people." He estimated that "of all the countries and places of dispersion that have been left to the Jewish people ... the only source today from which a stream of pioneering *aliyah* can and should erupt is South American Jewry." Sprinzak felt that the pioneering immigrants "should rise and renew the days of the Second and Third *Aliyah*—without questions or conditions they will come, toil, and highly elevate the message of the redemption of the people."[46] In this manner, as noted above in the wake of the Lapa Conference, Nahum Fassa described the spirit surging among the members of Dror, and the historical sequence that illuminated their decision to abandon their academic studies on the way to realizing two missions—*aliyah* and kibbutz. At the same time, Sharett's statement regarding the unique quality inherent in the pioneering youth from South America, as well as that of Sprinzak quoted above, did little to refute Ben-Gurion's disparaging remark that, in fully representing the life and place of the kibbutz in the Israeli society in the first decade of the existence of the State of Israel, he was "deeply ashamed" of the kibbutz movement because of the excessive focus on the politically left turn taken by *Hakibbutz Hameuhad* and *Hakibbutz Haartzi*. Following the Holocaust, the ability to mobilize pioneering efforts dissipated, and the establishment of the State of Israel marked the beginning of the end of the pioneering driving force that had pushed Zionism to its political and social

---

45 Letter of Yosef Burg to the editorial board of the monthly *Brazil–Israel*, February 6, 1952, *Brazil-Israel*, April 1953.

46 Letter of Sprinzak to Yosef Perlmutter, December 20, 1951, in Sprinzak, *Letters*, vol. 3, 46–47.

achievements. However, the pioneering urge continued to make ripples at the geographically remote ends of the Zionist reality. This source of pioneering energy was utilized only to a limited degree; among other reasons, because the revolutionary and pioneering emphases were constantly being eroded in the process of shaping the Labor movement.

In the context of the discussion of the great *aliyah* of the 1950s, it is appropriate, therefore, to clarify. These historical events teach us that even when—according to the evaluation of senior activists at the top political echelon of the Labor movement—there was a pioneering human reservoir that could have been developed and expanded according to the circumstances of that time in a manner that clearly and directly would have benefited the realization of the worldview of the kibbutz and the Labor movement, it was done only covertly. The real gap between the knowledge and understanding in principle, and the actual ability to realize the promising potential of the pioneering *aliyah* from South America in general, and from Brazil in particular, seems to indicate that there is a need for "more caution, less arrogance, and a lot more intellectual modesty" than what has become common in academic research regarding the description and analysis of the hidden desires, the statements made in documented forums, and the operational steps taken, in the area of *aliyah* from various countries in the 1950s. These patterns of thought and conduct were precisely those that Dov Tsamir, the "prophet" of the Dror revolution in the 1950s, asked to adopt when examining the bridge that was being built between Jewish communities in the Diaspora—in Brazil, in this case—and Israel since, through that bridge and relying on those patterns, "the great reservoir, from which the country will draw its powers," was going to be created. Tsamir spoke in a symposium about Israel and the North and South American Jewry that took place at the Hebrew University in early May 1967, when the imminent war was not yet visible on the horizon.[47]

Two years later, in May 1969, sixteen years after Sharett's visit to Brazil, the eighty-two- year-old Ben-Gurion also visited. Ben-Gurion used to apologize, at the beginning of his speeches in Rio de Janeiro and São Paulo, for the fact that he did not understand what had been said before his turn to speak came, since it was usually in Portuguese. He noted that even a Jew could not understand the languages of all peoples. Ben-Gurion, who had a great fondness for studying

---

47 "Israel Likrat Tafkideha Batfutzot" ("Israel Facing Its Tasks in the Diaspora"), a conference held at the Hebrew University of Jerusalem on May 2–3, 1967, *Bitfutzot Hagola* (Winter 1968), 81.

a variety of languages, never learned Portuguese. In a speech he delivered at a public assembly at the "Hebraica" club in Rio de Janeiro on May 19, Ben-Gurion said, in a similar spirit to that of the words of Dov Tsamir, two years earlier, that the integrity of the Jewish people depended on the intimate relations that Jewish communities in the Diaspora would maintain with Israel. A sociologist once asked—Ben-Gurion told his listeners—whether distinguished scientists, such as Albert Einstein, for example, would be willing to immigrate to Israel, or whether they would prefer America, England, or France. Ben-Gurion answered: "there are those who want to receive and enjoy, and those who want to create and give."[48] These words of Ben-Gurion were accurately relevant to the personal choice and to the decisions made by the members of Dror movement in Brazil in the 1950s.

---

48 "Speech of MK David Ben-Gurion while Visiting Brazil," May 18–25, 1969, BGA, Division of Speeches and Articles.

CHAPTER 13

The World Jewish Congress, the Jews of Argentina, and the Military Junta, 1976–83

Yitzhak MUALEM

INTRODUCTION

This study examines the impact of the World Jewish Congress (WJC), a non-state entity, in the international arena, in relation to the central roles played by Israel and Argentina, as sovereign states, in shaping the character and nature of the processes in this arena. The research issue examined here is the extent of influence of nongovernment organizations (NGOs) on world politics in an area where the state is the key player.

Our focal point is the extent of the WJC's ability and scope of activity as an NGO in the inter-state sphere, in comparison to that of a sovereign state, and whether the activities of the WJC, as a cross-national organization, are characterized by its influence in the areas on its political agenda, and its ability to arouse international public opinion, and to create coalitions and a communications system between different elites. In the context of the case study here, the research question posed is whether, to what extent, and in what way, the WJC had any impact on the status and welfare of the Jews of Argentina from 1976–83, during the regime of the military junta.

The World Jewish Congress, as a non-state entity, operates within the extensive field of Jewish politics in humanitarian and political aid worldwide. This organization has widespread ties with institutes and governments all over the world: in the West (United States and western Europe), the East (Russia and CIS), among third-world countries, and Arab countries.[1] These relations

---

1 Avi Beker, "Sixty Years of Diplomacy of the World Jewish Congress," *Gesher* (Journal of Jewish Affairs) [Heb], 42, no. 132 (1996–97): 11–25; *Protocol Du Premier Congrès Juif*

serve the WJC in its activities on behalf of Jewish communities around the world in providing material, political, and cultural aid.

The WJC commenced its activities as an international Jewish organization in the 1930s. Shortly after its inauguration, it was already lending assistance to the Jews of the world in general and the Jews of Europe in particular by assisting German Jews under the Nazi regime.[2] Its activity continued throughout World War II and intensified after the war, with an agenda of rescuing and rehabilitating Holocaust survivors. After the establishment of the State of Israel, the WJC focused on aiding Jewish communities in Arab countries, in North Africa, Ethiopia, the Soviet Union, South America, and elsewhere.

Nahum Goldmann, WJC President from 1949 to 1977, described the nature of the organization's activities and its goals:

> First, as giving real content to the abstract notion of the unity of the Jewish people and to use its leverage to achieve this goal in practice; second, to ensure cooperation between all parts of the Jewish people anywhere in the diaspora, over their common issues.[3]

As a worldwide Jewish organization representing the Jewish communities of the world, the WJC placed on its agenda the constitution of a framework for Jewish communities around the world to converge and act collectively for Jewish survival, materially, spiritually, and culturally. Such a policy was enabled by the existence of the WJC as a trans-state, nongovernmental organization, which allowed it to operate beyond territorial boundaries.[4] This capacity was implemented in WJC activities for Moroccan Jews in the 1950s, for the Jews of Algeria in the early 1960s, and for Soviet Jewry from the late 1960s to the early

---

Mondial (Geneva: Le Comité Exécutif, 1936); *Congress 50th Jubilee 1936–1986* (Jerusalem: WJC, 1986); Leon A. Kubovitzki, *Unity in Desperation* (New York: Institute of Jewish Affairs, 1948); Itzhak Mualem, "The WJC: Influence Without Power," *Jewish Culture and History* 5, no. 2 (Winter 2002): 95–113.

2   Elizabeth Apler, "Rescue and Aid Missions between 1933–1945 by the World Jewish Congress," *Gesher* 16, nos. 2–3 (1970): 173–207; Avi Beker, "Diplomacy without Sovereignty: Rescue Missions of the World Jewish Congress," in *National Jewish Solidarity in the Modern Period* [Heb], ed. Benjamin Pinkus and Selwyn Ilan Troen (Kiryat Sdeh Boker: Ben-Gurion University, 1988), 304–18.

3   Nahum Goldmann, *Memories* [Heb] (Jerusalem: Weidenfeld and Nicolson, 1969), 114.

4   Robert O. Keohane and Joseph S. Nye, *Power and Interdependence* (Boston: Little Brown and Company, 1977), 25; Samuel Huntington, "Transnational Organizations in World Politics," in *Perspectives on World Politics*, ed. Richard Little and Michael Smith, 2nd ed. (New York: Routledge, 1991), 212–28.

1980s.[5] This capacity was also put to use in the struggle on behalf of the Jews of Argentina from 1976–83, during the regime of the military junta.

In the context of this study, we argue that as concern increased regarding the junta regime adopting an official collective anti-Semitic policy, thus grew the tendency among leaders of the WJC to adopt a peaceful and cooperative diplomacy both vis-à-vis the junta regime and the Jewish organizations, *Delegación de Asociaciones Israelitas Argentina* (DAIA), and *Amit Asociacion Mutual Israelita Argentina* (AMIA). Moreover, this study argues that, as a federal organization, the WJC tended to cooperate with the Jewish organizations in Argentina according to the objectives defined by the leaders of the local community.

Argentinean society is characterized by two major approaches regarding Jews: the liberal approach, which allows Jews to integrate into Argentinean society; and the conservative approach, whose prominent component is anti-Semitism as propagated by the Catholic church.[6] However, in this case it should be noted that anti-Semitism was not collective but expressed on the individual level.[7] Shmuel Ettinger distinguishes between these two levels of anti-Semitism. He claims that European nations sometimes directed anti-Semitism against the individual and sometimes against all Jews. Such a policy had an impact on the very existence of the Jewish collective in that particular country, as was the case in Russia during the latter half of the nineteenth, and the twentieth century, and in Germany in the 1930s and '40s. In this context, Haim Avni suggests an additional classification. He claims that the anti-Semitic policies in Argentina can be viewed on three levels.[8]

---

5 Yitzhak Mualem, *The Global Politics of the World Jewish Congress* [Heb] (MA thesis, Bar-Ilan University, 1988); Shneor Lowenberg, "The World Jewish Congress—Success or Failure?" *Gesher* [Heb] 113, no. 2 (1986): 42–44.

6 Garciela Ben-Dor, "Three Antisemitic Priests in the Catholic Church: Deviation or Norm," in *Society and Identity in Argentina*: The *European Context, ed.* Zvi Medin and Raanan Rein (*Tel Aviv*: Ibero-America and the School of History, Tel Aviv University, 1997), 231–67; *Haim Avni, "Anti-Semitism in Argentina: Dimensions of Danger," in Medin and Rein, Society and Identity in Argentina,* 168–97.

7 Shmuel Ettinger, *Anti-Semitism in the Modern Era* [Heb] (Tel Aviv: Moreshet Sifriyat Poalim Hakibbutz Ha-artzi, 1989), 223–40; Yaakov Reuveni, "On Anti-Semitism: Concept and Theory," *Gesher* [Heb] 134 (1996): 64–73.

8 Haim Avni, *From the End of the Inquisition to "Law of Return"—The History of Jewish Immigration to Argentina* [Heb] (Jerusalem: Magnes Press, 1985), 109; Efraim Zadoff, "The Jews of Argentina: Achievements, Challenges and Uncertainty," *Gesher* [Heb] 141 (2000): 79–93; Haim Avni, "Antisemitismo en Argentina: Los dimensiones del peligro," in *El Legado Del Autoritarismo,* ed. Leonardo Senkman and Mario Sznajder (Jerusalem: Instituto Harry Truman–Universidad Hebrea de Jerusalem, 1995), 197–216.

First, anti-Semitism can be seen as a popular phenomenon, initiated by the unorganized public out of religious and social hatred, commonplace among the non-Jewish society. The second level, of institutionalized anti-Semitism, originated from organizations and institutions operating against Jews as individuals and as a collective. At the third level, anti-Semitism was the outcome of deliberate government policy, which differentiated between individually directed and collective anti-Semitism.[9]

The junta regime persecuted young Argentinean Jews who were members of left-wing groups like the People's Revolutionary Army, *Ejército Revolucionario del Pueblo* (ERP), and the Montoneros.[10] To this, we should add the anti-Semitism in Argentina at the time, which originated in the government and was directed mostly at individuals. This meant that despite the above, Jewish life and Jewish institutions continued to exist unabated. Yet, the WJC was apprehensive of any step that would make the community's situation worse, and therefore strived to bring about a positive change in the policy of the military regime while refraining from any act that would induce the anti-Semitic policy to revert from an individually based one to a collective one against the Jews.[11]

The structure of the WJC as a democratic, federal organization granted each member organization full authority for activity in its own country. Thus, the WJC accepted the guidelines laid down by the Jewish organizations in Argentina and acted accordingly. The DAIA, as the umbrella organization of the Jewish communities in Argentina, is a federal body representing the community organizations operating in Buenos Aires and other city provinces in Argentina. As such, it gives expression to all the organizations in making

---

9   Haim Avni, *Emancipation and Jewish Education* (Jerusalem: Zalman Shazar Center, 1986); Haim Avni, Government Anti-Semitism in Argentina?" in *Anti-Semitism through the Ages* [Heb], ed. Shmuel Almog (Jerusalem: Zalman Shazar Center, 1980), 323–42; Aharon Vinias, "Analysis of Anti-Semitism in Argentina," *Bi-tfutzot Ha-Gola* [Heb] 81–82 (1977): 134–47; Aharon Vinias, "Jewish Presence and Identity in Argentina," *Bi-tfutzot Ha-Gola* 83–84 (1978): 144–62.

10 Raanan Rein, "The Miracle that Never Occurred: The Return of Peronism to Power in Argentine, 1973–1976," *Zmanim* [Heb] 71 (Summer 2000): 66–93; MargerateFeitlowitz, "Codigos Del Terror: Argentina y Los Legados De Lu Tortura," in *El Legado Del Autoritarismo*, ed. Senkman and Sznajder, 79–94.

11 Collective anti-Semitism was implemented earlier by President Isabel Péron and Jose Vega, her right-hand man; see Luis Roniger and Mario Sznajder, "Military Rule and Politics in Argentina in the Twentieth Century against the 1976–1983 Events," in *The Israeli Inter-Ministerial Commission Inquiry into the Case of the Jewish Vanished under Military Dictatorship in Argentina* (Jerusalem: The Foreign Office and the Ministry of Justice, July 2003),17–35; Avni, *Emancipation and Jewish Education*, 154; Laster A. Sobel, *Argentina and Peron 1970–1975* (New York: Facts On File Inc., 1975),149–52.

decisions and setting policy. A president and deputies, who implement the organization's policy, head the DAIA.

THEORETICAL FRAMEWORK

The international reality is characterized by a varied web of relationships based on ties between states and between non-state units. This phenomenon has implications for the nature of the institutions and processes in the global political arena. The non-state units maintain autonomy in their activities in this arena, and occasionally are able to influence areas of activity they share with state units.

Tools from two central theoretical approaches in international relations will be applied in this study. The first, political realism, focuses on the objectives, power, and function of the state actor.[12] The second, complementary approach of neo-liberalism focuses on the complex and comprehensive relations governing world politics. This approach focuses on the activity, impact, and contribution of nongovernmental entities operating in this arena and their impact on nonmilitary existential areas.[13]

Political realism is based on a state-centric view of international politics. The nation-state is the key player in the international arena, doing its best to realize its self-defined national interest. Political realism has three basic assumptions. First, states operate as rational units and constitute the dominant players in world politics. Second, empowerment is the effective tool for the global political arena. Third, mutual interactions between states are founded on constant struggle. Therefore, states aim to increase their power so that they can survive in an anarchic existential power struggle between states.[14]

The political logic underlying this theoretical approach is that states operate out of a desire to exist and survive as independent, sovereign entities in the international system. Thus, their aim is to enhance their relative power. A state checking its own empowerment will not survive and will be defeated by other

---

12 See the six principles of classical political realism in Hans Morgenthau, *Politics Among Nations*, trans. Yosef Nedavah, vol. 1 (Tel Aviv: Yachdav, 1968), 1–16.

13 Donald J. Puchala and Raymond F. Hopkins, "International Regimes: Lessons from Inductive Analysis," *International Organization* 36, no. 2 (Spring 1982): 245–75; Oran R. Young, "Regime Dynamics: The Rise and Fall of International Regimes," *International Organization* 36, no. 2 (Spring 1982): 277–97; Joseph S. Nye, "The Changing Nature of World Power," *Political Science Quarterly* 105, no. 2 (1990): 177–92; Stephan D. Kresner, "Global Communication and National Power: Life on Pareto Frontier," *World Politics* 43 (April 1998): 336–66.

14 Richard Mansbach and John Vasquez, *In Search of Theory: A Paradigm for Global Politics* (New York: Columbia University Press, 1981), 5.

states in the existential international struggle. Therefore, sovereign states are significant players in the global political system due to their ability to constitute powerful entities in relation to non-state actors and entities. In this case study, Israel and Argentina are the state actors affecting processes in the global political arena, with the aim of enhancing their power and maximizing their national interests. This fact has an impact on the conduct of the WJC as a non-state actor in its endeavors on behalf of the Jews of Argentina.

Robert Keohane and Joseph Nye argue that the classical perspective of political realism does not provide a complete picture of the political processes in the international arena and therefore that one must widen the perspective to overcome the problems posed by the limitations of the sovereign state.[15] They claim that reciprocal relations are neither unique nor exclusive to nation states, and that world politics are a web of relations between state and non-state actor–entities in the framework of cross-state politics.[16] Therefore, this framework constitutes the theoretical basis for the study of the WJC's ability to operate within world politics in relation to the power and impact of the state-actor.

Even though the State of Israel developed good relations with Argentina, and acted on behalf of detainees in various prisons throughout Argentina, there is room to examine the unique contribution and influence of the WJC on behalf of the welfare of the Jews of Argentina. The theoretical premise regarding the WJC is that its activities have no impact on the course of events of high politics, such as military and security issues.[17] However, it does have an impact in the sphere of low politics, i.e., social and economic affairs in general, and in preserving Jews' rights and, in particular, providing aid to Jewish communities in distress.

The distinction between spheres of high and low politics allows for the examination of the WJC's activity in the area of low politics, as specified above. The contribution of this approach to the study of international organizations in the global political arena is in the area of conduct analysis of non-state actors focused on specific areas of activity.[18] That is, the politics conducted by these

15 Robert O. Keohane and Joseph S. Nye, "Trans-National Organizations and Processes," in *International Relations* [Heb], ed. Eytan Gilboa (Tel Aviv: Am Oved, 1978), 183–99; see also Paul R. Viotti and Mark V. Kauppi, *International Relations and World Politics* (New Jersey: Prentice Hall, 2009), 90–95.

16 Charles Pentland, "International Organizations and Their Roles," in *Perspectives on World Politics*, ed. Little and Smith, 242–49; Oran R. Young, "The Actors in World Politics," in *The Analysis of International Politics*, ed. James Rosenau, Vincent Davis, and Maurice East (New York: The Free Press, 1977), 125–44.

17 Keohane and Nye, *Power and Interdependence*, 25.

18 Ibid., 65; Viotti and Kauppi, *International Relations and World Politics*, 11–13.

organizations are institutional and interinstitutional, aimed at promoting their objectives as defined by their agenda.[19]

In this study, we examine the WJC's influence in low politics, where the nation-state has neither dominance nor influence on processes in the global political arena in the context of the organization's agenda. In the period discussed, significant diplomatic relations did exist between Israel and Argentina, as well as good relations between the Jewish organizations, such as the DAIA and the AMIA, and the elite of the ruling Argentinean military junta. We examine how the WJC acted on behalf of the Argentine Jews from the spiritual aspect, facilitating continued Jewish existence, and from a physical aspect, preventing persecution and arrests of young Argentinean Jews, and endeavoring to prevent anti-Semitic publications and activity on the part of governmental institutions and other factors toward the Jews, from the political, economic, and social aspects.

The primary source of information for assessing the activities and impact of the WJC is the relevant documentation found in the Central Zionist Archives. Despite the fact that these documents originate in the WJC, the purpose of their examination is not to take a moral stand on the WJC's conduct with regard to the Jews of Argentina, but to shed light on the activity of this NGO. This will be accomplished by focusing on three areas of activity, through which this author will attempt to diagnose and define the activities of the WJC in the campaign for the Argentine Jews: quiet diplomacy; cooperation between the WJC and the DAIA; and the Timmerman affair.

QUIET DIPLOMACY

As a cross-state NGO, the WJC can develop cross-state ties with regimes and governments. The WJC had the ability to use its global reach through its branches in Jewish communities around the world to influence the Argentine government by having these representatives exert pressure on Argentina's embassies in various countries. But the political reality of the time in Argentina forced the WJC to conduct quiet diplomacy.[20] The campaign for Soviet Jewry differed in the sense

---

19 Richard Mansbach, Yale H. Ferguson, and Donald Lampart, *The Web of World Politics* (New Jersey: Prentice-Hall, 1976), 37–39; Nye, "The Changing Nature of World Power."

20 On quiet diplomacy, see Aharon Kleiman, "Arms Sales: The Secret Cultivation of the National Interest," in *Wars and Arrangements* [Heb], ed. Benjamin Neuberger (Tel Aviv: Open University, 1992), 215–32; Sasson Sofer, "Old and New Diplomacy," *Review of International Studies* 14 (1988): 195–211; Aharon Kliemán, *Statecraft in the Dark* (Jerusalem: JCSS Studies, 1988), 55–74.

that, in addition to quiet diplomacy, the WJC also launched a public, worldwide campaign.[21] The decision to resort only to quiet diplomacy resulted from fear that a vocal campaign might be detrimental to the Jewish community as a whole: it was feared that the junta might change its approach from individual to collective anti-Semitism. In the words of Philip Klutznick, WZO president in the 1970s, it was important to act in a way that would not antagonize the military junta in Argentina.[22]

Management of the campaign was given to the international department, located in Paris, headed by Armand Kaplan.[23] Kaplan developed a personal relationship with the local ambassador of Argentina, Tomas J. de Anchorena, thereby creating open channels of communication between leaders of the WJC and the leaders of the military regime in Argentina,[24] in the hope of creating positive change toward the Jews of Argentina in general and, in particular, in relation to the *Desaparecidos* ("Disappeared") and detainees. In July 1977, news of torture and anti-Semitic conduct toward Jewish detainees reached the WJC. Armand Kaplan addressed the Argentine ambassador to have this policy stopped.[25]

In a 1977 memorandum, from the WJC international department to the Argentine embassy in Paris, Armand Kaplan addressed the Argentine ambassador, entreating him to act for the Jews of his country, whose situation had deteriorated over the recent months. Kaplan wrote that the Jews of Argentina felt fear and insecurity, and that this situation should be rectified by introducing a legislative change in Argentine law. In view of the importance attributed by the junta regime during this period to foreign public opinion, the ambassador summoned the WJC heads to a meeting with him in Paris. During this meeting, held on July 13, 1977, the delegation described the dire situation of the Jews in Argentina and their suffering from anti-Semitism and neo-Nazi attacks, derogatory publications, and acts of violence. Their demand was to alleviate the situation, to lift the Jews'

---

21 See on this matter a letter sent on September 28, 1977, from Paul Warshawski to Max Melmet at the New York branch of the WJC, Central Zionist Archive, file no. c10/2802; See also *Activities of the WJC January 1970-June 1973* (Geneva: Secretary General, 1973); *Activities of The WJC February 1975-October 1977* (Geneva: Secretary General, 1977).

22 See letter from Philip Klutznick to Gerhart Riegner, WJC secretary general, of September 25, 1978, Central Zionist Archive, file no. c10/2556.

23 See letter from Philip Klutznick to Armand Kaplan of October 17, 1978, Central Zionist Archives, file no. c10/2556.

24 See memorandum on this issue of July 11, 1977, Central Zionist Archive, file no. c10/2807.

25 See memorandum of the WJC international department of July 15, 1977, Central Zionist Archive, file no. c10/2807; see letter from Armand Kaplan to WJC heads of October 6, 1978, Central Zionist Archive.

spirits, and to remove their sense of uncertainty, by having the government of Argentina take legal and administrative measures to prevent such attacks. The Argentine ambassador's response was positive. He promised personally to deliver the delegation's message to President Jorge Videla and his government.[26] The ties between the Argentine ambassador and Kaplan continued throughout 1978. In October of that year, the ambassador conveyed to Kaplan a commitment by the government of Argentina pertaining to the Jews, even though the regime's constitution restricted their human rights as a minority.[27] The ambassador assured Kaplan that since the rights of the Jews were a sensitive matter, he considered this matter to be of paramount importance.

Diplomacy refers to the interaction between the representatives of two actors in the international arena. Quiet diplomacy was, as noted, the foundation stone of the WJC's campaign for the Jews of Argentina. This activity[28] is reflected also against the backdrop of the activities of Professor Leon Schwarzenberg, a Jew and a world expert on cancer. He used his professional status to influence the heads of the military junta on the issue of the Jews in general and on the status of the missing detainees in particular. His concern for the Jews in Argentina pushed him to seek an opportunity to bring this matter to the world's attention. An opportune moment was an international conference on cancer research, scheduled for early October 1978, which was to convene in Buenos Aires, Argentina. He traveled to Argentina at the head of a preparatory delegation of Jewish cancer specialists.[29] On arrival in Argentina in late September, he requested a meeting with President Videla to demand the release of the Jewish detainees and the publication of a report on the whereabouts of the absentees. When his request for a meeting was denied, Schwarzenberg threatened that he would cancel the all-important conference if his request for a meeting with President Videla in Buenos Aires was not granted.[30]

---

26 See memorandum of July 15, 1977, Central Zionist Archive, file no. c10/2807.

27 See letter from Argentine ambassador to Armand Kaplan from October 20, 1978, Central Zionist Archive, file no. c10/2556.

28 On Prof. Leon Schwarzenberg's activities, see Charlotte Jacobs, *Henry Kaplan and the Story of Hodgkin's Disease* (Stanford, CA: Stanford University Press, 2010), 226–338; Douglas Johnson, "León Chwarzenberg: Surgeon Whose Controversial Views on Patient Care Shook France," *The Guardian*, October 24 2003, accessed May 23, 2017, www.theguardian.com/news/2003/oct/24/guardianobituaries.france.

29 "Le professeur León Schwarzenberg dénonce l'extermination des intellectuels en Argentine," *Le Monde*, October 30, 1978.

30 See report written by Armand Kaplan to WJC heads of September 26, 1978, Central Zionist Archive, file no. c10/2556.

Prof. Schwarzenberg returned to Paris empty-handed and fuming. On his return, he convened a press conference in which he criticized the junta regime and accused it of violation of human rights and its persecution of Jews. He demanded that the regime release the detainees and inform the general public of the fate of the *Desaparecidos*. At this press conference, he also called on the WJC to raise an outcry and take aggressive steps on the issue at hand.[31]

Armand Kaplan's response to this was that the WJC must work together with the junta leaders toward a solution, rather than against them. The WJC believed that it should act discreetly with respect to the Jews of Argentina rather than in a public, vocal manner. Kaplan conceded that Prof. Schwarzenberg did have a point, but the WJC decided, nevertheless, to utilize quiet diplomatic tools and use the organization as an NGO working within the framework of cross-national relations and low politics, initiating activities such as Armand Kaplan's ties with the Argentine ambassador in Paris.

Following the press conference and publicized criticism by Prof. Schwarzenberg, the Argentine ambassador asked to meet with Armand Kaplan, to learn to what extent the WJC was involved or associated with the policy presented by Prof. Schwarzenberg.[32] To wit—was the WJC planning to take steps to influence Jewish and general public opinion worldwide? The ambassador wished to clarify his government's policy to the Jewish world through the WJC, and the aim of the meeting was, therefore, to resolve the questions that were raised on the issue. In their meeting in September 1978, Armand Kaplan reiterated the WJC's key policy principles pertaining to the Argentine government: that it must take action against all manifestations of anti-Semitism, and neo-Nazi and anti-Zionist trends in Argentina. Kaplan received assurances and agreement from Ambassador de Anchorena in three areas, namely that:

1) The Argentine regime would act to minimize the impact of neo-Nazi and anti-Semitic factors.
2) The Argentine authorities would act on behalf of anyone arrested or who had disappeared, and would pass on information about them to their family or community leaders, as well as release those against whom no charges had been brought.

---

31 Ibid.
32 Ibid.

3) The Argentine authorities were committed to changing legislation, such as Law No. 21745—National Registry of Religious Groups—which hindered religious minorities (legislation that, in the opinion of the ambassador, was an act of folly and unnecessary and therefore should be retracted).[33]

The commitment of the Argentine government to these steps was reinforced in a letter conveyed by Ambassador de Anchorena to Kaplan in January 1979, which reiterated its commitment to release detainees unrelated to anti-regime terrorist activities, as well as a claim of non-implementation of Law No. 21745, by finding a way to refrain from applying the law against Jews.[34] The letter goes on to describe a positive and amicable meeting between head of AMIA, Mario Gorenstein, and a chargé d'affaires at the Foreign Ministry, aimed at emphasizing the open policy of the regime in relation to Jewish religious observance.

Thus, the aim of the WJC was to continue with the line of quiet diplomacy to bring about political achievements for the Argentine community through such agreements and commitments, and to prevent the regime from escalating its policy to collective anti-Semitism, including legislation that would impinge on Jewish religious observance, injure the Jews' civil rights, and cause economic harm. In this, despite its nongovernmental status, the WJC had a unique influence on the situation of the Jews in Argentina, as it did not take aggressive measures against the regime.

The State of Israel also had influence over the junta regime. However, this influence stemmed from its relative position of power, where Israel had an advantage over the WJC, enabling, in practice, the escape and extraction of Jews from Argentina, and the release of some of the prisoners. In contrast, as a cross-national NGO, the WJC's influence was reflected in its interpersonal abilities of persuasion and its ability to ensure that the Argentine government did not exacerbate its policies and approach toward the Jewish community by adopting a collective anti-Semitic policy—thus achieving economic and social benefits for the Jewish community, which was able to continue to exist and even prosper, despite all. This ability of the WJC is expressed in the framework of its cooperation with DAIA in the campaign for the Jews of Argentina.

---

33 Ibid.
34 See letter written by Argentine ambassador to Mr. Kaplan of January 16, 1979, Central Zionist Archive, file no. c10/2852; see earlier letter sent on October 20, 1978, containing report and explanation of recent legislation implemented by the junta regime, Central Zionist Archive, file no. c10/2556; see n. 30.

WJC-DAIA COOPERATION

In the period examined in this case study, the Jewish community in Argentina numbered about three hundred thousand, and had formal, active institutions, vital to the community.[35] The activities of these organizations were unaffected by government policy. Herzl Inbar, chargé d'affaires at the Israeli embassy in Buenos Aires, described the situation at the time as one of suffering for the Jews, particularly for the detainees and their families, but the community as a whole was not in distress. The community leaders acted on behalf of the prisoners' families through an aid foundation established for this purpose.[36] Besides the desire to improve the status of the Argentine Jews, the WJC and the DAIA had an additional goal, to prevent the deterioration of the approach of the junta regime toward the Jews into a collective anti-Semitic policy.

Rabbi Marshall Meyer, the Conservative rabbi of the Jewish community of Buenos Aires, said that while it was far-fetched to think of Jews being killed on the streets, or Jews not being able to lead a normal life, one should not overlook the fact that the extreme, negative treatment of the Jews arrested was due merely to the fact that they were Jewish.[37] He strongly criticized the WJC and the DAIA for their approach on this matter. He blamed their overly low-key manner and submissiveness for the inaction in the matter of saving detainees and disappeared persons.[38] Against this, the WJC and DAIA leaders claimed that they chose to follow an opposite course of action due to their fear that adopting a public course of action would result in the implementation of a collective anti-Semitic policy by the military junta. DAIA president Nehemiah Resnizky and the heads of the WJC vociferously supported this policy.[39]

According to the constitution of the WJC, its member organizations were autonomous and could exercise independent decision making. Under these conditions, the WJC leadership was unable to establish a policy contrary to the interests of the local community organizations, since these bodies were the authentic representatives of the communities and were familiar with the

---

35 See Moshe Kimchi, DAIA representative at *The 30th Zionist Congress* [Heb] (Jerusalem: World Zionist Organization, 1982), 301; Zadoff, "The Jews of Argentina."
36 Herzl Inbar, Center for *Oral Documentation,* The *Institute* for the Study of *Contemporary Judaism,* The *Hebrew University,* file no. 51 (216).
37 *The 30th Zionist Congress,* 281.
38 Marguerate Feitlowitz, *A Lexicon of Terror* (Oxford: Oxford University Press, 2011), 99.
39 See letter from Nehemiah Resnizky to the European Department of the WJC, June 29, 1979, Central Zionist Archive, file no. c10/2852.

nature and problems of the communities. In this case, the WJC leadership's continuous policy was to refrain from acting against the interests of the Jews in Argentina, as defined by the local community leaders.

DAIA president Resnizky explained that this relationship was complex. There existed a fundamental right and even a moral duty on the part of the different organizations in the Jewish world, including the WJC, to help Jewish communities around the world. However, the Argentine case was unique because of the fear that the government would adopt a collective anti-Semitic policy.[40] Therefore, the DAIA should be enabled to operate in an independent and legitimate manner against the junta regime. In a communication from WJC president, Philip Klutznick, to the organization's secretary general, Gerhart Riegner, and to Armand Kaplan, Klutznick demanded unequivocally that the WJC's activity be coordinated with the DAIA pertaining to the community's status and security, in regard to the *Decaparecidos* and detainees. This was because the DAIA knew how to operate in this problematic reality without causing harm to be inflicted on the Jews by the authorities.[41]

Paul Warshawski, VP of the Latin American Department, recommended a two-way course of action in Argentina, as presented in his summary report on the WJC's activities in 1977:[42] first, strengthening the community's identity; second, strengthening ties between the community and government in order to lessen the tragedy's magnitude in the eyes of the detainees' families. This was because of the decreasing sensitivity of the government to internal and external pressures, and the desire to keep the unharmed status of the communities and institutions intact. Therefore, in a report presented to the WJC in 1978, Nehemiah Resnizky claimed that the DAIA had succeeded in its mission to preserve the condition of Jews and Jewish life in Argentina, and efforts had been made to prevent a situation where the anti-Semitic institutions would have grounds to adopt a collective anti-Semitic policy.[43] Therefore, he stated, both Jewish and non-Jewish factors should be approached to avoid taking any stand or action against the junta regime. When journalist Mark Heller published an article in which he claimed that the Jews of Argentina were in

---

40 See 1978 report sent by Nehemiah Resnizky to heads of WJC in March 1979, Central Zionist Archive, file no. c10/2852.
41 See letter from Philip Klutznick, WJC president, to Secretary General Gerhart Riegner, of July 27, 1979, Central Zionist Archive, file no. c10/2852.
42 See letter from Riegner to the organization board members, of February 7, 1978, Central Zionist Archive, file no. c10/2852.
43 See Resnizky's 1978 report, n. 40.

a greater state of fear than the Hungarian Jews living under the Communist regime, the Argentine interior minister, General Albano Harguindenguy, demanded that the president of the DAIA publicize a denial, refuting this. And, indeed, the latter stated that this article was untrue, and was damaging to the Jews of Argentina.[44] He reiterated this statement at a board meeting that took place in Israel, in which he implored the WJC to beware acting hastily so as not to damage the positive relationships he had created with the junta leadership.[45]

Due to the sensitivity to change and the implications of activities initiated by external parties, the WJC and DAIA leaders avoided collaborating with international Jewish organizations in order to circumvent any impression of an anti-Argentinean joint front. The adoption of this policy was a deviation from the WJC's usual approach, which was characterized largely by cooperation with international and global entities.[46] However, in this case, the WJC complied with the demand of the local community leaders, who objected to any moves that could endanger the community. Accordingly, the WJC supported the joint conference of Jewish organizations from the United States and Canada (American Jewish Committee, B'nai B'rith, American Jewish Congress), whose goal was to create a quiet dialogue to find solutions for the Jews of Argentina.[47] While the WJC cooperated with Amnesty International in Paris,[48] it refrained from cooperating with organizations that adopted loud and aggressive activities such as the Anti-Defamation League (ADL).

Aaron Kleiman, in his research on the Israeli defense exports to South America, argues that one of the incentives was the Jewish interest.[49] These countries had Jewish communities both large and small. Therefore, the Israeli arms export policy took into account the status of the Jews in these countries. For the leaders of the WJC and especially the DAIA, this policy failed the test when the Beagel crisis

44 Feitlowitz, A Lexicon of Terror, 101; Noni Meyer, "Argentina," American Jewish Yearbook 1979 79 (1979): 209.
45 Feitlowitz, A Lexicon of Terror, 101–102.
46 Mualem, "The WJC: Influence Without Power," see n. 1.
47 See n. 41; see also DAIA dispute and struggle with the Jewish organizations in the United States over the status of the Jews of Argentina in general and that of Jacob Timmerman in particular, in Victor A. Mirelman, "Las organizaciones Internacionales Judias ante La Represion y El Antisemitismo En Argentina," in El Legado Del Autoritarismo, ed. Senkman and Sznajder, 239–71.
48 See report written by Serge Cwajgenbaum, member of International Department in Paris, to WJC President Klutznik and board members, July 11, 1979, Central Zionist Archive, file no. c10/2852; see letter from Zak Lazarus, WJC board member in Paris of August 2, 1979, Central Zionist Archive, file no. c10/2852.
49 Aharon Kleiman, Double-Edged Sword [Heb] (Tel Aviv: Am-Oved, 1992), 200.

erupted in 1978 between Argentina and Chile concerning sovereignty over the Picton islands in the Beagel Channel.[50] According to military sources in Argentina, Israel backed the government of Chile diplomatically, economically, and militarily. Relations between Argentina and Israel deteriorated at that time following this crisis.[51] The crisis increased concerns among the local Jewish leadership, and they made vigorous conciliatory efforts vis-à-vis the leaders of the junta.

The same occurred when Israeli deputy defense minister Mordechai Tzipori, while visiting Chile, declared that Israel had offered that country military assistance and arms. This declaration amounted to a slap in the face for the leaders of the junta, as the crisis situation between the two countries had not yet been resolved. The heads of DAIA therefore sent an urgent letter to Prime Minister Menachem Begin requesting him to change this policy, and members of the WJC advocated toward this end among the Israeli diplomats in Buenos Aires.[52]

In a report submitted by Manuel Tenenbaum, WJC head of Latin America to WJC secretary general Gerhart Riegner, DAIA leaders called on the ministers of the interior, foreign affairs, international trade, and religion, on behalf of the WJC, to prevent extremist right-wingers from harming the community due to the inter-state crisis and the vocal activity of the American Jews.[53] They feared that this situation might bring harm to the Jewish community as a collective. The quiet policy of the WJC was also reflected in the adoption of the DAIA line. The fear of the junta regime adopting a worse policy increased the sensitivity among WJC leaders, and they therefore took extreme care in this area not only in quiet diplomacy but also in building close cooperation and agreement with the DAIA.

THE TIMMERMAN CASE

The Timmerman case is presented here to illuminate the difficulties accompanying the activities of the WJC in Argentina. This episode eclipsed all other activities conducted by state and non-state actors operating in the field

---

50 "Dispute between Argentina and Chile Concerning the Beagle Channel," in *Reports of International Arbitral Awards* 21 (February 18, 1977): 53–264; Alejandro Corbacho, "Predicting the Probability of War during Brinkmanship Crisis: The Beagle and the Malvinas Conflicts" (Buenos Aires: Universidad del CEMA, 2003), accessed May 23, 2017, www.ucema.edu.ar/publicaciones/download/documentos/244.pdf.

51 See report written by Manuel Tennenbaum, head of WJC Latin American Department to Riegner ofSeptember 25, 1978, Central Zionist Archive, file no. c10/2556.

52 See letter from Nathan Lerner to WJC heads, February 7, 1979, Central Zionist Archive, file no. c10/2852.

53 See n. 52.

of rescue and relief. The WJC had problems acting on this matter. As neither a governmental nor a sovereign actor, the question of whether it could or would wish to conduct a rescue did not arise. However, in this instance, even they played a role in the release of Jacob Timmerman, whose case represented the condition of all the detainees and imprisoned Jews in Argentina. In the political reality and modern history of Argentina, in which anti-Semitism played a prominent and significant role, the various institutions and actors were compelled to adopt controlled and responsible policies. Nevertheless, once the Timmerman case was placed on the public agenda, the leadership of the local Jewish community had to defend itself against accusations of cooperation with the authorities. Timmerman himself compared the conduct of the Jewish community to that of the *Judenrat* in the ghettos during World War II.[54]

Jacob Timmerman, an Argentine Jew, was chief editor of *La Opinion* newspaper in Argentina. He was arrested on April 14, 1977, and confined to house arrest on April 17, 1978. On September 25, 1979, he left the country and immigrated to Israel.[55] According to the findings of the court, there were no clear, unequivocal grounds for his arrest and detention. Furthermore, the pressure exerted by interior minister General Harguindenguy led to his release and exodus from Argentina.[56] Therefore, it cannot be claimed that external factors brought about Timmerman's release. The pressure brought to bear by the United States actually exacerbated Timmerman's situation, while Israeli attempts to bring about his release were successful only after continuous, protracted negotiations.[57] Against this backdrop, one can understand the poor ability of the WJC as an NGO to influence his release. Through the discussion of the controversy surrounding Timmerman's arrest, we will attempt to establish further the nature and conduct of the activities by the WJC and DAIA on behalf of the Jews of Argentina.

---

54 Jacob Timmerman, *Prisoner without a Name, Cell without a Number* [Heb] (Jerusalem: Domino, 1981), 73; Mordechai Bar-On, "Timmerman and the Jewish Question," *Gesher* 28, no. 106 (1982): 91.

55 Joel Barromi, "Were the Jews of Argentina Abandoned?" *Gesher* 4, no. 133 (1996): 61–64; Raanan Rein and Efraim Davidi, "A Jewish Hero Becomes an Enemy of the People of Israel: The Timmerman Affair, the Israeli Establishment, and the Hebrew Press," *Israel (Studies in Zionism and the State of Israel)* [Heb] 15 (2009): 167–91.

56 See report written by Paul Warshawski, co-director of WJC Latin American Department to board members, in October 1979, Central Zionist Archive, file no. c10/2852; Barromi, "Were the Jews of Argentina Abandoned?" 65.

57 Later on, Israel did have a covert influence on his release; see Barromi, "Were the Jews of Argentina Abandoned?" 63–65.

Timmerman was arrested because of his relationship with his partner David Graiver, a Jewish financier, who was in contact with the underground Montoneros.[58] According to Timmerman, his harsh treatment in prison derived from anti-Semitic motives.[59] He claimed that the Jewish community, led by the DAIA, did not help him while in jail and did not strive for his quick release but, rather, ignored his plight. In truth, his story greatly affected the Jewish community and the WJC. Nahum Goldman, former president of the WJC, addressed a personal letter to Argentine president Videla, requesting Timmerman's release.[60] The community leaders acted discreetly as they feared that the entire community would be labeled supporters of Timmerman's actions and his indirect connections with the Montoneros.

After his release, Timmerman criticized all those who acted for his release: the American government, the government of Israel, and the Jewish leadership in Argentina.[61] The local leadership was faced with the dilemma whether or not to actively support Timmerman. In this context, Herzl Inbar argues that this was not due to cowardice or fear on the part of the DAIA president.[62] Rather, this was due to the limited political influence of the WJC and the other Jewish organizations. The WJC, as an NGO, was unable to influence the political processes at the national and international levels, and, against this backdrop, it is easier to understand the conduct of the WJC on behalf of the Jews of Argentina during the period under discussion. Because Argentina as a sovereign state was not affected by the power of other sovereign states, like the United States and Israel, as this could allow its vital interests to be harmed, so the WJC, as an NGO, and the DAIA were compelled to take the route of more conservative action.

The conduct of the DAIA and the WJC was based on the principle of humanitarian activity, and preventing the violation of Timmerman's rights as a journalist and publisher of the newspaper *La Opinion*.[63] The DAIA turned to the WJC to spread the word on Timmerman's behalf among Jewish communities around the world, to get the latter to approach the Argentine diplomatic

---

58 Ibid., 61; Bar-On, "Timmerman and the Jewish Question," ibid.; Benno Vizer-Yaron, "Do Not Save Latin American Jewry," *Tefutzot Yisrael (Israel Diaspora)* [Heb] 23, no. 2 (1985): 112–25.
59 See memorandum sent by Lerner to heads of WJC on October 14, 1979, Central Zionist Archive, file no. c10/2852.
60 See letter from Nachum Goldmann to Rafael Videla of January 12, 1979, Central Zionist Archive, file no. c10/2852.
61 Jacob Timmerman, "Coming Home," *Congress Monthly* 47, no. 2 (February 1980): 9–10.
62 See n. 36.
63 See letter from Stephen Roth of the WJC Legal Department to Michael Fidler, London board member, of December 12, 1979, Central Zionist Archive, file no. c10/2807.

missions in their respective countries and to advocate for Timmerman's immediate release from what they regarded as an illegal arrest.[64] The DAIA, which initiated this activity, demanded that their approach to the world Jewish communities not be made public, as they feared that publicity about their involvement in the endeavors for Timmerman's release would exacerbate the junta's policy toward the Jewish community.

At a meeting in the UK between the leaders of the Committee of Jewish Delegations with the chargé d'affaires of the Argentine embassy in London, the latter suggested that they provide him with a petition signed by Jews and world leaders calling for Timmerman's release, which he would convey to the junta heads in Argentina.[65] The Committee leaders objected, on the grounds that it would take too long to accomplish. Instead, the chargé d'affaires agreed to accept a letter written by them addressed to the junta leaders, demanding that Timmerman be released and permitted to leave Argentina.

The Timmerman affair was a charged and difficult one for the leaders of the Jewish community since Timmerman vented his anger and frustration on them, accusing the Jewish community heads of forsaking him and the rest of the Jewish detainees in prisons in Argentina. He claimed he had been arrested and imprisoned only for being a Jew, although his Jewish identity was shown to be irrelevant as reflected during his court case and sentencing. Politically, the heads of the WJC and the DAIA were limited in their ability to operate and to influence. They maintained that they had followed a responsible, complex, and quiet policy, as claimed by Manuel Tenenbaum, a policy that took into account the plight of the Argentine Jews as a vibrant, social community and collective.[66]

CONCLUSION

The basic goals of the World Jewish Congress are the continued Jewish survival in the Diaspora, prevention of persecution, and prevention of physical and spiritual harm from befalling the Jewish communities worldwide. This study examined the conduct of the WJC on behalf of the Jews of Argentina from 1976–83, during the rule of the military junta. The aim of this study was

---

64 See letter from Armand Kaplan to Pietro Blair of the Union of Italian Jewish Communities, of January 26, 1978, Central Zionist Archive, file no. c10/2454.

65 Letter sent from WJC heads in London to international headquarters, from March 7, 1979, Central Zionist Archive, file no. c10/2852.

66 See report written by Tennenbaum to WJC heads, in October 1979, Central Zionist Archive, file no. c10/2852.

to examine the activities and influence of a nongovernmental organization in the international and inter-state arena. The WJC, then and now, conducts itself in different world arenas using tools of quiet diplomacy and advocacy. The political reality in Argentina at the time compelled the WJC to achieve its goals through quiet diplomacy. Quiet diplomacy served the general Jewish interest, and allowed this NGO to operate effectively in achieving its goals, and enabled its increased level of cooperation with the representatives of the Argentine government of the time.

The cooperation between the WJC and the DAIA reflected the nature of the former as a federative NGO. Its ability to operate in Argentina without restriction and to cooperate with community leaders and junta heads enabled the WJC to realize its all-Jewish humanitarian goals in the framework of the release of detainees, changes in legislation, and the continuation of the regime's policy and positive attitude toward the Jewish community as a collective, but not necessarily in its conduct toward individuals. The activities conducted in the particular case of Jacob Timmerman did not have a real influence on his eventual release from house arrest and imprisonment. Nevertheless, they did express the measure of balance between concern for his safety and freedom versus the community's needs as seen by the WJC. The WJC as an NGO endeavored to apply the tools of diplomatic negotiation to persuade the junta to release Timmerman. Timmerman was eventually released in the framework of a deal between the sovereign governments of Argentina and Israel. The aim of the WJC and the DAIA's endeavors was indeed to bring about Timmerman's release, and simultaneously prevent a situation whereby the regime would blame the community and implement collective, governmental anti-Semitism toward it.

The World Jewish Congress is a cross-national, nongovernmental organization that places on its agenda concern for all Jewish communities in the world. Yet, due to its nongovernmental status, it is limited in power and function, so it has to adopt a policy in which it can express its unique social and economic skills. There is criticism by politicians and various scholars of its conduct, which, they claim, resulted in the abandonment of the Jews of Argentina.[67] The aim of this study was not to examine the morality of the WJC's actions,

---

67 See Members of Knesset on this matter: Yair Zaban, *Knesset Reports* [Heb], June 26, 1983, 2810–12; Yossi Sarid, "J'accuse," *Haaretz* (Hebrew daily newspaper), August 31, 1989; Shulamit Aloni, "Indeed Ethics in Defense," *Haaretz*, May 26, 2006; Marcel Zohar, *Let My People Go to Hell—Blue and White Betrayal* [Heb] (Tel Aviv: Zitrin, 1990); Feitlowitz, *A Lexicon of Terror*, 101–102.

but to present and examine the ability of this organization to operate under a military regime that adopted an aggressive policy both domestically and externally. In practical terms, this organization worked and influenced the junta's policy in relation to the Jews of Argentina pertaining to the release of Jewish detainees and the welfare of the community. It also prevented the exacerbation by the regime of the Jewish community's social and economic conditions, as well as aiming to continue the positive approach of the regime with regard to the Jewish community in the future.

CHAPTER 14

Educational Excellence Program in South America—Case Study

MARGALIT YOSIFON

"... the Jews are a perennial forest reserve
where the trees densely stand."
Yehuda Amichai (*The Jews*, 1989)

INTRODUCTION

From 1996–2004, a determined effort was made to improve the system of Jewish education in South America by sending educationalists from Israel to countries on that continent, and bringing educational staff from there to Israel to participate in professional improvement courses. The program encompassed Jewish institutions and educational personnel from several countries in South America and was funded by a number of Jewish organizations. During its eight years of operation, about one thousand teachers participated in the program.

The qualitative research method was used to perform case study analysis—describing, analyzing, and presenting the considerations and principles underlying the planning and implementation of the project in the various countries. The research contributes to an understanding of the importance to their communities of Jewish schools in South America, the feasibility of applying universal educational principles, and the cultural differences that are significant in the world of education.

The research is based on interviews that were conducted with educational personnel from Israel who participated in the project, in addition to an analysis of documents and testimonies. The case study analysis describes and clarifies the professional bonds that were formed and the nature of these bonds. It details the ability to "export" implementable educational-pedagogic expertise from Israel, and sheds light on the capability of educationalists in the Jewish communities to assimilate innovative approaches in education in order to improve the Jewish educational systems in their countries.

The name given to the project by the planners in South America and Israel jointly was *Programa de Apoyo a la Excelencia Educativa* (Educational Excellence Program)—a name that sought to emphasize the innovative nature of the educational activities and the desire to raise the status of the schools participating in the program.

The project was implemented with the help of professionals in the field of education who were sent from Israel, some of whom traveled up to fifteen times to South America in the framework of the project, headed by Ms. Esther Hacham.[1] These personnel worked in the Unit for Adaptive Teaching and Learning of the Center for Educational Technology. Working together with these personnel were educationalists from those locations in South America where the program was being implemented.

A steering committee, named *Coalición de Escuelas para la Excelencia de la Educación*, was set up in South America together with personnel from the Center for Educational Technology to plan and run the project.

Originally, the project was planned to run for a period of two years only, but ultimately it ran for eight years, with a total of thirty-seven schools and about a thousand teachers participating. Most of the participants passed courses and underwent training in South America, while some came to Israel specifically to participate in professional improvement courses and to visit schools in the country.

The project was carried out in three stages, with only schools in Buenos Aires taking part in the first stage. In the second stage, schools in the provincial towns around Buenos Aires were added, while school principals from other countries, who had come especially to take part in improvement courses in Buenos Aires, also conducted independent studies. In the third stage, the project spread to other countries based on the successes of the first stage (see Appendix 14.1). It is of interest to note that non-Jewish schools also expressed an interest in the project.

---

1 Ms. Hacham participated in the first team to develop differential instruction (part of the "individual instruction" approach, which came to be known as "adaptive instruction"), and headed the unit that was instrumental in incorporating the system in education in Israel.

METHODOLOGY

The aim of the present research is to describe the program, collect data that was not documented in the past, analyze implementation of the project steps, and determine the operational success within an educational system that sought to incorporate pedagogic innovations under multicultural conditions.

The research questions were:

1) How was the project conducted and what were its characteristics?
2) According to which overt or covert model did the project operate?
3) What characterized the interdependencies between the universal innovative educational-pedagogic processes and the improvement of the Jewish educational system in the Jewish community?

The study was conducted according to the qualitative research method, in the form of a case study,[2] which consists in gaining an understanding of human activity in a particular place at a particular time.[3] Hammel[4] claims that data collection, including interpretations that the researcher brings to an understanding of the case study, serves as a basis for constructing epistemological forms and knowledge about social life. This is descriptive theory, which is necessary for all explanations in behavioral science. The more unique is the case study and the more special the case, the more things can be learned about human, personal, and/or organizational behavior, as well as about processes taking place in the case under investigation. Yin[5] states that the case study is an experimental study that seeks to investigate a phenomenon within the fabric of everyday living, with the boundaries of the case being defined only partially. Thus, Yin emphasizes the fact of the research being empirical in nature.

The *Programa de Apoyo a la Excelencia Educativa* presented in this article is defined as the "case" under investigation. It includes educational activities in a number of countries in South America, as detailed below.

---

2 M. Yosifon, "The Case Study," in *Traditions and Strems in Qualitative Research* [Heb], ed. Tsabar Ben-Yehoshua (Lod, IL: Dvir, 2001), 257–305.

3 R. E. Stake, "Case Studies," in *Handbook of Qualitative Research*, ed. N. K. Denzin and Y. S. Lincoln, 2nd ed. (Thousand Oaks, CA: Sage, 2000), 435–54.

4 J. Hammel, "The Case Study Method in Sociology—New Theoretical and Methodological Issues," *Current Sociology* 40, no. 1 (1992): 1–7.

5 R. K. Yin, *The Case Study Research—Design and Methods*, 2nd ed. (Thousand Oaks, CA: Sage, 1989).

In-depth interviews were conducted with Israeli interviewees who participated in the project (all of whom traveled to South America from Israel some thirteen to fifteen times during the course of the project for this specific purpose). Some were specialists in a particular field, such as linguistics or evaluation. Among them were individuals who were responsible for the improvement courses held in Israel to train teachers from South America each time a new group of teachers arrived in Israel in the framework of the program.

At this stage, no interviews were conducted with the overseas personnel who participated in the project.

A content analysis was carried out on the texts gathered, including documents that were distributed in Israel and abroad summing up the project activities: annual reports, reports produced by the schools in South America (written in Spanish or Portuguese and translated into English, or written in Hebrew), and evaluation reports that were written in Israel or abroad. Photographs that were taken during the course of the project were also collected and treated in the same manner as textual–visual information.

THEORETICAL BACKGROUND

Understanding and analysis of the project steps were based on the research and theoretical literature that deal with three aspects of the field of education: 1) professional development of teachers; 2) modern pedagogic theories; and 3) studies on educational reforms and changes.

The above three aspects are interrelated, with the project involving them all. Accordingly, the questions used in the interview, analysis of findings, discussion, and conclusions are based on the knowledge gained in connection with these aspects. Details on each of the subjects are presented below.

1. Professional Development of Teachers

Professionalization and empowerment of teachers[6] have been on the public-educational agenda in most of the Western world for more than three decades. Numerous research studies have tried to interpret the interrelationship and interdependency between the teacher's professionalism and his knowledge,

---

6 M. Yosifon, "Empowerment as an Agent and Result of Change: A New Look to Professional Development in the School" [Heb], in *Teachers in a World of Change: Trends and Challenges*, ed. S. Guri-Rosenblit (Tel Aviv: The Open University, 2004), 38–73.

class techniques, and impact on students[7] as well as changes in the school setup in order to adapt it to societal, technological, and economic changes.

The McKinsey Report[8] [9] emphasizes that the factor most influencing students' achievements is the quality of the teachers. Following this report, and indeed even prior to it, many countries, including Israel, allocated extensive budgets with a view to raising the professional level of their teaching staff (Cloyer and Klozminsky 2012; Avidav-Unger 2013; Shimoni and Avidav-Unger 2013). In addition to the fact that professional development can influence students in the short term, widespread reforms have been introduced in this field worldwide and in Israel, in view of the need to prepare teachers for their roles under the complex educational conditions prevailing in the twenty-first century (Yosifon and Shmida 2006). The classic traditional concept of teaching as a profession has assumed that teachers must have professional training, subject matter, and pedagogic knowledge in order to impart knowledge to their students connected with the relevant disciplines. At present, under the influence of postmodernism, innovative educational theories, and technological developments, the assumption is that teachers' professionalism is expressed not only in their command of the subject matter but also in their ability to incorporate additional bodies of knowledge into their instruction, and apply them in the classroom with their students and with other teachers in the school. As far back as the mid-1980s, Shulman[10] claimed that the time had come to change the perception of the teaching profession and to transform the teacher into an "expert pedagogue"; in so doing, he both broadened and focused the diverse knowledge required for

---

7 C. Day, ed., *The Routledge International Handbook of Teacher and School Development. Routledge International Handbooks of Education* (Florence, KY: Routledge, Taylor and Francis Group, 2011); L. Darling-Hammond, "Keeping Good Teachers: Why It Matters, What Leaders Can Do," *Educational Leadership* 60, no. 8 (2003): 6–13; L. Darling Hammond, "The Story of Gloria as a Future Vision of the New Teacher," *Journal of Staff Development* 28, no. 3 (2007): 25–26; Robert C. Pianta, *Teaching Children Well: New Evidence-Based Approached to Teacher Professional Development and Training* (Washington, DC: Center for American Progress, 2011); E. Villegas-Reimers, *Teacher Professional Development: An International Review of the Literature* (Paris: International Institute for Educational Planning, 2003).

8 M. Barber and M. Mourshed, *How the World's Best-Performing School Systems Come Out on Top* (Dubai: McKinsey & Company, 2007).

9 McKinsey & Company. *How the World's Best-Performing School Systems Come Out* (September 2007), accessed May 23, 2017, http://mckinseyonsociety.com/how-the-worlds-best-performing-schools-come-out-on-top/.

10 L. S. Shulman, "Those Who Understand: Knowledge Growth in Teaching," *Educational Researcher* 15, no. 2 (1986): 4–14.

the teaching profession. Teachers today are required to cope with educational challenges that did not exist in the past. They need to teach under multicultural conditions; advance minority groups; extend the concept of equal opportunity to underachievers; act in unforeseen situations involving conflicts, stress, and ambiguity created in communities with various interest groups; as well as reflect on their own actions in order to improve their professionalism. These factors have resulted in increased professional demands on the teachers, and to expectations regarding their ability to achieve independent learning throughout their professional career.

Additional macro-processes that have influenced the reorientation necessary for the professional development of teachers are the legitimization given in postmodern society to individual differences and social heterogeneity, to processes of educational decentralization, and to strengthening the status of teachers vis-à-vis central authorities. Current perceptions view professional teachers as those who learn, are intellectuals, investigate, and plan syllabuses according to the needs of their students[11] and their individual differences (Drexler 2011).

The above facts reinforce the need for professional teachers who are able to assume educational responsibilities and authority, and have a high awareness of their professional competence. These teachers will tend to rely on their own professional discretion, and make autonomous decisions in their classrooms and their schools.

Thus, research studies conducted worldwide place an emphasis on teacher training and learning throughout the teacher's lifetime. This includes reference to: 1) teacher quality: education, experience, educational beliefs, and perception of the role of teacher; 2) teacher performance: behavior and activities in the classroom and the school; 3) teacher effectiveness: influence on the students, e.g., in terms of their achievements and motivation; and 4) teacher functioning as part of a team, including participation in professional networks.

It was found that professional development is effective when it: 1) is an ongoing process to which time and resources are devoted uninterruptedly;[12]

---

11 Y. Nevo and T. Levine. "Teacher and Student Metaphors in Schools in the Process of Change" [Heb]. In *Research in Education and Its Application in a Changing World*, ed. F. Nasser, N. Hativa, and Z. Schartz, 122–27 (Even Yehuda, IL: Reches, 2000).

12 L. Darling-Hammond and M. W. McLaughlin, "Policies That Support Professional Development in an Era of Reform," *Phi Delta Kappan* 92, no. 6 (2011): 81–92; 76, no. 8 (1995): 597–604; T. R. Guskey, "Does it Make a Difference? Evaluating Professional Development," *Educational Leadership* 59, no. 6 (2002): 45–51; R. F. Elmore, *Bridging the Gap between Standards and Achievement: The Imperative for Professional Development in Education* (Washington, DC: Albert Shanker Institute, 2002).

2) is directed to the needs of the teacher;[13] 3) includes a definition of clear aims with respect to professional development;[14] 4) focuses on improvement of student performance;[15] and 5) is conducted according to a holistic approach, i.e., is coherent with general school policy and with other aspects of change taking place in the school,[16] while including study by the organization, peer learning, and support through personal mentoring.[17]

Because of the importance of professional development on the part of the teacher, it is not surprising that the primary purpose of the project was to focus on this aspect in general, and on differential treatment of students in the classroom in particular. We may interpret high professionalism on the part of teachers as the use of innovative educational concepts and an intimate knowledge of new educational theories, leading to changes in instructional techniques and to creating a teacher who has a high awareness of correct learning processes, including differential instruction and the need to cater to diversity in students.

2. Innovative Pedagogy

In the project under investigation, innovative pedagogy served as the principal basis for the pedagogic changes that were incorporated, and for professional development of the teachers.

Two educational ideologies currently dominate educational systems worldwide:[18] the traditional stream and the progressive stream. The differences between the two are manifested in basic questions regarding education, such as: What are the aims of education? What should be taught? How does one learn, where, and in what manner? Additional factors that may be instrumental in influencing this development are: changes in the status of the child in the family and in society; development of the field of psychology and understanding of learning processes; and the extensive research in teaching

---

13 Darling-Hammond and McLaughlin, "Policies That Support Professional Development"; Elmore, *Bridging the Gap between Standards and Achievement.*
14 Elmore, *Bridging the Gap between Standards and Achievement.*
15 Guskey, "Does It Make a Difference?"
16 Ibid.; Darling-Hammond and McLaughlin, "Policies That Support Professional Development."
17 NIET. *Beyond "Job-Embedded": Ensuring That Good Professional Development Gets Results.* (Santa Monica, CA: NIET National Institute for Excellence in Teaching, 2012).
18 M. Yosifon and M. Schmida, *Towards a New Educational Paradigm in Israel's Educational System in the Postmodern Age* [Heb] (Tel Aviv: Matach, 2006).

and learning processes that have resulted in recommendations for changes in teaching methods and professional development of teachers.

Although the traditional stream is the more common one, there is an increasing awareness in educational systems of the need to adopt innovative pedagogic theories in order to prepare students for the twenty-first century.[19] Progressive pedagogy, also known as innovative pedagogy, principally addresses issues such as: development of high-level thought processes; building of student knowledge (constructivism); multiple intelligences; learning strategies and styles; development of an active learner with self-determination; adaptation to student diversity;[20] and the significance of teaching methods geared to these approaches.

Diversity in the population, embracing all its aspects, is today a recognized fact and one that is well established scientifically. Diversity stems from personal, biological, and psychological differences that exist in people as well as from the heterogeneous social and cultural makeup existing in every society. Educational systems throughout the world are coping with the challenges of imparting a proper education that is suited to students who differ from one another, and who live and learn in heterogeneous societies that are attempting to meet needs deriving from personal, social, and cultural differences.[21] The State of Israel, which developed as an immigrant-absorbing society, has had to contend since its establishment with the challenge of advancing and providing equal opportunities to students learning in a pluralistic, multicultural society. An important part of innovative pedagogy is recognition of the existence of differences as a natural component in every group of learners.[22] This basic assumption emphasizes the need for a deeper understanding of all aspects of the concept as a basis for educational proaction. It necessitates in-depth examination of theoretical, ideological, and practical questions that address issues such as teaching and learning methods, and advancement of individual students, while ensuring equal learning opportunities for all.

Different theories that explain learning processes against a biological, psychological, social, and cultural background have served as a basis for the development of approaches, methods, and means for teaching and learning

---

19 M. Levine, "The Essential Cognitive Backpack," *Educational Leadership* 64, no. 7 (2007): 16–22; V. Stewart, "Becoming Citizens of the World," *Educational Leadership* 64, no. 7 (2007): 8–14.

20 R. E. Snow, "Individual Differences." In *Instructional Design: International Perspectives: Theory, Research and Models*, vol. 1, ed. R. D. Tennyson, F. Schott, N. M. Seel, and S. Dijkstrs (Mahwah, NJ: Lawrence Erlbaum Associates Inc. Publishers, 2009), 215–42.

21 A. Hargreaves and M. G. Fullan, eds., *Change Wars* (Bloomington, IN: Solution Tree, 2009).

22 R. D. Kahlenberg, ed., *The Future of School Integration—Socioeconomic Diversity as an Education Reform Strategy* (New York: The Century Foundation Press, 2012).

in a society that respects diversity in its students. In recent decades, efforts have been made in Israel and abroad to develop educational approaches, teaching, and learning methods in an attempt to implement equal opportunity in education while providing students with a platform to realize their own personal potential through differential instruction.[23]

Social and cultural backgrounds also influence the environment in which the student is brought up, as do the ways in which society, economy, and culture shape personal identity and influence realization of one's individual potential for learning. Among the social and cultural variables, those such as religion, language, customs, and social status create differences between students. Every society has different cultural repertoires and these are generally associated with well-defined groups (e.g., new immigrants, the ultra-Orthodox, Arabs). Each culture influences in myriad ways variables that are relevant to learning and the results of learning, such as: perception of learning types (e.g., rote versus investigative learning), preferred subjects for study, preferred study groups (women as opposed to men), expectations of the student, ability to choose, etc. The sum total of the influences creates life situations that shape realization of the personal potential of each student in different ways, this too necessitating adaptation of teaching methods on the part of teachers according to innovative pedagogical concepts. Research studies report that the use of these methods has a positive effect on factors such as raising motivation for study.[24]

Research question No. 3 was formulated in line with this factor. It attempted, among other things, to address the differences existing between the culture of the trainers (Israelis) and that of the trainees (South American), while also interpreting the connection between innovative educational concepts (the foundation for whose formulation is universal, based on research in various countries), and the diverse cultural, Jewish and/ or national–local reality.

---

23 W. Drexler, "Empowering Students with Personal Learning Environments," *Independent School* 71, no. 1 (2011): 2–20; M. Rock, M. Gregg, and R. A. Goble, "REACH: A Framework for Differentiating Classroom Instruction." *Preventing School Failure* 52, no. 2 (2008): 31–46; C. Tomlinson, C. Brighton, H. Hertberg, and C. Callahan, "Differentiating Instruction in Response to Student Readiness, Interest, and Learning Profile in Academically Diverse Classroom: A Review of Literature," *Journal for Education of the Gifted* 27, nos. 2–3 (2003): 54–119.

24 R. Ben-Ari and L. Eliasi, "Between Frontal Teaching Strategy and Complex Teaching Strategy: The Differential Influence of Learning Environment on the Student's Motivation to Achieve" [Heb], *Megamot* 45, no. 3 (2008): 531–54.

3. Educational Reforms and Changes

Recent decades have witnessed extensive educational changes in most countries.[25] In a modern society, the educational system serves as an agent for social change, being a mechanism for improving the achievements of groups, thus allowing equal opportunity. The principal trend in educational reforms and changes has been the achievement of social, ideological, political, technological, or economic goals.[26] In addition, twenty-first-century society expects the educational system to act in accordance with its expectations of the future adult entering its portals.[27] The expectation is that the educational system will influence personal changes in the lives of those joining it as well as changes in society. Graduates of the educational system are at present required to demonstrate thought processes and skills to a more significant degree than in the past, with this requirement expected to acquire even greater emphasis in the future. These include autonomy, lifelong self-learning, use of high-level cognitive skills, and an ability to adapt to frequently changing conditions. Even today, they are required to act in an environment in which a plethora of information and knowledge sources exists, stored in a range of technological media. This requires teachers to deal with changes and uncertainties, and to act as professionals providing answers in unforeseen situations. Shulman refers to the teacher's ability to cope with these demands as the "pedagogy of uncertainty."[28]

Recent years have seen a revision of the strategy used to implement changes, from those defined as "top-down" to those combining "top-down" and "bottom-up" principles. These are characterized by collaboration or decentralization, based on the understanding that a centralized policy of

25 M. G. Fullan, *The New Meaning of Educational Change*, 4th ed. (New York: Teachers College Press, 2007).

26 J. W. Guthrie and L. C. Piercel, "The International Economy and National Education Reform: A Comparison of Education Reforms in the United States and Great Britain," *Oxford Review of Education* 12, no. 2 (1990): 1–27.

27 R. Aviram, "The Educational System in Postmodern Society: An Anomalous Organization in a Chaotic World," in *Education in an Era of Postmodern Dialogue* [Heb], ed. A. Gur-Zeev (Jerusalem: Magnus, 1996, 103–20); *Navigating the Storm—Education in the Postmodern Democracy* [Heb] (Tel Aviv: Massada, 1999); *The Futuristic School—A Research Journey to the Future of Education* [Heb] (Tel Aviv: Massada, 2004); *The School as a Communications Center: A Model of Optimal Humanistic Education* [Heb] (Haifa: Pardes, 2010); Yosifon and Schmida, *Towards a New Educational Paradigm*; Levine, "The Essential Cognitive Backpack"; Stewart, "Becoming Citizens of the World."

28 L. S. Shulman, "To Dignify the Profession of the Teacher: The Carnegie Foundation Celebrates 100 Years," *Change* 37, no. 5 (2005): 22–29.

change does not achieve its aims, and that considerable leeway must be allowed for the individual interpretations of the participants.[29] Researchers of educational changes suggest that planners take into account the fact that the preferred model for implementing changes is allowing the individual, the teacher, and the collective to create a common educational and social energy that will enable the process of change to be fleshed out in the short term, while also lasting through the long term.

As stated, the Educational Excellence Program addressed professional development of the teacher, employing innovative pedagogic techniques. The project thus was transformed into a process of educational change that sought to alter the professional world of teachers, in terms of both their pedagogic perceptions and the practices applied by them in the classroom.

BACKGROUND TO PROJECT IMPLEMENTATION

Large numbers of the Jewish population in South America send their children to Jewish schools. These schools belong to a private network and operate according to a "long day" framework: study based on the public school syllabus until the afternoon hours and Jewish studies from the afternoon on, when they learn about religious holidays, study the Hebrew language, and discuss consolidation of Jewish identity, customs, traditions, etc. Through education in such schools, parents hope to ensure, as far as possible, continuity of Jewish identity in the next generation as well.

The governments of the different countries, the parents, wealthy members of the community, and funds from Israel provide the budget for these schools— as was the case both before and during implementation of the project. The budgets allocated by Israeli and Jewish entities were intended both for study scholarships for needy families and for reducing the number of students per class, in keeping with the norm in many private schools.

It should be noted that many Jewish families were sending their children to private non-Jewish schools when the project commenced. The less affluent Jewish families registered their children in regular public schools.

The important role of Jewish education in the life of the South American communities is manifested in the following ways: a strong emphasis on the

---

29 M. Yosifon, *Reshaping Teaching Patterns: Study of the Process of Change in a Middle School in Israel* [Heb] (PhD diss., Tel Aviv University, 1996); Yosifon, "Empowerment as an Agent and Result of Change"; M. G. Fullan, *Change Forces—Probing the Depth of Educational Reform* (London: The Falmer Press, 1993); Fullan, *The New Meaning of Educational Change.*

study of Hebrew, close involvement by parents in school activities, donations by wealthy members of the community to the community's educational systems, and employment of an educational-organizational advisor.[30]

In the early 1990s, Argentina faced a severe economic crisis, which resulted in many families seeing their assets eroded, preventing them from sending their children to private schools. At the same time, affluent members of the community significantly reduced their donations to the Jewish educational system. In order for the Jewish schools to continue to function, there was a need to strengthen them, principally in terms of budget.

Until 1995, representatives of communities in South America used to visit Israel to participate in symposia as guests of the Jewish Agency, the World Zionist Federation, and the Labor party. Various issues relating to Jewish-Zionist education in South America were aired, including, among other things, the worldwide phenomenon of assimilation in Jewish communities. The communities would request and receive budgets for scholarships for children from families with meager means.

The economic crisis intensified the difficulty in maintaining the schools. Thus, at the onset of the crisis, talks were held between the community representatives and the entities in Israel, at which a request was made for support.

In the mid-1990s, in the wake of the economic crisis, Mr. Yitzhak Rabin, the then prime minister, decided to support the schools through educational-professional means that would lead to improving the quality of teaching and learning, rather than through additional budgetary allocations. Raising the professional level of the schools would, it was believed, draw additional groups of families with means (families who were sending their children to private non-Jewish schools), and would encourage them to change their minds in light of the improvement that would be felt in the community's educational system. The assumption was that increasing the number of students in schools would also enable them to be bolstered financially.

Dr. Shimshon Shoshani, at the time director-general of the Jewish Agency, was called upon to handle the issue.[31] In 1995, he sent Balchinsky to check out the situation and make recommendations for further action. In wake of the report, Shoshani decided to go a step further and make a trip to Argentina (at that time, the area of concern was the educational system in Buenos Aires only)

---

30 In Argentina, for example, this role was filled by Mr. Balchinsky, former Jerusalem District Director of the Ministry of Education.

31 Mr. Shoshani had served in the past as Director-General of the Ministry of Education and head of ORT in South America.

in order to assess the situation there, map the schools and their condition, and carry out a feasibility study to implement an educational project. He approached Ms. Esther Hacham from the Center for Educational Technology, as well as Ms. Sarah Lotan, ministry of education supervisor, and Ms. Dina Bankler, principal of the Nature School in Tel Aviv, and asked them to travel to Argentina and, in their professional capacity, submit a report to him with recommendations for effective investment in the local educational system. The visit took place in 1996.

In planning processes of change, it is common to perform a preliminary situation assessment aimed at gathering data on the educational institution or organization, analyzing the data and diagnosing the situation, and allowing an examination of alternatives for making improvements. Thus, the sojourn there included visits to schools, observation of lessons, discussions with school principals (mostly female), talks with parents, students, and teachers, as well as discussions with community heads in Buenos Aires.

FINDINGS AND CONCLUSIONS FROM THE VISIT AND EVALUATION OF THE SITUATION

The principal conclusion from the first visit to evaluate the situation was that there was room for a two-year educational project in elementary schools. The recommendation was that ten Buenos Aires schools interested in the project should begin activities. Supporting this conclusion were the following factors:

Subject matter teachers—The teachers were familiar with innovative educational theories but did not know how to put them into practice in the classroom. Some of the teachers had advanced degrees in the subjects they taught.

Love of children—This seems to be taken for granted as a teacher's trait since children are the object of their work and the reason they chose the profession. Nevertheless, it is not a factor that can be assumed, and complaints in this connection are at times heard in the educational system in Israel. The impression was that teachers in South America treat their students with particular sensitivity and fondness.

Frontal lessons—The standard system of teaching in all the classes was the frontal method: the teacher relates to the entire class as a single unit without taking into consideration differences between the students; subjects are taught in a uniform manner to everyone, with all students being allotted an equal amount of time, irrespective of their individual learning abilities. There was no differential treatment in the classroom based on professional pedagogic considerations.

Jewish pride—The message conveyed by the schools and the teaching staff was that they were proud to be Jewish and were willing to invest considerable pedagogical efforts to improve the effectiveness of teaching and transmitting a Jewish/Zionist message to their students.

Command of Hebrew—Many of the educational staff in Argentina had a good command of Hebrew.

Openness to pedagogic innovations—The teachers expressed their desire to learn and apply innovative pedagogic concepts, in particular those pertaining to development of their professional capabilities to deal with differences in their students.

Politicization of education—The political life of the community was reflected in its education: school principals and/or teachers were hired or dismissed by the community committee, which also participated in preparing content and developing pedagogic methods.

Distance between teacher and principal—A distance was found to exist between the principal and school officials on the one hand, and the class teachers on the other, in terms of conduct and actions; this was a feature of the local culture. Meetings with the teachers were held separately from those with the principals, even though it was clear to the visitors from Israel who were carrying out the situation evaluation that joint thinking and planning could yield good results.

Hierarchical structure and authority—In accordance with the local culture, a strict hierarchy was observed with respect to decision-making powers, with a clear differentiation being made between principals and decision makers on the one hand, and teachers on the other. Thus, teachers generally were not partners in the pedagogic decision-making process in their schools.

Inter-school rivalry—It was found that rivalry existed between schools, originating in a competition over the student population. As a result, there was no collaboration between principals, as they regarded this as being to their detriment.

The above observations were part of the insights that served as a basis for the project planners in aiming to improve pedagogic performance and ensure the success of the project.

CRITERIA FOR PARTICIPATION IN THE PROJECT

The criteria for accepting schools to participate in the project were determined by the school officers. The criteria were (as cited from the program's articles of association):

Participants will include schools that believe in innovative pedagogy, whose principals and staff are prepared for pedagogical changes; elementary schools with at least 200 students; schools located in a Jewish area with potential for expansion; schools with a physical structure suited to innovative teaching methods; executive committees that are willing to accept commitments involving budget allocations; schools that have received the community's approval for inclusion in the program.

Determination of the criteria at the outset was important, and served as a means of selection: only schools that were willing to assume responsibility for implementing the pedagogical changes were included in the project. It was thus possible to allocate the necessary budgetary resources with a degree of certainty that they would be utilized efficiently. In addition, the criteria were instrumental in conveying a message of transparency and integrity to the members of the community.

At the initial stage, there was indeed an emphasis on observing the criteria. However, these were somewhat relaxed at later stages, when additional countries joined the project, and especially when principals from countries outside Argentina arrived for professional improvement courses, becoming independent agents of change in their respective schools.

PROJECT AIMS

A document reviewing the first year of the project included reference to two project objectives, one of which was to bring about professionalization of the teachers. In the words of the report: "The purpose of the *Programa de Apoyo a la Excelencia Educativa* is to introduce changes in teaching–learning processes and in the school as an educational organization." The second objective was: "to adapt Jewish schools to their changing role in the development of graduates on the threshold of the twenty-first century."

The objectives of the project are thus adoption of innovative pedagogic methods, awareness of student diversity, and teaching students to become independent learners. Realization of these goals would bring the student to a better state of readiness vis-à-vis the twenty-first century.

The objectives were defined following a process of situation assessment in collaboration with members of the community in Argentina. The purpose of defining the goals was to determine the project direction, establish criteria for project evaluation, and set a new educational vision for the schools that would also be attainable. The above two goals constituted the basis for project planning, and determining the subjects for training, the model for professional development in Israel and abroad, and the specialization of the professionals sent from Israel for the purposes of training, consultation, and consolidation of the evaluation process.

> S: "I understood that the aim was to transform the schools into magnet schools through innovative pedagogy."

Based on the interviews, it could be understood that there was an additional objective that remained unstated: pedagogical marketing of the schools in order to increase registration.

> A: "That was what was implied, it was in the air, it was clear that improving the schools would attract interested parents, it was a huge motivation."

The assumption was that parents in the community, especially the wealthy ones, would make every effort to have their children enrolled in those schools that had undergone revitalization after meeting the above goals.

FORMULATION OF THE PROJECT AND ITS STRUCTURE

The structure of the project points to advance planning of an active partnership, with respect to both design and implementation, between representatives from Israel, representatives from the Jewish Agency (which initiated and funded the principal part of the program),[32] and representatives of the local communities. Because of the special nature of the project and the many visits to South America from Israel and vice-versa, there was a need for a special budget, which is the reason that funding was provided by several entities collaboratively.

Appointment of a local coordinator for the project facilitated implementation of the program when the representatives from Israel were not present.

The trips to South America took place twice a year and generally lasted for two weeks. Each time they included visits to the schools and guidance to the

---

32 The project was funded by Jewish communities in South America, the World Zionist Federation, the Jewish Agency, the Joint Distribution Committee (JDC); the Pinkus Foundation, and the Doron-Rich Foundation (some during the course of project implementation).

teachers in the classrooms; professional improvement courses for the executive cadre; meetings with members of the community and the parents; participation in the steering committee; planning of future activities with all the partners in the project; and determination of solutions with respect to various professional issues.

> G: "In the mornings I observed lessons in the classrooms, each time in a different school, following which I conducted training courses for all the schoolteachers. I also conducted intensive four-day courses for all the Hebrew teachers in the city. I was astonished to see that all of them came after a day's work. There was a huge thirst for validated content."

The professional improvement courses that were given in Israel to teachers from South America addressed subjects such as theoretical learning, workshops for applying pedagogic techniques with Israeli specialists, visits to schools that had succeeded in implementing pedagogic innovations, visits to other educational institutions, and tours of the country.

> A: "For from Zion shall come forth Torah! The fact that the people came from Israel made the innovations something that was worth adopting, and the visits to Israel showed that introducing a different method in the classroom was possible."
> B: "During visits to Israel they were awestruck by the level of implementation; they saw that it was possible; the principals especially inquired about processes taking place in the school."

Many teachers had relatives in Israel, and they took advantage of their visits for family get-togethers. Participating in the courses in Israel were also non-Jewish teachers who were on the staff of the Jewish schools in South America.

ANALYSIS OF PROJECT PRINCIPLES AND ACTIVITIES

This section includes an analysis of the principles that served as a basis for project planning and implementation. The identified components were not presented as such in the documents outlining the project proposal and design. In hindsight, based on the interviews, generalizations can be made regarding the components that were presented. Altogether, seven principles were identified that constituted the covert and overt model for implementation of the project:

1. Application of Innovative Pedagogy

The application of educational pedagogy through training is based on the premise that teachers possess professional skills, knowledge, and ability in frameworks involving traditional frontal instruction, but need to acquire new knowledge in fields such as differential instruction, planning of lessons for heterogeneous groups, and learning processes that develop high-level cognitive and investigative skills.

> A: "The teachers wanted very much to learn ... they wanted to understand the theories and not only the techniques. Teachers of grades one to ten were especially interested in learning."
>
> H: "The teachers did not object to the process in the way we experienced it in Israel, even though this meant a lot of work for them, because they had a sense of mission. They understood that this greatly benefited the children."
>
> B: "There was no case where a principal was not interested ... relative to the age of the teachers, who were veterans, objections were few."

The counseling included theoretical knowledge for application in the classroom. Analysis of the information obtained from the interviews—including photographs of the classrooms and other study areas in the schools during the course of implementation—shows that teachers who participated in the project actively applied innovative pedagogic principles. In particular, these processes pertained to differential instruction, learning, and evaluation through:

1) relaxation of time restrictions in the classroom;
2) emphasis on effective teaching, learning, and evaluation processes;
3) planning of lessons in the different subjects and their adaptation to the students' needs;
4) selection of topics that were of relevance to the students;
5) incorporation of variety in learning assignments;

6) development of a meaningful learning environment (some of the buildings were renovated expressly for this purpose);

7) individual support to the students; and

8) renewal of technological equipment (computers, video sets, and printers) and assimilation of their operation.

H: "There was quite a large number of teachers who were extremely taken up with active instruction, and, after they had experienced it, actually waited for us to ask us questions about it and get advice from us. They understood that it was a help to them. There was something very magnetic and attractive about the process."

A: "They were familiar with the theories of innovative education but did not know how to apply them. They were shown how, and especially saw that the students enjoyed it. It worked."

N: "I worked with them on the differences in acquiring a second language, how to teach Hebrew (e.g., vocabulary, syntax) in a differential manner. It all went smoothly; they were very eager to learn. It is a different experience from undergoing a professional improvement course in Israel. There was a great willingness to try new things."

Shulman (1986) claimed that the professional teacher adapts his teaching to innovative pedagogy (he is the "expert pedagogue") by acquiring knowledge of the following components: 1) familiarity with the subject matter; (2) knowledge about instruction in the subject matter; (3) knowledge about learning processes. A command of all these types of knowledge thus makes the teacher an expert. The process undergone by a substantial number of teachers in the project in applying innovative pedagogy resulted in their professional development and their transformation into "expert pedagogues."

2. Jewish Identity

The molding of a Jewish identity is one of the principal aims of the Jewish educational system in South America. In their special position as schools for the community's children that also impart unique study content, the schools reflect the wish of the parents and the community to preserve a Jewish identity, especially in light of global influences (which tend to blur identities) and the society as a whole in which they live. The concern for continuity and for preserving the Jewish ethos for future generations has spurred most parents in the community to register their children in these frameworks despite the difficulty in financing their share of the tuition fees in the semi-private system, which calls for a major investment of resources on their part. In addition, the educational system is perceived as a principal means for internalizing values; the parents view the school as a social institution that helps them and their children shape their complex world. On the one hand, they are citizens in a non-Jewish society and act within this culture; on the other, they are interested in maintaining a separate identity as Jews. Schner[33] claims that the uneasiness inherent in the awareness of Jewish identity today stems from the natural bond that exists with the surrounding non-Jewish society, unlike the "classic mold" that once existed to preserve this identity.

The model that was developed in the project was a combination of general study content and Jewish studies. The teachers in the project used additional ways to strengthen and consolidate a Jewish identity by means of innovative studies that had not been tried before, the intention being that these instructional activities would raise academic achievements in general, and intensify Jewish identity in particular.

As such, it was natural that the question of Jewish identity would be a dominant theme in the pedagogic activities of the teachers.

> H: "There was an emphasis on subjects associated with Jewish identity: Bible studies, Hebrew, history, Yiddish in Shalom Aleichem... on looking back, it was the right thing to do because it reinforced the parents' decision to send them there. In retrospect, it may be said that it was also used as a marketing strategy."
>
> N: "The teachers had no knowledge of how to teach Hebrew as a foreign language. They wished to hear how Israeli Hebrew was taught and to be infused with the Israeli spirit. This connected very strongly with Jewish identity and the bond with Israel."

---

33 M. Schner, "The Jewish Education Dialogue—Wandering Between Contradictory Concepts" [Heb], in *Pathways in Pluralistic Jewish Education*, ed. Hamo and Dror (Tel Aviv: Mofet Institute and Tel Aviv University School of Education, 2012), 33–68.

In all the pedagogic activities, the teachers generally were given the choice of dealing with the subject matter according to their needs. The teachers (even the non-Jewish ones) mostly chose to engage in content that was related to consolidation of a Jewish identity: religious festivals, Jewish customs, the Hebrew calendar, Israel, and Jerusalem were referred to repeatedly. This emphasis was a constant in all the schools that participated in the project.

> K: "Most of the content chosen for the learning environment reflected the subject matter: Jerusalem, connection with the State of Israel, Jewish customs and religious festivals, the Hebrew calendar, the Hebrew language, etc."
>
> N: "In the classrooms the learning environment conveyed a host of messages on Jewish identity. On the walls—Jewish and Israeli content: a map of Israel, the seven species, religious festivals, traditional songs."

This model placed the emphasis on Jewish cultural characteristics and less on religious–halakhic or textual references. In addition, it was found that a consensus existed in every school with respect to teaching about Israel. This finding reflects the close bond that existed between the communities in the various countries that participated in the project and Israel. The desire to learn about Israel was an expression of both the support given by the Jewish communities to the Zionist concept, as well as the fact that they see no contradiction between life in the Diaspora and the strong bond with Israel and its representatives as contributors of Jewish identity to the school.

The teachers in the schools that participated in the project bore several identities: Jewish, professional, and national in relation to the country of which they were citizens. The combination of these three elements of identity in a single arena and the consciously flexible manner in which they were used are not unique to these teachers: it is a characteristic of almost every Jew who lives in the Diaspora. It is possible that the focus on the educational change they experienced in the project facilitated consolidation of their identities, with some being suppressed and others emphasized, and shedding additional light on their roles. Nevertheless, this issue invites further research.

It should be noted that an additional project (Pele 2003–2005) was conducted as a sequel to the present one, dealing with the development of study materials for subjects associated with Jewish identity. This activity was particularly conspicuous in subjects like Bible studies, Hebrew, history, and Yiddish.

3. Development of Local Leadership

With teachers, acceptance of a function in addition to that of teaching constitutes a catalyst for a change in role orientation.[34] Role orientation may be related to a change in tasks, a change in position in the framework of the same organization, a change in workplace, and even a professional change.[35]

From the project's outset, the development of a local leadership constituted a principal focal point. First, planning and activities in collaboration with local entities reflect the partners' strong points; secondly, development of a local training force to ensure the community's independent continuation of the system once the project is over (and the Israeli representatives are no longer present to provide professional support) imparts a sense of proprietorship over the change and empowers the participants. The assumption was that preparations should be made already from the commencement of activities for a severance from the Israeli representatives; the fact that a period of only two years was allocated for the project required the Israeli representatives to expedite this process as far as possible.

Among other things, planning of the project was based on the assumption that a fundamental educational change is a difficult one to implement, and that its assimilation cannot be taken for granted. The interested parties must therefore receive appropriate training.

> H: "We expected a lot of objections, as we had experienced in Israel. Because in their culture there is high acceptance of hierarchy and authority, the teachers came and were compliant. This made it easy from the beginning."

An additional assumption was that the school principal and officers would be a key factor in the success of the change.[36] During the course of applying

---

34 L. Darling-Hammond and G. Sykes, "Wanted: A National Teacher Supply Policy for Education: The Right Way to Meet the 'Highly Qualified Teacher' Challenge," *Journal of Education Policy Analysis* 11, no. 33 (2003).

35 Yosifon, "Empowerment as an Agent and Result of Change."

36 D. L. Duke, "Keys to Sustaining Successful School Turnarounds," *ERS Spectrum* 24, no. 4 (2006): 21–35.

innovative pedagogical concepts, principals and teachers were identified who stood out from the others in terms of implementation, motivation to change behavior patterns, and leadership qualities, as expressed in their interpersonal communication and in their relationships with others.

> N: "When I arrived (not at the start of the project), the principals had already been taken on. They participated in all the professional improvement courses, acted as hosts in the schools and were present and involved in everything. Even the principals who did not speak Hebrew took part in the courses for the schoolteachers."

The following activities took place as part of the development of local leadership:

Principals mentoring principals—A number of outstanding principals were identified who were trained and assumed responsibility for transferring the knowledge and experience they had gained to other principals.

> H: "Principals participated in the courses and stood out. Afterwards we saw them in the classrooms; there were principals who appeared to be suitable for counseling others, and they were selected for this. I don't know if they received any monetary remuneration for it, but I do know that there were some who came to Israel more than once in order to acquire additional learning. The visit to Israel was a bonus, a reinforcement, the opening of a window to new things. The tours of the schools were important."

Training of counselors (outstanding teachers)—As in the case of the principals, outstanding teachers were identified who were given training for a period of about two years with a view to counseling other teachers in their schools or in other schools. The team from Israel gave several demonstrations in classrooms in order to show how things could be implemented.

> S: "They spoke a lot about our demonstrations, because they said we don't only talk about ... but also do ... and they also saw the strength of the teamwork between us."

Routine counselor meetings—The group of counselors worked as a team and met once a month for refresher courses where they shared knowledge, organized the cumulative knowledge gained, and learned new subjects, while also discussing professional matters relating to counseling. Research today encourages concerted peer learning of this kind (Nieto 2009).

Professional improvement courses for teachers—This arrangement took place once a year in Buenos Aires under the responsibility of local lecturers. Responsibility for counseling the teachers generally devolved on to the local representatives.

Professional improvement courses for teachers—One course was held each year in South America under the responsibility of the Israeli team, generally in countries with many schools that were participating in the project.

> H: "The professional improvement courses were conducted each
> time in a different school, which hosted everyone. It gave one a
> good feeling and, besides, training was adapted to the needs of
> each school."

Internal professional improvement courses in each school—The school was responsible for this arrangement, and it too encompassed development of local leadership and transfer of responsibility for pedagogic change to the local representatives.

Professional improvement courses for a number of schools together, under the responsibility of the local team—In this case, there was a desire for efficiency and an economical use of the counseling capability, as well as for bringing together a number of schools for the purpose of mutual professional exchange. The ingathering of a number of representatives from different schools was intended to allow exposure to varied experiences, collaboration in educational practices, and opportunities for educational cooperation in the future.

The subject of innovative pedagogy continues to be studied in higher education frameworks in universities in Brazil and Argentina. Because of the extended duration of the project, some of the project leaders began to study the subject with an in-depth theoretical–academic orientation, and eventually, based on the academic knowledge gained and on-the-ground experience, became lecturers in the subject. Issues such as educational changes and reforms, pedagogic innovativeness, and differential instruction—subjects that were addressed as part of the project activities and are commonplace in academic teaching—became part of the knowledge base of these lecturers.

4. Holistic Approach

Based on research studies carried out in recent years, Postholm (2012)[37] found that one of the elements most influencing learning by teachers in terms of their professional development is learning in a social–professional framework. Moreover, according to him, individual and organizational development of the school go hand in hand. His recommendation is that it is appropriate for the teacher's professional development processes to be conducted inside the school or in the framework of peer learning. His view reflects the holistic approach, which is the recommended approach today for implementation of educational changes at the level of the school, the community (the city), and the country. The holistic approach assumes that a view of the entire picture (the student, class, school, or community) is essential for implementing a meaningful change.[38]

The holistic approach used in the project was planned in advance, manifested at all levels, and implemented using a number of mechanisms:

Steering committee—The steering committee was an important mechanism for consolidation of the holistic approach. It included the various entities that were involved in planning, budgeting, and implementing the project (representatives of the school, the Jewish Agency, the Joint, the Organization of Jewish Communities in South America, the education committee, and others). Decision-making by the committee served as a means for expressing the wishes and interests of all the entities and aimed at achieving the aims of the project with maximum efficiency and transparency.

Professional improvement of principals planned jointly with the teachers—The holistic approach is manifested in the fact that all teaching staff and principals at the school studied and implemented the subjects learned in a single system. It should be borne in mind that, according to the management culture in South America, it was not a common practice for teachers and principals to study together.

---

37 M. B. Postholm, "Teachers' Professional Development: A Theoretical Review," *Educational Research* 54, no. 4 (2012): 405–29.

38 Duke, "Keys to Sustaining Successful School Turnarounds"; G. Fisher, "Holistic Leadership" [Heb], *Hed Hachinuch* 83, no. 4 (2009): 66–68; D. O'Leary and J. Craig, *System Leadership: Lessons from the Literature* (Nottingham, UK: National College for School Leadership, 2007); V. Chrisman, "How Schools Sustain Success." *Educational Leadership*, 62, no. 5 (2005): 16–20.

A: "It was not usual for principals and teachers to sit together. The teachers accept what they are told to do, and the principals do not take part in workshops."

It was necessary to explain the importance of joint learning, which contributes to mutual observation and to concerted holistic action, as well as to incorporate changes—based on consensus—in the strict hierarchical structure that existed before the commencement of the project.

H: "The togetherness, everyone doing, everyone coming, specializing together was good for them and personal interest was expressed even by those who in the beginning were apprehensive (i.e., the principals and officials)."

Principals' forum—This forum met twice a month for the purpose of planning, peer learning, and discussions on implementation. The principals, as important decision makers and school leaders, represented an important forum for consultation, planning, and collaboration in these sessions. The forum greatly reduced the competition that had existed between them before the project. In the course of the joint activity, a team was formed with common objectives that saw the advantages to be gained in joining forces.

H: "The trips around Israel had a huge effect on the principals. In visits to the schools, they saw that this worked, even when there was a large number of students in the class, and this affected their support and their management techniques."

Peer learning in the schools—Peer learning and collaboration for advancement of instruction in schools is today one of the most significant elements in the professional development of teachers.[39] Support and encouragement in the teachers' room have been observed in numerous research studies on schools, including the fact that the teachers' feelings vis-à-vis the school affect the level of teaching in the classroom.[40]

---

39 B. Levin, *Improving All Schools* (2010), accessed February 1, 2017, www.avneyrosha.org.il.
40 Yosifon, *Reshaping Teaching Patterns*; A. Keinan, *The Teachers' Room—The Professional Culture of Teachers* [Heb]. (Beer Sheva, IL: Bar-Ilan University, 1996).

S: "Each visit to a school involved the entire staff of principals and officials, and was carried out with a holistic orientation. At first they were not used to working in teams, while the coordinators also did no teaching."

Among other things, peer learning included demonstration lessons. Shulman (1993) was one of the first to emphasize the connection between the pedagogic beliefs and practical experiences of the individual teacher on the one hand, and his professional community on the other, thus shedding additional light on the consolidation of his identity while in the process of professional development.[41] Like the meaningful learning processes undergone by students in a social context,[42] the teachers also learned from one another while discussing experiences in the classroom, thus advancing professional development.

In the view of some of the interviewees, the various activities that were carried out in a holistic framework by all the schoolteachers, and the collaborative activities as described above, created a team spirit in terms of both the school and the community. This was due to the consolidation of an innovative educational ethos and an intensification of professionalism on the part of both the teachers and the principals.

Support and facilitation circles—Figure 14.1[43] presents the circles involved in the holistic approach adopted in the framework of the project:

Personal operator circle—This circle refers to the personal level of the teacher in his classroom, applying innovative instruction–learning–evaluation processes. At this level, the individual—namely, the teacher—operates as a person who is willing to adopt whatever is necessary in his opinion from the concept/program/project in order to change his teaching methods in the classroom.

School support circle—This is the school circle, which provides conceptual–moral support for the desired change in classroom teaching–learning processes, while also allocating additional resources in time, experts, and budget. At this level, a collective innovative pedagogic identity is formed for the school and a professional practice that the teachers can discuss. Thus,

---

41 L. S. Shulman, *Where Genius Can Thrive* (paper presented at the International Conference on Teachers' Cognition and Pedagogical Knowledge, Tel Aviv University, 1993).

42 L. Wigotsky, *Learning in a Social Context—Development of High Level Psychological Processes* [Heb] (Tel Aviv: Hakibbutz Hameuhad, 2004).

43 Yosifon, *Reshaping Teaching Patterns.*

the change in this circle is of a social–group nature. The collaboration that exists when the support circle operates also becomes a cultural process in which values and goals become a joint creation of the group as a whole.[44]

District/town facilitating circle—In this circle, the proper conditions are created for change on a holistic level, such as granting of legitimacy, autonomy, and allocation of resources. This circle includes the community, officials involved in education on the town level, etc. Thanks to resources and a decision-making ability, it facilitates intensification of activities in the two inner circles. The very fact that officials in this circle discussed the processes taking place in the schools, visited the schools in order to gain an impression of the changes in the classrooms, and allocated resources motivated the teachers and the school staff to perform by investing greater effort to ensure the success of the change.

5. Provision of Practical Tools

The principal difficulty in assimilating an innovative educational concept is to find ways in which ideas, values, educational approaches, and theories underlying them can be proposed to teachers, and to show them how to adapt their application to practical instruction in the classroom. Because of this, emphasis must be placed on techniques where changes are intended to be instilled,[45] as was done in the present project. Further, it is recommended today that programs for professional development of teachers not deal with consolidation of knowledge in the subject matter alone, but that they relate to the teachers' professional practice.[46] Teaching is a practical profession and, accordingly, teacher training, as also other frameworks for professional development, should include components such as an understanding of student characteristics and the differences between them, the teaching context, learning approaches, diverse methods for activating students in the learning process, the significance of interaction during the lesson, meta-learning, and reflection on teaching.[47]

In many cases, as in the present project, the pedagogical changes alter the instructional technique in the classroom. The team from Israel

---

44 Keinan, *The Teachers' Room.*

45 Levin, *Improving All Schools.*

46 Duke, "Keys to Sustaining Successful School Turnarounds"; J. H. Van Driel and A. Berry, "Teacher Professional Development Focusing on Pedagogical Content Knowledge," *Educational Researcher* 41 (2012): 26–28.

47 J. B. Biggs and P. J. Moore. *The Process of Learning* (New York: Prentice Hall, 1993).

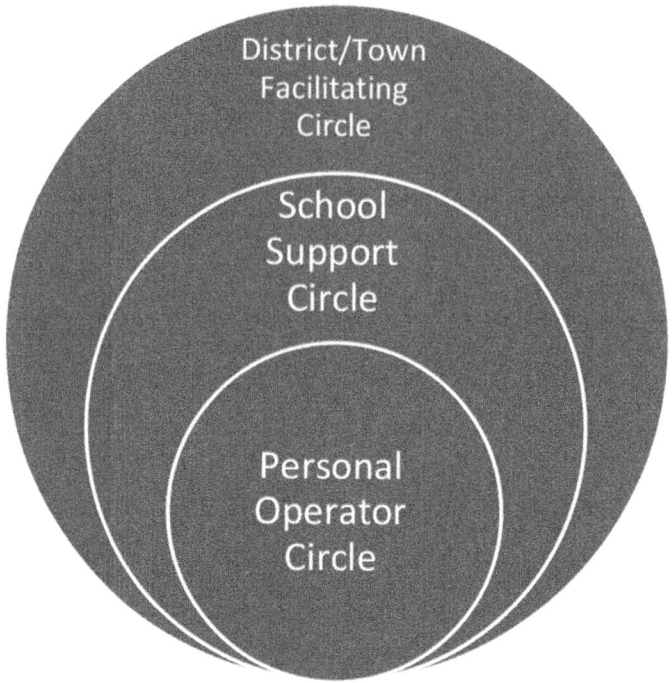

Figure 14.1 Support and Facilitation Circles.

had many years of experience in differential instruction, and transferred their knowledge and experience to the local staff. During the course of their participation in the program, the teachers—who had used the frontal teaching style prior to joining the program—received tools to deal with the diversity in their students and provide differential solutions to suit their needs. These innovative tools represented a significant change in the teachers' instructional methods as well as in the students' learning methods. Through the courses, practical tools were provided for innovative learning methods, support and guidance at both the individual and school level, and granting of legitimacy to student success according to their own pace. They discussed the pedagogic changes they had undergone:

> K: "We began with a change in the learning environment. It was at first difficult for them to think anything other than frontal ... it was initially orderly and clean, but the learning environment was not meaningful ... it was merely decorative ... there was no internalization of the fact that other learning resources existed ... when they came to instituting a flexible schedule,

they had a better understanding of the connection with the learning environment, which must be customized and rich and not just teacher-dependent. It was difficult at first."

N: "It was a meeting place of knowledge—the teachers came with their knowledge and familiarity with their students and I brought modern content that was different, new, graded, and validated by experience, and we created a new practice."

In the course of acquiring teaching methods considered to be innovative, the teachers in the project underwent professional development—from the need for and an understanding of the teaching profession as "transferring material," through a realization by the teachers that this was not sufficiently effective, to a consolidation of an educational perception of "adapting" and "educating," representing an understanding of the profession according to a broader and more professional interpretation. An evaluation report, supported by a statement of one of the interviewees, found that feedback from the students encouraged the teachers to continue with innovations, and that satisfaction was expressed with the practical tools that were extended to the teachers and the differential methods adopted. The teachers found that by using these methods they were succeeding in providing answers to the diversity between the students. Satisfaction was tempered, however, by numerous testimonies by the teachers on the amount of time that had to be invested to achieve this goal.

Some of the interviewees stated that differences could be discerned among schools in this area between schools that were participating formally in the project and those where only the principals were taking part in professional improvement courses (see point 7 below).

6. Adaptation to the Local Culture

Communities in South America exhibit a variety of identities. Schools that serve the communities reflect communal dynamics, and an approach that is based on cultural pluralism is therefore essential.[48]

The communities that participated in the project represent a diverse and complex reality, given the fact that there is no one formula for living life

---

48 Y. J. Goldstein, "Jewish Education in Latin-America: A Socio-Historical Comparative Perspective," in *Paths in Pluralistic Jewish Education*, ed. N. Chamo and Y. Dror. (Tel Aviv: Mofet, 2012), 23–42.

as a Jew and that, by definition, the Jewish people constitute a collective with very vague boundaries. Differences include aspects such as religious streams, language, social and cultural fabric, economic differences both within the community and between communities, ethnic backgrounds, as well as a wide range of views on the subject of Jewish identity and the role of Jewish education in the community. In the course of the research, it was therefore interesting to observe how the professional development of the teachers took place despite the possible cultural differences between the Israeli advisors–counselors and the principals and teaching staff in South America, with their own cultural diversity.

The personnel from Israel needed to familiarize themselves with this multiculturalism and operate within it, while taking into consideration the culture unique to each community in the wide range that existed.

> S: "It is an accepted fact that criticism should not be voiced, but if one wants to learn then feedback is needed, and in order to be professional one must develop reflection, self-criticism, and criticism of others, when the message is understood. They asked reflective questions—what would succeed, what must be improved, plunging into the depths of the subject matter."

The interviewees dwelt considerably on the thought processes occurring around these subjects, and took into account the prevailing cultural pluralism in planning the project together with the local teams, in order to ensure compatibility between the educational concepts and the local culture.

> H: "One had to get used to the pace, which was slower. Only in Israel does one race all the time. We soon realized that we had set the bar for sprinting and we slowed down."
>
> S: "The teachers had a conceptual difficulty in imagining that the student is able to study on his own, independently. One of the goals of the project was preparing the graduate for the future, or in other words independent learning. This was difficult for them, but they saw that the students were enjoying it and this gave them an incentive. This was undoubtedly a difficulty that had to be overcome."

Throughout the program, the teachers chose the subject matter that was suited to them and was in line with the aims and culture of the school. Cooperation with the schoolteachers and principals, as well as with the steering committee, imparted a sense of ownership over the educational changes initiated by the teachers, thus enabling their assimilation with little resistance. This is indeed a recommended strategy for mitigating resistance.[49]

> H: "The presence of absence helped. Some of the time we were situated at a distance and were less available, they developed an autonomous approach, created new things, and became independent pedagogues."

The low resistance also stemmed from the fact that the change was of the "first order,"[50] i.e., change that is brought about in the framework of commonly accepted values, interests, assumptions, and norms (versus "second order" change, which brings about paradigmatic change).

The principle of adaptation to the local culture was also reflected in the adjustment of implementation to the individual pace of each teacher.

In processes involving pedagogic change, where teachers differ from one another in terms of the pace at which they adopt changes in their instructional techniques, the tempo that each teacher develops vis-à-vis the pedagogic changes that he wishes to implement once he develops confidence in them is of great importance. The fact that guidance was not given on a one-on-one basis (personal meetings were held only three times a year) allowed the local teams to adjust their initiatives by themselves and according to their own professional, social, and cultural perceptions. This process may be referred to as the "presence of absence":[51] in implementing educational changes, the planner frequently may find himself assuming an intensive "in the field" presence, aimed at ensuring incorporation of the educational concept to which he is devoting his efforts. Intense involvement often becomes burdensome for teachers, making them feel patronized, and limiting their autonomy and their own professional discretion regarding implementation. The "presence of absence" concept emphasizes the need to allow the teacher an autonomous professional breathing space, and

---

49 S. Fuchs, *The Psychology of Opposing Change* [Heb] (Ramat Gan, IL: Bar-Ilan University, 1998).
50 Vatzlavik, Wickland, and Fish 1979 in Fuchs, *The Psychology of Opposing Change.*
51 Yosifon, *Reshaping Teaching Patterns.*

claims that this will bring about a more satisfactory assimilation of changes, especially among teams with high functional maturity.[52]

7. Flexibility

Analysis of the data collected on project progress shows that one of its characteristics was the principle of flexibility. This principle was manifested in a number of ways, initially with respect to participation by schools in the project, because of the choice of schools in different countries and geographic areas (e.g., center, periphery) that could take part according to their needs.

The following is a description of the different models for participation in the project:

Schools that participated with the support of sponsors—Schools, especially newly founded ones, that participated intensively in the project thanks to the budget allocated by the project funders. Intensive participation included visits to them by representatives from Israel and teachers who traveled to Israel for professional improvement courses.

Schools that joined the project later without sponsorship—About ten schools were able to join the project despite their lack of budget; the budget (e.g., to send representatives to South America and/or teachers to Israel for courses) was made available by the school principals and their communities.

Schools that received counseling from local personnel—About two years into the project, after local representatives had been suitably trained, additional personnel were allowed to join the project, receiving guidance from those who had undergone training during the first two years.

Principals from various regions in Argentina who studied with principals from Buenos Aires and returned to implement procedures in their own schools—According to this model, principals from the various regions joined the program for the purpose of the professional improvement courses held for principals who were participating formally in the project. The circle of participants was expanded to include principals who came by themselves, volunteering to study and to convey the knowledge gained to the teachers in their own schools and, in so doing, becoming secondary agents of change.

---

52 Popper, M. *On Principals as Leaders* [Heb]. Tel Aviv: Ramot, Tel Aviv University, 1994.

Sporadic participation—There were schools that began to take part in the program but stopped after a time. There were also principals who wished to participate in the project, secured the necessary budget and then dropped out, usually after one year. These were few in number, and no accurate information was obtained on these schools.

In addition, the principle of flexibility in project planning and implementation with the teachers was applied. Flexibility was manifested in different circles, in particular those associated with the implementation of educational–pedagogic changes.

Selection of the subject content and methods of implementation or learning have changed since the early 1990s, because many researchers of educational reforms have recommended viewing the central role of the teacher in implementing changes in the classroom, taking into consideration his needs, culture, and social and professional environment. In addition, emphasis is placed on the autonomy that must be granted to teaching staff, enabling them to participate in planning the course of the change and putting it into practice. Every change is an expression of educational, social, and cultural values;[53] accordingly, without a moral and ideological commitment on the part of the teacher, no educational change is possible.[54]

The principle of flexibility was also evident in the voluntary manner in which the schools in general, and the teachers in particular, joined the project. The voluntary nature of the participation allowed negotiations to be conducted free of pressure between the partners. The assumption was that the teacher's professional acumen cannot be improved merely through a program that dictates or binds, imposing on him a blueprint for teaching that is not to his liking, or co-opting him to a program with whose aims he cannot identify. Underlying the counseling was the question as to what extent the teachers felt that counseling was indeed helping them. From a review of the school reports, we can observe that the principals and officials answered this question in the positive in a relatively large percentage of the cases.

> S: "There were practically no objections. The teachers wanted more and more to attend the professional improvement courses.

---

53 Fullan, *Probing the Depth of Educational Reform.*
54 L. Cuban, "Why Some Reforms Last? The Case of the Kindergarten," *American Journal of Education* 100 (February 1992): 166–94.

We focused on cultivating high-order thinking; the questions that were given to the students were analyzed; there were demonstrations; it interested them greatly."

Counseling too expressed the principle of flexibility since it was customized, in terms of its content and methods, to the differing needs of the teachers. The counselor's response to a problem that appeared to the teacher to be an urgent one had a decisive effect on the favorable attitude of the teacher toward receiving guidance.[55] The teachers felt that they had been given institutional legitimization for the pedagogic changes and adapted what they saw fit in their respective classrooms.

The counselors from Israel, like the local counselors, established new knowledge and an ethos, each in his own way but through joint planning and in accordance with the principal aims of the project.

Research Conclusions

The research study had two main objectives: to investigate and understand educational actions and processes; and to derive conclusions that would enable improvement of the educational system in the future. Conspicuous in researches on the processes of change is the second function. Key researchers such as Fullan and Cuban investigate processes of change, and constantly refresh our understanding of the appropriate actions to be taken to implement them.[56] To this end, it is important to analyze the main conclusions of the present research in order to gain an understanding of the project.

In addition to what has been stated above, the conclusions may be summed up in terms of two main factors: 1) achievement of the project objectives; and 2) implementation of the processes of change.

---

55 E. Shremer, "Guiding and Counselling Teachers: A Critical Perspective" [Heb], in *Training of Teachers*, ed. N. Peles and S. Orion (Jerusalem: Ministry of Education, Pedagogical Secretariat, 1994), 7–28; M. Yosifon, "From Theory to Practice: The Impact of Study Planning and Counselling on the Shaping of New Teaching Patterns" [Heb], in *Curricula as a Social Construction*, ed. H. Eilon (Tel Aviv: Ramot, Tel Aviv University, 1998), 109–36.

56 Fullan, *The New Meaning of Educational Change*; L. Cuban, "Why So Many Structural Changes in Schools and So Little Reform in Teaching Practice?" *Journal of Educational Administration* 51, no. 2 (2013): 109–25.

Achievement of the project objectives—Based on the interviews conducted in Israel, on evaluation reports, and on additional narratives, we may state that the project achieved its primary objective, namely, the professional development of the teachers. Feedback was also obtained from professional improvement courses held for some of the teachers in Israel. A review of the feedback forms carried out at the time shows great satisfaction on the part of the participants.

The second objective is difficult to measure or evaluate due to its long-term nature. Nevertheless, though quantification of future development of values and skills by students is problematic, we may assert with reasonable confidence that students who experience investigative methods of instruction, autonomy, and development of high-order thinking processes, will indeed adopt superior cognitive skills. Numerous research studies on the subject support this train of thought.

Implementation of the processes of change—An analysis of the data shows that the process of change was conducted in line with the numerous recommendations of researchers, based on a familiarity with the relevant professional literature. The holistic approach was operative throughout the duration of the project, and at all levels. Collaboration in planning and implementation at all levels was carried out with single-mindedness, resulting in both a sense of ownership of the educational change on the part of the trainees, and in the creation of a change that involves a combination of top-down and bottom-up principles that has the greatest chance of success. A culture of innovation was initiated through flexibility, discussion, and trials, learning from successes and encouragement of local initiatives. Counseling was not intensive and left much room for local autonomy. The cultural adaptations prevented patronization, and allowed each teacher, school, and community to match what was desirable to them and to the local culture. Judicious use was made of resources (time, budget, and professional knowledge). In addition, finally, although the voice of students is not generally heard in researches on educational reforms and changes, in the present case study it was found that student satisfaction also served as a factor in motivating the teachers to implement new techniques in the classroom.

In summation, a few further comments may be added:

Cross-linking of interests—Conspicuous in the project was an element that is seen to bring about successful educational changes: there was a cross-linking of interests,[57] which facilitated implementation of the

---

57 Yosifon 1996.

educational changes. The desire of the teachers to be more professional tied in with the interest of the principals to improve their schools, which in turn meshed with the interest of the community and other stakeholders. The project managers knew how to emphasize common interests, and the holistic approach that was adopted served as a primary tool in giving prominence to this aspect.

Can the change be preserved?—Did the project succeed in being long lasting? It is difficult to answer this question based on the data of the present research, both because no teachers from South America have been interviewed for some years following completion of the project, and because of the turnover of teachers in the schools.

One of the questions most asked by researchers of change is whether it is possible—and if so, for how long—for the change to be preserved in schools after so much effort has been invested in developing and assimilating it. Most reforms, even when successful, do not survive the test of time. Fullan[58] suggests the use of the phrase "ongoing process of change" in order to emphasize the fact that long-term "preservation of change" should not be expected unless the change is actively maintained over time. Fuchs[59] claims that change in the school will succeed only if it becomes a way of life. Some use the expression "school culture" under the premise that change will be recognized as successful if it transforms the school culture to the extent that it becomes a daily routine.[60]

Consolidation of Jewish identity—The focus on innovative pedagogy led to the teachers rethinking things they had taken for granted in their classes, even when it came to teaching subjects with Jewish content. Pedagogic questions included: What does one teach? What content is relevant for the students? Which teaching and learning methods should one adopt? These questions were asked particularly in connection with the second objective—development of a school graduate with skills suited to the twenty-first century.

Assimilation of innovative pedagogy thus involved questions of this nature, causing the teachers to search for ways and means to intensify the awareness of Jewish identity among the students. The teachers wished to

---

58 Fullan, *Change Forces.*
59 A. Fuchs, *Change as a Way of Life in Educational Institutions* [Heb] (Tel Aviv: Cherikover, 1995).
60 Ibid.

be influential in shaping the Jewish identity of the students (and perhaps their own?), which is nourished to a considerable degree by historical and religious–halakhic perceptions. The pedagogic questions posed brought additional questions to the surface regarding the search for a real modern identity that would tie in with innovative approaches and would not stand in opposition to the surrounding society—a kind of key to orientation in the present, based on the past, and with an eye to the future. The contact with representatives from Israel served both for connecting with a culture that is associated with a modern, contemporary Jewish identity,[61] and for attaching themselves to a territory that defines the identity of the Jewish people. One of the interviewees (a linguist) stated that she had met with young parents at one of the schools who had pressured her to emphasize the study of English at the expense of Hebrew—an indication of the desire to consolidate a global identity over a Jewish one.

Intercultural dialogue circles—There are considerable differences, manifested in the educational systems, between the various countries that participated in the project as well as between the various communities in those countries. These differences came to the fore in applying educational concepts, some of which were mentioned earlier. There is also a vast cultural difference between the Israeli staff and the educational staff in the countries reported in the project. Despite these differences, however, a large number of dialogue circles were formed: between the teachers and their counselors, between the school staff and their students, between the teachers and representatives of their communities, and between the representatives from Israel and the members of the various communities. Two common foundations existed for dialogue. First and foremost, there was the language of Jewish culture, to which must be added the sound knowledge of the Hebrew language on the part of a very large number of teachers and principals in South America, to the extent that there was frequently no need for translation from one language to the other. Secondly, there was the educational-professional language and joint thinking as to how to maximize the students' successes. The spotlight on innovative pedagogy placed the teachers' view of the students' circles of affiliation in sharper focus, making them find ways in which they could influence the

---

61 Most had relatives living in Israel; some had tried living in Israel but had returned to South America after a few years.

students in this regard. The student's first circle of affiliation in elementary school is his family, and the Jewish school wished to strengthen this affiliation. The second circle is his affiliation with the community. Through the project, the school sought ways to tell the story of establishing a Jewish identity together with development of the student, one who will function successfully in the future as a Jew, and also as a citizen of his country and as a member of his near and distant community.

APPENDIX 14.1

Schools and Cities Participating in the Project

Argentina: Buenos Aires—13 schools
Argentina: Provincial towns around Buenos Aires—Mendoza, Córdoba, Santa Fe, Paraná, Tucumán—5 schools
Brazil: Rio de Janeiro—5 schools
Brazil: São Paulo, Recife, Curitiba—schools
Mexico: Mexico City—4 schools
One school in each of the following countries: Uruguay—Montevideo; Paraguay—Asunción; San Jose, Costa Rica; Quito, Ecuador; Lima, Peru; Chile —Santiago; Colombia—Medellín, Barranquilla—7 schools

REFERENCES

Amihai, Y. "The Jews." In *The Fist Too Was Once an Open Hand and Fingers* [Heb], 139. New York: Schocken Books, 1989.

Avidav-Unger, A. "Professional Development in an Age of Reforms and Changes—The Significance of Perceiving Continuity." In *On Continuity: Specialization and Professional Development of Teachers—Policy, Theory and Practice* [Heb], edited by S. Shimoni and A. Avidav-Unger, 197–227. Tel Aviv: Mofet, 2013.

Aviram, R. "The Educational System in Postmodern Society: An Anomalous Organization in a Chaotic World." In *Education in an Era of Postmodern Dialogue* [Heb], edited by A. Gur-Zeev, 103–20. Jerusalem: Magnes Press, 1996.

———.*Navigating the Storm—Education in the Postmodern Democracy* [Heb]. Tel Aviv: Massada, 1999.

———.*The Futuristic School—A Research Journey to the Future of Education* [Heb]. Tel Aviv: Massada, 2004.

———.*The School as a Communications Center: A Model of Optimal Humanistic Education* [Heb]. Haifa, IL: Pardes, 2010.

Balanga, A., Landler-Pardo, G., Shachar, M. *Teacher Learning communities (TLC)—Literature review* [Heb]. Jerusalem: The Israel Academy of Sciences and Humanities, 2011.

Barber, M., and M. Mourshed. *How the World's Best-Performing School Systems Come Out on Top.* Dubai: McKinsey & Company, 2007.

Ben-Ari, R., and L. Eliasi. "Between Frontal Teaching Strategy and Complex Teaching Strategy: The Differential Influence of Learning Environment on the Student's Motivation to Achieve" [Heb]. *Megamot*, 45, no. 3 (2008): 531–54.

Biggs J. B., and P. J. Moore. *The Process of Learning.* New York: Prentice Hall, 1993.

Boker-Cohen, Y. *Professional learning communities for teachers—Literature review* [Heb]. Tel Aviv: Mofet, 2016.

Chrisman, V. "How Schools Sustain Success." *Educational Leadership*, 62, no. 5 (2005): 16–20.

Cloyer, R., and L. Kozminsky, eds. *Constructing a Professional Identity: Training and Professional Development Processes of Teachers in Israel* [Heb]. Tel Aviv: Mofet, 2012.

Cuban, L. "Why Some Reforms Last? The Case of the Kindergarten." *American Journal of Education* 100 (February 1992): 166–94.

———."Why So Many Structural Changes in Schools and So Little Reform in Teaching Practice?" Legacy Paper. *Journal of Educational Administration* 51, no. 2 (2013): 109–25.

Darling-Hammond, L., and M. W. McLaughlin. "Policies That Support Professional Development in an Era of Reform." *Phi Delta Kappan* 76, no. 8 (1995): 597–604.

———.Policies That Support Professional Development in an Era of Reform. *Phi Delta Kappan* 92, no. 6 (2011): 81–92.

Darling-Hammond, L., and G. Sykes. "Wanted: A National Teacher Supply Policy for Education: The Right Way to Meet the 'Highly Qualified Teacher' Challenge." *Journal of Education Policy Analysis* 11, no. 33 (2003).

Darling-Hammond, L. "Keeping Good Teachers: Why It Matters, What Leaders Can Do." *Educational Leadership* 60, no. 8 (2003): 6–13.

———. "The Story of Gloria as a Future Vision of the New Teacher." *Journal of Staff Development* 28, no. 3 (2007): 25–26.

Day, C., ed. *The Routledge International Handbook of Teacher and School Development. Routledge International Handbooks of Education.* Florence, KY: Routledge, Taylor and Francis Group, 2011.

Drexler, W. "Empowering Students with Personal Learning Environments." *Independent School* 71, no. 1 (2011): 2–20.

Duke, D. L. "Keys to Sustaining Successful School Turnarounds." *ERS Spectrum* 24, no. 4 (2006): 21–35.

Elmore, R.F. *Bridging the Gap between Standards and Achievement: The Imperative for Professional Development in Education.* Washington, DC: Albert Shanker Institute, 2002.

Fisher, G. "Holistic Leadership" [Heb]. *Hed Hachinuch* 83, no. 4 (2009): 66–68.

Fuchs, A. *Change as a Way of Life in Educational Institutions* [Heb]. Tel Aviv: Cherikover, 1995.

Fuchs, S. *The Psychology of Opposing Change* [Heb]. Ramat Gan, IL: Bar-Ilan University, 1998.

Fullan, M. G. "Leading professional learning." *The School Administrator* 63 (November 2006): 10–14.

———.*Change Forces—Probing the Depth of Educational Reform*. London: The Falmer Press, 1993.

———. *The New Meaning of Educational Change*. New York: Teachers College Press, 2007, 4th ed.

Goldstein, Y. J. "Jewish Education in Latin-America: A Socio-Historical Comparative Perspective." In *Paths in Pluralistic Jewish Education*, ed. N. Chamo and Y. Dror. Tel Aviv: Mofet, 2012, 23–42.

Guthrie, J. W., and L. C. Piercel. "The International Economy and National Education Reform: A Comparison of Education Reforms in the United States and Great Britain." *Oxford Review of Education* 12, no. 2 (1990): 1–27.

Guskey T. R. "Does It Make a Difference? Evaluating Professional Development." *Educational Leadership* 59, no. 6 (2002): 45–51.

Hammel, J. "The Case Study Method in Sociology—New Theoretical and Methodological Issues." *Current Sociology* 40, no. 1 (1992): 1–7.

Hargreaves, A., and M. G. Fullan, eds. *Change Wars*. Bloomington, IN: Solution Tree, 2009.

Kahlenberg, R. D., ed. *The Future of School Integration—Socioeconomic Diversity as an Education Reform Strategy*. New York: The Century Foundation Press, 2012.

Keinan, A. *The Teachers' Room—The Professional Culture of Teachers* [Heb]. Beer Sheva, IL: Bar-Ilan University, 1996.

Levin, B. *Improving All Schools*. 2010. Accessed February 1, 2017. www.avneyrosha.org.il.

Levine, M. "The Essential Cognitive Backpack." *Educational Leadership* 64, no. 7 (2007): 16–22.

McKinsey & Company. *How the World's Best-Performing School Systems Come Out* (2007). Accessed May 23, 2017. http://mckinseyonsociety.com/how-the-worlds-best-performing-schools-come-out-on-top/.

McLaughlin, M. W. and Talbert, J. E. *Building Schools-Based Teacher Learning Communities: Professional Strategies to Improve Student Achievement*. New York: Teachers College Press, (2006).

Nevo, Y., and T. Levine. "Teacher and Student Metaphors in Schools in the Process of Change" [Heb]. In *Research in Education and Its Application in a Changing World*, ed. F. Nasser, N. Hativa, and Z. Schartz, 122–27. Even Yehuda, IL: Reches, 2000.

NIET. *Beyond "Job-Embedded": Ensuring That Good Professional Development Gets Results*. Santa Monica, CA: National Institute for Excellence in Teaching, 2012.

Nieto, S. "From Surviving to Thriving." *Educational Leadership* 66, no. 5 (2009): 8–13.

O'Leary, D., and J. Craig. *System Leadership: Lessons from the Literature*. Nottingham, UK: National College for School Leadership, 2007. In Hebrew, on website www.avneyrosha.org.il, accessed on 15 February 2013.

Popper, M. *On Principals as Leaders* [Heb]. Tel Aviv: Ramot, Tel Aviv University, 1994.

Postholm, M. B. "Teachers' Professional Development: A Theoretical Review." *Educational Research* 54, no. 4 (2012): 405–29.

Pianta, Robert C. *Teaching Children Well: New Evidence-Based Approaches to Teacher Professional Development and Training*. Washington, DC: Center for American Progress, 2011.

Rock, M., M. Gregg, and R. A. Goble. "REACH: A Framework for Differentiating Classroom Instruction." *Preventing School Failure* 52, no. 2 (2008): 31–46.

Schner, M. "The Jewish Education Dialogue—Wandering Between Contradictory Concepts" [Heb]. In *Pathways in Pluralistic Jewish Education,* ed. Hamo and Dror. Tel Aviv: Mofet Institute and Tel Aviv University School of Education, 2012, 33–68.

Shimoni, S., and A. Avidav-Unger, eds. *On Continuity: Specialization and Professional Development of Teachers—Policy, Theory and Practice* [Heb]. Tel Aviv: Mofet, 2013, 197–227.

Shremer, E. "Guiding and Counselling Teachers: A Critical Perspective" [Heb]. In *Training of Teachers,* ed. N. Peles and S. Orion. Jerusalem: Ministry of Education, Pedagogical Secretariat, 1994, 7–28.

Shulman, L. S. "Those Who Understand: Knowledge Growth in Teaching." *Educational Researcher* 15, no. 2 (1986): 4–14.

———. *Where Genius Can Thrive.* Paper presented at the International Conference on Teachers' Cognition and Pedagogical Knowledge. Tel Aviv University, 1993.

———. "To Dignify the Profession of the Teacher: The Carnegie Foundation Celebrates 100 Years." *Change* 37, no. 5) (2005): 22–29.

Snow, R. E. "Individual Differences." In *Instructional Design: International Perspectives: Theory, Research and Models,* vol. 1, ed. R. D. Tennyson, F. Schott, N. M. Seel, and S. Dijkstrs. Lawrence Erlbaum Associates Inc. Publishers, 2009, 215–42.

Stake, R. E. "Case Studies." In *Handbook of Qualitative Research,* ed. N. K. Denzin and Y. S. Lincoln. Thousand Oaks, CA: Sage, 2000; 2nd ed., 435–54.

Stewart, V. "Becoming Citizens of the World." *Educational Leadership* 64, no. 7 (2007): 8–14.

Tomlinson, C., C. Brighton, H. Hertberg, and C. Callahan. "Differentiating Instruction in Response to Student Readiness, Interest, and Learning Profile in Academically Diverse Classroom: A Review of Literature." *Journal for Education of the Gifted* 27, nos. 2–3 (2003): 54–119.

Van Driel, J. H., and A. Berry. "Teacher Professional Development Focusing on Pedagogical Content Knowledge." *Educational Researcher* 41 (2012): 26–28.

Vatslavsky, P., G. Winkland, and R. Fish. *Change—Principles of Creating and Solving Problems* [Heb]. Tel Aviv: Sifriat Hapoalim, 1979.

Villegas-Reimers, E. *Teacher Professional Development: An International Review of the Literature.* Paris: UNESCO: International Institute for Educational Planning, 2003. On websitehttp://www.unesco.org/iiep, accessed on 1 December 2012.

Wigotsky, L. *Learning in a Social Context—Development of High Level Psychological Processes* [Heb]. Tel Aviv: Hakibbutz Hameuhad, 2004.

Yin, R. K. *The Case Study Research—Design and Methods.* Thousand Oaks, CA: Sage, 1989, 2nd ed.

Yosifon, M. *Reshaping Teaching Patterns: Study of the Process of Change in a Middle School in Israel* [Heb]. PhD diss. Tel Aviv: Tel Aviv University, 1996.

Yosifon, M. "From Theory to Practice: The Impact of Study Planning and Counselling on the Shaping of New Teaching Patterns" [Heb]. In *Curricula as a Social Construction,* ed. H. Eilon. Tel Aviv: Ramot, Tel Aviv University, 1998, 109–36.

Yosifon, M. "The Case Study." In *Traditions and Streams in Qualitative Research* [Heb], ed. Tsabar Ben-Yehoshua. Lod: Dvir, 2001, 257–305.

Yosifon, M. "Empowerment as an Agent and Result of Change: A New Look to Professional Development in the School" [Heb]. In *Teachers in a World of Change: Trends and Challenges*, ed. S. Guri-Rosenblit. Tel Aviv: The Open University, 2004, 38–73.

Yosifon, M., and M. Schmida. *Towards a New Educational Paradigm in Israel's Educational System in the Postmodern Age* [Heb]. Tel Aviv: Matach, 2006.

CHAPTER 15

The Local Role of the Mordechai Anielewicz Movement in Uruguay during and after the Six-Day War

GRACIELA BEN DROR AND VICTOR BEN DROR

INTRODUCTION

Uruguay witnessed the establishment of Zionist youth movements from across the Zionist political spectrum in the mid-twentieth century. These included the left-wing kibbutz-affiliated movements of Habonim, Dror, and Hashomer Hatzair, through the centrist Hanoar Hatzioni movement and the religious Bnei Akiva movement, to the nationalist right-wing Betar movement—all of which educated youth between the ages of eight and eighteen according to the principles of Zionism and toward immigration to Israel. A number of Zionist parties also established young adult divisions, which worked with Jews over the age of eighteen, with an emphasis on students. These organizations, the majority of whose members immigrated to Israel after the establishment of the state, have yet to be the subject of detailed monographic research or more comprehensive study. This article examines one of these movements—the Zionist–socialist Mordechai Anielewicz movement, which operated in Uruguay from the early 1950s through the mid-1970s—with an emphasis on the years prior to, during, and following the Arab–Israeli war of 1967. It focuses on the factors that led to the establishment and rapid development of the movement from 1965 onward; its role as a Zionist–socialist movement within the Uruguayan left; and the extent to which the 1967 Arab–Israeli War, known in Israeli historiography as the "Six-Day War," constituted a watershed for the movement's role in the local Zionist movement.

We begin with a characterization of the Mordechai Anielewicz Movement, which focused its efforts both internally on its own membership and externally on political activity and information campaigns outside the movement. Its activities had two primary emphases. The first was Jewish activity, aimed at building the internal ideological strength of the movement and expanding its ranks through the recruitment of young Jews. In the Jewish realm, the movement viewed itself as a relevant and attractive framework for Jewish students active in various left-wing frameworks, such as student unions, labor unions, and left-wing political parties, who— without choosing to do so—had moved away from their Jewish identity. Despite being the children of immigrants, these young Jews underwent assimilation within a society that, at the outset of the twentieth century, enforced a separation between the state and the Christian religion, thus enabling them full social integration. Some of these young Jews, who had still not found a common language with the existing Jewish frameworks, began to gravitate toward the Mordechai Anielewicz Movement after it began to make its voice heard and became known to the public. The movement's overall goal was to constitute an attractive Zionist alternative for young Jews associated with the political left who had begun integrating into general society, and to draw them back into the bosom of Judaism and Zionism. It was also joined by some who came from homes characterized by a greater observance of Jewish culture, who found the combination of Zionism and socialism captivating and well suited to their worldview.

The second emphasis of movement activities was reflected in its work vis-à-vis frameworks of the local left wing, aimed at disseminating ideological and political information to benefit the Jewish people, Zionism, and the State of Israel. The movement's views were consistent with, though not always identical to, those of Mapam (the United Workers Party) in Israel, and exhibited a strong identification with the anti-imperialist liberation movement throughout the world. This article, which is based primarily on archival material and personal interviews that fill out the historical picture, focuses on the extent to which the Mordechai Anielewicz Movement fulfilled the role it assigned itself in this public realm of the local Uruguayan context.

THE ROLE OF IDEOLOGY AND THE HUMAN FACTOR IN THE DEVELOPMENT OF THE MORDECHAI ANIELEWICZ MOVEMENT

The Mordechai Anielewicz movement was established in Montevideo in 1954 as a young adult division linked to the Mapam party and the Kibbutz Artzi and Hashomer Hatzair movements in Israel. During this period of democratic rule, which mainly characterized the country's historical development during the twentieth century, Uruguay was referred to by the country's democratic regime as the "Switzerland of South America." In 1973, like most other Latin American countries, Uruguay experienced an authoritarian coup that ultimately evolved into military rule. The Anielewicz movement was shut down three years later, in 1976, at the height of Uruguay's military dictatorship. Throughout its existence, dozens of the movement's young adult members immigrated to Israel to kibbutzim (plural of kibbutz), and to Israel's cities and towns.

The movement's rapid evolution from 1965 onward stemmed from a number of factors. The first was its embracement of the Zionist–socialist ideology associated with Ber Borochov, who was not only a Marxist and one of the founders of the early Zionist–socialist party Poalei Zion, but whose writings defined Zionism as the liberation movement of the Jewish people. An additional and complementary factor was the reality then prevailing in Latin America in general, and Uruguay in particular, following the twentieth congress of the Communist party of the Soviet Union and the implementation of a policy of coexistence with the West, which raised fundamental questions among leftists in Latin America. The emergence of the new left, the uprising of students in Europe and the United States, and—perhaps most importantly—the establishment of the Non-Aligned Movement bloc heralding the birth of the Third World, as well as the revolution in Cuba and the support it received among leftists in Latin America, were all factors that led to the emergence of an independent local left that was unaffiliated with the Soviet Union and the Communist party, and which adopted a unique model of nation-based socialism. Members of this new left in Latin America were not guided by the internationalist socialism of the Communist party, but rather by a new brand of socialism. This new socialism emphasized the role of the "nation" as the basis for, and a necessary phase in, the development of the anti-imperialist struggle toward the achievement of socialism and social justice. In this reality, the Mordechai Anielewicz Movement in Uruguay found an attentive ear and fertile ground for its Zionist–socialist message, and was able to defend Zionism and the State of Israel using language that was understandable to the local left. Understanding Zionism as the liberation movement of the Jewish people during this period, similar to other liberation movements, was a concept that was difficult to reject. The resurrection of the ideological approach of Ber Borochov—a Zionist-socialist thinker who regarded the nation as the foundation of socialism—served as a useful tool for the Mordechai Anielewicz Movement in Latin America in the mid-1960s.[1]

---

1 See for instance the following material from the weekly *Nueva Sión*, published in Buenos Aires by the Mordechai Anielewitz Movement in Argentina: *Enfoque no. 1, Suplemento de Nueva Sión,*

Another factor stimulating the movement's rapid development was the human one. Dozens of Jewish students with socialist views gravitated toward the Anielewicz movement during a period in which its utopian aspirations appeared to be almost immediately attainable, and worked energetically to achieve their goals. In addition to the Anielewicz movement emissaries and members from Buenos Aires and their newspaper *Nueva Sion*, the movement in Israel sent Mapam and the Anielewicz movement in Uruguay emissaries of high intellectual caliber, who made a qualitative contribution to the establishment of the movement's Zionist–socialist ideology. The movement's members were led by their faith in their methods, their work, and the fertile conditions that existed in Uruguay for the left wing's reception of the movement's messages to adopt Zionist maximalism and socialist radicalism. These were manifested in an uncompromising position that viewed Zionism as a movement concerned solely with Jewish immigration to Israel, and socialism as dictating a preference for settlement on kibbutz and as a source of identification with the worldwide anti-imperialist struggle. Some movement members cut short their university studies in order to immigrate to Israel and settle on kibbutzim, whereas others immigrated only after completing their studies and still live and work in Israel as physicians, engineers, architects, and experts in other professions in different cities throughout the country.

At the beginning of 1966, in accordance with the explicit decision of its institutions, the organization changed its name from the Mordechai Anielewicz Division to the Mordechai Anielewicz Movement. This change was a conscious product of the members' desire to engage in activity that enjoyed greater independence—i.e., to cease merely being an appendix to the international

---

Año XVI, no. 363, Buenos Aires; "La Cuestión Judía"; "El Kibutz," *Enfoque no. 2, Suplemento de Nueva Sión* (n.d.); "Israel, La construccíon y las fuerzas en pugna," *Enfoque no. 3, Suplemento de Nueva Sión* (n.d.); "El hombre enajenado," *Enfoque no. 4, Suplemento de Nueva Sión,* March 15, 1963; "El pueblo judío en lucha por su vida y su dignidad," *Enfoque no. 5, Suplemento de Nueva Sión,* Buenos Aires, April 15, 1963; "Argentina, el antisemitismo y los judíos," *Enfoque no. 6, Suplemento de Nueva Sión* (n.d.); "Neonazismo," *Enfoque no.7, Suplemento de Nueva Sión,* Buenos Aires, April 1967; "De la Rebelión de los Ghettos al El pueblo judío en lucha por su vida y su dignidad," *Nueva Sión* (n.d.); "La URSS ante Israel—La Union Soviética y la creación del Estado de Israel," *Enfoque no. 8, Suplemento de Nueva Sión,* August 1967. Also see "La mujer en el kibutz," *Al Hamishmar, Suplemento especial,* Hanhaga Eliona del Hashomer Hatzair, Israel, October 1966; *La Cuestión judía y el Socialismo—El Sionismo y la Tricontinental* (Montevideo: Juventud Sionista Socialista Mordejai Anilevich, 1966); *La crisis del Cercano Oriente, Acerca del conflicto árabe-israelí. Imperialismo y anti-imperialismo* (Montevideo: Movimiento Mordejai Anilevich, June 1967); *Polonia. Antisionismo y antisemitismo* (Montevideo: Movimientos Sionistas Socialistas Mordejai Anilevich y Hashomer Hatzair, May 1968).

Mapam movement, and to begin work that would prove more relevant to current local needs. Its members recognized the movement's unique place within the local Zionist movement, and were determined to work vigorously in order to achieve their goals.

THE ANIELEWICZ MOVEMENT'S INFORMATION CAMPAIGNS AND PUBLIC RELATIONS WORK

In the realm of information dissemination and public activity, the Anielewicz movement was fully cognizant of its unique ability to serve as a Zionist mouthpiece vis-à-vis the local left by means that were intended for the general public. The movement's information campaigns and public relations work dealt with a number of primary themes.

MOVEMENT ACTIVITY IN THE DAYS OF THE TRI-CONTINENTAL CONFERENCE IN HAVANA

A tri-continental conference was held in Havana in January 1966, and, when the conference's organizers refused to allow the participation of the Israeli left—Mapam, Maki (the Israeli Communist Party), and *Achdut Ha'Avoda*—the Anielewicz division took emergency measures and instituted a mobilization of members of the left wing in Uruguay, the general media in the country, and other public intra- and extra-movement realms.

On January 5, 1966, at the initiative of the Anielewicz division, well-known intellectuals and left-wing figures throughout Latin America signed a telegram that was sent to Havana, to Cuban leader Fidel Castro personally, and to *Casa de las Américas* (a major Cuban institution that maintained the country's extensive relations with the countries of Latin America, particularly in the realm of public relations and cultural ties). The telegram called on Castro to reconsider the Israeli political movements' non-invitation to the Havana conference as follows:

> We are concerned by the denial of the request to invite the political forces of the Israeli left to the Tri-Continental Conference in Havana and by the fact that this rejection may benefit imperialism, which has an interest in sowing division among the forces of the left and isolating them around issues of tension. As representatives of the only forces capable of actualizing a path of understanding for the national and social liberation of the nations, we hereby request that this decision be reconsidered.

[Signed:] Carlos Quijano, editor in chief of the weekly newspaper *Marcha*; Eduardo Galeano, editor in chief of the newspaper *Época*; Prof. Gastón Blanco; Prof. Ángel Rama; journalist Carlos Machado; journalist Guillermo Chifflet; theater director and manager Atahualpa del Cioppo; parliamentarian Enrique Martínez Moreno; Senator Hugo Batalla; former socialist parliamentarian German D'Elía; and sociologist German Rama.[2]

These signatories were all prominent intellectuals and public figures in Uruguay who, at the time, played leading roles in the shaping of public opinion within political streams associated with the center–left of the political spectrum.

The telegram was written in a positive tone, in the form of a request for reconsideration, and contained no element of protest (at least not at this stage), in order to ease the recruitment of desired individuals to sign the letter; some may have refused to sign had the text been formulated in a more antagonistic manner.

Communist senator Enrique Rodríguez, a leader of the "Leftist Front of Liberation" (*Frente Izquierda de Liberación*, or FIDEL—a front consisting of various left-wing parties but dominated by the Communist party), informed the movement that the members of the committee who had been sent to Havana would not sign the telegram, even if they had no reservations concerning its formulation, but that other FIDEL members would do so.

The Anielewicz movement itself sent two additional telegrams. The first was addressed to the Uruguayan delegation to the conference and proposed the creation of a bloc of Latin American countries that would act to thwart the anti-Israeli decision, and requested that Castro himself be personally informed of the concern that such a position had the potential to spark serious protest in communities around the world. The second letter was sent to Rodney Arismendi, a Communist party parliament member in Uruguay and the party's decades-long undisputed leader in the country. Anielewicz movement members also took advantage of the presence in Montevideo of one of their own members from Buenos Aires to motivate the movement in Argentina to mobilize itself accordingly, to appeal to public opinion in the country, and to send a letter to Havana and to Chile on their own behalf. The Communists whom the Anielewicz division approached in Montevideo were essentially in agreement with them and their request, but nonetheless refrained from adding their signatures to the telegrams.

---

2 *Marcha*, January 14, 1966. The members of the Mordechai Anielewicz Movement worked hard to achieve their aims.

In addition to their work vis-à-vis local Uruguayan political forces, Anielewicz movement members published a public statement regarding the tri-continental conference in *Marcha*, an independent weekly publication that published the writings of most of the left-wing intellectuals. It was the most popular publication of its kind in Uruguay and one of the most prestigious such journals in Latin America. On January 14, 1966, the readers' section ran the following open letter under the headline "Expulsions from the Tri-Continental Conference":

In light of the convening of the Tri-Continental Conference in Havana, the Mordechai Anielewicz Zionist–socialist Youth regards itself obligated to articulate publicly the following positions:

The Tri-Continental Conference constitutes a fundamental milestone in the struggle of the nations for their national and social liberation. At this stage, such a struggle is based on and conducted by means of the positive internationalism of all the revolutionary and anti-imperialist movements, whose strength stems from solidarity among nations. This was articulated explicitly by Fidel Castro on the occasion of the seventh anniversary celebrations of the victory of the Cuban Revolution in his statement that "this will be a year of solidarity," to which we add: a year of international anti-imperialist solidarity, national solidarity, and unity. From this perspective, we are expressing our unequivocal support of this conference…. However, like all realities, this one has a dark side that harms us directly and requires us to intervene and express our position: [specifically,] the deliberate expulsion of Israel's left-wing parties, following their explicit request to be invited to the event. Why do we regard it as our obligation to formulate our position and assert it publicly? Because such an act runs completely counter to the essence of the conference in that it serves imperialism using one of its preferred methods: the sowing of division and the prevention of the unity of the nations in their just struggle. What are the factors that resulted in this expulsion? Was it a one-time act or one more link in a chain? … Thus far, this has been the general nature of all the assemblies—at every level —that include the participation of delegations from the Arab countries, in which Israel's right to exist, and that of the different segments of its population, is systematically denied. Such positions become particularly difficult when asserted at meetings of forces of the left or anti-imperialist fronts, as is currently occurring at the conference in question. What kind of internationalism can serve to justify the rejection and isolation of the leftist forces of a specific people? Israel today is an irreversible fact, and, peace in the Middle East eventually will become a reality based on the joint efforts of Arab and the Israeli peoples. The objective of our activities in this area—for us—represents an existential issue. On this basis, it is important to facilitate the meeting of all the forces fighting for peace and socialism, both in Israel and in the Arab states.... Nothing can be achieved by means of such expulsions, except the weakening of the forces of progress in Israel on the domestic front, and a limiting of the anti-imperialist struggle in the Middle East. The Arab states are therefore contributing nothing to the Tri-Continental Conference with this position. They are intensifying the passivity of the other delegations around the world with their incessant repetition of such occurrences at international meetings, serving only to strengthen these contradictions. In this manner, international forums become party to this mistake and to preventing it from being overturned. It is for this reason that we have written this public statement. In conclusion, the expulsion of the left-wing Israeli parties from the Tri-Continental Conference is destructive to its essence, and blocks the paths of understanding in the Middle East. Only progressive movements among the peoples of the Arab countries and Israel can pave a way to the reality of peace and mutual support for the sake of the national and social liberation of their peoples. The above formulation has been understood and adopted by public figures with a proven anti-imperialist orientation in Uruguay, and on this basis it was decided to send a telegram using this language to the leadership of the Tri-Continental Conference.

Signed: The Mordechai Anielewicz Movement[3]

As we have seen, alongside this letter from the Anielewicz movement, the same issue of *Marcha* contained the abovementioned telegram signed by Uruguayan intellectuals and shapers of public opinion, which was also initiated by members of the movement.

The intensive activity that led up to and continued during the assembly in Havana resulted in sharp disagreements with the Young Zionist Federation (FJS) and the local Zionist organization (OSU). In a report submitted on January 30, 1966, to Chaike Grossman, who had recently replaced Yehuda Tubin as chairperson of the World Union of Mapam, the Anielewicz movement and Mapam emissary Zelig Shoshan explained the events that had taken place leading up to and during the tri-continental conference as follows: the Mapam and Hashomer Hatzair–affiliated movement "family" to which the Anielewicz movement belonged was "facing an attack of the Zionist right." Shoshan also reported that the broader Hashomer Hatzair movement had not been authorized

---

3 Ibid.

by the Zionist establishment to intervene in political affairs in the non-Jewish community. In his opinion, the explanations of the Anielewicz movement and its broader affiliated family had been rejected by the establishment based not on doubt regarding the importance of its Zionist activity, but because the movement's "broad socialist support at the conference" had had the potential to create the impression that "all Jews are associated with the left"—which was the focus of the Jewish establishment's concerns. Shoshan made special note of the fact that the Israeli embassy in Montevideo had conducted itself wisely and had refrained from contributing to or encouraging anti-Castro hysteria. The embassy's first consul took care to enumerate all the virtues of the Cuban leader vis-à-vis Israel, and argued that there was no logic in attacking him, "at least not at this point."[4] Overall, concluded the report, it was abundantly clear that the movement supported the anti-imperialist struggle but denounced the organizing committee's decisions, the unequivocal discrimination they reflected, and its willingness to be extorted by Arab parties.

In the meantime, on January 28, 1966, the Anielewicz movement mounted a nighttime placard-posting campaign throughout the city, this time on a particularly massive scale, to denounce the discrimination against the parties of the Israeli left. The placards bore such slogans as "Peace and socialism in the Middle East will be achieved with Israel or will not be achieved at all," and "the Jewish People demands its role in the worldwide anti-imperialist struggle," and were signed: "Zionist–socialist youth, the Mordechai Anielewicz Movement."[5] Movement members composed and disseminated the Marxist interpretation of the Jewish question based on Zionist–socialist Borochovist ideology, as discussed above. It was probably the first time that the fundamental documents of this interpretation of Zionism—beyond the books that also dealt with the national issue of the Jewish people, published by a press named after Mordechai Anielewicz—had ever been disseminated in Uruguay by the press of the political left in Montevideo, particularly by *Marcha* and *Época*.[6]

For the first time ever, according to the assessment of the Israeli embassy in Montevideo, the Uruguayan delegation abstained from the vote against Israel at the tri-continental conference in Havana, which also influenced the abstention of the Argentinean delegation. According to the Israeli ambassador in Montevideo, these positions were related to the work of the Anielewicz movement.

---

4   Zelig Shoshan to Chaike Grossman, January 30, 1966, Hashomer Hatzair Archive 85.31 (2).
5   Interview with Eduardo Bartfeld, August 4, 2014, in Montevideo, and interview with Aharon Melika, the Hashomer Hatzair Emissary to Uruguay from 1965–67, at Kibbutz Dan, March 13, 2012.
6   See, for instance, in the intellectual journal *Marcha*, January 14, 1966 and February 2, 1966.

When disagreements intensified, the Israeli embassy in Uruguay offered its assistance in reaching compromise. However, resolving the never-ending disputes that characterized the movement's operations required the periodic intervention of institutions in Israel—the Israel-based institutions of the Kibbutz Artzi settlement movement and Mapam (the senior leadership of world Hashomer Hatzair and the World Union of Mapam in Tel Aviv) on the one hand, and the major institutions of the World Zionist Organization in Jerusalem, from the organization department of the Zionist Organization to requests for the intervention of Zionist executive chairman Louis A. Pincus, and even WZO president Nahum Goldmann, on the other.[7]

THE ROLE AND ACTIVITY OF THE ANIELEWICZ MOVEMENT DURING THE SIX-DAY WAR

The Anielewicz movement was extremely active in the "days of waiting" that preceded the outbreak of the war, including publishing letters from Israel calling on Jewish youth to mobilize and come to Israel. During this period, the movement issued a manifesto that was published in booklet form and by the local press, which enumerated the basic principles for supporting the State of Israel as a means of promoting peace in the Middle East. The text was divided into three subtopics, and was signed by the Mordechai Anielewicz Movement in Montevideo, Uruguay.[8] The goal of this declaration was to facilitate better understanding of the problems of the people in Israel in light of the crisis caused by the days of waiting, and to cause Jews on the one hand, and the local left wing on the other, to support the State of Israel in the conflict. To this end, it employed language familiar to the local left wing. As we will see below, the movement also engaged in other types of activity.

In the meantime, a telex had reached the country calling on the Jewish youth to mobilize and come to Israel.[9] During a meeting held that same evening, the central movement institutions decided that all members of the central committee would leave for Israel immediately. Within twenty-four hours, they all informed their families that they had been mobilized as volunteers to go to Israel in preparation for the imminent war. Hostilities finally broke out on Monday, June 5, 1967, as clearly reflected in the

---

7 Zelig Shoshan to Chaike Grossman, January 30, 1966 Hashomer Hatzair Archive, 37.93 A (1).

8 June 1967, *The Crisis in the Middle East: The Israeli-Arab Conflict, Imperialism and Anti-Imperialism*, signed by the Mordechai Anielewicz Movement, Victor Blit (Ben-Dror) Personal Archive, Kibbutz Ramot Menashe.

9 Hashomer Hatzair Archive, 85.31 (2), and The Jewish People Archive, The Hebrew University of Jerusalem, Givat Ram, UR/MO 39.

newspaper *El Plata*, which reported "war has already broken out between Israel and the United Arab Republic," and continued to provide general information on what was happening in the region from various sources. The Uruguayan press conveyed the following information, which originated in Tel Aviv: war had broken out that morning in the Middle East, with fierce battles between Egyptian and Israeli tanks and artillery and Israeli air attacks against Egyptian military airfields. Tel Aviv and Cairo reported casualties resulting from aggression by the other side, and the UN secretary general decided to convene the organization's security council urgently. A number of Arab countries announced that they had initiated military action against Israel, and, by midday, hostilities were also underway on the Israeli–Jordanian border in Jerusalem. Additional newspaper headlines expanded the coverage and provided information under headlines such as "Johnson and the Pope Face the Conflict," "Cairo Bombed," and "The U.N.: A Discussion on the War."[10] The major commercial newspaper reflected a sense of sympathy with Israel during the period of waiting, as well as with the members of the Anielewicz movement who had decided to leave for Israel immediately at the end of May 1967. The press contained extensive coverage on the subject. The war was to last only six days. Delays originating in Israel meant that before the volunteers left for Israel by plane, as planned, another group of volunteers, consisting of the central activists of the Anielewicz movement and many other mobilized young adults (approximately one-third of all the volunteers who left Uruguay for Israel in June 1967), set out for Israel by ship on June 8. As noted, large numbers of young Jews visited the Anielewicz movement's headquarters during the period of waiting that led up to the war and during the war itself, and the entire process was extensively photographed and covered by the local press.[11]

The movement's activity, and the fact that some movement members spent six months working on kibbutzim in Israel—with some members remaining in the country as immigrants and others returning to Uruguay and immigrating to Israel later, in 1969—endowed the Anielewicz movement with senior status among the Zionist youth movements in Uruguay. When they returned to the country, an *aliyah* (a Hebrew term referring to Jewish immigration to Israel) movement was established, in which Anielewicz movement members played a central role, and the Uruguayan Zionist establishment's attitude toward the Anielewicz movement reflected significant change. Aharon Melika, a Hashomer Hatzair emissary in Montevideo reflected on how, during the Six-Day War, the Anielewicz movement

---

10   "Ya estalló la guera entre Israel y RAU," "Johnson y el Papa ante la contienda," "El Cairo fue bombardeado," "Un Debate sobre la guerra," *El Plata*, June 5, 1967.

11   Report from Shabtai Avni and Aharon Melika to Shaike Wainer, June 5, 1967, Hashomer Hatzair Archive, 85.31 (2).

had succeeded in playing a central role in the Jewish community. It had become the major recruiter of volunteers from within the community, even though all its major activists had already left for Israel as volunteers. One of the factors he noted was the sense of persecution that had characterized the movement until that point, which had forced it to go to great lengths to prove itself. In the mid-1960s, when the Anielewicz movement was still in its early stages, the movement was no more than a signature. However, sometimes, when effectively managed and cultivated, a signature can create a dynamic and a chain reaction that, in the right constellation, can be more decisive than the phenomenon itself.[12]

The mass mobilization of the central activists of the Anielewicz movement, and the extensive work conducted to promote the mobilization of volunteers during the days of waiting that led up to the Six-Day War, provided the movement with a respected position within the community in general and within the organized Zionist movement in particular. The Mordechai Anielewicz Movement now enjoyed a much higher standing and could no longer be ignored or restricted in statement or action. As we have seen, its members played a central role in the work of the *aliyah* movement that was established in the country in 1968. The fact that the Anielewicz movement addressed a different, hitherto non-Zionist population, consisting primarily of young Jews oriented toward the political left, was also important. These members did not always possess a deeply rooted or explicit Jewish identity, and some had been assimilated before they joined the ranks of the movement. Certainly, they had never before been affiliated organizationally with the World Zionist Organization.

IDEOLOGICAL-POLITICAL VIEWS: THE MORDECHAI ANIELEWICZ PUBLISHING HOUSE (EDITORIAL MORDEJAI ANILEVICH)

Following the Six-Day War, an atmosphere that was antagonistic to Israel rapidly took hold in leftist circles, and criticism was quick to come. Between 1967 and 1970, movement members worked in conjunction with Israeli emissaries to produce and distribute books that the movement wished to use to disseminate the messages of the Israeli left, and to have local impact. Movement emissary Shabtai Avni was particularly active in the realm of book production, which included books on ideology, politics, international current affairs, the Holocaust, the kibbutz, the Arab–Israeli conflict, Zionism and the left, and other

---

12 Interview with Carmela and Aharon Melika, March 13, 2012, at Kibbutz Dan, Israel, and interview with Eduardo Bartfeld, August 4, 2014, Montevideo.

relevant subjects. The Mordechai Anielewicz Publishing House in Uruguay produced eleven books in three years. Some were of critical importance to external Zionist information dissemination among intellectuals and Jewish students, and to the dissemination of the message of the Uruguayan left. One such book was *A Visit to Israel: Jean-Paul Sartre and Simone de Beauvoir* (*Visita a Israel, Jean Paul Sartre–Simone de Beauvoir*), published and distributed in July 1967, which documented Simone de Beauvoir's and Jean-Paul Sartre's visit to Israel before the Six-Day War. As a result of the war and the atmosphere that emerged among the left, movement members thought it necessary to engage in an information campaign, and materials from various sources were combined even before the arrival of *Modern Times* (*Temps Modernes*) to Montevideo.[13] The book covers the visit of the two French philosophers in Israel in April–May 1967, and was produced and disseminated the same year, just after the war. In a report of September 14, 1967, submitted to Akiva Wasserman, a member of the senior leadership of world Hashomer Hatzair, Avni reported that a thousand copies of the book had been purchased by the Israeli embassy with the intention of distributing them throughout Latin America.[14]

Another title published by the Anielewicz movement in 1967, *Pages of Jewish Heroism* (*Páginas de heroismo judío*), was devoted to the subject of the Holocaust and instances of Jewish heroism during the period.[15] In this case, two thousand copies were printed.[16]

One of the most important books published dealt with the nationalist question, which was the main issue employed by Anielewicz movement members to convince young Jews to leave the ranks of the left and join Zionism, and to convince the left-wing parties in Uruguay of the legitimacy of Zionism and the State of Israel. This book, entitled *The National Question* (*La cuestión nacional*), was published in February 1968.[17]

One of the most important of the other titles that were published was a short book by Meir Yaari, the leader of Mapam and Hashomer Hatzair in Israel, entitled

---

13 Jean Paul Sartre and Simone de Beauvoir, *Visita a Israel* (Montevideo: Ediciones Mordejai Anilevich, 1967).

14 Report from Shabtai Avni to Akiva Wasserman, August 14, 1967, Hashomer Hatzair Archive, 85.31 (2).

15 Yehuda Bauer, Shalom Cholavski, Itzjak Rabin, et al., *Páginas de heroismo judío* (Montevideo: Ediciones Mordejai Anilevich, 1967).

16 Letter from Shabtai Avni to Akiva Wasserman, September 14, 1967, Hashomer Hatzair Archive, 85.31 (2).

17 Ber Borojov, Meir Iaari, and Daniel Ben Nahum, *La cuestión nacional* (Montevideo: Ediciones Mordejai Anilevich, 1968).

Under the Slogan of Unity and Independence (*Bajo el signo de unidad e independencia*). The Anielewicz movement also dealt extensively with Soviet Jewry as a persecuted minority, which brought it into conflict with the Jewish Communists of the ICUF.[18] One such book was *An Oppressed Nationality: The Jewish Minority in the Soviet Union* (*Nacionalidad oprimida—La minoría judía en la URSS*), which was produced and published in 1968, just as the struggle for Soviet Jewry was intensifying,[19] and was ultimately distributed throughout Latin America. Another book produced in 1968 was an anthology containing articles on the Soviet invasion of Czechoslovakia entitled *Czechoslovakia 1968* (*Checoslovaquia 1968*).[20]

The movement's publishing apparatus was extremely active later as well. In 1969, it published *Arab Socialism* (*El socialismo árabe*) by Avraham Ben-Tzur, a scholar of the Middle East and a member of Kibbutz Lehavot Habashan,[21] which diligently explored the theory and activities related to this phenomenon. Members of the Anielewicz movement believed in the importance of exposing the false mythology underlying the term "Arab Socialism." The book was received warmly by non-Jewish circles with an interest in deepening their knowledge on the subject.[22] In 1968, the movement published *Israel: A Subject for the Left* (*Israel: Un tema para la izquierda*), edited by Bernardo Kliksberg. This book contained a collection of articles written by influential political and intellectual figures from around the world addressing the Arab-Israeli conflict from a left-wing perspective.[23] The following year witnessed the publication of *The Kibbutz: A Socialist Challenge* (*El kibuts—Un desafío socialista*),[24] written by Dan León, a member of Kibbutz Yasur. Another book published by the Mordechai Anielewicz Publishing House in 1969 was Nessia Orolovitz

---

18 Meir Iaari, *Bajo el Signo de la Unidad e Independencia* (Tesis ante la 5ª. Convención del Partido MAPAM—Israel) (Montevideo: Ediciones Mordejai Anilevich, 1969).

19 Julio Adin and Nahum Goldmann et al., *Nacionalidad Oprimida. La minoría judía en la URSS* (Montevideo: Ediciones Mordejai Anilevich, 1968).

20 Jean Paul Sartre, Bertrand Russell, Jean Daniel, et al., *Checoslovaquia 1968* (Montevideo: Ediciones Mordejai Anilevich, 1968).

21 Abraham BenTzur, *El socialismo árabe. Teoría y práctica* (Montevideo: Ediciones Mordejai Anilevich, 1969).

22 Report from Shabtai Avni to Chaike Grossman, December 26, 1969, Hashomer Hatzair Archive 37.93 A (1).

23 *Israel: Un tema para la Izquierda* (Montevideo: Ediciones Mordejai Anilevich, 1969).

24 Dan Leon, *El Kibuts: un desafío socialista* (Montevideo: Ediciones Mordejai Anilevich, 1970). See also Report from Shabtai Avni to Chaike Grossman, December 26, 1969, Hashomer Hatzair Archive, 37.93 A (1).

Reznik's well-known testimony *Mama, Are We Already Allowed to Cry?* (*Ya puedo llorar, mamá?*), about life in the ghetto.[25]

In 1970, the Mordechai Anielewicz Publishing House produced its last book. It was an ideological text entitled *Zionism and the Left* (*El sionismo y la izquierda*) by Dov Bar-Nir,[26] an ideologue who had served as secretary of the Hashomer Hatzair Workers Party, a member of the first Knesset for the Mapam party and secretary of the party's Central Committee, and secretary of the World Union of Mapam. Bar-Nir was considered to be knowledgeable on the new streams of leftist thinking in the world, and well informed regarding recent developments in international politics.

In addition to the books published and distributed by the Mordechai Anielewicz Publishing House, the movement also felt the need to produce materials that were accessible to young Jews in general, as well as to university students, Jews and non-Jews alike. To this end, it produced two such publications entitled *Anielewicz Notebooks* (*Cuadernos Anilevich*), the first in July–August 1967 and the second in March 1968.[27]

An overview of the activity of the Mordechai Anielewicz Publishing House between 1967 and 1970 reveals a number of factors that assured the economic feasibility and survival of the publication enterprise. First, the Israeli embassy in Montevideo typically purchased their books in large quantities and took care to distribute them effectively throughout Latin America. In addition, the fact that the Anielewicz movement in Montevideo was the only element within the Zionist movement engaged in such work helped ensure the movement's dominance in this realm.[28]

The very existence of the publishing enterprise made the Mordechai Anielewicz Movement an organization that commanded the respect of the Jewish and non-Jewish public in Uruguay. With regard to the Jewish population, the publishing enterprise also had a positive impact on those who disagreed with the movement's worldview and political aims; such legitimization was

---

25 Nessia Orlovitz Reznik, *Ya puedo llorar, mamá?* (Montevideo: Ediciones Mordejai Anilevich, 1969).

26 Dov Bar Nir, *El Sionismo y la Izquierda* (Montevideo: Ediciones Mordejai Anilevich, 1970). Also see interview with Shabtai Avni, April 8, 2012, at Kibbutz Ga'ash.

27 *Cuadernos Anilevich, Radiografía de un conflicto, Que es el socialismo árabe, Nasserismo y socialismo* 1, 1 (Montevideo: Ediciones Mordejai Anilevich, July–August 1967); *Cuadernos Anilevich, Israel: los mitos de la Izquierda* 2 (Montevideo: Ediciones Mordejai Anilevich, March 1968).

28 Interview with Shabtai Avni, February 10, 2012, at Kibbutz Ga'ash.

particularly important in light of the crises and conflicts that for years had characterized its interactions with the local Jewish establishment.

THE RADIO BROADCASTS OF THE "HASHOMER FAMILY" IN MONTEVIDEO

The "Hashomer Family" (*Hamishpacha Hashomrit*)—an expression used at times to refer collectively to Hashomer Hatzair, the Mordechai Anielewicz Movement, and the Mapam party—had one hour each week, on Saturday afternoons, to articulate its views over the radio in Montevideo. During these broadcasts, which could be picked up in several parts of the city, Mapam personnel typically spoke in Yiddish and Anielewicz movement personnel in Spanish. In some years, Hashomer Hatzair members also conducted radio broadcasts. Because the movement activists who took part in the effort were not professionals, they found it difficult to prepare a weekly program that lasted a full hour. The activists on the radio committees usually had to work extremely hard for an entire week to prepare a program for broadcast, and from time to time resorted to playing tracks from records they had received from Israel over and over again. Reports and stories were based on content published in *Nueva Sion*, the newspaper published by the Hashomer family in Buenos Aires; responses to articles that appeared in *Marcha*; and stories from the Israeli press translated by the movement emissary, especially from the Hebrew-language Israeli movement newspaper *Al Hamishmar*. Surprisingly, unequivocal unanimity exists regarding the importance of the movement's radio broadcasts over the course of many years as a mouthpiece for the dissemination of its views. On the one hand, as the ratings of these radio broadcasts have never been examined professionally, it is difficult to reach an objective assessment of their effectiveness in disseminating the approach and insights of the movement in Montevideo. On the other hand, there is no doubt that the obligation to meet the weekly broadcast schedule, within an organization that operated entirely on a volunteer basis, required its activists to carry out their work systematically and with a unique sense of devotion. As a result, over the years, the movement's radio broadcasts constituted the longest running movement activity in Montevideo. At times, and particularly during the period of persecution under the dictatorship in Uruguay, no alternative channels existed to ensure that the voice of the movement would continue to be heard by the Jewish community, even if—under the circumstances—the content underwent change and was adapted to the constraints of the situation.[29]

---

29 Interview with Leonardo and Iris Ziman, November 20, 2011, at Kibbutz Ramot Menashe.

Movement emissaries also made use of local Yiddish- and Spanish-language newspapers to convey the messages of the movement, primarily to address the issue of Jewish identity, in order to draw young Uruguayan Jews into the ranks of socialist Zionism. In this way, Zelig Shoshan, who served as an Israeli emissary to the Anielewicz movement and Mapam in Uruguay between 1963 and 1966, and who led the movement's rapid development and recognized its potential to attract young assimilated Jews, tried to reach out not only to members of the movement but to young Jews in general—those who, in an era of cosmopolitanism, had theoretically rejected their connection to the nation and to the Jewish people, and had chosen to assimilate. Articles in the Spanish-language Jewish press offered a convenient way to pursue this task.[30]

REJECTION OF THE COMMUNIST PARTY LINE

Movement members also engaged in defending the State of Israel from complete, en bloc rejection, primarily from the orthodox Communist world bloc and the local Communist party, including the Jewish Communists. The Anielewicz movement opposed the approach of the international Communist party, not only because of its a-national cosmopolitan ideology, which rejected the Zionist movement altogether, but also due to the practical activity of the Communist bloc in Europe. This included the invasion of Hungary in 1956, the invasion of the Czech Republic in 1968, and the Soviet Union's treatment of its own internal Jewish population (including the denial of their freedom of expression and their freedom to immigrate to Israel). Criticism also resulted from the non-Marxist analysis (as Anielewicz members viewed it), which negated the nationality of an entire people—the Jewish people. As a result, it also tended to negate Israel en bloc, without focused criticism, and without taking account of the complexity and internal political divisions that existed within Israel with regard to socioeconomic issues and factors related to peace in the Middle East. Members of the Anielewicz movement believed that with regard to all-embracing strategic issues, time was not to be wasted on a focused information campaign vis-à-vis the Communist party in Uruguay, as it was abundantly clear that its positions were determined in Moscow, not in Montevideo.

---

30 Zelig Shoshan, "Diálogo con la juventud judía," *Semanario Hebreo* 1–2, from Zelig Shoshan, personal archive, no date mentioned (probably from 1964 or 1965). We would like to thank his wife, Esther Shoshan, for putting his personal archive at our disposal.

As for the Communist party and all the affiliated circles, including the non-Zionist Jewish left, the state of affairs in Uruguay was no different from that in the rest of the world. The Jews who were linked ideologically to the Communist party were organized within a Jewish organization known as the ICUF, which had an adult division, a youth movement, a supplementary school for instruction of the Yiddish language, and published a daily newspaper in Yiddish known as *Undzer Fraint* (*Our Friend*). The institutions of the ICUF engaged in fierce arguments with the Anielewicz movement as a movement that defined itself as leftist but that belonged to the Zionist camp, which they regarded as reactionary. Most Anielewicz movement members did not espouse the ideology of the Communist party for the reasons explained above, which were related in essence to both Zionist–socialist ideology and to approaches regarding definitions of socialism in the new era, following the twentieth congress of the Communist party in the Soviet Union. The ideological aspect was the fundamental cause of disagreement. It is interesting to note that the parents of a small number of Anielewicz movement members were either Jewish Communists, taught in the organization's Zhitlowsky School, or had ties to the group and received its Yiddish-language newspaper. Nonetheless, the struggle with the Jewish Communists intensified, particularly around the ideological issue, as a result of the Anielewicz movement's efforts (the success of which was extremely partial) to attract young left-wing Jews to defect from the orthodox cosmopolitan Communism of the ICUF to the ranks of the Zionists, to espouse socialist Zionism, and to immigrate to Israel. In most cases, as noted, these young Jews reached the Anielewicz movement via student activities at the university. These activities were characterized also by a strict adherence to leftist conceptions and an opposition to socioeconomic policies that worked to the detriment of the students and the working class, and were closely associated with what was then understood as Uruguayan government support for imperialism, which deleteriously affected the rights of the people.

POSITIVE RELATIONS WITH THE SOCIALIST PARTY

The new perspective of the young Jews on the political left in Latin America and in Montevideo, particularly after the Cuban revolution, drew them closer to movements that were independent in the formulation of their positions, such as the Uruguayan socialist party. The Anielewicz movement in Montevideo was particularly sympathetic to post-revolution Cuba, as was the rest of the left wing in Uruguay and Latin America and the newly awakening Third World. It had a Marxist-Borochovist answer to the development and crystallization of socialism, as was typical of anti-imperialist movements of the Third World and the new left. It remained loyal to its anti-imperialist approaches and, as we have seen, did indeed espouse nation-based socialism. Like the leaders of many other anti-imperialist movements, leaders of the Uruguayan socialist party, like Vivian Trías, naturally gravitated toward the nation-based socialism of Borochov and at times sounded almost as if they were quoting him. As a result, the Anielewicz movement established closer relations with the Uruguayan socialist party, which was obligated not to the Soviet Union but to nation-based socialism as it understood it, and with which the movement maintained a running dialogue of respect.[31]

A few movement members recall that on the night of November 27, 1966, the day of the national general elections, a number of members of the Anielewicz leadership paid a visit to the socialist party's headquarters at "People's House." The party had just suffered one of the most staggering defeats in its history after receiving only 11,559 votes, or 9 percent of the total votes. It remained without parliamentary representation, putting an end to a parliamentary presence that had lasted decades. Within the movement, it was decided to meet with party representatives immediately at the time of crisis, and a group of movement members made their way to the building, which was empty except for them and a handful of socialist party leaders, including Vivian Trías and José Pedro Cardoso, for whom they had come to show their solidarity. The movement invested great efforts in explaining to the socialists in Uruguay the positions of the Israeli left, especially those of Mapam, on the conflict in the Middle East. Faithful to the battle slogan that accompanied movement activity during that period, "Only peace is revolutionary in the Middle East," movement members used a number of channels of information dissemination. These included posting placards, publishing letters in the readers' sections of the independent left-wing newspapers *Marcha* and *Época*, organizing "roundtable" discussions on a number of occasions to clarify major issues related to the conflict in the Middle East, and conducting personal meetings with leading influential left-wing figures and intellectuals.[32]

---

31 Vivián Trías, *Socialismo Nacional* (Montevideo: Ediciones El Sol, n.d.), 7–9.
32 Interview with Eduardo Bartfeld, August 4, 2014, Montevideo, and also photo album of Aharon Melika, personal archive.

THE ANIELEWICZ MOVEMENT'S TIES WITH PARTIES, MOVEMENTS, AND INTELLECTUALS OF THE URUGUAYAN LEFT

Between 1964 and 1973, the year the Uruguayan dictatorship was established, the Anielewicz movement had extensive contacts with political parties of the Uruguayan center and left, as well as with movements and prominent Uruguayan intellectuals and public figures. The work of the Anielewicz movement was relatively easier and its information dissemination and persuasion efforts made more sense with regard to circles associated with the independent left, which lacked a quasi-religious ideological center that authoritatively decided upon dogmas and ways of thinking that were closely coordinated with instructions issued from Moscow. Cuba did not necessarily follow policies that were identical to those espoused by the Soviet Union, but rather adopted more independent positions. The Cubans were not party to the declarations of complete rejection of the State of Israel, based on their recognition of the rights of small nations to fight for their existence. The approach within Uruguay to elements in the press with sympathies for the local independent left and intellectuals was also relatively convenient for the Anielewicz movement, which managed to publish a number of articles in their publications. From the tri-continental conference in Havana in 1966 onward, during the Six-Day War and in its aftermath, the movement and its Israeli emissary Shabtai Avni published letters in the readers' section of *Marcha* that explained the positions of the Mapam party in Israel and of the Anielewicz movement in Montevideo. In October 1967, this weekly paper took the movement's declarations seriously, and the public reverberations caused by their publication in this venue were considerable. Also influential was the fact that the Anielewicz movement was the only Zionist–socialist party operating on the ground; its views were well known to Jewish and non-Jewish students in all faculties.[33]

Avni also developed special ties with an anarchist Marxist group known as Commune of the South (Comunidad del Sur). This relationship began to take form when Zelig Shoshan was the movement emissary in Montevideo, as reflected in the publication of *The Goals and the Path: Comunidad del Sur— A Cooperative and Integral Life Experience*. The book opens with the familiar words of Meir Yaari: "not pens, paper, and ink; not odes and anthems;

---

33 Interviews with Eduardo Bartfeld, August 4, 2014, Leonardo and Iris Ziman, November 20, 2012, and Shabtai Avni, April 8, 2012.

not confessions and the spilling of the soul; but rather saws, axes, hoes, and, first and foremost— hands! Give us your hands!" Shoshan published articles in *Al Hamishmar* under the title "Kibbutz in Montevideo," which not only highlighted the kibbutz, but which also reflected the fact that the movement had maintained a close relationship with Comunidad del Sur for many years prior to the beginning of Avni's stint as an emissary in Montevideo. Shoshan met the members after coming across a booklet that had been published by the Uruguayan kibbutz to attract supporters for it and its ideas. The booklet included excerpts from Erich Fromm, Bertrand Russell, and others, as well as articles by Meir Yaari and Yaakov Hazan, the leaders of Mapam in Israel.[34]

From a social and cultural perspective, the cultural activities conducted on Saturdays at the Anielewicz movement club facilitated unique encounters with intellectuals and artists, who mostly were just starting their careers, and resulted in relationships that lasted for many years. Of the prominent figures who visited and gave lectures at the club, all on a voluntary basis, we single out Gastón Blanco, a Uruguayan intellectual, a teacher of history, and a leading figure in the history and criticism of cinema. He visited the movement club a number of times, delivering lectures to audiences that sometimes numbered over a hundred people. Gradually, Blanco became like one of the family in the movement club and, on more than one occasion, took part in information dissemination and political work on the part of the movement.

Abraham Guillén, who lived as an exile in Uruguay after fighting in the Spanish Civil War, and who wrote a number of books that were well known primarily in Argentina and Uruguay, including *The Theory of Violence* (*Teoría de la Violencia*), was also a frequent visitor, and gave lectures at the Anielewicz movement club. According to Avni, Guillén once visited the club with his son and, on seeing a large picture of Mordechai Anielewicz hanging above the stairs at the entrance to the building, said to him: "You see? He's one of ours." Guillén always related to the young movement members differently than to other visitors at the movement club. Everyone was received warmly and expressed some level of identification with the movement, but, according to Avni in a personal interview, Guillén's attitude toward the movement and its members was unique.

Another visitor who gave lectures at the movement club was playwright, journalist, and poet Mauricio Rosencof. As he advanced in years, Rosencof became

---

34 Zelig Shoshan, "A Kibbutz in Montevideo," *Al Hamishmar* (the Mapam newspaper in Israel, n.d.), personal archive of Zelig Shoshan.

a prominent journalist and a renowned figure in the theater, both within Uruguay and outside its borders, and a leading political activist in the Tupamaros guerilla movement (FLN). Before the beginning of the dictatorship, Rosencof was invited periodically to visit the movement club for its cultural evenings. As a guerilla leader, he was incarcerated in brutal conditions for thirteen years under the dictatorship that ruled Uruguay between 1973 and 1985. Another figure who paid periodic visits to the Anielewicz movement club at the beginning of his career, when he was less well known, was Alfredo Zitarrosa, who subsequently became one of Uruguay's most influential musicians and artists. During his visits, Zitarrosa typically would not sing or perform, but rather converse with the members.[35]

The Anielewicz movement's relationship with the Israeli embassy was understandably strong, as the ambassador and his staff understood the movement's role and appreciated and supported the movement's activity in the local arena. In the context of the anti-Israel atmosphere that prevailed in left-wing circles in Uruguay following the Six-Day War, the Israeli embassy approached Avni and proposed inviting representative personalities to visit Israel. Avni was granted the authority to decide on a suitable figure and came up with Mario Benedetti, one of the country's best known and admired writers. Avni subsequently met with Benedetti and extended an invitation on behalf of Mapam and the Mordechai Anielewicz Movement, but Benedetti refused the offer. His opposition, he explained, was based on Israel's relationship with the United States. Indeed, he had also never visited the United States and had even refused a personal invitation to do so by parties from the American left.[36]

As 1970 approached, *Marcha* planned a supplement entitled "Marcha Notebooks" (*Cuadernos de Marcha*), which would focus on the Middle East. Against this background, Avni invited Carlos Quijano, the weekly newspaper's mythological editor, to visit Israel. Quijano, however, suggested instead that he invite Leopoldo Muller, who had been charged with editing the supplement.[37] After visiting Israel for several months, Muller prepared a professional, sympathetic supplement containing various views of the left in Israel and around the world regarding the conflict. Ultimately, as a result of internal disagreements within *Marcha*—and perhaps due to the high quality of the supplement itself—it was decided to publish two supplements: No. 42 on

---

35 Interview with Shabtai Avni, February 10, 2012. There were several interviews with Shabtai Avni—on three different dates.

36 About the stand of the Israeli Embassy, see letter from Zelig Shoshan to Chaike Grossman, February 16, 1966, Hashomer Hatzair Archive, 37.93 A (1); and report from Shabtai Avni to Chaike Grossman, December 26, 1969, Hashomer Hatzair Archive, 37.93 A (1).

37 Interview with Shabtai Avni, February 10, 2012.

behalf of "Israel" in October 1970, edited by Muller; and No. 43, entitled "The Arabs–Palestine," in November 1970, edited by the pro-Palestinian Uruguayan intellectual Sofia Magariños, whose work favored the Arab perspective.

When the first supplement was published, *Marcha* readers had already been informed that the "Israel" supplement would reflect only the views of the Israeli left, based on Muller's visit to Israel. It would include an explanation of the reasons and solutions for the conflict from the perspective of the Israeli left. The newspaper's next supplement, on "The Arabs–Palestine," would highlight the views of the Arab left as presented by Magariños. Even then, the publication appears to have been attempting to maintain a degree of balance to ensure that the supplement would not be seen as reflecting a pro-Israel orientation. The list of Israeli and non-Israeli left-wing figures whose views were included in the first supplement—Dov Bar-Nir, Meir Yaari, Aharon Cohen, Abdul Aziz Zuabi, Mordechai Bentov, Moshe Sneh, Tawfik Toubi, Uri Avnery, and others[38]—speaks for itself. The views of Mapam and the Anielewicz movement in Montevideo regarding the Middle East, and the prominent and respectful attention it was paid on such issues, endowed it with influence on local left-wing public opinion, as reflected in the dedication of an entire supplement to the positions of the Israeli Zionist left. It can be assumed that the "balance" sought by some members of *Marcha*'s editorial board was what yielded the compromise that facilitated the presentation of voices of Arab intellectuals who opposed these views in the next issue.

TAKING A STAND ON THE CONFLICT IN THE MIDDLE EAST

After the Six-Day War, Israel was subject to severe criticism by the left. For this reason, an additional effort to engage with the issue took the form of an attempt to establish a movement for Middle East peace in Uruguay, in addition to personal conversations with leaders of the left and the organizing of roundtable discussions on subjects related to the conflict in the Middle East. This was done in coordination with similar efforts conducted by sister movements in Argentina and Chile. In 1960, Hashomer Hatzair and the Anielewicz movement in Montevideo disseminated the fundamental declaration of the Argentine Committee for Peace in the Middle East, which articulated the following principles:

> The conflict in question is one of the most complicated problems of the day, primarily because in involves authentic and legitimate interests of both

---

38 Ibid.—all very well known intellectuals from Israel and the Arab countries.

Israelis and Palestinians, alongside the foreign interests of the powers in the region. Foreign interests in the region do not view the fate of the two peoples suffering injury as a result of war to be a major fundamental concern. For this reason, the Argentine Committee for Peace in the Middle East permits itself to warn the national left that all overly simplistic analyses, falsified analogies, and one-sided interpretations of the conflict in the Middle East not only distort reality, the facts, and the "actors" involved, but serve the interests of imperialism in general, and imperialism based on the control of oil in particular. Such views may weaken the left, particularly on both sides of the ceasefire line: Palestinian Arabs and Israelis. This unfortunate situation exists at a time when everything indicates that only through understanding and the coordinated action of left-wing Arab and Israeli forces in support of the left in the world will it be possible to move toward a solution based on the genuine interests of both peoples.

The Argentine Committee for Peace in the Middle East once again resolves that the revolutionary changes in the Middle East cannot occur with the destruction of the State of Israel or the annihilation of its People, but only through the achievement of a just and sustainable peace between Israel and its Arab neighbors.

The Argentine Committee for Peace in the Middle East adopts the following three decisions formulated in Paris in February 1969 by the "Leftist Committee for an Agreed-Upon Peace in the Middle East":

1) Recognition of Israel's right to exist.
2) Recognition of the national rights of the Palestinian Arabs.
3) Understanding that, in the conditions currently existing in the Middle East, the achievement of social change is dependent on the achievement of peace between Arabs and Israelis.[39]

Members of the Anielewicz movement and Hashomer Hatzair in Uruguay also disseminated the call of Chilean intellectuals and politicians to establish a committee for peace in the Middle East in a document entitled "The Chilean Left and the Conflict in the Middle East—A Call for Peace!" Following are the main points of this appeal, based on a declaration that was published in *El Mercurio* above the signatures of thirty-three major activists of the Chilean left. The declaration began as follows:

---

39 "Declaration of the Argentine Committee for Peace in the Middle East," Hashomer Hatzair Archive, DD1–4417.

Our position in favor of peace in the Middle East is based on a deep solidarity with the peoples of the region. Such a peace does not mean relinquishing the nations' struggles to overcome hardship, backwardness, and imperialist exclusion. On the contrary, peace will constitute a positive incentive for the activity of the peoples of the region for the sake of national and social liberation.

It then proposed the following principles for a solution:

1) A just, wise, and sustainable peace in the Middle East can be based only on recognition of the legitimate rights of Israel and the certainty of the right to national self-determination of the Palestinian Arab People.

2) The achievement of peace requires understandings between the peoples involved that cannot be forced upon them from the outside and that necessarily must lead to direct talks between them. Negotiations offer the only possible path toward reaching a solution to the territorial dispute and the tragedy of the Arab refugees.

3) Effective solidarity between the enlightened forces of the world and the true Israeli and Arab left could provide substantial encouragement for the persistent adherence to a path of peace, just as unilateral and opportunistic tendencies can encourage measures of war.

4) A state of war between the Arab peoples and Israel objectively hinders the cultivation of a genuine anti-imperialist struggle. Only a sustainable peace can help disconnect the region from imperialist influence and open channels toward a just society that will benefit the peoples of the region.[40]

The Anielewicz movement believed in the importance of the dissemination of manifestos and the initiatives of left-wing activists in neighboring countries and around the world. They regarded such measures as being extremely valuable for Israel's defense and for proving to the Uruguayan left that not all initiatives had to detract from Israel's right to exist—and that some taken elsewhere actually strengthened it. On this basis, it grabbed on to every declaration issued by leftist elements on the American continent and around the world, and worked toward similar efforts in Uruguay—though with little success. Nonetheless, movement members regarded such efforts as a ray of hope for a dialogue toward peace in the Middle East, and therefore publicized and disseminated these statements as well.

---

40 "The Chilean Left and the Conflict in the Middle East—A Call for Peace!" Hashomer Hatzair Archive, DD1-4417.

INFORMATION CAMPAIGNS IN SOUTH AMERICA INVOLVING
ISRAELI MAPAM AND HASHOMER HATZAIR LEADERS

In addition to the visits described above, other visits made an important impact on movement information campaigns in Montevideo. One such visit was that made by Yechiel Harari, a member of Kibbutz Ein Shemer, a prominent intellectual of the Kibbutz Artzi settlement movement and Hashomer Hatzair, a long-time force within the Kibbutz Artzi's ideological seminary at Givat Haviva, and a former movement emissary to Buenos Aires. Harari was sent to Latin America to engage in an information campaign following an assembly of the pro-Cuban Organization of Latin American Solidarity (OLAS) in Havana, which discussed, for the first time ever, the organization's support of armed resistance against the State of Israel. Harari's primary task was to promote the State of Israel's right to exist among the forces of the left on the continent, to ensure that the voice of the Zionist left in Israel was being heard and taken into consideration, and to defend the existence of the State of Israel. In Montevideo, Harari enjoyed the benefit of the already existing ties with the local left, which been established over the years through the regular activity of the Mordechai Anielewicz Movement, and out of the respect stemming from his years as an emissary in Argentina. Also beneficial was his command of Spanish and the informality that was typical of Uruguay, where meetings could be scheduled by telephone with no special ceremony. In addition to these advantages, Harari was also a Renaissance man with an extensive education and a vast knowledge of the conflict in the Middle East.[41] The combination of these factors ultimately provided Harari with a full schedule of meetings with influential left-wing figures. In Uruguay, it was a relatively simple matter to set up a meeting with a politician at his home, regardless of the importance or the status of the host. Still, in terms of subject matter, the disagreements with left-wing figures in Uruguay were now much more severe than in the past. This came as no surprise to Harari, as intensely anti-Israel views were not uncommon in the world in light of Israel's policy and the new reality in the country following the Six-Day War.

In 1969, Israeli poet Avraham Shlonsky also paid a visit to Montevideo. In addition to being one of Israel's most prominent poets at the time, Shlonsky was associated with the Mapam party, as was obvious during his visit. During his time in Montevideo, *Marcha* conducted an interview with Shlonsky, and the

---

41 Interview with Carmela and Aharon Melika, March 13, 2012, at Kibbutz Dan.

Israeli embassy purchased 300 copies of the issue with the aim of disseminating the interview with Shlonsky throughout the continent.[42]

A number of additional visits by members of Kibbutz Artzi and Hashomer Hatzair in Israel are of particular relevance to our discussion in that they bolstered the reputation of the Anielewicz movement. Examples include the visits of Holocaust survivors and ghetto fighters such as Chaike Grossman and Shalom Cholawski, who succeeded in moving the local Jewish community using the Yiddish language. Dov Bar-Nir's visit was of great value since the Uruguayan left was already familiar with his views based on the Spanish translations of his articles.[43]

PLACARD-POSTING CAMPAIGNS IN THE STREETS OF MONTEVIDEO

For the Anielewicz movement, posting placards throughout the city was the most inexpensive way of asserting its presence and drawing attention to issues that were consistent with the aims of the movement. Due to the constant state of financial hardship in which the movement operated, finances were an important concern. Posting placards also enabled the movement to distinguish itself from the other Zionist youth movements, which lacked the skills necessary to operate on the streets of the city after dark, and whose activities did not usually venture outside the confines of the Jewish community. Two dates on which movement members would demonstrate a major presence in the streets of the city were quickly decided upon each year: in April, placards were posted bearing the slogan "Praise to the Heroes of the Warsaw Ghetto," and, leading up to the First of May, members posted placards that read "Long Live the First of May!" The First of May, the holiday of the working class, was an official holiday in Uruguay; schools and businesses closed, and public transportation did not operate. The night before the holiday, Anielewicz movement members posted placards throughout the city, signed by the Socialist Zionist Mordechai Anielewicz Movement, expressing their solidarity with the working class.

In addition to these two regular annual campaigns, one or two additional placard-posting campaigns were carried out as dictated by international and local events. However, the two occasions mentioned previously—the anniversary of the Warsaw Ghetto Uprising (which was the movement's major

---

42 Report from Shabtai Avni to Chaike Grossman, December 26, 1969, Hashomer Hatzair Archive 37.93 A (1).

43 Letter from Nadav Meirav, Hashomer Hatzair Emissary in Montevideo to Haini Borenstein, director of the Hashomer Hatzair Movement in Tel Aviv, August 9, 1970, Hashomer Hatzair Archive, 85.31 (2).

annual event), and the celebrations of the working class in Montevideo—became symbols of the movement and marks of recognition. The Anielewicz movement made sure it took part in the large annual First of May rally that was organized in central Montevideo, generally by the National Convention of Workers (*Convención Nacional de Trabajadores*, or CNT).[44]

The following anecdote from the period illustrates the importance of the placard-posting campaigns in shaping the image of the movement. In 1966, three members of the Anielewicz movement were invited to meet with the leading forum of the country's socialist party. During a spontaneous informal conversation among a small group that preceded the formal meeting, a number of movement members were surprised to hear one party activist say to them matter-of-factly, "Okay, you have the capacity to get things done due to your 2,500 members." Although the movement members did not respond, they knew all too well that even during the period leading up to the Six-Day War and during the war itself, the movement had never had more than 150 members. Although it is unclear how they arrived at such an unrealistically high number, the experienced socialist activists appear to believe that the overnight posting of placards on all the walls of the city required the mobilization of large numbers of people. After all, the campaigns did not involve posting placards that had been prepared ahead of time. Rather, they began with the independent production of glue (made from water and flour) and then moved on to the posting of large sheets of paper (three to six meters long) on the walls of the city, and the painting of slogans that had been decided upon ahead of time. These campaigns were carried out by no more than eight to twelve members, who worked on the project from sunset to sunrise using a 1940s-model car (which was the only car owned by a movement member—in this case, Mario Hojman), sometimes benefiting from the assistance of one of the older Mapam activists' cars. Without a doubt, the movement's massive presence on the city streets, achieved by its posting of placards and its weekly radio broadcasts, played a major role in creating an awareness of the existence of the socialist Zionist movement in Uruguay.[45]

In 1971, as the general elections in Uruguay approached, the movement expressed its solidarity with the broad leftist front. The movement's declarations during this period reflected ideological solidarity with the Broad Front (*Frente*

---

44 Interview with Aharon Melika, March 13, 2012, at Kibbutz Dan. For the radio broadcast see interview with Iris and Leonardo Ziman, October 27, 2012, and November 20, 2012, at Kibbutz Ramot Menashe.

45 Interview with Eduardo Bartfeld, August 4, 2014, in Montevideo.

Amplio), and support for the unification of the forces of the left in the country, even if the movement's aims were immigration to Israel and not political activity in Uruguay.[46] Two years later, in 1973, Uruguay's democracy was annulled, and the country's unprecedented dictatorship took action against all those who until that point had constituted opposition within the leftist and centrist movements, and within the student and labor unions. All political parties were disbanded, and a regime of intimidation and terrorism reigned in the country. Although murders of individuals due to their opinions did not take place in Uruguay on the same scale as in Argentina and Chile, Uruguay was the Latin American country with the largest number of political arrests and imprisonments.[47]

CONCLUSION

The personal element played a significant role in the growth and expansion of the Mordechai Anielewicz Movement in Uruguay. In the movement, young Jews hailing from the ranks of the left met young Jewish students, typically the children of immigrants, who were born in Uruguay and who, because of its open and secular character, had successfully integrated into Uruguayan society. These second-generation immigrants had made their way into the movement and, in some cases, into Judaism in general, through externalized political activity within student and labor unions. The movement became radically Zionist–socialist in ideology, and, due to their worldview and young age, its members sought to actualize the full meaning of the maximalist Zionist–socialist imperative, which included the revolution of *aliyah* to Israel and self-realization through settlement on kibbutz. These young Jews, who had left the ranks of the local left, decided to immigrate to Israel full of revolutionary fervor, as reflected in the extensive correspondence between Hashomer Hatzair and the emissaries on the ground.[48] In addition, infused with ideology

---

46 Gabriel Hojman, "Elecciones de 1971. Las Instituciones Judías de Izquierda y el Comité Judío del Frente Amplio," Maestría en Historia Rioplatense, Facultad de Humanidades y Ciencias de la Educación, Universidad de la República, Montevideo, Uruguay.

47 Benjamin Nahum, *Breve Historia del Uruguay Independiente* (Montevideo: Banda Oriental, 1999), 171–83.

48 See, for instance, Shaike Wainer to Zelig Shoshan, February 10, 1966, Hashomer Hatzair Archive, 85.31 (2); Zelig Shoshan to Chaike Grossman, Hashomer Hatzair Archive, January 16, 1966, Hashomer Hatzair Archive, 37.93 A (1). See also a letter from Zvi Bodnovsky, Jewish Agency delegate, to Menachem Gelerter, responsible for the Latin America section in the Jewish Agency, March 14, 1966, The Zionist Central Archive, Jerusalem, S5–12.693; telegram from Zvi Luria of the Jewish Agency to Israel Nemirovski, head of the Uruguay

that was relevant to the period, Anielewicz movement members served as a mouthpiece for, and operated in the service of Zionism and the State of Israel vis-à-vis the forces of the left in Uruguay; that is, for as long as they were able to operate freely within a democratic state. The democratic reality within Uruguay, which enabled individuals, parties, and movements to operate freely within its borders, was an important factor that helps explain the emergence and rapid expansion of the Mordechai Anielewicz Movement in the country.

By the end of the 1960s, however, the political situation in Uruguay had grown increasingly volatile and continued to deteriorate. On June 27, 1973, after years of social instability, economic and political crisis, and the emergence of urban guerilla activity against the regime, which was brutally repressed, President Juan María Bordaberry issued an order disbanding the two houses of parliament and other laws that terminated democracy in the country. A mass demonstration against the coup was held less than two weeks later on July 9, but the democracy that had been one of the major attributes of the Uruguayan state during the twentieth century had ceased to exist. The dictatorship was strengthened further in February 1974, when all political parties were outlawed and individuals associated with the left— including teachers, university professors, and others—were dismissed from public service. This period also witnessed the torture of civilians who had been arrested and jailed, and the enactment of laws aimed at suppressing civil society. In 1976, prior to the date on which elections were scheduled to be held, the army seized power, and a military dictatorship replaced the authoritarian civil-military rule of the president in office.[49]

In the prevailing atmosphere of internal terrorism against the left, the Mordechai Anielewicz Movement could no longer function. Members, aware that the movement club was now operating under the watchful eye of the police, burned all books and materials that could link them to the left. The police raided the club on more than one occasion, and, according to their own testimony, movement emissary Meir Retner and movement member Anita Zalcberg were detained for interrogation one night after leaving the club.[50]

Due to this drastic change in conditions, the movement's voice went silent. In the days of democracy, movement members had been permitted to

---

Zionist Organization, February 16, 1966, The Zionist Central Archive, S5 12.693.

49 Benjamin Nahum, *Breve Historia del Uruguay Independiente* (Montevideo: Ediciones de la Banda Oriental, 1999), 161–83.

50 Interview with Meir Retner, emissary from the Kibbutz Artzi to Montevideo in Kibbutz Metzer, and with Anita Zalcberg, in Ra'anana. She was a member of the Anielewitcz Movement until she came to Israel in 1976.

publish, to conduct radio broadcasts, to appear before Jewish students, and to express themselves freely on the subject of Borochovist Zionist–socialist ideology. Under the conditions of military dictatorship—in which terror was used against the local left, freedom of speech and assembly were denied, movement activists were viewed by the police as suspects, and the Hashomer Hatzair emissary and a number of movement activists found themselves being interrogated by the police—it was pointless to go on operating. Without public reverberation and the ability to articulate its view in public in order to attract young Jews to the Zionist camp, the movement had no reason to take its work underground. In these circumstances, in 1976, the Hashomer Hatzair emissary closed the doors of the movement club at 1212 Andes Street for good.[51]

Nonetheless, the work of the Mordechai Anielewicz Movement in Uruguay and the memory of the commander of the Warsaw Ghetto Uprising remain ingrained in the memory of Uruguayan intellectuals and leaders to this day. On May 15, 2013, the lower house of the Uruguayan parliament held a special session in honor of "Mordechai Anielewicz and the Warsaw Ghetto Uprising" to mark the seventieth anniversary of the event. The words of the speakers clearly reflected that the subject was not new to them, that they were familiar with its historic detail, and that their deep identification with the event had transformed it from a subject with specifically Jewish import to a universal theme with values that Uruguayan leaders deemed valuable to society. The parliamentary session concluded in an extremely moving manner, with the playing of the Spanish version of a familiar anthem—the anthem of the Jewish partisans. Some of the attendees stood out of respect as they sang the anthem, and thundering applause accompanied its final verse: "Therefore never say the road now ends for you, though leaden skies may cover over days of blue. As the hour that we longed for is so near, our step beats out the message: we are here!"[52]

---

51 Interview with Helena and Alberto Korkin, who were emissaries from the Kibbutz Artzi to the Hashomer Hatzair Movement in Uruguay during the dictatorship. Alberto Korkin described how he closed the doors of the Anielewicz movement because of the danger to their members, according to his understanding, in those days.

52 Protocol from the Uruguayan Parliament, May 15, 2013.

Part Four

From Jewish Writers in Latin America to Latin America in Israeli Contemporary Literature

CHAPTER 16

But at Night, at Night, I Still Dream in Spanish—The Map of Imagination of Israeli Literature: South America

YIGAL SCHWARTZ

DREAMING IN SPANISH

I get up in the morning in Hebrew
And drink coffee in Hebrew,
Pay dearly in Hebrew
For everything I buy.

In the language of King David
I live and make myself heard,
And read stories to my child—
Yes, always from right to left. . . .

I think and I write Hebrew without difficulty
And love to love you exclusively in Hebrew.
It's a wonderful language, I will never have another
But at night, at night, I still dream in Spanish. . . .

Ehud Manor

I

As Benedict Anderson argues in his influential book, *Imagined Communities*,[1] nationalism is not another ideology, like socialism or fascism, but a self-generating phenomenon, a product of the act of reimagining the nation that involves the development of methods of production and media. This act of the imagination is carried out through the renewal and/or invention of internal tradition. There is a conscious–emotional need to present the new nation as an ancient one that is being renewed,[2] and also the necessity, pointed out by Mircea Eliade,[3] of creating a mechanism of repetition of the founding moment of the nation. That is to say, nationalism entails the establishment of a ritual event devoted to confirming the primary covenant—at once physical and metaphysical—between community members, the land, and their God.[4]

However, the act of reimagining a nation cannot be based only on the inwardly directed creative observation of the reserve of traditions and images of the community itself, rich and diverse though it may be. This act of reimagination is also based, as Itamar Even-Zohar[5] noted, on outwardly directed creative observation, an act mainly based, as Edward Said[6] showed us,

1 Benedict Anderson, *Imagined Communities: Reflections on the Origin and Spread of Nationalism* (London: Verso, 2006).

2 See, among others, Hugh Trevor Roper, "The Highland Tradition of Scotland," in *The Invention of Tradition*, ed. Eric Hobsbawm and Terence Ranger (Cambridge: Cambridge University Press, 2012), 15–42; Larry McMurtry, "Inventing the West," *The New York Review of Books*, August 10, 2000, accessed May 23, 2017, http://www.nybooks.com/articles/archives/2000/aug/10/inventing-the-west/?pagination=false.

3 Mircea Eliade, *The Myth of the Eternal Return: Or, Cosmos and History*, trans. Willard R. Trask (Princeton, NJ: Princeton University Press, 1954); idem, *Rites and Symbols of Initiation: The Mysteries of Birth and Rebirth*, trans. Willard R. Trask (San Francisco: Harper and Row, 1975).

4 See also my book, Yigal Schwartz, *Zemer Nogeh shel Amos Oz: Pulhan Hasofer Vedat Hamedina* (*The Cult of the Author and the Religion of the State*) (Tel Aviv: Dvir, 2011),9–41.

5 Itamar Even-Zohar, "Hasifrut Haivrit Haisraelit"("Israeli Hebrew Literature"), *Hasifrut 4*, no. 3 (1972–73): 427–40.

6 Edward Said, *Orientalism* (London: Penguin, 1977).

on a subjugating projection of the "Other," which, as his successors and critics[7] have demonstrated, is always also a projection subjugated by the "Other."

Thus, for example, Europe, "the Old World," imagined itself through subjugating and subjugated projections of America, the "New World,"[8] which, in turn, imagined itself through parallel projections of the "Old World," of "the European mother countries."[9] The phenomenon of modern Jewish nationalism can be described also as the product of a dual act of the imagination: the renewal of internal traditions and the subjugating and subjugated projection of "Others." This act of the imagination was realized repeatedly in hundreds of texts that were intended to achieve a twofold goal: to present the philosophy of an old–new national space— *altneuland*, and to outline the engineering of a new man: *altneumann*.[10] Naturally, this corpus was influenced by the utopian genre, which experienced an amazing boom, as Rachel Elboim Dror[11] aptly explains, during the second half of the nineteenth century.

The most prominent pioneer of this trend, Avraham Mapu, reimagined the Land of Israel, which he never got to see with his own eyes, in all his books, particularly in his foundational work *The Love of Zion* (1852), perceived by many young people at the time as a cult object, a holy book, something like a new Bible.

---

7 For example, Homi K. Bhabha, "Remembering Fanon: Self, Psyche and the Colonial Condition," in *Colonial Discourse and Postcolonial Theory*, ed. P. Williams and L. Chrisman (New York: Columbia University Press, 1994), 125–33.

8 This is apparent, for example, in an allegorical way in Vladimir Nabokov's Lolita. This point, among others, was made by Menachem Perry in his afterword to the Hebrew edition, which was translated by Dvora Steinhart. See also Menachem Perry, "Tzilo Shel Hazeev Habadui: Lolita Betzelem Humbert" ("The Shadow of the Fabricated Wolf, Lolita in the Image of Humbert"), in Lolita (Jerusalem: Siman Kriya Keter Publishing, 1986),334–52. See also Jean Baudrillard's wonderful book, *America*, trans. Chris Turner (London: Verso, 1988); Matan Hermoni, "Kol Hanehalim Zormim Leamerica: Al Tafkid Haolam Hehadash Besifrut Tkufat Hathiya" ("All Rivers Flow to America: On the Role of the New World in the Literature of the Renaissance Period") (PhD diss., Ben-Gurion University of the Negev, n.d.).

9 This is apparent, for example, in some of the essays in the anthology *Visions of America: Personal Narratives from the Promised Land*, ed. Wesley Brown and Amy Ling (New York: Persea Books, 1993).

10 On this point see, among others, Anita Shapira, *Yehudim Yeshanim, Yehudim Chadashim* (*New Jews, Old Jews*) (Tel Aviv: Am Oved, 1997); Yigal Schwartz, *Hayadata et Haaretz Sham Halimon Poreach?: Handasat Haadam Veitzuv Hamerhav Hehadash* (*Do You Know the Land Where the Lemon Blooms?: Human Engineering and Designing the New Space*) (Tel Aviv: Dvir, 2007).

11 Rachel Elboim-Dror, *Hamahar shel Haetmol*: 1. *Hautopia Hatzionit*, 2. *Mivchar Hautopia Hatzionit*. (*Yesterday's Tomorrow*, vol.1: *The Zionist Utopia*, vol. 2: *Selections from The Zionist Utopia*) (Jerusalem: Yad Izhak Ben-Zvi, 1993). See also Leah Hadomi, "Haroman Hautopi ve Hautopia Hatzionit" ("The Utopian Novel and the Zionist Utopia"), *Bikoret Ufarshanut* 13–14 (1979): 131–68.

Many noted that, because of this little book, they had packed up their belongings, abandoned their homes and families, and immigrated to the Land of Israel.[12]

For the perspective of Mapu and his contemporaries, and from the point of view of writers and poets of the *Hibbat Zion* movement who followed them, there was no doubt about the identity of the "place" where the process of the renaissance, the rebirth, would take place. Or, in the words of Zali Gurevitch and Gideon Aran,[13] "the place" is the space that represents in the best possible way the regulative idea of the nation, the focus of its identity, and its specific uniqueness.[14]

In this context, Mapu and his successors, the people of the Enlightenment and *Hibbat Zion*, went the way of their predecessors. They took upon themselves the direction of the vector of national desire, which had developed in exile and found its most refined expression in Yehuda Halevi's famous poem "My Heart is the East and I in the Uttermost West." They lived in Lithuania, in the towns of the Pale of Settlement in Ukraine, and elsewhere in eastern and central Europe. They created for themselves and for their readers "a Promised Land,"[15] an imagined Land of Israel. This was based on blends of slivers of information from books by travelers to the Land of Israel: popular geography books, the realization of fragments of verses from the Bible, the landscape that surrounded them, and the landscapes of the magical places familiar to them from literature that shaped the dreams of their youth.[16]

The exclusivity of the Land of Israel as "the place" was undermined in the late nineteenth century and the first decade of the twentieth century. This undermining, this deviation from the direction of the traditional "vector of national

---

12 On this matter, see Schwartz, *Hayadata et Haaretz Sham Halimon Poreach?*29–34.

13 Zali Gurevich and Gideon Aran, "Al Hamakom: Antropologia Israelit," *Alpayim* 4 (1991): 9–44.

14 On this issue, see Dan Miron's comments on Jerusalem as a "locus," a "place," in "Hatrilogia Hayerushalmit shel Aharon Reuveni" ("Aharon Reuveni's Jerusalem Trilogy"), in *Kivun Orot* (New York: Schocken Books, 1979), 395–430 and "Im Lo Tehiyeh Yerushalayim" ("If There Is No Jerusalem"), in *Massot al Sifrut Ivrit Baheksher Hapoliti-tarbuti* (*Essays on Hebrew Literature in the Political-Cultural Context*), 227–35.

15 See Eliezer Shavid, *Moledet Ve'eretz Yeuda: Eretz Yisrael Bahagut shel Am Yisrael* (*Homeland and a Land of Promise: The Land of Israel in the Philosophy of the Nation of Israel*) (Tel Aviv: Am Oved, 1997).

16 And see in this context Tova Cohen, *Mehalom Lemitziut: Eretz Yisrael Besifrut Hahaskala* (*From Dream to Reality: The Land of Israel in Enlightenment Literature*) (Ramat Gan: Bar-Ilan University, 1982); Shmuel Werses, "Darkei Hasipur shel Avraham Mapu be 'Ahavat Tzion'" ("Ways of Telling in Abraham Mapu's 'Ahavat Tzion'"), *Sipur Veshorsho: Iyunim Behitpathut Haproza Haivrit* (Ramat Gan: Massada, 1971),46–59; Dan Miron, "Hatzipui Hamazhir: Haomanut Hamilitzit shel Avraham Mapu be *Ahavat Tzion*" ("The Glowing Cover: The Poetic Art of Abraham Mapu in *The Love of Zion*"), in *Beyn Hazon Le'emet: Nitzani Haroman Haivri Vehayidi Bamea Hatisha'asar*(*Between Vision and Truth: the Buds of the Hebrew and Yiddish Novel in the Nineteenth Century*) (Jerusalem: Mossad Bialik, 1979), 15–151.

desire," could have changed the map of the national imagination as a whole had it been more solidly and deeply based. As Benjamin Harshav aptly noted,[17] it was the product of an enormous cultural and political revolution, especially, but not only, among the Jews of the Russian Pale of Settlement, a revolution whose results were, he said: "The greatest contribution to our culture since the Bible."[18]

Harshav claims that this cultural and political revolution—and this is his main point for us here—was not marked by one historical–ideological process, Zionism, but rather by a modernist revolution, of which Zionism, i.e., the Zionists' declaration of the exclusivity of the Land of Israel as the focus of the vector of national desire, is only one of its derivatives. According to Harshav, this inclusive revolution took advantage of the dynamic opportunities of the modern world in Europe and the United States. It gave rise to what appeared at the time to be a Jewish people different from its predecessor, built with two heads with different natures: Israel and the new Diaspora.[19] By "new Diaspora," Harshav probably meant the massive settlement of Jews in the United States. However, it must include, of course, the massive settlement of Jews during the same period in various places in Latin America, including Argentina, beginning in 1891, as part of the vision, initiative, and diverse activities of Baron Hirsch.

In this context of the emergence of two heads with different natures, Israel and the "new Diaspora," cloaked in the modern Jewish revolution, Harshav argues that the accepted history of modern Hebrew literature has been distorted. This is a "historiography of the winners," in which the history of literature is described from end to beginning, from the stage seen by (Zionist) historians as a victory for Zionism, and back. This has resulted, he claims, in a distortion of the historical truth, a reduction and diminishment of the literary corpus, and a diminution of the richness of contacts between writers and their works.

Harshav's strong words must be qualified, in this context, regarding two points. The first of these qualifications is that it is easy to see that positioning the Land of Israel as "the place," constituted a conscious decision on the part of many writers and thinkers "from the start"—at the latest from the 1880—and, accordingly, the exclusion of the "new Diaspora" was also a conscious decision "from the beginning." In other words, what we have here is not only

---

17 Benjamin Harshav, "Thiyata shel Eretz Yisrael Vehamahapecha Hayehudit: Hamodernit: Hirhurim al Tmunat Matzav" ("The Rebirth of the Land of Israel and the Modern Jewish Revolution: Thoughts on the Situation") in *Nekudat Tatzpit: Tarbut Vehevra Be'eretz Yisrael* (*Observation Point: Culture and Society in the Land of Israel*), ed. Nurit Gertz (The Open University, 1987–88),7–31.
18 Harshav, ibid., 16.
19 Ibid., 11.

a "historiography of winners," but also an *ab ovo* move, from the beginning, a calculated and deliberate move that succeeded—at least for a few decades.

The second qualification is that at the formative time that Harshav is discussing, a cultural–linguistic phenomenon that we can call "territorial diglossia" was permanently established. Most of the writers who chose to write in Hebrew chose the Land of Israel as "the place," while most of the writers who chose Yiddish, English, Spanish, and so on, chose the "new Diaspora" as "the place." This is a reasonable phenomenon. Authors who chose a different path—for example, the Hebrew writers in the United States at the beginning of the twentieth century, created a heroic, but somewhat bizarre corpus. On the other hand, many Hebrew writers who came to Israel by choice or as a result of their parents' choice carried on "secret affairs" with the language of the lands of their birth.[20]

We may learn much about the validity of both parts of the first qualification of Harshav's claim, the decision regarding the exclusivity of the Land of Israel as "the place," on the one hand, and the decision regarding the exclusion of competing places, on the other, from the opening chapter of *Altneuland*, Herzl's foundational book.[21]

The chapter opens with a description of the book's protagonist, Dr. Friedrich Loewenberg, who "was sunk in deep melancholy,"[22] that is, "spleen," the disease of that generation of detached central European Jews. This Loewenberg spends most of his time sitting in a Viennese café called Birkenreis. There, he ponders the existential possibilities open to him, and dismisses them one by one:

> [O]nce upon a time, there had been lighthearted talk. Now only dreams were left, for the two good comrades with whom he had been wont to while away the idle, pleasant evening hours at this café had died several months previously. Both had been older than he, and it was, as Heinrich had written to him just before sending a bullet into his temple, "chronologically reasonable" that they should yield to despair sooner than he. *Oswald went to Brazil to help in founding a Jewish labor settlement, and there succumbed to the yellow fever.*[23]

Herzl rules out the option of settlement in South America—that is, the settlement enterprise that was the brainchild of Baron Hirsch and his ilk—with the

---

20 See on this matter Nili Scharf Gold's pioneering study, *Yehuda Amichai, The Making of Israel's National Poet* (Waltham, MA: Brandeis University Press, 2008).

21 Theodor Herzl, *Old–New Land (Altneuland)*, trans. Lotta Levensohn (Princeton, NJ: Marcus Wiener, 1941 [1902]).

22 Ibid., 3.

23 Ibid. (emphasis mine).

same stroke of his pen with which he rejects the option of suicide, as if these options are of equal status and significance. Later, he also rejects the option of the intellectual and detached European Jew and the option of bourgeois Judaism in its nouveau riche version.

After these disqualifications, to which we can also add the option of emigration to the United States, whose absolute negation the industrialist Kingscourt, Loewenberg's benefactor, presents—there supposedly remains only one suitable existential option: settlement in the old–new country, the Land of Israel, represented by David Litvak, a Jewish boy from a poor eastern European home. Loewenberg is charmed by Litvak and his commitment to the idea of the revival of the nation in the old–new country, so he helps him in his studies, through which the boy, the son of a notions peddler, will eventually become the president of the "new society" in Israel. Loewenberg himself is found to be worthy of the "winning" Zionist option only after he goes through a lengthy "process of repair," both physical and psychological, on an isolated island in the Indian Ocean.[24]

The choice of the Land of Israel as "the place," as the ultimate objective vector of national desire, underwent a process of institutionalization and became permanently established in the prose and poetry written by most artists who settled in the Land of Israel in the three great waves of pioneering Zionist immigration (1882–1928). These artists, who took upon themselves the "Zionist narrative" in different ways, privileging the Land of Israel while negating the Diaspora,[25] included Moshe Smilansky, Joseph Lavidor, Israel Zarchi, Joseph Aricha, S. Y. Agnon, Y. Brenner, Aryeh Arieli-Orloff, Aharon Reuveni, Haim Hazaz, Yehuda Yaari, Natan Bistritzky, and many others.

Control over the unidirectional plot structure on the national map of the imagination of Hebrew literature began to be undermined in the late 1940s, in the writings of the "Palmach generation." These writers, among them Moshe Shamir, Yigal Mossinson, Shlomo Nitzan, Nathan Shaham, and others, were

---

24 See Schwartz, *Hayadata et Haaretz Sham Halimon Poreach?*159–83.
25 See Yigal Schwartz, "Ma Sheroim Mikan Lo Roim Misham, Aval Gam Lehefekh: Siporet Haaliyah Hashniyah Beshtei Perspectivot Historiot" ("What You See from Here You Don't See from There, but the Opposite Is Also True: The Fiction of the Second Aliyah from Two Historical Perspectives"), in *Ma Sheroim Mikan: Sugiot Bahistoriografia shel Hasifrut Haivrit Hahadasha* (*What You See from Here: Issues in the Historiography of Modern Hebrew Literature*) (Tel Aviv: Dvir, 2005),125–47.
    See also the first and second chapters of the previously mentioned book. And, from another angle, Amnon Raz-Kraotzkin, "Galut Betoch Ribonut: Lebikoret 'Shlilat Hagalut' Batarbut Hayisraelit" ("Exile within Sovereignty: Toward a Critique of the 'Negation of Exile' in Israeli Culture"), *Teoria Uvikoret* 4 (1993): 23–55; *Teoria Uvikoret* 5 (1994): 113–32.

born in Israel or came as young children. They realized the "Zionist dream" in the stories of their lives, but also dreamed of places outside the Promised Land. One of these places was, as Nurit Gertz[26] has demonstrated, the American Wild West, which served as the site of desire of the "silver platter youth," mainly through the mediation of the books they read, and especially through the movies they watched. Gertz notes that we may learn about the role played by the western in constructing the contemporary ethos from—among other things—songs that featured fighters as horsemen riding alone in deserted areas, from street posters that told the stories of brave warriors in the form of wanted posters in westerns, and even in a joke that was prevalent at the time, according to which two people founded the Palmach—Yitzhak Sadeh and Gary Cooper.[27] Another site of desire through which the "Palmach generation" constructed its national identity was the Russian space, including the "Wild East" of Asia, the Cossacks,[28] and the cultural space of revolutionary Russia.[29]

Another objection, far more radical, emerges in the writings of "the first Israelis." I refer to the group of writers known as the "Generation of the State," born in and outside Israel in the 1930s, which largely determined the characteristics of Israeli identity. This group includes Amos Oz, A. B. Yehoshua, Aharon Appelfeld, Yehoshua Kenaz, Ruth Almog, Haim Beer, and others.

One characteristic of the fiction written during this period, particularly the fiction of Amos Oz, who is perceived as the most typical Israeli author, is

---

26 Nurit Gertz, *Sipur Mehasratim: Siporet Yisraelit Veibuda Lakolnoa* (*A Story from the Movies: Israeli Fiction and Its Adaptation to Cinema*) (The Open University, 1993), 70–82.

27 Gertz, ibid., 71.

28 The figure of the Cossack, and, similarly, the figure of the "Bedouin" as models of identification were inherited by the "Palmach Generation" from the generation of the Second *Aliyah*, which to a large degree created the identity paradigm that the members of the "Generation of the State" realized in their bodies and souls. See also in this context Itamar Even-Zohar, "Hasifrut Hayisraelit Haivrit: Model Histori" ("Israeli Hebrew Literature: A Historical Model"), ibid.; Israel Bar-Tal, *Kozak Ubedoui* (*Cossack and Bedouin*) (Tel Aviv: Am Oved, 2007), 68–79.

29 Mediated by two foundational books, among others: *Yalkut Shirat Haamim: Shirei Rusia* (*An Anthology of National Poetry: Russian Poetry* (1942)), ed. Avraham Shlonsky and Leah Goldberg; and *General Panfilov's Reserve* by Alexander Bek, which were said to have been carried in the pocket of every Palmach fighter. *General Panfilov's Reserve* was also a foundational book of the Israel Defense Forces (IDF), and was required reading in officers' courses. See on this matter, among others, Uri Simchoni, *Livyatan Lavan* (*White Whale*) (Glory Publishers, 2006),123–24; Gershon Shaked, "Haim al Kav Haketz" ("Life on the Razor's Edge"), the introduction to the book *Haim al Kav Haketz: Antologia Lesiporet Yisraelit* (*Life on the Razor's Edge: An Anthology of Israeli Fiction*) (Bnei Brak: Hakibbutz Hameuchad, 1982), 9–44.

a dramatic change in direction of the vector of national territorial desire. The place of the Land of Israel as the ultimate destination of sovereign national desire is overtaken by "another place" (like the title of Oz's first novel, published in 1966), a "new–old" destination – Europe.[30]

Thus, it is precisely in the stories of "The First Israelis," who began writing after the establishment of the sovereign Jewish state for the first time after the "big bang"—the cultural and political revolution of the late nineteenth century as pointed out above by Benjamin Harshav—that the automatic correlation between writing in Hebrew and the concept of "the Promised Land" was broken down.

The undermining of Israel as "the place" created a serious vacuum in the national imagination—a vacuum filled partially and for a limited time by Europe. The position of the Land of Israel as "the place," and the position of Europe as "the alternative place," began to be filled, from the early 1980s onward, by places that had been marginalized until that time. One of those places was South America, which gradually came to occupy an important place on the map of the national imagination.

II

South America fulfills several functions on the map of the Israeli imagination. Some are not very significant, while others are more so. I will present a few of them here, in ascending order of importance.

For some writers of the "Generation of the State," South America appears mainly as an extreme existential image. This kind of situation is a desperate yearning for an "authentic" way of life that would allow indirect contact with the "pristine era" of the *Yishuv* in the Land of Israel before the "shock of statehood."[31] We can see a typical example of such a situation in the chapter "Hadrom Americanim" ("The South Americans") in *Al Tagidi Laila* (*Don't Call it Night*) (1994)[32] by Amos Oz. Theo, the protagonist, abandons Israel and sails to South America. He travels from place to place, developing "a few models of rural areas that suited the tropical climate and were not at odds with the existing way of life" for the "locals."[33]

---

30 Schwartz, *Hayadata et Haaretz Sham Halimon Poreach?* 367–461 and *idem, Ma Sheroim Mikan,* 137–43.
31 See Yigal Schwartz, "Le choc de la création de l'État" ("The Shock of the Creation of the State"), *Yod* 14 (Paris: Inalco, 2009), 13–30.
32 Amos Oz, *Don't Call it Night,* trans. Nicholas de Lange (San Francisco: Harcourt Brace, 1997).
33 Ibid., 98. Compare, also, to the opening, of Oz's first novel, *Makom Aher* (*Another Place*), which includes detailed settlement planning—except that he is writing there about a

Alongside his development work, which naturally takes into account both the environment and the human landscape, Theo occupies himself mainly with wandering—he is a kind of adult backpacker—always alone. This aloneness is interrupted by two kinds of events—encounters with "the place" and localness ("Women were easy to find, like food, like a hammock to spend the night in, all lavished on him everywhere out of curiosity or hospitality"[34]), and "conversations late into the night ... with strangers or chance acquaintances."[35] The meetings with "the place," the nature scenes, and "localness" have a clearly colonial character:

> He despatched most of his monthly salary to a bank in Toronto, because his expenses were negligible. Like a travelling artisan, he wandered in those years from one godforsaken place to another that was even more so. He stayed in wretched villages at the foot of extinct volcanoes and once he saw one of them erupting in flames. Sometimes he journeyed under thick canopies of ferns and creepers through sensuous jungles. Here and there, he would befriend for a while a desolate river or steep mountain range that the forest seemed to be invading with the savage claws of its roots. Here and there, he would stop for a couple of weeks and surrender to total idleness, laying in a hammock all day watching birds of prey in the depths of the empty sky. A girl or a young woman would come in the night to share his hammock, bringing huge earthenware cups of coffee for them both.[36]

The landscapes here are portrayed like the backdrops of an African film being shot in Hollywood. The details that are supposed to represent the South American space—"wretched villages," "volcanoes," "forests," "ferns," "creepers," "desolate river[s] or steep mountain range[s]"—play, first and foremost, a figurative–emotional role. The extinct volcanoes mark the state of Theo's libidinal passions, which awaken from time to time and erupt like the volcano he sees "erupting in flames." Ferns and creepers are important because they create "canopies," which hint at Theo's libidinal nature. The forest "seems to be invading [the steep mountain range] with the savage claws of its roots," in order to express indirectly,

---

kibbutz, a pioneering socialistic Zionist settlement in northern Israel, and here they are random sites in South America.

34 Ibid., 98.
35 Ibid., 98–99.
36 Ibid., 99.

in a "natural," male–female way, his detachment and emotional sterility, and so on. The sexual encounters themselves bring to mind the women of Gauguin's paintings from his Tahiti period. But here, the strong plasticity that is present and so necessary in Gauguin's paintings is lacking. Reuven Miran is a writer who has not received the attention he deserves, and an additional example of the use of the South American province as an extreme existential image can be found in his novella, *Dromit Leantartica* (*South of Antarctica*) (1990).[37] At the center of the book is the story of the total, vital, and, at the same time, destructive relationship of a man and woman, "the Italian" and "the Frenchwoman," two mysterious protagonists, probably spies. The high points of the story occur at the last meeting in two geographical extremities that have obvious symbolic existential value. The first: "the edge of Patagonia, at the jagged margins of the Land of Fire,"[38] symbolizes in the book the limit of human existence. The second, "the 70th parallel south,"[39] symbolizes the place of the material stripped down to pure spirituality and also the realization of the existential paradox that serves as the novella's metaphorical bolt. These two things are connected since, according to the "Italian": "When you are here . . . the North is any place except the place you're stepping on. You can't go any further south. What more do you want, damn it? You won't be able to lose the North even if you have to make an effort."[40]

Other functions that South America serves on the map of the Israeli national imagination are related to two events that seem very distant from one another, at least at a superficial glance. One is an extra-literary event, the return of the Sinai region, which was occupied by Israel between 1967 and 1982, to Egypt. The second event is inter-literary: the publication of the Hebrew translation in Israel in 1972 of Gabriel Garcia Marquez's monumental work, *One Hundred Years of Solitude*.[41]

In the 1950s and until the Six-Day War, many young people dreamed of going to Petra, the "Red Rock," the Nabatean temple on the other side of the River Jordan.

---

37 Reuven Miran, *Dromit Leantartica* (*South of Antarctica*) (Jersualem: Keter, Tzad Hatefer, 1990). A similar symbolic use of the South American promise characterizes Reuven Miran's novella *Marak Tzabim Laaruhat Boker* (*Turtle Soup for Breakfast*)(Jerusalem: Keter, Tzad Hatefer, 1995), 7–22.

38 Miran, *Dromit Leantartica*, 94 (all translations from this text: Hannah Komy Ofir).

39 Ibid., 96.

40 Ibid., p. 97.

41 Gabriel Garcia Marquez, *Mea Shanim Shel Bedidut* (*One Hundred Years of Solitude*) (Tel Aviv: Am Oved, 1972).

Some of them, including for example Meir Har-Zion and Rachel Savorai, even realized the dream. At the time, the Red Rock functioned as a magical place on the map of the Israeli national imagination, the product of an ancient civilization, the secret of whose charm also lay, without a doubt, in the fact that it was a dangerous site to reach.[42] Literary expressions of this phenomenon may be found in Oz's *Menucha Nechona (A Perfect Peace)*[43] (1982) and Ayelet Gondar-Goshen's book *Laila Echad, Markovitz (One Night, Markowitz)* (2012).[44]

After the Six-Day War, the place of the Red Rock on the map of the Israeli national imagination was inherited, in a different way, by the Sinai desert. Many Israelis saw this huge space—especially its eastern shore from Eilat to Sharm el Sheikh—as the ultimate realization of borderless free space; blending into it was in line with the hippie spirit that arrived from the West after 1968.

The return of the Sinai Peninsula to Egypt wounded the Israeli national imagination, in much the same way as it was wounded with the declaration of the establishment of the state, an event that brought about the destruction of the culture of the Israeli *Yishuv*.[45] After the evacuation of Sinai, as after the establishment of the state, nostalgic literature that mourned the "lost place" and the "time that would never return" was created. The writer who expressed this phenomenon most convincingly is Tsur Shezaf, in his book *Namer Beharim (Tiger in the Mountains)*, published in 1988.[46]

The function of the space of absolute freedom, with all its components: liberation from everyday troubles and the pressure of the security situation and the economic situation, as well as the link to spiritual experiences, drug use,

---

42　Haim Hefer wrote a well-known song entitled "Red Rock" in the 1950s. The tune was composed by Yohanan Zarai, and was performed by singer Arik Lavi. According to Hefer, he demanded that the song not be played on the radio, because he was afraid that it would encourage young Israelis to make the dangerous journey to Petra. And, indeed, on July 30, 1958, the song was banned from the radio, a decision that remained in force for several decades. See also Oz Almog, *Hatzabar, Diukan (The Sabra, A Portrait)* (Tel Aviv: Am Oved, 1997),268–88.

43　Amos Oz, *Menuha Nehona (A Perfect Peace)* (Tel Aviv: Am Oved, 1982).

44　Ayelet Gondar-Goshen, *Laila Ehad, Markovitz (One Night, Markowitz)* (Kinneret: Zmora-Bitan, 2012).

45　See note 32, above.

46　Tsur Shezaf, *Namer Beharim (Tiger in the Mountains)* (Jerusalem: Sifrei Siman Kria, Keter). See also in this connection Elchanan Raz, "Masah Le'eretz Hashatuach: al Namer Beharim, Roman Me'et Tsur Shezaf" ("Journey to the Flat Land: On *Tiger in the Mountains*, a Novel by Tsur Shezaf"), *Haaretz* Literary and Cultural Supplement, March 25, 1988. Shezaf also published an excellent travel guide entitled *Sinai Umitzrayim (Sinai and Egypt)* (Keter, no year of publication). He also published several travel guides to other exotic sites around the world and other books that straddle the line between travel guides and literature.

sexual freedom, and so on, which Sinai had fulfilled, was fulfilled from the late 1980s and early '90s by two competing, similar, yet different sites—the East, in particular India,[47] and South America.

Eshkol Nevo addresses the relationship between the space of Sinai and that of South America in his latest book, *Neuland* (2011),[48] to which I will return below. The narrator, Dori, goes looking for his father (who has disappeared) all over the Latin continent. He is impressed by the "breathtaking landscape"[49] revealed to him through the wide window of the vehicle in which he is traveling. A landscape open "to infinity, and in the middle it's not even split by an interchange, or a new city with high-rise buildings, or a line of vehicles with four-wheel drives."[50]

Nevo's protagonist asks himself "when the last time was that such enthusiasm for beauty had caught in his throat."[51] And he replies: "In Sinai, apparently,"[52] adding:

> But they killed Sinai for him, too. Two years ago, when the first images of the attack arrived and he realized that it had happened on "his" beach, he began to cry. Strange. Even at his mother's funeral he hadn't cried. But when he saw the destruction in Ras al-Satan—the huts that had collapsed, shattered plates—his shoulders began to shake.[53]

And to his wife, Ronnie, he explains: "I had one place, Ronnie, you understand? A place I could escape to. I haven't gone there for years. But I knew that if I needed to, the mountains would still be there. The water."[54]

---

47 See also in this context the books of A.B. Yehoshua, *Hashiva Mehodu* (*The Return from India*) (Jerusalem: Hasifria Hahadasha, 1994); Haim Beer, *El Makom Sheharuah Holekh* (*To Where the Wind Goes*) (Tel Aviv: Am Oved, 2010); and Assaf Gavron, *Min Beveit Ha'almin* (*Sex in the Cemetery*) (Yehud: Zamora Bitan, 2000). Sites with similar potentiality that have not yet been appropriated by the map of the Israeli imagination, at least not significantly, are Australia and New Zealand. An exception to this rule is the brilliant use that Amos Kenan makes of the imagined Australian space in his novella *Mahol Cherkesi Besidney* (*A Circassian Dance in Sydney*), which is included in his novella collection: *Tzvivonim Aheinu* (*Tulips Our Brothers*) (Jerusalem: Keter, Tzad Hatefer, 1989).

48 Eshkol Nevo, *Neuland* (Yehud: Zmora Bitan, Amudim Lesifrut Ivrit, 2011). All translations from this text are by Hannah Komy Ofir.

49 Nevo, *Neuland*, 70.

50 Ibid.

51 Ibid.

52 Ibid.

53 Ibid., 70–71.

54 Ibid., 71.

Thus, along with the East, especially India, the South American space fills the role of a space of ultimate freedom on the map of the Israeli national imagination, especially of the young, but also of a certain group of adults. South American literature has occupied a similar place on the literary map of the national imagination since the early 1970s.

This is a spiritual process, which is elusive by nature. Nevertheless, and this is a relatively rare phenomenon, it is very easy to point to the moment that instigated it. I refer to the publication of the Hebrew translation of *One Hundred Years of Solitude* by the Colombian author Gabriel Garcia Marquez. Published in Buenos Aires in 1967, the novel had amazing international success.[55] Yeshayahu Austridan translated it into Hebrew, and 22,500 copies were printed in February 1972. In July of that year, 4,000 additional copies were printed, and five years later 80,000 more copies. In total, approximately 150,000 copies were printed in the 1970s and '80s—a staggering number relative to the size of the local community of readers, and certainly for a translated work.[56] In retrospect, it is possible to say that the Israeli literary imagination was thirsty for an intoxicating brew of the kind that Marquez and his South American magical realists offered in abundance.[57] This richly imaginative literature—boundary

---

55 According to Bilha Rubinstein, *Hedvat Hahaim Mool Hemdat Hamavet* (*The Joy of Life versus the Delight of Death*) (Jerusalem: Carmel, 1999), 159.

56 For comparison, works that received a similarly enthusiastic reception are *Hu Halakh Basadot* (*He Walked Through the Fields*) (1947) by Moshe Shamir, and *Sipur al Ahava Vehoshech* (*A Tale of Love and Darkness*) (2002) by Amos Oz. In this context, Eitan Glass wrote that "the literary world in Israel is split into two, more or less, those influenced by Gabriel Garcia Marquez, on the one hand, and those influenced by Keret, Auster, Vonnegut, on the other." See also Eitan Glass, "Bikoret Sefer: Min Beveit Ha'almin: Zakuf Vaamiti" (Book Review: "Sex in the Cemetery—Straight and Real") *Ynet*, July 4, 2000.

57 The depth of the need of the Israeli literary scene for a South American "version" was expressed then, for example, in the establishment of the *Sidrat Latino* (*The Latino Series*), edited by Tal Nitzan. Hebrew translations of the following books, among others, were included in it: The Holy Innocents by Miguel Delibes (2003); *Finished Symphony* by Augusto Monterroso (2003); *On this Night, in this World: A Selection of Poems and Diary Entries* by Alejandra Pizarnik (2005); *The Other Sky* by Julio Courtazár (2006); *The Olive Labyrinth* by Eduardo Mendoza (2007). Another Israeli writer who is devoted to enriching the dialogue between Israeli literature and culture and Central and South American literature and culture is Yaron Avitov. Avitov published many lists after his travels in South America and his visits to book fairs, lists of books by South American writers published in Hebrew, interviews with South American writers, and so on. In addition, he published literature connected, for example, with life in Cuba and South America, including, among others: *Ha Laila Shel Santiago* (*Santiago Night*) (Astrolog, 2001); *Yuma* (Glory, 2004); *Haorot Shel Miami* (*The Lights of Miami*) (Carmel, Emda, 2005). In addition, he published three books from Ecuador, to which he added a preface or afterword: *Sipurim*

breaking, almost hallucinatory—offered Israeli writers a liberated, joyful, winged, and sometimes crazy way out of the terribly serious literature of the West. They found an escape route from social realism, the legacy of "Mother Russia," the seriously explained hyperrealism, Kafka-style, and the intense, sometimes suffocating, stream of consciousness of Faulkner's style. Moreover, the colorful South American family sagas allowed them to "rethink" Jewish historiography in general and Zionism in particular from a liberated position, without fear of judges, prophets, rabbis, commissars of all the ideologies of the Zionist movement, and so on— in short, without fear of the judgmental eyes of the current representatives of "the Jewish audience." Two books that express this trend are: *Zelig Mainz Vegaaguav Elhamavet* (*Zelig Mainz and His Longings for Death*) (1985),[58] Itamar Levy's first book, and *Roman Rusi* (*A Russian Novel*) (1988),[59] Meir Shalev's first and most successful novel.

In *Zelig Mainz and His Longings for Death*, Itamar Levy wrote a hallucinatory alternative historiography of the story of the Jewish people. The plot's lack of logic, the strange dynasties and the syntactic tapestry all correspond with the school of magical realism, especially with the exciting option offered

Me'emtza Haolam (*Stories from the Middle of the World*) (Carmel, 2005); *Yerushalayim Shel Ha'andim* (*Jerusalem of the Andes*) (which also included one of Avitov's stories) (Carmel, 2008); *Indiani Alhahar* (*Indian on the Mountain*) (Carmel, 2009). He also published several anthologies of Israeli literature published in South America.The books of Nahum Megged also contributed significantly to the intercultural dialogue on the ancient cultures of South America, shamanism, and magic in Central and South America, and more. See Nahum Megged, *Ha'aztekim: Mehanit Hashemesh Lehanitot Shvurot* (*The Aztecs: From the Sun Spear to Broken Spears*) (Ma? Da! Dvir, 1996); idem, *Shaarei Tikva Veshaarei Eima: Shamanism, Magia, Vekishuf Bedrom Umercaz America* (*Portals of Hope and Gates of Terror: Shamanism, Magic and Witchcraft—Journey in South and Central America*) (Modan, 1998); idem, *Tarbuyot Kdumot Beyabeshet America* (*Ancient Civilizations on the American Continent*) (The Broadcast University, Israel Ministry of Defense, 1999); idem, *Hamitologia Haindianit* (*Indian Mythology*) (Mapa, 2001); idem, *Keshe Hazman Nisdak Vehaetzim Bokhim* (*When Time Is Cracked and the Trees Cry*), a novel (Xargol, 2004); idem, *Malinche, Hatzeira Haindianit Shekavsha Imperia* (*Malinche, The Young Indian Woman Who Conquered an Empire*) (Tel Aviv: Modan, 2008).

See also Sagi Green, (interviewer), "Siha Im Gabriel Garcia Marquez" ("A Talk with Gabriel Garcia Marquez"), *Haaretz*, April 9, 1996; Luiz Landau, "Gabriel Garcia Marquez Kebaal Utopia Chasar Ashlayot" ("Gabriel Garcia Marquez as Having a Utopia without Illusions"), *Alei Siah* 15–16 (1982), 178–81; Gabriel Garcia Marquez, "Mea Shanim Shel Bedidut: Hizdamnut Shniya" ("One Hundred Years of Solitude: A Second Chance"), *Alei Siah* 19–20 (1983): 199–200.

58 Itamar Levy, *Zelig Mainz Vega'aguav Elhamavet* (*Zelig Mainz and His Longings for Death*) (Sifriat Hapoalim, Hakibbuta Hartzi, 1985).
59 Meir Shalev, *Roman Rusi* (*A Russian Novel*) (Tel Aviv: Am Oved, 1988).

by Peruvian writer Manuel Skorza in his book *Drums for Rancas* (published in Hebrew as *Trua Lerancas* in 1975).[60]

Meir Shalev's book creatively uses similar artistic tools perfected in the same school. He describes the period of the founding of the Zionist project, the days of the Second *Aliyah*, with two kinds of brushes, a precise realistic brush and a frenetic imaginary brush. This combination no doubt was made possible for him due to his exposure to the works of Marquez, and primarily *One Hundred Years of Solitude*, which allowed him to probe and thoroughly search the inner workings of Zionist mythology without shattering it.[61]

The writers whose works I have discussed drew from the South American scene without referring to the hundreds of thousands of Jews who came there in the framework of highly significant historical and ideological processes. The writer who broke through this egocentric–Zionist concept was Gabriela Avigur-Rotem. Avigur-Rotem was born in Buenos Aires, immigrated with her parents to Israel, and decided, as early as in her first novel, *Mozart Lo Haya Yehudi (Mozart Was Not a Jew)* (1992),[62] to give a renewed mandate to what Harshav called the "new Diaspora."

Avigur-Rotem's novel opens at the outbreak of the late nineteenth-century Jewish modernist revolution in the Pale of Settlement in Russia, and from there it outlines a complicated, two-tracked plot whose vector of desire is aimed not toward the Land Israel, not toward the United States, but rather toward Latin America. She unfolds the chronicles of two families of Jewish immigrants in early twentieth-century South America. One of the families settles in Buenos Aires and the other in Mar de Oro. Blood ties are formed between the two families, but in accordance with the best of the traditions of South

---

60 Manuel Skorza, *Trua Lerancas (Drums for Rancas)* (Tel Aviv: Dora Publishers, 1975). The book addresses the history of a violent struggle that took place in the central Andes between poor Andean villagers and wealthy estate owners and other capital owners, which ended in the annihilation of the Rancas community by the Peruvian assault forces with the assistance of the estate owners.

61 In this context, see also Smadar Shiffman, "On the Possibility of Impossible Worlds: Meir Shalev and the Fantastic in Israel literature," *Prooftexts* 13, no. 3 (1993): 253–67; Robert Alter, "Magic Realism in the Israeli Novel," in *The Boom in Contemporary Israeli Fiction*, ed. Alan Mintz (Hanover, MA: Brandeis University Press, 1997), 17–34. Incidentally, the publication in Hebrew of *The Garden of Forking Paths* by the Argentinean author Jorge Luis Borges (trans. Yoram Bronowsky) had a real, though modest and subtle, cultural and literary influence in the 1980s and '90s (Hakibbutz Hameuchad, 1978).

62 Gabriela Avigur-Rotem, *Mozart Lo Haya Yehudi (Mozart Was Not a Jew)* (Jerusalem: Keter, Tzad Hatefer, 1992).

American magical realism,[63] spiritual and mysterious ties are formed as well. The novel's plot comprises the daily trials and tribulations of raising sons and daughters, educating them, and providing for them. Beneath the sane, realistic social–psychological textures, however, a dark and unknown force occasionally emerges, causing night wanderings and performing miracles, wreaking damage, and creating music.

The book opens with an attempt to trace the nature of the obscure force agitating Aryeh-Yehuda Leib (one of the heads of the two main families in the novel), "from glorified Odessa ... [and] taking hold of him to move him to the other side of the world to seek a dimmed land between sun and shadow at the edge of the anticlinorium of the ocean."[64] The book follows the growth of the magnetic attraction South America exerts on Aryeh-Yehuda Leib, and associates it with Abraham's intention to go to the Land of Israel and to the event of "the sacrifice." Zionist literature changed the meaning of this from an event marking the covenant between man and "the place" in the theological sense, to an event that marks the covenant between man and "the place" in the territorial sense.[65]

> Sometimes he [Aryeh-Yehuda Leib,] dares to enter the *biblioteca*, where he finds the great globe leaning on its side, and he reaches out, touches it, and the ball spins seas and lands and mountains and rivers under his fingertips. *Get thee out*, whispers a voice in his heart, *get thee out*, and the dizzy ball freezes when his fingers rest on a distant land in the shape of a salamander, and his head leans to the side, and his lips pluck the syllables of the sound playing on his tongue, Tierra del Fuego. Go, go, the voice throbs, and the sound of his finger teaches its lesson: *"Here I am."*[66]

Avigur-Rotem's pioneering literary initiative in *Mozart Was Not a Jew*—to try and track the attempt to realize the vector of desire for South America, which had been foiled for decades due to literary–ideological censorship of the

---

63 Adi Ofir (*Maariv*, February 14, 1992, 14) characterized the book as *One Hundred Years of Jewish Solitude*—Marquez circumcised and brought into the Hebrew covenant" (trans. Hannah Adelman Komy Ofir). See in this context also Avigur-Rotem's excellent article "Al Mea Shnot Bedidut shel G.G. Marquez" ("On One Hundred Years of Solitude by G.G. Marquez"), *Akhshav* 39–40 (1979): 351–61.

64 Avigur-Rotem, *Mozart Lo Haya Yehudi*, 15.

65 See also on this matter: Schwartz, "Handasat Haadam Veitsuv Hamerchav" ("Human Engineering and Shaping Space") in *Ma Sheroim Mikan*, 25–49.

66 Avigur-Rotem, *Mozart Lo Haya Yehudi*, 16.

dominant vector of desire—was not followed up until recently. In recent years, three broad-scoped books that address this issue intensively have been published, *Maaseh Betabaat (The Tale of a Ring)* (2007),[67] and *Keshehametim Chazru (When the Dead Returned)* (2012) by Ilan Sheinfeld,[68] who is currently working on a third "South American" novel. The other is Eshkol Nevo's *Neuland* (2011). All three books attracted considerable public attention.

The Tale of a Ring deals with a sad part of the history of the Jews of South America. The protagonist, Esperanza Ganz, reveals her secret to her daughter: she, her mother, and her grandmother were Jewish prostitutes and their lives were bound by the passing of a magic ring from mother to daughter. The true story about the Jewish pimps' organization "Zvi Migdal," which operated in Buenos Aires from 1870 to 1930,[69] provides the backdrop to the book.

When the Dead Returned is a Jewish fantasy of the return of the messiah to the People of Israel—a messiah of the flesh, a messiah against his will, who does not even know what he is going to cause to happen. The book begins with a history of an extensive Jewish family in a Polish town. It continues with the description of the various incarnations of some of the family members in Argentina and several places in Peru. In one of them, Iquitos, at the edge of the Amazon forest, a baby is born, and the inheritance of his fathers and the influence of the forest make him into the messiah. The book ends in the Land of Israel, where, before our eyes, a grotesque version of the end of days is realized.

At the center of *Neuland* is the story of a father and son. The son travels to South America to find his father, who has disappeared. The father, shell-shocked from the Yom Kippur War, gave up the path of implementing the Zionist project, and decided to rebuild Herzl's vision precisely in the place rejected by Herzl: the province in Argentina where Hirsch founded his own Jewish outposts.

These three books—all products of the spirit of the transitional period between the end of the twentieth century and the early twenty-first

---

67 Ilan Sheinfeld, *Maaseh Betabaat.*
68 Ilan Sheinfeld, *Keshehametim Hazru.*
69 See also Haim Avni, *Tmeim, Sahar Benashim Yehudiot Beargentina (Unclean: White Slavery of Jewish Women in Argentina)* (Yediot Aharonot, Hemed Books, Miskal, 2009); Isabelle Vincent, *Bodies and Souls: The Tragic Plight of Three Jewish Women Forced into Prostitution in the Americas* (New York: HarperCollins, 2005) (translated into Hebrew as *Begufan Ubenafshan: Sipuran Hatragi Shel Nashim Yehudiot Shenimkeru Liznut Bidrom America* by Haim Amit and published in Israel in 2008 by Keter). There is reason to assume that a connection exists between the dizzying success of Scheinfeld's book and the later appearance of these reference books.

century—are linked by several significant similarities. First, all three of them continue along the path of Avigur-Rotem, and return to the point of "in the beginning," the modern Jewish Revolution of the late nineteenth century, and grant a renewed mandate to the South American version of the "new diaspora." In addition, in all three of them, Baron Hirsch's option is rejuvenated after more than a hundred and twenty years of almost complete exclusion.[70]

Second—in a deviation from Avigur-Rotem's path, which provides the Jewish South American option with a separate and independent place and real vitality—in all three of these books it is apparent that this existential settlement option serves primarily as a mirror, reflecting the Zionist option that was put into practice in the Land of Israel, and strayed from its original purpose in the views of Nevo and Scheinfeld. This phenomenon is particularly evident in *Neuland*, where South American Judaism is represented as "archeological" and nothing more; the father in the novel establishes his "Neuland" community on the ruins of one of Baron Hirsch's settlements. In other words, in these books, the South American option has the status, and again this is especially obvious in Nevo's book, of a secondary story, a story that makes it possible to represent, using different comparative techniques, the dystopian nature of the great Zionist story to which it is subjected.

Another common denominator of these books is the use that both authors make of the toolbox of the school of magical realism in order to reimagine Jewish historiography in general and its Zionist chapter in particular, and, in this, they

---

70 Through the use of various maneuvers, Eshkol Nevo repeatedly creates equivalency between the option formulated by Baron Hirsch and that formulated by Herzl. One is anchored in the words of Cecilia-Aharona, who serves as an official tour guide in the renewed Jewish settlement of *Neuland*, a role that exists in every utopia—including Herzl's, of course. Cecilia-Aharona opens her speech thus: "Peace and blessings upon you, my friend from the Land of Israel. I am happy to welcome you here in Moisesville, which is, indeed, the Jerusalem of Argentina, and to show you the way to Neuland" (441). She continues: "Bueno, I talked so much about myself that I didn't talk to you about our Moisesville. At this very moment, we are approaching the intersection of Theodor Herzl Street and Baron Hirsch Street" (ibid.). This intersection is the topographical–ideological junction of "the Jerusalem of Argentina," and, as such, it places the two "prophets" on equal footing. Moreover, this intersection "corresponds," as I learned from Nili Gold, through a kind of backward logic, with the absence of such an intersection in Moisesville's twin city—Haifa, which is the city most exemplary of Herzl's topographical–ideological vision. And here, and this is almost certainly a deliberate ironic sign, in the actual Haifa there does exist an intersection of Baron HirschandRothschildStreets, and there is, of course, a Herzl Street, but it does not intersect anywhere with Baron Hirsch Street (translations in this note: Hannah Komy Ofir).

follow in the footsteps of those who preceded them in this creative channel: Meir Shalev, Itamar Levy, and Gabriela Avigur-Rotem. I agree with Sheinfeld's statement made, in this context, in an interview about his *A Tale of a Ring*:

> The subject that interests me in my writing in general, and in this novel in particular, is the construction of Jewish collective memory and the way in which personal memory conducts itself. For me, this matter [the story of the Jewish pimps' organization, "Zvi Migdal"] allowed me to sail to the provinces of imagination and magic and attempt to reconnect my life and Israeli existence to provinces that once existed and no longer do.[71]

Schoenfeld's comments on the possibility that opened up and allowed him to "sail to the provinces of imagination and magic and attempt to reconnect [his] life and Israeli existence to provinces that once existed and no longer do" are connected to two additional and particularly interesting similarities that link his novels to Eshkol Nevo's *Neuland*.

For Avigur-Rotem, the Russian Pale of Settlement serves as a womb out of which the South American Jewish option bursts. In contrast, in the works of Sheinfeld and Nevo, the South American Jewish option, the one that was, or even better, the one whose existence Sheinfeld restores, and the one that Dori's father reinvents and attempts to implement in an area previously acquired by Baron Hirsch, serves as *an alternative womb*. In both, the land of South America serves as a *fertile surrogate mother*, whose role is to regerminate the Zionist option, whose growth medium in Israel has been destroyed.

The climax in this context is the identity of the connection that becomes clear in the three novels, which were written by two different Israeli authors, one born in 1960 and the other born in 1971, when we attempt to clarify what, for them, makes the South American province such a suitable womb.

One factor is, as mentioned above, "historical justice," righting the injustice inadvertently and/or intentionally done to the Jewish settlement in South America, which was marginalized in the Israeli national imagination. Other very significant factors are, as noted, "the borderless space" and magical realism. However, all these factors, each on its own, and all together, could not fulfill their mission in the novels of Nevo and Sheinfeld without the inclusion of another, surprising factor: *shamanism*.

---

71 www.text.org.il/index.php?book=0701051, accessed May 23, 2017.

When we examine the life stories of the protagonists of the two books, *Neuland* and *When the Dead Returned*, it turns out that both Dori's father and Solomon, Sheinfeld's messiah, are sanctified for their roles—messiah and prophet—by means of "qualified" shamanic mentors. These shamans serve as guides to life in every respect, and they play the role played by all such life guides in Zionist utopias and dystopias.[72] The two have very different biographical backgrounds; one is a "standard" sabra, shell-shocked, the other the son of a Jewish father who grew up in Poland with a Gentile family and a mother who may be Indian or Jewish. Both are constructed in the generic tradition of the bildungsroman or, more precisely, in the generic tradition of the genre that preceded it and continued to develop parallel to it, the "legend," the genre of sanctification, which Christianity cultivated and enhanced. The life guides in Zionist fiction—who lead the protagonists to the old–new land with the power of the vision of the prophets and modernist progress (and a perfect example in this regard is David Litvak, the young, educated, enthusiastic Zionist who serves in *Altneuland* as a life guide to Friedrich, the "Diaspora Jew")—are replaced in *Neuland* and *When the Dead Returned* by shamans. Both straddle the line between utopia and dystopia, and are reminiscent more than anything of Don Juan Matus, the old Mexican wizard and sage, who serves as a life guide to the Peruvian-born American author Carlos Castaneda in twelve books, including *Journey to Ixtlan* (1972),[73] and *The Lessons of Don Juan* (1969).[74]

Furthermore, the literary historical process presented here also has an interesting circular logic. Herzl signified the Diaspora as *elend*, a not-place,[75] in the framework of which South America was a place of death. Now, a hundred years later, South America is perceived in Israeli fiction as a place by means of which Jewish nationalism can survive, live, and thrive.

This strength is attributed to South America due to a strange and fascinating combination of factors: "virgin space," which replaces the pre-state Land of Israel

---

72 Rachel Elboim-Dror, *Hamachar shel Haetmol*, vol. 1. *Hautopia Hatzionit* (*Yesterday's Tomorrow*, vol. 1: *The Zionist Utopia*) (Jerusalem: Yad Izhak Ben-Zvi, 1993), 71. See also Leah Hadomi, "Haroman Hautopi ve Hautopia Hatzionit" ("The Utopian Novel and the Zionist Utopia"), *Bikoret Ufarshanut* 13–14 (1979): 131–68.

73 Carlos Castaneda, *Journey to Ixtlan: The Lessons of Don Juan* (New York: Washington Square Press, 1972).

74 Carlos Castaneda, *The Teachings of Don Juan: A Yaqui Way of Knowledge* (Berkeley, CA: University of California Press, 1969).

75 "And all that time Judaism had sunk lower and lower. It was an 'eland' in the full sense of the Old German word that had meant 'out-land,'—the limbo of the banished," *Altneuland* (*Old–New Land*), 189.

and the Sinai desert and is an alternative space in which it is possible to talk about the Israeli experience and space indirectly;[76] Jewishness that managed to escape, at least partially, the major traumas of the twentieth century, including the Holocaust and Israel's wars, and, as mentioned, and perhaps especially, a new and rejuvenating spirituality, which is based on the power of shamanism, which completely deviates from the Jewish rabbinic tradition.[77]

---

76 In an interview with Moshe Natan, when asked why he did not write about Israel in his plays, Nissim Aloni replied: "Who doesn't write about his own place? I don't write about my place? I come from a little neighborhood in Tel Aviv, no? But I cannot write about the Land of Israel directly." See also, Moshe Natan, *Kishuf Neged Hamavet: Hateatron shel Nissim Aloni* (*Magic against Death: The Theater of Nissim Aloni*) (Tel Aviv: Hakibbutz Hameuchad, 1996), 42.

77 And see, on the matter of the use of shamanic and pagan practices in the "alternative" Jewish tradition (folk, feminine, etc.) in Tamar Alexander and Eliezer Papo: "Lekhokha Shel Mila: Lahashei Ripui Sfaradiim Mipi Neshot Sarayevo" ("On the Power of the Word: Sephardi Healing Incantations according to Jewish Women from Sarajevo"), *Mehkarei Yerushalayim Befoklor* 24–25: 303–48.

CHAPTER 17

From Batiste Linen to the Empire at Palatnik Villa— Centennial Records of Economic Life in Natal's First Jewish Community

NANCY ROZENCHAN

Fate, irony, or luck? Who knows what happens in somebody else's life, or why a person allows himself to be led in one direction and not another?

Since, obviously, there are no answers to these formulations, it would seem preferable to reveal what the directions were, who the people were, how they behaved, and why they headed one way or another.

Some of the Ukrainian Palatnik family's records[1] from Podolia, and the path the Palatnik brothers trailed to Natal, the capital city of the state of Rio Grande do Norte in northeastern Brazil, are herein presented. The emphasis is on the economic aspects linked to this family's activity and establishment in Brazil from 1912. These records were disclosed, written, and published in Hebrew by Tuvia Palatnik (1890–1972) in his book *Binetive Hanedudim* (Palatnik 1970).[2] The records were supplemented with comments and interviews carried out by Egon and Frieda Wolf, Brazilian researchers, and published in *Natal: A Singular Community* (Wolf et al. 1984).

---

1 Several years ago, I wrote an essay about the Jewish community in the city of Natal, as developed by the Palatnik brothers, namely "Os judeus de Natal: Uma comunidade segundo o registro de seu fundador" ("The Jews in Natal: A Community, according to Its Founder's Logs"), published in *Revista Herança Judaica* 106 (April 2000).

2 I am extremely indebted to Prof. Ethel W. Kosminsky, a native from Natal, for offering some key material for my research.

This immigration celebrated its centennial in 2012. That alone, along with the unique character of this community and its records, justifies our work here.

Jewish immigration took place over three periods: the **first** being the colonial era (1500–1808), when converts or New Christians set foot in Brazil. It includes the brief period under Dutch rule, when a Jewish community settled in Recife, where the first synagogue in the Americas was set up.

The **second** immigration period, known as the Imperial period (1808–89), divides into three stages. The **first** phase (1808–22) includes the Opening of Ports to Friendly Nations on the part of King João VI, on January 28, 1808, and the signing of a commercial treaty with England in 1810, which encouraged the inflow of foreigners into Brazil, among them many Jews. Those arriving from England enjoyed freedom of religion, as advocated in the 1824 Constitution. All Jews enjoyed full freedom of religion in 1889, when Brazil adopted a constitution assuring this right. Jews also came from Germany, and a large wave of migration arrived from the Alsace-Lorraine in the second half of the century. A large migration from Morocco then flowed into the north of the country before and during the "rubber boom" phase, which led to the formation of Jewish nuclei in various parts of the Amazon and Pará states. The first organized community, the Israeli Association of *Gemilut Hassadim*, in Rio de Janeiro, highlighted the **second** phase of the imperial period (1822–48). The **third** phase, from 1848 to 1889, covers the immigration waves flowing from western and central Europe resulting from the 1848 revolutions and the Franco–Prussian War. It ended with the Proclamation of the Brazilian Republic.

Finally, the republican or contemporary period runs from 1889 to this day. Two stages stand out during this period. The first, unfolding from 1889 to 1904, includes the immigration flow beginning in 1891, coinciding with the First Republican Constitution and colonization projects of the early republic. From 1904 to 1914, with the help of the Jewish Colonization Association (hereafter JCA), the agricultural colonies of "Philipson" and "Quatro Irmãos" settled in the state of Rio Grande do Sul. The state government promoted agricultural colonization in the hinterlands of São Paulo State (Nova Odessa, Campos Salles, and Jorge Tibiriçá), which were settled in 1905.[3] Such projects attracted Jewish immigrants. The second stage is of Jews coming from eastern Europe and, to a lesser extent, from the Ottoman Empire, with regard to no specific project.

Tens of thousands of eastern European Jews came to Brazil seeking new prospects for survival and life. Mostly, they were trying to avoid

---

3 "História de Nova Odessa" (2013).

military service, discrimination, and the oppression that affected them from all sides. Or else, they were just trying to make a living, looking for economic and social mobility, and seeking new opportunities. In the early days, most became suppliers and door-to-door sales representatives working in new urban neighborhoods poorly served by trade. They were known as *clienteltchikes* in Yiddish. Following the abolition of slavery in 1888, markets expanded in the country without a parallel growth in the distribution system of goods. Usually with no trade or professional skills, most Jewish immigrants managed to fit their livelihoods into this niche.

Most Jewish immigrants in the 1910s and '20s were aided by Jewish organizations in Europe and the United States like the aforementioned JCA, the Joint Distribution Committee for the Relief of Jewish War Sufferers (hereafter JDC), and the Hebrew Immigrant Aid Society (hereafter HIAS).

Several scholars from Brazil and other countries, engrossed in the various study aspects of Jewish immigration and the Jewish presence in Brazil, have provided interesting and revealing information regarding such help and covering over five hundred years of Jewish presence in the country, including also the "New Christians."[4] Many of these scholars discuss the most controversial aspects of the various periods of immigration, particularly those involving political issues and discrimination.

Jewish immigration to Natal presented certain unique characteristics that did not fall within the general framework concerning most other Brazilian cities or specific immigration projects. This was perhaps because those immigrants arrived on a known recorded date, or maybe because they had an ideological and concrete project in mind, or perhaps due to the small number of their members. The one book about this family and the community remains unknown to Brazilian researchers since it was written in Hebrew, is no longer available, is very little known and virtually inaccessible.

As previously mentioned, there are only two primary sources concerning this immigration, the book by Palatnik and that written by the Wolf couple, based on reports from Palatnik's second-generation descendants. Apart from

---

4 See studies by Henrique Rattner, Nachman Falbel, Helena Lewin, Roberto Grün, Jeffrey Lesser, Roney Cytrynowicz, Marcelo Gruman, Ieda Gutfreind, Bernardo Sorj, Bila Sorj, Anita Brumer, Monica Grin, Nelson Vieira, Boris Fausto, Tania Kaufman, Keila Grinberg, Fabio Koifman, Maria Luiza Tucci Carneiro, Ethel W. Kosminsky, René Decol, Mirian Goldenberg, Marta F. Topel, Samuel Malamud, Avraham Milgram, Elias Lipiner, Eva Blay, Robert Levine, Marcos Chor Maio, Arnold Wiznitzer, Anita Novinsky, Lina Gorenstein Ferreira da Silva, and Reginaldo Heller, among others.

these books, the folklorist Câmara Cascudo[5,6] briefly recorded the presence of Jews in the city.

The aforementioned involvement in trade highlights records and unique perspectives of the author's and his brothers' process of immigration—the motivation and justification for their trip to Brazil, their social and economic integration into local life, the boldness of their incursions, their upward mobility and his family's role in the consolidation of their status. It thus dwells on some cases that did not take place and were not recorded in any other community of Jewish immigrants in Brazil.[7]

Although they came from a small town, like most immigrants, the Palatniks' motives and intentions on leaving Europe and their subsequent progress in Brazil differed from those of many other immigrants who came at that time. They had been land leasers and traders for generations. They were primarily farmers or otherwise connected to agriculture. Not only did they raise cereal crops, grains, beets, and potatoes, but also took care of related activities, such as milling. Their family's history discloses edicts of expulsion from the villages where they lived and the loss of leasing rights. They had to outwit the decrees by using two contracts with the property's owner—a pro forma one to be used before the authorities and another undisclosed one, stating the real business relations. By 1911,[8] no longer able to evade the land lease laws, or to make a

---

5   In Luís da Câmara Cascudo, *História da Cidade do Natal*, 2nd ed. (Rio de Janeiro: Civilização Brasileira; Brasília: INL; Natal: Universidade Federal do Rio Grande do Norte, 1980,) 389, the four Palatnik brothers—Tobias, Jacob, Adolfo, and Joseph—were the first Jews to settle in the city of Natal who practiced Judaism, on November 14, 1912. The Jewish community of Natal was founded on January 12, 1919. Later, in 1925, an Israeli center operating as a synagogue was set up, though it was only registered on August 18, 1929. The synagogue celebrates all Jewish festivals, i.e., New Year, The Day of Atonement, Pentecost, Feast of Tabernacles, Passover.

6   Following my late 1990s presentation of the abovementioned academic paper about the Jewish community in Natal and its activities, based on Palatnik's work—attended by some members of the second or third generations of the Palatnik family—I was told that they were unaware of most events. In my more recent contacts with the third-generation family members, I came to understand just how little these people knew of their family's history.

7   It should be noted that recent studies on Jews in Natal, the capital of Rio Grande do Norte, do not generally refer to the local Jewish community in the early twentieth century, but only to the contemporary groups that consider themselves Jews.

8   From the entry on "Agriculture" in the YIVO Encyclopedia (September 2013), one learns that Jews were forbidden to own land: "In the early days, few Eastern European Jews engaged in agriculture. They only got involved in agricultural economy in the late sixteenth century. Many Jews leased the great *latifundia* in Ukraine, paying noble landowners large sums, recouped by the lessees when running the estates. Thus, some Jews became involved

living, David, the patriarch and father of four sons and four daughters born between 1888 and 1908, decided that the family had to leave Staraia-Utshitsa. They eventually emigrated in 1912, over a century ago.

Like most immigrants, they did not have the means for all of them to leave. These particular Jews were instilled with the Zionist ideal. The purpose of the trip, therefore, was to reach Palestine and there alone. They would thus fulfill the ideals of the youth movement that had taught and trained them in agriculture, comprising acquisition of land and devotion to the work that employed some of the new inhabitants, namely, soil recovery and plantation of orchards and orange groves.

Faced with insurmountable difficulties, they reconsidered their plans, and the target of immigration—not for the parents or daughters, but that of the young men—pointed to Brazil. Their goal was to engage in agriculture and accumulate money in order to fulfill their desire to settle in Palestine.

This family chose Brazil as the result of an announcement in eastern European newspapers that offered about 500 acres of fertile land to farming families—water and forest for free, as well as equipment worth five million *reis* (the Brazilian currency at that time), to be repaid in ten annual installments from the third year on, interest-free and tax-free for five years.

Tuvia (aka Tobias in Portuguese) Palatnik did not specify these land locations on his records. As the first city where the first Palatnik brother landed was Salvador, on a regular navigation route from north to south, one might conclude that it meant south of Salvador, to areas in need of and interested in immigrants. In an interview with Egon and Frieda Wolf, one of the descendants reported that the land worked on was in southern Brazil, in the JCA agricultural colonies in Rio Grande do Sul State. According to Tuvia, this propaganda attracted crowds of Italian, Portuguese, Spanish, Polish, and Ukrainian farmers, among others, to Brazil. So, he might have been speaking of immigration in a general way.

At any rate, it should not be surprising that the Palatniks sought an agricultural project and location to settle. They were accustomed to landwork,

---

in agricultural management ... from 1859 until 1891, a series of edicts forbade Jews to rent or purchase farmland anywhere in the Empire. Russian Jews had to bribe or otherwise manipulate laws in order to farm ... Jews' contributions to the agricultural economy were significant, and noble estate owners effectively blocked attempts to amend this situation ... discriminatory legislation restricted Jewish access to land. Authorities in the Russian Empire tried to isolate Jews from the peasants, for the former were considered a destabilizing force that might end up taking over the countryside. Toward the end of the 1800s, the belief of Jews being agents of a coming revolution stepped up such policies."

though not in such a practical and direct way, such as actually handling agricultural tools.

Early in 1912, the family organized the first expedition, which did not include the oldest son, twenty-two-year-old Tuvia, as one might have expected. Instead, they sent Yaacov, who would soon be twenty and had to avoid military service. He crossed the Russian border illegally, along with two friends and an uncle added to the expedition at the very last moment. After setting out from Hamburg, and sailing for twenty-three days, Yaacov's ship docked in Salvador, the capital city of the State of Bahia, where he met several eastern European Jews living in the old city. This, however, was not his final destination.[9]

Tuvia was fortunate to receive good education at an above-average level for that time and place. So probably did the other brothers. He had studied languages (Hebrew, Russian, French, German, and Latin) and basic accounting—not to mention the traditional Jewish studies (Bible, prayers, laws). Notions of agriculture and land administration were most likely not at all strange to him.

Yaacov sought out the local Jews at the first Brazilian port, in order to get information on potential areas offered for agriculture. In the opinion of already seasoned veterans, the soils were unsuitable for agriculture, not to mention the fact that Jews were generally unfamiliar with agriculture. Without more ado, Yaacov gave up on the idea of continuing the trip to fulfill the original purpose. On top of not knowing the language, the region he was seeking was undeveloped and offered no roads or transport, the climate and environment was strange, and agriculture itself was very different. The idea of traveling toward the offered land was postponed. The suggestion was to start with what was most accessible: Yaacov should become an itinerant sales representative, an activity representing little risk and generating some real profit. Yaacov and his brothers could, if they so wished, acquire a farm at the outskirts of a town at a later time and plant fruit.

A week after arriving, Yaacov joined the *clienteltchik*'s activity, selling fabrics to men and women, for cash or in installments. He was aided by a handler, who carried the goods in a chest. The handler also served as an interpreter,

---

9 Jeffrey Lesser, *O Brasil e a Questão Judaica* (Rio de Janeiro: Imago, 1995). The entry "Jewish immigrants in Brazil" is flawed. Lesser maintains that the ports of Recife and Salvador kept no inventory of the immigrants who arrived in the 1910s or '20s. The records started from 1928. Thus, it is only through records such as Palatnik's that one can obtain information about this immigration. The way the story goes, it is not strange at all that Yaacov interrupted the journey before reaching the final destination and also failed to return to the ship.

since his boss did not yet know Portuguese. Even though the beautiful city of Salvador, with its warm and humid climate and its bumpy roads, was unfriendly to a peddler, Yaacov soon realized that if he lived modestly, he could amass resources. He immediately wrote to his brothers, advising them to hurry up and come. If they all worked together, it was clear that they could accomplish their father's ideals, and purchase land in Palestine.

On arrival in 1912, Tuvia found his brother in yet another city, just as hot as Salvador, though less mountainous: Recife, the capital of Pernambuco State, an agriculture-based economy, where animals still pulled the trams. The four brothers arrived in the same year.

Certain aspects of Tuvia's report draw our attention at this point: the need to assume the physical role of being a tradesman, while having to deal with feelings toward this undesired and unplanned situation. On the third day following his arrival and a "crash course" on commodities, prices, payments, customer's behavior, and management, it was essential to practice it all on the streets. Despite the first days of despair at having to go out and knock on strangers' doors, Tuvia soon convinced himself that he could manage. There was no way out, or any other starting point. They had all come to Brazil with the intention of reaching the final goal—the *aliyah* of the whole family to Palestine. As an additional practical measure, they began to read the *Diário de Pernambuco* every evening, even without understanding it. They wanted to get used to reading Portuguese; they used to write down each new word they learned daily, with translations into Hebrew and Yiddish, in a notebook.

Their diligent work soon bore fruit: after the first week, each one of them was already working independently. Together they created their first "installment business enterprise." They ordered printed letter pads, client forms, and company receipts. They began to acquire more goods. They left every day with three chests and three handlers, who not only helped them carry the goods but also with the language. They lived in a boarding house, leaving at 7:00 a.m. for a twelve-hour-day's work, a brief break for a snack – some canned sardines or a cheese sandwich, accompanied by the local *guaraná* soft drink or fruit. Most sales were on credit. Back at the boarding house after dinner, they assessed their activities. Just two weeks after arrival, they decided to rent a more comfortable house. There, they put aside a room for bookkeeping and storing commodities. They also hired a cook to prepare their meals.

The clientele grew. A known Jewish trader from Recife endorsed their request for additional capital resources and credit. The four Palatnik brothers felt that their business could develop, but realized that they faced considerable and fierce competition. They considered abandoning the itinerant trade and taking on some other more stable business, which was impracticable at that time. In Recife, about eighty young Jewish men were street traders, a newly developed activity. They dealt with the same goods and chased after the same customers. Almost all young men were single, willing to return to their families in Europe with a substantial amount of money.

As the trip to Brazil rather than to Palestine represented an unexpected shift in the lives of the Palatniks, an event in the business field is regarded to have been a turning point in their decision-making. This is where the business of batiste linen fits in.

What people wore a century ago provided information about their identity. The Brazilian elites wanted to dress like the Europeans, mostly French women's wear and men's English style. The imported way of life, however, did not mean that Brazil had not created its own identity. The hot weather demanded the precious batiste linen and the Panama hat, which became indispensable to those who could afford them. Without dwelling on details, circumstances, or economic calculations, the brothers had the audacity to take on the sale of a ten-chest stock of this precious fabric, two additional chests of French silk, and a hundred Panama hats that had recently been brought to the city by the son of an English tradesman. They accomplished and concluded the sale in just three weeks—quicker than they had ever imagined. They were aware that no *clienteltchik* owned this class of material and that together they represented a superior sales force. They knew that they could sell such sophisticated goods for cash to an affluent clientele. They also foresaw they would be able to win over such customers for future business. They learned the skills very quickly and became more confident and capable.

Casual circumstances added to curiosity also carry weight in business, and can change directions or unexpectedly create new opportunities. After examining a rail map on a wall in a client's house, Tuvia asked for details about the itinerary of the Great Western Railway Company train lines. In his poor Portuguese, he understood that there was a line leading to the north, to the city of Natal—the capital city of the Rio Grande do Norte State—and that it had been inaugurated a few years earlier. Some hours later, he tried to persuade the brothers that due to the harsh competition in Recife, their skills could be useful in Natal. The idea did not enthrall them, nor did all the brothers accept it—for several reasons. They considered it inconvenient to restart the development of a new market. In addition, they did not know the characteristics of that city—or what it had to offer. They evaluated travel costs and losses for interrupting work for a week, for not getting new customers, for not selling, and for not collecting installments. Tuvia eventually managed to persuade them. Having settled in Brazil only three months earlier, he left on a long second-class train ride to Natal, carrying various items of batiste linen, silk, and hats. The distance today is merely 286 km. Then, it was an adventure. Travelers were at the mercy of wild animals. Trains did not run at night, in order to avoid being attacked by animals.

What is most interesting about Natal is how Tuvia got acquainted with the new market. He first discovered that there were no carts, trolleys, cars, or trucks. Unlike Recife, the three streetcar transportation lines did not depend on animal traction but on electricity. During his first day in the new city, Tuvia traveled to the final stop of each of the lines. In this way, he was able to evaluate a large part of the city. On the second day, he already took along some silk fabric cuts and folded hats, and traveled along the Upper City neighborhood. Before seven in the morning, he approached a potential first client in the street, who invited him home. There he was told that no such merchandise was to be found in Natal. The record of this first contact calls attention to the type of relationship that developed between the Jewish tradesman and the customer from Natal. It indicates the standard of those with whom he came into contact: he was invited to have breakfast at the client's home, before showing the goods to the customer's wife, and was served coffee, milk, butter, cheese, and yams. Properties and the mode of preparation and consumption are explained in detail. The first sale already paid half his expenses for the trip back, and set the standard for some of his future clientele, who bought fabrics and hats. He also sealed an agreement with the owner of the hotel where he stayed, by offering him commission for potential clients. That brought him considerable earnings. Furthermore, he learned that men inland would not buy silk, because the women could not wear it in the hinterlands. On the third day, he set out to evaluate the goods offered by local wholesalers and retailers. He found out that they did not offer as many products as in Recife, and that the goods were more expensive.

In his wanderings, he found only Arab peddlers (probably Turks[10]), who sold haberdashery. His investigations revealed that, among the local 23,000 inhabitants, there were few foreigners. There were no more than five Arab–Turks, and there were no Jews (he asked if there were "Russians," because that was how Ashkenazi Jewish immigrants were known). Moreover, no one sold clothing on credit. Natal housed some industry, a power plant,

---

10 Reference to Turkish passport holders, even if the immigrants were not from that country. The Ashkenazi Jews, in turn, were generically referred to as "Russians," whether or not they held passports from that country.

a textile mill, two soap factories, an ice factory, an oil press for cottonseed, and a cigarette factory. Public and private workshops supplied other jobs. He then decided that Natal would be the base for the Palatnik brothers, and rented a house right away. On the two remaining days before he returned, he also visited the suburbs where laborers and anglers lived. He concluded that the more modest population would probably yield him some 200 clients for inexpensive goods. In other districts, he would be able to trade goods that were more expensive. He estimated that they would reach about one thousand potential customers within four to five months, which would enable the brothers to achieve their goals to acquire land and settle in Palestine in a few years. He did not miss Sundays or leisure days—when people wore their fanciest suits—in order to evaluate the population's profile. Whether at Mass, in the cathedral, or over a silent movie at the cinema, he relentlessly assessed fashion habits.

After moving in with his brothers to this new and unexplored market, he took the following steps. Within two to three months he had dissolved the company in Recife; he settled his debts; he purchased new goods and settled a new business in Natal—named "Zion House of Tobias Palatnik and Brothers," obviously alluding to the Zionist ideal. Tuvia called on his brother Adolfo to join him immediately in the new city, bringing along five chests and several goods. In addition, he obtained a vendor's license, hired helpers and salesmen, and prepared a work schedule. He alternated activities, ensuring that one of them was available to travel to Rio de Janeiro to purchase fabric; men's and women's umbrellas; raincoats; silk blouses; linen and woolen skirts; blankets for different seasons; curtains; gold jewelry (brooches, earrings, bracelets, pocket watches, chains with or without a Christian cross, and wedding rings); wall clocks; gramophones, pictures of Jesus, Mary, and the saints; and scarves.

As a result of their hard work, they achieved a secure position in one year. They had no competition whatsoever. The choice of Natal proved correct. As part of their clientele was the elite, they were soon known by prominent people and enjoyed the proximity to governors and authorities. Tobias Palatnik recorded all the top names he contacted, their positions, and the events during which they had met, especially the various rulers, members of the sugar oligarchy (The Maranhãos), and the cotton oligarchy (The Bezerra de Medeiros).

Among his clients in Natal were the head of the department of education and editor of the government newspaper, a Presbyterian minister, judges, and the president of the superior court in the city.

At the same time, the brothers did not neglect the clientele in the hinterlands, to where they sent cheaper goods.

As their enterprise already indicates, almost all missions and goals described in the book —including economic and community activities not covered here—were developed jointly by the brothers even when conducted under the leadership of one of them. They were strongly bonded to each other and that alone, along with the role played by their family both in Brazil and in Palestine, considerably contributed to the brothers' success—forever aiming for the goal they had in mind. "In the transition from the Old to the New World, the family played an important role as an economic unit, the main socializing agent in charge of the preservation of traditions," as stated by Yans-McLaughlin.[11] One can conclude that without this intimate relationship, the Palatniks would not have been able to reach the success they achieved, in Brazil or in Palestine.

Taken unaware by World War I, like everyone else, the Palatniks of Natal needed to stay in Natal and get used to the new reality. Access to Europe became difficult and Palestine, where the other part of the family lived, became an unreachable dream. They postponed for a few years the opportunity to visit their family and to marry prospective brides in Palestine, as would eventually happen.

Aware of the role they played in the family project of acquiring land and devoting themselves to agriculture in Palestine and, simultaneously, aware of the status they occupied in Rio Grande do Norte, they would later try to settle down more consistently and not to depend on commerce alone. This plan played a part in their attachment to farming. Only three years after their arrival, in 1915, they purchased a farm in the state of Rio Grande do Norte. The farm comprised a main house and a factory to produce sugar and *cachaça*—a distilled spirit made from sugarcane juice—along with fields, woods, and water. By that time, the other members of the family in Palestine had already established an orange grove in Petach Tikva.

Some historical knowledge is now required to understand the local political and economic background as well as its process of modernization. When first colonized, Rio Grande do Norte was mainly dependent on fisheries,

11 Virginia Yans-McLaughlin, *Family and Community: Italian Immigrants in Buffalo, 1880–1930* (Ithaca, NY: Cornell University Press, 1982), 22–24; E. W. Kosminsky, "Perspectivas e Valores de Homens Judeus de São Paulo" ("Sociability and Values of Jewish Men in São Paulo"), in *Ways of Men: Gender and Movements*, ed. M. N. Strey, Bruna Krimberg Von Muhlen, and Kelly Cristina Kohn (Porto Alegre, BR: ediPUCRS, 2014).

livestock, and agriculture. The exploitation of Brazilwood—an important Brazilian resource and virtually the first Brazilian export product from Rio Grande do Norte to Europe—represented the most important economic activity in colonial times (1530–1815).

By the end of the Imperial period (1822–89), the economic hub of the state moved from the coastal region, with its production of sugar and salt, to the hinterlands—cotton production and livestock. At each new step, new oligarchies tried to rise above the previous ones, generating predictable political and social dissent.

Livestock was the most developed local subsistence activity. Cattle were raised on large farms in order to supply neighboring regions. In the twentieth century, the main activities focused on agricultural land, planting cotton, rice, bananas, cashew nuts, sugarcane, coconut, beans, cassava, maize, sweet potato, sisal, tobacco, castor beans, and pineapple.

The Palatnik brothers worked in Natal—the capital city founded on December 25, 1599,[12] by João Rodrigues Colaço—in the period known as the First Republic or the Old Republic of Brazil, which began with the promulgation of the Republican Constitution (February 24, 1891) and lasted until the Revolution of 1930 (November 3, 1930). Some political decentralization of the federal system characterized the period, comprising a series of landmark events in the history of Rio Grande do Norte.

The main characteristic of the Old Republic (also known as the Republic of Coffee) was the political predominance of the agricultural export sector, based on the coffee economy prevalent in other states. After independence in 1822, the culture and commerce of coffee began to define itself as a new dynamic center of the Brazilian economy. To the extent that its culture was developing in the center–south of the country, especially in western part of São Paulo State, local farmers depended less on slaves and more on immigrants. Brazil practically held a monopoly of the product. São Paulo State solved its need for skilled labor by hiring Italian, Portuguese, Spanish, and Japanese immigrants. The government built a transportation network. They counted on fertile and largely uncultivated soil, and established direct ties with international financial groups, especially English ones. At the beginning of the twentieth century, milk and dairy products prevailed in the State of Minas Gerais. Being geographically and economically close, the states associated in the so-called "coffee and milk"

---

12 Natal means "Christmas." Other names of cities in Brazil refer to Christian celebrations.

policy regarding both economy and politics (coffee and milk being the most popular Brazilian breakfast drink in a large part of the country).

Under the new *decentralization* system, each of the states belonging to the federal system (former Imperial provinces) had the right to borrow money abroad, to enact taxes on exports, and to maintain military corporations, a constitution, a judiciary, and an electoral code. The new tax provisions greatly benefited the federative units (particularly the most prosperous ones). The non-interference policy of this system in the regional policies offered the oligarchic heads of state some electoral warranties against the opposition, allowing the empowered situation to perpetuate itself through the choice of successors. Hence, the strong consolidation of the "Colonels' Regime"[13]—which defined the political and social organization of the First Republic.

The undiversified economy in the late nineteenth century characterized Rio Grande do Norte as an underdeveloped state. This condition affected its urban demographic index as a trade center and hub of activities benefiting from production. When the sugar economy entered a slow process of stagnation, cotton began to establish itself as the new major activity in Natal's *"potiguar"*[14] economy.

From the first decade of the twentieth century on, the urbanization process gained greater momentum. However, alongside urbanization, several problems surfaced—famine, drought, and poor living conditions in the hinterlands, along with the rural exodus. In addition to these problems, frequent epidemics led to the emergence of several popular religious movements. Furthermore, the *cangaço* (highway bandits)[15] were also a force to be reckoned with in this

---

13 The colonels' rule was a typical facet of the early years of the Brazilian republic. Building an agriculture-based society on large properties is the mark of historical events responsible for the onset of the so-called "Colonels." The property owners received the rank of colonel in order to recruit people well aligned with the interests of the government and the elites. The term "colonel" in the republican period simply meant a political leader in a particular location. He was either a landowner or a merchant. By providing services to the executive, the colonels earned prestige and power. They supported the mainstays of political exclusion and control of large areas of political representation. At the local level, the colonels used the police force to maintain order. The militia served the colonels' private interests. In a society where the countryside was the scene of major political decisions, control of the police turned the colonel into an almost unquestioned authority. The colonels' rule was a period of violent and authoritarian practices. The colonels controlled the people in the region and forced them to support their actions and decisions.

14 *Potiguar*: a Tupi word used for the locals born in Natal, Rio Grande do Norte. It means shrimp eater—initially designating the indigenous tribe of Potiguares.

15 In the backlands of northeastern Brazil, the violent disputes between powerful families and the lack of prospects for social mobility in a region of great misery led to the emergence of

period, particularly in the hinterlands. Where the colonels lived, deprived people had three options: to depend eternally on the colonels' families; to join the highwaymen; or to enter the mystical world where believers stopped considering the colonels, and turned into groups of "fanatics."

Within this context, after succeeding in commerce, the Palatniks tried a new way to expand their activities while engaging in agriculture. On their farm, Tuvia followed the criteria of economic management and planting that his conscience and knowledge pointed out to him. He determined the work steps to be developed, priorities, costs, forecasts, and means of production. While dealing with diverse settlers and employees, one could clearly see the principles of social justice that guided him. Definitions of wages, benefits, housing, and employment are detailed thoroughly in his book. Wages were paid in cash and not in goods as was common at that time, workers received Sunday clothing, and men's wages were twice as high as those of the women or youths. The forty-two dwelling houses on the farm housed 223 people; 162 were workers. Since workers were in short supply, others had to be hired. As many people who had fled conscription in their homelands now lived in Natal, the other brothers managed to send additional workers from among these people.

Nonetheless, Tuvia was not a "colonel"—nor did he behave as such, receiving no support from anyone in this position. The safety measures promised by the governor were ineffective. Despite the good results of their hard work, and the prospect of excellent profits, the brothers feared for their lives and decided to sell the farm. Tuvia, the brother who worked and managed the farm, and lived there, could not cope with the neighboring populations, who were described as lazy, and who preferred to rob or plunder instead of

---

armed bands, creating the phenomenon of banditry known as *cangaço*. There were three types of banditry in the history of the hinterland: 1) defensive—sporadic activity guarding farms due to threats of Indians, land disputes, and feuding families; 2) political—the expression of the power of the big landowners; and 3) the independent bands that emerged in the late nineteenth century. By the end of the nineteenth century, these independent bands were not subordinate to any local chief, since their origins lay in the problems of land monopoly, the colonels' rule, revolting against the misery in the northeast, and indifference to public power. The bandits terrorized towns, carrying out robberies, extorting money from the population, kidnapping major figures in addition to looting farms. The most famous of all *cangaceiros* was Virgulino Ferreira, the Lantern (*Lampião*). Because of the organization and discipline he imposed on his flock, he was rarely defeated. He appeared before the people in the region as an instrument of social justice, seeking thereby to justify his crimes, which struck rich and poor alike. He died in combat in 1938, when the phenomenon ended.

working or earning money. Although he does not explicitly mention the *cangaço* bandits, he gave up this fourteen-month venture in agriculture.[16]

The following decade offered new momentum to the business in Natal. All the brothers, by then, were married to girls they had met in Palestine, to where they had traveled, one by one, in order to visit their family. They created the first furniture factory in Natal (the wood came from the northern states of Amazonas and Pará). They produced wicker chairs (out of raw material from Madeira Island) and manufactured mattresses, marble tiles for home use and for cemeteries, tiles, and carbonated soft drinks. They hired professionals in Recife, Rio de Janeiro, and even in Israel for all these fields, in which they were the pioneers in the city. The construction industry came next, with the building of houses for rent. Meanwhile, in 1921, they had acquired at auction a 14,000-square-meter block, at 274 Ulysses Caldas Street, in the Upper City neighborhood. The house there was refurbished and enlarged. Other houses were built around it, and it became known as the Palatnik Villa. The four brothers' families lived there, and it was there that the Jewish communal life first developed in Natal. Later, in 1942, this first Jewish community consisted of twenty-four families.

The family's farming dream that developed powerfully among the other Palatniks on the other side of the world, took shape once again in Natal in 1924. The brothers purchased a tract of uncultivated land south of Natal from the town hall, of which a small part was used for grazing animals belonging to the municipality. The brothers developed a plantation of tropical and subtropical fruit on half the land. On the second half, they planted coconut. This plantation, which yielded good results, was called "Renaissance." Again, the Zionist allusion is obvious.

Another site that owed its development to the Palatnik family was Praia do Meio (Middle Beach), not far from Natal, where they built beach homes in 1925. The vacation spot became known as Palatinópolis Beach, named after the family.

Due both to chance and to hard work, and bearing in mind their project in another country, Tuvia's and part of this family's economic activities in Natal began in 1912 and lasted for thirty-four years. The reasons for the departure of Tuvia and the brothers are diverse.

---

16 His successor, the new owner of the farm, was killed shortly thereafter. The security problems encountered in rural labor also greatly hindered the Quatro Irmãos colony in Rio Grande do Sul, which eventually led to its abandonment.

The 1929 stock market crash in New York worsened the Brazilian economic situation, especially in the 1930s. Not only did it follow the global trend in this period, but it also suffered local economic problems.

After the rise of Getúlio Vargas as president, and as a result of the military revolution in October 1930, changes took place in the Brazilian system. The parliament and the senate were dissolved. Mediators formerly subordinate to the president were nominated for the states. Many mediators as well as ministers were military personnel. A tense mood prevailed between the old oligarchies and the mediator lieutenants. The economic crisis in Rio Grande do Norte, as well as in other states, significantly hit by the situation, therefore deteriorated and declined over the following two years. The mediators were unable to pay off the debts to the government employees, suppliers, dealers, or contractors—among whom now were also the Palatniks, who painstakingly tried to recover what the government owed them.

Facing the economic and political difficulties that engulfed the country, though still hoping to emigrate to Palestine in order to implement their elderly father's agricultural projects, the brothers seriously considered the dissolution of their business in Natal. They knew, however, that the economic crisis would hamper the shutting down of their enterprises. Two of the brothers moved to Palestine in 1934—Tuvia was one of them—while one brother remained in Natal, and the other moved definitively to Rio de Janeiro, where he already had contacts and businesses. The city also offered better education options for his children. Tuvia, however, was asked to return to Natal for a brief period: if starting up a small business required the commitment of all the brothers, closing it—now a big business—was also a task for more than one person. Again, he would stay in Natal for long periods. To the various projects mentioned above, some others had been added, namely, a pottery barn and a cattle ranch. These projects were no longer operated by all the brothers, though. The political environment, which was hostile to Jews, was also one of the depressing factors that hastened the dissolution of the empire: the anti-Semitic campaigns of the Brazilian Integralist–fascist[17] press and the newspaper *Ofensiva* (*Offensive*)

---

17 Originating in Portugal, the integralism developed in Brazil in the 1930s, when the country was ruled by the dictator Getúlio Vargas, who advocated a traditionalist, ultra-conservative policy, founded in the defense of a structured society based on religion and family, grounded in the social doctrine of the Catholic church. The integralist movement gained prominence in Brazil drawing a growing number of followers. Once influenced by Italian fascism, their party fought against supporters of leftist thought. The fundamentalists accused the Communists of corrupting the idea of family, for their beliefs threatened the

played out their roles in Natal. Old acquaintances, the now so-called "Integralists," turned their backs to them and pretended not to know them.

In 1934, Tuvia and his family settled in Tel Aviv. He was responsible for the family farm in Bnei Brak. In 1935, this plot was sold, and the family acquired a larger one in the northern Sharon region. Some years later, part was transferred to the *Keren haKayemet LeIsrael (KKL)*, which established a *moshav* there.

Tuvia Palatnik wrote his records and memoirs from 1962 to 1967, initially in Teresópolis and Rio de Janeiro State, and later concluded in Israel. One of the streets in Natal is named after the Palatnik brothers. In 1962, fifty years after his arrival, Tuvia decided he could no longer travel back and forth between Brazil and Israel. The Jewish Communal Center in Natal, founded and developed by the brothers, closed its operations in 1968. Its assets, in particular the headquarters, were transferred to the League of Rio Grande do Norte to Fight Cancer, with its property deed drawn up in Rio de Janeiro, as recorded by Egon and Frieda Wolff.

REFERENCES

"Agriculture." *The YIVO Encyclopedia of Jews in Eastern Europe.* Accessed September 22, 2104. http://www.yivoencyclopedia.org/article.aspx/Agriculture.

Cascudo, Luís da Câmara. *História da Cidade do Natal*, 2nd ed. Rio de Janeiro: Civilização Brasileira; Brasília: INL; Natal: Universidade Federal do Rio Grande do Norte, 1980.

Kosminsky, E. W. "Perspectivas e Valores de Homens Judeus de São Paulo" ("Sociability and Values of Jewish Men in São Paulo"). In *Ways of Men: Gender and Movements*, ed. M. N. Strey, Bruna Krimberg Von Muhlen, and Kelly Cristina Kohn, 177–235. Porto Alegre, BR: ediPUCRS, 2014.

Lesser, Jeffrey. *O Brasil e a Questão Judaica: imigração, diplomacia e preconceito.* Rio de Janeiro: Imago, 1995.

Monteiro, Denise Mattos. *Introdução à História do Rio Grande do Norte.* Natal: EDUFRN, 2007.

Nova Odessa's City hall site. "História de Nova Odessa." Accessed September 22, 2013. http://www.novaodessa.sp.gov.br/Historia.aspx.

Palatnik, Tuvia. *Binetive hanedudim. Sefer Zichronot. Bein Hadniester shebeUkraina uvein HaPotengi shebiTsefon Brasil (Meandering Paths—Memories—Between the Dniester in Ukraine and Potengi in North Brazil).* Tel Aviv: author's edition, 1970.

Rozenchan, Nancy. "Os judeus de Natal: Uma comunidade segundo o registro de seu fundador." *Revista Herança Judaica* 106. São Paulo: B'nai B'rith, April 2000.

---

religious formation of people. Strong anti-Semitic feelings and attitudes prevailed among the leadership of the movement.

Spinelli, José Antonio. *Coronéis e oligarquias na Primeira República.* 2005. Accessed September 22, 2013. http://www.fundaj.gov.br/geral/observanordeste/spinelli_05.pdf. Formerly published under the title *Da oligarquia Maranhão à política do Seridó; O Rio Grande do Norte na Velha República.* Natal: CCHLA, 1992.

Wolf, Egon and Frieda. *Natal: Uma Comunidade Singular.* Rio de Janeiro: Ed. Cemitério Comunal Israelita, 1984.

Yans-McLaughlin, Virginia. *Family and Community: Italian Immigrants in Buffalo, 1880–1930.* Ithaca, NY: Cornell University Press, 1982.

CHAPTER 18

Between Nostalgia and Utopia: Stefan Zweig in Brazil

LUIS S. KRAUSZ

This article discusses three of Stefan Zweig's later books—*Die Welt von gestern, Brasilien: ein Land der Zukunft*, and *Montaigne*, all of which he wrote in Brazil. These three works point to Zweig's feelings of nostalgia toward the vanishing world of European humanism during World War II. They also reflect his unfulfilled hopes of reconstructing a homeland for himself in a country ruled by a proto-fascist dictator, Getulio Vargas, with its policy of restricting the entrance of Jewish refugees to those who could be considered "useful" to the state—like Zweig himself.

The irreconcilable contradictions between the view of Brazil as a country where the concept of "race" played no role, as expressed by Zweig in *Brasilien: ein Land der Zukunft*, and the fact that tens of thousands of Jewish refugees from Europe were denied entrance merely because they were "Jewish," as I attempt to show, played a key role in Zweig's split consciousness and in his final refusal to accept Brazil as a new home for himself.

Stefan Zweig (1891–1942) was an Austrian Jew who died in Brazil over seventy years ago. He was a writer who regarded himself as a European before anything else. The cosmopolitan identity he sought during his entire life was also a matter of personal choice: Zweig assumed that a strong European identity would be an effective antidote against the belligerent nationalistic tendencies that had led to the destruction of his native Austro-Hungarian Empire, and also had led Europe to its two world wars in the twentieth century. His cosmopolitanism, however, had become entirely outdated in Europe in the 1930s, at a time when the only ones still interested in being Europeans appear to have been the Jews. All other groups emphasized their identification with the national ideas of their countries of birth, putting nationalism before cosmopolitanism. Zweig's cosmopolitanism is also directly associated to the Catholic legacy of Zweig's country of birth— Catholic in the sense that the Austro-Hungarian Empire saw itself as an heir to the legacy of the Holy Roman Empire of the German nation, an empire constructed on the idea that its spiritual values were directed toward the entire world, i.e., *kat'holos*.

If, in the nineteenth century, France was a national state and Prussia was a dynastic territorial state, Zweig's Austro-Hungarian Empire was a state of many peoples, ethnical groups, cultures, languages, and religions. As Arnold Bauer states,

> Austria-Hungary was a State of many peoples and its capital a melting pot in which, next to the leading Germans, several other nationalities resided and gave the city (Vienna) its unique flavor. Magyar, Slavic and Roman spirit encountered each other in Vienna.... Seen as a whole ... the city's intellectual and social upper class was cosmopolitan.[1]

German-speaking Austrians played the role of leaders in this multinational state, but they coexisted in higher or lower degrees of harmony with Hungarians, Czechs, Slovenes, Slovaks, Italians, Poles, Ukrainians, Romanians and Croats—as well as Jews who, during the first decades of Emancipation, belonged to none of these nationalities, but who had mostly integrated successfully into Viennese life. In the second half of the nineteenth century, Jews played a significant role in the economical, artistic, social, and cultural life of Vienna, the capital of Europe's largest and most important empire.

A faithful follower of the belief in progress and science, which had almost gained the status of a new religion in Vienna at the time of his youth, Zweig firmly believed that Austria-Hungary and Europe as a whole were swiftly approaching an era of peace and long-lasting prosperity. In his book of memoirs written in Petrópolis, in Brazil, entitled *Die Welt von gestern*, Zweig writes that

---

1 Arnold Bauer, *Stefan Zweig* (Berlin: Colloquium Verlag, 1961), 7: "Frankreich war im 19. Jahrhundert ein Nationalstaat und Preußen ein dynastischer Territorialstaat, aber Österreich-Ungarn war ein Viel-Völker Staat und seine Hauptstadt ein Schmelztiegel, in dem neben den tonangebenden Deutschen die Angehörige vieler anderer Nationalistäten lebten und der Stadt ihr Gepräge gaben. Magyarisches, slawisches und romanisches Wesen begegnete sich in Wien.... Im Ganzen ... war die geistige und soziale Oberschicht kosmopolitisch."

he grew up with the belief that progress would heal humanity of all its ills, and that it was an open and secure road toward redemption:

> It would be just a question of decades until all evil and all violence would be finally be overcome and this belief in a continuous and unstoppable "progress" had the power of a true religion for that era. Faith in progress had already become more important than faith in the Bible.[2]

Zweig's youth in Vienna was spent under the aegis of what he calls the "Golden Age of Security." The Habsburg monarchy had existed for almost a thousand years, and the illusion that the Empire was destined to last forever marked every aspect of existence. The palaces, monuments, and public buildings erected in Vienna in the final decades of the nineteenth century express, by means of architecture, this will toward duration. The illusion was that history and its calamities could be avoided by means of the advancement of civilization, culture, and science, which predominated in a society that viewed itself as definitive. Thus, Zweig writes in *Die Welt von gestern*:

> Everything in our almost millenary Austrian monarchy seemed to have been built in order to last, and the State itself was the highest guarantee of this durability. The rights the Emperor granted to his citizens were ratified by a freely elected Parliament, and each of the obligations of every subject was precisely determined. Our currency, the Austrian Crown, was circulated in massive gold coins, and this was a guarantee of its immutability. Everyone knew exactly how much he owned and what was allowed to him. There was a norm, a weight, and a measure for everything.[3]

In the same book, Zweig writes, "The Habsburg Monarchy was an ancient State, ruled by a grey-haired Emperor, who was assisted by old ministers, a state free of any ambition other than maintaining itself, by means of radical opposition to any kind of radical change in the European realm."[4] A policy of conciliation and agreement sustained the project of overcoming history

---

2 Stefan Zweig, *Die Welt von gestern* (Detmold, DE: Bertelsmann, 1961), 16: "Jetzt war es doch nur eine Angelegenheit von Jahrzehnten, bis das letzte Böse und Gewalttätige endgültig überwunden sein würde, und dieser Glaube an den ununterbrochenen, unaufhaltsamen 'Fortschritt' hatte für jenes Zeitalter wahrhaftig die Kraft einer Religion; man glaubte an diesen 'Fortschritt' schon mehr als an die Bibel."
3 Ibid., 13.
4 Ibid., 48.

and its calamities. People imagined that within a few decades all tendencies toward violence would be overcome within the realm of civilization. "People believed as little in the return of barbarity and in the possibility of war between the peoples of Europe as they believed in witches or ghosts: our ancestors were firmly persuaded that tolerance and conciliation had infallible powers."[5]

As far as the situation of the Jews is concerned, Zweig states that only the Golden Age of Spain could be seen as a paradigm of what happened in Vienna at the time of his youth. He was referring to Andalusia in the eleventh and twelfth centuries, an era of flourishing artistic and intellectual creativity, and poetic and philosophical fertility. During these centuries, the Jews benefited from cultural interchange with the surrounding cultures, just like their Muslim and Christian neighbors, and absorbed the paradigms of classical culture, then preserved in Arabic, which functioned as the basis for the development of humanistic culture.

It is no coincidence that this Spanish paradigm should be a frequent theme in nineteenth-century German-Jewish literature, and also a frequent research theme in Jewish scholarship. It represented an era of cultural exuberance, when peace, quiet, and a home for Jews seemed to be guaranteed. It was also an era during which Jews occupied important social positions, and took part in all their country's political and social spheres. Zweig built his identity as an Austrian and as a European, as a man of the nineteenth century, inspired by the lofty idealism of the German *Aufklärung*, based on these seemingly unshakable guarantees.

***

The history of Zweig's adult life, and of his exile and death in Brazil, is also the history of the shattering of the humanistic beliefs fundamental to his identity. The nationalistic insanity that dismembered the Austro-Hungarian Empire between 1914 and 1918 replaced the ideas of tolerance with the different kinds of fanaticism that proliferated in twentieth-century Europe. Nothing could be further removed from the European reality o f the 1930s and '40s than that the "Golden Age of Security" that Zweig remembers nostalgically in the book of memoirs he wrote in Pertropolis, shortly before his death. In a letter to French Jewish novelist André Maurois (1886–1967), written in 1939

---

5 Ibid., p. 17.

in England, where Zweig had taken refuge from Nazism before emigrating to South America, he wrote: "Now you are beginning your life in exile. You will see how the world renounces its expatriates. You will get to know a life that is no longer *our* life—a life that may not even be worth living."[6]

Zweig began to see himself and the ethical values on which he had built his *Weltanschauung* as anachronisms. "We will become homeless men," he wrote, "We are nothing but ghosts and memories." In *Die Welt von gestern*, Zweig recalls the instant he left Austria with the following words: "The minute our train crossed the border, I understood, like Lot, our ancestor from the Bible, that everything that I had left behind would turn into ashes and dust, into petrified past and into bitter salt."[7]

This desolate nostalgia brings Zweig close to another Jewish novelist from the Austro-Hungarian Empire, namely Joseph Roth, who was his close friend and whose oeuvre is also a long and sorrowful meditation about the safe and well-ordered universe of the Austro-Hungarian Empire and of that empire as the repository of transcendent values that twentieth-century Europe would forget.

Neither Roth nor Zweig were able to accept Europe's moral bankruptcy, and the triumph of fanaticism and nationalism over those values of civility and humanity that had been inherited from the Jewish–Christian tradition. Both of them regarded the social Darwinism that replaced the rules of coexistence between different national and religious groups as a catastrophe, and as the moral—or rather immoral—counterpart to the triumph of a new ruling class whose power derived solely from the exercise of violence. As Roth wrote in a newspaper article published in 1937, Europe, within a short span of time, had described a trajectory that went from humanity to nationality and from nationality to bestiality.

Roth viewed the twentieth century as the century of tragedy, the century of the so-called modern man, in which all ethical, philosophical, political, and economical rules and certainties that had served as guidelines for humanity collapsed, leaving behind them nothing but debris, dust, and ashes.

Roth's and Zweig's *Austria Felix* should also be understood as a kind of metaphysical refuge, conceived by authors who faced despair when their homeland fell prey to Nazism. The agony of the world frequently generates nostalgic views of the past that are not always realistic. Yet this idealization of the past is always revealing of the distortions and aberrations of the present. Zweig and Roth have become the creators of what Claudio Magris has named "the Habsburg Myth," and

---

6 George Prochnik, *The Impossible Exile: Stefan Zweig at the End of the World* (London: Granta, 2014), 10.

7 Stefan Zweig, *Die Welt von gestern* (Detmold, DE: Bertelsmann, 1961), 358.

their memories of the lost world of their origin tend to represent it as a lost paradise. Their Austro-Hungarian books can also be understood as portable sanctuaries and repositories of vanished spiritual values. According to Magris,

> For Roth and Zweig, who have seen the emergence of a new Europe, dom-
> inated by racial hatred, the old Habsburg Monarchy seemed to be an ideal
> home, even though it was not free from the defect of anti-Semitism—a
> home that offered a serene and safe life. That is the reason why they have
> written the most passionate and emotional memories of the old Empire.[8]

The despair of Roth and Zweig in the final years of their lives—Roth died in Paris as an alcoholic in 1939 and Zweig committed suicide in Petrópolis in 1942—cannot be separated from their attachment to this lost and idealized place, and from their inability to accept their own exile.

It is no surprise, therefore, that in *Brasilien: ein Land der Zukunft*, a book published in 1941, Zweig never ceases to praise the harmony in which descendants of natives and immigrants from all countries of the world lived in the South American country he chose as a refuge from the destruction of Europe. "How would it be possible," he writes,

> to reach, in our planet, the peaceful coexistence between different people,
> in spite of all racial, social, religious and ideological differences? This is a
> problem all countries of the world have faced, and nowhere in this world
> has this problem been solved more successfully than in Brazil. This is the
> reason why I am writing this book.[9]

Fleeing fratricidal Europe, Zweig saw in the cordiality of Brazilian society in the 1940s a continuation of a story of optimism that has its origins in the images, memories, and idealizations he had brought with himself from Imperial

---

8 Cláudio Magris, *Der habsburgische Mythos in der modernen österreichischen Literatur* (Vienna: Paul Zsolnay Verlag, 2000), 317.

9 Stefan Zweig, *Brasilien: ein Land der Zukunft* (Frankfurt am Main, DE: Insel Verlag, 1981), 12: "Wie ist auf unserer Erde ein friedliches Zusammenleben der Menschen trotz aller disparaten Rassen, Klassen, Farben, Religionen und Überzeugungen zu erreichen? Es ist das Problem, das an jede Gemeinschaft, jeden Staat immer wieder von neuem gebieterisch herantritt. Keinem Lande hat es sich durch eine besonders komplizierte Konstellation gefährlicher gestellt als Brasilien, und keines hat es—und dies dankbar zu bezeugen, schreibe ich dieses Buch—in so glücklicher und vorbildlicher Weise gelöst wie Brasilien. In einer Weise, die nach meiner persönlichen Meinung nicht nur die Aufmerksamkeit, sondern auch die Bewunderung der Welt für sich fordert."

Austria. "For in Brazil," wrote Zweig, "the disposition toward conciliation and the humane attitude are the results of an innate sense of tolerance, which was kept intact all along the country's history." Further, he writes: "Brazil has made the problem of races, that is destroying Europe in our time, entirely absurd insofar as it has completely ignored its validity."[10]

***

Besides *Die Welt von Gestern, Brasilien: ein Land der Zukunft,* the *Schachnovelle, Clarissa,* and his Balzac biography, written during his Brazilian years, Zweig also worked on a book that has received little scholarly attention so far, maybe because it was left unfinished at the time of his death, and has reached us only as a fragment. This book is entitled *Montaigne,* and it is a biographical essay about the French philosopher Michel de Montaigne. It is akin in spirit to so many of the historical novels responsible for Zweig's world renown, such as *Balzac, Marie Antoinette,* and *Erasmus of Rotterdam.*

In sixteenth-century France, Michel de Montaigne acted as mediator in the bloody conflicts between Catholics and Huguenots that led to thousands of deaths. A man in search of himself who lived in a time of destruction, hatred, and mass murder, Montaigne was someone with whom Zweig could identify during his exile in Petrópolis. In fact, as Zweig states at the opening of his book, his encounter with the *philosophe* was almost incidental. Zweig and his wife had rented a cottage in Petrópolis and, in its basement, he found an edition of Montaigne's complete works, which he had already known from Europe but had never actually had a chance to read properly.

Montaigne is Zweig's last book, written in an era of fanaticism as a kind of consolation and spiritual testament, and as a confirmation of Zweig's faith in the values of conciliation and tolerance. Michel de Montaigne spent his adult life isolated in a tower in his own castle, surrounded by books and in a constant search for wisdom.

---

10 Ibid., 13: "Nach europäischer Einstellung wäre zu erwarten, daß jede dieser Gruppen sich feindlich gegen die andere stellte, die früher Gekommenen gegen die später Gekommenen, Weiße gegen Schwarze, Amerikaner gegen Europäer, Braune gegen Gelbe, daß Mehrheiten und Minderheiten in ständigem Kampf um ihre Rechte und Vorrechte einander befeindeten. Zum größten Erstaunen wird man nun gewahr, daß alle diese schon durch die Farbe sichtbar voneinander abgezeicheneten Rassen in vollster Eintracht miteinander leben und trotz ihrer individuellen Herkunft einzig in der Ambition wetteifern, die einstigen Sonderheiten abzutun, um möglichst rasch und möglichst vollkommen Brasilianer, eine neue und einheitliche Nation zu werden. Brasilien hat … das Rassenproblem, das unsere europäische Welt verstört, auf die einfachste Weise ad absurdum geführt: indem es seine angebliche Gültigkeit einfach ignorierte."

He would become an example and a paradigm for Zweig's isolation in Petrópolis. Just like Zweig, he was a man who strove to preserve his freedom and lucidity in times of chaos and darkness. The parallels between the history of sixteenth-century France and twentieth-century Europe seemed quite evident to Zweig.

In a letter to his first wife, Friederike, who was exiled in the United States, and who belonged to the group of German intellectuals who fought against Nazi Germany abroad, he wrote: "I feel seduced to write about Montaigne, whose works I have been reading very intensively and with much pleasure. Montaigne is another, better Erasmus, a very consoling spirit."[11]

In November 1941, Zweig received a series of books about the French philosopher in Petrópolis, as a gift sent from New York by Friederike, and he immediately started work on this unfinished biography.

This final work can be seen also as an attempt to make a new beginning in his career, by working in the genre that had made him one of the most important authors of world literature in the first half of the twentieth century. In December 1941, Zweig also had the opportunity to meet Fortunat Strowski, a very well-known French literary critic and editor of Montaigne's *Essays*, who was visiting Rio de Janeiro at a time when French intellectuals still dominated the study of humanities in Brazil, having been responsible for the creation of the nation's leading universities.

According to Zweig, Montaigne's crucial question is how to preserve inner integrity in face of the attacks of the outside world, and how to maintain the "interior citadel" of which Goethe speaks in his works. Montaigne renounces the outside world; he retreats to his library and to his meditation, searches his inner world, and thus ends up playing a key role in the pacification of France, a nation torn apart by the bloody conflicts between the Catholics and the Huguenots.

The horrors of Europe's history in the 1940s, however, and the feeling of isolation and abandonment that Zweig and his wife faced during their exile in Petrópolis, living in the modest bungalow that recently has been turned into a museum, on Rua Gonçalves Dias, led him to relinquish life. At the age of sixty, he felt he was already too old to start a new existence in Brazil, while a return to Europe, at that time, would be something he could never achieve.

Zweig voluntarily departed from this world in February 1942, and left his *Montaigne* unfinished. The optimism toward Brazil that appears in

---

11   Knut Beck, "Nachbemerkung," in Stefan Zweig, *Montaigne* (Frankfurt am Main, DE: Fischer Taschenbuch Verlag), 95: "Mich lockte sehr über Montaigne zu schreiben, den ich jetzt mit viel und großem Genuß lese, ein anderer (besserer) Erasmus, ganz ein tröstlicher Geist."

Brasilien: ein Land der Zukunft obviously contrasts with the fact, doubtlessly known by Zweig, that while he was writing that book, tens of thousands of Jewish refugees from Europe were being denied visas to enter Brazil, for no reason other than being Jews.

From 1937, Getulio Vargas's government categorically prohibited all Brazilian diplomats from issuing visas for Jews, who were seen as undesirable immigrants. Exceptions, such as that Zweig had benefited from, were granted only to owners of significant capital or to Jews who could be of benefit to the country. Zweig also failed to take into consideration, in *Brasilien: ein Land der Zukunft*, that until 1881, the year of his own birth, black people were still being enslaved in Brazil.

Zweig's political opponents, including several of Brazil's leading intellectuals who opposed the Vargas regime, accused him of collaboration with Vargas's proto-fascist dictatorship. They suspected that his book was a kind of bargaining chip in exchange for a permanent visa, a deal by means of which the Vargas regime would take advantage of Zweig's international renown to foster a positive image of the country abroad. In fact, Vargas's government was greatly interested in the book, which, due to Zweig's international prestige, could be used effectively as propaganda for the regime. Zweig received official support in his trips around the country and in the publication of the book.

The imperial ideals of conciliation and understanding brought from the old empire, which Zweig projected onto Brazilian reality, were considerably removed from what was actually taking place in Brazil, certainly as far as Jewish refugees from Europe were concerned. In spite of this, however, Zweig's discussion of the racial question in Brazil could be understood as an attempt to recover his lost homeland in the tropics. We should not forget that Petrópolis, his last dwelling place on earth, was also the seat of the summer palace of Pedro II, Brazil's last emperor. Nor should we forget that Pedro II, a humanist who had been deposed from the throne only fifty-three years prior to Zweig's arrival, was the son of Leopoldine von Habsburg, the great-aunt of the Kaiser Franz Joseph I, the arcane figure of the "Golden Age of Security."

Yet Zweig's dream of Brazil as a new homeland, where the lost values of the empire could be reconstructed, quickly vanished. Being depressed and pessimistic regarding Europe's future, he committed suicide together with his second wife, Lotte Altmann, during the carnival of 1942.

REFERENCES

Bauer, Arnold. *Stefan Zweig*. Berlin: Colloquium Verlag, 1961.

Magris, Claudio. *Der habsburgische Mythos in der modernen österreichischen Literatur*. Vienna: Paul Zsolnay Verlag, 2000.

Prochnik, George. *The Impossible Exile: Stefan Zweig at the End of the World*. London: Granta, 2014.

Zweig, Stefan. *Brasilien: ein Land der Zukunft*. Frankfurt am Main, DE: Insel Verlag, 1981.

———. *Die Welt von gestern*. Detmold, DE: Bertelsmann, 1961.

———. *Montaigne*. Frankfurt am Main, DE: Fischer Taschenbuch Verlag.

CHAPTER 19

Representation of the *Shoah* in Brazilian Literature

BERTA WALDMAN

The present paper aims to show examples of how Brazilian literature portrayed the atrocities committed during World War II, and how different generations of writers, at different moments, represented them.

1) The first Brazilian text about the *Shoah* was published by Jacó Guinsburg, an editor, essayist, translator, writer of fiction, and professor of literature and drama, who was born in Bessarabia and immigrated to Brazil in 1924 at the age of three. Jacó Guinsburg was the first to publish fiction about the *Shoah* in Portuguese: his short story, "The Portrait," written in 1946 and published in 1949,[1] inaugurated the genre.

The narrative focus is the war as seen from Brazil, probably from São Paulo. It is a first-person account by a young character–narrator, born to Romanian immigrants.

The short story centers around a family consisting of an only child, his mother and his father, divided between their place of birth, a country at war, and Brazil, their new homeland. News of the war arrives in the country mainly via newspapers. Their bombastic, reverberating headlines serve as a contrast to a more restricted, silent, and individual means of communication: the letter, expected by the family from the very beginning of the story, presumably to be written by an uncle who used to live with the nuclear family in Bessarabia. This letter would justify their survival. The story encompasses the entire duration of the war in four pages.

---

1 Review, *O reflexo,* n. 8.

Apart from Guinsburg, Samuel Rawet also wrote some short stories in Portuguese about the *Shoah*; and some other writers, who wrote in Yiddish, were translated (e.g., Meir Kucinski). They wrote the texts we collected as being representative of the first generation. The texts generally deal with the tendency to refuse to hear the accounts of suffering that those who experienced the *Shoah* sought to tell, in conformity with Primo Levi's account in *If This Is a Man*.[2]

2) The second generation is defined by an impulse toward bringing the *Shoah* to Brazil, and creating a synthesis between the oppressors and the oppressed. One example is the work of Moacyr Scliar, who uses intermingled cultures, as may be seen in a fragment of *A guerra no Bom Fim*[3] (*The War in Bom Fim*—"Good End," a Jewish-established town in the southernmost state of Brazil, Rio Grande do Sul, where the author was born), in which the author brings the Nazi atrocities to the capital, Porto Alegre. In the story, the sons of the German immigrant Ralph Schmidt arrest and kill an elderly Jew named Samuel, and, not knowing what to do with the corpse, end up using it to prepare a Sunday barbecue. The German, Polish, and dark characters in the novel repeatedly threaten to burn the Jews—in a clear allusion to the Nazi crematoria. The third-person narrator also informs us that Brazil sheltered a group of German Nazis immediately after World War II. Thus, when Ralph Schmidt's sons decide to capture old Samuel, and give him to their father as a birthday present, verisimilitude has already been constructed. Nevertheless, the author needs to draw on the fantastic and insert the episode within the Carnival, in a moment of subverted order, to carry out the grotesque and morbid aspects of the events.

When Ralph's sons gratuitously murder the old Jew and broil him, it is Maria, the mulatto mother of the criminal children, who, ignoring what her sons and the reader know, begins to eat old Samuel's flesh. Beyond the macabre aspects presented by the episode, we may interpret it also from an anthropophagical point of view. When Maria eats human flesh, the author makes her a native cannibal. As an autochthonous character, she is contrasted with her husband and their sons, who took after him, i.e., the civilized European white men. The contrasting behaviors of the white European and the native woman lead the reader into evaluating an

---

2 Primo Lévi, *É isto um homem?* (Rio de Janeiro: Rocco, 2000).
3 Moacyr Scliar, *A guerra no Bom Fim* (Rio de Janeiro: Expressão e Cultura, 1972).

ordinary consequence of colonialism: the corruption of natives by Europeans—the true barbarians—in a clear inversion of colonialist views. In this episode, the author illustrates the Nazi genocide through a macabre crime, as well as taking a stance in relation to the barbaric colonization process imposed by the white Europeans in Brazil and all of Latin America. Samuel Reibscheid and Roney Cytrynowich are among other authors belonging to this second generation.

3)   Several changes are seen in the third generation of post-*Shoah* writers, as can be clearly perceived in Cíntia Moscovich's fiction. Judaism is one of the constructive elements of the work of this writer from Porto Alegre. In this context, "being a Jew" is a changing concept, and many of the conflicts between parents and children are related to this transformation. The author describes the Jews in Brazil, the immigration, the different customs and language, the mixed marriages—along with the memories of the ancestors—with accuracy and humor. The experience of the *Shoah*, and its effects on third-generation Jews, traverse the writer's narratives. Highlighted below are certain scenes built on characteristic figures of speech that produce new and multiple meanings, for instance: "Counting forkfuls. Like in a concentration camp."[4]

In the cited passage, the statement heightens the obese protagonist's sufferings as she starves to lose weight in the novel *Por que sou gorda, mamãe?* (*Why am I Fat, Mom?*) The doctor has recommended she eat three forkfuls less at each meal—a minimum of six forkfuls less each day. Food is abundant and the compulsive protagonist must cut down, yet food was scarce, almost nonexistent, for the neglected concentration camp interns. In the camps, there was scarcity of food; in the story, there is excess. The comparison ("like in a concentration camp") establishes an ironic tone, and creates a homology to designate two intertwined antagonistic realities. Such irony applies to objects out of place. The essential ambiguity of the ironic discourse lies in accepting, simultaneously, intertwined meanings that mislead the reader, now responsible for finding the path into irony.

The same occurs in the following passage: "The father, like an extermination camp commander, took control of the (luggage) cart and said he would take them to the hotel."[5]

---

4   *Por que sou gorda, mamãe?* (Rio de Janeiro: Record, 2006), 231.
5   *Anotações durante o incêndio* (*Notes Taken during the Fire*), 2nd ed. (Porto Alegre, BR: L&PM, 2001), 36.

Excerpted from the short story *O homem que voltou ao frio*[6] (*The Man Who Returned to the Cold*), the quotation above is one of many such passages throughout this narrative, used to mark the undesired stay of a Finn in Porto Alegre and the portrayal of the character as a victim of a misunderstanding. By mentioning the Nazi concentration camps, the narrative evokes the disgrace of this young man who extemporaneously arrives in Porto Alegre to get married to the young woman he had met in Israel and stay there. From his arrival, there is the premonition of his death at the end of the story. The young Finn, non-Jewish, thin and with an unhealthy look, fails to convert to Judaism, yet wants to marry the young woman he briefly got to know on a *kibbutz*, and with whom he wishes to have Jewish children. The intended bride's father will do whatever possible to frustrate the young man's intentions. The cart mentioned in the quote above, for instance, is the one containing the Finn's suitcase. It allows the father to lead the guest where he wishes: to a hotel, not to their house. The youth, who has come to stay, will be turned away on the third day of his stay in Porto Alegre. Many years later, the now married woman will receive a letter from her sister with an account of the young man's death.

Some other passages that employ concentration-camp imagery include:

I felt as if I was under a shower that, instead of flowing water, threatened to *suffocate me with a lethal gas.*[7]

We went to the parking lot together in strained silence—the silence of a *crematory oven.*[8]

The Ford Galaxy was a *private Auschwitz.*[9]

I felt bad for letting him fall into a trap: there was *gas coming out of the shower.*[10]

Again the feeling that the shower would produce no water, *but a lethal gas.*[11]

I felt I was the cursed one, who had led a man into a *concentration camp.* [12]

Do such constructions, based on litotes (the negative for the affirmative, the large for the small, the terrible for the banal), in the

6 Ibid., 36.
7 Ibid., 32.
8 "O homem que voltou ao frio," in *Anotações durante o incêndio*, op. cit., p. 32.
9 Ibid., 36.
10 Ibid., 37.
11 Ibid., 37.
12 Ibid., 43.

end, bring the *Shoah* to mind as a place of *remembrance* or as a place of *forgetting?* The constant evocation reflects a gravity (albeit a mocked one) that stems from the referent *Shoah*, which is, nevertheless, effaced. Thus, the dimension of the tragedy suffered by the Jews, homosexuals, Gypsies, and other minorities during World War II, becomes a cliché. In fact, the reader is left somewhere along the way between memory and oblivion, for language fails to bring back to life the fossilized history that involves neither the fictional character nor the reader.

Individuals belonging to a group may even forget events that have taken place during their own lives, yet cannot forget their collective past. Therefore, when we say a people "remembers," it really means that a specific past has been transmitted to the contemporary generations by means of "channels and receptacles of memory," as Yossef Yerushalmi calls it in his book,[13] and what Pierre Nora rightly refers to as "places of memory."[14] Therefore, a people "forgets" when the generation that received the past does not pass it on, or when this generation ceases to transmit it. The discontinuing of the transmission may occur abruptly, or may involve several generations. The new generations may also adapt the memory legacy into unusual situations, in which case the reader, as in the quotes above, asks himself whether the catastrophe is being remembered or forgotten.

The *Shoah*, in Cíntia Moscovich's works, appears not merely as a figure of speech, but also as a subject. This is the case in the traumatic story of Dona Dora,[15] who survived the concentration camps and lives in her house as a recluse, with her husband and their son, a deaf mute, a skinny and unapproachable boy. The windows of their house have been boarded up with bricks and boards, shelves covering all the inside walls, windows included, to store their victuals. The windows were shut to a world that had changed; no longer the concentration camp, but twenty-first-century Brazil, Porto Alegre.

Here, the *excessive*—the overflowing experience of the Holocaust—reaches the immeasurable: the construction of a hyperbole and a displacement.

---

13 Cf. Yossef Hayim Yerushalmi, *Zakhor: Jewish History and Jewish Memory* (Seattle, WA: University of Washington Press, 1982). See also Maurice Halbwachs's concept of "collective memory," i.e., a continuous flow of thought in a community that has no artificiality, for it keeps nothing from the past except what is still alive or capable of living in the conscience of the group that preserves it. See M. Halbwachs, *La mémoire collective*, 2nd rev. ed. (Paris: PUF, 1968), 70.

14 Pierre Nora, *Les lieux de la mémoire* (Paris: Gallimard, 1984).

15 In Cíntia Moscowich, *Por que sou gorda, mamãe?*, op. cit.

The trauma imposed by the suffering and privation is inserted into a wider narration, in which *moderation* is the exemplary nucleus from which originate the precepts transmitted by the father. It is to emphasize the father's righteousness that the excesses of a family which anachronically lives the *Shoah* in another place and time are so overstated: "It was not a mere motto; the gravity with which my father uttered it was in the proper and right place. *There was a measure to things, and we ought to learn it*" (emphasis mine).[16]

In the aforementioned examples, it is remarkable that the *Shoah* is used to construct metaphors, hyperboles, and litotes, aiming to address subjects other than the Holocaust itself. Representative of the third-generation post-catastrophe, the author's action is ambiguous. She shakes off a history marked by the destruction and consequent trauma, which she has inherited. Yet, at the same time, she uses it to embody her figures of speech—which are springboards to reach grace and irony, based on the disproportion between the World War II genocide and the more or less prosaic events of a relatively wealthy and bourgeois Jewish family in Porto Alegre. The huge time gap between World War II and the narrative present becomes patent, and the sentences are inscribed on a history that no longer exists. The past is not recovered, cannot be rescued, but is brought to stage in a theatrical sense; namely, it once again becomes present through the re-presentation, which sets its tone and imprints the intention, without being a mandatory remembrance.

Another book, *Diary of the Fall*,[17] starts from a central event that provides meaning to the novel as a whole. It is a violent episode experienced by the narrator, together with a group of boys, that will mark not only his adolescent life, but also his life as an adult — a past of distressed relationships, including his own family history. The process of remembering leads to soul-searching, as the boy gradually comes to understand the hatred that he and his colleagues, registered at a Jewish school, directed at the only non-Jew in their class. The collective contempt for João (the boy's name), who is repeatedly buried and humiliated in the school sandpit, reveals to the narrator the emptiness of his father's discourse on anti-Semitism. The construction of the plot is bold; in its continuous transition between delicate poles of the human nature, it shows how the excluded can take on the role of the oppressor and, in general, how these roles are interchangeable.

Along the way, the novel alludes to multiple sensations: the lack of a protective net, as a result of which the characters plunge into unimaginable places;

---

16 Ibid., 214–19.
17 Michel Laub, *Diário da queda* (São Paulo: Companhia das Letras, 2011).

the exploration of the "biographical space" that gives voice to experience; different forms of annihilation; unfathomable and unsuspected depths of humanity; a traumatic memory transformed into an object of inquiry; oblivion; and a discussion of the ethical duty to remember. The diversity of registers thus traces an intricate cartography that signals the paths of the fall and its recognition.

In order to merge so many threads, the novel interweaves three diaries. The account presents the confrontation of three generations, represented by the grandfather, the father, and the son—who is the narrator.

Written in the first person, it does not make clear whether this is a true autobiography or a fictional autobiography, since the author mixes in his own data, also attributed to the narrator–protagonist, which could lead the reader to believe that it is an autobiography. Even though the narrator gives the floor to another individual, it is from his point of view that the story is told. He is responsible for the selection of facts, for assembling the text, for what is said—and for what remains unsaid—in the novel.

The generation clash originates a thematic segment directed at both individual and collective memory. Since his grandfather came from the Auschwitz concentration camp, there is an exhausting repetition of the idea that "we" (perhaps more the Jews than the non-Jews) cannot forget the mass murders committed by Nazi fascism. His grandfather escapes from the concentration camp, travels to Porto Alegre in Brazil, and marries a non-Jew who converts to Judaism; he never mentions his experience as a prisoner and survivor. He ends up committing suicide, leaving sixteen volumes of written memories. His fourteen-year-old son is the one who opens the door and discovers his father shot dead. As the grandfather did not mention his life in Auschwitz, the reader could have expected the volumes to reveal what so far had been concealed. However, this does not happen. The volumes deal with how life *should be*, not with how life is or was. In the same way that the entries of Gustave Flaubert's *Bouvard and Pécuchet* make up a dictionary of ideas through citations, the grandfather's texts also are written based on commonplaces—but they deal with hygiene, primarily building a fictional present, a speechless act, in which the fundamental remains silent, to the detriment of any realistic account of what happened. Notably, all the information about his grandfather given by the narrator comes from a third party. In addition, the cleanness, the asepsis, in the grandfather's text negatively reflects a past cast in a blind spot, which he is unable to digest and disclose. Observe the following entry: "Wife—person who is in charge of the housework, ensuring that the most rigorous hygiene procedures are employed in the house and also that there are no disturbances in the husband's day when he wishes to be alone."[18]

Also, note the sugared history of Brazil, told from the grandfather's point of view: "1945 Brazil was a country that had not experienced slavery—where no agent of the government imposed any restrictions on the entrance of immigrants fleeing the war. A place full of opportunities."[19]

If the grandfather does not mention his condition as an immigrant and his victimization by Nazism, the father does, determining what cannot be forgotten: what a wildly politicized majority is able to do with a minority in a rigid scheme of perpetrator and victim. Ironically, he will suffer from Alzheimer's disease and lose his memory, diluted by the degenerative disease.

The son/narrator composes his book as a collection of numbered fragments, which allow him to move between stories and times. Thus, he shifts easily between narrative blocks, which sometimes have the grandfather, or the father, or himself and his peers, as central figures. The notable experience is that of his adolescence at the Jewish school, against a pupil who was poor, a non-Jew, and the child of a bus collector. This brings out the other side of the coin. In this community, the Jews are the majority and João, the non-Jew, is made the target of mockery by his schoolmates. They bury him every day in the sandpit and make fun of him, until his thirteenth birthday, when his father decides to have a party to reciprocate the invitations from the schoolmates, who always included him in their parties celebrating the Jewish rite of passage to adulthood, which occurs, for boys, at the age of thirteen—the *bar mitzvah*. Poor party, poor food—the guests of the family were poor people. João's schoolmates agree to throw him up in the air thirteen times, as they were accustomed to do with the other boys. On the thirteenth time, however, they would let him fall to the ground. The narrator wonders whether he participated in this ambush because of the other boys, whether he was active in the development of the idea, or whether it was his fault or that of the others.

> I don't know if I did it just to copy my colleagues. João was thrown up once, twice, I held on to him until the thirteenth time and then, when he was still going up, I withdrew my arms and took a step back. I saw João still in the air and starting to fall—or maybe it was the opposite. Perhaps I'd had this idea days before, something I had said or an attitude I had voiced, even if just once, even if in front of just one person, regardless of the circumstances

---

18 Ibid., 31.
19 Ibid., 26.

and excuses, if in fact they were also copying me.... [I]t would have been enough just to stretch out an arm, to cushion the impact, and João would have stood up. I would never have seen again the unfolding of events, of what I had done, for so long until I left the school there. The break, the stairs and the patio, and the wall where João used to sit to have his snack, the sandwich flung far away and João buried in the sand, and me getting carried away with the others, repeating the verses, the cadence, everybody together and at the same time—the music that you chant because it is the only thing you can do when you are 13. Eat sand, eat sand, eat sand, goy son of a bitch.[20]

Instead of stories about the extermination of Jews during World War II, which the narrator knows only abstractly, it is the experience of having caused João's fall that becomes decisive for him. Now, he is part of the group that attacks the "other," and he will not be immune. This moment changes his point of view about himself and his colleagues, marking the loss of the innocence of the narrator–protagonist, and his fall. Thereafter, he will have to confront who he is, what he did, what he must or can do; that is, his own limits. His inadequacy becomes visible from this moment on, in conflicts with himself, with his father who can neither see him nor save him, with the world and its rules; from this moment on, his moral and existential hell starts to grow.

The sensitivity and delicacy in dealing with complex issues of daily life and the richness of details, of the sensorial descriptions, of the digressions,- provide the text with a rich and disturbing dimension, with gradual revelations that interconnect at different points.

> After I became friends with João, I also started looking at my friends without understanding why they had done that, and how they had co-opted me, and I began to feel ashamed for screaming *goy son of a bitch*. This mingled with an increasing discomfort in my father's presence, and a rejection of his talk about anti-Semitism. I had nothing in common with those people, beyond the fact of having been born Jewish, and I did not know anything about those people beyond the fact that they were Jews, and even though so many people had died in concentration camps, it did not make any sense to me that I had to remember this every day.

Since his grandfather, who had been in Auschwitz, did not mention the past, the narrator always refers to Primo Levi's work *É isto um homem?* (*If This Is*

---

20 Ibid., 22.

a Man?). The analysis of the political gesture of writing appears throughout this author's textual references. Levi defended the necessity to testify, to prevent the atrocities of Nazism and the reification of man from oblivion. For this author, it is an imperative of ethical order to articulate a discourse that can recover this passage of the survivors' lives, however painful the act of narrating can be. The grandfather in the novel, who insists on running away from his past, obliterating this experience and, ultimately, eliminating himself in the act of committing suicide, rejects this alleged duty. Both Primo Levi and the grandfather commit suicide—and their motivations may be the same, or not. However, what is certain is that both reveal their difficulty in remaining alive.

On the other hand, when João falls and is hurt, then hospitalized, and has difficulties walking again, the narrator cannot face what he has done, and seeks relief in drinking. This addiction begins for him in adolescence, and will last until his father's disease is confirmed, and the life of the narrator moves on to another stage—with the birth of a child on the horizon.

Following the fall, the narrator goes to public school and gets closer to João. They are now in the same class. Now, it is João who, feeling stronger, denounces his friend to their new schoolmates, telling them how disloyal he was, having participated in planning the accident.

From actions that recur, the author builds up a courageous reflection on identities, emotions, and losses, highlighting not only the grandfather's silence about his own experiences at Auschwitz, but also about the experiences of fatherhood: "a single word from those we usually see in the memories of survivors of concentration camps, life that goes on after one leaves a camp such as Auschwitz, the joy that you have again from seeing a child growing up as a response to everything seen in Auschwitz."[21]

By means of prose that oscillates between violence, lyricism, and irony, with pauses for an almost documentary neutrality in the description of smells, tastes, sounds, facts, and feelings, the novel outlines the unusual trip of a man who needs to make a decisive choice in order to give direction to his life.[22]

Since Laub's novel deals with questions related to testimony and the Holocaust, it is important also to discuss the book *Homo sacer*.[23] Here, Giorgio Agamben portrays the deep transformations in the contemporary

---

21 Ibid., 37.
22 Ibid., 47.
23 It is important to emphasize that the novel brings into focus the third generation after the *Shoah*, and highlights different aspects of how this heritage marks the protagonist.

political scenario with the institution of what he calls biopolitics—the man seen as a body—and the appearance of the concentration camp as a paradigm of power.

The author examines World War II, a time when the emancipated reason of the Enlightenment was reduced successfully to the mere instrumental rationality of the logic of annihilation. Thus, the author's approach to the camps and the Holocaust provides an abstract understanding of the fact, alluding less to their historical components than to their structural nucleus, in order to extend his interpretation from Auschwitz to other twentieth-century events of oppression.

The same seems to happen with *Diary of the Fall*, by Michel Laub. Although Nazism is presented through the grandfather's biography, and Auschwitz is mentioned, these elements echo in other moments of the novel that deal with the suffering and physical destruction caused by *human evil* that man has inside himself, demanding the monitoring of *good* or the repair of evil. Laub uses notes to introduce information that *corrects* the history of the extermination of Jews, obtained by searching the Internet; the 52 existing cremating furnaces at Auschwitz would not have had the capacity to burn 4,756 bodies a day, the necessary average to reach the total number of deaths according to official statistics. Notably, the revisionists use this type of argument to prove that the Holocaust did not exist, that it is all an invention of the Jews. Is this true or false? This makes no difference to his father, for whom Auschwitz was, above all, a *concept* in which you may believe or not. And the son is reluctant to believe:

> When I was a child, I used to dream about these stories, the swastikas or the torches of the Cossacks outside the window, as if anyone in the street could put pajamas with a star on me, and put me on a train going to the chimneys. But this changed as time went by. I realized that the stories were repeated. My father told them in the same way, with the same intonation, and I can still cite examples that frequently made his voice stop, the arrest of a little girl, the separation of two brothers, the doctor and the teacher and the postman and the pregnant woman who crossed Poland before being caught in an ambush in the woods. Something changes when you see your father repeating the same thing one, two, or five hundred times. Suddenly you cannot follow him anymore. You feel so affected by something that, little by little, as you get older, at age 13, in Porto Alegre, living in a house with a swimming pool and having been

able to let a schoolmate fall on his back on his birthday, little by little you realize that all this has very little to do with your life.[24]

Bringing into the discussion the philosopher Theodor Adorno,[25] also cited in the novel, he approaches memory in a subtle way. He does not state that we should always remember Auschwitz, but rather that we should ensure that a similar event does not happen again. He does not defend the celebrations and homages, but the struggle against oblivion. If this struggle is necessary, it is not only because the tendency to forget is strong, but also the desire to forget. There is a natural forgetting, necessary in life, said Nietzsche. But there are other negative ways to forget: to deny, to repress, to pretend not to know. It is not about making the past present so that it remains in the memory as a record of complaints, recrimination, and accusation. Those who accuse and complain occupy a superior position in relation to the accused, and are exempt from having a clear performance, reproducing the vicious circle of perpetrators and victims. This does not mean to abstract the issue of guilt, but rather to remember, with Primo Levi, that we have a paradoxical analogy between victim and oppressor, and that it is important to be clear: "both are in the same trap, but it is the oppressor, and he alone, who prepared and triggered it."[26]

If the blame lies in the system, the totalitarian state as a whole, who is to judge? Basically—nobody, says Primo Levi,[27] for whom it is not possible "to reduce the net of the human relations of the *Lager* to only two blocks, the one of the victims and the one of the oppressors." The Manichean tendency to simplification is inclined to consider the division of humanity into two clearly distinct groups: that of good and that of evil. The lesson of the camp, in contrast, was that "the enemy was around but also inside, the 'we' lost its borders and the contenders were not two; one could not discern a single frontier, but rather many confused, perhaps innumerable

---

24 Giorgio Agamben, *Homo sacer. El poder soberano y la nuda vida,* trans. Antonio Gimeno (Valencia: Pre-Textos, 1998). The book was translated into Portuguese by Minas Gerais, *Homo sacer* (Ed. UFMG, 2006).

25 Ibid., 36.

26 See the chapter "O que significa elaborar o passado" ("What It Means to Elaborate the Past"), by Jeanne Marie Gagnebin, *Lembrar escrever esquecer* (*Remember Write Forget*) (São Paulo: Editora 34, 2006), which summarizes and discusses the *Dialect of Enlightenment* by Theodor Adorno.

27 Primo Levi, *Os afogados e os sobreviventes* (*The Drowned and the Saved*): *Os delitos, os castigos, as penas e as impunidades* (*The Offenses, Punishments, Penalties and Impunities*), trans. by Luís Sérgio Henriques (São Paulo: Paz e Terra, 1990), 10.

frontiers, which stretched between each one of us."[28] To define the human being as being from an *essence* is, to some extent, to repeat the SS logic and its sovereign division between German humanity and Jewish inhumanity, between German human morality and Jewish sub-human venality, between the genetic heritage of the German people and the "naked life" of the "Jewish lice," exterminated in the gas chambers. Perhaps the new imperative is not merely to remember or to forget, but rather to map a new ethics that prevents the circuit of repetition. This is the proposal that underlies Laub's book. He brings back all the abstract questions experienced within the family, and deals with memory and oblivion, with different levels of the fall. However, he also unmasks the rigid separation between good and evil, us and them, showing how the characters slide into their roles, make choices, suffer, commit cruelties, have contradictory and overlapping feelings. In the meantime, identities are produced and dismantled.[29] Laub's work is a coming-of-age novel, and three generations are intertwined within its framework. If the grandfather's diary presents what life should be, the father's diary "fixes" it, since it deals with things that matter, symbolically directed at the son, who has to deal with that legacy, as an existence in progress:

> The memories of my grandfather can be summarized in the sentence: how the world should be. It is possible to say that those of my father were something like how things actually were. If both are somehow complementary texts that deal with the same theme —the impossibility of human experience in all times and places—my grandfather being immobilized by this, my father being able to carry on despite this, and if it is impossible to talk about both without also having to affirm a position, the fact is that, since the beginning, I write this text as a justification for this position.

---

28 Levi, op. cit., 17.

29 I refer the reader to the book by Hans Keilson, *Comédia em tom menor* (*Comedy in a Minor Key*), translated by Luiz A. de Araújo (São Paulo: Companhia das Letras, 2011), originally published in 1947, where the author presents the story of a Jewish refugee who had been hidden by a non-Jewish couple in Holland, after the German occupation. The Jew dies a year later and the couple leaves clues that will lead to their identification as betrayers of the system, since they helped a Jew. This fact makes them hide and live as refugees—ironically putting them in the same position as the Jews. These exchanges of situations are of interest for breaking schematic oppositions that often hinder our reflections about what happened during World War II.

Highlighting the darkroom of memory and the observations that design a type of family topography, in which the immediate and the remote mingle, the narrator's choice of life marks the end of the account.

Along the way, however, he questions family relationships, the functioning of his community, intensifying the doubt in relation to a cultural and religious past founded on the maintenance of a dogmatic system. The frozen instant, the static portrait, images often used to describe the memory and the writing of memories proving insufficient when treated as something stable, loose pieces of time, which only acquire meaning amid the dizzying multiplicity of stimuli that constitute life.

In *Diary of the Fall,* Laub addresses this material with maturity and rigor, revealing an author whose work presents new questions about tradition and human nature.

REFERENCES

Agamben, Giorgio. *Profanações*. São Paulo: Boitempo, 2007.

————. *Homo sacer. El poder soberano y la nuda vida*. Translated by Antonio Gimeno. Valencia: Pre-Textos, 1998.

————. *Lo que queda de Auschwitz*. Valencia: Pre-Textos, 2000.

Bellemin-Nöel, Jean. *Psicanálise e literatura*. São Paulo: Cultrix, 1983.

Benjamin, Walter. *Magia e técnica, arte e política*. São Paulo: Brasiliense, 1985.

Blixen, Carina. *Palabras rigurosamente vigiladas: Dictadura, lenguaje, literatura. La obra de Carlos Liscano*. Montevideo: Ed. del Caballo Perdido, 2006.

Chiarelli, Stefania. Review of *Diário da queda*. http://glo.bo/gOEvFE

Deleuze, Gilles. *A imagem-tempo*. São Paulo: Brasiliense, 1990.

Derrida, Jacques. *Dar (el) tiempo*. Buenos Aires: Paidós, 1995.

Gagnebin, Jeanne Marie. "O que significa elaborar o passado" ("What It Means to Elaborate the Past"). In *Lembrar escrever esquecer* São Paulo: Editora 34, 2006.

Halbwachs, Maurice. *La mémoire collective*. 2nd rev. ed. Paris: PUF, 1968.

Henriques, Luís Sérgio. São Paulo: Paz e Terra, 1990.

Laub, Michel. *Diário da queda* (São Paulo: Companhia das Letras, 2011).

Levi, Primo. *É isto um homem?* Rio de Janeiro: Rocco, 2000.

————. *Os afogados e os sobreviventes* (*The Drowned and the Saved*): *Os delitos, os castigos, as penas e as impunidades* (*The Offenses, Punishments, Penalties and Impunities*). Translated by Cintia Moscowich. *Por que sou gorda, mamãe?* Rio de Janeiro: Record, 2006.

Nora, Pierre. *Les lieux de la mémoire*. Paris, Gallimard, 1984.

Yerushalmi, Yossef Hayim. *Zakhor: Jewish History and Jewish Memory*. Seattle, WA: University of Washington Press, 1982.

CHAPTER 20

Samuel Rawet and the Representation of the Holocaust

SAUL KIRSCHBAUM

The Jewish writer Samuel Rawet was born in Poland in 1929, and moved to Brazil with his family in 1936. In Brazil, he developed a prolific literary career that included short stories, novellas, essays, plays, and literary and theatrical criticism. He is reputed to have been one of the authors responsible for the renewal of the short story genre in Brazilian literature in the 1950s.

Although he did not experience the horrors of the Holocaust (*Shoah*) at firsthand, that is, not personally being a witness, Rawet was among the first writers active in Brazil to thematize the subject. His first collection, *Contos do Imigrante* (*Tales of the Immigrant*), contains five short stories whose protagonists are Jews, survivors of the *Shoah*, or, who somehow had their lives dramatically affected by the tragedy.

In this article, I will try to show how the author represents the *Shoah*. His unique style— the telegraphic, elliptical text, which is more allusive than descriptive—accounts for the fragmentation of the characters. Their language and the recourse to free indirect discourse highlight the massive difficulties they faced in order to rebuild their lives in a situation of strangeness, in an unwelcoming and even hostile environment, be it the medium in which they try to integrate, composed of residents of a tenement, or the Jewish community, or even the survivor's own family.

When Samuel Rawet published his first collection of short stories in 1956, Holocaust literature was a practically unknown genre in Brazil. In a comprehensive study of Jewish Brazilian literature, Regina Igel points out that the first writings by the survivors began to appear only three decades after their arrival in Brazil.[1] Indeed, we may say that the genre is not one of those most exploited by Jewish Brazilian writers. Its relevance is hardly comparable to the importance it reached among authors writing in Hebrew, like Aharon Appelfeld and David Grossman, or in English, like Cynthia Ozick, Art Spiegelman, Saul Bellow and Chaim Potok, or even in European languages, like Primo Levi, Andre Schwarz-Bart, Elie Wiesel, and Jurek Becker.

Thus, the space devoted by Samuel Rawet to the representation of the *Shoah*, notably in his earlier short stories, composed when he was a young man, is even more significant. Rawet was not a direct victim of the Holocaust: he came to Brazil in 1936 at age seven, joining his mother and brothers; his father had already immigrated in 1932.

In the same work, Igel points to the so-called "witnesses through the imagination," authors of literary fiction who were not direct victims of the *Shoah*.[2] In Brazil, Igel points to Jacó Guinsburg's short story "O Retrato" ("The Portrait"), published in *O reflexo—Revista Juvenil* (*The Reflex – Juvenile Magazine*) in 1946.[3] According the researcher, after Guinsburg's youthful experience, the issue would only return several decades later, in the writing of other authors.

In "Contos do Imigrante," published by Livraria José Olympio Editora in 1956, Rawet deals with the tragedy that befell central and eastern European Jewry. As we shall see, Rawet's short stories anticipate some of the main themes of the genre, which would be treated later by the most distinguished authors, including foreign ones. Obviously, the impact of the *Shoah* and the way of treating these themes would change throughout the following generations of writers, be they survivors or "witnesses through the imagination."

Unlike Guinsburg's short story, whose protagonist is a young Jewish Brazilian who attempts to understand what happened to a mysterious cousin who stayed in Europe with his family ("On a certain day I read that the Germans had massacred a great part of the Jewish population in Bessarabia"[4]), Rawet's protagonists are survivors themselves, still under the unbearable burden of the facts. The state of shock in which they find themselves, the difficulty of mourning,[5] as well as the imperative of restarting their lives amid the feeling

---

1 Regina Igel, *Imigrantes Judeus / Escritores Brasileiros* (São Paulo: Perspectiva, 1997), 211.

2 Ibid., 221.

3 Ibid., 218; this short story, the first work of fiction by the author, was included in this collection: Jacó Guinsburg, *O que aconteceu, aconteceu* (São Paulo: Ateliê Editorial, 2000), 59–65.

4 Guinsburg, *O que aconteceu, aconteceu*, 63.

5 As Ruth Klüger discovered, "where there's no grave, the work of mourning never ends"; Ruth Klüger, *Paisagens da memória. Autobiografia de uma sobrevivente do Holocausto* (*Still Alive: A Holocaust Girlhood Remembered*) (São Paulo: Editora 34, 2005), 87.

of strangeness, make these "human tatters" voiceless. This allows Rawet to use highly subjective narrative strategies, frequent interruptions, and inversions in the temporal flow of the story, as well as free indirect speech and interior monologue techniques that force the reader to participate actively, bringing the reader closer to the characters' minds, in all their puzzlement and vulnerability, thus gaining the reader's sympathy.

All of Samuel Rawet's short stories analyzed in this article belong to the *Contos do imigrante* (*Tales of the Immigrant*) collection, published in 1956.[6]

The protagonist of the short story "The Prophet," whom "the war had stripped ... of all his prior illusions and had confirmed the precariousness of what once had been solid,"[7] arrives in Brazil expecting to be received by his brother, who had come before the war, and his family. He "expected to find on this side of the ocean the comfort of those like him who had suffered, but whom chance had marginally saved from the worst."[8] However, little by little, "the sensation that their world was really something other than his—that they had not participated in anything that (for him) had been the horrible night—was being slowly transformed into concrete reality."[9]

The impossibility of rebuilding his life in an indifferent and even hostile family environment ("a year had scarcely gone by and he found himself still repeating monotonously what he imagined to be over and done with"[10]) leads him to the extreme decision of returning to Europe, without any expectations. This protagonist's attitude updates the image of the wandering Jew:[11] "Plans? He didn't have any. He was simply going in search of the company of people who were the same, the same, yes. Perhaps in search of the end."[12]

---

6 And republished in 2004 by Civilização Brasileira, in a book that contains all the short stories and novels written by Rawet. Some of these short stories were translated by Nelson H. Vieira, and were published in the collection *The Prophet and Other Stories*. Whenever possible, I have used Vieira's translation.

7 Samuel Rawet, "The Prophet" (1–8), in *The Prophet and Other Stories* (Albuquerque, NM: University of New Mexico Press, 1998), 4–5.

8 Ibid., 3.

9 Ibid., 4; the metaphorical language should be noted: "saved from the worst," "the horrible night."

10 Ibid., 5.

11 The theme of the "wandering Jew" is present throughout Rawet's work, reaching its peak in the novella *The Travels of Ahasverus to a Land of Others in Search of a Past That Doesn't Exist because It's Already Future and of a Future That's Already Past because It Was Dreamed*, published in 1970.

12 Rawet, "The Prophet," 8. As is typical in Rawet's work, the short story begins at its end, with a description of the protagonist travelling back to Europe: "All illusions lost, the only thing really left for him to do was to take that step. The gangplank already hauled off, and the last whistle blown, the steamship would weigh anchor" (1).

One of the aspects that probably caused the greatest astonishment to the reader in 1956 is the difficulty the main character had to face in order to share the horror he had lived through with his relatives and other people who were close to him. At the beginning, when he first arrives in Brazil, everyone wants to know what happened "there," but he cannot answer: "To the onslaught of questions, he responded with gestures, evasions, or else silence."[13] After some time has passed, he concludes that his isolation may be a result of this behavior, and musters up the courage to talk about his experiences—but then he realizes that the reality has changed:

> He thought about changing a little his topics of conversation and began to narrate stories about what he had once denied. But now it didn't seem to interest them. Condescendingly (they didn't understand what degree of sacrifice that meant to him) they listened to him at first and no tears were missing from the women's eyes. Afterwards, noticing their annoyance, indignation, he thought he discovered reproof in some looks and second guessed sentences like these: "What do you expect from all this talk? Why do you torment us with stuff that has nothing to do with us?"[14]

Years later, this situation would become familiar to the most renowned former interns of concentration camps who published their memoirs. For example, in *The Drowned and the Saved* (1986), Primo Levi[15] pointed out:

> Strangely enough, this same thought ("even if we were to tell it, we would not be believed") arose in the form of nocturnal dreams produced by the prisoners' despair. Almost all the survivors, orally or in their written memoirs, remember

---

13   Ibid., 2.

14   Ibid., 5–6. A very similar situation is reported by Ruth Klüger in 1992, when she describes a "disagreeably long" dinner hosted by relatives who had been living in the United States for a long time: "We were taken back home in a big and portentous car. In the dark, sitting in the comfortable back seat, the distant aunt told me: 'You have to erase from your mind what happened back in Germany and have a new beginning. Erase, just like you erase chalk from the board with an eraser'. . . . I thought she wanted to take away from me the only thing I had, that is, my life, the life I had lived"; Klüger, *Paisagens da memória*, 203.

15   Primo Levi was born in 1919 in Turim, where he received a degree in chemistry. On September 13, 1943, he was arrested by the fascist militia as a partisan; identified as Jewish, he was deported in January 1944 to Auschwitz, to leave it only at the end of the war. His first work about his concentration camp experience, *If This Is a Man*, was published in 1947, but was not widely read; only the second edition, printed in 1958, had a large circulation.

a dream which frequently recurred during the nights of imprisonment, varied in its details but uniform in its substance: they had returned home and with passion and relief were describing their past sufferings, addressing themselves to a loved one, and were not believed, indeed were not even listened to. In the most typical (and cruelest) form, the interlocutor turned and left in silence.[16]

The conversation recorded by Jorge Semprun[17] between a group of recently liberated prisoners—a group to which he himself belonged—in *Literature or Life*, published in 1994, goes in the same direction:

> — Anyway, it is good that you are here, said Yves, now that I joined the group of the future repatriated. We were thinking of how we would have to tell our story, so that they will understand us.
>
> I nod, it is a good question: one of the good questions.
>
> — That is not the problem, someone quickly exclaims, the true problem is not telling, whatever difficulties there are. The problem is listening.... Will they want to listen to our stories, even if they are well told?[18]

Ruth Klüger[19] also observed this phenomenon, in *Still Alive: A Holocaust Girlhood Remembered*, from 1992:

> I always thought I would have something interesting and important to tell after the war. But people don't want to listen, or only listen with a certain pose, a certain attitude, not as interlocutors but as someone who has to submit to an unpleasant task, with a type of reverence that easily becomes disgust, two sensations that are complementary in any case, since both the object of reverence and the one of disgust are always kept at distance.[20]

---

16 Primo Levi, *The Drowned and the Saved* (New York: Vintage International, 1989), 12.
17 In 1943, the Spaniard Jorge Semprun was a young militant Communist exiled in Paris; he was arrested by the Gestapo and deported to the concentration camp in Buchenwald, where he was incarcerated until April 1945, when the camp was liberated by the North American troops.
18 Jorge Semprun, *A escrita ou a vida* (São Paulo: Companhia das Letras, 1995), 124–25.
19 Ruth Klüger was born in 1931, in Vienna. In 1942, she was deported with her mother to the concentration camp in Terezin, from where she was taken, in 1944, to Auschwitz-Birkenau; she escaped in 1945, after being chosen to be part of a forced labor group in Christianstadt.
20 Klüger, *Paisagens da memória*, 102.

It should be noted that due to this impossibility of communication, to the silence imposed on the survivors, the Holocaust is frequently more alluded to than represented in Rawet's stories.[21] For example, the protagonist of "The Prophet," in one of the most explicit passages, says, in an internal monologue:

> The forms in the dimness of the room (he slept with the grandson) composed scenes he didn't expect to see again. Horrible and skeletal daybreaks. Anguished faces and prayers flying away from human ashes. His wife's figure wrapping her shawl at the last minute. Where are the eyes, where are the muted eyes that disclosed the animal cry?[22]

Ida, the protagonist of the short story "The Prayer," came to Brazil without a family waiting for her. Why exactly did she come to Brazil? It is a mystery even to herself, a free wanderer with no destination; the narrator tells us that:

> Without knowing how, she disembarked in this port. She was leaving a whole existence behind. … At the beginning they invited her to stay at somebody's house, but as a novelty, a rare beast from other lands who has stories lasting for more than a month. The stories wore out. So did the kindness. Then came the tenement with a language she did not understand, kids making fun of her, the packages burdening her arms, and her legs registering sidewalks and rubbing together daily over a hundred doormats.[23]

The Jewish community received her; some days later, feeling that they had met their obligations, her benefactors got tired of her and her stories. They gave her a package of goods and sent her away to make a living as a peddler (a "profession" she, surely, had never had) and live in a slum, despite her difficulty with

---

21 About this, see Nelson Vieira's comment on Rawet's work: "His shifts among signifiers and his elliptical language evoke rather than represent. As literary innovations, his revolutionary prose demonstrates the emerging crisis in representation"; Vieira, *Jewish Voices in Brazilian Literature: A Prophetic Discourse of Alterity* (Gainesville, FL: University Press of Florida, 1995), 66–67.

22 Rawet, ibid., 7.

23 "The Prayer," 12. The short story starts with the protagonist living in a slum: "At the entrance to the courtyard, the remains of a wall nobody ever bothered to raise after it was knocked down by a truck, Zico assembled the gang of boys. 'There, the old woman, over there!'" (9).

the language and the strangeness that she presented to her new neighbors—the same impossibility of narrating, the same rejection by the possible listeners.

Rawet projects the psychological disaggregation of the protagonist in her physical aspect, in expressionistic tones: "The light from a streetlamp split Ida's face in two, diagonally. One eye blinded by the flash of light glowed moistlessly."[24]

The reference to the Holocaust in "The Prayer" is even more allusive than in "The Prophet"; in an excerpt of strong visual appeal, in which the narrator's discourse and the main character's interior monologue merge in an almost inextricable way, we can envision what "the whole existence she left behind" must have been:

> On the wall Isaiah's praying eyes had been startled by the click of the photograph. Ida remembered the trouble in convincing him to keep the photo that was taken by surprise. Now, all yellowed, it hung on the wall, showing the blot of his beard, his arched eyebrows and those startled eyes. From the others nothing more had remained. Ida's eyes quivered with the memory. What a nightmare! On Fridays, Isaiah would come home more happy, his face shining, and one drop of water or another from his beard would be a sign of the ritual bath. He would gently slap her on the back a few times, (Ida's face was red from the wood in the stove), and would go pray. Now only the photograph.

And, a little further on:

> Children, she had already had them, husband as well. From all that, only the photo on the wall remained. And herself. On her wrinkled face, a crushed suffering. She was forgetting. All of them died in the war.[25]

In the present time of the narrative, the first Friday in the tenement, Ida, despite everything, finds the strength to overcome her tiredness and accomplish her obligations as a devoted Jewess: she cleans and sweeps the floor, covers the table with a white cloth, prepares the ritual Shabbat meal, lights the candles, and begins to recite the traditional prayers. But her spirit is not at peace. The burning candles and the tone of her voice when the prayer "gushes" out of her mouth generate great amazement in the children

---

24 Ibid., 12.
25 Ibid., 11–12.

who are watching her, and, because of this, they call the other residents of the slum to observe the scene:

> A stream of language in a strange dialect, a wailing lament, escaped from Ida's door. Her voice was fiery and strong, nobody had heard her like this, and it produced a lump in the throat of the crowd that was squeezing into the hallway. The suspicions increased. Rosa, of rugged hand and robust figure, struck her fist against the wood:

> "Knock the door down!"[26]

In contrast to the nameless protagonist of "The Prophet," who was met in Brazil by close relatives, the short story "The Prayer" presents another possible response to the reconstruction of a life torn to pieces by the tragedy. Ida, who does not have family in Brazil and who has been discarded by the Jewish community at the first opportunity, will not get desperate and will not go back to Europe. Ida is a survivor who will be accepted by the Brazilian population and adapt to the new life:

> "– Let's leave, my friends. It's nothing at all!"

> A man's voice resounded, giving the signal to withdraw, and the squeaking of shoes through the doorway turned into a growing murmur outside the apartment.

> "—That's what prayer is over there in their country." The same voice. On the stairs going up to the next floor, the womenfolk milled around and Brito's mother gave him a beating:

> "—That will teach you to spy into other people's window, that'll teach you!"

In the short story "Little Gringo," there is no explicit reference to the Holocaust. The memory of his arrival in Brazil, with his family, is still present in the "rope from the improvised swing," which "had remained of the heavy crate that his family had brought over."[27] However, a dissonant keynote is introduced by the

---

26 Ibid., 13–14.
27 Ibid., "Little Gringo," 25.

memory of a life lost in the shtetl, and a grandfather he no longer has news from, alluding again to an obscure past, of which the protagonist himself does not have a very clear view:

> Way back when, before the ship, he had his gang of friends. . . .
> In the wintertime there was the sled that was carried up the river, the
> frozen river where his ironclad boots slid like skates. At home, the hot
> soup of beets, or the steaming cabbage. He would sit on the lap of
> his grandfather who had just come from prayers and enthusiastically
> would repeat what he had learned in school. Where is grandfather?[28]

The narrative, in lengthy paragraphs, articulates the voice of a third-person narrator with free indirect speech, interior monologue, and stream of consciousness, constructing a mosaic that interweaves memories of facts from different times in a chaotic sequence, showing the difficulty of the protagonist in dealing with the new situation.

As in the short stories previously discussed, "Little Gringo" also starts at its end, when the boy, after a conflict with the teacher that prevents him from returning to school, goes back home and tries to find a solution to the crisis: "He was crying. Not really out of fear of the possible spanking, despite his torn uniform."[29] The solution must have a magical nature: evoking the freedom of the past. He goes out to buy the onions his mother asked for, running, seeking to reach adulthood.

> When he crossed the gate, he quickened his step spurred on by the
> will to become a man right there and then. He thought that by running
> he would speed up time. His feet skipped over the wet cement, like a
> long time ago when, with his ironclad boots, they slid across the frozen
> river in the wintertime.[30]

In the short story "Réquiem para um solitário" ("Requiem for a Lonely Man"), Rawet addresses another issue that came to have great impact on the Holocaust literature due to the frequency of its occurrence and the influence it has had over the people involved: the survivors' sense of guilt. As Regina Igel says, "the survivors' sensation of guilt, in its complexity and ramifications, is one of the

---

28 Ibid., 26–27. Regina Igel argues that "some narratives bring back memories of happy times, previous to the Holocaust facts" (Igel, *Imigrantes Judeus*, 213).
29 "Little Gringo," 25.
30 "Little Gringo," 29.

feelings that psychologists who treat survivors most observe."[31] Here, it is not the case of those who were imprisoned in extermination camps and were lucky enough not to die, but of those who emigrated before the war, when they were already adults, leaving family and friends in Europe, and later did not exert enough effort to remove them from there. It is not the case of "Little Gringo," who came as a child.

The protagonist, confronted by his son, who read an old letter sent by relatives who died in the Holocaust, creates a mental picture contrasting their situation and his relative prosperity:

> He now stood there in the well-illuminated room, where the reflections in the crystal pendants had already allowed him to spend a long time in a state of absorption and amusement. Today, they painfully injured his retina, as if searing it. They hurt more than his son's words from the corner of the office, after dinner. He could never conceive such events. The recent abundance had blunted even his former dexterity of thinking.[32]

The face of his son in front of him reminded him of another son, his pregnant wife, and the rest of the family, who had not been as bold as he had been. In his mind, sensations of the successful present clashed with oppressive memories of an alluded to and unresolved past, in a magnificent stream of consciousness:

> The letter lying on the table—a merciless report of a world that had disappeared. Two o'clock. Dawn. The sounds of tires hissing on the asphalt. An almost mute radio somewhere. (Heavens! How not to go crazy! ...) Of the houses, nothing else remains. And in the woods nearby, there are mass graves of hearts destroyed by bullets, and there are chestnut tree branches that resist the swinging of bulging eyes. A horn. The remains of a bohemian in a drunken voice. The short and deep bell's toll of the quarter hour. A procession of faces, some smoky, others painfully visible, grandfather, uncle, cousin, sparse and majestic beards in a hesitation of prayers on Doomsday. (Heavens! How not to go crazy!) Why hadn't they left, like him, in the hold of a ship? Why, at the pier, instead of waving handkerchiefs, hadn't they run across the gangplank?[33]

---

31 Igel, *Imigrantes Judeus*, 230.
32 Samuel Rawet, "Réquiem para um solitário," in *Contos e novelas reunidos* (46–52), ed. André Seffrin (Rio de Janeiro: Civilização Brasileira, 2004), 46.
33 Ibid., 48–49.

Sleepless, he cannot come to terms with the indifference with which, so far, he had been dealing with the destiny of his first family; reacting to the wife's remark that his insomnia was caused by his preoccupation with some new company he must be thinking about, he reflects, in interior monologue:

> Another company. Yes. Why not? Was there any other reason, except for disease, which could make a man spend the dawn lonely in a room? Once he had done that, years ago. The letter arrived and with it a wave of remorse and images. Then—the mitigation. The question of why they had died had never even been outlined by him.[34]

The issue of Nazism, of the Holocaust, would be treated again by Samuel Rawet in later works, as in the short story "Lisbon by Night," published in 1969 in the collection *O terreno de uma polegada quadrada* (*The One Square Inch Land*), in the 1970 novel *The Travels of Ahasverus to a Land of Others in Search of a Past that Doesn't Exist because it's Already Future and of a Future that's already Past because it was Dreamed*, and in the plays *O papa do Gueto* (*The Ghetto's Pope*), *Miriam*, and *O lance de dados* (*A Roll of Dices*), unpublished.

Commenting on the publication of *Contos do Imigrante* (*Tales of the Immigrant*), Jacó Guinsburg pointed out that the nature of Jewish immigration (to Brazil) underwent profound changes due to the war and Nazism. These changes brought the images of the refugee, the displaced person, the ex-inmate of concentration camps, the survivor, with their poignant tragedies, with their shattered souls floating on a sea of ashes and bloody memories.[35]

In this article I have sought, through the analysis of some short stories published in 1956, to focus on the precursor role played by Samuel Rawet in the Holocaust literature in Brazil, together with Jacó Guinsburg. I have also tried to show how this new situation is captured by Rawet's artistic sensibility, anticipating themes and daring to create innovative narrative forms that could successfully meet the demands of the challenge of representing the unrepresentable.

---

34 Ibid. 52.
35 Jacó Guinsburg, "Os imigrantes de Samuel Rawet" ("The Immigrants of Samuel Rawet") (75–84), in *Samuel Rawet: fortuna crítica em jornais e revistas*, ed. Francisco Venceslau dos Santos (Rio de Janeiro: Editora Caetés, 2008), 79–80.

REFERENCES

Guinsburg, Jacó. "O retrato." In *O que aconteceu, aconteceu*, 59–65. São Paulo: Ateliê Editorial, 2000.

Igel, Regina. *Imigrantes Judeus / Escritores Brasileiros*. São Paulo: Perspectiva, 1997.

Klüger, Ruth. *Paisagens da memória. Autobiografia de uma sobrevivente do Holocausto* São Paulo: Editora 34, 2005.

Levi, Primo. *É isto um homem?* Rio de Janeiro: Rocco, 1988.

————. *The Drowned and the Saved*. New York: Vintage International, 1989.

Rawet, Samuel. *The Prophet and Other Stories*. Translated and with an introduction by Nelson H. Vieira. Albuquerque, NM: University of New Mexico Press, 1998.

————. *Contos e novelas reunidos*. Edited by André Seffrin. Rio de Janeiro: Civilização Brasileira, 2004.

————. *Samuel Rawet: ensaios reunidos*. Edited by Rosana Kohl Bines and José Leonardo Tônus. Rio de Janeiro: Civilização Brasileira, 2008.

Santos, Francisco Venceslau dos, ed. *Samuel Rawet: fortuna crítica em jornais e revistas*. Rio de Janeiro: Editora Caetés.

Schwarz, Daniel R. *Imagining the Holocaust*. New York: St. Martin's Press, 1999.

Semprun, Jorge. *A escrita ou a vida*. Translated by Rosa Freire D'Aguiar. São Paulo: Companhia das Letras, 1995.

Vieira, Nelson. "Ser judeu e escritor: três casos brasileiros." *Papéis Avulsos* 25 (1990): 1–20.

————. *Jewish Voices in Brazilian Literature: A Prophetic Discourse of Alterity*. Gainesville, FL: University Press of Florida, 1995, 256p.

————. "Translator's Note and Acknowledgments." In *The Prophet and Other Stories*. xi–xiii. Albuquerque, NM: University of New Mexico Press, 1998.

Waldman, Berta. *Entre passos e rastros: presença judaica na literatura brasileira contemporânea*. São Paulo: Perspectiva, 2003.

Index

Note: Page numbers followed by 'n' denotes notes

CPSIA information can be obtained
at www.ICGtesting.com
Printed in the USA
BVOW06*1950261117
501284BV00003B/10/P